HOLT SCIENCE & TECHNOLOGY

Earth
Science

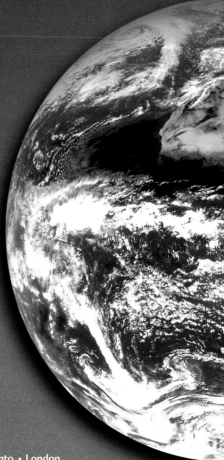

HOLT, RINEHART AND WINSTON

A Harcourt Classroom Education Company

Austin · New York · Orlando · Atlanta · San Francisco · Boston · Dallas · Toronto · London

Acknowledgments

Contributing Authors

Kathleen Meehan Berry
Science Chairman
Canon-McMillan School District
Canonsburg, Pennsylvania

Robert H. Fronk, Ph.D.
Chair of Science and Mathematics Education Department
Florida Institute of Technology
West Melbourne, Florida

Mary Kay Hemenway, Ph.D.
Research Associate and Senior Lecturer
Department of Astronomy
The University of Texas
Austin, Texas

Kathleen Kaska
Life and Earth Science Teacher
Lake Travis Middle School
Austin, Texas

Peter E. Malin, Ph.D.
Professor of Geology
Division of Earth and Ocean Sciences
Duke University
Durham, North Carolina

Karen J. Meech, Ph.D.
Associate Astronomer
Institute for Astronomy
University of Hawaii
Honolulu, Hawaii

Robert J. Sager
Chair and Professor of Earth Sciences
Pierce College
Lakewood, Washington

Lab Writers

Kenneth Creese
Science Teacher
White Mountain Junior High School
Rock Springs, Wyoming

Linda A. Culp
Science Teacher and Dept. Chair
Thorndale High School
Thorndale, Texas

Bruce M. Jones
Science Teacher and Dept. Chair
The Blake School
Minneapolis, Minnesota

Shannon Miller
Science and Math Teacher
Llano Junior High School
Llano, Texas

Robert Stephen Ricks
Special Services Teacher
Department of Classroom Improvement
Alabama State Department of Education
Montgomery, Alabama

James J. Secosky
Science Teacher
Bloomfield Central School
Bloomfield, New York

Academic Reviewers

Mead Allison, Ph.D.
Assistant Professor of Oceanography
Texas A&M University
Galveston, Texas

Alissa Arp, Ph.D.
Director and Professor of Environmental Studies
Romberg Tiburon Center
San Francisco State University
Tiburon, California

Paul D. Asimow, Ph.D.
Assistant Professor of Geology and Geochemistry
Department of Physics and Planetary Sciences
California Institute of Technology
Pasadena, California

G. Fritz Benedict, Ph.D.
Senior Research Scientist and Astronomer
McDonald Observatory
The University of Texas
Austin, Texas

Russell M. Brengelman, Ph.D.
Professor of Physics
Morehead State University
Morehead, Kentucky

John A. Brockhaus, Ph.D.
Director—Mapping, Charting, and Geodesy Program
Department of Geography and Environmental Engineering
United States Military Academy
West Point, New York

Michael Brown, Ph.D.
Assistant Professor of Planetary Astronomy
Department of Physics and Astronomy
California Institute of Technology
Pasadena, California

Wesley N. Colley, Ph.D.
Postdoctoral Fellow
Harvard-Smithsonian Center for Astrophysics
Cambridge, Massachusetts

Andrew J. Davis, Ph.D.
Manager—ACE Science Data Center
Physics Department
California Institute of Technology
Pasadena, California

Peter E. Demmin, Ed.D.
Former Science Teacher and Department Chair
Amherst Central High School
Amherst, New York

James Denbow, Ph.D.
Associate Professor
Department of Anthropology
The University of Texas
Austin, Texas

Roy W. Hann, Jr., Ph.D.
Professor of Civil Engineering
Texas A&M University
College Station, Texas

Frederick R. Heck, Ph.D.
Professor of Geology
Ferris State University
Big Rapids, Michigan

Richard Hey, Ph.D.
Professor of Geophysics
Hawaii Institute of Geophysics and Planetology
University of Hawaii
Honolulu, Hawaii

John E. Hoover, Ph.D.
Associate Professor of Biology
Millersville University
Millersville, Pennsylvania

Acknowledgments (cont.)

Robert W. Houghton, Ph.D.
Senior Staff Associate
Lamont-Doherty Earth
  Observatory
Columbia University
Palisades, New York

Steven A. Jennings, Ph.D.
Assistant Professor
Department of Geography &
  Environmental Studies
University of Colorado
Colorado Springs, Colorado

Eric L. Johnson, Ph.D.
Assistant Professor of Geology
Central Michigan University
Mount Pleasant, Michigan

John Kermond, Ph.D.
Visiting Scientist
NOAA–Office of Global
  Programs
Silver Spring, Maryland

Zavareh Kothavala, Ph.D.
Postdoctoral Associate Scientist
Department of Geology and
  Geophysics
Yale University
New Haven, Connecticut

Karen Kwitter, Ph.D.
*Ebenezer Fitch Professor of
  Astronomy*
Williams College
Williamstown, Massachusetts

Valerie Lang, Ph.D.
*Project Leader of
  Environmental Programs*
The Aerospace Corporation
Los Angeles, California

Philip LaRoe
Professor
Helena College of
  Technology
Helena, Montana

Julie Lutz, Ph.D.
Astronomy Program
Washington State University
Pullman, Washington

Duane F. Marble, Ph.D.
Professor Emeritus
Department of Geography
  and Natural Resources
Ohio State University
Columbus, Ohio

Joseph A. McClure, Ph.D.
Associate Professor
Department of Physics
Georgetown University
Washington, D.C.

Frank K. McKinney, Ph.D.
Professor of Geology
Appalachian State University
Boone, North Carolina

Joann Mossa, Ph.D.
*Associate Professor of
  Geography*
University of Florida
Gainesville, Florida

LaMoine L. Motz, Ph.D.
*Coordinator of Science
  Education*
Department of Learning
  Services
Oakland County Schools
Waterford, Michigan

Barbara Murck, Ph.D.
*Assistant Professor of Earth
  Science*
Erindale College
University of Toronto
Mississauga, Ontario
  CANADA

Hilary Clement Olson, Ph.D.
Research Associate
Institute for Geophysics
The University of Texas
Austin, Texas

Andre Potochnik
Geologist
Grand Canyon Field Institute
Flagstaff, Arizona

John R. Reid, Ph.D.
Professor Emeritus
Department of Geology and
  Geological Engineering
University of North Dakota
Grand Forks, North Dakota

Gary Rottman, Ph.D.
Associate Director
Laboratory for Atmosphere
  and Space Physics
University of Colorado
Boulder, Colorado

Dork L. Sahagian, Ph.D.
Professor
Institute for the Study of
  Earth, Oceans, and Space
University of New Hampshire
Durham, New Hampshire

Peter Sheridan, Ph.D.
Professor of Chemistry
Colgate University
Hamilton, New York

David Sprayberry, Ph.D.
*Assistant Director for
  Observing Support*
W.M. Keck Observatory
California Association for
  Research in Astronomy
Kamuela, Hawaii

Lynne Talley, Ph.D.
Professor
Scripps Institution of
  Oceanography
University of California
La Jolla, California

Glenn Thompson, Ph.D.
Scientist
Geophysical Institute
University of Alaska
Fairbanks, Alaska

Martin VanDyke, Ph.D.
Professor of Chemistry Emeritus
Front Range Community
  College
Westminister, Colorado

Thad A. Wasklewicz, Ph.D.
*Assistant Professor of
  Geography*
University of Memphis
Memphis, Tennessee

Hans Rudolf Wenk, Ph.D.
*Professor of Geology and
  Geophysical Sciences*
University of California
Berkeley, California

Lisa D. White, Ph.D.
*Associate Professor of
  Geosciences*
San Francisco State University
San Francisco, California

Lorraine W. Wolf, Ph.D.
Associate Professor of Geology
Auburn University
Auburn, Alabama

Charles A. Wood, Ph.D.
*Chairman and Professor of
  Space Studies*
University of North Dakota
Grand Forks, North Dakota

Safety Reviewer

Jack Gerlovich, Ph.D.
Associate Professor
School of Education
Drake University
Des Moines, Iowa

Teacher Reviewers

Barry L. Bishop
Science Teacher and Dept. Chair
San Rafael Junior High
  School
Ferron, Utah

Yvonne Brannum
*Science Teacher and Dept.
  Chair*
Hine Junior High School
Washington, D.C.

Daniel L. Bugenhagen
*Science Teacher and Dept.
  Chair*
Yutan Junior & Senior High
  School
Yutan, Nebraska

Kenneth Creese
Science Teacher
White Mountain Junior High
  School
Rock Springs, Wyoming

Linda A. Culp
*Science Teacher and Dept.
  Chair*
Thorndale High School
Thorndale, Texas

Alonda Droege
Science Teacher
Pioneer Middle School
Steilacom, Washington

Laura Fleet
Science Teacher
Alice B. Landrum Middle
  School
Ponte Vedra Beach, Florida

Susan Gorman
Science Teacher
Northridge Middle School
North Richland Hills, Texas

C. John Graves
Science Teacher
Monforton Middle School
Bozeman, Montana

Janel Guse
*Science Teacher and Dept.
  Chair*
West Central Middle School
Hartford, South Dakota

Gary Habeeb
Science Mentor
Sierra–Plumas Joint Unified
  School District
Downieville, California

Dennis Hanson
*Science Teacher and Dept.
  Chair*
Big Bear Middle School
Big Bear Lake, California

iii

Acknowledgments (cont.)

Norman E. Holcomb
Science Teacher
Marion Local Schools
Maria Stein, Ohio

Tracy Jahn
Science Teacher
Berkshire Junior-Senior High
  School
Canaan, New York

David D. Jones
Science Teacher
Andrew Jackson Middle
  School
Cross Lanes, West Virginia

Howard A. Knodle
Science Teacher
Belvidere High School
Belvidere, Illinois

Michael E. Kral
Science Teacher
West Hardin Middle School
Cecilia, Kentucky

Kathy LaRoe
Science Teacher
East Valley Middle School
East Helena, Montana

Scott Mandel, Ph.D.
*Director and Educational
  Consultant*
Teachers Helping Teachers
Los Angeles, California

Kathy McKee
Science Teacher
Hoyt Middle School
Des Moines, Iowa

Michael Minium
*Vice President of Program
  Development*
United States Orienteering
  Federation
Forest Park, Georgia

Jan Nelson
Science Teacher
East Valley Middle School
East Helena, Montana

Dwight C. Patton
Science Teacher
Carroll T. Welch Middle
  School
Horizon City, Texas

Joseph Price
*Chairman—Science
  Department*
H. M. Brown Junior High
  School
Washington, D.C.

Terry J. Rakes
Science Teacher
Elmwood Junior High School
Rogers, Arkansas

Steven Ramig
Science Teacher
West Point High School
West Point, Nebraska

Helen P. Schiller
Science Teacher
Northwood Middle School
Taylors, South Carolina

Bert J. Sherwood
Science Teacher
Socorro Middle School
El Paso, Texas

Larry Tackett
Science Teacher and Dept. Chair
Andrew Jackson Middle
  School
Cross Lanes, West Virginia

Walter Woolbaugh
Science Teacher
Manhattan Junior High
  School
Manhattan, Montana

Alexis S. Wright
*Middle School Science
  Coordinator*
Rye Country Day School
Rye, New York

Gordon Zibelman
Science Teacher
Drexel Hill Middle School
Drexel Hill, Pennsylvania

Staff Credits

Editorial

Robert W. Todd, Associate
  Director, Secondary Science
Debbie Starr, Managing Editor
Robert V. Tucek, Senior Editor

ANNOTATED TEACHER'S EDITION
Jim Ratcliffe

COPYEDITORS
Dawn Spinozza, Copyediting
  Manager

EDITORIAL SUPPORT STAFF
**Jeanne Graham, Mary Helbling,
Kenneth G. Raymond, Tanu'e
White**

EDITORIAL PERMISSIONS
Cathy Paré, Permissions Manager
Jan Harrington, Permissions
  Editor

Art, Design, and Photo

BOOK DESIGN
Richard Metzger, Design Director
Marc Cooper, Senior Designer
Jose Garza, Designer
David Hernandez, Designer
Alicia Sullivan, Designer (ATE),
Cristina Bowerman, Design
Associate (ATE), **Holly Whittaker**,
Traffic Coordinator

IMAGE ACQUISITIONS
Elaine Tate, Art Buyer Supervisor
Erin Cone, Art Buyer
Jeannie Taylor, Photo Research
  Supervisor
Andy Christiansen, Photo
  Researcher
Jackie Berger, Assistant Photo
  Researcher

PHOTO STUDIO
Sam Dudgeon, Senior Staff
  Photographer
Victoria Smith, Photo Specialist
Lauren Eischen, Photo
  Coordinator

Production

Mimi Stockdell, Senior
  Production Manager
Adriana Bardin Prestwood,
  Senior Production Coordinator
Beth Sample, Production
  Coordinator
**Suzanne Brooks, Sara Carroll-
Downs**

Contents in Brief

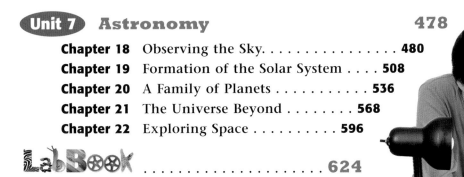

Contents

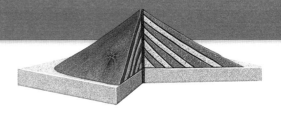

The more labs, the better!
Take a minute to browse the **LabBook** located at the end of this textbook. You'll find a wide variety of exciting labs that will help you experience science firsthand. But please don't forget to be safe. Read the "Safety First!" section before starting any of the labs.

Start your engines with an activity!

Science is an activity in which investigation leads to information and understanding. The **Start-Up Activity** at the beginning of each chapter helps you gain scientific understading of the topic through hands-on experience.

START-UP Activity

QuickLab

Not all laboratory investigations have to be long and involved.

The **QuickLabs** found throughout the chapters in this book require only a small amount of time and limited equipment. But just because they are quick, don't skimp on the safety.

$$\div \;\; 5 \;\div\;\; \Omega \;\; \leq \;\; \infty \;\; +\Omega \;\; ^{\sqrt{}} \;\; 9 \;\; _\infty \;\; ^{\leq} \;\; \Sigma \; 2$$

MATH BREAK

Science and math go hand in hand.

The **MathBreaks** in the margins of the chapters show you many ways that math applies directly to science and vice versa.

Science can be very useful in the real world.

It is interesting to learn how scientific information is being used in the real world. You can see for yourself in the **Apply** features. You will also be asked to apply your own knowledge. This is a good way to learn!

Connections

One science leads to another.

You may not realize it at first, but different areas of science are related to each other in many ways. Each **Connection** explores a topic from the viewpoint of another science discipline. In this way, areas of science merge to improve your understanding of the world around you.

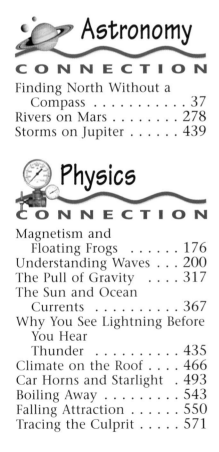

Astronomy
CONNECTION

Physics
CONNECTION

Biology
CONNECTION

Chemistry
CONNECTION

Environment
CONNECTION

Feature Articles

CAREERS

ACROSS THE SCIENCES

Science, Technology, and Society

EYE ON THE ENVIRONMENT

Feature articles for any appetite!

Science and technology affect us all in many ways. The following articles will give you an idea of just how interesting, strange, helpful, and action-packed science and technology are. At the end of each chapter, you will find two feature articles. Read them and you will be surprised at what you learn.

Eureka!

Health WATCH

SCIENTIFIC DEBATE

Science Fiction

WEIRD SCIENCE

How to Use Your Textbook

Your Roadmap for Success with *Holt Science & Technology*

Study the Terms to Learn

Key Terms are listed for each section. Learn the definitions of these terms because you will most likely be tested on them. Use the glossary to locate definitions quickly.

STUDY TIP If you don't understand a definition, reread the page where the term is introduced. The surrounding text should help make the definition easier to understand.

Read What You'll Do

Objectives tell you what you'll need to know.

STUDY TIP Reread the objectives when studying for a test to be sure you know the material.

Take Notes and Get Organized

Keep a science notebook so that you are ready to take notes when your teacher reviews the material in class. Keep your assignments in this notebook so that you can review them when studying for the chapter test. In addition, you will be asked to keep a *ScienceLog*, in which you will write your answers to certain questions. Your *ScienceLog* may be a section of your science notebook.

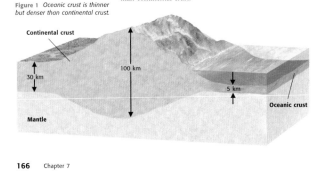

Section 1

Inside the Earth

The Earth is not just a ball of solid rock. It is made of several layers with different physical properties and compositions. As you will discover, scientists think about the Earth's layers in two ways—by their *composition* and by their *physical properties*.

Earth's layers are made of different mixtures of elements. This is what is meant by differences in composition. Many of the Earth's layers also have different physical properties. Physical properties include temperature, density, and ability to flow. Let's first take a look at the composition of the Earth.

The Composition of the Earth

The Earth is divided into three layers—the *crust, mantle,* and *core*—based on what each one is made of. The lightest materials make up the outermost layer, and the densest materials make up the inner layers. This is because lighter materials tend to float up, while heavier materials sink.

The Crust The **crust** is the outermost layer of the Earth. Ranging from 5 to 100 km thick, it is also the thinnest layer of the Earth. And because it is the layer we live on, we know more about this layer than we know about the other two.

There are two types of crust—continental and oceanic. *Continental crust* has a composition similar to granite. It has an average thickness of 30 km. *Oceanic crust* has a composition similar to basalt. It is generally between 5 and 8 km thick. Because basalt is denser than granite, oceanic crust is denser than continental crust.

Figure 1 *Oceanic crust is thinner but denser than continental crust.*

166 Chapter 7

Terms to Learn

crust   mesosphere
mantle   outer core
core   inner core
lithosphere tectonic plate
asthenosphere

What You'll Do

◆ Identify and describe the layers of the Earth by what they are made of.
◆ Identify and describe the layers of the Earth by their physical properties.
◆ Define *tectonic plate.*
◆ Explain how scientists know about the structure of Earth's interior.

Be Resourceful, Use the Web

Internet Connect boxes in your textbook take you to resources that you can use for science projects, reports, and research papers. Go to **scilinks.org** and type in the SciLinks code to get information on a topic.

Visit **go.hrw.com** Find worksheets and other materials that go with your textbook at **go.hrw.com**. Click on the textbook icon and the table of contents to see all of the resources for each chapter.

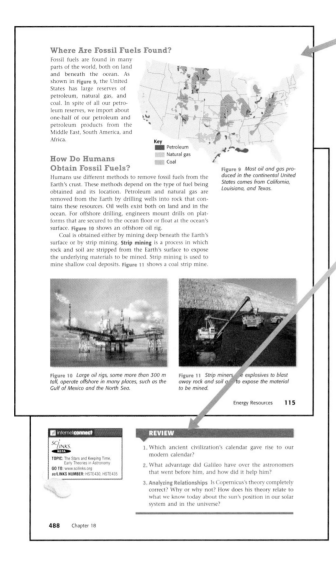

Where Are Fossil Fuels Found?

Fossil fuels are found in many parts of the world, both on land and beneath the ocean. As shown in **Figure 9**, the United States has large reserves of petroleum, natural gas, and coal. In spite of all our petroleum reserves, we import about one-half of our petroleum and petroleum products from the Middle East, South America, and Africa.

How Do Humans Obtain Fossil Fuels?

Humans use different methods to remove fossil fuels from the Earth's crust. These methods depend on the type of fuel being obtained and its location. Petroleum and natural gas are removed from the Earth by drilling wells into rock that contains these resources. Oil wells exist both on land and in the ocean. For offshore drilling, engineers mount drills on platforms that are secured to the ocean floor or float at the ocean's surface. **Figure 10** shows an offshore oil rig.

Coal is obtained either by mining deep beneath the Earth's surface or by strip mining. **Strip mining** is a process in which rock and soil are stripped from the Earth's surface to expose the underlying materials to be mined. Strip mining is used to mine shallow coal deposits. **Figure 11** shows a coal strip mine.

Key
Petroleum
Natural gas
Coal

Figure 9 *Most oil and gas produced in the continental United States comes from California, Louisiana, and Texas.*

Figure 10 *Large oil rigs, some more than 300 m tall, operate offshore in many places, such as the Gulf of Mexico and the North Sea.*

Figure 11 *Strip miners use explosives to blast away rock and soil and to expose the material to be mined.*

Energy Resources **115**

internetconnect

SC*LINKS*
NSTA

TOPIC: The Stars and Keeping Time, Early Theories in Astronomy
GO TO: www.scilinks.org
sciLINKS NUMBER: HSTE430, HSTE435

REVIEW

1. Which ancient civilization's calendar gave rise to our modern calendar?

2. What advantage did Galileo have over the astronomers that went before him, and how did it help him?

3. **Analyzing Relationships** Is Copernicus's theory completely correct? Why or why not? How does his theory relate to what we know today about the sun's position in our solar system and in the universe?

488 Chapter 18

Use the Illustrations and Photos

Art shows complex ideas and processes. Learn to analyze the art so that you better understand the material you read in the text.

Tables and graphs display important information in an organized way to help you see relationships.

A picture is worth a thousand words. Look at the photographs to see relevant examples of science concepts you are reading about.

Answer the Section Reviews

Section Reviews test your knowledge over the main points of the section. Critical Thinking items challenge you to think about the material in greater depth and to find connections that you infer from the text.

STUDY TIP When you can't answer a question, reread the section. The answer is usually there.

Do Your Homework

Your teacher may assign worksheets to help you understand and remember the material in the chapter.

STUDY TIP Don't try to answer the questions without reading the text and reviewing your class notes. A little preparation up front will make your homework assignments a lot easier. Answering the items in the Chapter Review will help prepare you for the chapter test.

Holt Online Learning

Visit Holt Online Learning

If your teacher gives you a special password to log onto the **Holt Online Learning** site, you'll find your complete textbook on the Web. In addition, you'll find some great learning tools and practice quizzes. You'll be able to see how well you know the material from your textbook.

Visit CNN Student News

You'll find up-to-date events in science at **cnnstudentnews.com**.

UNIT 1

Introduction to Earth Science

In this unit, you will start your own investigation of the planet Earth and of the regions of space beyond it. But first you should prepare yourself by learning about the tools and methods used by Earth scientists. As you can imagine, it is not easy to study something as large as the Earth or as far away as Venus. Yet that is what Earth scientists do. The timeline shown here identifies a few of the events that have helped shape our understanding of Earth.

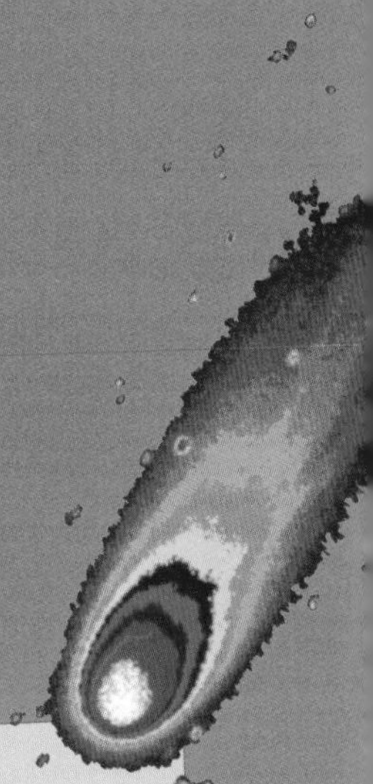

1669
Nicolaus Steno accurately describes the process by which living organisms become fossils.

1758
Halley's comet makes a reappearance, confirming Edmond Halley's 1705 prediction. Unfortunately, the comet reappeared 16 years after his death.

1943
The volcano *Paricutín* grows more than 150 m tall during its first six days of eruption.

1960
The first weather satellite, *Tiros I*, is launched by the United States.

1962
By reaching an altitude of 95 km, the *X-15* becomes the first fixed-wing plane to reach outer space.

1896

The first modern Olympic Games are held in Athens, Greece.

1899

The Rosetta stone is discovered in Egypt. It enables scholars to decipher Egyptian hieroglyphics.

1906

Roald Amundsen determines the position of the magnetic north pole.

1922

Roy Chapman Andrews discovers fossilized dinosaur eggs in the Gobi Desert. They are the first such eggs to be found.

1997

China begins construction of Three Gorges Dam, the world's largest dam. Designed to control the Yangtze River, the dam will supply 84 billion kilowatt-hours of hydroelectric power per year.

1970

The United States holds its first Earth Day on April 22. More than 20 million people participate in peaceful demonstrations to show their concern for the environment.

1990

The Hubble Space Telescope is launched into orbit. Three years later, faulty optics are repaired during a space walk.

Pre-Reading
Questions

1. What are scientific
   methods?
2. What is a model, and
   what are the limitations
   of models?
3. What tools are used to
   measure mass and volume?

WHAT IS THAT?

Did you ask this question when you first saw the image
on this page? This image shows what scientists think some
living things on Earth looked like over 540 million years
ago! Remains of living things found in rocks, such as the
one shown at right, help scientists find answers to their
questions about what an organism might have looked
like. In this chapter, you will learn about science. You
will also learn about the process used to help answer
questions such as, What IS that?

These are thought to be the remains of one of the first large multicellular living things on Earth!

MISSION IMPOSSIBLE?

In this activity, you will do some creative thinking to solve what might seem like an impossible problem.

Procedure

1. Examine an **index card.** Take note of its size and shape. Your mission is to fit yourself through the card.

2. Brainstorm with a partner about ways to complete your mission. Keep the following rules in mind: You can only tear and fold the card. You cannot use tape, glue, or anything else to hold the card together.

3. When you and your partner have a plan, write your procedure in your ScienceLog.

4. Test your plan. Did it work? If necessary, get another index card and try again. Record your new plan and results in your ScienceLog.

5. Share your plans and results with other groups in your class.

Analysis

6. Why was it helpful to come up with a plan in advance?

7. How did testing your plan help you complete your mission?

8. How did sharing your ideas with your classmates help you complete your mission? What did your classmates do differently?

The World of Earth Science   **5**

Branches of Earth Science

Planet Earth! How can anyone study something as large and complicated as our planet? One way is to divide the study of Earth into smaller areas of study. The most common areas of study are *geology, oceanography,* and *meteorology.* However, Earth science does not stop at our planet. *Astronomy* is the study of all physical things beyond planet Earth. Let's take a look at each of these four sciences and at some of the people who work within them.

Geology—Science that Rocks

Geology is the study of the solid Earth. Anything and everything that has to do with the solid Earth is part of geology. Most geologists specialize in a particular aspect of the Earth.

Would you like to put on an insulated suit and walk to the edge of a 1,000°C pool of lava? If so, you could be a *volcanologist,* a geologist who studies volcanoes. Are earthquakes more to your liking? Then you could be a *seismologist,* a geologist who studies earthquakes. How about digging up dinosaurs? You could be a *paleontologist,* a geologist who studies fossils. These are only a few of the careers you could have as a geologist.

Specialized Exploration Some geologists become highly specialized. For instance, geologist Robert Fronk, at the Florida Institute of Technology, explores the subsurface of Earth by scuba-diving in underwater caves in Florida and the Bahamas. Underwater caves often contain evidence that sea level was once much lower than it is now. They contain *stalagmites* and *stalactites,* as shown in **Figure 1.** These formations develop from minerals in dripping water in air-filled caves. When Fronk sees these kinds of geologic formations in underwater caves, he knows that the caves were once above sea level.

Figure 1 *Stalagmites grow upward from the floors of caves, and stalactites grow downward from the ceilings of caves.*

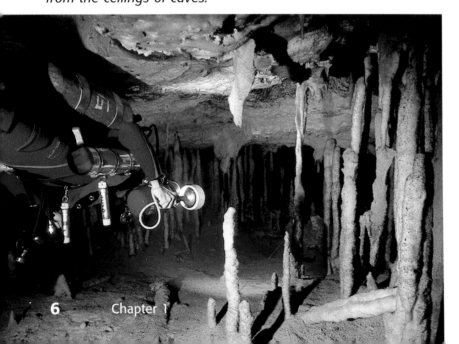

Oceanography—Water, Water Everywhere

Oceanography, which is the study of the ocean, is often divided into special areas. Physical oceanographers study things like waves and ocean currents. Biological oceanographers study the plants and animals that live in the ocean. Geological oceanographers study the ocean floor. Chemical oceanographers study natural chemicals and chemicals from pollution in the ocean.

Not long ago, people studied the ocean only from the surface. But as technology has advanced, scientists have worked with engineers to build miniature research submarines. Now oceanographers can go practically anywhere in the oceans. Below, oceanographer John Trefry talks about a trip he took in the minisub *Alvin*.

QuickLab

How Hot Is 300°C?

1. Use a **thermometer** to measure the air's temperature in the room in degrees Celsius. Record your reading.

2. Hold the thermometer near a **heat source** in the room, such as a light bulb or a heating vent. Be careful not to burn yourself. Record your reading.

3. How do the temperatures you recorded compare with the 300°C temperature of the water from a black smoker?

"We move through the darkness of the Pacific Ocean at a depth of almost one and a half miles with the lights of the submersible shining on the glassy black rock that is new ocean crust. Then, in a magic moment, we can peer ahead through a small porthole at a 300°C black smoker surrounded by an oasis of beautiful and exotic life-forms. The feeling of exhilaration inspires renewed wonderment and makes the many years of study in oceanography seem so satisfying and worthwhile."

Exploring the Ocean Floor Trefry and other oceanographers have discovered the world of the black smokers. *Black smokers* are rock chimneys on the ocean floor that spew black clouds of minerals. Black smokers are a type of *hydrothermal vent,* which is a crack in the ocean floor that releases very hot water from beneath the Earth's surface. The minerals and hot water from these vents support a biological community that includes blood-red tube worms that are 3.5 m long, clams that are 30 cm in diameter, and blind white crabs.

Figure 2 *This satellite photo traces Hurricane Andrew's path from the Atlantic Ocean (right) to the Gulf of Mexico (left).*

Figure 3 *These meteorologists are risking their lives to gather data about tornadoes.*

Meteorology—It's a Gas!

The study of the entire atmosphere is called **meteorology.** When you ask, "Is it going to rain today?" you are asking a meteorological question. One of the most common careers in meteorology is weather forecasting. Sometimes knowing what the weather is going to be like makes our lives more comfortable. And occasionally our lives depend on these forecasts.

Hurricanes In 1928, a major hurricane hit Florida and killed 1,836 people. In comparison, a hurricane of similar strength—Hurricane Andrew, shown in **Figure 2**—hit Florida in 1992, killing only 48 people. Why were there far fewer deaths in 1992? Two major reasons were hurricane tracking and weather forecasting.

Meteorologists began tracking Hurricane Andrew on Monday, August 17. By the following Sunday morning, most South Floridians had left the coast because the National Hurricane Center had warned them that Andrew was headed their way. Hurricane Andrew hit southern Florida early on Monday morning, August 24. The hurricane caused a lot of damage, but it killed very few people thanks to meteorologists' warnings.

Tornadoes Another dangerous weather element is the tornado. An average of 780 tornadoes touch down each year in the United States. What do you think about a meteorologist who chases tornadoes as a career? Howard Bluestein does just that. Bluestein predicts where tornadoes are likely to form and then drives to within a couple of kilometers of the site to gather data, as shown in **Figure 3.** By gathering data this way, scientists like Bluestein hope to understand tornadoes better. The better they understand them, the better they can predict how these violent storms will behave.

Astronomy—Far, Far Away

How do you study things that are far away in space? That's a question that astronomers can answer. **Astronomy** is the study of all physical things beyond Earth. Astronomers study stars, asteroids, planets, and everything else in space.

Because most things in space are too far away to sense directly, astronomers depend on technology to help them study objects in space. Optical telescopes have been used for hundreds of years—Galileo built one in 1609. Astronomers still use optical telescopes to look into space, but they also use other types of telescopes. For example, the radio telescopes shown in **Figure 4** allow astronomers to study objects that are too far away to be seen using optical telescopes or that do not give off visible light.

Figure 4 *These radio telescopes receive radio waves from space.*

Star Struck Astronomers spend much of their time studying stars. Astronomers estimate that there are 100 billion billion stars in the sky. That's a lot of stars! Try the MathBreak at right to get an idea of how many stars there are. The most familiar star in the universe is the sun, which is the closest star to Earth. Astronomers have studied the sun more than any other star. Astronomers have also studied planets that are close to Earth. **Figure 5** illustrates the sun, the Earth, and some nearby planets. Can you name these planets?

Figure 5 *Astronomers have spent more time studying objects near Earth than objects that are farther away in space.*

Lots of Zeros!

Astronomers estimate that there are more than 100 billion billion stars in the sky! One billion written out in numerals looks like this:

1,000,000,000

1. How many zeros do you need in order to write 100 billion billion in numerals? To find out, multiply 1 billion by 1 billion, then multiply your answer by 100. Count the zeros in the final answer.
2. Now time how long it takes you to count to 100. How long would it take you to count to 100 a billion billion times?

Special Branches of Earth Science

In addition to the main branches of Earth science, there are branches that depend more heavily on other areas of science. Earth scientists often find themselves in careers that rely on life science, chemistry, physics, and many other areas of science. Let's take a look at some Earth science careers with strong ties to other sciences.

Ecology   It is difficult to understand the behavior of certain organisms without studying the relationships between these organisms and their surroundings. Ecologists study ecosystems, like the one in **Figure 6.** An **ecosystem** is a community of organisms and their nonliving environment. The principles of ecology are useful in many related fields, such as wildlife management, agriculture, forestry, and conservation. The science of ecology requires people trained in many disciplines, such as biology, geology, chemistry, climatology, mathematics, and computer technology.

Geochemistry   As the name implies, geochemistry combines the studies of geology and chemistry. Geochemists, like the one in **Figure 7,** specialize in the chemistry of rocks, minerals, and soil. They study the chemistry of these materials to determine their economic value, interpret what the environment was like when they formed, and learn what has happened to them since they first formed.

Figure 6 *Because beavers spend time in water as well as on land, they share their ecosystem with many plants and other animals.*

Is there water on Mars? Turn to page 31 to see how one geophysicist is finding out.

Figure 7 *This geochemist is taking rock samples from the field so she can perform chemical analyses of them in her laboratory.*

Environmental Science Humans have recently begun to examine their relationship with their surroundings, or *environment,* more closely. The study of how humans interact with the environment is called *environmental science.* As shown in **Figure 8,** one common task of an environmental scientist is trying to find out whether humans are damaging the environment. Pollution of the air, water, and land can harm natural resources, such as wildlife, drinking water, and soil. Environmental science, which relies on life science, chemistry, physics, and geology, is helping us to preserve Earth's resources and to use them more wisely.

Figure 8 *This environmental scientist is testing the effects of industry on the environment.*

Geography and Cartography Geographers, who are educated in geology, life science, and physics, study the surface features of the Earth. Cartographers make maps of those features. Have you ever wondered why our cities are located where they are? Often, the location of a city is determined by geography. Many cities, such as the one in **Figure 9,** were built near rivers, lakes, or oceans because boats were used for transporting people and items of trade. Rivers and lakes also provide communities with plenty of water for drinking and for raising crops and animals. We make maps to record the geography of our world. Maps help us keep track of natural resources and navigate the surface of the Earth.

Figure 9 *The easily accessible Mississippi River helped St. Louis become the large city it is today.*

REVIEW

1. List three major branches of Earth Science.

2. Name two branches of Earth science that rely heavily on other areas of science. Explain how the branches rely on the other areas of science.

3. List and describe three Earth-science careers.

4. **Inferring Relationships** If you were a *hydrogeologist,* what kind of work would you do?

internetconnect

*SCi*LINKS.
NSTA

TOPIC: Branches of Earth Science
GO TO: www.scilinks.org
*sci*LINKS NUMBER: HSTE005

What You'll Do

◆ Explain the scientific method and how scientists use it.
◆ Apply the scientific method to an Earth science investigation.
◆ Identify the importance of communicating the results of a scientific investigation.
◆ Describe how scientific investigations often lead to new investigations.

The Scientific Method in Earth Science

Imagine that you are standing in a thick forest on the bank of a river. The sun is shining through the needles of the trees. Insects are buzzing, but no birds are flying because they don't yet exist. It is the Jurassic period, 150 million years ago.

Wading in the shallow water, several long-necked dinosaurs quietly munch on vegetation. As you peer through the trees, you spot a different type of dinosaur on the prowl for prey. It is an allosaur, the most common meat-eating predator of this time.

Suddenly you feel the ground begin to shake. You begin to hear a booming noise that accompanies the tremors. The allosaur stops and looks in the direction of the sound. The booming gets louder, and the tremors get stronger.

Suddenly you notice a creature's head looming over the treetops. The creature's head is so high that its neck must be 20 m long! Then the entire animal comes into view. You understand why the ground is shaking. The animal is *Seismosaurus hallorum* (SEIZ moh SAWR uhs hah LOHR uhm), the "earth shaker." You are looking at one of the largest dinosaurs known.

Seismosaurus hallorum

The scene you just witnessed is not based on imagination alone. Scientists have been studying dinosaurs for years. From the bits and pieces of information they gather about dinosaurs and their environment, scientists re-create what the Earth might have been like 150 million years ago. But how do scientists tell one dinosaur species from another? How do they know if they have discovered a new species? The answers to these questions are related to the methods that scientists use.

Steps of the Scientific Method

When scientists make observations about the natural world, they are often presented with a question or problem. But scientists don't just throw out random answers. Instead, they follow a series of steps called the *scientific method*. The **scientific method** is a series of steps that scientists use to answer questions and solve problems. The most basic steps are illustrated in **Figure 10.**

Although the scientific method has several distinct steps, it is not a rigid procedure. Scientists may use all of the steps or just some of the steps of the scientific method. They may even repeat some of the steps or do them in a different order. The goal of the scientific method is to come up with reliable answers and solutions. As long as scientists use the scientific method effectively, the overall result is the same—they gain more insight into the problems they investigate.

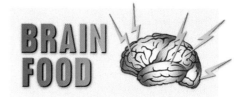

BRAIN FOOD

Several species of dinosaurs are claimed to be the largest known. So which is the largest? Good scientists look carefully at the information available and judge for themselves.

Figure 10 *The scientific method is illustrated in this flowchart. Notice that there are several ways to follow the paths.*

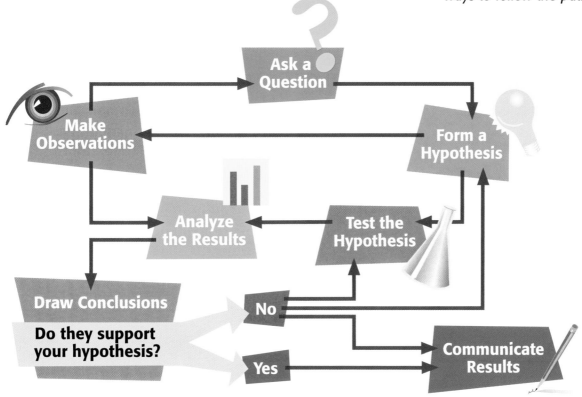

Dino Discovery—A Case for the Scientific Method

One of the first things a scientist does, even before starting an investigation, is make observations. An **observation** is any use of the senses to gather information. Observations are made throughout scientific investigations.

Remember the hikers at the beginning of this chapter and their discovery of dinosaur bones in the desert? Those hikers may have been the first to examine the bones, but they weren't the last. In May 1985, paleontologist David D. Gillette visited the site and began to wonder what type of dinosaur these huge bones came from. This started him on the path to using the scientific method.

Ask a Question

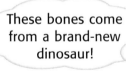

What kind of dinosaur do these bones come from?

Ask a question that needs a scientific answer.

Ask a Question When scientists make observations, they often have questions that they would like answered. Gillette may have asked, "What type of dinosaur did these bones come from?" Gillette knew that in order to answer this question, he would have to use the scientific method. So Gillette moved to the next step.

Form a Hypothesis

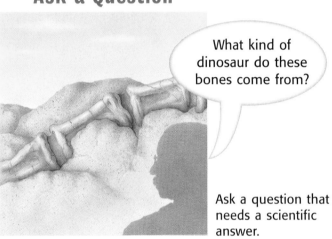

These bones come from a brand-new dinosaur!

Propose a possible answer to the question.

Form a Hypothesis When scientists want to investigate a question, they form a *hypothesis*. A **hypothesis** is a possible explanation or answer to the question. Sometimes called an *educated guess,* the hypothesis represents a scientist's best answer to the question. But it can't be just any answer. It has to be a testable explanation.

Based on his observations and on what he already knew, Gillette formed a hypothesis—the bones came from a type of dinosaur unknown to science. This was Gillette's best testable explanation of what type of dinosaur the fossil bones came from. If correct, it would answer his question. To test his hypothesis, Gillette would have to do a lot of research.

Making Hypotheses

Scientists exploring the Texas Gulf Coast have discovered American Indian artifacts that are thousands of years old. The odd thing about it is that the artifacts were buried in the sea floor several meters below sea level. These artifacts were in-place, meaning that they had not been moved since they were originally buried. The *observation* is that there are American Indian artifacts several meters below sea level, and the *question* is, "Why are they there?" Your job is to *form a hypothesis* that answers this question. Remember, your hypothesis must be stated in such a way that it can be tested using the scientific method.

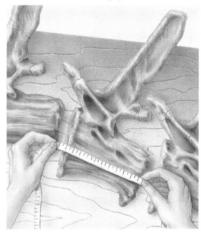

Test the Hypothesis Once a hypothesis is established, it must be tested. Scientists test hypotheses by gathering data that can help determine whether the hypotheses are valid or not. Often a scientist will run experiments to test a hypothesis.

To test a hypothesis, a scientist may conduct a controlled experiment. *A controlled experiment* is an experiment that tests only one factor at a time. By changing only one factor (the *variable*), scientists can see the results of just that one change. Earth scientists, however, usually rely more heavily on observations to test their hypotheses. Instead of trying to control nature, Earth scientists more often observe nature and collect large amounts of data to test their hypotheses.

To test his hypothesis, Gillette took hundreds of measurements of the bones and compared his measurements with those of bones from known dinosaurs. He visited museums and talked with other paleontologists. His testing took more than a year to complete.

Analyze the Results Once scientists finish their tests, they must analyze the results. In this step, scientists often create tables and graphs to organize their data. When Gillette analyzed the results of the bone comparisons, he found that the bones of the mystery dinosaur were either too large or shaped too differently to have belonged to any of the dinosaurs he used for comparison.

Test the Hypothesis

Test the hypothesis with observations or experiments.

Analyze the Results

The new bones don't match any others known.

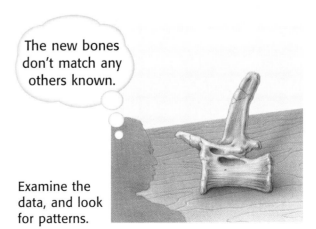

Examine the data, and look for patterns.

Draw Conclusions

This *is* a brand-new kind of dinosaur.

Seismosaurus hallorum

Decide if the original hypothesis is supported.

Draw Conclusions Finally, after carefully analyzing the results of their tests, scientists must draw conclusions. Scientists must conclude whether the results supported the hypothesis. If the hypothesis was not supported, scientists may repeat the investigation to check for errors. Or they may ask new questions and form a new hypothesis.

Based on all his analyses, Gillette concluded that the eight bones found in New Mexico were indeed from a newly discovered dinosaur species that was probably 45 m long and weighed at least 100 tons. The creature certainly fit the name Gillette gave it—*Seismosaurus hallorum*, the "earth shaker."

Communicate Results

I'd like to introduce *Seismosaurus*!

Share your discoveries with other scientists.

Communicate Results Upon completing an investigation, scientists communicate their results. In this way, scientists share what they have learned with other scientists, who may want to repeat the investigation to see if they get the same results. Science depends on the sharing of information.

Scientists share information by publishing reports in scientific journals. Scientists also give lectures on the results of their scientific investigations at professional meetings.

Gillette announced his discovery of *Seismosaurus* at a press conference at the New Mexico Museum of Natural History and Science. He later submitted a report to the *Journal of Vertebrate Paleontology* that summarized his investigation.

Figure 11 *This reconstruction of the skeleton of* Seismosaurus hallorum *is based on Gillette's research. The bones shown in the darker color are those that have so far been identified.*

2 m

Case Closed?

All of the *Seismosaurus* bones that Gillette found have been dug up, but the *Seismosaurus* project continues in a laboratory phase as the remains of one of the largest dinosaurs ever discovered are still being studied. Like so many other scientific investigations, Gillette's work led to new problems to be explored using the scientific method.

To try your hand at using the scientific method, turn to page 630 in the LabBook.

Figure 12 *David Gillette continues to study the bones of* Seismosaurus *for new insights into the past.*

REVIEW

1. What is the scientific method? How do scientists use it?

2. After observing eight tailbones, Gillette hypothesized that they were from a newly discovered dinosaur species. What was his hypothesis based on?

3. Why do scientists communicate the results of their investigations?

4. **Applying Concepts** Why might two scientists develop different hypotheses based on the same observations?

internetconnect

SC*LINKS*
NSTA

TOPIC: The Scientific Method
GO TO: www.scilinks.org
*sci*LINKS NUMBER: HSTE004

What You'll Do

◆ Demonstrate how models are used in science.
◆ Compare mathematical models with physical models.
◆ Determine limitations of models.

Life in a Warmer World— An Earth Science Model

There has been a lot of talk lately about changes in Earth's climate. Some people think the world is getting dangerously warm; others say it is only a natural cycle. But what would happen if Earth's average surface-air temperature rose only a few degrees? Look at **Figure 13;** the answers might surprise you.

A worldwide increase in temperature is called **global warming.** Is global warming really happening? What would cause global warming? To answer these questions, many scientists are studying the concept of global warming. One way they study global warming is by making a model of it.

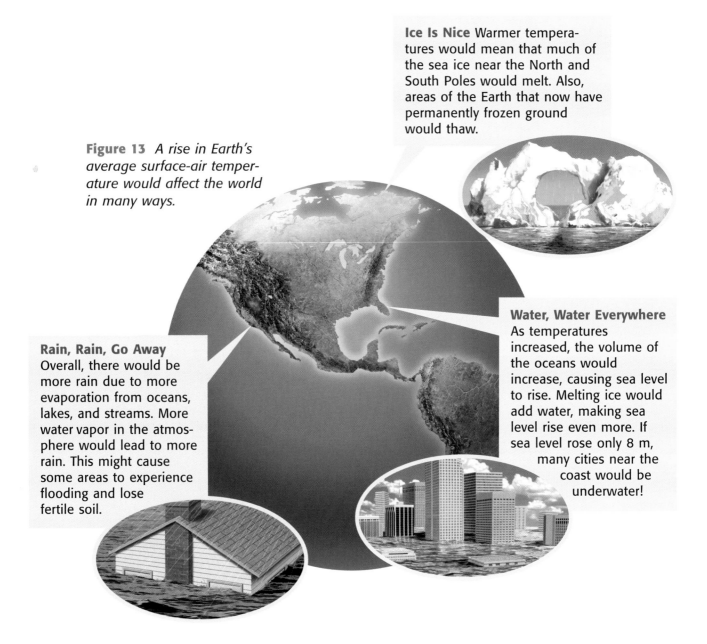

Ice Is Nice Warmer temperatures would mean that much of the sea ice near the North and South Poles would melt. Also, areas of the Earth that now have permanently frozen ground would thaw.

Figure 13 *A rise in Earth's average surface-air temperature would affect the world in many ways.*

Rain, Rain, Go Away Overall, there would be more rain due to more evaporation from oceans, lakes, and streams. More water vapor in the atmosphere would lead to more rain. This might cause some areas to experience flooding and lose fertile soil.

Water, Water Everywhere As temperatures increased, the volume of the oceans would increase, causing sea level to rise. Melting ice would add water, making sea level rise even more. If sea level rose only 8 m, many cities near the coast would be underwater!

Types of Scientific Models

You are probably familiar with many types of models—models of ships, cars, planes, buildings, and other objects. **Models** are representations of objects or systems. Models are used to represent things that are too small to see, such as atoms, or too large to completely see, like the Earth or the solar system. Models can also be used to explain the past and present as well as to predict the future. Scientific models come in three major types.

Physical Models Physical models are models that you can touch. Model airplanes, car kits, and dolls are all physical models. Physical models should look and act just like the real thing. For example, engineers put very accurate models of new airplanes in wind tunnels, as shown in **Figure 14,** to see how aerodynamic they are. It is safer and less expensive to discover problems with models than with real planes.

Figure 14 *Models of airplanes are tested in models of wind, as shown here by a prototype jet inside a wind tunnel.*

Mathematical Models Every day, people try to predict the weather. One way they do this is by using mathematical models. A mathematical model is made up of mathematical equations and data. Some mathematical models are so complex that only supercomputers can handle them. These models are complicated, but then so is trying to predict the weather!

Conceptual Models The third type of model is a conceptual model, or system of ideas. These take the form of theories. A **theory** is a unifying explanation for a broad range of hypotheses and observations that have been supported by testing. Atomic theory and the big bang theory can be thought of as conceptual models. Conceptual models are composed of many hypotheses, each of which has found support through the scientific method.

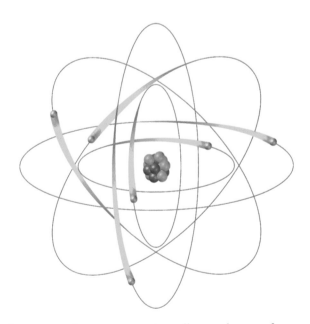

Figure 15 *Atoms are not really made up of tiny colored balls, but using a model like this helps scientists understand atoms.*

The Global-Warming Model

All models have pieces. A model ship, for example, may contain hundreds of pieces that are glued together. Mathematical models also contain pieces. The pieces are numbers representing information that describe real events. The global-warming model is a mathematical model designed to help scientists predict future temperature changes of the Earth's atmosphere. One of the pieces used in the global-warming model is the *greenhouse effect.*

Greenhouse Effect A greenhouse is a building made mostly of glass in which plants are grown. If you have been in a greenhouse, you know that it is usually warmer inside than outside. This is because sunlight not only heats the greenhouse directly after passing through the glass, but the glass also traps thermal energy created by plants and other objects inside the greenhouse. The greenhouse effect, shown in **Figure 16,** works a lot like a greenhouse made of glass.

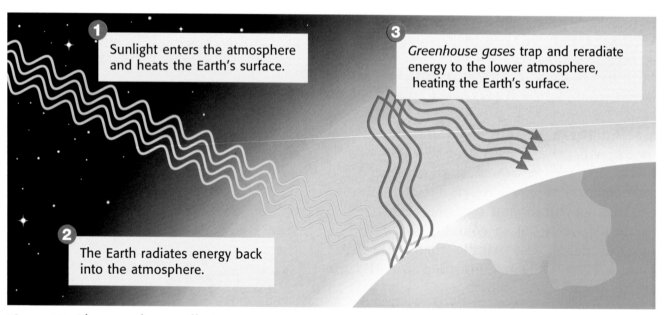

1 Sunlight enters the atmosphere and heats the Earth's surface.

3 *Greenhouse gases* trap and reradiate energy to the lower atmosphere, heating the Earth's surface.

2 The Earth radiates energy back into the atmosphere.

Figure 16 *The greenhouse effect is partly responsible for the Earth's moderate temperatures, which are suitable to support life.*

Testing the Global-Warming Model

Models are used to try to explain the present. But how do we know if models are accurate? Physical, mathematical, and conceptual models can be tested. For instance, we can compare the model of a car with the real car. Similarly, we can compare a prediction of Earth's temperature changes made by a global-warming model generated by a computer with Earth's actual temperature changes. If the model can accurately explain the present, then we can be more confident that the model will be able to accurately predict the future.

Scientists have estimated the amount of carbon dioxide that has been added to the atmosphere over the last 100 years. The model should therefore be able to predict how much warmer the atmosphere is today than it was 100 years ago. Most global-warming models tell us that overall temperature change due to increased greenhouse gases during the last 100 years should be between 0.5°C and 1.5°C. Now comes the test: How much global warming has actually taken place? The answer is 0.5°C. So far so good!

Using the Global-Warming Model

Models are used to predict the future and are good for answering, "What if?"

These are the kinds of questions that many scientists are asking as they enter the new millennium. The global-warming model can give them answers, but will these answers be accurate? The more complicated models are, the more careful scientists must be when using them to make predictions. The global-warming model is extremely complicated, so scientists often use words like *possible* and *probable* when making predictions. The only certain test of this model is the test of time.

REVIEW

1. How might a scientist use a model to test a new airplane design?

2. How are astronomers limited when they design models of the universe?

3. **Analyzing Relationships** Name one advantage of physical models and one advantage of mathematical models.

internet**connect**

SC**i**LINKS
NSTA

TOPIC: Using Models in Earth Science
GO TO: www.scilinks.org
*sci*LINKS NUMBER: HSTE015

What You'll Do

◆ Explain the importance of the International System of Units.
◆ Determine appropriate units to use for particular measurements.
◆ Identify lab safety symbols and determine what they mean.

Measurement and Safety

Hundreds of years ago, different countries used different systems of measurement. At one time in England, the standard for an inch was three grains of barley placed end to end. Other standardized units were based on parts of the body, such as the foot. Such units were not very accurate because they were based on objects that varied in size.

Eventually people recognized that there was a need for a global measurement system that was simple and accurate. In the late 1700s, the French Academy of Sciences set out to develop that system. Over the next 200 years, the metric system, now called the International System of Units (SI), was refined.

Using the SI System

Today most scientists and almost all countries use the International System of Units. One advantage of using SI measurements is that it helps all scientists to share and compare their observations and results. Another advantage of SI is that all units are based on the number 10, which is a number that is easy to use in calculations. The table in **Figure 17** contains the commonly used SI units for length, volume, mass, and temperature.

Figure 17 *Prefixes are used with SI units to convert them to larger or smaller units. The prefix used depends on the size of the object being measured.*

Common SI Units		
Length	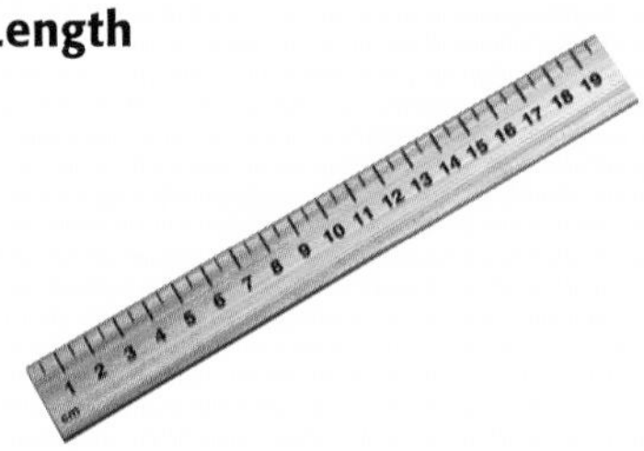 **meter (m)**	
	kilometer (km)	1 km = 1,000 m
	decimeter (dm)	1 dm = 0.1 m
	centimeter (cm)	1 cm = 0.01 m
	millimeter (mm)	1 mm = 0.001 m
	micrometer (μm)	1 μm = 0.000001 m
	nanometer (nm)	1 nm = 0.000 000 001 m
Volume 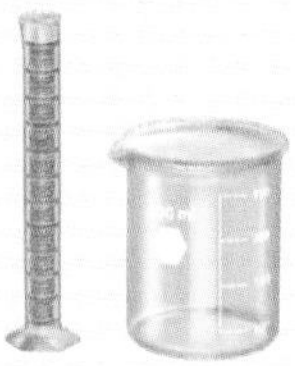	**cubic meter (m³)**	
	cubic centimeter (cm³)	1 cm³ = 0.000 001 m³
	liter (L)	1 L = 1 dm³ = 0.001 m³
	milliliter (mL)	1 mL = 0.001 L = 1 cm³
Mass	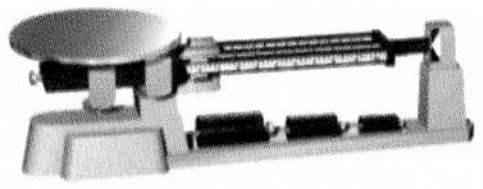 **kilogram (kg)**	
	gram (g)	1 g = 0.001 kg
	milligram (mg)	1 mg = 0.000 001 kg
Temperature	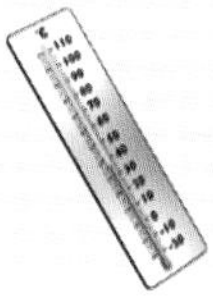 **Kelvin (K)**	
	Celsius (°C)	0°C = 273 K
		100°C = 373 K

Measuring Length How thick is the ice sheet in **Figure 18?** To describe this length, an Earth scientist would probably use meters (m). A **meter** is the basic unit of length in the SI system. A meter is divided or multiplied by powers of 10 to produce the other SI units of length. If you divide 1 m into 100 parts, for example, each part equals 1 cm. In other words, 1 cm is one-hundredth of a meter. Some objects are so tiny that even smaller units must be used. To describe the length of microscopic objects, micrometers (μm) or nanometers (nm) are used. Going the other way, 1,000 m is equal to one kilometer. **Figure 19** shows how the units of length relate to various objects.

Figure 18 *This scientist is measuring the thickness of an ice sheet.*

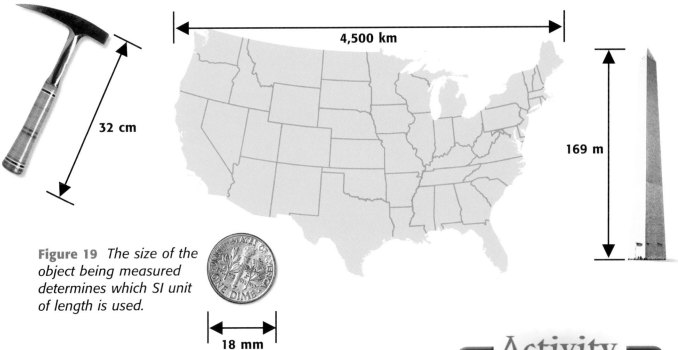

4,500 km

32 cm

169 m

Figure 19 *The size of the object being measured determines which SI unit of length is used.*

18 mm

Measuring Volume Imagine that you're a scientist who needs to move some fossils to a museum. How many fossils will fit into a crate? That depends on the volume of the crate and the volume of each fossil. **Volume** is the amount of space that something occupies, or, as in the case of the crate, the amount of space that something contains.

The volume of a liquid is often given in liters (L). Liters are based on the meter. A cubic meter (m^3) is equal to 1,000 L. In other words, 1,000 L of liquid will fit into a box 1 m on each side. Just like the meter, the liter can be divided into smaller units. A milliliter (mL) is one-thousandth of a liter and is equal to one cubic centimeter (1 cm^3). A microliter (μL) is one-millionth of a liter. Graduated cylinders are used to measure the volume of liquids.

Activity

Measure the width of your desk, but do not use a ruler or a tape measure. Pick an object to use as your unit of measurement. It could be a pencil, your hand, or anything else. Find how many units wide your desk is, and compare your measurement with those of your classmates. In your ScienceLog, explain why it is important to use standard units of measurement.

Figure 20 *The volume of the crate can be calculated by multiplying its length by its width by its height.*

Measuring Volume of Solids The volume of a large solid object is given in cubic meters (m³). The volumes of smaller objects, such as the crate in **Figure 20,** can be given in cubic centimeters (cm³) or cubic millimeters (mm³). To calculate the volume of a box-shaped object, multiply the object's length by its width by its height.

Objects like fossils and rocks have irregular shapes. If you multiplied only their length, width, and height, you would not get a very accurate measure of their volume. One way to determine the volume of an irregularly shaped object is to measure how much liquid the object displaces. The student in **Figure 21** is measuring the volume of a rock by placing it in a graduated cylinder that contains a known quantity of water. The student can find the volume of the rock by subtracting the volume of the water alone from the volume of the water and the rock.

Figure 21 *This graduated cylinder contains 70 mL of water. After the rock was added, the water level moved to 80 mL. Because the rock displaced 10 mL of water, and because 1 mL = 1 cm³, the volume of the rock is 10 cm³.*

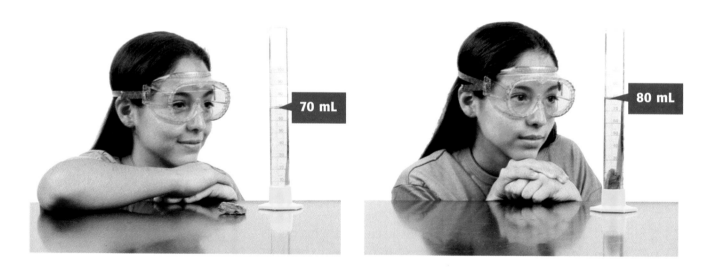

70 mL

80 mL

Mass How large of a boulder can a rushing stream move? That depends on the energy of the stream and the mass of the boulder. **Mass** is the amount of matter that something is made of. The kilogram (kg) is the basic unit for mass and is used to describe the mass of things like boulders. Many common objects are not so large, however. Grams are used to describe the mass of smaller objects, such as an apple. The mass of large objects, such as an elephant, is given in metric tons. A metric ton equals 1,000 kg.

Temperature How hot is a lava flow? To answer this question, an Earth scientist would need to measure the temperature of the lava. **Temperature** is a measure of how hot (or cold) something is. You are probably used to describing temperature with degrees Fahrenheit (°F). Scientists use degrees Celsius (°C) and kelvins, which is the SI unit for temperature. The thermometer at right shows the relationship between °F and °C. Degrees Celsius is the unit you will most often see in this book.

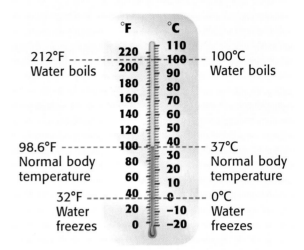

Safety Rules!

Earth science is exciting and fun, but it can also be dangerous. So don't take any chances! Always follow your teacher's instructions, and don't take short-cuts—even when you think there is little or no danger.

Before starting any science investigation, get your teacher's permission and read the lab procedures carefully. Pay particular attention to safety information and caution statements. The table below shows the safety symbols used in this book. Get to know these symbols and what they mean. Do this by reading the safety information starting on page 626. **This is important!** If you are still unsure about what a safety symbol means, ask your teacher.

Stay on the safe side by reading the safety information on page 626. **This is a must before doing any science activity!**

Safety Symbols		
Eye protection	Clothing protection	Hand safety
Heating safety	Electric safety	Sharp object
Chemical safety	Animal safety	Plant safety

REVIEW

1. What are two benefits of using the International System of Units?

2. Which SI unit best describes the volume of gasoline in a car?

3. **Doing Calculations** What is the minimum length and width (in meters) of a box that can contain an object 56 cm wide and 843 mm long?

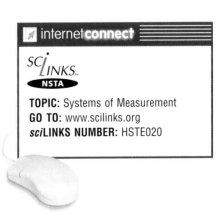

internet**connect**

SC*i*LINKS
NSTA

TOPIC: Systems of Measurement
GO TO: www.scilinks.org
sciLINKS NUMBER: HSTE020

Chapter Highlights

SECTION 1

Vocabulary
> **geology** (p. 6)
> **oceanography** (p. 7)
> **meteorology** (p. 8)
> **astronomy** (p. 9)
> **ecosystem** (p. 10)

Section Notes

- Earth science can be divided into three general categories: geology, oceanography, and meteorology.

- Astronomy is the study of physical things beyond planet Earth.

- Careers in Earth science often require knowledge of more than one science.

SECTION 2

Vocabulary
> **scientific method** (p. 13)
> **observation** (p. 14)
> **hypothesis** (p. 14)

Section Notes

- The scientific method is essential for proper scientific investigation.

- Scientists may use the scientific method differently.

- The discovery of *Seismosaurus hallorum* as a new kind of dinosaur was made using the scientific method.

- When scientists finish investigations, it is important that they communicate the results to other scientists.

Labs
> **Using the Scientific Method** (p. 630)

☑ Skills Check

Math Concepts

CONVERTING SI UNITS Take another look at the SI chart on page 22. The SI units for most categories of measurement, such as length and mass, are all expressed in terms of a single unit. For example, the unit *centimeter* is expressed in terms of the unit *meter*. To write 50 cm in terms of meters, divide 50 by 100 (there are 100 cm in 1 m).

$$50 \text{ cm} \times \frac{1 \text{ m}}{100 \text{ cm}} = 0.5 \text{ m}$$

Visual Understanding

WHICH PATH SHOULD YOU FOLLOW? Review the flowchart on page 13. The scientific method can follow many paths. For example, a scientist may make observations before asking a question or after forming a hypothesis.

Make Observations

SECTION 3

Vocabulary

global warming *(p. 18)*

model *(p. 19)*

theory *(p. 19)*

Section Notes

- Models are used in science to represent physical things and systems.

- Typically, physical models represent objects, and mathematical models represent systems.

- The greenhouse effect is an important part of the global-warming model.

- Scientists use models to explain the past and present as well as to predict the future.

- The only way to measure the accuracy of a model is to compare predictions based on the model with what actually occurs.

SECTION 4

Vocabulary

meter *(p. 23)*

volume *(p. 23)*

mass *(p. 24)*

temperature *(p. 25)*

Section Notes

- The International System of Units (SI) helps all scientists share and compare their work.

- The basic SI units of measurement for length, volume, and mass are the meter, cubic meter, and kilogram, respectively.

The World of Earth Science **27**

Chapter Review

Use the following terms in a sentence to show that you know what they mean:

1. hypothesis, scientific method

2. meteorology, model

3. geology, ecosystem

4. global warming, oceanography

UNDERSTANDING CONCEPTS

Multiple Choice

5. Earth science can be divided into three general categories: meteorology, oceanography, and
   a. geography.
   b. geology.
   c. geochemistry.
   d. ecology.

6. The science that deals with fossils is
   a. paleontology.
   b. ecology.
   c. seismology.
   d. volcanology.

7. Meteorology is the study of
   a. meteors.
   b. meteorites.
   c. the atmosphere.
   d. maps.

8. Gillette's hypothesis was
   a. supported by his results.
   b. not supported by his results.
   c. based only on observations.
   d. based only on what he already knew.

9. Atomic theory is an example of which type of model?
   a. physical
   b. mathematical
   c. conceptual
   d. global warming

10. According to global warming models, the average temperature of Earth's atmosphere has risen about
    a. 10°C.   c. 1°C.
    b. 5°C.   d. 0.5°C.

11. The greenhouse effect is used to explain
    a. volcanoes.
    b. earthquakes.
    c. fossilization.
    d. global warming.

12. Global warming would cause
    a. some polar ice to melt.
    b. more rain.
    c. overall rise in sea level.
    d. All of the above

13. An ecosystem can include
    a. plants and animals.
    b. weather and climate.
    c. humans.
    d. All of the above

Short Answer

14. How did Gillette determine that the dinosaur he found was new to science?

15. How and why do scientists use models?

16. Why is the temperature inside a greenhouse usually warmer than the temperature outside?

Concept Mapping

17. Use the following terms to create a concept map: Earth science, model, the scientific method, geology, hypothesis, meteorology, oceanography, observation, International System of Units.

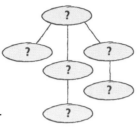

CRITICAL THINKING AND PROBLEM SOLVING

Write one or two sentences to answer the following questions:

18. A rock that contains fossil seashells might be studied by scientists in at least two branches of Earth science. Name those branches. Why did you choose those two?

19. Why might two scientists working on the same problem draw different conclusions?

20. The scientific method often begins with observation. How does observation limit what scientists can study?

21. Why are scientists so careful about making predictions from certain models, such as a global-warming model?

MATH IN SCIENCE

22. Scientists often use scientific laws when constructing models. According to Boyle's law, if you increase the pressure outside a balloon at a constant temperature, the balloon will get smaller. This law is expressed as the following formula:

$$P_1 \times V_1 = P_2 \times V_2$$

If the pressure on a balloon (P_1) is one atmosphere (1 atm) and the volume of air in the balloon (V_1) is one liter (1 L), what will the volume be (in liters) if the pressure is increased to 3 atm?

INTERPRETING GRAPHICS

Examine the graph below, and answer the questions that follow.

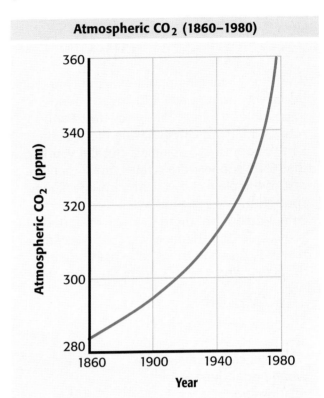

Atmospheric CO₂ (1860–1980)

23. Has the amount of CO_2 in the atmosphere increased or decreased since 1860?

24. The line on the graph is curved. What does this mean?

25. Was the rate of change in the level of CO_2 between 1940 and 1960 higher or lower than it was between 1880 and 1900? How can you tell?

Reading Check-up

Take a minute to review your answers to the Pre-Reading Questions found at the bottom of page 4. Have your answers changed? If necessary, revise your answers based on what you have learned since you began this chapter.

All the Earth's a Magnet

If you were standing on the equator, you would be moving around at 1,670 km/h. Sound impossible? It's true. That's how fast Earth rotates on its axis. Deep inside the planet, Earth's core is also spinning. But did you know that Earth's inner core rotates *faster* than the rest of the planet? If you stood in the same spot on the equator for a year, Earth's inner core would travel more than 20 km farther than you would! But the inner core is 5,150 km below Earth's surface. What makes scientists think they know what's going on down there?

The Core of the Matter

Scientists start looking for answers by asking questions. For instance, scientists have wondered if there is some relationship between Earth's core and Earth's magnetic field. To build their hypothesis, scientists started with what they knew: Earth has a dense, solid inner core and a molten outer core. They then created a computer model to simulate how Earth's magnetic field is generated. The model predicted that Earth's inner core spins in the same direction as the rest of the Earth but slightly faster than the surface. If that theory is correct, it might explain how Earth's magnetic field is generated. But how could the researchers test the theory?

Because scientists couldn't drill down to the core, they had to get their information indirectly. They decided to track seismic waves created by earthquakes.

Upper mantle
Crust
Lower mantle
Outer core
Inner core

Catch the Waves

Scientists analyzed 30 years' worth of earthquake seismic data. They knew that seismic waves traveling through the inner core along a north-south path travel faster than waves passing through it along an east-west line. Scientists searched seismic data records to see if the orientation of the "fast path" for seismic waves changed over time. They found that in the last 30 years, the direction of the "fast path" for seismic waves had indeed shifted. This is strong evidence that Earth's core does travel faster than the surface, and it strengthens the theory that the spinning core creates Earth's magnetic field.

Now That We Know . . .

This discovery will lead to more research into how Earth's magnetic field changes and how the north and south poles "wander" and even occasionally reverse. The new information may also lead to a better understanding of the role that heat plays in moving tectonic plates on Earth's surface.

Write About It

▶ Imagine what would happen if the magnetic poles were suddenly reversed or if magnetism disappeared completely. How would you be affected personally? How would it affect our civilization? Write a funny story describing a world with no magnetism.

CAREERS

GEOPHYSICIST

Bob Grimm is looking for water on Mars. Grimm is a geophysicist, a scientist who uses the science of physics to study Earth, its structure, and its atmosphere. Some geophysicists try to answer questions about the origin and history of Earth, while others use their knowledge of Earth to answer questions about other planets. One of those questions is whether there is water on Mars.

It isn't likely that humans will be living on Mars anytime soon, so why try to find water there? Bob Grimm explains the importance of his work this way: "The search for water on Mars really is the search for life. Are there microorganisms, algae, or other primitive life-forms beneath the surface? By finding liquid water, we will know where to look for life."

Probing Mars

Grimm isn't going to Mars in person. Instead, he and others are developing instruments to send to Mars to try to locate water beneath that planet's surface. These instruments work by reading patterns of electromagnetic waves reflected by formations beneath the surface. When electromagnetic waves hit something under the surface that conducts electricity, the pattern of the waves changes. By looking at the patterns in the waves as they are reflected back to the equipment, Grimm and others will be able to "see" what lies beneath Mars's surface. If there is underground water on Mars, it should show up as a change in the wave patterns.

Meanwhile, Back on Earth

The same procedures Grimm is using to find water on Mars can be used to locate objects, such as land mines, buried beneath the ground here on Earth. Standard metal detectors are useful, but they can't tell the difference between a mine and a piece of scrap metal. Along with electromagnetic pulses, Grimm uses imaging technologies similar to medical scanners to create images of objects buried beneath the ground. Once their location is pinpointed, mines can be safely removed or detonated.

An Interesting Career

Being a geophysicist has been rewarding for Grimm. "The sense of exploration really appeals to me," he explains. "It's like a hunt—I try to figure something out to bring some relationships together, and soon I have a story to tell!"

Think It Over

▶ Think of ways to locate objects buried more than 2 m below the surface. Could you use sound, light, X rays, or something else? What problems would you have to solve to make a useful detector to send to Mars?

▲ *The surface of Mars*

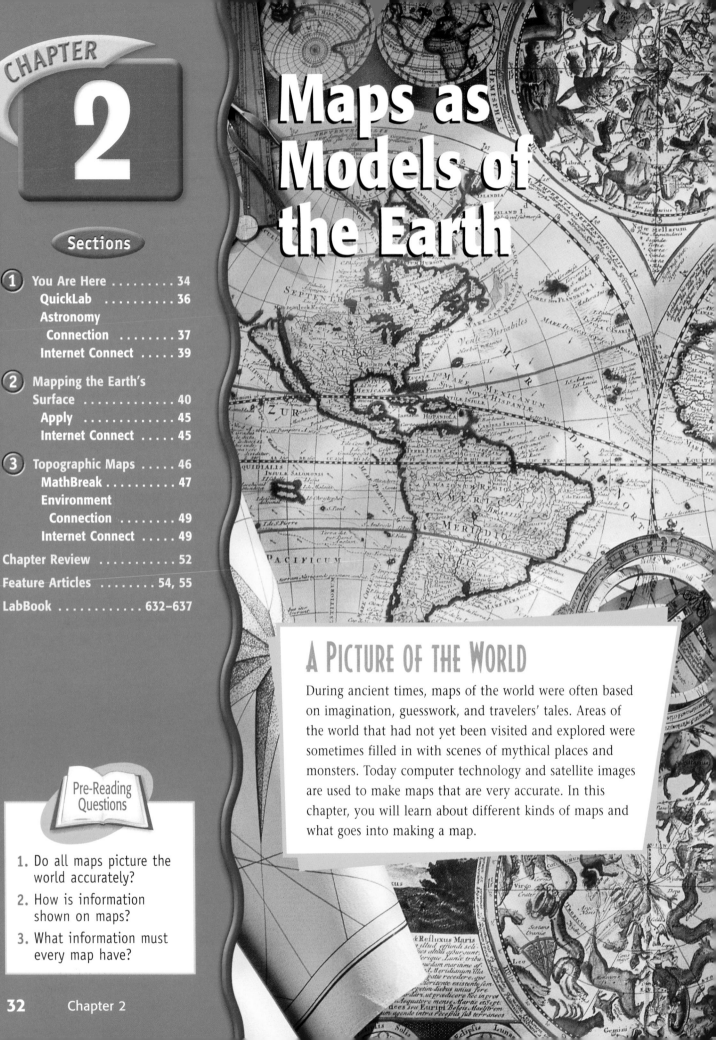

CHAPTER 2

Maps as Models of the Earth

Pre-Reading Questions

1. Do all maps picture the world accurately?

2. How is information shown on maps?

3. What information must every map have?

A Picture of the World

During ancient times, maps of the world were often based on imagination, guesswork, and travelers' tales. Areas of the world that had not yet been visited and explored were sometimes filled in with scenes of mythical places and monsters. Today computer technology and satellite images are used to make maps that are very accurate. In this chapter, you will learn about different kinds of maps and what goes into making a map.

Activity

FOLLOW THE YELLOW BRICK ROAD

In this activity, you not only will learn how to read a map but also make a map that someone else can read.

Procedure

1. With a **computer drawing program** or **colored pencils** and **paper,** draw a map showing how to get from your classroom to another place in your school, such as the gym. Make sure you include enough information for someone unfamiliar with your school to find his or her way.

2. After you finish drawing your map, switch maps with a partner. Examine your classmate's map, and try to figure out where the map is leading you.

Analysis

3. Is your map an accurate picture of your school? Explain your answer.

4. How do you think your map could be made better? What are some limitations of your map?

5. Compare your map with your partner's map. How are your maps alike? How are they different?

You Are Here

When you walk across the Earth's surface, the Earth does not appear to be curved. It looks flat. In the past, beliefs about the Earth's shape changed. Maps reflected the time's knowledge and views of the world as well as the current technology. A **map** is a model or representation of the Earth's surface. If you look at Ptolemy's world map from the second century, as shown in **Figure 1,** you probably will not recognize what you are looking at. Today satellites in space provide us with true images of what the Earth looks like. In this section you will learn how early scientists knew the Earth was round long before pictures from space were taken. You will also learn how to determine location and direction on the Earth's surface.

What Does the Earth Really Look Like?

The Greeks thought of the Earth as a sphere almost 2,000 years before Christopher Columbus made his voyage in 1492. The observation that a ship sinks below the horizon as it sails into the distance supported the idea of a round Earth. If the Earth were flat the ship would appear smaller as it moved away.

Figure 1 *This map shows what people thought the world looked like 1,800 years ago.*

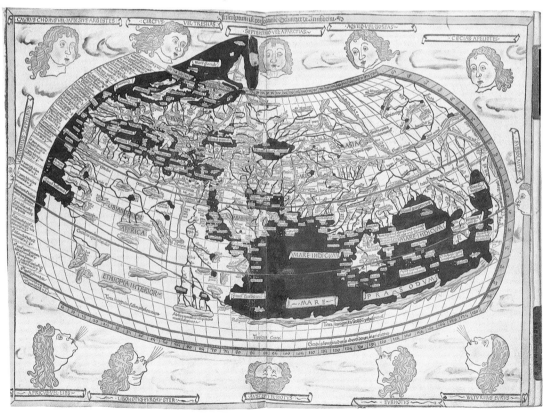

Eratosthenes (ER uh TAHS thuh NEEZ), a Greek mathematician, wanted to know how big the Earth was. In about 240 B.C., he calculated the Earth's circumference using geometry and observations of the sun. We now know his estimation was off by only 6,250 km, an error of 15 percent. That's not bad for someone who lived more than 2,000 years ago, in a time when computer and satellite technology did not exist!

Finding Direction on Earth

How would you give a friend from school directions to your home? You might mention a landmark, such as a grocery store or a restaurant, as a reference point. A *reference point* is a fixed place on the Earth's surface from which direction and location can be described.

Because the Earth is round, it has no top, bottom, or sides for people to use as reference points for determining locations on its surface. The Earth does, however, turn on its axis. The Earth's axis is an imaginary line that runs through the Earth. At either end of the axis is a geographic pole. The North and South Poles, as shown in **Figure 2,** are used as reference points when describing direction and location on Earth.

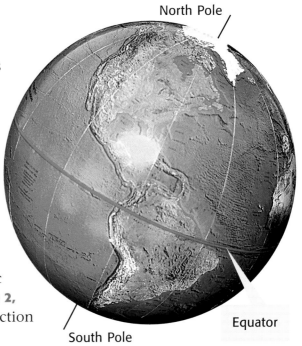

Figure 2 *Like the poles, the equator can be used as a reference.*

Cardinal Directions North, south, east, and west are called *cardinal directions*. **Figure 3** shows these basic cardinal directions and various combinations of these directions. Using these directions is much more precise than using directions such as turn left, go straight, and turn right. Unfortunately for most of us, using cardinal directions requires the use of a compass.

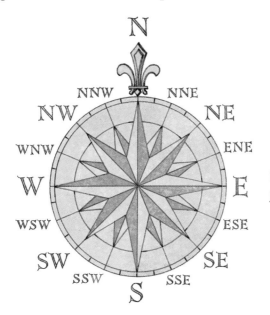

Figure 3 *A compass rose helps you orient yourself on a map.*

Quick Lab

Finding Directions with a Compass

1. This lab should be done outside. Hold a **compass** flat in your hand until the needle stops moving. Rotate the dial of the compass until the letter *N* on the case lines up with the painted or colored end of the needle.

2. While holding the compass steady, identify objects that line up with each of the cardinal points. List them in your ScienceLog.

3. See if you can locate objects at the various combinations of cardinal directions, such as SW and NE. Record your observations in your ScienceLog.

TRY at HOME

It's better than a scavenger hunt! Interested? Turn to page 634 of your LabBook.

Using a Compass One way to determine north is by using a magnetic compass. The compass uses the natural magnetism of the Earth to indicate direction. A compass needle points to the magnetic north pole. The Earth has two different sets of poles—the geographic poles and the magnetic poles. As you can see in **Figure 4,** the magnetic poles have a slightly different location than the geographic poles.

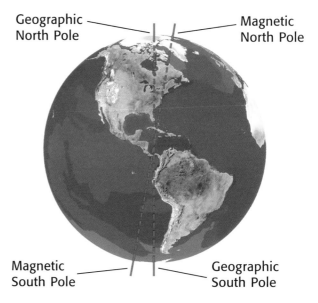

Geographic North Pole — Magnetic North Pole

Magnetic South Pole — Geographic South Pole

Figure 4 *Unlike the geographic poles, which are always in the same place, the magnetic poles have changed location throughout the history of the Earth.*

✓ Self-Check

Does the Earth rotate around the geographic poles or the magnetic poles? *(See page 726 to check your answer.)*

True North and Magnetic Declination Because the geographic North Pole never changes, it is called **true north.** The difference between the location of true north and the magnetic north pole requires that one more step be added to using a compass. When using a compass to map or explore the Earth's surface, you need to make a correction for the difference between geographic north and magnetic north. This angle of correction is called **magnetic declination.** Magnetic declination is measured in degrees east or west of true north.

Magnetic declination has been determined for different points on the Earth's surface. Once you know the declination for your area, you can use a compass to determine true north.

This adjustment is like the adjustment you would make to the handlebars of a bike with a bent front wheel. You know how much you have to turn the handlebars to make the bike go straight.

As **Figure 5** shows, a compass needle at Pittsburgh, Pennsylvania, points about 7° west of true north. Can you determine the magnetic declination of San Diego?

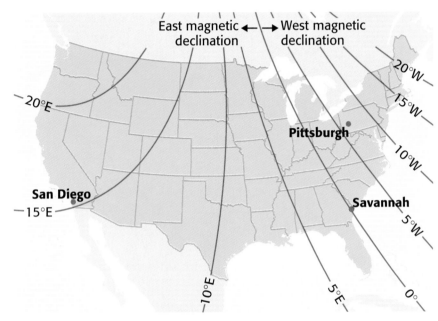

Figure 5 *The red lines on the map connect points with the same magnetic declination.*

Finding Locations on the Earth

The houses and buildings in your neighborhood all have addresses that identify their location. But how would you find the location of something like a city or an island? These places can be given an "address" using *latitude* and *longitude*. Latitude and longitude are intersecting lines on a globe or map that allow you to find exact locations. They are used in combination to create global addresses.

Latitude Imaginary lines drawn around the Earth parallel to the equator are called lines of latitude, or *parallels*. The **equator** is a circle halfway between the poles that divides the Earth into the Northern and Southern Hemispheres. It represents 0° latitude. **Latitude** is the distance north or south, measured in degrees, from the equator, as shown in **Figure 6**. The North Pole is 90° north latitude, and the South Pole is 90° south latitude.

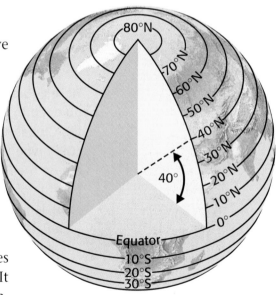

Figure 6 *The degree measure of latitude is the angle created by the equator, the center of the Earth, and the location on the Earth's surface.*

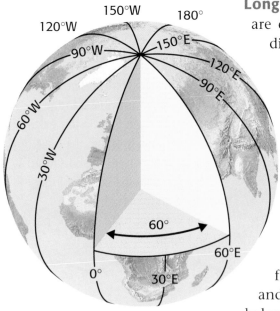

150°W
120°W
180°
90°W
150°E
120°E
90°E
60°W
60°E
30°W
60°
60°E
0°
30°E

Figure 7 *The degree measure of longitude is the angle created by the prime meridian, the center of the Earth, and the location on the Earth's surface.*

Longitude Imaginary lines that pass through the poles are called lines of longitude, or *meridians.* **Longitude** is the distance east and west, measured in degrees, from the prime meridian, as shown in **Figure 7.** By international agreement, one meridian was selected to be 0°. The **prime meridian,** which passes through Greenwich, England, is the line that represents 0° longitude. Unlike lines of latitude, lines of longitude are not parallel. They touch at the poles and are farthest apart at the equator.

The prime meridian does not completely circle the globe like the equator does. It runs from the North Pole through Greenwich, England, to the South Pole. The 180° meridian lies on the opposite side of the Earth from the prime meridian. Together, the prime meridian and the 180° meridian divide the Earth into two equal halves—the Eastern and Western Hemispheres. East lines of longitude are found east of the prime meridian, between 0° and 180°. West lines of longitude are found west of the prime meridian, between 0° and 180°.

Using Latitude and Longitude Points on the Earth's surface can be located using latitude and longitude. Lines of latitude and lines of longitude intersect, forming a grid system on globes and maps. This grid system can be used to find locations north or south of the equator and east or west of the prime meridian.

Finding Your Way

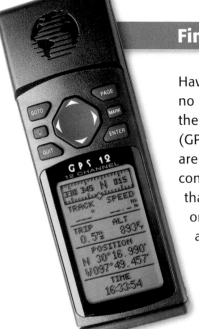

Have you ever been lost? There's no need to worry anymore. With the Global Positioning System (GPS), you can find where you are on the Earth's surface. GPS consists of 25 orbiting satellites that send radio signals to receivers on Earth in order to calculate a given location's latitude, longitude, and elevation.

GPS was invented in the 1970s by the United States Department of Defense for military purposes. During the last 20 years, this technology has made its way into many people's daily lives. Today GPS is used in a variety of ways. Airplane and boat pilots use it for navigation, and industry uses include mining and resource mapping as well as environmental planning. Even some cars are equipped with a GPS unit that can display the vehicle's specific location on a computer screen on the dashboard.

Figure 8 shows you how latitude and longitude can be used to find the location of your state capital. First locate the star symbol representing your state capital on the appropriate map. Find the lines of latitude and longitude closest to your state capital. From here you can estimate your capital's approximate latitude and longitude.

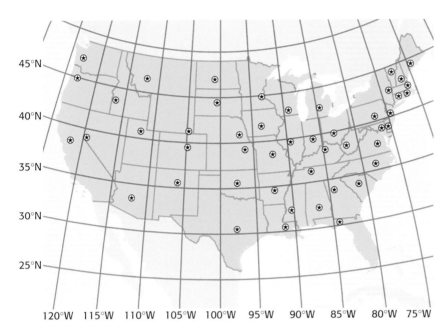

Figure 8 *The grid pattern formed by lines of latitude and longitude allows you to pinpoint any location on the Earth's surface.*

REVIEW

1. Explain the difference between true north and magnetic north.

2. When using a compass to map an area, why is it important to know an area's magnetic declination?

3. In what three ways is the equator different from the prime meridian?

4. How do lines of latitude and longitude help you find locations on the Earth's surface?

5. **Applying Concepts** While digging through an old trunk, you find a treasure map. The map shows that the treasure is buried at 97° north and 188° east. Explain why this is impossible.

internet**connect**

SC*i*LINKS
NSTA

TOPIC: Latitude and Longitude
GO TO: www.scilinks.org
*sci*LINKS NUMBER: HSTE035

Mapping the Earth's Surface

What You'll Do

- Compare a map with a globe.
- Describe the three types of map projections.
- Describe recent technological advances that have helped the science of mapmaking progress.
- List the parts of a map.

Models are often used to represent real objects. For example, architects use models of buildings to give their clients an idea of what a building will look like before it is completed. Likewise, Earth scientists often make models of the Earth. These models are globes and maps.

Because a globe is a sphere, a globe is probably the most accurate model of the Earth. Also, a globe accurately represents the sizes and shapes of the continents and oceans in relation to one another. But a globe is not always the best model to use when studying the Earth's surface. For example, a globe is too small to show a lot of detail, such as roads and rivers. It is much easier to show details on maps. Maps can show the entire Earth or parts of it. But how do you represent the Earth's curved surface on a flat surface? Read on to find out.

A Flat Sphere?

A map is a flat representation of the Earth's curved surface. However, when you transfer information from a curved surface to a flat surface, you lose some accuracy. Changes called distortions occur in the shapes and sizes of landmasses and oceans. These distortions make some landmasses appear larger than they really are. Direction and distance can also be distorted. Consider the example of the orange peel shown in **Figure 9**.

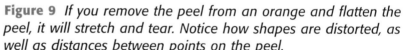

Figure 9 *If you remove the peel from an orange and flatten the peel, it will stretch and tear. Notice how shapes are distorted, as well as distances between points on the peel.*

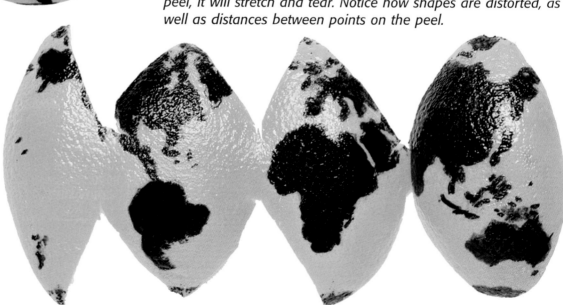

Map Projections Mapmakers use map projections to transfer the image of Earth's curved surface onto a flat surface. No map projection of the Earth can represent the surface of a sphere exactly. All flat maps have some amount of distortion. A map showing a smaller area, such as a city, has much less distortion than a map showing a larger area, such as the entire world.

To understand how map projections are made, imagine the Earth as a transparent globe with a light inside. If you hold a piece of paper up against the globe, shadows appear on the paper that show markings on the globe, such as continents, lines of latitude, and lines of longitude. The way the paper is held against the globe determines the kind of projection that is made. The most common projections are based on three geometric shapes—cylinders, cones, and planes.

Mercator Projection A **Mercator projection** is a map projection that results when the contents of the globe are transferred onto a cylinder of paper, as shown in **Figure 10.**

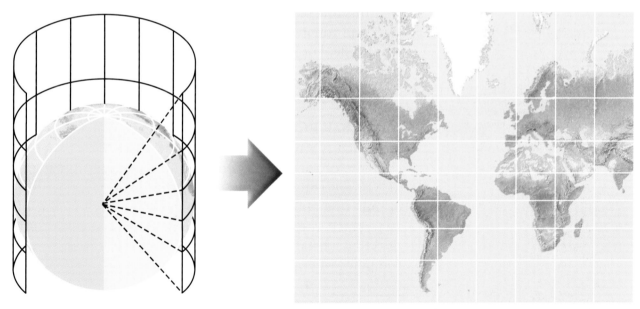

Figure 10 *A Mercator projection is accurate near the equator but distorts distances and sizes of areas near the poles.*

The Mercator projection shows the Earth's latitude and longitude as straight, parallel lines. Lines of longitude are plotted with an equal amount of space between each line. Lines of latitude are spaced farther apart north and south of the equator. Making the lines parallel widens and lengthens the size of areas near the poles. For example, on the Mercator projection in the map shown above, Greenland appears almost as large as Africa. Actually, Africa is 15 times larger than Greenland.

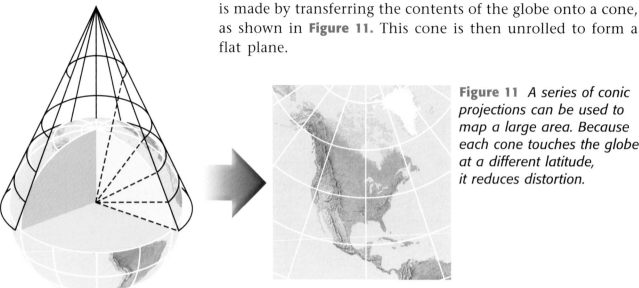

Conic Projection A **conic projection** is a map projection that is made by transferring the contents of the globe onto a cone, as shown in **Figure 11.** This cone is then unrolled to form a flat plane.

Figure 11 *A series of conic projections can be used to map a large area. Because each cone touches the globe at a different latitude, it reduces distortion.*

The cone touches the globe at each line of longitude but only one line of latitude. There is no distortion along the line of latitude where the globe comes in contact with the cone. Areas near this line of latitude are distorted the least amount. Because the cone touches many lines of longitude and only one line of latitude, conic projections are best for mapping landmasses that have more area east to west, such as the United States, than north to south, such as South America.

Azimuthal Projection An **azimuthal** (AZ i MYOOTH uhl) **projection** is a map projection that is made by transferring the contents of the globe onto a plane, as shown in **Figure 12.**

On an azimuthal projection, the plane touches the globe at only one point. Little distortion occurs at the point of contact, which is usually one of the poles. However, distortion of direction, distance, and shape increases as the distance from the point of contact increases.

Figure 12 *On this azimuthal projection, distortion increases as you move further away from the North Pole.*

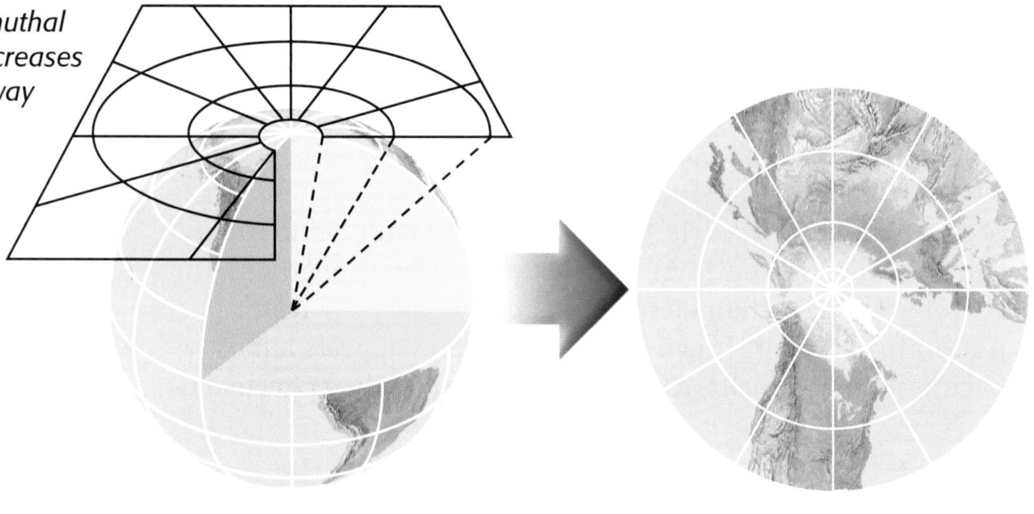

Modern Mapmaking

The science of mapmaking has changed more since the beginning of the 1900s than during any other time in history. This has been due to many technological advances in the twentieth century, such as the airplane, photography, computers, and space exploration.

Airplanes and Cameras The development of the airplane and advancements in photography have had the biggest effect on modern mapmaking. Airplanes give people a bird's-eye view of the Earth's surface. Photographs from the air are called **aerial photographs.** These photographs are important in helping mapmakers make accurate maps.

Remote Sensing The combined use of airplanes and photography led to the science of remote sensing. **Remote sensing** is gathering information about something without actually being there. Remote sensing can be as basic as cameras in planes or as sophisticated as satellites with sensors that can sense and record what our eyes cannot see. Remotely sensed images allow a mapmaker to map the surface of the Earth more accurately.

Our eyes can detect only a small part of the sun's energy. The part we see is called visible light. Remote sensors on satellites can detect energy that we cannot see. Satellites do not take photographs with film like cameras do. A satellite collects information about energy coming from the Earth's surface and sends it back to receiving stations on Earth. A computer is then used to process the information to create an image we can see, like the one shown in **Figure 13.**

Figure 13 *Satellites can detect objects the size of a baseball stadium. The satellite that took this picture was 220 km above the Earth's surface!*

Information Shown on Maps

As you have already learned, there are many different ways of making maps. It is also true that there are many types of maps. You might already be familiar with some, such as road maps or political maps of the United States. But regardless of its type, each map should contain the information shown in **Figure 14.**

Figure 14 **Road Map of Connecticut**

The **title** tells you what area is being shown on the map or gives you information about the subject of the map.

A **map's scale** shows the relationship between the distance on the Earth's surface and the distance on the map.

A **graphic scale** is like a ruler. The distance on the Earth's surface is represented by a bar graph that shows units of distance.

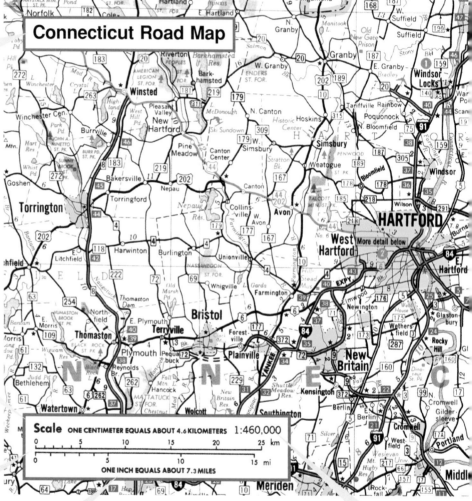

A **verbal scale** is a phrase that describes the measure of distance on the map relative to the distance on the Earth's surface.

A **representative fraction** is a fraction or ratio that shows the relationship between the distance on the map and the distance on the Earth's surface. It is unitless, meaning it stays the same no matter what units of measurement you are using.

Reading a Map

Imagine that you are a trip planner for an automobile club. A couple of people come in who want to travel from Torrington, Connecticut, to Bristol, Connecticut. Using the map in Figure 14, describe the shortest travel route you would suggest they take between the two cities. List the roads they would take, the direction they would travel, and the towns they would pass through. Use the map scale to determine approximately how many miles there are between Torrington and Bristol.

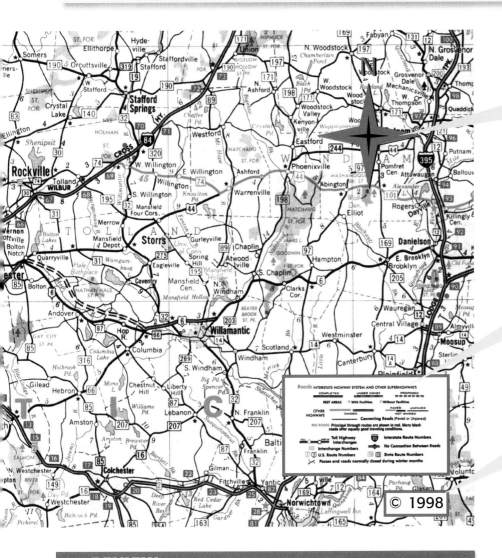

A **compass rose** shows you how the map is positioned in relation to true north.

A **legend** is a list of the symbols used in the map and their explanations.

The **date** gives the time at which the information on the map was accurate.

REVIEW

1. A globe is a fairly accurate model of the Earth, yet it has some weaknesses. What is one weakness?

2. What is distortion on a map, and why does it occur?

3. What is remote sensing? How has it changed mapmaking?

4. **Summarizing Data** List five items found on maps. Explain how each item is important to reading a map.

internet**connect**

SC/LINKS™
NSTA

TOPIC: Mapmaking
GO TO: www.scilinks.org
sciLINKS NUMBER: HSTE040

What You'll Do

- ◆ Describe how contour lines show elevation and landforms on a map.
- ◆ List the rules of contour lines.
- ◆ Interpret a topographic map.

Topographic Maps

Imagine that you are on an outdoor adventure trip. The trip's purpose is to improve your survival skills by having you travel across undeveloped territory with only a compass and a map. What kind of map will you be using? Well, it's not a road map—you won't be seeing a lot of roads where you are going. You will need a topographic map. A **topographic map** is a map that shows surface features, or topography, of the Earth. Topographic maps show both natural features, such as rivers, lakes and mountains, and features made by humans, such as cities, roads, and bridges. Topographic maps also show elevation. **Elevation** is the height of an object above sea level. The elevation at sea level is 0. In this section you will learn how to interpret a topographic map.

Elements of Elevation

The United States Geological Survey (USGS), a federal government agency, has made topographic maps for all of the United States. Each of these maps is a detailed description of a small area of the Earth's surface. Because the topographic maps produced by the USGS use feet as their unit of measure rather than meters, we will follow their example.

Contour Lines On a topographic map, contour lines are used to show elevation. **Contour lines** are lines that connect points of equal elevation. For example, one contour line would connect points on a map that have an elevation of 100 ft. Another line would connect points on a map that have an elevation of 200 ft. **Figure 15** illustrates how contour lines appear on a map.

Figure 15 *Because contour lines connect points of equal elevation, the shape of the contour lines reflects the shape of the land.*

Contour Interval   The difference in elevation between one contour line and the next is called the **contour interval.** For example, a map with a contour interval of 20 ft would have contour lines every 20 ft of elevation change, such as 0 ft, 20 ft, 40 ft, 60 ft, and so on. A mapmaker chooses a contour interval based on the area's relief. **Relief** is the difference in elevation between the highest and lowest points of the area being mapped. Because the relief of a mountainous area is high, it might be shown on a map using a large contour interval, such as 100 ft. However, a flat area has low relief and might be shown on a map using a small contour interval, such as 10 ft.

The spacing of contour lines also indicates slope, as shown in **Figure 16.** Contour lines that are close together, with little space between them, usually show a steep slope. Contour lines that are spaced far apart generally represent a gentle slope.

Index Contour   On many topographic maps, the mapmaker uses an index contour to make reading the map a little easier. An **index contour** is a darker, heavier contour line that is usually every fifth line and that is labeled by elevation. Find an index contour on both of the topographic maps.

MATH BREAK

Counting Contours

Calculate the contour interval for the map shown in Figure 15 on the previous page. (Hint: Find the difference between two bold lines found next to each other. Subtract the lower marked elevation from the higher marked elevation. Divide by 5.)

Figure 16 *The portion of the topographic map on the left shows Pikes Peak, in Colorado. The map above shows a valley in Big Bend Ranch State Park, in Texas.*

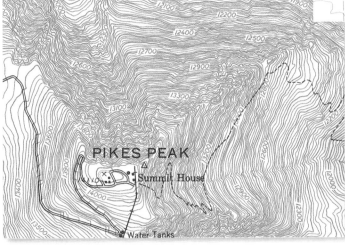

✓ Self-Check

If elevation is not labeled on a map, how can you determine if the mapped area is steep or not? *(See page 726 to check your answer.)*

Reading a Topographic Map

Topographic maps, like other maps, use symbols to represent parts of the Earth's surface. The legend from the USGS topographic map in **Figure 17** shows some of the common symbols used to represent certain features in topographic maps.

Different colors are also used to represent different features of the Earth's surface. In general, buildings, roads, bridges, and railroads are black. Contour lines are brown. Major highways are red. Cities and towns are pink. Bodies of water, such as rivers, lakes, and oceans, are shown in blue, and wooded areas are represented by the color green.

Figure 17 *All USGS topographic maps use the same legend to represent natural features and features made by humans.*

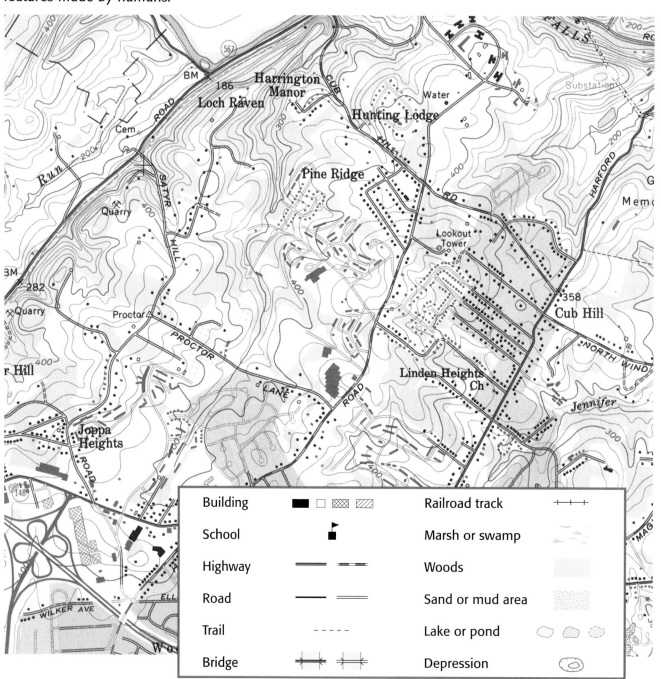

Building	▪ ▫ ▨ ▨	Railroad track	+++++
School	⚑	Marsh or swamp	
Highway		Woods	
Road		Sand or mud area	
Trail	-----	Lake or pond	
Bridge		Depression	

The Golden Rules of Contour Lines Contour lines are the key to interpreting the size and shape of landforms on a topographic map. When you first look at a topographic map, it might seem confusing. Accurately reading a topographic map requires training and practice. The following rules will help you understand how to read topographic maps:

Environment
C O N N E C T I O N

State agencies, such as the Texas Parks and Wildlife Department, use topographic maps to plot the distribution and occurrence of endangered plant and animal species. By marking the location of endangered species on a map, these agencies can record and protect these habitats.

1. Contour lines never cross. All points along a contour line represent a single elevation.

2. The spacing of contour lines depends on slope characteristics. Closely spaced contour lines represent a steep slope. Widely spaced contour lines represent a gentle slope.

3. Contour lines that cross a valley or stream are V-shaped. The V points toward the area of higher elevation. If a stream or river flows through the valley, the V points upstream.

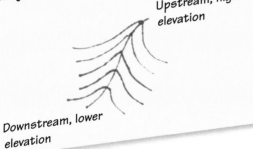

Upstream, higher elevation

Downstream, lower elevation

4. Contour lines form closed circles around the tops of hills, mountains, and depressions. One way to tell hills and depressions apart is that depressions are marked with short, straight lines inside the circle, pointing downslope toward the center of the depression.

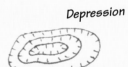

Hill   Depression

REVIEW

1. How do topographic maps represent the Earth's surface?

2. If a contour map contains streams, can you tell where the higher ground is even if all of the numbers are removed?

3. Why can't contour lines cross?

4. **Inferring Conclusions** Why isn't the highest point on a hill or a mountain represented by a contour line?

internet connect

SC*LINKS*
NSTA

TOPIC: Topographic Maps
GO TO: www.scilinks.org
***sci*LINKS NUMBER:** HSTE045

Chapter Highlights

Vocabulary

map *(p. 34)*

true north *(p. 36)*

magnetic declination *(p. 36)*

equator *(p. 37)*

latitude *(p. 37)*

longitude *(p. 38)*

prime meridian *(p. 38)*

Section Notes

- The North and South Poles are used as reference points for describing direction and location on the Earth.

- The cardinal directions— north, south, east, and west—are used for describing direction.

- Magnetic compasses are used to determine direction on the Earth's surface. The north needle on the compass points to the magnetic north pole.

- Because the geographic North Pole never changes location, it is called true north. The magnetic poles are different from the Earth's geographic poles and have changed location throughout the Earth's history.

- The magnetic declination is the adjustment or difference between magnetic north and geographic north.

- Latitude and longitude are intersecting lines that help you find locations on a map or a globe. Lines of latitude run east-west. Lines of longitude run north-south through the poles.

Labs

Round or Flat? *(p. 632)*

Orient Yourself! *(p. 634)*

Vocabulary

Mercator projection *(p. 41)*

conic projection *(p. 42)*

azimuthal projection *(p. 42)*

aerial photograph *(p. 43)*

remote sensing *(p. 43)*

Section Notes

- A globe is the most accurate representation of the Earth's surface.

- Maps have built-in distortion because some information is lost when mapmakers transfer images from a curved surface to a flat surface.

☑ Skills Check

Math Concepts

REPRESENTATIVE FRACTION One type of map scale is a representative fraction. A representative fraction is a fraction or ratio that shows the relationship between the distance on the map and the distance on the Earth's surface. It is unitless, meaning it stays the same no matter what units of measurement you are using. For example, say you are using a map with a representative fraction scale that is 1:12,000. If you are measuring distance on the map in centimeters, 1 cm on the map represents 12,000 cm on the Earth's surface. A measure of 3 cm on the map represents 12,000 × 3 cm = 36,000 cm on the Earth's surface.

Visual Understanding

THE POLES The Earth has two different sets of poles—the geographic poles and the magnetic poles. See Figure 4 on page 36 to review how the geographic poles and the magnetic poles differ.

INFORMATION SHOWN ON MAPS Study Figure 14 on pages 44 and 45 to review the necessary information each map should contain.

- Mapmakers use map projections to transfer images of the Earth's curved surface to a flat surface.

- The most common map projections are based on three geometric shapes—cylinders, cones, and planes.

- Remote sensing has allowed mapmakers to make more accurate maps.

- All maps should have a title, date, scale, legend, and north arrow.

Vocabulary

topographic map *(p. 46)*

elevation *(p. 46)*

contour lines *(p. 46)*

contour interval *(p. 47)*

relief *(p. 47)*

index contour *(p. 47)*

Section Notes

- Topographic maps use contour lines to show a mapped area's elevation and the shape and size of landforms.

- The shape of contour lines reflects the shape of the land.

- The contour interval and the spacing of contour lines indicate the slope of the land.

- Like all maps, topographic maps use a set of symbols to represent features of the Earth's surface.

- Contour lines never cross. Contour lines that cross a valley or stream are V-shaped. Contour lines form closed circles around the tops of hills, mountains, and depressions.

Labs

Topographic Tuber *(p. 636)*

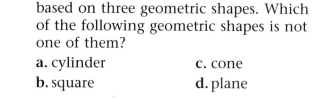

Chapter Review

USING VOCABULARY

Explain the difference between the following sets of words:

1. true north/magnetic north

2. latitude/longitude

3. equator/prime meridian

4. Mercator projection/azimuthal projection

5. contour interval/index contour

6. elevation/relief

UNDERSTANDING CONCEPTS

Multiple Choice

7. A point whose latitude is 0° is located on the
   a. North Pole.   **c.** South Pole.
   b. equator.   **d.** prime meridian.

8. The distance in degrees east or west of the prime meridian is
   a. latitude.   **c.** longitude.
   b. declination.   **d.** projection.

9. The needle of a magnetic compass points toward the
   a. meridians.
   b. parallels.
   c. geographic North Pole.
   d. magnetic north pole.

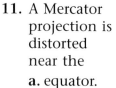

10. The most common map projections are based on three geometric shapes. Which of the following geometric shapes is not one of them?
    a. cylinder   **c.** cone
    b. square   **d.** plane

11. A Mercator projection is distorted near the
    a. equator.
    b. poles.
    c. prime meridian.
    d. date line.

12. What kind of scale does not have written units of measure?
    a. representative fraction
    b. verbal
    c. graphic
    d. mathematical

13. What is the relationship between the distance on a map and the actual distance on the Earth called?
    a. legend
    b. elevation
    c. relief
    d. scale

14. The latitude of the North Pole is
    a. 100° north.   **c.** 180° north.
    b. 90° north.   **d.** 90° south.

15. Widely spaced contour lines indicate a
    a. steep slope.
    b. gentle slope.
    c. hill.
    d. river.

16. ___?___ is the height of an object above sea level.
   a. Contour interval
   b. Elevation
   c. Declination
   d. Index contour

Short Answer

17. How can a magnetic compass be used to find direction on the Earth's surface?

18. Why is a map legend important?

19. Why does Greenland appear so large in relation to other landmasses on a map with a Mercator projection?

20. What is the function of contour lines on a topographic map?

Concept Mapping

21. Use the following terms to create a concept map: maps, legend, map projection, map parts, scale, cylinder, title, cone, plane, date, north arrow.

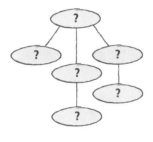

Write one or two sentences to answer the following questions:

22. One of the important parts of a map is its date. Why is this so important?

23. A mapmaker has to draw one map for three different countries that do not share a common unit of measure. What type of scale would this mapmaker use? Why?

24. How would a topographic map of the Rocky Mountains differ from a topographic map of the Great Plains?

MATH IN SCIENCE

25. A map has a verbal scale of 1 cm equals 200 m. If the actual distance between two points is 12,000 m, how far apart will they appear on the map?

26. On a topographic map, the contour interval is 50 ft. The bottom of a mountain begins on a contour line marked with a value of 1050 ft. The top of the mountain is within a contour line that is 12 lines higher than the bottom of the mountain. What is the elevation of the top of the mountain?

INTERPRETING GRAPHICS

Use the topographic map below to answer the questions that follow.

27. What is the elevation change between two adjacent lines on this map?

28. What type of relief does this area have?

29. What surface features are shown on this map?

30. What is the elevation at the top of Ore Hill?

Reading Check-up

Take a minute to review your answers to the Pre-Reading Questions found at the bottom of page 32. Have your answers changed? If necessary, revise your answers based on what you have learned since you began this chapter.

Science, Technology, and Society

The Lost City of Ubar

Can you imagine tree sap being more valuable than gold? Well, about 2,000 years ago, a tree sap called frankincense was just that! Frankincense was used to treat illnesses and to disguise body odor. Ancient civilizations from Rome to India treasured it. While the name of the city that was the center of frankincense production and export had been known for generations—Ubar—there was just one problem: No one knew where it was! But now the mystery is solved. Using remote sensing, scientists have found clues hidden beneath desert sand dunes.

▲ *Trails and roads appear as purple lines on this computer-generated remote-sensing image.*

Using Eyes in the Sky

The process of remote sensing uses satellites to take pictures of large areas of land. The satellite records images as sets of data and sends these data to a receiver on Earth. A computer processes the data and displays the images. These remote sensing images can then be used to reveal differences unseen by the naked eye.

Remote-sensing images reveal modern roads as well as ancient caravan routes hidden beneath sand dunes in the Sahara Desert. But how could researchers tell the difference between the two? Everything on Earth reflects or radiates energy. Soil, vegetation, cities, and roads all emit a unique wavelength of energy. The problem is, sometimes modern roads and ancient roads are difficult to distinguish. The differences between similar objects can be enhanced by assigning color to an area and then displaying the area on a computer screen. Researchers used differences in color to distinguish between the roads of Ubar and modern roads. When researchers found ancient caravan routes and discovered that all the routes met at one location, they knew they had discovered the lost city of Ubar!

Continuing Discovery

Archaeologists continue to investigate the region around Ubar. They believe the great city may have collapsed into a limestone cavern beneath its foundation. Researchers are continuing to use remote sensing to study more images for clues to aid their investigation.

Think About It!

▶ Do modern civilizations value certain products or resources enough to establish elaborate trade routes for their transport? If so, what makes these products so valuable? Record your thoughts in your ScienceLog.

CAREERS

WATERSHED PLANNER

Have you ever wondered if the water you drink is safe or what you could do to make sure it stays safe? As a watershed planner, **Nancy Charbeneau** identifies and solves land-use problems that may affect water quality.

Nancy Charbeneau enjoys using her teaching, biology, and landscape architecture background in her current career as a watershed planner. A watershed is any area of land where water drains into a stream, river, lake, or ocean. Charbeneau spends a lot of time writing publications and developing programs that explain the effects of land use on the quality of water.

Land is used in hundreds of ways. Some of these land uses can have negative effects on water resources. Charbeneau produces educational materials to inform the public about threats to water quality.

Mapping the Problems

Charbeneau uses Geographic Information System (GIS) maps to determine types of vegetation and the functions of different sections of land. GIS is a computer-based tool that allows people to store, access, and display geographic information collected through remote-sensing, field work, global positioning systems, and other sources. Maps and mapping systems play an important role in identifying land areas with water problems.

Maps tell Charbeneau whether an area has problems with soil erosion that could threaten water quality. Often the type of soil plays an important role in erosion. Thin or sandy soil does not hold water well, allowing for faster runoff and erosion. Flat land with heavy vegetation holds more water and is less prone to erosion.

Understanding the Importance

Charbeneau's biggest challenge is increasing understanding of the link between land use and water quality. If a harmful substance is introduced into a watershed, it may contaminate an aquifer or a well. As Charbeneau puts it, "Most people want to do the right thing, but they need information about land management practices that will protect water quality but still allow them to earn a decent living off their land."

Reading the Possibilities

▶ Map out your nearest watershed. Can you find any potential sources of contamination?

▲ *This GIS map shows the location of water in blue.*

UNIT 2

Earth's Resources

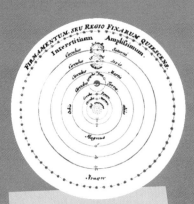

In this unit, you will learn about the basic components of the solid Earth—rocks and the minerals from which they are made. The ground beneath your feet is a treasure-trove of interesting materials, some of which are very valuable. Secrets of the past are also hidden within its depths. This timeline shows some of the events that have occurred through history as scientists have come to understand more about our planet.

1533

Nicolaus Copernicus argues that the sun is the center of the universe rather than the Earth, as was commonly believed, but does not publish his findings for another 10 years.

1680

The dodo, a flightless bird, is driven to extinction by hunters. It is the first extinction of a species in recorded history.

1955

Using 1 million pounds of pressure and temperatures of more than 3,000°F, General Electric creates the first artificial diamonds from graphite.

1969

Apollo 11 astronauts Neil Armstrong and Edwin "Buzz" Aldrin bring 20 kg of moon rocks back to Earth.

1975

Junko Tabei becomes the first woman to successfully climb Mount Everest, 22 years after Edmund Hillary and Tenzing Norgay first conquered the mountain in 1953.

1848

Gold is discovered in California. Prospectors during the gold rush of the following year are referred to as "forty-niners."

1735

George Brandt identifies a new element and names it cobalt. This is the first metal to be discovered since ancient times.

1861

Fossil remains of *Archaeopteryx,* a possible link between reptiles and birds, are discovered in Germany.

1936

Hoover Dam is completed. This massive hydroelectric dam, standing more than 72 stories high, required 450,000 cement-truck loads of concrete to build.

1946

Willard F. Libby develops a method of dating prehistoric objects by using radioactive carbon.

1997

Sojourner, a roving probe on Mars, investigates a Martian boulder nicknamed Yogi.

1984

Russian engineers drill a borehole 12 km into the Earth's crust, three times deeper than the deepest mine shaft.

CHAPTER 3

Minerals of the Earth's Crust

Pre-Reading Questions

1. What is a mineral?
2. How do minerals form?

CAVE CURTAINS

Look at the lacy hanging mineral formations in this photo of a limestone cavern. These *stalactites* were formed from dripping water that contained a dissolved mineral, calcium bicarbonate. The mineral reacted with air and hardened into another mineral compound, calcium carbonate. Sometimes called dripstone, such mineral formations may have many colors caused by the presence of yet other minerals in the dripping water. In this chapter, you will learn how mineral compounds form and how they are classified.

RIDING A MINERAL?

More than 3,000 different minerals occur naturally on Earth. What is a mineral? Do the following activity, and see if you can figure it out.

Procedure

1. In your ScienceLog, make two columns—one for minerals and one for nonminerals.

2. Ask your classmates what ideas they have about the materials that make up a motorcycle. Take notes as you gather information.

3. Based on what you already know about minerals, classify the materials in a motorcycle into things that come from minerals and things that come from nonminerals.

Analysis

4. Based on your list, is most of a motorcycle made of minerals or nonminerals?

5. Where do you think the minerals that make a motorcycle come from?

Terms to Learn

mineral   crystal
element   silicate mineral
atom   nonsilicate mineral
compound

What You'll Do

◆ Explain the four characteristics of a mineral.

◆ Classify minerals according to the two major compositional groups.

What Is a Mineral?

Not all minerals look like gems. In fact, most of them look more like rocks. But are minerals the same as rocks? Well, not really. So what's the difference? For one thing, rocks are made of minerals, but minerals are not made of rocks. Then what exactly is a mineral? By asking the following four questions, you can tell whether something is a mineral:

Is it formed in nature?
Crystalline materials made by people aren't classified as minerals.

Is it a solid?
Minerals can't be gases or liquids.

Does it have a crystalline structure?
Minerals are crystals, which have a repeating inner structure that is often reflected in the shape of the crystal. Minerals generally have the same chemical composition throughout.

Is it nonliving material?
A mineral is inorganic, meaning it isn't made of living things.

A **mineral** is a naturally formed, inorganic solid with a crystalline structure. If you cannot answer "yes" to all four questions above, you don't have a mineral.

Minerals: From the Inside Out

Three of the four questions might be easy to answer. The one about crystalline structure may be more difficult. In order to understand what crystalline structure is, you need to know a little about the elements that make up a mineral. **Elements** are pure substances that cannot be broken down into simpler substances by ordinary chemical means. All minerals contain one or more of the 92 elements present in the Earth's crust.

How many elements does it take to "set" the periodic table? Find out by turning to page 744.

Atoms and Compounds Each element is made of only one kind of atom. An **atom,** as you may recall, is the smallest part of an element that has all the properties of that element. Like all other substances, minerals are made up of atoms of one or more elements.

Most minerals are made of compounds of several different elements. A **compound** is a substance made of two or more elements that have been chemically joined, or bonded together. Halite, for example, is a compound of sodium and chlorine, as shown in **Figure 1.** A few minerals, such as gold and silver, are composed of only one element. For example, pure gold is made up of only one kind of atom—gold.

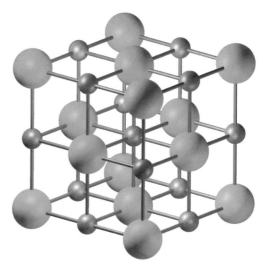

Figure 1 *Atoms of sodium and chlorine are joined together in a compound commonly known as rock salt, or the mineral halite.*

Crystals A mineral is also made up of one or more crystals. **Crystals** are solid, geometric forms of minerals produced by a repeating pattern of atoms that is present throughout the mineral. A crystal's shape is determined by the arrangement of the atoms within the crystal. The arrangement of atoms in turn is determined by the kinds of atoms that make up the mineral. Each mineral has a definite crystalline structure. All minerals can be grouped into crystal classes according to the kinds of crystals they form. **Figure 2** shows how the atomic structure of gold gives rise to cubic crystals.

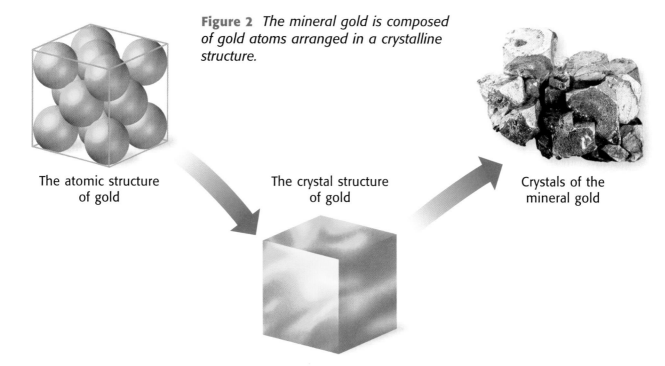

Figure 2 *The mineral gold is composed of gold atoms arranged in a crystalline structure.*

The atomic structure of gold

The crystal structure of gold

Crystals of the mineral gold

Biology
CONNECTION

Several species of animals have a brain that contains the mineral magnetite. Magnetite has a special property—it is magnetic. Scientists have shown that certain fish can sense magnetic fields because they have magnetite in their brain. The magnetite gives the fish a sense of direction.

Types of Minerals

Minerals can be classified by a number of different characteristics. The most common classification of minerals is based on chemical composition. Minerals are divided into two groups based on the elements they are composed of. These groups are the silicate minerals and the nonsilicate minerals.

Silicate Minerals Silicon and oxygen are the two most common elements in the Earth's crust. Minerals that contain a combination of these two elements are called **silicate minerals.** Silicate minerals make up more than 90 percent of the Earth's crust—the rest is made up of nonsilicate minerals. Silicon and oxygen usually combine with other elements, such as aluminum, iron, magnesium, and potassium, to make up silicate minerals. Some of the more common silicate minerals are shown in **Figure 3.**

Feldspar Feldspar minerals make up about half the Earth's crust, and they are the main component of most rocks on the Earth's surface. They contain the elements silicon and oxygen along with aluminum, potassium, sodium, and calcium.

Biotite Mica Mica minerals are shiny and soft, and they separate easily into sheets when they break. Biotite is but one of several varieties of mica.

Quartz Quartz (silicon dioxide, SiO_2) is the basic building block of many rocks. If you look closely at the piece of granite, you can see the quartz crystals.

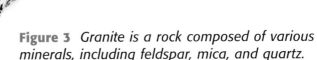

Figure 3 *Granite is a rock composed of various minerals, including feldspar, mica, and quartz.*

Nonsilicate Minerals Minerals that do not contain a combination of the elements silicon and oxygen form a group called the **nonsilicate minerals.** Some of these minerals are made up of elements such as carbon, oxygen, iron, and sulfur. Below are several categories of nonsilicate minerals.

Classes of Nonsilicate Minerals

Native elements are minerals that are composed of only one element. About 20 minerals are native elements. Some examples are gold (Au), platinum (Pt), diamond (C), copper (Cu), sulfur (S), and silver (Ag).

Native copper

Carbonates are minerals that contain combinations of carbon and oxygen in their chemical structure. Calcite ($CaCO_3$) is an example of a carbonate mineral. We use carbonate minerals in cement, building stones, and fireworks.

Calcite

Halides are compounds that form when atoms of the elements fluorine, chlorine, iodine, or bromine combine with sodium, potassium, or calcium. Halite (NaCl) is better known as rock salt. Fluorite (CaF_2) can have many different colors. Halide minerals are often used to make fertilizer.

Fluorite

Oxides are compounds that form when an element, such as aluminum or iron, combines chemically with oxygen. Corundum (Al_2O_3) and magnetite (Fe_3O_4) are important oxide minerals. Oxide minerals are used to make abrasives and aircraft parts.

Corundum

Sulfates contain sulfur and oxygen (SO_4). The mineral gypsum ($CaSO_4 \cdot 2H_2O$) is a common sulfate. It makes up the white sand at White Sands National Monument, in New Mexico. Sulfates are used in cosmetics, toothpaste, and paint.

Gypsum

Sulfides are minerals that contain one or more elements, such as lead, iron, or nickel, combined with sulfur. Galena (PbS) is a sulfide. Sulfide minerals are used to make batteries, medicines, and electronic parts.

Galena

REVIEW

1. What are the differences between atoms, compounds, and minerals?

2. Which two elements are most common in minerals?

3. How are silicate minerals different from nonsilicate minerals?

4. **Making Inferences** Explain why each of the following is not considered a mineral: a cupcake, water, teeth, oxygen.

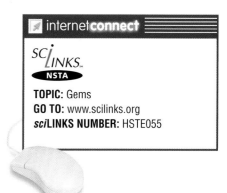

internet connect

SC*i*LINKS

NSTA

TOPIC: Gems
GO TO: www.scilinks.org
*sci*LINKS NUMBER: HSTE055

What You'll Do

◆ Classify minerals using common mineral-identification techniques.
◆ Explain special properties of minerals.

Identifying Minerals

If you found the two mineral samples below, how would you know if they were the same mineral?

By looking at these minerals, you can easily see physical similarities. But how can you tell whether they are the same mineral? Moreover, how can you determine the identity of a mineral? In this section you will learn about the different properties that can help you identify minerals.

Luster Chart

Metallic   **Submetallic**

Nonmetallic

Vitreous   **Silky**
glassy, brilliant   swirly, fibrous

Resinous   **Waxy**
plastic   greasy, oily

Pearly   **Earthy**
creamy   rough, dull

Color

Minerals come in many different colors and shades. The same mineral can come in a variety of colors. For example, in its purest state quartz is clear. Quartz that contains small amounts of impurities, however, can be a variety of colors. Rose quartz gets its color from certain kinds of impurities. Amethyst, another variety of quartz, is purple because it contains other kinds of impurities.

Besides impurities, other factors can change the appearance of minerals. The mineral pyrite, often called fool's gold, normally has a golden color. But if pyrite is exposed to weather for a long period, it turns black. Because of factors such as weathering and impurities, color usually is not a reliable indicator of a mineral's identity.

Luster

The way a surface reflects light is called **luster.** When you say an object is shiny or dull, you are describing its luster. Minerals have metallic, submetallic, or nonmetallic luster. If a mineral is shiny, it may have either a glassy or a metallic luster. If the mineral is dull, its luster is either submetallic or nonmetallic. The different types of lusters are shown in the chart at left.

Streak

The color of a mineral in powdered form is called the mineral's **streak.** To find a mineral's streak, the mineral is rubbed against a piece of unglazed porcelain called a streak plate. The mark left on the streak plate is the streak. The color of a mineral's streak is not always the same as the color of the mineral sample, as shown in **Figure 4.** Unlike the surface of a mineral sample, the streak is not affected by weathering. For this reason, streak is more reliable than color as an indicator of a mineral's identity.

Figure 4 *The color of the mineral hematite may vary, but its streak is always red-brown.*

Cleavage and Fracture

Different types of minerals break in different ways. The way a mineral breaks is determined by the arrangement of its atoms. **Cleavage** is the tendency of some minerals to break along flat surfaces. Gem cutters take advantage of natural cleavage to remove flaws from certain minerals, such as diamonds and rubies, and to shape them into beautiful gemstones. **Figure 5** shows minerals with different cleavage patterns.

Fracture is the tendency of some minerals to break unevenly along curved or irregular surfaces. One type of fracture is shown in **Figure 6.**

Once you've learned about the properties of minerals, put your knowledge to the test! To find out how, turn to page 638 in your LabBook.

Figure 5 *Cleavage varies with mineral type. Mica breaks easily into distinct sheets. Halite breaks at 90° angles in three directions. Diamond breaks in four different directions.*

Diamond   **Halite**

Mica

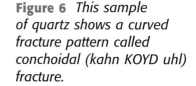

Figure 6 *This sample of quartz shows a curved fracture pattern called conchoidal (kahn KOYD uhl) fracture.*

Hardness

Hardness refers to a mineral's resistance to being scratched. If you try to scratch a diamond, you will have a tough time because diamond is the hardest mineral. Talc, on the other hand, is one of the softest minerals. You can scratch it with your fingernail. To determine the hardness of minerals, scientists use *Mohs' hardness scale,* shown below. Notice that talc has a rating of 1 and diamond has a rating of 10. Between these two extremes are other minerals with progressively greater hardness.

To identify a mineral using Mohs' scale, try to scratch the surface of a mineral with the edge of one of the 10 reference minerals. If the reference mineral scratches your mineral, it is harder than your mineral. Continue trying to scratch the mineral until you find a reference mineral that cannot scratch your mineral.

Mohs' Hardness Scale

1 Talc   **2** Gypsum   **3** Calcite

4 Fluorite   **5** Apatite   **6** Orthoclase   **7** Quartz

8 Topaz   **9** Corundum   **10** Diamond

Density

Figure 7 *Because a golf ball has a greater density than a table-tennis ball, more table-tennis balls are needed to balance the scale.*

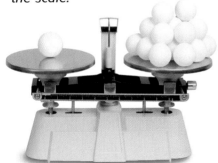

If you pick up a golf ball and a table-tennis ball, which will feel heavier? Although the balls are of similar size, the golf ball will feel heavier because it is denser, as shown in **Figure 7.** **Density** is the measure of how much matter there is in a given amount of space. In other words, density is a ratio of an object's mass to its volume. Density is usually measured in grams per cubic centimeter. Because water has a density of 1 g/cm^3, it is used as a reference point for other substances. The ratio of an object's density to the density of water is called the object's *specific gravity.* The specific gravity of gold, for example, is 19. This means that gold has a density of 19 g/cm^3. In other words, there is 19 times more matter in 1 cm^3 of gold than in 1 cm^3 of water.

Special Properties

Some properties are particular to only a few types of minerals. The properties below can quickly help you identify the minerals shown. To identify some properties, however, you will need specialized equipment.

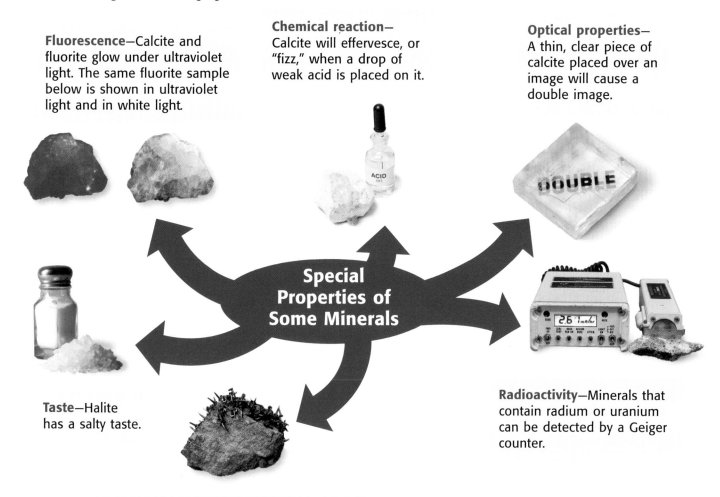

Fluorescence—Calcite and fluorite glow under ultraviolet light. The same fluorite sample below is shown in ultraviolet light and in white light.

Chemical reaction—Calcite will effervesce, or "fizz," when a drop of weak acid is placed on it.

Optical properties—A thin, clear piece of calcite placed over an image will cause a double image.

Special Properties of Some Minerals

Taste—Halite has a salty taste.

Radioactivity—Minerals that contain radium or uranium can be detected by a Geiger counter.

Magnetism—Magnetite and pyrrhotite are both natural magnets that attract iron.

REVIEW

1. How do you determine a mineral's streak?

2. What is the difference between cleavage and fracture?

3. How would you determine the hardness of an unidentified mineral sample?

4. **Applying Concepts** Suppose you have two minerals that have the same hardness. Which other mineral properties would you use to determine whether the samples are the same mineral?

For a list of minerals and their properties, see page 750.

The Formation and Mining of Minerals

Terms to Learn

ore
reclamation

What You'll Do

◆ Describe the environments in which minerals are formed.
◆ Compare and contrast the different types of mining.

Almost all known minerals can be found in the Earth's crust. They form in a large variety of environments under a variety of physical and chemical conditions. The environment in which a mineral forms determines the mineral's properties. Minerals form both deep beneath the Earth's surface and on or near the Earth's surface.

Evaporating Saltwater When a body of salt water dries up, minerals such as gypsum and halite are left behind. As the salt water evaporates, these minerals crystallize.

Limestones Surface water and ground water carry dissolved materials into lakes and seas, where they crystallize on the bottom. Minerals that form in this environment include calcite and dolomite.

Metamorphic Rocks When changes in pressure, temperature, or chemical makeup alter a rock, *metamorphism* takes place. Minerals that form in metamorphic rock include calcite, garnet, graphite, hematite, magnetite, mica, and talc.

Heat and Pressure

Self-Check

Where do minerals such as gypsum and halite form? *(See page 726 to check your answer.)*

Hot-water Solutions Ground water works its way downward and is heated by magma. It then reacts with minerals to form a hot liquid solution. Dissolved metals and other elements crystallize out of the hot fluid to form new minerals. Gold, copper, sulfur, pyrite, and galena form in such hot-water environments.

Pegmatites As magma moves upward it can form teardrop-shaped bodies called *pegmatites.* The presence of hot fluids causes the mineral crystals to become extremely large, sometimes growing to several meters across! Many gems, such as topaz and tourmaline, form in pegmatites.

Plutons As magma rises upward through the crust, it sometimes stops moving before it reaches the surface and cools slowly, forming millions of mineral crystals. Eventually, the entire magma body solidifies to form a *pluton.* Mica, feldspar, magnetite, and quartz are some of the minerals that form from magma.

Magma

MATH BREAK

How Pure Is Pure?

Gold classified as 24-karat is 100 percent gold. Gold classified as 18-karat is 18 parts gold and 6 parts another, similar metal. It is therefore $18/24$ or $3/4$ pure. What is the percentage of pure gold in 18-karat gold?

Mining

Many kinds of rocks and minerals must be mined in order to extract the valuable elements they contain. Geologists use the term **ore** to describe a mineral deposit large enough and pure enough to be mined for a profit. Rocks and minerals are removed from the ground by one of two methods—surface mining or deep mining. The method miners choose depends on how far down in the Earth the mineral is located and how valuable the ore is. The two types of mining are illustrated below.

Surface mining is the removal of minerals or other materials at or near the Earth's surface. Types of surface mines include open pits, strip mines, and quarries. Materials mined in this way include copper ores and bauxite, a mixture of minerals rich in aluminum.

Deep mining is the removal of minerals or other materials from deep within the Earth. Passageways must be dug underground to reach the ore. The retrieval of diamonds and coal commonly requires deep mining.

The Value of Minerals

Many of the metals you are familiar with originally came from mineral ores. You may not be familiar with the minerals, but you will probably recognize the metals extracted from the minerals. The table at right lists some mineral ores and some of the familiar metals that come from them.

As you have seen, some minerals are highly valued for their beauty rather than for their usefulness. Mineral crystals that are attractive and rare are called gems, or gemstones. An example of a gem is shown in **Figure 8.** Gems must be hard enough to be cut and polished.

Common Uses of Minerals		
Mineral	**Metal**	**Uses**
Chalcopyrite	copper	coins, electrical wire
Galena	lead	batteries, paints
Beryl	beryllium	bicycle frames, airplanes
Chromite	chromium	stainless steel, cast iron, leather tanners

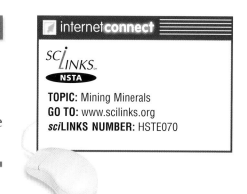

Figure 8 *The Cullinan diamond, at the center of this scepter, is part of the largest diamond ever found.*

Responsible Mining

Mining gives us the minerals we need, but it also creates problems. Mining can destroy or disturb the habitats of plants and animals. The waste products from a mine can get into water sources, polluting both surface water and ground water.

One way to reduce the harmful effects of mining is to return the land to its original state after the mining is completed. This process is called **reclamation.** Reclamation of mined public land has been required by law since the mid-1970s. But reclamation is an expensive and time-consuming process. Another way to reduce the effects of mining is to reduce our need for minerals. We do this by recycling many of the mineral products we currently use, such as aluminum and iron. Mineral ores are *nonrenewable resources;* therefore, the more we recycle, the more we will have in the future.

REVIEW

1. Describe how minerals form underground.

2. What are the two main types of mining?

3. **Analyzing Ideas** How does reclamation protect the environment around a mine?

Chapter Highlights

SECTION 1

Vocabulary

mineral (p. 60)

element (p. 60)

atom (p. 61)

compound (p. 61)

crystal (p. 61)

silicate mineral (p. 62)

nonsilicate mineral (p. 63)

Section Notes

- A mineral is a naturally formed, inorganic solid with a definite crystalline structure.

- An atom is the smallest unit of an element that retains the properties of the element.

- A compound forms when atoms of two or more elements bond together chemically.

- Every mineral has a unique crystalline structure. The crystal class a mineral belongs to is directly related to the mineral's chemical composition.

- Minerals are classified as either silicates or nonsilicates. Each group includes different types of minerals.

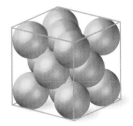 

SECTION 2

Vocabulary

luster (p. 64)

streak (p. 65)

cleavage (p. 65)

fracture (p. 65)

hardness (p. 66)

density (p. 66)

Section Notes

- Color is not a reliable indicator for identifying minerals.

- The luster of a mineral can be metallic, submetallic, or nonmetallic.

- A mineral's streak does not necessarily match its surface color.

- The way a mineral breaks can be used to determine its identity. Cleavage and fracture are two ways that minerals break.

☑ Skills Check

Math Concepts

THE PURITY OF GOLD The karat is a measure of the purity of gold. Gold that is 24 karats is 100 percent gold. But gold that is less than 24 karats is mixed with other elements, so it is less than 100 percent gold. If you have a gold nugget that is 16 karats, then 16 parts out of 24 are pure gold—the other 8 parts are composed of other elements.

$$24 \text{ karats} = 100\% \text{ gold}$$
$$16 \text{ karats} = 24 \text{ karats} - 8 \text{ karats}$$
$$\frac{16}{24} = \frac{2}{3} = 0.67 = 67\% \text{ gold}$$

Visual Understanding

ATOMIC STRUCTURE This illustration of the atomic structure of the mineral halite shows that halite is made of two elements—sodium and chlorine. The large spheres represent atoms of chlorine, and the small spheres represent atoms of sodium. The bars between the atoms represent the chemical bonds that hold them together.

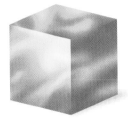

SECTION 2

- Mohs' hardness scale provides a numerical rating for the hardness of minerals.

- The density of a mineral can be used to identify it.

- Some minerals have special properties that can be used to quickly identify them.

Labs

Mysterious Minerals *(p. 638)*

Is It Fool's Gold?—A Dense Situation *(p. 640)*

SECTION 3

Vocabulary

ore *(p. 70)*

reclamation *(p. 71)*

Section Notes

- Minerals form in both underground environments and surface environments.

- Two main types of mining are surface mining and deep mining.

- Minerals are valuable because metals can be extracted from them and because some of them can be cut to form gems.

- Reclamation is the process of returning mined land to its original state.

---

internetconnect

GO TO: go.hrw.com

Visit the **HRW** Web site for a variety of learning tools related to this chapter. Just type in the keyword:

KEYWORD: HSTMIN

GO TO: www.scilinks.org

Visit the **National Science Teachers Association** on-line Web site for Internet resources related to this chapter. Just type in the *sci*LINKS number for more information about the topic:

TOPIC: Gems	*sci*LINKS NUMBER: HSTE055
TOPIC: Birthstones	*sci*LINKS NUMBER: HSTE060
TOPIC: Identifying Minerals	*sci*LINKS NUMBER: HSTE065
TOPIC: Mining Minerals	*sci*LINKS NUMBER: HSTE070

Chapter Review

USING VOCABULARY

For each pair of terms, explain the difference in their meaning.

1. fracture/cleavage

2. element/ compound

3. color/streak

4. density/hardness

5. silicate mineral/nonsilicate mineral

6. mineral/atom

UNDERSTANDING CONCEPTS

Multiple Choice

7. On Mohs' hardness scale, which of the following minerals is harder than quartz?
   a. talc   c. gypsum
   b. apatite   d. topaz

8. A mineral's streak
   a. is more reliable than color in identifying a mineral.
   b. reveals the mineral's specific gravity.
   c. is the same as a luster test.
   d. reveals the mineral's crystal structure.

9. Which of the following factors is **not** important in the formation of minerals?
   a. heat
   b. volcanic activity
   c. presence of ground water
   d. wind

10. Which of the following terms is **not** used to describe a mineral's luster?
    a. pearly   c. dull
    b. waxy   d. hexagonal

11. Which of the following is considered a special property that applies to only a few minerals?
    a. color   c. streak
    b. luster   d. magnetism

12. Which of the following physical properties can be expressed in numbers?
    a. luster
    b. hardness
    c. color
    d. reaction to acid

13. Which of the following minerals would scratch fluorite?
    a. talc
    b. quartz
    c. gypsum
    d. calcite

Short Answer

14. Using no more than 25 words, define the term *mineral.*

15. In one sentence, describe how density is used to identify a mineral.

16. What methods of mineral identification are the most reliable? Explain.

Concept Mapping

17. Use the following terms to create a concept map: minerals, oxides, nonsilicates, carbonates, silicates, hematite, calcite, quartz.

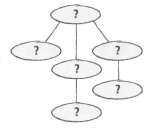

Write one or two sentences to answer the following questions:

18. Suppose you have three rings, each with a different gem. One has a diamond, one has an amethyst (purple quartz), and one has a topaz. You mail the rings in a small box to your friend who lives five states away. When the box arrives at its destination, two of the gems are damaged. One gem, however, is damaged much worse than the other. What scientific reason can you give for the difference in damage?

19. While trying to determine the identity of a mineral, you decide to do a streak test. You rub the mineral across the plate, but it does not leave a streak. Does this mean your test failed? Explain your answer.

20. Imagine that you work at a jeweler's shop and someone brings in some "gold nuggets" that they want to sell. The person claims that an old prospector found the gold nuggets during the California gold rush. You are not sure if the nuggets are real gold. How would you decide whether to buy the nuggets? Which identification tests would help you decide the nuggets' identity?

21. Suppose that you find a mineral crystal that is as tall as you are. What kinds of environmental factors would cause such a crystal to form?

22. Gold has a specific gravity of 19. Pyrite's specific gravity is 5. How much denser is gold than pyrite?

23. In a quartz crystal there is one silicon atom for every two oxygen atoms. That means that the ratio of silicon atoms to oxygen atoms is 1:2. If there were 8 million oxygen atoms in a sample of quartz, how many silicon atoms would there be?

Imagine that you had a sample of feldspar and analyzed it to find out what it is made of. The results of your analysis are shown below.

Composition of Orthoclase (Pink Feldspar)

Percent of Mass vs *Elements* (K, Al, Si, O)

24. Your sample consists of four elements. What percentage of each one is your sample made of?

25. If your mineral sample has a mass of 10 g, how many grams of oxygen does it contain?

26. Make a circle graph showing how much of each of the four elements the feldspar contains. (You will find help on making circle graphs in the Appendix of this book.)

Reading Check-up

Take a minute to review your answers to the Pre-Reading Questions found at the bottom of page 58. Have your answers changed? If necessary, revise your answers based on what you have learned since you began this chapter.

LIGHTNING LEFTOVERS

Without warning, a bolt of lightning lashes out from a storm cloud and strikes a sandy shoreline with a crash. Almost instantly, the sky is dark again—the lightning has disappeared without a trace. Or has it?

Nature's Glass Factory

Fulgurites are a rare type of natural glass formed when lightning strikes silica-rich minerals that occur commonly in sand, soil, and some rocks. *Tubular fulgurites* are found in areas with a lot of silica, such as beaches or deserts. Lightning creates a tubular fulgurite when a bolt penetrates the sand and melts silica into a liquid. The liquid silica cools and hardens quickly, leaving behind a thin glassy tube, usually with a rough outer surface and a smooth inner surface. Underground, a fulgurite may be shaped like the roots of a tree. It branches out with many arms that trace the zigzag path of the lightning bolt. Some fulgurites are as short as your little finger, while others stretch 20 m into the ground.

Underground Puzzles

So should you expect to run across a fulgurite on your next trip to the beach? Don't count on it. Scientists and collectors search long and hard for the dark glass formations, which often form with little or no surface evidence pointing to their underground location. Even when a fulgurite is located, removing it in one piece is difficult. They are quite delicate, with walls no thicker than 1–2 mm. Some of the largest fulgurites are removed from the ground in many pieces then glued back into their original shape.

Rock Fulgurites

Rock fulgurites are extremely rare, usually occurring only on high mountains. These oddities are created when lightning strikes the surface of a silica-rich rock. A rock fulgurite often looks like a bubbly glass case 1–3 mm thick around the rock. Lightning travels around the outside of the rock, fusing silica-rich minerals on its surface. Depending on which minerals melt, a rock fulgurite's color can range from glassy black to light gray or even bright yellow.

Find Out More

▶ Investigate how scientists studying the formation of fulgurites try to make lightning bolts strike a precise location to create a new fulgurite. You may also want to do some research to find out about companies that will *create* a fulgurite just for you!

◀ *A Tubular Fulgurite*

Science Fiction

"The Metal Man"

by Jack Williamson

In a dark, dusty corner of Tyburn College Museum stands a life-sized statue of a man. Except for its strange greenish color, the statue looks pretty ordinary. But if you look closely, you will marvel at the perfect detail of the hair and skin. You will also see a strange mark on the statue's chest, a dark crimson shape with six sides.

No one knows how the statue ended up in the dark corner. Everyone believes that the Metal Man is, or once was, Professor Thomas Kelvin of the Geology Department. Professor Kelvin had for many years spent his summer vacations along the Pacific coast of Mexico, prospecting for radium. Then at the end of one summer, Kelvin did not return to Tyburn. He had been more successful than he ever dreamed, and he had become very rich. But high in the mountains, he had also found something else . . .

Now there is only one person who knows what really happened to Professor Kelvin, and he tells the professor's story in "The Metal Man," by Jack Williamson. The tale involves Kelvin's expedition to search for the source of El Rio de la Sangre, the River of Blood, and the radium that makes the river radioactive. Did he find it? Is that what made Kelvin so rich? And what else did Professor Kelvin find there in the remote mountain valley?

Read for yourself the strange story of Professor Kelvin and the Metal Man in the *Holt Anthology of Science Fiction.*

Rocks: Mineral Mixtures

Pre-Reading Questions

1. What is the difference between a rock and a mineral?

2. What are some modern uses of rocks?

3. How does rock form?

STEPS FOR A GIANT?

Irish legend claims that the mythical hero Finn MacCool built the Giant's Causeway, shown here. According to legend, these stepping stones were used to cross the sea in order to invade a neighboring island. Actually, this rock formation is the result of the cooling of huge amounts of molten rock. As the molten rock cooled, it formed tall, hexagonal pillars called *columnar joints*. Columnar joints can be seen in basalt rocks around the world. In this chapter, you will learn more about how rocks form.

CLASSIFYING OBJECTS

Scientists use the physical and chemical properties of rocks to classify them. Classifying objects such as rocks requires close attention to many properties. Do this exercise to get some classifying practice.

Procedure

1. Your teacher will give you a **bag containing several objects**. Examine the objects and note features such as size, color, shape, texture, smell, and any unique properties.

2. Invent three different ways to sort these objects. You may have only one group or as many as 14.

3. Create an identification key explaining how you organized the objects into each group.

Analysis

4. What properties did you use to sort the items?

5. Were there any objects that could fit into more than one group? How did you solve this problem?

6. Which properties might you use to classify rocks? Explain your answer.

Terms to Learn

rock   texture
rock cycle   igneous rock
magma   sedimentary rock
composition   metamorphic rock

What You'll Do

- Describe two ways rocks were used by early humans, and describe two ways they are used today.
- Describe how each type of rock changes into another as it moves through the rock cycle.
- List two characteristics of rock that are used to help classify it.

Understanding Rock

The Earth's crust is made up mostly of rock. But what exactly is rock? **Rock** is simply a solid mixture of crystals of one or more minerals. However, some types of rock, such as coal, are made of organic materials. Rocks come in all sizes—from pebbles to formations thousands of kilometers long!

The Value of Rock

Rock has been an important natural resource as long as humans have existed. Early humans used rocks as hammers to make other tools. They discovered that they could make arrowheads, spear points, knives, and scrapers by carefully hammering flint, chert, and obsidian rocks. See **Figure 1**. These rocks were shaped to form extremely sharp edges and points. Even today, obsidian is used to form special scalpels, as shown in **Figure 2**.

Rock has also been used for centuries to make buildings, roads, and monuments. **Figure 3** shows some inventive uses of rock by both ancient and modern civilizations. Buildings have been made out of marble, granite, sandstone, limestone, and slate. Modern buildings also use concrete, in which rock is an important ingredient. Concrete is one of the most common building materials used today.

Figure 1 *This stone tool was made and used more than 5,000 years ago.*

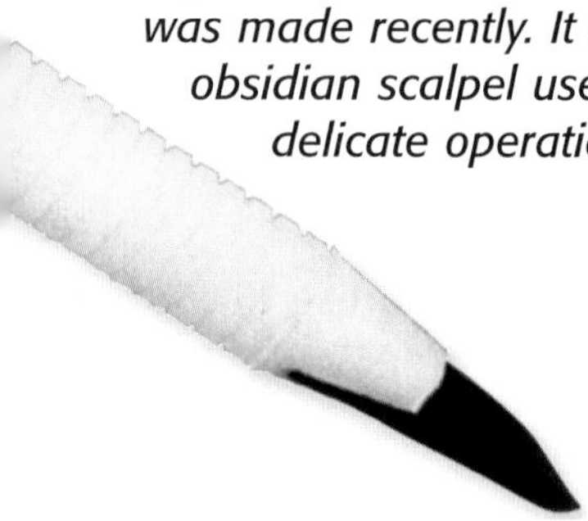

Figure 2 *This stone tool was made recently. It is an obsidian scalpel used in delicate operations.*

Figure 3 *These photos show a few samples of structures built with rock. On this page are structures built by ancient civilizations. On the facing page are some more-modern examples.*

Machu Picchu, Peru (A.D. 600)

Pyramids at Giza, Egypt (3000 B.C.)

Humans have a long history with rock. Certain types of rock have helped us to survive and to develop both our ancient and modern civilizations. Rock is also very important to scientists. The study of rocks helps answer questions about the history of the Earth and our solar system. Rocks provide a record of what the Earth and other planets were like before recorded history.

The fossils some rocks contain also provide clues about life-forms that lived billions of years ago, long before dinosaurs walked the Earth. **Figure 4** shows how rocks can capture evidence of life that became extinct long ago. Without such fossils, scientists would know very little about the history of life on Earth. The answers we get from studying rocks often cause us to ask even more questions!

BRAIN FOOD

Some meteorites are actually rocks that come from other planets. Below is a microscopic view of a meteorite that came from Mars. The tiny structures may indicate that microscopic life once existed on Mars.

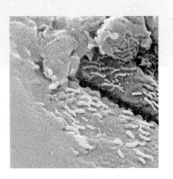

Figure 4 *These fossils were found on a mountaintop. Their presence indicates that what is now a mountaintop was once the bottom of a shallow sea.*

Exeter Cathedral, Exeter, England (A.D. 1120–1520)

LBJ Library, Austin, Texas (1972)

The Rock Cycle

The rocks in the Earth's crust are constantly changing. Rock changes its shape and composition in a variety of ways. The way rock forms determines what type of rock it is. The three main types of rock are *igneous, sedimentary,* and *metamorphic.* Each type of rock is a part of the *rock cycle.* The **rock cycle** is the process by which one rock type changes into another. Follow this diagram to see one way sand grains can change as they travel through the rock cycle.

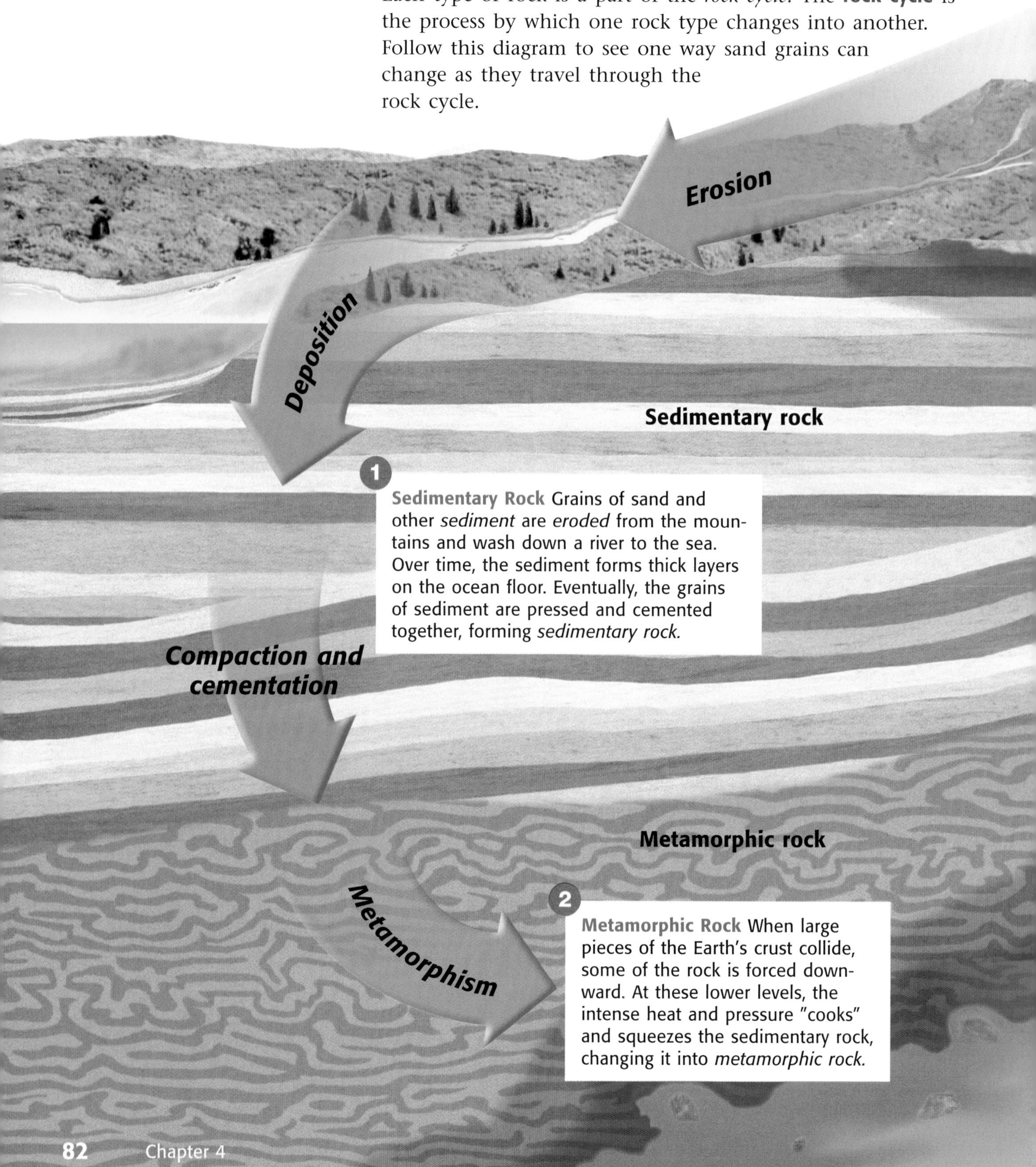

Erosion

Deposition

Sedimentary rock

1

Sedimentary Rock Grains of sand and other *sediment* are *eroded* from the mountains and wash down a river to the sea. Over time, the sediment forms thick layers on the ocean floor. Eventually, the grains of sediment are pressed and cemented together, forming *sedimentary rock.*

Compaction and cementation

Metamorphic rock

Metamorphism

2

Metamorphic Rock When large pieces of the Earth's crust collide, some of the rock is forced downward. At these lower levels, the intense heat and pressure "cooks" and squeezes the sedimentary rock, changing it into *metamorphic rock.*

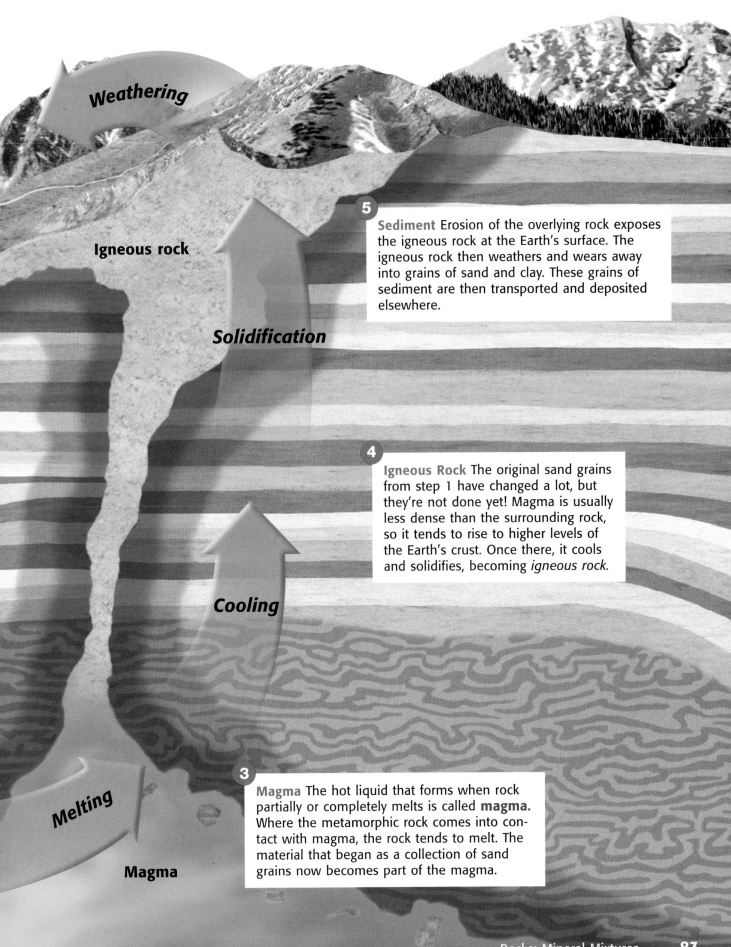

Weathering

Igneous rock

Solidification

Cooling

Melting

Magma

5 **Sediment** Erosion of the overlying rock exposes the igneous rock at the Earth's surface. The igneous rock then weathers and wears away into grains of sand and clay. These grains of sediment are then transported and deposited elsewhere.

4 **Igneous Rock** The original sand grains from step 1 have changed a lot, but they're not done yet! Magma is usually less dense than the surrounding rock, so it tends to rise to higher levels of the Earth's crust. Once there, it cools and solidifies, becoming *igneous rock.*

3 **Magma** The hot liquid that forms when rock partially or completely melts is called **magma.** Where the metamorphic rock comes into contact with magma, the rock tends to melt. The material that began as a collection of sand grains now becomes part of the magma.

Now that you know something about the natural processes that make the three major rock types, you can see that each type of rock can become any other type of rock. This is why it is called a cycle—there is no beginning or end. All rocks are at some stage of the rock cycle and can change into a different rock type. **Figure 5** shows how the three types of rock change form.

Figure 5 The Rock Cycle

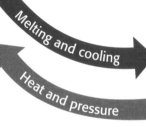

Sedimentary rock is rock that forms when sediments are compacted and cemented together. The sediments that form sedimentary rock come from the weathering and erosion of igneous, metamorphic, or even other sedimentary rock.

Metamorphic rock is rock that forms when the texture and composition of a preexisting rock is changed by heat or pressure deep underground. Igneous and sedimentary rock can change into metamorphic rock, and metamorphic rock can even change into another metamorphic rock.

Igneous rock is rock that forms from the cooling of *magma.* When magma cools and solidifies, it forms igneous rock. Magma forms in Earth's lower crust and upper mantle. When magma flows out onto the Earth's surface, it is called **lava.**

Weathering and erosion

Heat and pressure

Weathering and erosion

Melting and cooling

Weathering and erosion

Melting and cooling

Heat and pressure

Heat and pressure

Melting and cooling

Classifying Objects

Suppose you have an apple, a tomato, a peach, a kiwi fruit, a pineapple, a banana, a lemon, a cactus, a blue ball, a coconut, a brick, a sugar cube, a pair of sunglasses, and a garden hose. Use your imagination to invent three different ways to classify these objects into groups with similar characteristics. You may have only 1 group or as many as 14. What criteria did you use for each of your classification schemes? Which criteria would you use to classify rocks?

The Nitty-Gritty on Rock Classification

You now know that scientists classify all rock into three main types based on how they formed. But did you know that each type of rock is divided into even smaller groups? These smaller groups are also based on differences in the way rocks form. For example, all igneous rock forms when hot liquid cools and solidifies. But some igneous rocks form when lava cools on the Earth's surface, while others form when magma cools deep beneath the surface. Therefore, igneous rock is divided into two smaller groups, depending on how and where it forms. In the same way, sedimentary and metamorphic rocks are also divided into smaller groups. How do Earth scientists know how to classify different rocks? They study them in detail using two important criteria—*composition* and *texture*.

Composition The minerals a rock is made of determine the **composition** of the rock. For example, a rock that is made up mostly of the mineral quartz will have a composition very similar to quartz. A rock that is made of 50 percent quartz and 50 percent feldspar will have a very different overall composition. Use this idea to compare the examples given in **Figure 6.**

MATH BREAK

What's in It?

Assume that a granite rock you are studying is made of 30 percent quartz, 55 percent feldspar, and the rest biotite mica. What percentage of the rock is biotite mica?

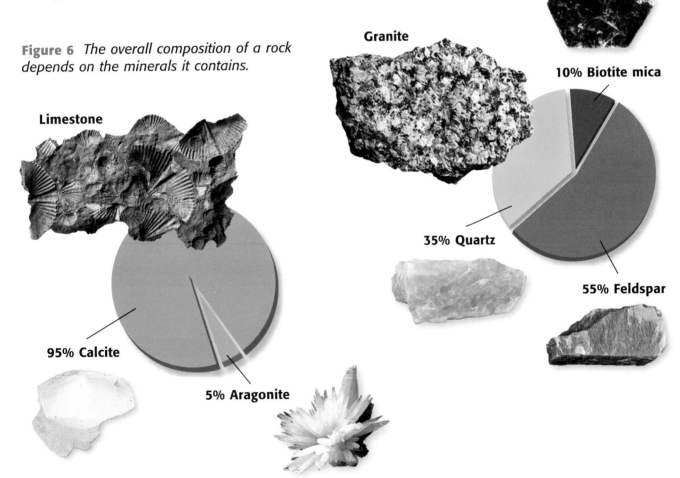

Figure 6 *The overall composition of a rock depends on the minerals it contains.*

Granite

10% Biotite mica

35% Quartz

55% Feldspar

Limestone

95% Calcite

5% Aragonite

Texture The **texture** of a rock is determined by the sizes, shapes, and positions of the grains of which it is made. Rocks that are made entirely of small grains, such as silt or clay particles, are said to have a *fine-grained* texture. Rocks that are made of large grains, such as pebbles, are said to have a *coarse-grained* texture. Rocks that have a texture between fine- and coarse-grained are said to have a *medium-grained* texture. Examples of these textures are shown in **Figure 7.**

Figure 7 *These three sedimentary rocks are made up of grains of different sizes. Can you see the differences in their textures?*

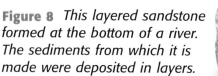

Fine-grained	**Medium-grained**	**Coarse-grained**

Siltstone   Sandstone   Conglomerate

Each rock type has a different kind of texture that can provide good clues to how and where the rock formed. For example, the rock shown in **Figure 8** has a texture that reflects how it formed. Both texture and composition are important characteristics that scientists use to understand the origin and history of rocks. Keep these characteristics in mind as you continue reading through this chapter.

Figure 8 *This layered sandstone formed at the bottom of a river. The sediments from which it is made were deposited in layers.*

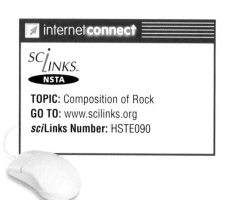

internet connect

SC/
LINKS
NSTA

TOPIC: Composition of Rock
GO TO: www.scilinks.org
*sci*Links Number: HSTE090

REVIEW

1. List two ways rock is important to humans today.

2. What are the three major rock types, and how can they change from one type to another type?

3. How is lava different from magma?

4. **Comparing Concepts** Explain the difference between texture and composition.

Igneous Rock

The word *igneous* comes from the Latin word for "fire." Magma cools into various types of igneous rock depending on the composition of the magma and the amount of time it takes the magma to cool and solidify. Like all other rock, igneous rock is classified according to its composition and texture.

Terms to Learn

intrusive
extrusive

What You'll Do

◆ Explain how the cooling rate of magma affects the properties of igneous rock.
◆ Distinguish between igneous rock that cools deep within the crust and igneous rock that cools at the surface.
◆ Identify common igneous rock formations.

Origins of Igneous Rock

Magma and lava solidify in much the same way that water freezes. When magma or lava cools down enough, it solidifies, or "freezes," to form igneous rock. One difference between water freezing and magma freezing is that water freezes at 0°C and magma and lava freeze at between 700°C and 1,250°C.

There are three ways magma can form: when rock is heated, when pressure is released, or when rock changes composition. To see how this can happen, follow along with **Figure 9.**

Figure 9 *There are three ways a rock can melt.*

Temperature An increase in temperature deep within the Earth's crust can cause the minerals in a rock to melt. Different minerals melt at different temperatures. So depending on how hot a rock gets, some of the minerals can melt while other minerals remain solid.

Pressure The high pressure deep within the Earth forces minerals to stay in the solid state, when otherwise they would melt from the intense heat. When hot rocks rise to shallow depths, the pressure is finally released and the minerals can melt.

Composition Sometimes fluids like water and carbon dioxide enter a rock that is close to its melting point. When these fluids combine with the rock, they can lower the melting point of the rock enough for it to melt and form magma.

Composition and Texture of Igneous Rock

Look at the rocks in **Figure 10.** All of these are igneous rocks, even though they look very different from one another. These rocks differ from one another in what they are made of and how fast they cooled.

The light-colored rocks are not only lighter in color but also less dense. They are rich in elements such as silicon, aluminum, sodium, and potassium. These lightweight rocks are called *felsic.* The darker rocks are denser than the felsic rocks. These rocks are rich in iron, magnesium, and calcium and are called *mafic.*

Figure 10 *Light-colored igneous rock generally has a felsic composition. Dark-colored igneous rock generally has a mafic composition.*

	Coarse-grained	**Fine-grained**
Felsic	Granite	Rhyolite
Mafic	Gabbro	Basalt

Now look at **Figure 11.** This illustration shows what happens to magma when it cools at different rates. The longer it takes for the magma or lava to cool, the more time mineral crystals have to grow. And the more time the crystals have to grow, the coarser the texture of the resulting igneous rock.

Fast-cooling lava

Fine-grained igneous rock

Magma

Slow-cooling magma

Coarse-grained igneous rock

Figure 11 *The amount of time it takes for magma or lava to cool determines the texture of igneous rock.*

✔ Self-Check

Rank the rocks shown in Figure 10 by how fast they cooled. Hint: Pay attention to their texture. *(See page 726 to check your answer.)*

Igneous Rock Formations

You have probably seen igneous rock formations that were caused by lava cooling on the Earth's surface. But not all magma reaches the surface. Some magma cools and solidifies deep within the Earth's crust.

Intrusive Igneous Rock When magma cools beneath the Earth's surface, the resulting rock is called **intrusive.** Intrusive rock usually has a coarse-grained texture. This is because it is well insulated by the surrounding rock and thus cools very slowly.

Intrusive rock formations are named for their size and the way in which they intrude, or push into, the surrounding rock. *Plutons* are large, balloon-shaped intrusive formations that result when magma cools at great depths. Intrusive rocks are also called *plutonic rocks,* after Pluto, the Roman god of the underworld. **Figure 12** shows an example of an intrusive formation that has been exposed on the Earth's surface. Some common intrusive rock formations are shown in **Figure 13.**

Figure 12 *Enchanted Rock, near Llano, Texas, is an exposed pluton made of granite.*

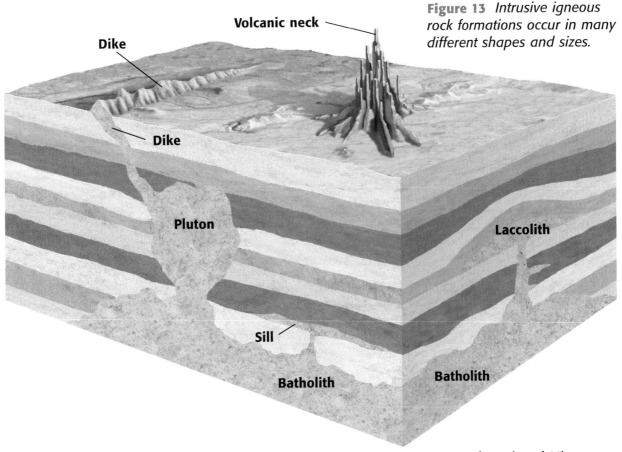

Figure 13 *Intrusive igneous rock formations occur in many different shapes and sizes.*

Volcanic neck

Dike

Dike

Pluton

Laccolith

Sill

Batholith

Batholith

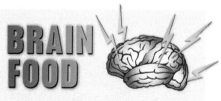

Extrusive Igneous Rock Igneous rock that forms on the Earth's surface is called **extrusive.** Most volcanic rock is extrusive. Extrusive rock cools quickly on the surface and contains either very small crystals or none at all.

When lava erupts from a volcano, a formation called a *lava flow* is made. You can see an active lava flow in **Figure 14.** But lava does not always come from volcanoes. Sometimes lava erupts from long cracks in the Earth's surface called *fissures.* When a large amount of lava flows out of a fissure, it can cover a vast area, forming a plain called a *lava plateau.* Preexisting landforms are often buried by extrusive igneous rock formations.

Figure 14 *Below is an active lava flow. When exposed to surface conditions, lava quickly cools and solidifies, forming a fine-grained igneous rock.*

internetconnect

SCi*LINKS.*
NSTA

TOPIC: Igneous Rock
GO TO: www.scilinks.org
*sci*LINKS **NUMBER:** HSTE093

REVIEW

1. What two properties are used to classify igneous rock?

2. How does the cooling rate of lava or magma affect the texture of an igneous rock?

3. **Interpreting Illustrations** Use the diagram in Figure 13 to compare a sill with a dike. What makes them different from each other?

What You'll Do

◆ Describe how the three types of sedimentary rock form.
◆ Explain how sedimentary rocks record Earth's history.

Sedimentary Rock

Wind, water, ice, sunlight, and gravity all cause rock to *weather* into fragments. **Figure 15** shows how some sedimentary rocks form. Through the process of erosion, rock fragments, called sediment, are transported from one place to another. Eventually the sediment is deposited in layers. Sedimentary rock then forms as sediments become compacted and cemented together.

Origins of Sedimentary Rock

As new layers of sediment are deposited, the layers eventually become compressed, or compacted. Dissolved minerals separate out of the water to form a natural glue that binds the sediments together into sedimentary rock. Sedimentary rock forms at or near the Earth's surface, without the heat and pressure involved in the formation of igneous and metamorphic rocks. The physical features of sedimentary rock tell part of its history. The most noticeable feature of sedimentary rock is its layers, or **strata.** Road cuts and construction zones are good places to observe sedimentary rock formations, and as you can see in **Figure 16,** canyons carved by rivers provide some spectacular views.

Figure 15 A Sedimentary Rock Cycle

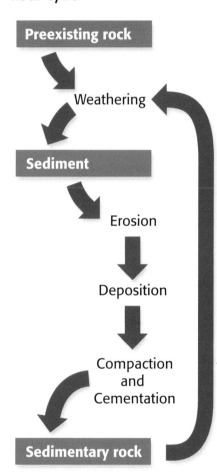

Figure 16 *Millions of years of erosion by the Colorado River have revealed the rock strata in the walls of the Grand Canyon.*

Conglomerate

Coarse-grained

Breccia

Sandstone

Composition of Sedimentary Rock

Sedimentary rock is also classified by the way it forms. There are three main categories of sedimentary rock—clastic, chemical, and organic. *Clastic* sedimentary rock forms when rock or mineral fragments, called clasts, stick together. *Chemical* sedimentary rock forms when minerals crystallize out of a solution, such as sea water, to become rock. *Organic* sedimentary rock forms from the remains of organisms.

Clastic Sedimentary Rock Clastic sedimentary rock is made of fragments of other rocks and minerals. As you can see in **Figure 17,** the size and shape of the rock fragments that make up clastic sedimentary rock influence their names.

Siltstone

Shale

Fine-grained

Figure 17 *Clastic sedimentary rock is classified by the sizes of fragments it is made of.*

Chemical Sedimentary Rock Chemical sedimentary rock forms from *solutions* of minerals and water. As rainwater slowly makes its way to the ocean, it dissolves some of the rock material it passes through. Some of this dissolved material eventually forms the minerals that make up chemical sedimentary rock. One type of chemical sedimentary rock, chemical limestone, is made of calcium carbonate ($CaCO_3$), or the mineral calcite. It forms when calcium and carbonate become so concentrated in the sea water that calcite crystallizes out of the sea water solution, as shown in **Figure 18.**

Figure 18 *Both salt water and fresh water contain dissolved calcium and carbonate. Chemical limestone forms on the ocean floor.*

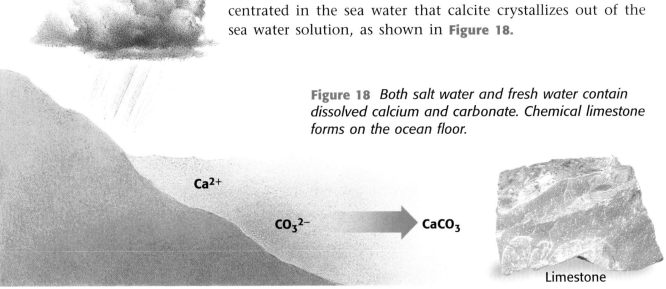

Ca^{2+}

CO_3^{2-} → $CaCO_3$

Limestone

Organic Sedimentary Rock

Most limestone forms from the remains of animals that once lived in the ocean. This organic material consists of shells or skeletons, which are made of calcium carbonate that the animals get from sea water.

For example, some limestone is made of the skeletons of tiny organisms called coral. Coral are very small, but they live in huge colonies, as shown in **Figure 19.** Over time, the remains of these sea animals accumulate on the ocean floor. These animal remains eventually become cemented together to form *fossiliferous* (FAHS uhl IF uhr uhs) *limestone.*

Fossils are the remains or traces of plants and animals that have been preserved in sedimentary rock. Fossils have given us enormous amounts of information about ancient life-forms and how they lived. Most fossils come from animals that lived in the oceans. Another type of organic limestone, shown in **Figure 20,** forms from organisms that leave their shells in the mud on the ocean floor.

Figure 19 *Sea animals called coral create huge deposits of limestone. As they die, their skeletons accumulate on the ocean floor.*

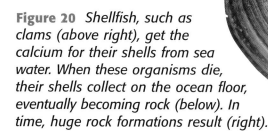

Figure 20 *Shellfish, such as clams (above right), get the calcium for their shells from sea water. When these organisms die, their shells collect on the ocean floor, eventually becoming rock (below). In time, huge rock formations result (right).*

Figure 21 *Wind caused these slanted deposits, called* cross-beds, *but water can also cause them.*

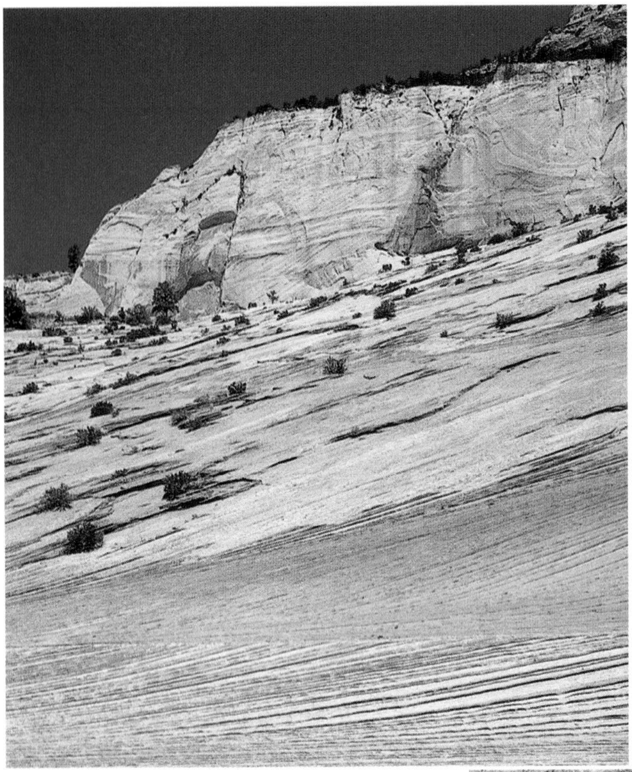

Sedimentary Rock Structures

Many sedimentary rock features can tell you about the way the rock formed. The most characteristic feature of sedimentary rock is **stratification,** or layering. Strata differ from one another depending on the kind, size, and color of their sediment. The rate of deposition can also affect the thickness of the layers. Sedimentary rocks sometimes record the motion of wind and water waves on lakes, seas, rivers, and sand dunes. Some of these features are shown in **Figures 21** and **22.**

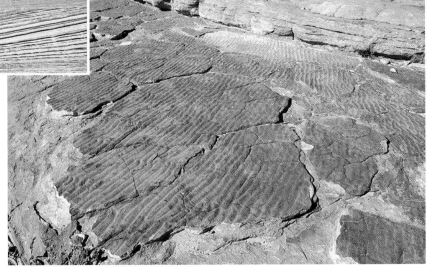

Figure 22 *These* ripple marks *were made by flowing water and were preserved when the sediments became sedimentary rock. Ripple marks can also form from the action of wind.*

internetconnect

SCILINKS NSTA

TOPIC: Sedimentary Rock
GO TO: www.scilinks.org
***sci*LINKS NUMBER:** HSTE095

REVIEW

1. Describe the process by which clastic sedimentary rock forms.
2. List three sedimentary rock structures, and explain how they record geologic processes.
3. **Analyzing Relationships** Both clastic and chemical sedimentary rocks are classified according to texture and composition. Which property is more important for each sedimentary rock type? Explain.

Metamorphic Rock

Terms to Learn

foliated
nonfoliated

What You'll Do

◆ Describe two ways a rock can undergo metamorphism.
◆ Explain how the mineral composition of rocks changes as they undergo metamorphism.
◆ Describe the difference between foliated and nonfoliated metamorphic rock.

The word *metamorphic* comes from *meta,* meaning "changed," and *morphos,* meaning "shape." Remember, metamorphic rocks are those in which the structure, texture, or composition of the rock has changed. Rock can undergo metamorphism by heat or pressure acting alone or by a combination of the two. All three types of rock—igneous, sedimentary, and even metamorphic—can change into metamorphic rock.

Origins of Metamorphic Rock

The texture or mineral composition of a rock can change when its surroundings change. If the temperature or pressure of the new environment is different from the one the rock formed in, the rock will undergo metamorphism.

Most metamorphic change is caused by increased pressure that takes place at depths greater than 2 km. At depths greater than 16 km, the pressure can be more than 4,000 times the pressure of the atmosphere! Look at **Figure 23.** This rock, called garnet schist, formed at a depth of about 30 km. At this depth, some of the crystals the rock is made of change as a result of the extreme pressure. Other types of schist form at much shallower depths.

The temperature at which metamorphism occurs ranges from 50°C to 1,000°C. At temperatures higher than 1,000°C, most rocks will melt. Metamorphism does not melt rock—when rock melts, it becomes magma and then igneous rock. In **Figure 24** you can see that this rock was deformed by intense pressure.

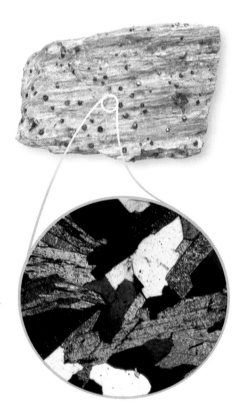

Figure 23 *At top is a metamorphic rock called garnet schist. At bottom is a microscopic view of a thin slice of a garnet schist.*

Figure 24 *In this outcrop, you can see an example of how sedimentary rock was deformed as it underwent metamorphism.*

Quick Lab

Stretching Out

1. Draw your version of a granite rock on a **piece of paper** with a **black-ink pen.** Be sure to include the outline of the rock, and fill it in with different crystal shapes.

2. Mash some **plastic play putty** over the "granite," and slowly peel it off.

3. After making sure that the outline of your "granite" has been transferred to the putty, push and pull on the putty. What happened to the "crystals"? What happened to the "granite"?

TRY at HOME

Contact Metamorphism   One way rock can undergo metamorphism is by coming into contact with magma. When magma moves through the crust, it heats the surrounding rock and "cooks" it. As a result, the magma changes some of the minerals in the surrounding rock into other minerals. The greatest change takes place where magma comes into direct contact with the surrounding rock. The effect of heat gradually lessens with distance from the magma. As you can see in **Figure 25,** *contact metamorphism* only happens next to igneous intrusions.

Regional Metamorphism   When enormous pressure builds up in rock that is deeply buried under other rock formations, or when large pieces of the Earth's crust collide with each other, *regional metamorphism* occurs. The pressure and increased temperature that exist under these conditions cause rock to become deformed and chemically changed. This kind of metamorphic rock is underneath most continental rock formations.

✓ Self-Check

How could a rock undergo both contact and regional metamorphism? *(See page 726 to check your answer.)*

Figure 25 *Metamorphism occurs over small areas, such as next to bodies of magma, and large areas, such as mountain ranges.*

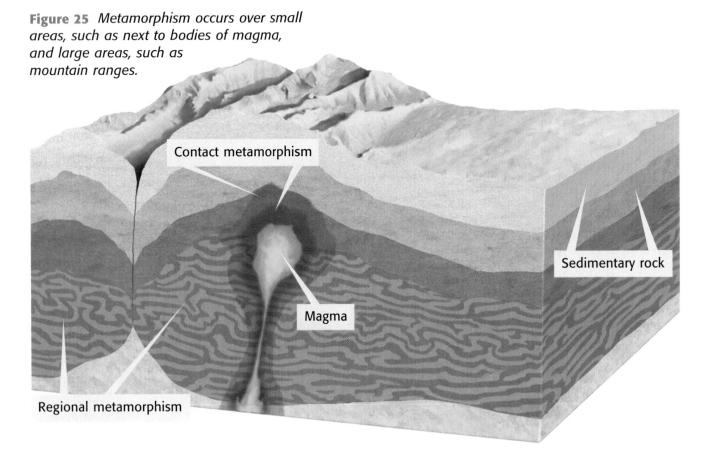

Composition of Metamorphic Rock

When conditions within the Earth's crust change because of collisions between continents or the intrusion of magma, the temperature and pressure of the existing rock change. Minerals that were present in the rock when it formed may no longer be stable in the new environment. The original minerals change into minerals that are more stable in the new temperature and pressure conditions. Look at **Figure 26** to see an example of how this happens.

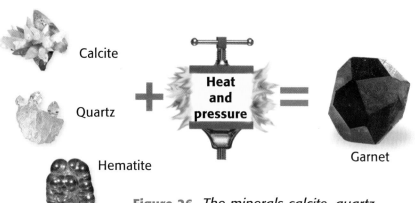

Figure 26 *The minerals calcite, quartz, and hematite combine and recrystallize to form the metamorphic mineral garnet.*

Calcite
Quartz
Hematite
Heat and pressure
Garnet

Many of these new minerals occur only in metamorphic rock. As shown in **Figure 27,** some metamorphic minerals form only within a specific range of temperature and pressure conditions. When scientists observe these metamorphic minerals in a rock, they can estimate the temperature and depth (pressure) at which recently exposed rock underwent metamorphism.

Figure 27 *Scientists can understand a metamorphic rock's history by observing the minerals it contains. For example, metamorphic rock containing garnet formed at a greater depth than one that contains only chlorite.*

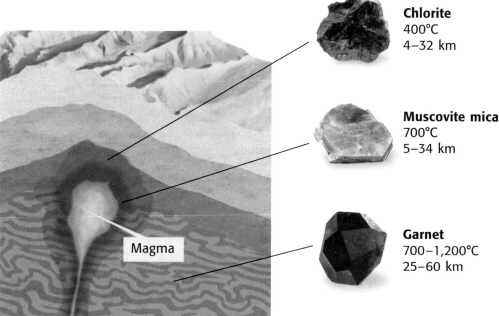

Magma

Chlorite
400°C
4–32 km

Muscovite mica
700°C
5–34 km

Garnet
700–1,200°C
25–60 km

Textures of Metamorphic Rock

As you know, texture helps to classify igneous and sedimentary rock. The same is true of metamorphic rock. All metamorphic rock has one of two textures—*foliated* or *nonfoliated*. **Foliated** metamorphic rock consists of minerals that are aligned and look almost like pages in a book. **Nonfoliated** metamorphic rock does not appear to have any regular pattern. Let's take a closer look at each of these types of metamorphic rock to find out how they form.

Foliated Metamorphic Rock   Foliated metamorphic rock contains mineral grains that are aligned by pressure. Strongly foliated rocks usually contain flat minerals, like biotite mica. Look at **Figure 28.** Shale consists of layers of clay minerals. When subjected to slight heat and pressure, the clay minerals change into mica minerals and the shale becomes a fine-grained, foliated metamorphic rock called slate.

Metamorphic rocks can become other metamorphic rocks if the environment changes again. With additional heat and pressure, slate can change into phyllite, another metamorphic rock. When phyllite is exposed to additional heat and pressure, it can change into a metamorphic rock called schist.

As the degree of metamorphism increases, the arrangement of minerals in the rock changes. With additional heat and pressure, coarse-grained minerals separate into bands in a metamorphic rock called *gneiss* (pronounced "nice").

Sedimentary shale

Slate

Phyllite

Figure 28 *The effects of metamorphism depend on the heat and pressure applied to the rock. Here you can see what happens to shale when it is exposed to more and more heat and pressure.*

Schist

Gneiss

Wouldn't it be "gneiss" to make your own foliated rock? Turn to page 647 in your LabBook to find out how.

Nonfoliated Metamorphic Rock Nonfoliated metamorphic rocks are shown in **Figure 29.** Do you notice anything missing? The lack of aligned mineral grains makes them nonfoliated. They are rocks commonly made of only one, or just a few, minerals.

Sandstone is a sedimentary rock made of distinct quartz sand grains. But when sandstone is subjected to the heat and pressure of metamorphism, the spaces between the sand grains disappear as they recrystallize, forming quartzite. Quartzite has a shiny, glittery appearance. It is still made of quartz, but the mineral grains are larger. When limestone undergoes metamorphism, the same process happens to the mineral calcite, and the limestone becomes marble. Marble has larger calcite crystals than limestone. You have probably seen marble in buildings and statues.

Biology
C O N N E C T I O N

The term *metamorphosis* means "change in form." When certain animals undergo a dramatic change in the shape of their body, they are said to have undergone a metamorphosis. As part of their natural life cycle, moths and butterflies go through four stages of life. After they hatch from an egg, they are in the larval stage in the form of a caterpillar. In the next stage they build a cocoon or become a chrysalis. This is called the pupal stage. They finally emerge into the adult stage of their life, complete with wings, antennae, and legs!

Marble

Quartzite

Figure 29 *Marble and quartzite are nonfoliated metamorphic rocks. As you can see in the microscopic views, none of the mineral crystals are aligned.*

REVIEW

1. What environmental factors cause rock to undergo metamorphism?

2. What is the difference between foliated and nonfoliated metamorphic rock?

3. **Making Inferences** If you had two metamorphic rocks, one with garnet crystals and the other with chlorite crystals, which one would have formed at a deeper level in the Earth's crust? Explain.

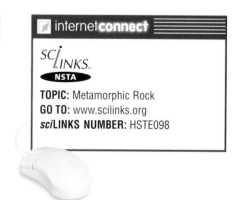

internet**connect**

SC/LINKS
NSTA

TOPIC: Metamorphic Rock
GO TO: www.scilinks.org
***sci*LINKS NUMBER:** HSTE098

Chapter Highlights

SECTION 1

Vocabulary

rock (*p. 80*)

rock cycle (*p. 82*)

magma (*p. 83*)

sedimentary rock (*p. 84*)

metamorphic rock (*p. 84*)

igneous rock (*p. 84*)

composition (*p. 85*)

texture (*p. 86*)

Section Notes

- Rocks have been used by humans for thousands of years, and they are just as valuable today.

- Rocks are classified into three main types—igneous, sedimentary, and metamorphic—depending on how they formed.

- The rock cycle describes the process by which a rock can change from one rock type to another.

- Scientists further classify rocks according to two criteria—composition and texture.

- Molten igneous material creates rock formations both below and above ground.

SECTION 2

Vocabulary

intrusive (*p. 89*)

extrusive (*p. 90*)

Section Notes

- The texture of igneous rock is determined by the rate at which it cools. The slower magma cools, the larger the crystals are.

- Felsic igneous rock is light-colored and lightweight, while mafic igneous rock is dark-colored and heavy.

- Igneous material that solidifies at the Earth's surface is called extrusive, while igneous material that solidifies within the crust is called intrusive.

Lab

Crystal Growth (*p. 642*)

☑ Skills Check

Math Concepts

MINERAL COMPOSITION Rocks are classified not only by the minerals they contain but also by the amounts of those minerals. Suppose a particular kind of granite is made of feldspar, biotite mica, and quartz. If you know that feldspar makes up 55 percent of the rock and biotite mica makes up 15 percent of the rock, the remaining 30 percent must be made of quartz.

55% feldspar + 15% biotite mica + 30% quartz = 100% of granite	100% of granite − 55% feldspar − 15% biotite mica = 30% quartz

or

Visual Understanding

PIE CHARTS The pie charts on page 85 help you visualize the relative amounts of minerals in different types of rock. The circle represents the whole rock, or 100 percent. Each part, or "slice," of the circle represents a fraction of the rock.

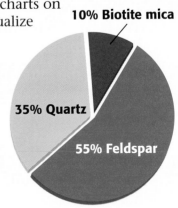

10% Biotite mica

35% Quartz

55% Feldspar

Vocabulary

strata *(p. 91)*

stratification *(p. 94)*

Section Notes

- Clastic sedimentary rock is made of rock and mineral fragments that are compacted and cemented together. Chemical sedimentary rock forms when minerals crystallize out of a solution such as sea water. Organic sedimentary rock forms from the remains of organisms.

- Sedimentary rocks record the history of their formation in their features. Some common features are strata, ripple marks, and fossils.

Lab

Let's Get Sedimental *(p. 645)*

Vocabulary

foliated *(p. 98)*

nonfoliated *(p. 98)*

Section Notes

- One kind of metamorphism is the result of magma heating small areas of surrounding rock, changing its texture and composition.

- Most metamorphism is the product of heat and pressure acting on large regions of the Earth's crust.

- The mineral composition of a rock changes when the minerals it is made of recrystallize to form new minerals. These new minerals are more stable under increased temperature and pressure.

- Metamorphic rock that contains aligned mineral grains is called foliated, and metamorphic rock that does not contain aligned mineral grains is called nonfoliated.

Lab

Metamorphic Mash *(p. 647)*

---

 internetconnect

GO TO: go.hrw.com

Visit the **HRW** Web site for a variety of learning tools related to this chapter. Just type in the keyword:

KEYWORD: HSTRCK

 **SCiLINKS**

NSTA

GO TO: www.scilinks.org

Visit the **National Science Teachers Association** on-line Web site for Internet resources related to this chapter. Just type in the *sci*LINKS number for more information about the topic:

TOPIC: Composition of Rock	*sci*LINKS NUMBER: HSTE090
TOPIC: Igneous Rock	*sci*LINKS NUMBER: HSTE093
TOPIC: Sedimentary Rock	*sci*LINKS NUMBER: HSTE095
TOPIC: Metamorphic Rock	*sci*LINKS NUMBER: HSTE098
TOPIC: Rock Formations	*sci*LINKS NUMBER: HSTE100

Chapter Review

USING VOCABULARY

To complete the following sentences, choose the correct term from each pair of terms listed below:

1. __?__ igneous rock is more likely to have coarse-grained texture than __?__ igneous rock. (*Extrusive/intrusive* or *Intrusive/extrusive*)

2. __?__ metamorphic rock texture consists of parallel alignment of mineral grains. (*Foliated* or *Nonfoliated*)

3. __?__ sedimentary rock forms when grains of sand become cemented together. (*Clastic* or *Chemical*)

4. __?__ cools quickly on the Earth's surface. (*Lava* or *Magma*)

5. Strata are found in __?__ rock. (*igneous* or *sedimentary*)

UNDERSTANDING CONCEPTS

Multiple Choice

6. A type of rock that forms deep within the Earth when magma solidifies is called
   a. sedimentary.
   b. metamorphic.
   c. organic.
   d. igneous.

7. A type of rock that forms under high temperature and pressure but is not exposed to enough heat to melt the rock is
   a. sedimentary.
   b. metamorphic.
   c. organic.
   d. igneous.

8. After they are deposited, sediments, such as sand, are turned into sedimentary rock when they are compacted and
   a. cemented.
   b. metamorphosed.
   c. melted.
   d. weathered.

9. An igneous rock with a coarse-grained texture forms when
   a. magma cools very slowly.
   b. magma cools very quickly.
   c. magma cools quickly, then slowly.
   d. magma cools slowly, then quickly.

10. The layering that occurs in sedimentary rock is called
    a. foliation.
    b. ripple marks.
    c. stratification.
    d. compaction.

11. An example of a clastic sedimentary rock is
    a. obsidian.
    b. sandstone.
    c. gneiss.
    d. marble.

12. A common sedimentary rock structure is
    a. a sill.
    b. a pluton.
    c. cross-bedding.
    d. a lava flow.

13. An example of mafic igneous rock is
    a. granite.
    b. basalt.
    c. quartzite.
    d. pumice.

14. Chemical sedimentary rock forms when
    a. magma cools and solidifies.
    b. minerals are twisted into a new arrangement.
    c. minerals crystallize from a solution.
    d. sand grains are cemented together.

15. Which of the following is a foliated metamorphic rock?
    a. sandstone
    b. gneiss
    c. shale
    d. basalt

Short Answer

16. In no more than three sentences, explain the rock cycle.

17. How are sandstone and siltstone different from one another? How are they the same?

18. In one or two sentences, explain how the cooling rate of magma affects the texture of the igneous rock that forms.

Concept Mapping

19. Use the following terms to create a concept map: rocks, clastic, metamorphic, nonfoliated, igneous, intrusive, chemical, foliated, organic, extrusive, sedimentary.

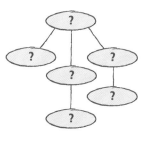

CRITICAL THINKING AND PROBLEM SOLVING

Write one or two sentences to answer the following questions:

20. The sedimentary rock coquina is made up of pieces of seashells. Which of the three kinds of sedimentary rock could it be? Explain.

21. If you were looking for fossils in the rocks around your home and the rock type that was closest to your home was metamorphic, would you find many fossils? Why or why not?

22. Suppose you are writing a book about another planet. In your book, you mention that the planet has no atmosphere or weather. Which type of rock will you not find on the planet? Explain.

23. Imagine that you want to quarry or mine granite. You have all of the equipment, but you need a place to quarry. You have two pieces of land to choose from. One piece is described as having a granite batholith under it, and the other has a granite sill. If both plutonic bodies were at the same depth, which one would be a better buy for you? Explain your answer.

MATH IN SCIENCE

24. If a 60 kg granite boulder were broken down into sand grains and if quartz made up 35 percent of the boulder's mass, how many kilograms of the resulting sand would be quartz grains?

INTERPRETING GRAPHICS

The red curve on the graph below shows how the melting point of a particular rock changes with increasing temperature and pressure. Use the graph to answer the questions below.

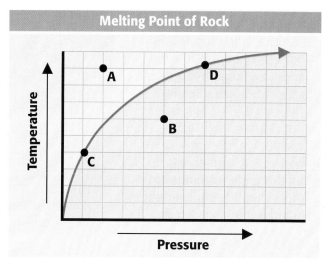

25. What type of material, liquid or solid, would you find at point **A**? Why?

26. What would you find at point **B**?

27. Points **C** and **D** represent different temperature and pressure conditions for a single, solid rock. Why does this rock have a higher melting temperature at point **D** than it does at point **C**?

Reading Check-up

Take a minute to review your answers to the Pre-Reading Questions found at the bottom of page 78. Have your answers changed? If necessary, revise your answers based on what you have learned since you began this chapter.

Science, Technology, and Society

Rock City

Today when we dig into a mountainside to build a highway or make room for a building, we use heavy machinery and explosives. Can you imagine doing the same job with just a hammer and chisel? Well, between about 300 B.C. and A.D. 200, an Arab tribe called the Nabataeans (nab uh TEE uhns) did just that. In fact, they carved a whole city—homes, storage areas, monuments, administrative offices, and temples—right into the mountainsides!

▲ *Petra's most famous building, the Treasury, was shown in the movie* Indiana Jones and the Last Crusade.

Rose-Red City

This amazing city in southern Jordan is Petra (named by the Roman emperor Hadrian Petra during a visit in A.D. 131). A poet once described Petra as "the rose-red city" because all the buildings and monuments were carved from the pink sandstone mountains surrounding Petra.

Using this reddish stone, the Nabataeans lined the main street in the center of the city with tall stone columns. The street ends at what was once the foot of a mountain but is now known as the Great Temple—a two-story stone religious complex larger than a football field!

The High Place of Sacrifice, another site near the center of the city, was a mountaintop. The Nabataeans leveled the top and created a place of worship more than 1,000 m above the valley floor. Today visitors climb stairs to the top. Along the way, they pass dozens of tombs carved into the pink rock walls.

Tombs and More Tombs

There are more than 800 other tombs dug into the mountainsides in and around Petra. One of them, the Treasury (created for a Nabataean ruler), stands more than 40 m high! It is a magnificent building with an elaborate facade. Behind the massive stone front, the Nabataeans carved one large room and two smaller rooms deeper into the mountain.

Petra Declines

The Nabataeans once ruled an area extending from Petra to Damascus. They grew wealthy and powerful by controlling important trade routes near Petra. But their wealth attracted the Roman Empire, and in A.D. 106, Petra became a Roman province. Though the city prospered under Roman rule for almost another century, a gradual decline in Nabataean power began. The trade routes by land that the Nabataeans controlled for hundreds of years were abandoned in favor of a route by the Red Sea. People moved and the city faded. By the seventh century, nothing was left of Petra but empty stone structures.

Think About It!

▶ Petra is sometimes referred to as a city "from the rock as if by magic grown." Why might such a city seem "magic" to us today? What might have encouraged the Nabataeans to create this city? Share your thoughts with a classmate.

Health Watch

Glass Scalpels

Would you want your surgeon to use a scalpel that was thousands of years old? Probably not, unless it was a razor-sharp knife blade made of obsidian, a natural volcanic glass. Such blades and arrowheads were used for nearly 18,000 years by our ancestors. Recently, physicians have found a new use for these Stone Age tools. Obsidian blades, once used to hunt woolly mammoths, are now being used as scalpels in the operating room!

Obsidian or Stainless Steel?

Traditionally, physicians have used inexpensive stainless-steel scalpel blades for surgical procedures. Steel scalpels cost about $2 each, and surgeons use them just once and throw them away. Obsidian scalpels are more expensive— about $20 each—but they can be used many times before they lose their keen edge. And obsidian scalpel blades can be 100 times sharper than traditional scalpel blades!

During surgery, steel scalpels actually tear the skin apart. Obsidian scalpels divide the skin and cause much less damage. Some plastic surgeons use obsidian blades to make extremely fine incisions that leave almost no scarring. An obsidian-scalpel incision heals more quickly because the blade causes less damage to the skin and other tissues.

▲ *An obsidian scalpel can have an edge as fine as a single molecule.*

Many patients have allergic reactions to mineral components in steel blades. These patients often do not have an allergic reaction when obsidian scalpels are used. Given all of these advantages, it is not surprising that some physicians have made the change to obsidian scalpels.

A Long Tradition

Early Native Americans were among the first people to recognize that chipped obsidian has extremely sharp edges. Native Americans made obsidian arrowheads and knife blades by flaking away chips of rock by hand. Today obsidian scalpels are fashioned in much the same way by a *knapper,* a person who makes stone tools by hand. Knappers use the same basic technique that people have used for thousands of years to make obsidian blades and other stone tools.

Find Out for Yourself!

▶ Making obsidian blades and other stone tools requires a great deal of skill. Find out about the steps a knapper follows to create a stone tool. Find a piece of rock, and see if you can follow the steps to create a stone tool of your own. Be careful not to hit your fingers, and wear safety goggles.

105

Energy Resources

LIVING INSIDE YOUR TRASH?

Would you believe that this house is made from empty soda cans and old tires? Well, it is! Not only does this house use recycled materials, but it also saves Earth's energy resources. This house gets all its energy from the sun and uses rainwater for household activities. In this chapter, you will learn about what Earth's energy resources are and how we can conserve them.

Architect Mike Reynolds designed The Castle *in Taos, New Mexico.*

Pre-Reading
Questions

1. List four nonrenewable resources.

2. On which energy resources do humans currently depend the most?

3. What is the difference between a solar cell and a solar panel?

Activity

WHAT IS THE SUN'S FAVORITE COLOR?

Are some colors better than others at absorbing the sun's energy? If so, how might this relate to collecting solar energy? Try the following activity to answer these questions.

Procedure

1. Obtain **at least five balloons** that are the same size and shape. One of the balloons should be white, and one should be black.

2. Place **one large ice cube or several small cubes** in each balloon. Each balloon should contain the same amount of ice.

3. Line the balloons up on a flat, uniformly colored surface that receives direct sunlight. Make sure that all the balloons receive the same amount of sunlight and that the openings in the balloons are not facing directly toward the sun.

4. Keep track of how much time it takes for the ice to melt completely in each of the balloons. You can tell how much ice has melted in each balloon by pinching the balloon's opening and then gently squeezing the balloon.

Analysis

5. In which balloon did the ice melt first? Why?

6. What color would you paint a device used to collect solar energy?

Natural Resources

Terms to Learn

natural resource
renewable resource
nonrenewable resource
recycling

What You'll Do

◆ Determine how humans use natural resources.
◆ Contrast renewable resources with nonrenewable resources.
◆ Explain how humans can conserve natural resources.

Think of the Earth as a giant life-support system for all of humanity. The Earth's atmosphere, waters, and solid crust provide almost everything we need to survive. The atmosphere provides the air we need to breathe, maintains air temperatures, and produces rain. The oceans and other waters of the Earth provide food and needed fluids. The solid part of the Earth provides nutrients and minerals.

Interactions between the Earth's systems can cause changes in the Earth's environments. Organisms must adapt to these changes if they are to survive. Humans have found ways to survive by using natural resources to change their immediate surroundings. A **natural resource** is any natural substance, organism, or energy form that living things use. Few of the Earth's natural resources are used in their unaltered state. Most resources are made into products that make people's lives more comfortable and convenient, as shown in **Figure 1**.

Figure 1 *Lumber, gasoline, and electricity are all products that come from natural resources.*

This pile of lumber is made of wood, which comes from trees.

The gasoline in this can is made from oil pumped from the Earth's crust.

Electricity generated by these wind turbines ultimately comes from the sun's energy.

Renewable Resources

Some natural resources are renewable. A **renewable resource** is a natural resource that can be used and replaced over a relatively short time. **Figure 2** shows two examples of renewable resources. Although many resources are renewable, humans often use them more quickly than they can be replaced. Trees, for example, are renewable, but humans are currently cutting trees down more quickly than other trees can grow to replace them.

Figure 2 *Fresh water and trees are just a few of the renewable resources available on Earth.*

Nonrenewable Resources

Not all of Earth's natural resources are renewable. A **nonrenewable resource** is a natural resource that cannot be replaced or that can be replaced only over thousands or millions of years. Examples of nonrenewable resources are shown in **Figure 3.** The amounts of nonrenewable resources on Earth are fixed with respect to their availability for human use. Once nonrenewable resources are used up, they are no longer available. Oil and natural gas, for example, exist in limited quantities. When these resources become scarce, humans will have to find other resources to replace them.

Figure 3 *Nonrenewable resources, such as coal and natural gas, can be replaced only over thousands or millions of years once they are used up.*

Renewable or Nonrenewable?

Find five products in your home that were made from natural resources. List the resource or resources from which each product was made. Label each resource as renewable or nonrenewable.

Are the products made from mostly renewable or nonrenewable resources? Are those renewable resources plentiful on Earth? Do humans use those renewable resources more quickly than the resources can be replaced? What can you do to help conserve nonrenewable resources and renewable resources that are becoming more scarce?

Figure 4 *You can recycle many household items to help conserve natural resources.*

Conserving Natural Resources

Whether the natural resources we use are renewable or nonrenewable, we should be careful how we use them. To conserve natural resources, we should try to use them only when necessary. For example, leaving the faucet running while brushing your teeth wastes clean water. Turning the faucet on only to rinse your brush saves a lot of water that you or others need for other uses.

Another way to conserve natural resources is to recycle, as shown in **Figure 4**. **Recycling** is the process by which used or discarded materials are treated for reuse. Recycling allows manufacturers to reuse natural resources when making new products. This in turn reduces the amount of natural resources that must be obtained from the Earth. For example, recycling aluminum cans reduces the amount of aluminum that must be mined from the Earth's crust to make new cans.

internetconnect

SCiLINKS
NSTA

TOPIC: Natural Resources
GO TO: www.scilinks.org
*sci*LINKS NUMBER: HSTE105

REVIEW

1. How do humans use most natural resources?

2. What is the difference between renewable and nonrenewable resources?

3. Name two ways to conserve natural resources.

4. **Applying Concepts** List three renewable resources not mentioned in this section.

Fossil Fuels

What You'll Do

◆ Classify the different forms of fossil fuels.

◆ Explain how fossil fuels are obtained.

◆ Identify problems with fossil fuels.

◆ List ways to deal with fossil-fuel problems.

Energy resources are natural resources that humans use to produce energy. There are many types of renewable and nonrenewable energy resources, and all of the energy released from these resources ultimately comes from the sun. The energy resources on which humans currently depend the most are fossil fuels. **Fossil fuels** are nonrenewable energy resources that form in the Earth's crust over millions of years from the buried remains of once-living organisms. Energy is released from fossil fuels when they are burned. There are many types of fossil fuels, which exist as liquids, gases, and solids, and humans use a variety of methods to obtain and process them. These methods depend on the type of fossil fuel, where the fossil fuel is located, and how the fossil fuel formed. Unfortunately, the methods of obtaining and using fossil fuels can have negative effects on the environment. Read on to learn about fossil fuels and the role they play in our lives.

Liquid Fossil Fuels—Petroleum

Petroleum, or crude oil, is an oily mixture of flammable organic compounds from which liquid fossil fuels and other products, such as asphalt, are separated. Petroleum is separated into several types of fossil fuels and other products in refineries, such as the one shown in **Figure 5.** Among the types of fossil fuels separated from petroleum are gasoline, jet fuel, kerosene, diesel fuel, and fuel oil.

Figure 5 *Fossil fuels and other products are separated from petroleum in a process called* fractionation. *In this process, petroleum is gradually heated in a tower so that different components boil and vaporize at different temperatures.*

Chemistry
CONNECTION

Petroleum and natural gas are both made of compounds called hydrocarbons. A *hydrocarbon* is an organic compound containing only carbon and hydrogen.

Gaseous Fossil Fuels—Natural Gas

Gaseous fossil fuels are classified as **natural gas.** Most natural gas is used for heating and for generating electricity. The stove in your kitchen may be powered by natural gas. Many motor vehicles, such as the van in **Figure 6,** are fueled by liquefied natural gas. Vehicles like these produce less air pollution than vehicles powered by gasoline.

Methane is the main component of natural gas. But other natural-gas components, such as butane and propane, can be separated and used by humans. Butane is often used as fuel for camp stoves. Propane is used as a heating fuel and as a cooking fuel, especially for outdoor grills.

Figure 6 *Vehicles powered by liquefied natural gas are becoming more common.*

Figure 7 *This coal is being gathered so that it may be burned in the power plant shown in the background.*

Solid Fossil Fuels—Coal

The solid fossil fuel that humans use most is coal. **Coal** is a solid fossil fuel formed underground from buried, decomposed plant material. Coal, the only fossil fuel that is a rock, was once the leading source of energy in the United States. People burned coal for heating and transportation. Many trains in the 1800s and early 1900s were powered by coal-burning steam locomotives.

People began to use coal less because burning coal often produces large amounts of air pollution and because better energy resources were discovered. Coal is no longer used much as a fuel for heating or transportation in the United States. However, many power plants, like the one shown in **Figure 7,** burn coal to produce electricity.

How Do Fossil Fuels Form?

All fossil fuels form from the buried remains of ancient organisms. But different types of fossil fuels form in different ways and from different types of organisms. Petroleum and natural gas form mainly from the remains of microscopic sea life. When these organisms die, their remains settle on the ocean floor, where they decay and become part of the ocean sediment. Over time, the sediment slowly becomes rock, trapping the decayed remains. Through physical and chemical changes over millions of years, the remains become petroleum and gas. Gradually, more rocks form above the rocks that contain the fossil fuels. Under the pressure of overlying rocks and sediments, the fossil fuels are squeezed out of their source rocks and into permeable rocks. As shown in **Figure 8,** these permeable rocks become reservoirs for petroleum and natural gas. The formation of petroleum and natural gas is an ongoing process. Part of the remains of today's sea life will probably become petroleum and natural gas millions of years from now.

Rock Sponge

1. Place samples of **sandstone, limestone,** and **shale** in separate **Petri dishes.**

2. Place 5 drops of light **machine oil** on each rock sample.

3. Observe and record the time required for the oil to be absorbed by each of the rock samples.

4. Which rock sample absorbed the oil fastest? Why?

5. Based on your findings, describe a property that allows for easy removal of fossil fuels from reservoir rock.

To obtain petroleum and gas, engineers must drill wells into the reservoir rock.

After fuels are successfully tapped, pumps must sometimes be installed to remove them.

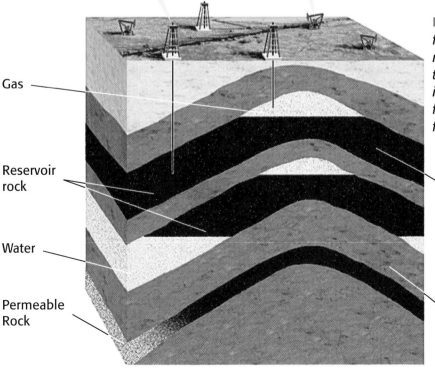

Gas

Reservoir rock

Water

Permeable Rock

Petroleum

Impermeable Rock

Figure 8 *Petroleum and gas rise from source rock into reservoir rock. Sometimes the fuels are trapped by overlying rock that is impermeable. Rocks that are folded upward are excellent fossil-fuel traps.*

Coal Formation Coal forms differently from petroleum and natural gas. Coal forms underground over millions of years from decayed swamp plants. When swamp plants die, they sink to the bottom of the swamps. This begins the process of coal formation, which is illustrated below. Notice that the percentage of carbon increases with each stage. The higher the carbon content, the cleaner the material burns. However, all grades of coal will pollute the air when burned.

The Process of Coal Formation

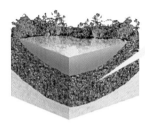

Stage 1: Peat
Bacteria and fungi transform sunken swamp plants into peat. Peat is about **60 percent carbon.**

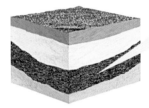

Stage 2: Lignite
Sediment buries the peat, increasing the pressure and temperature. This gradually turns the peat into lignite, which is about **70 percent carbon.**

Stage 3: Bituminous coal
The temperature and pressure continue to increase. Eventually lignite turns into bituminous coal. Bituminous coal is about **80 percent carbon.**

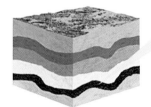

Stage 4: Anthracite
With more heat and pressure, bituminous coal eventually turns into anthracite, which is about **90 percent carbon.**

REVIEW

1. Name a solid, liquid, and gaseous fossil fuel.

2. What component of coal-forming organic material increases with each step in coal formation?

3. **Comparing Concepts** What is the difference between the organic material from which coal forms and the organic material from which petroleum and natural gas mainly form?

Where Are Fossil Fuels Found?

Fossil fuels are found in many parts of the world, both on land and beneath the ocean. As shown in **Figure 9,** the United States has large reserves of petroleum, natural gas, and coal. In spite of all our petroleum reserves, we import about one-half of our petroleum and petroleum products from the Middle East, South America, and Africa.

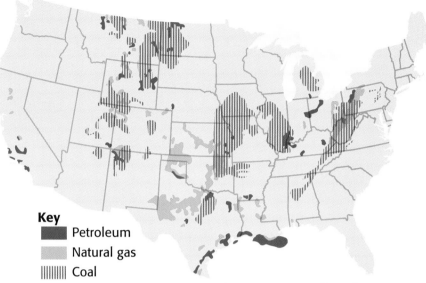

Key
■ Petroleum
■ Natural gas
||||||| Coal

Figure 9 *Most oil and gas produced in the continental United States comes from California, Louisiana, and Texas.*

How Do Humans Obtain Fossil Fuels?

Humans use different methods to remove fossil fuels from the Earth's crust. These methods depend on the type of fuel being obtained and its location. Petroleum and natural gas are removed from the Earth by drilling wells into rock that contains these resources. Oil wells exist both on land and in the ocean. For offshore drilling, engineers mount drills on platforms that are secured to the ocean floor or float at the ocean's surface. **Figure 10** shows an offshore oil rig.

Coal is obtained either by mining deep beneath the Earth's surface or by strip mining. **Strip mining** is a process in which rock and soil are stripped from the Earth's surface to expose the underlying materials to be mined. Strip mining is used to mine shallow coal deposits. **Figure 11** shows a coal strip mine.

Figure 10 *Large oil rigs, some more than 300 m tall, operate offshore in many places, such as the Gulf of Mexico and the North Sea.*

Figure 11 *Strip miners use explosives to blast away rock and soil and to expose the material to be mined.*

Problems with Fossil Fuels

Although fossil fuels provide energy for our technological world, the methods of obtaining and using them can have negative consequences. For example, when coal is burned, sulfur dioxide is released. Sulfur dioxide combines with moisture in the air to produce sulfuric acid, which is one of the acids in acid precipitation. **Acid precipitation** is rain or snow that has a high acid content due to air pollutants. Acid precipitation negatively affects wildlife, plants, buildings, and statues, as shown in **Figure 12.**

Figure 12 *Acid precipitation can dissolve parts of statues.*

Coal Mining The mining of coal can also create environmental problems. Strip mining removes soil, which plants need for growth and some animals need for shelter. If land is not properly repaired afterward, strip mining can destroy wildlife habitats. Coal mines that are deep underground, such as the one shown in **Figure 13,** can be hazardous to the men and women working in them. Coal mining can also lower local water tables, pollute water supplies, and cause the overlying earth to collapse.

Petroleum Problems Obtaining petroleum can also cause environmental problems. In 1989, the supertanker *Exxon Valdez* spilled about 257,000 barrels of crude oil into the water when it ran aground off the coast of Alaska. The oil killed hundreds of thousands of animals and damaged the local fishing industry.

Figure 13 *Coal dust can damage the human respiratory system. And because coal dust is flammable, it increases the danger of fire and explosion in coal mines.*

Smog Burning petroleum products causes a big environmental problem called smog. **Smog** is a photochemical fog produced by the reaction of sunlight and air pollutants. Smog is particularly serious in places such as Denver and Los Angeles. In these cities, the sun shines most of the time, there are millions of automobiles, and surrounding mountains prevent the wind from blowing pollutants away. Smog levels in some cities, including Denver and Los Angeles, have begun to decrease in recent years.

Dealing with Fossil-Fuel Problems

So what can be done to solve fossil-fuel problems? Obviously we can't stop using fossil fuels any time soon—we are too dependent on them. But there are things we can do to minimize the negative effects of fossil fuels. By traveling in automobiles only when absolutely necessary, people can cut down on car exhaust in the air. Carpooling, riding a bike, walking, and using mass-transit systems also help by reducing the number of cars on the road. These measures help reduce the negative effects of using fossil fuels, but they do not eliminate the problems. Only by using certain alternative energy resources, which you will learn about in the next section, can we eliminate them.

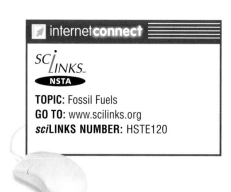

Figure 14 *Using mass transit, walking, or riding your bike can help reduce air pollution due to burning fossil fuels.*

REVIEW

1. Name a state with petroleum, natural-gas, and coal reserves.

2. How do we obtain petroleum and natural gas? How do we obtain coal?

3. Name three problems with fossil fuels. Name three ways to minimize the negative effects of fossil fuels.

4. **Making Inferences** Why does the United States import petroleum from other regions even though the United States has its own petroleum reserves?

internet**connect**

SC**LINKS**
NSTA

TOPIC: Fossil Fuels
GO TO: www.scilinks.org
*sci***LINKS NUMBER:** HSTE120

Alternative Resources

Terms to Learn

nuclear energy   biomass
solar energy   gasohol
wind energy   geothermal
hydroelectric   energy
  energy

What You'll Do

◆ Describe alternatives to the use of fossil fuels.
◆ List advantages and disadvantages of using alternative energy resources.

The energy needs of industry, transportation, and housing are increasingly met by electricity. However, most electricity is currently produced from fossil fuels, which are nonrenewable and cause pollution when burned. For people to continue their present lifestyles, new sources of energy must become available.

Splitting the Atom

Nuclear energy is an alternative source of energy that comes from the nuclei of atoms. Most often it is produced by a process called *fission*. Fission is a process in which the nuclei of radioactive atoms are split and energy is released, as shown in **Figure 15**. Nuclear power plants use radioactive atoms as fuel. When fission takes place, a large amount of energy is released. The energy is used to produce steam to run electric generators in the power plant.

Figure 15 *The process of fission generates a tremendous amount of energy.*

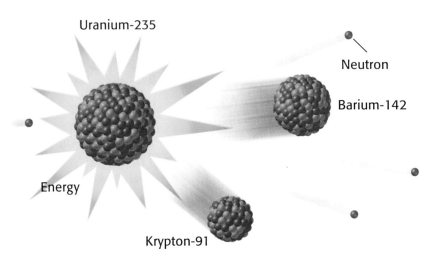

Uranium-235

Neutron

Barium-142

Energy

Krypton-91

Pros and Cons Nuclear power plants provide alternative sources of energy without the problems that come with fossil fuels. So why don't we use nuclear energy instead of fossil fuels? Nuclear power plants produce dangerous wastes. The wastes are unsafe because they are radioactive. Radioactive wastes must be removed from the plant and stored until they lose their radioactivity. But nuclear wastes can remain dangerously radioactive for thousands of years. A safe place must be found to store these wastes so that radiation cannot escape into the environment.

Figure 16 *Areas or objects marked with this symbol should be approached only after taking proper precautions.*

Because nuclear power plants generate a lot of energy, large amounts of water are used in cooling towers, like the ones shown in **Figure 17,** to cool the plants. If a plant's cooling system were to stop working, the plant would overheat, and its reactor could possibly melt. Then a large amount of radiation could escape into the environment, as it did at Chernobyl, Ukraine, in 1986.

Combining Atoms

Another type of nuclear energy is produced by *fusion.* Fusion is the joining of nuclei of small atoms to form larger atoms. This is the same process that is thought to produce energy in the sun.

The main advantage of fusion is that it produces few dangerous wastes. The main disadvantage of fusion is that very high temperatures are required for the reaction to take place. No known material can withstand temperatures that high, so the reaction must occur within a special environment, such as a magnetic field. So far, fusion reactions have been limited to laboratory experiments.

Figure 17 *Cooling towers are one of many safety mechanisms used in nuclear power plants. Their purpose is to prevent the plant from overheating.*

Sitting in the Sun

When sunlight falls on your skin, the warmth you feel is part of solar energy. **Solar energy** is energy from the sun. Every day, the Earth receives more than enough solar energy to meet all of our energy needs. And because the Earth continuously receives solar energy, the energy is a renewable resource.

There are two common ways that we use solar energy. Sunlight can be changed into electricity by the use of solar cells. You may have used a calculator, like the one shown in **Figure 18,** that was powered by solar cells.

Figure 18 *This solar calculator receives all the energy it needs through the four solar cells located above its screen.*

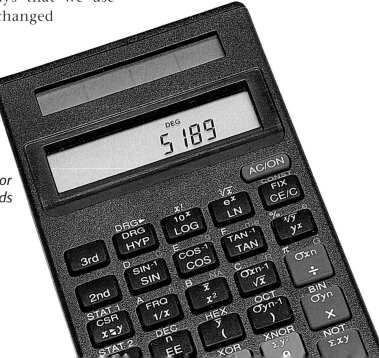

119

Solar Cells A single solar cell produces only a tiny amount of electricity. For small electronic devices, such as calculators, this is not a problem because enough energy can be obtained with only a few cells. But in order to provide enough electricity for larger objects, such as a house, thousands of cells are needed. Many homes and businesses use solar panels mounted on their roof to provide much of their needed electricity. Solar panels are large panels made up of many solar cells wired together. **Figure 19** shows a building with solar panels.

Figure 19 *Although they are expensive to install, solar panels are good investments in the long run.*

Counting the Cost Solar cells are reliable and quiet, have no moving parts, and can last for years with little maintenance. They produce no pollution during use, and pollution created by their manufacturing process is very low.

So why doesn't everyone use solar cells? The answer is cost. While solar energy itself is free, solar cells are relatively expensive to make. The cost of a solar-power system could account for one-third of the cost of an entire house. But in remote areas where it is difficult and costly to run electric wires, solar-power systems can be a realistic option. In the United States today, tens of thousands of homes use solar panels to produce electricity. Can you think of other places that you have seen solar panels? Take a look at **Figure 20.**

Figure 20 *Perhaps you have seen solar panels used in this manner in your town.*

Solar Heating Another use of solar energy is direct heating through solar collectors. Solar collectors are dark-colored boxes with glass or plastic tops. A common use of solar collectors is heating water, as shown in **Figure 21.** Over 1 million solar water heaters have been installed in the United States. They are especially common in Florida, California, and some southwestern states.

As with solar cells, the problem with solar collectors is cost. But solar collectors quickly pay for themselves—heating water is one of the major uses of electricity in American homes. Also, solar collectors can be used to generate electricity.

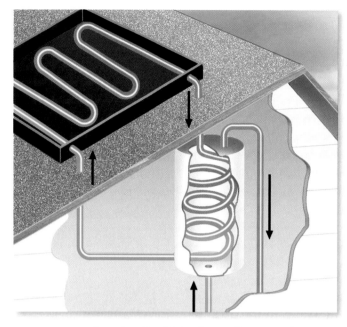

Figure 21 *After the liquid in the collector is heated by the sun, it is pumped through tubes that run through a water heater, causing the temperature of the water to rise.*

Large-Scale Solar Power Experimental solar-power facilities, such as the one shown in **Figure 22,** have shown that it is possible to generate electricity for an entire city. Facilities like this one are designed to use mirrors to focus sunlight onto coated steel pipes filled with synthetic oil. The oil is heated by the sunlight and is then used to heat water. The heated liquid water turns to steam, which is used to drive electric generators.

An alternative design for solar-power facilities is one that uses mirrors to reflect sunlight onto a receiver on a central tower. The receiver captures the sunlight's energy and stores it in tanks of molten salt. The stored energy is then used to create steam, which drives a turbine in an electric generator. *Solar Two,* a solar-power facility designed in this manner, was capable of generating enough energy to power 10,000 homes in southern California.

Turn to page 650 to calculate the power of the sun.

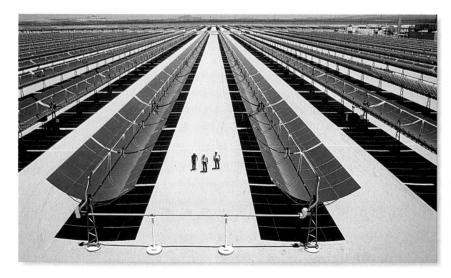

Figure 22 *This solar-power facility in the Mojave Desert used sun-tracking mirrors called heliostats.*

Capture the Wind

Wind is created indirectly by solar energy through the uneven heating of air. There is a tremendous amount of energy in wind, called **wind energy.** You can see the effects of this energy unleashed in a hurricane or tornado. Wind energy can also be used productively by humans. Wind energy can turn a windmill that pumps water or produces electricity.

Figure 23 *Wind turbines take up only a small part of the ground's surface. This allows the land on wind farms to be used for more than one purpose.*

Wind Turbines Today, fields of modern wind turbines—technological updates of the old windmills—generate significant amounts of electricity. Clusters of these turbines are often called wind farms. Wind farms are located in areas where winds are strong and steady. Most of the wind farms in the United States are in California. The amount of energy produced by California wind farms could power all of the homes in San Francisco.

Steady Breezes There are many benefits of using wind energy. Wind energy is renewable. Wind farms can be built in only 3–6 months. Wind turbines produce no carbon dioxide or other air pollutants during operation. The land used for wind farms can also be used for other purposes, such as cattle grazing, as shown in **Figure 23.** However, the wind blows strongly and steadily enough to produce electricity on a large scale only in certain places. Currently, wind energy accounts for only a small percentage of the energy used in the United States.

internetconnect

SCI*LINKS*
NSTA

TOPIC: Renewable Resources
GO TO: www.scilinks.org
*sci*LINKS **NUMBER:** HSTE110

REVIEW

1. Briefly describe two ways of using solar energy.

2. In addition to multiple turbines, what is needed to produce electricity from wind energy on a large scale?

3. **Analyzing Methods** Nuclear power plants are rarely found in the middle of deserts or other extremely dry areas. If you were going to build a nuclear plant, why would you not build it in the middle of a desert?

Hydroelectric Energy

The energy of falling water has been used by humans for thousands of years. Water wheels, such as the one shown in **Figure 24,** have been around since ancient times. In the early years of the Industrial Revolution, water wheels provided energy for many factories. More recently, the energy of falling water has been used to generate electricity. Electricity produced by falling water is called **hydroelectric energy.**

Harnessing the Water Cycle Hydroelectric energy is inexpensive and produces little pollution, and it is renewable because water constantly cycles from the ocean to the air, to the land, and back to the ocean. But like wind energy, hydroelectric energy is not available everywhere. Hydroelectric energy can be produced only where large volumes of falling water can be harnessed. Huge dams, like the one in **Figure 25,** must be built on major rivers to capture enough water to generate significant amounts of electricity.

Figure 24 *Falling water turns water wheels, which turn giant millstones used to grind grain into flour.*

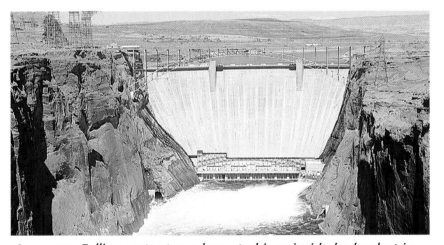

Figure 25 *Falling water turns huge turbines inside hydroelectric dams, generating electricity for millions of people.*

Turn to page 648 to make your own water wheel.

At What Price? Increased use of hydroelectric energy could reduce the demand for fossil fuels, but there are trade-offs. Construction of the large dams necessary for hydroelectric power plants often destroys other resources, such as forests and wildlife habitats. For example, hydroelectric dams on the Lower Snake and Columbia Rivers in Washington disrupt the migratory paths of local populations of salmon and steelhead. Large numbers of these fish die each year because their life cycle is disrupted. Dams can also decrease water quality and create erosion problems.

Self-Check

How are ancient water wheels like modern hydroelectric dams? *(See page 726 to check your answer.)*

Powerful Plants

Plants are similar to solar collectors, absorbing energy from the sun and storing it for later use. Leaves, wood, and other parts of plants contain the stored energy. Even the dung of plant-grazing animals is high in stored energy. These sources of energy are called biomass. **Biomass** is organic matter that contains stored energy.

Burning Biomass Biomass energy can be released in several ways. The most common is the burning of biomass. Approximately 70 percent of people living in developing countries heat their homes and cook their food by burning wood or charcoal. In the United States this number is about 5 percent. Scientists estimate that the burning of wood and animal dung accounts for approximately 14 percent of the world's total energy use.

Figure 26 *In many parts of the world where firewood is scarce, people burn animal dung for energy. This woman is preparing cow dung that will be dried and used as fuel.*

Miles per Acre

Imagine that you own a car that runs on alcohol made from corn that you grow. You drive your car about 15,000 miles in a year, and you get 240 gallons of alcohol from each acre of corn that you process. If your car gets 25 mi/gal, how many acres of corn would you have to grow to fuel your car for a year?

Gasohol Plant material can also be changed into liquid fuel. Plants containing sugar or starch, for example, can be made into alcohol. The alcohol is burned as a fuel or mixed with gasoline to make a fuel mixture called **gasohol.** An acre of corn can produce more than 1,000 L of alcohol. But in the United States we use a lot of fuel for our cars. It would take about 40 percent of the entire United States corn harvest to produce enough alcohol to make just 10 percent of the fuel we use in our cars! Biomass is obviously a renewable source of energy, but producing biomass requires land that could be used for growing food.

Deep Heat

Imagine being able to tap into the energy of the Earth. In a few places this is possible. This type of energy is called geothermal energy. **Geothermal energy** is energy from within the Earth.

Geothermal Energy In some locations, rainwater penetrates porous rock near a source of magma. The heat from the magma heats the water, often turning it to steam. The steam and hot water escape through natural vents called geysers, or through wells drilled into the rock. The steam and water contain geothermal energy. Some geothermal power plants use primarily steam to generate electricity. This process is illustrated in **Figure 27.** In recent years, geothermal power plants that use primarily hot water instead of steam have become more common.

Geothermal energy can also be used as a direct source of heat. In this process, hot water and steam are used to heat a fluid that is pumped through a building in order to heat the building. Buildings in Iceland are heated in this way from the country's many geothermal sites.

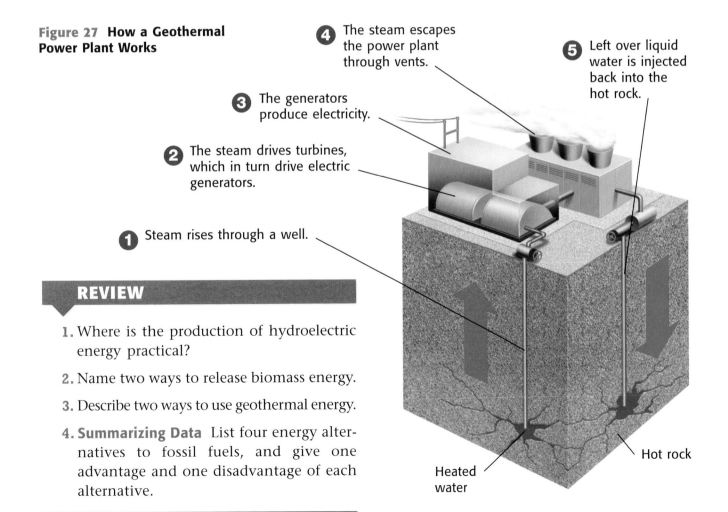

Figure 27 How a Geothermal Power Plant Works

④ The steam escapes the power plant through vents.

⑤ Left over liquid water is injected back into the hot rock.

③ The generators produce electricity.

② The steam drives turbines, which in turn drive electric generators.

① Steam rises through a well.

Heated water

Hot rock

REVIEW

1. Where is the production of hydroelectric energy practical?

2. Name two ways to release biomass energy.

3. Describe two ways to use geothermal energy.

4. **Summarizing Data** List four energy alternatives to fossil fuels, and give one advantage and one disadvantage of each alternative.

Chapter Highlights

SECTION 1

Vocabulary

natural resource *(p. 108)*

renewable resource *(p. 109)*

nonrenewable resource *(p. 109)*

recycling *(p. 110)*

Section Notes

• Natural resources include everything that is not made by humans and that can be used by organisms.

• Renewable resources, like trees and water, can be replaced in a relatively short period of time.

• Nonrenewable resources cannot be replaced, or they take a very long time to replace.

• Recycling reduces the amount of natural resources that must be obtained from the Earth.

SECTION 2

Vocabulary

energy resource *(p. 111)*

fossil fuel *(p. 111)*

petroleum *(p. 111)*

natural gas *(p. 112)*

coal *(p. 112)*

strip mining *(p. 115)*

acid precipitation *(p. 116)*

smog *(p. 117)*

Section Notes

• Fossil fuels, including petroleum, natural gas, and coal, form from the buried remains of once-living organisms.

• Petroleum and natural gas form mainly from the remains of microscopic sea life.

• Coal forms from decayed swamp plants and varies in quality based on its percentage of carbon.

• Petroleum and natural gas are obtained through drilling, while coal is obtained through mining.

• Obtaining and using fossil fuels can cause many environmental problems, including acid precipitation, water pollution, and smog.

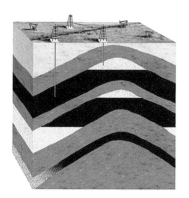

☑ Skills Check

Math Concepts

THE CARBON CONTENT OF COAL Turn back to page 114 to study the process of coal formation. Notice that at each stage, 10% more of the organic material becomes carbon. To calculate the percentage of carbon present at the next stage, just add 10%, or 0.10. For example:

$$\text{peat} \rightarrow \text{lignite}$$
$$60\% \rightarrow 70\%$$
$$0.60 + 0.10 = 0.70, \text{ or } 70\%$$

Visual Understanding

NO DIRECT CONTACT Take another look at Figure 21 on page 121. It is important to realize that the heated liquid inside the solar collector's tubes never comes in direct contact with the water in the tank. Cold water enters the tank, receives energy from the hot, coiled tube, and leaves the tank when someone turns on the hot-water tap.

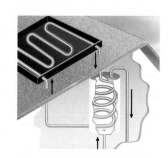

126 Chapter 5

Vocabulary

nuclear energy *(p. 118)*

solar energy *(p. 119)*

wind energy *(p. 122)*

hydroelectric energy *(p. 123)*

biomass *(p. 124)*

gasohol *(p. 124)*

geothermal energy *(p. 125)*

Section Notes

- Nuclear energy is most often produced by fission.

- Radioactive wastes and the threat of overheating in nuclear power plants are among the major problems associated with using nuclear energy.

- Solar energy can be converted to electricity by using solar cells.

- Solar energy can be used for direct heating by using solar collectors.

- Solar energy can be converted to electricity on both a small and large scale.

- Although harnessing wind energy is practical only in certain areas, the process produces no air pollutants, and land on wind farms can be used for more than one purpose.

- Hydroelectric energy is inexpensive, renewable, and produces little pollution. However, hydroelectric dams can damage wildlife habitats, create erosion problems, and decrease water quality.

- Plant material and animal dung that contains plant material can be burned to release energy.

- Some plant material can be converted to alcohol. This alcohol can be mixed with gasoline to make a fuel mixture called gasohol.

- Geothermal energy can be harnessed from hot, liquid water and steam that escape through natural vents or through wells drilled into the Earth's crust. This energy can be used for direct heating or can be converted to electricity.

Labs

Make a Water Wheel *(p. 648)*

Power of the Sun *(p. 650)*

---

internet connect

GO TO: go.hrw.com

Visit the **HRW** Web site for a variety of learning tools related to this chapter. Just type in the keyword:

KEYWORD: HSTENR

GO TO: www.scilinks.org

Visit the **National Science Teachers Association** on-line Web site for Internet resources related to this chapter. Just type in the *sci*LINKS number for more information about the topic:

TOPIC:	Natural Resources	*sci*LINKS NUMBER:	HSTE105
TOPIC:	Renewable Resources	*sci*LINKS NUMBER:	HSTE110
TOPIC:	Nonrenewable Resources	*sci*LINKS NUMBER:	HSTE115
TOPIC:	Fossil Fuels	*sci*LINKS NUMBER:	HSTE120
TOPIC:	Nuclear Energy	*sci*LINKS NUMBER:	HSTE122

Chapter Review

USING VOCABULARY

For each pair of terms, explain the difference in their meanings.

1. natural resource/energy resource

2. acid precipitation/smog

3. biomass/gasohol

4. hydroelectric energy/ geothermal energy

UNDERSTANDING CONCEPTS

Multiple Choice

5. Of the following, the one that is a renewable resource is
   a. coal.
   c. oil.
   b. trees.
   d. natural gas.

6. All of the following are separated from petroleum except
   a. jet fuel.
   c. kerosene.
   b. lignite.
   d. fuel oil.

7. Which of the following is a component of natural gas?
   a. gasohol.
   c. kerosene
   b. methane
   d. gasoline

8. Peat, lignite, and anthracite are all stages in the formation of
   a. petroleum.
   c. coal.
   b. natural gas.
   d. gasohol.

9. Which of the following factors contribute to smog problems?
   a. high numbers of automobiles
   b. lots of sunlight
   c. mountains surrounding urban areas
   d. all of the above

10. Which of the following resources produces the least pollution?
    a. solar energy
    b. natural gas
    c. nuclear energy
    d. petroleum

11. Nuclear power plants use a process called ____?____ to produce energy.
    a. fission
    b. fusion
    c. fractionation
    d. None of the above

12. A solar-powered calculator uses
    a. solar collectors.
    b. solar panels.
    c. solar mirrors.
    d. solar cells.

13. Which of the following is a problem with using wind energy?
    a. air pollution
    b. amount of land required for wind turbines
    c. limited locations for wind farms
    d. none of the above

14. Dung is a type of
    a. geothermal energy.
    b. gasohol.
    c. biomass.
    d. None of the above

Short Answer

15. Because renewable resources can be replaced, why do we need to conserve them?

16. How does acid precipitation form?

17. If sunlight is free, why is electricity from solar cells expensive?

Concept Mapping

18. Use the following terms to create a concept map: fossil fuels, wind energy, energy resources, biomass, renewable resources, solar energy, nonrenewable resources, natural gas, gasohol, coal, oil.

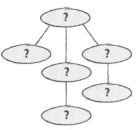

Write one or two sentences to answer the following questions:

19. How would your life be different if all fossil fuels suddenly disappeared?

20. Are fossil fuels really nonrenewable? Explain.

21. What solutions are there for the problems associated with nuclear waste?

22. How could the problems associated with the dams in Washington and local fish populations be solved?

23. What limits might there be on the productivity of a geothermal power plant?

MATH IN SCIENCE

24. Imagine that you are designing a solar car. If you mount solar cells on the underside of the car as well as on the top in direct sunlight, and it takes five times as many cells underneath to generate the same amount of electricity generated by the cells on top, what percentage of the sunlight is reflected back off the pavement?

INTERPRETING GRAPHICS

The chart below shows how various energy resources meet the world's energy needs. Use the chart to answer the following questions:

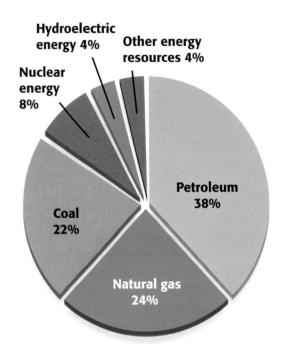

25. What percentage of the world's total energy needs is met by coal? by natural gas? by hydroelectric energy?

26. What percentage of the world's total energy needs is met by fossil fuels?

27. How much more of the world's total energy needs is met by petroleum than by natural gas?

Reading Check-up

Take a minute to review your answers to the Pre-Reading Questions found at the bottom of page 106. Have your answers changed? If necessary, revise your answers based on what you have learned since you began this chapter.

EYE ON THE ENVIRONMENT

Sitting on Your Trash

Did you know that the average person creates about 2 kg of waste every day? About 7 percent of this waste is composed of plastic products that can be recycled. Instead of adding to the landfill problem, why not recycle your plastic trash so you can sit on it? Well you can, you know! Today plastic is recycled into products like picnic tables, park benches, and even highchairs! But how on Earth does the plastic you throw away become a park bench?

Sort It Out

Once collected and taken to a recycling center, plastic must be sorted. This process involves the coded symbols that are printed on every recyclable plastic product we use. Each product falls into one of two types of plastic—*polyethylene* or *polymer*. The plastic mainly used to make furniture includes the polyethylene plastics called *high density polyethylene,* or HDPE, and *low density polyethylene,* or LDPE. These are items such as milk jugs, detergent bottles, plastic bags, and grocery bags.

Grind It and Wash It

The recycling processes for HDPE and LDPE are fairly simple. Once it reaches the processing facility, HDPE plastic is ground into small flakes about 1 cm in diameter. In the case of LDPE plastic, which are thin films, a special grinder is used to break it down. From that point on, the recycling process is pretty much the same for LDPE and HDPE. The pieces are then washed with hot water and detergent. In this step, dirt and things like labels are removed. After the wash, the flakes are dried with blasts of hot air.

Recycle It!

Some recycling plants sell the recycled flakes. But others may reheat the flakes, change the color by adding a pigment, and then put the material in a *pelletizer.* The little pellets that result are then purchased by a company that molds the pellets into pieces of plastic lumber. This plastic lumber is used to create flowerpots, trash cans, pipes, picnic tables, park benches, toys, mats, and many other products!

From waste...

to plastic lumber...

to a park bench!

Can You Recycle It?

▶ The coded symbol on a plastic container tells you what type of plastic the item is made from, but it doesn't mean that you can recycle it in your area. Find out which plastics can be recycled in your state.

Eureka!

Oil Rush!

You may have heard of the great California gold rush. In 1849, thousands of people moved to the West hoping to strike gold. But you may not have heard about another rush that followed 10 years later. What lured people to northwestern Pennsylvania in 1859? The thrill of striking oil!

Demand for Petroleum

People began using oil as early as 3000 B.C., and oil has been a valuable substance ever since. In Mesopotamia, people used oil to waterproof their ships. The Egyptians and Chinese used oil as a medicine. It was not until the late 1700s and early 1800s that people began to use oil as a fuel. Oil was used to light homes and factories.

Petroleum Collection

But what about the oil in northwestern Pennsylvania? Did people use the oil in Pennsylvania before the rush of 1859? Native Americans were the first to dig pits to collect oil near Titusville, Pennsylvania. Early settlers used the oil as a medicine and as a fuel to light their homes. But their methods for collecting the oil were very inefficient.

The First Oil Well

In 1859, "Colonel" Edwin L. Drake came up with a better method of collecting oil from the ground. Drilling for oil! Drake hired salt-well drillers to burrow to the bedrock where oil deposits lay. But each effort was unsuccessful because water seeped into the wells, causing them to cave in. Then Drake came up with a unique idea that would make him a very wealthy man. Drake suggested that the drillers drive an iron pipe down to the bedrock 21.2 m below the surface. Then they could drill through the inner diameter of the pipe. The morning after the iron pipe was drilled, Drake woke to find that the pipe had filled with oil!

Oil City

Within 3 months, nearly 10,000 people rushed to Oil City, Pennsylvania, in search of the wealth that oil promised. Within 2 years, the small village became a bustling oil town of 50,000 people! In 1861, the first gusher well was drilled nearby, and some 3,000 barrels of oil spouted out daily. Four years later, the first oil pipeline carried crude oil a distance of 8 km.

▲ *Edwin Drake (right) and his friend Peter Wilson (left) in front of Drake Oil Well, near Titusville, Pennsylvania*

Find Out for Yourself!

▶ Drake's oil well was the first well used to collect oil from the ground. Research the oil wells today. How are they similar to Drake's well?

The Rock and Fossil Record

Pre-Reading Questions

1. How can you determine if some rocks and fossils are older than others?

2. Are fossils always made up of parts of plants or animals?

3. How do scientists study the Earth's history?

TIME STANDS STILL

Sealed in darkness for 49 million years, this beetle still shimmers with the same metallic hues that once helped it hide among ancient plants. This rare fossil was found in Messel, Germany. In the same rock formation, scientists have found fossilized crocodiles, bats, birds, and frogs. A living stag beetle *(below)* has a similar form and color. Do you think that these two beetles would live in similar environments? What do you think Messel, Germany, was like 49 million years ago? In this chapter, you will learn how scientists answer questions like these.

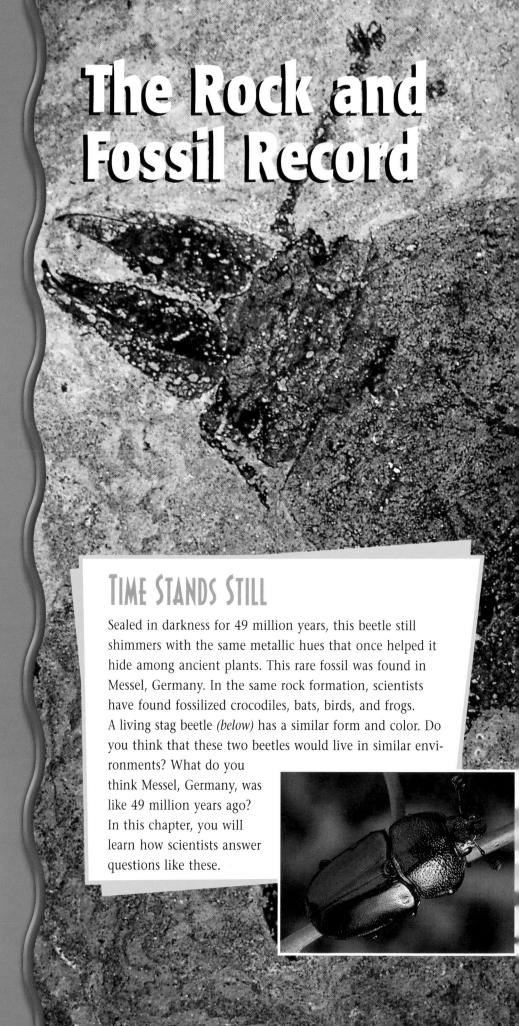

Activity

MAKING FOSSILS

How do scientists learn from fossils? In this activity, you will study "fossils" and identify the object that made each.

Procedure

1. You and three or four of your classmates will be given several pieces of **modeling clay** and a paper sack containing a few **small objects.**

2. Press each object firmly into a piece of clay. Try to leave a fossil imprint showing as much detail as possible.

3. After you have made an imprint of each object, exchange your model fossils with another group.

4. In your ScienceLog, describe the fossils you have received. List as many details as possible. What patterns and textures do you observe?

5. Work as a group to identify each fossil and check your results. Were you right?

Analysis

6. What kinds of details were important in identifying your fossils? What kinds of details were not preserved in the imprints? For example, can you tell the color of the objects?

7. Explain how Earth scientists follow similar methods when studying fossils.

Terms to Learn

uniformitarianism
catastrophism

What You'll Do

- Identify the role of uniformitarianism in Earth science.
- Contrast uniformitarianism with catastrophism.
- Describe how the role of catastrophism in Earth science has changed.

Earth's Story and Those Who First Listened

Humans have wondered about Earth's history for thousands of years. But the branch of Earth science called *geology,* which involves the study of Earth's history, got a late start. The main concept of modern geology was not outlined until the late eighteenth century. Within a few decades, this concept replaced a more traditional concept of Earth's history. Today, both concepts are an essential part of Earth science.

The Principle of Uniformitarianism

In 1795, a philosopher and scientist named James Hutton published *Theory of the Earth,* in which he wrote that Earth's landforms are constantly changing. As shown in **Figure 1,** Hutton assumed that these changes result from geologic processes—such as the breakdown of rock and the transport of sediment—that remain uniform, or do not change, over time. This assumption is now called uniformitarianism. **Uniformitarianism** is a principle that states that the same geologic processes shaping the Earth today have been at work throughout Earth's history. "The present is the key to the past" is a phrase that best summarizes uniformitarianism.

Figure 1 *Hutton observed gradual, uniform geologic processes at work. Judging by the slowness of the processes, he concluded that the Earth must be incredibly old.*

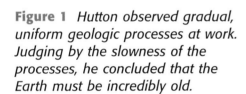

❶ Hutton observed natural forces breaking down rock into smaller particles.

❷ He watched as rivers carried rock particles downstream.

❸ He saw that rock particles are deposited and that they form new layers of sediment. He predicted that these deposits would eventually form new rock.

❹ Hutton thought that in time the new rock would be uplifted, creating new landforms, and that the cycle would start over again.

Making Assumptions

Examine the photographs at right. List the letters of the photos in the order you think the photos were taken. Now think of all the assumptions that you made to infer that order. Write down as many of these assumptions as you can. Compare notes with your classmates. Did you get the same sequence? Were your assumptions similar?

In science, assumptions must also be made. For example, you assume that the sun will rise each day. Briefly explain the importance of being able to count on certain things always being the same. How does this apply to uniformitarianism?

Uniformitarianism Versus Catastrophism In Hutton's time most people thought that the Earth had existed for only thousands of years. This was not nearly enough time for the gradual geologic processes that Hutton described to have shaped our planet. But uniformitarianism was not immediately accepted. Instead, most scientists believed in catastrophism. **Catastrophism** is a principle that states that all geologic change occurs suddenly. Supporters of catastrophism claimed that the formation of all Earth's features, such as its mountains, canyons, and seas, could be explained by rare, sudden events called *catastrophes*. These unpredictable catastrophes caused rapid geologic changes over large areas—sometimes even globally.

Uniformitarianism Wins! Despite Hutton's observations, catastrophism remained geology's guiding principle for decades. It took the work of Charles Lyell, another scientist, for people to seriously consider uniformitarianism.

From 1830 to 1833, Lyell published three volumes collectively titled *Principles of Geology,* in which he reintroduced uniformitarianism. Armed with Hutton's notes and new evidence of his own, Lyell successfully challenged the principle of catastrophism. Lyell saw no reason to doubt that major geologic change happened the same way in the past as it does in the present—gradually.

As a friend of Charles Lyell, Charles Darwin was greatly influenced by Lyell's uniformitarian ideas. Lyell's influence became clear when Darwin published *On the Origin of Species by Natural Selection* in 1859. Similar to uniformitarianism, Darwin's theory of evolution proposes that changes in species occur gradually over long periods of time.

Modern Geology—A Happy Medium

Today scientists realize that neither uniformitarianism nor catastrophism accounts for all of Earth's history. Although most geologic change is gradual and uniform, catastrophes do occur occasionally. For example, huge craters have been found where asteroids and comets are thought to have struck Earth in the past. Some of these strikes indeed may have been catastrophic. Some scientists think one such asteroid strike led to the extinction of the dinosaurs, as explained in **Figure 2.** The impact of an asteroid is thought to have spread debris into the atmosphere around the entire planet, blocking the sun's rays and causing major changes in the global climate.

Figure 2 *Today scientists think that sudden events are responsible for some changes in Earth's past. An asteroid hitting Earth, for example, may have led to the extinction of the dinosaurs 65 million years ago.*

REVIEW

1. Why do Earth scientists need the principle of uniformitarianism in order to make predictions?

2. What is the difference between uniformitarianism and catastrophism?

3. **Summarizing Data** How has the role of catastrophism in Earth science changed?

Terms to Learn

relative dating
superposition
geologic column
unconformity

What You'll Do

- ◆ Explain how relative dating is used in geology.
- ◆ Explain the principle of superposition.
- ◆ Demonstrate an understanding of the geologic column.
- ◆ Identify two events and two features that disrupt rock sequences.
- ◆ Explain how physical features are used to determine relative ages.

Relative Dating: Which Came First?

Imagine that you are a detective investigating a crime scene. What is the first thing you would do? You might begin by dusting the scene for fingerprints or by searching for witnesses. As a detective, your goal is to figure out the sequence of events that took place before you arrived at the scene.

Geologists have a similar goal when investigating the Earth. They try to determine the order of events that led to how the Earth looks today. But instead of fingerprints and witnesses, geologists rely on rocks and fossils. Determining whether an object or event is older or younger than other objects or events is called **relative dating.**

The Principle of Superposition

Suppose you have an older brother who takes a lot of photographs of your family but never puts them into an album. He just piles them in a box. Over the years, he keeps adding new pictures to the top of the stack. Think about the family history recorded in those pictures. Where are the oldest pictures—the ones taken when you were a baby? Where are the most recent pictures—those taken last week?

Rock layers, such as the ones shown in **Figure 3,** are like stacked pictures. The oldest layers are at the bottom. As you move from bottom to top, the layers get more recent, or younger. Scientists call this superposition. **Superposition** is a principle that states that younger rocks lie above older rocks in undisturbed sequences. "Younger over older" is a phrase you can use to remember this principle.

Figure 3 *Rock layers are like photos stacked over time— the younger ones lie above the older ones.*

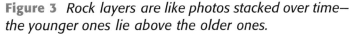

Activity

1. Write the titles of 10 chapters of this book on 10 note cards (one title on each note card).

2. Shuffle the cards and exchange them with a partner. Try to put your partner's titles in the correct order without using your book.

3. Compare your order with the order in the book.

4. Your work would have been easier if you had been allowed to use your book. How does this relate to geologists using the geologic column to put rock layers in order?

Disturbing Forces Some rock-layer sequences, however, are disturbed by forces from within the Earth. These forces can push other rocks into a sequence, tilt or fold rock layers, and break sequences into movable parts. Sometimes these forces even put older layers above younger layers, which goes against superposition. The disruptions of rock sequences caused by these forces pose a great challenge to geologists trying to determine the relative ages of rocks. Fortunately, geologists can get help from a very valuable tool—the geologic column.

The Geologic Column

To make their job easier, geologists combine data from all the known undisturbed rock sequences around the world. From this information, geologists create the *geologic column*. The **geologic column** is an ideal sequence of rock layers that contains all the known fossils and rock formations on Earth arranged from oldest to youngest.

Geologists rely on the geologic column to interpret rock sequences. For example, when geologists are not sure about the age of a rock sequence they are studying, they gather information about the sequence and compare it to the geologic column. Geologists also use the geologic column to identify the layers in puzzling rock sequences, such as sequences that have been folded over.

Constructing the Geologic Column

Here you can see three rock sequences (**a, b,** and **c**) from three different locations. Some rock layers appear in more than one sequence. Geologists construct the geologic column by piecing together different rock sequences from all over the world.

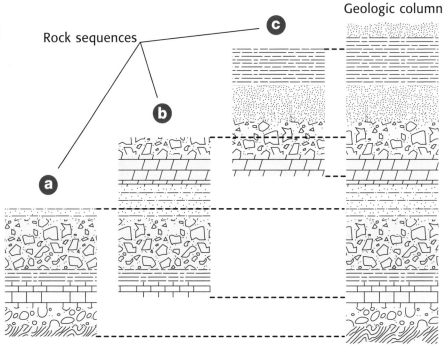

Rock sequences

Geologic column

Disturbed Rock Layers

Geologists often find features that cut through existing rock layers. Geologists use the relationships between rock layers and the features that cut across them to assign relative ages to the features and the layers. They know that those features are younger than the rock layers because the rock layers had to be present before the features could cut across them.

Faults and intrusions are examples of features that cut across rock layers. A *fault* is a break in the Earth's crust along which blocks of the crust slide relative to one another. Another cross-cutting feature is an intrusion. An *intrusion* is molten rock from the Earth's interior that squeezes into existing rock and cools. **Figure 4** illustrates both of these features.

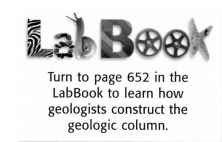

Turn to page 652 in the LabBook to learn how geologists construct the geologic column.

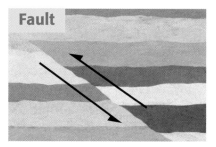 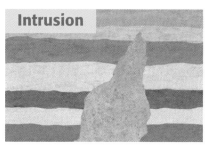

Figure 4 *A fault (left) and an intrusion (right) are always younger than the layers they cut across.*

Geologists assume that the way sediment is deposited to form rock layers—in horizontal layers—has not changed over time. According to this principle, if rock layers are not horizontal, something must have disturbed them after they formed. This principle allows geologists to determine the relative ages of rock layers and the events that disturbed them.

Folding and tilting are two additional types of events that disturb rock layers. *Folding* occurs when rock layers bend and buckle from Earth's internal forces. *Tilting* occurs when internal forces in the Earth slant rock layers without folding them. **Figure 5** illustrates the results of folding and tilting.

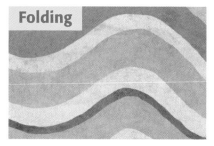 

Figure 5 *Folding (left) and tilting (right) are events that are always younger than the rock layers they affect.*

Gaps in the Record—Unconformities

Faults, intrusions, and the effects of folding and tilting can make dating rock layers a challenge. But sometimes layers of rock are missing altogether, creating a gap in the geologic record. To think of this another way, let's say that you stack your newspapers every day after reading them. Now let's suppose you want to look at a paper you read 10 days ago. You know that the paper you want should be 10 papers deep in the stack. But when you look, the paper is not there. What happened? Perhaps you forgot to put the paper in the stack. Now instead of a missing newspaper, imagine a missing rock layer.

Missing Evidence Missing rock layers create gaps in rock-layer sequences called unconformities. An **unconformity** is a surface that represents a missing part of the geologic column. Unconformities also represent missing time—time that was not recorded in layers of rock. When geologists find unconformities, they must question whether the "missing layers" were actually present or whether they were somehow removed. **Figure 6** shows how *nondeposition* and *erosion* create unconformities.

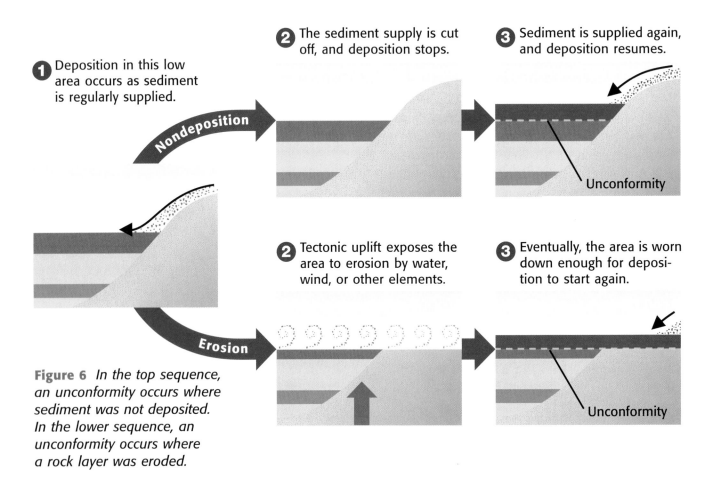

❶ Deposition in this low area occurs as sediment is regularly supplied.

Nondeposition

❷ The sediment supply is cut off, and deposition stops.

❸ Sediment is supplied again, and deposition resumes.

Unconformity

Erosion

❷ Tectonic uplift exposes the area to erosion by water, wind, or other elements.

❸ Eventually, the area is worn down enough for deposition to start again.

Unconformity

Figure 6 *In the top sequence, an unconformity occurs where sediment was not deposited. In the lower sequence, an unconformity occurs where a rock layer was eroded.*

Types of Unconformities

Most unconformities form by both erosion and nondeposition. But other factors can complicate matters. To simplify the study of unconformities, geologists put them in three major categories—disconformities, nonconformities, and angular unconformities. The three diagrams at right illustrate these three categories.

Rock-Layer Puzzles

Geologists often find rock-layer sequences that have been affected by more than one of the events and features mentioned in this section. For example, an intrusion may squeeze into rock layers that contain an unconformity and that have been cut across by a fault. Determining the order of events that led to such a sequence is like piecing together a jigsaw puzzle.

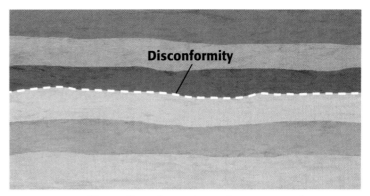

Figure 7 *A **disconformity** exists where part of a sequence of parallel rock layers is missing. While often hard to see, a disconformity is the most common type of unconformity.*

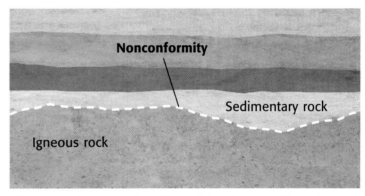

Figure 8 *A **nonconformity** exists where sedimentary rock layers lie on top of an eroded surface of non-layered igneous or metamorphic rock.*

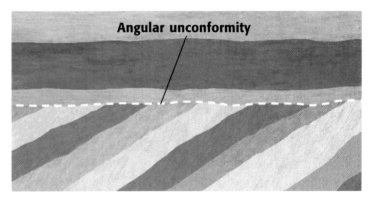

Figure 9 *An **angular unconformity** exists between horizontal rock layers and rock layers that are tilted or folded. The tilted or folded layers were eroded before horizontal layers formed above them.*

REVIEW

1. In a rock-layer sequence that hasn't been disturbed, are older layers found on top of younger layers? What rule do you use to answer this question?

2. List five events or features that can disturb rock-layer sequences.

3. Consider a fault that cuts through all the layers of a rock-layer sequence. Is the fault older or younger than the layers? Explain.

4. **Analyzing Methods** Unlike other types of unconformities, disconformities are hard to recognize because all the layers are horizontal. How does a geologist know when he or she is looking at a disconformity?

The Rock and Fossil Record **141**

What You'll Do

◆ Explain how radioactive decay occurs.
◆ Explain how radioactive decay relates to radiometric dating.
◆ List three types of radiometric dating.
◆ Determine the best type of radiometric dating to use to date an object.

Absolute Dating: A Measure of Time

By using relative dating, scientists can determine the relative ages of rock layers. To determine the actual age of a layer of rock or a fossil, however, scientists must rely on absolute dating. **Absolute dating** is a process of establishing the age of an object, such as a fossil or rock layer, by determining the number of years it has existed. In this section, we will concentrate on radiometric dating, which is the most common method of absolute dating.

Radioactive Decay

To determine the absolute ages of fossils and rocks, scientists most often analyze radioactive isotopes. **Isotopes** are atoms of the same element that have the same number of protons but have different numbers of neutrons. Most isotopes are stable, meaning that they stay in their original form. But some isotopes are unstable. Scientists call unstable isotopes *radioactive.* Radioactive isotopes tend to break down into stable isotopes of other elements in a process called **radioactive decay. Figure 10** shows how one type of radioactive decay occurs. Because radioactive decay occurs at a steady pace, scientists can use the relative amounts of stable and unstable isotopes present in an object to determine the object's age.

Figure 10 *During radioactive decay, an unstable parent isotope breaks down into a stable daughter isotope.*

Unstable isotope
6 protons, 8 neutrons

Radioactive decay
When the unstable isotope decays, a neutron is converted into a proton. In the process, an electron is released.

Stable isotope
7 protons, 7 neutrons

Dating Rocks—How Does It Work? Consider a stream of molten lava flowing out of a volcano. As long as the lava is in liquid form, the daughter material that is already present and the parent material are free to mix and move around. But eventually the lava cools and becomes solid igneous rock. When this happens, the parent and daughter materials often end up in different minerals. Scientists know that any daughter material found in the same mineral as the parent material most likely formed after the lava became solid rock. Scientists compare the amount of new daughter material with the amount of parent material that remains. The more new daughter material there is, the older the rock is.

Radiometric Dating

If you know the rate of decay for an element in a rock, you can figure out the age of the rock. Determining the absolute age of a sample based on the ratio of parent material to daughter material is called **radiometric dating.** For example, let's say that it takes 10,000 years for half the parent material in a rock sample to decay into daughter material. You analyze the sample and find equal amounts of parent material and daughter material. This means that half the original radioactive isotope has decayed and that the sample must be about 10,000 years old.

What if one-fourth of your sample is parent material and three-fourths is daughter material? You would know that it took 10,000 years for half the original sample to decay and another 10,000 years for half of what remained to decay. The age of your sample would be $2 \times 10{,}000$, or 20,000, years. **Figure 11** shows how this steady decay works. The time it takes for one-half of a radioactive sample to decay is called a **half-life.**

÷ 5 ÷ Ω ≤ ∞ + Ω √ 9 ∞ ≤ Σ 2
+

MATH**BREAK**

Get a Half-Life!

After observing the process illustrated in Figure 11, complete the chart below in your ScienceLog.

Parent left	Half-life in years	Age in years
1/8	?	30,000
?	1.3 billion	3.9 billion
1/4	10,000	?

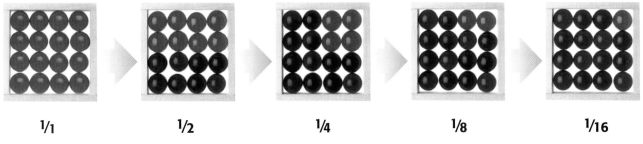

Figure 11 *After every half-life, the amount of parent material decreases by one-half.*

¹/₁   ¹/₂   ¹/₄   ¹/₈   ¹/₁₆

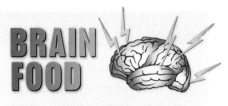
Types of Radiometric Dating

Imagine traveling back through the centuries to a time long before Columbus arrived in America. You are standing along the bluffs of what will one day be called the Mississippi River. You see dozens of people building large mounds. Who are these people, and what are they building?

The people you saw in your time travel were American Indians, and the structures they were building were burial mounds. The area you imagined is now an archaeological site called Effigy Mounds National Monument. **Figure 12** shows one of these mounds.

According to archaeologists, people lived at Effigy Mounds from 2,500 years ago to 600 years ago. How do archaeologists know these dates? They have dated bones and other objects in the mounds using radiometric dating. Scientists use different radiometric dating techniques based on the estimated age of an object. As you read on, think about how the half-life of an isotope relates to the age of the object being dated. Which technique would you use to date the burial mounds?

Figure 12 *This burial mound at Effigy Mounds resembles a snake.*

Uranium-Lead Method Uranium-238 is a radioactive isotope that eventually decays to lead-206. The half-life of uranium-238 is 4.5 billion years. The older the rock is, the more daughter material (lead-206) there will be in the rock. Uranium-lead dating can be used for rocks more than 10 million years old. Younger rocks do not contain enough daughter material to be accurately measured by this method.

Potassium-Argon Method Another isotope used for radiometric dating is potassium-40. Potassium-40 has a half-life of 1.3 billion years, and it eventually decays to argon and calcium. Geologists measure argon as the daughter material for radiometric dating. This method is mainly used to date rocks older than 100,000 years.

Carbon-14 Method The carbon-14 method works differently from the two methods already mentioned. The element carbon is normally found in three forms, the stable isotopes carbon-12 and carbon-13 and the radioactive isotope carbon-14. These carbon isotopes combine with oxygen to form the gas carbon dioxide, which is taken in by plants during photosynthesis. As long as a plant is alive, new carbon dioxide with a constant carbon-14 to carbon-12 ratio is continually taken in. Animals that eat plants contain the same ratio of carbon isotopes.

Once a plant or animal dies, however, no new carbon is taken in. The amount of carbon-14 begins to decrease as the plant or animal decays, and the ratio of carbon-14 to carbon-12 decreases. This decrease can be measured in a laboratory, such as the one shown in **Figure 13.** Because the half-life of carbon-14 is only 5,730 years, this dating method is mainly used for dating things that lived within the last 50,000 years.

Figure 13 *Some samples containing carbon must be cleaned and burned before their age can be determined.*

REVIEW

1. Explain how radioactive decay occurs.

2. How does radioactive decay relate to radiometric dating?

3. List three types of radiometric dating.

4. **Applying Concepts** Which radiometric-dating method would be most appropriate for dating artifacts found at Effigy Mounds? Explain.

internet connect

SC*i*LINKS.
NSTA

TOPIC: Absolute Dating
GO TO: www.scilinks.org
*sci*LINKS NUMBER: HSTE140

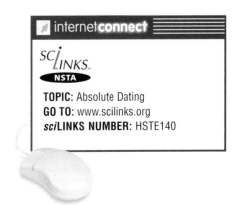

Looking at Fossils

Terms to Learn

fossil	coprolite
permineralization	mold
petrification	cast
trace fossil	index fossil

What You'll Do

- Describe how different types of fossils are formed.
- List the types of fossils that are not part of organisms.
- Demonstrate how fossils can be used to determine changes in environments and in the organisms the fossils came from.
- Describe index fossils, and explain how they are used.

Imagine you and your classmates are on a cross-country science field trip to Coralville, a town in east-central Iowa. Your teacher takes your class to a nearby stone quarry and points to a large rock wall that looks just like a coral reef. "This is how Coralville got its name," your teacher explains. "There used to be a living coral reef right here. What you see today is a fossilized coral reef." But you know that coral reefs are found in warm tropical oceans and that Iowa is more than 1,000 km away from any ocean! How did this huge coral reef end up in the middle of Iowa? To answer this question, you need to learn about fossils.

Fossilized Organisms

A **fossil** is any naturally preserved evidence of life. Fossils exist in many forms. The most easily recognizable fossils are preserved organisms, such as the stingray shown at right, or parts of organisms. Usually these fossils occur in rock. But as you will see, other materials can also preserve evidence of life.

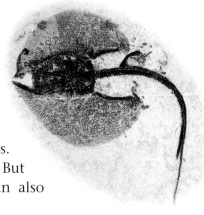

Fossils in Rocks When organisms die, the soft, fleshy parts of their bodies decompose, leaving only the hard parts. Occasionally, these hard parts get buried quickly in sediment and are preserved while the sediment turns to rock.

It takes more time for hard body parts such as bones, shells, and wood to decompose. For this reason, organisms with hard body parts are more likely to become fossils than those with only soft parts.

Mineral Replacement Organisms can also be preserved by **permineralization,** a process in which minerals fill in pore spaces of an organism's tissues. Minerals can also replace the original tissues of organisms. **Petrification** of an organism, shown in **Figure 14,** occurs when the organism's tissues are completely replaced by minerals.

Figure 14 *These pieces of petrified wood are made of stone.*

Fossils in Amber Imagine a fly or a mosquito landing in a drop of tree sap and getting stuck. Suppose that the insect gets covered by more sap. When the sap hardens, the insect will be preserved inside. Hardened tree sap is called *amber*. Some of our best insect fossils are found in amber, as shown in **Figure 15**.

Mummification When organisms die in dry places, such as deserts, they can sometimes dry out so fast that there isn't enough time for even their soft parts to decay. This process is called *mummification*. Mummified organisms don't decay because the bacteria that feed on dead organisms can't live without water. Some food, like dried fruit and beef jerky, is preserved in a similar way.

Figure 15 *This insect is perfectly preserved in amber.*

Frozen Fossils Imagine a huge animal that looks like an elephant with long hair walking along a glacier 12,000 years ago. It's a woolly mammoth. Suddenly, the beast slips and falls between two huge pieces of ice into a deep crack. With no way out, the animal freezes and is preserved until the glacier thaws thousands of years later. Scientists find fossils of woolly mammoths and many other organisms when glaciers thaw. These frozen specimens are some of the best fossils.

Fossils in Tar There are places where tar occurs naturally in thick, sticky pools. One such place is the La Brea tar pits, in Los Angeles County, California. These pits of thick oil and tar were present when saber-toothed cats roamed the Earth 40,000 years ago, as shown in **Figure 16.**

Much of what we know about these extinct cats comes from fossils found in the La Brea tar pits. But saber-toothed cats are not the only organisms found in the pits. Scientists have found fossils of many other mammals as well as plants, snails, birds, salamanders, and insects.

Figure 16 *Many animals, including saber-toothed cats, became fossils after sinking in tar pits.*

Other Types of Fossils

What happens when scientists cannot find any remains of plants or animals? Is there anything else that might indicate an organism's former presence?

Trace Fossils Any naturally preserved evidence of an animal's activity is called a **trace fossil.** An easily recognizable type of trace fossil is a *track.* Just like animals today, the animals in the past left tracks. These ancient tracks became fossils when they filled with sediment that eventually turned to rock.

Imagine that the tracks shown here were made by a ferocious *Tyrannosaurus rex.* While the animal that made them is long gone, the fossil tracks remain as evidence that it once prowled the Earth.

Burrows are another type of trace fossil. Burrows are shelters made by animals that dig into the ground. Like tracks, burrows are preserved when they are filled in with sediment and buried quickly.

Coprolites are a third type of trace fossil. The word *coprolite* (KAHP roh LIET) is from the Greek words meaning "dung stone." **Coprolites** are preserved feces, or dung, from animals. Coprolites can provide valuable information about the habits and diets of the animals that left them. **Figure 17** shows a coprolite that is more than 5 million years old.

Figure 17 *This coprolite came from a prehistoric mammal.*

 Self-Check

Why are tracks and coprolites considered trace fossils? *(See page 726 to check your answer.)*

Molds and Casts A **mold** is a cavity in the ground or rock where a plant or animal was buried. Often the cavity has been filled in, leaving a cast of the original organism. A **cast** is an object created when sediment fills a mold and becomes rock. A cast shows what the outside of the organism looked like. **Figure 18** shows a mold and cast from the same organism.

Figure 18 *The ammonite cast on the left formed when sediment filled the ammonite mold on the right and became rock.*

Using Fossils to Interpret the Past

By examining fossils, scientists can find out what was happening in the environment when the sediments surrounding the fossils were deposited. Scientists can also interpret how plants and animals have changed over time by studying fossils from different parts of the geologic column.

Changes in Environments

Fossils can reveal changes that have occurred in parts of the Earth. By studying the coral-reef fossils and applying the principle of uniformitarianism, for example, scientists have determined that Iowa was once covered by a shallow sea. This is hard to believe when you look at Iowa's landscape today!

Iowa is just one example of where inconsistent fossils have been found. Who would have expected fossils of coral to be found in the landlocked state of Iowa? Likewise, who would have expected fossils of marine organisms on the top of a mountain? But that is exactly what scientists found on mountaintops in Canada, as shown in **Figure 19.** The presence of these fossils means that these rocks were once below the surface of an ocean.

Figure 19 *Scientists often find rocks that contain marine fossils on mountaintops. These rocks were pushed up from below sea level millions of years ago.*

Changes in Life Older rock layers contain organisms different from those found in younger rock layers. The record stored in the rocks shows a change in life-forms over the years. For example, rock layers that contain fish fossils are found beneath the oldest rock layers that contain fossils of amphibians. Amphibians, such as frogs and salamanders, are animals with characteristics that allow them to live both on land and in water. On top of these rock layers are the oldest layers that contain fossils of reptiles, most of which lived only on land. Using the principle of superposition, we know that fish existed before amphibians because fish were found in a lower layer of rock. In the same way, we know that amphibians existed before reptiles.

Using Fossils to Date Rocks

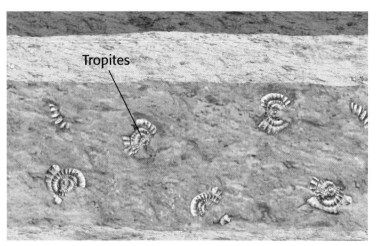

Geologists sometimes use *index fossils* to date rocks while in the field. **Index fossils** are fossils of organisms that lived during a relatively short, well-defined time span. Whenever geologists find an index fossil in a rock layer, they know where in the geologic column the rock layer fits. This enables them to give the layer a date without directly using radiometric dating. Good index fossils also have a wide distribution around the world.

An example of an index fossil is a genus of trilobites called *Phacops,* shown above. Trilobites are extinct, but they looked like a cross between a modern horseshoe crab and a pill bug. *Phacops* lived in shallow oceans about 400 million years ago. Where geologists find a fossil of this trilobite, they can assume that the surrounding rock is about 400 million years old.

Another good index fossil is a genus of ammonites called *Tropites,* shown in **Figure 20.** Ammonites were marine animals that looked a lot like modern squids, but they lived in coiled shells with complex inner walls. *Tropites* lived between 230 million and 208 million years ago. Where geologists find them in a rock layer, they know that the rock layer is between 208 million and 230 million years old.

Tropites

Figure 20 Tropites, *a genus of ammonites, existed for only about 20 million years, which makes it a good index fossil.*

internet**connect**

SCi*LINKS*
NSTA

TOPIC: Looking at Fossils
GO TO: www.scilinks.org
*sci*LINKS NUMBER: HSTE145

REVIEW

1. Describe two ways that fossils can form.

2. List two types of fossils that are not part of an organism.

3. What are index fossils? How do scientists use them to date rocks?

4. **Making Inferences** If you find rock layers containing fish fossils in a desert, what can you infer about that area of the desert?

Time Marches On

Terms to Learn

geologic time scale
eon   period
era   epoch

What You'll Do

◆ Demonstrate an understanding of the geologic time scale.
◆ Identify important dates on the geologic time scale.
◆ Identify the eon we know the most about, and explain why we know more about it than about other eons.

Remember the stack of family pictures mentioned in Section 2? The oldest pictures were on the bottom, and the newest ones were on the top. By looking through the pictures in order, you could see the sequence of events and changes that occurred in your family's history. In studying the history of the Earth, scientists follow a similar process. But instead of looking at pictures, they analyze rock layers and the fossils they contain.

Rock Layers and Geologic Time

One of the best places in North America to see the Earth's history recorded in rock layers is in Grand Canyon National Park, shown in **Figure 21.** The Colorado River has cut the canyon nearly 2 km deep in some places. During this process, countless layers of rock have been eroded by the river. These layers represent nearly 2 billion years of geologic time!

Figure 21 *The rock layers in the Grand Canyon correspond to a very large section of the geologic column.*

Biology
C O N N E C T I O N

The Grand Canyon is so wide and deep that organisms on either side of the canyon took different evolutionary paths. As the Colorado River formed the canyon, groups of individuals from the same species became separated and could no longer interact. Over millions of years, these groups developed differently and became different species.

The Geologic Time Scale

While the rock layers in the Grand Canyon represent the time that passed as they formed, the geologic column represents the billions of years that have passed since the first rocks formed on Earth. Geologists must grapple with the time represented by the geologic column as well as the time between Earth's formation and the formation of Earth's oldest known rocks. Altogether, geologists study 4.6 billion years of Earth's history! To make their job easier, geologists have created the geologic time scale. The **geologic time scale**, which is shown in **Figure 22**, is a scale that divides Earth's 4.6-billion-year history into distinct intervals of time.

Figure 22 *The geologic time scale accounts for Earth's entire history. It is divided into four major parts called* eons.

Phanerozoic eon

(540 million years ago– present)
The rock and fossil record mainly represents the Phanerozoic eon, which is the eon in which we live.

Proterozoic eon

(2.5 billion years ago– 540 million years ago)
The first organisms with well-developed cells appeared during this eon.

Archean eon

(3.8 billion years ago– 2.5 billion years ago)
The earliest known rocks on Earth formed during this eon.

Hadean eon

(4.6 billion years ago– 3.8 billion years ago)
The only rocks that scientists have found from this eon are meteorites and rocks from the moon.

Geologic Time Scale			
Era	**Period**	**Epoch**	**Millions of years ago**
Cenozoic	Quaternary	Holocene	0.01
		Pleistocene	1.8
	Tertiary	Pliocene	5.3
		Miocene	23.8
		Oligocene	33.7
		Eocene	54.8
		Paleocene	65
Mesozoic	Cretaceous		144
	Jurassic		206
	Triassic		248
Paleozoic	Permian		290
	Pennsylvanian		323
	Mississippian		354
	Devonian		417
	Silurian		443
	Ordovician		490
	Cambrian		540

PHANEROZOIC EON

PROTEROZOIC EON — 2,500

ARCHEAN EON — 3,800

HADEAN EON — 4,600

Divisions of Time Geologists have divided Earth's history into sections of time, as shown on the geologic time scale in Figure 22. The largest divisions of geologic time are **eons.** The four eons in turn are divided into **eras,** which are the second-largest divisions of geologic time. Eras are divided into **periods,** which are the third-largest divisions of geologic time. Some periods are divided into **epochs** (EP uhks), which are the fourth-largest division of geologic time. Look again at Figure 22. Can you figure out what epoch we live in?

The boundaries between geologic time intervals represent major changes on Earth. These changes include the appearance or disappearance of life-forms, changes in the global climate, and changes in rock types. For example, each of the three eras of the Phanerozoic eon are characterized by unique life-forms.

The Paleozoic Era *Paleozoic* means "old life." The Paleozoic era lasted from about 540 to 248 million years ago. It is the first era that is well represented by fossils.

At the beginning of the Paleozoic era, there were no land organisms. Imagine how empty the landscape must have looked! By the middle of the era, plants started appearing on land. By the end of the era, amphibians were living partially on the land, and insects were abundant. **Figure 23** shows what the land might have looked like late in the Paleozoic era. The Paleozoic era came to an end with a mass extinction—nearly 90 percent of all species perished.

Living in the Past
How do scientists know what life was like in prehistoric times? Turn to page 161 to learn how one paleontologist finds out.

Figure 23 *Jungles were present during the Paleozoic era, but there were no birds singing in the trees and no monkeys swinging from the branches. Birds and mammals didn't evolve until much later.*

The Mesozoic Era *Mesozoic* means "middle life." The Mesozoic era lasted from about 248 million years ago until about 65 million years ago. This era is also known as the Age of Reptiles. Dinosaurs, such as the ones shown in **Figure 24,** inhabited the land and the water.

Although reptiles dominated the Mesozoic era, birds and small mammals began to evolve late in the era. Most scientists think that birds evolved directly from a type of dinosaur. By the end of the Mesozoic era, about 50 percent of all species on Earth, including the dinosaurs, became extinct.

Figure 24 *Imagine walking in the desert and bumping into these fierce creatures! It's a good thing humans didn't evolve in the Mesozoic era, which was dominated by dinosaurs.*

The Cenozoic Era *Cenozoic* means "recent life." The Cenozoic era began about 65 million years ago and continues to the present. We live in the Cenozoic era.

Whereas the Mesozoic era is called the Age of Reptiles, the Cenozoic era is called the Age of Mammals. After the mass extinction at the end of the Mesozoic era, mammals became abundant on Earth, as shown in **Figure 25.** Many types of mammals that lived earlier in the Cenozoic era are now extinct, including woolly mammoths, saber-toothed cats, and giant sloths.

Figure 25 *Thousands of species of mammals evolved during the Cenozoic era. This scene shows species from the early Cenozoic era that are now extinct.*

Can You Imagine 4.6 Billion Years?

It's hard to picture 4.6 billion of anything, especially years. As humans, we do quite well to live to be 100 years old. Given this perspective, it is very difficult to think of Earth as being billions of years old. One way to do this is to organize the geologic time scale into the frame of 12 hours, with the first moment of Earth's history being noon and the present moment being midnight. This has been done on the Earth-history clock shown in **Figure 26.** On the Earth-history clock, the millions of years of evolution that you just read about occurred within the last hour. Human civilizations appeared within the last second! Perhaps you now have a better understanding of just how old the Earth is and just how brief humans' existence has been.

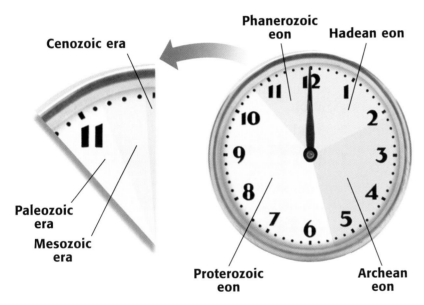

Figure 26 *On the Earth-history clock, which organizes Earth's history into the frame of 12 hours, 1 hour equals 383 million years, 1 minute equals 6.4 million years, and 1 second equals 106,000 years.*

QuickLab

Make a Time Scale

1. Using a pair of **scissors,** cut a length of **adding-machine tape** 46 cm long.

2. Starting at one end of the tape, use a **ruler** and a **black marker** to draw a line across the width of the tape at the following measurements: 5.4 cm, 25 cm, and 38 cm.

3. Using **colored markers,** color the sections of tape as follows:
   0 cm–5.4 cm = green
   5.4 cm–25 cm = blue
   25 cm–38 cm = red
   38 cm–46 cm = yellow

4. Your tape represents the geologic time scale, and the present moment is at 46 cm. What is the name of each time interval on your scale?

REVIEW

1. How many eras are in the Phanerozoic eon? List them.

2. In this section, extinctions at the end of two geologic time intervals are mentioned. What are these two intervals, and when did each interval end?

3. Which eon do we know the most about? Why?

4. **Making Predictions** What future event might mark the end of the Cenozoic era?

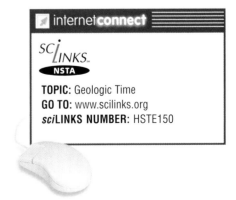

internet connect

SC*i*LINKS.
NSTA

TOPIC: Geologic Time
GO TO: www.scilinks.org
*sci*LINKS NUMBER: HSTE150

Chapter Highlights

SECTION 1

Vocabulary

uniformitarianism *(p. 134)*

catastrophism *(p. 135)*

Section Notes

- Scientists use the principle of uniformitarianism to interpret the past and make predictions.

- According to uniformitarianism, geologic change is gradual. According to catastrophism, geologic change is sudden.

- Before Hutton and Lyell, most scientists believed all geologic change was catastrophic. After Hutton and Lyell, most scientists rejected catastrophism. Today most scientists favor uniformitarianism, but they recognize some geologic change as catastrophic.

SECTION 2

Vocabulary

relative dating *(p. 137)*

superposition *(p. 137)*

geologic column *(p. 138)*

unconformity *(p. 140)*

Section Notes

- Geologists use relative dating to determine the relative age of objects.

- Geologists assume that younger layers lie above older layers in undisturbed rock-layer sequences. This is called superposition.

- The entire rock and fossil record is represented by the geologic column.

- Geologists examine the relationships between rock layers and the structures that cut across them in order to determine relative ages.

- Geologists also determine relative ages by assuming that all rock layers were originally horizontal.

- Unconformities form where rock layers are missing, and they represent time that is not recorded in the rock record.

Labs

How DO You Stack Up? *(p. 652)*

☑ Skills Check

Math Concepts

HALF-LIVES Remember from Figure 11 on page 143 that the ratio of parent material to daughter material decreases by one-half with each half-life. An easy way to think of this is to multiply the ratio by $1/2$ for each half-life. This is shown below.

$$\frac{1}{1} \times \frac{1}{2} = \frac{1}{2}; \quad \frac{1}{2} \times \frac{1}{2} = \frac{1}{4};$$

$$\frac{1}{4} \times \frac{1}{2} = \frac{1}{8}; \quad \text{and} \quad \frac{1}{8} \times \frac{1}{2} = \frac{1}{16}$$

Visual Understanding

FAULTS AND UNCONFORMITIES It is important to realize that faults and unconformities are not bodies of rock. They are types of surfaces where bodies of rock contact each other.

SECTION 3

Vocabulary

absolute dating *(p. 142)*
isotopes *(p. 142)*
radioactive decay *(p. 142)*
radiometric dating *(p. 143)*
half-life *(p. 143)*

Section Notes

- During radioactive decay, an unstable parent isotope of one element decays at a constant rate into a stable daughter isotope of a different element.

- The absolute age of samples of some rocks and fossils can be determined by the ratio of unstable isotopes to stable isotopes in the samples. This is called radiometric dating.

- The radiometric-dating method scientists use depends on the estimated age of the object they are dating.

SECTION 4

Vocabulary

fossil *(p. 146)*
permineralization *(p. 146)*
petrification *(p. 146)*
trace fossil *(p. 148)*
coprolite *(p. 148)*
mold *(p. 148)*
cast *(p. 148)*
index fossil *(p. 150)*

Section Notes

- Any naturally preserved evidence of life is considered a fossil.

- There are many ways fossils can form, such as mineral replacement, mummification, and freezing.

- Fossils can be used to show how environments and organisms have changed over time.

- Fossils, especially index fossils, can be used to date rocks.

SECTION 5

Vocabulary

geologic time scale *(p. 152)*
eon *(p. 153)*
era *(p. 153)*
period *(p. 153)*
epoch *(p. 153)*

Section Notes

- The history of the Earth is recorded in rock layers.

- The 4.6 billion years of Earth's history is represented on the geologic time scale, including the intervals not represented in the rock and fossil record.

- There are several different time intervals on the geologic time scale.

- Scientists know very little about the Earth's early history. This is because the rock and fossil record primarily represents the last eon of Earth's history.

---

internet**connect**

GO TO: go.hrw.com

Visit the **HRW** Web site for a variety of learning tools related to this chapter. Just type in the keyword:

KEYWORD: HSTFOS

GO TO: www.scilinks.org

Visit the **National Science Teachers Association** on-line Web site for Internet resources related to this chapter. Just type in the *sci*LINKS number for more information about the topic:

TOPIC:	Earth's Story	*sci*LINKS NUMBER: HSTE130
TOPIC:	Relative Dating	*sci*LINKS NUMBER: HSTE135
TOPIC:	Absolute Dating	*sci*LINKS NUMBER: HSTE140
TOPIC:	Looking at Fossils	*sci*LINKS NUMBER: HSTE145
TOPIC:	Geologic Time	*sci*LINKS NUMBER: HSTE150

Chapter Review

USING VOCABULARY

For each pair of terms, explain the difference in their meaning.

1. uniformitarianism/catastrophism

2. relative dating/absolute dating

3. mold/cast

4. eon/era

5. geologic time scale/geologic column

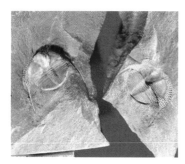

UNDERSTANDING CONCEPTS

Multiple Choice

6. Which of the following words does not describe catastrophic geologic change?
   a. sudden
   b. widespread
   c. gradual
   d. rare

7. Scientists assign relative ages by using
   a. potassium-argon dating.
   b. the principle of superposition.
   c. radioactive half-lives.
   d. the ratios of isotopes.

8. Rock layers cut by a fault formed
   a. after the fault.
   b. before the fault.
   c. at the same time as the fault.
   d. Cannot be determined

9. If the half-life of an unstable element is 5,000 years, what percentage of the parent material will be left after 10,000 years?
   a. 100   c. 50
   b. 75   d. 25

10. Of the following unstable isotopes, which has the longest half-life?
    a. uranium-238
    b. potassium-40
    c. carbon-14

11. Fossils can be
    a. petrified.
    b. dried out.
    c. frozen.
    d. All of the above

12. Of the following geologic time intervals, which is the shortest?
    a. an eon
    b. a period
    c. an era
    d. an epoch

13. If Earth's history is put on a scale of 12 hours, human civilizations would have been around for
    a. hours.
    b. minutes.
    c. less than 1 second.

Short Answer

14. What is the principle of superposition? How is it used by geologists?

15. Describe how plant and animal remains become petrified.

16. Explain how a fossil cast forms.

Concept Mapping

17. Use the following terms to create a concept map: age, absolute dating, half-life, radioactive decay, radiometric dating, relative dating, superposition, geologic column, isotopes.

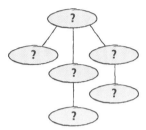

CRITICAL THINKING AND PROBLEM SOLVING

Write one or two sentences to answer the following questions:

18. You may have heard the term *petrified wood*. Why doesn't a "petrified" tree contain any wood?

19. How do tracks and burrows end up in the rock and fossil record?

20. How do you know that an intrusion is younger than its surrounding rock layers?

MATH IN SCIENCE

21. Copy the graph below onto a separate sheet of paper. Place a dot on the *y*-axis at 100 percent. Then place a dot on the graph at each half-life to show how much of the parent material is left. Connect the points with a curved line. Will the percentage of parent material ever reach zero? Explain.

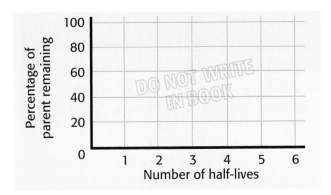

INTERPRETING GRAPHICS

Examine the drawing below, and answer the following questions.

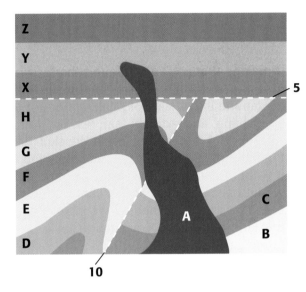

22. Is intrusion **A** younger or older than layer X?

23. What kind of unconformity is marked by **5**?

24. Is intrusion **A** younger or older than fault **10**? Why?

25. Other than the intrusion and faulting, what event occurred in layers **B**, **C**, **D**, **E**, **F**, **G**, and **H**? Number this event, the intrusion, and the faulting in the order they occurred.

Reading Check-up

Take a minute to review your answers to the Pre-Reading Questions found at the bottom of page 132. Have your answers changed? If necessary, revise your answers based on what you have learned since you began this chapter.

Science, Technology, and Society

CAT Scanning Fossils

Imagine that you've just found the fossilized skull of a small prehistoric mammal. You examine it very carefully, taking note of its size, shape, and external features. But you also want to look at features inside the skull, like the tiny bones of the middle ear. Can you do it without damaging the fossil? In the past it would have been impossible. Today, though, scientists are using medical technology to do this kind of detailed examination.

Breaking Bones

Paleontologists want to learn all they can about the fossils they study. They want to know about internal structures as well as external ones. Paleontologists usually grind a fossil away layer by layer, recording their observations as they go. Unfortunately, by the time they finish analyzing all the internal structures, the fossil is destroyed! This is a real problem if you want to show someone else your discovery.

Scientists with X-ray Vision

Now paleontologists have another choice. *Computerized axial tomography* (CAT scanning) is quickly replacing the more destructive method of studying internal structures. Originally designed as medical technology to examine the inside of the human skull, CAT scans provide interior views of a fossil without even touching its surface.

To understand how a CAT scan works, imagine a dolphin jumping through a hoop. As the dolphin passes through the hoop a CAT scan machine takes an X-ray picture of it from *every point around the hoop.* In effect, the machine takes a series of cross-section X-ray pictures of the dolphin. A computer then assembles these "slices" to create a three-dimensional picture of the dolphin. Every part of the dolphin's insides can then be studied without dissecting the dolphin.

When a paleontologist needs to reconstruct an entire skull, a series of two-dimensional "slice" shots is taken and the "slices" are combined through computer imaging to produce a three-dimensional image of the skull—inside and out!

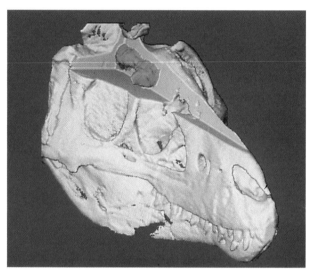

▲ *This CAT scan shows the size and location of the dinosaur* Nanotyrannosaurus rex's *brain.*

What's Hidden Inside?

Using CAT scans, scientists have learned much more about the internal structures of fossils. They have used CAT scans to look at the skeletons of embryos inside fossilized eggs and to study fragile bones still embedded in rock.

On Your Own

▶ What are the advantages of using CAT scans over conventional X rays? Find out by doing some research on your own.

CAREERS

PALEONTOLOGIST

Jack Horner found his first fossil bones at age 7 or 8 while collecting rocks at his father's quarry. From then on, he was hooked on dinosaurs. "I became a paleontologist because I like to dig in the dirt, discover things, and piece together puzzles," Horner says. As one of the world's leading experts on dinosaurs, Horner is curator of paleontology at the Museum of the Rockies, in Bozeman, Montana.

A mother nuzzles her babies in a nest. Nearby, another mother lets out a worried yelp; one of her babies has crawled out of its nest and is scampering away. The mother quickly captures her baby and returns it to safety. Puppies? Birds? No—dinosaurs! Or so Jack Horner believes.

Horner has come to this conclusion by comparing dinosaur fossils with modern alligators and birds. "I am studying how dinosaur bones developed, and I'm comparing them with the development of bones of alligators and birds so that we can learn more about dinosaur growth and nesting behaviors," Horner says. "I think that birds probably evolved from dinosaurs. If I find fossils of several nests close to each other, that tells me that the dinosaurs that built those nests may have lived together in a group."

Meeting the Challenge

As a child, Horner had difficulties in school because he had a learning disability called dyslexia. But no learning disability could dampen Horner's enthusiasm for science, especially the study of dinosaurs. "I like dinosaurs and figuring out what the world looked like at different times in the past. I've always liked the detective work that's involved in paleontology. You can't study a living dinosaur, so you have to figure out everything using clues from the past."

Boning Up on the Latest . . .

One of Horner's current projects is analyzing whether *Tyrannosaurus rex* was a vicious predator, as is often pictured, or a scavenger, eating other animals' kills. The more he studies fossil clues, the more Horner leans toward accepting the scavenger hypothesis. "Predatory animals require certain characteristics in order to be efficient killers. They need to be able to run fast, and they need to be able to maneuver and leap," Horner explains. "*T. rex* couldn't run fast, wasn't agile, and couldn't jump around or even fall down without doing serious damage to itself or even dying."

Decide for Yourself

▶ Observe the behavior of birds in your area. Focus on one or two species. Note their eating habits, the sounds they make, and their interactions with other birds. Do you think birds might have evolved from dinosaurs? Use your observations to support your theory.

▲ *A model of a* Maisasaura *hatching.*

UNIT 3

The Restless Earth

In this unit, you will learn about the Earth's internal structure. Many mysteries remain because we cannot see very far inside the Earth. The deepest holes we can dig barely scratch the planet's surface. If the Earth were an orange, our attempts to dig into it would not even break through the peel. One way scientists can learn about the Earth's interior is by studying earthquakes and volcanoes. This timeline shows some of the events that have occurred as scientists have tried to understand our dynamic Earth.

1864
Jules Verne's *A Journey to the Center of the Earth* is published. In this fictional story, the heroes enter and exit the Earth through volcanoes.

1883
Krakatau erupts, killing 36,000 people.

1966
A worldwide network of seismographs is established.

1979
Volcanoes are discovered on Io, one of Jupiter's moons.

1980
Mount St. Helens erupts.

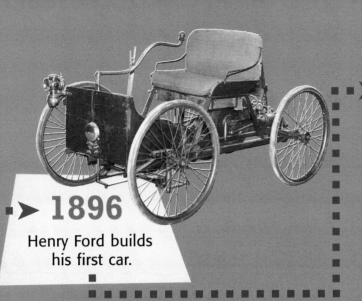

1896
Henry Ford builds his first car.

1906
San Francisco burns in the aftermath of an earthquake.

1935
Charles Richter devises a system of measuring the strength of earthquakes.

1912
Alfred Wegener proposes his continental-drift theory.

1951
Color television is introduced in the United States.

1994
An eight-legged robot named *Dante II* descends into the crater of an active volcano in Alaska.

1997
The population of the Caribbean island of Montserrat dwindles to less than half its original size as frequent eruptions of the Soufriere Hills volcano force evacuations.

1982
Compact discs (CDs) and compact-disc players are made available to the public.

Plate Tectonics

Pre-Reading
Questions

1. Why do entire mountain ranges move?
2. How do mountains form?

WHEN CONTINENTS COLLIDE

The Himalayas are the highest mountains on Earth. They are located between India and Asia in a region where two continents are slowly crashing into each other. This photo shows the highest mountain of all—Mount Everest. At an elevation of 8,848 m, the air at the top of Mount Everest is so thin that climbers must bring their own oxygen! In this chapter you will learn about how and where different types of mountains form. You will also learn about how scientists came up with *plate tectonics*, the theory that revolutionized geology.

Mountain climbers must brave extreme conditions when climbing mountains such as Mount Everest.

CONTINENTAL COLLISIONS

As you can see, continents not only move, but they can also crash into each other. In this activity, you will model the collision of two continents.

Procedure

1. Obtain **two stacks of paper,** each about 1 cm thick.

2. Place the two stacks of paper on a **flat surface,** such as a desk.

3. Very slowly, push the stacks of paper together so that they collide. Continue to push the stacks until the paper in one of the stacks folds over.

4. Repeat step 3, but this time push the two stacks together at a different angle. For example, if you pushed the flat edges together in step 3, try pushing the corners of the paper together this time.

Analysis

5. What happens to the stacks of paper when they collide with each other?

6. Do all of the pieces of paper get pushed upward? If not, what happens to those pieces that do not get pushed upward?

7. What type of landform does this model predict as the result of a continental collision?

Inside the Earth

What You'll Do

◆ Identify and describe the layers of the Earth by what they are made of.
◆ Identify and describe the layers of the Earth by their physical properties.
◆ Define *tectonic plate.*
◆ Explain how scientists know about the structure of Earth's interior.

The Earth is not just a ball of solid rock. It is made of several layers with different physical properties and compositions. As you will discover, scientists think about the Earth's layers in two ways—by their *composition* and by their *physical properties.*

Earth's layers are made of different mixtures of elements. This is what is meant by differences in composition. Many of the Earth's layers also have different physical properties. Physical properties include temperature, density, and ability to flow. Let's first take a look at the composition of the Earth.

The Composition of the Earth

The Earth is divided into three layers—the *crust, mantle,* and *core*—based on what each one is made of. The lightest materials make up the outermost layer, and the densest materials make up the inner layers. This is because lighter materials tend to float up, while heavier materials sink.

The Crust The **crust** is the outermost layer of the Earth. Ranging from 5 to 100 km thick, it is also the thinnest layer of the Earth. And because it is the layer we live on, we know more about this layer than we know about the other two.

There are two types of crust—continental and oceanic. *Continental crust* has a composition similar to granite. It has an average thickness of 30 km. *Oceanic crust* has a composition similar to basalt. It is generally between 5 and 8 km thick. Because basalt is denser than granite, oceanic crust is denser than continental crust.

Figure 1 *Oceanic crust is thinner but denser than continental crust.*

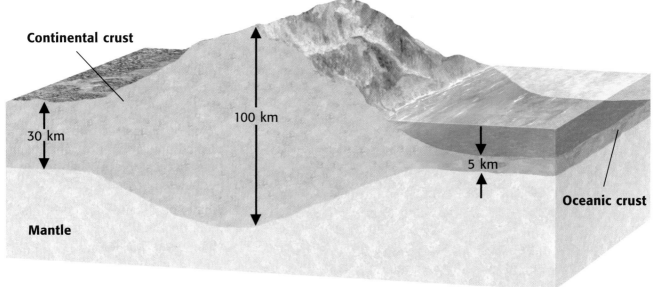

Continental crust

100 km

30 km

5 km

Oceanic crust

Mantle

The Mantle The **mantle** is the layer of the Earth between the crust and the core. Compared with the crust, the mantle is extremely thick and contains most of the Earth's mass.

No one has ever seen what the mantle really looks like. It is just too far down to drill for a sample. Scientists must infer what the composition and other characteristics of the mantle are from observations they make on the Earth's surface. In some places mantle rock has been pushed up to the surface by tectonic forces, allowing scientists to observe the rock directly.

As you can see in **Figure 2,** another place scientists look is on the ocean floor, where molten rock from the mantle flows out of active volcanoes. These underwater volcanoes are like windows through the crust into the mantle. The "windows" have given us strong clues about the composition of the mantle. Scientists have learned that the mantle's composition is similar to that of the mineral olivine, which has large amounts of iron and magnesium compared with other common minerals.

Figure 2 *Volcanic vents on the ocean floor, such as this one off the coast of Hawaii, allow magma to escape from the mantle beneath oceanic crust.*

The Core By studying the different layers that make up the Earth, geologists can get an idea of which elements each is made of. They think that the Earth's *core* is made mostly of iron, with smaller amounts of nickel and possibly some sulfur and oxygen. The **core** extends from the bottom of the mantle to the center of the Earth. As you can see in **Figure 3,** the diameter of the planet Mars is slightly smaller than that of the Earth's core.

Figure 3 *The Earth is made up of three layers, as shown here.*

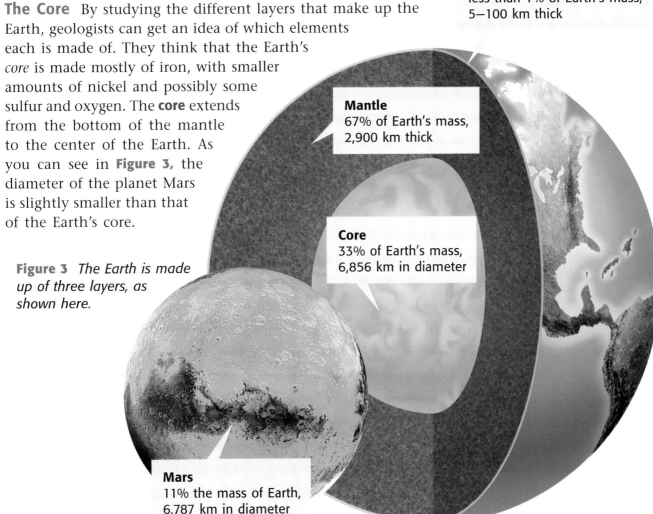

Crust
less than 1% of Earth's mass, 5–100 km thick

Mantle
67% of Earth's mass, 2,900 km thick

Core
33% of Earth's mass, 6,856 km in diameter

Mars
11% the mass of Earth, 6,787 km in diameter

Using Models

Imagine that you are building a model of the Earth that is going to have a radius of 1 m. You find out that the average radius of the Earth is 6,378 km and that the thickness of the lithosphere is about 150 km. What percentage of the Earth's radius is the lithosphere? How thick (in centimeters) would you make the lithosphere in your model?

The Structure of the Earth

So far we have talked about the composition of the Earth. Another way to look at how the Earth is made is to examine the physical properties of its layers. The Earth is divided into five main physical layers—the *lithosphere, asthenosphere, mesosphere, outer core,* and *inner core.* As shown below, each layer has its own set of physical properties.

Lithosphere The outermost, rigid layer of the Earth is called the **lithosphere** ("rock sphere"). The lithosphere is made of two parts—the crust and the rigid upper part of the mantle. The lithosphere is divided into pieces called *tectonic plates.*

Asthenosphere The **asthenosphere** ("weak sphere") is a soft layer of the mantle on which pieces of the lithosphere move. It is made of solid rock that, like putty, flows very slowly—at about the same rate your fingernails grow.

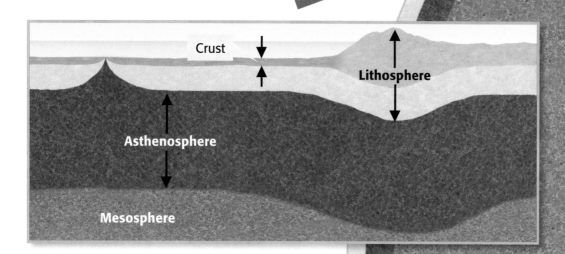

Mesosphere Beneath the asthenosphere is the strong, lower part of the mantle called the **mesosphere** ("middle sphere"). The mesosphere extends from the bottom of the asthenosphere down to the Earth's core.

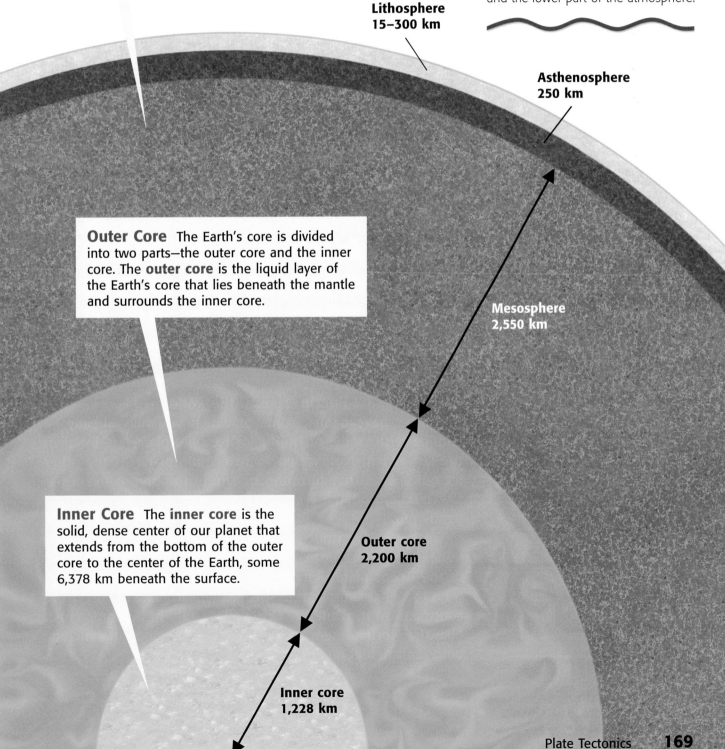

Lithosphere
15–300 km

Asthenosphere
250 km

Mesosphere
2,550 km

Outer Core The Earth's core is divided into two parts—the outer core and the inner core. The **outer core** is the liquid layer of the Earth's core that lies beneath the mantle and surrounds the inner core.

Inner Core The **inner core** is the solid, dense center of our planet that extends from the bottom of the outer core to the center of the Earth, some 6,378 km beneath the surface.

Outer core
2,200 km

Inner core
1,228 km

Tectonic Plates

Tectonic plates are pieces of the lithosphere that move around on top of the asthenosphere. But what exactly does a tectonic plate look like? How big are tectonic plates? How and why do they move around? To answer these questions, start by thinking of the lithosphere as a giant jigsaw puzzle.

Figure 4 *Tectonic plates fit together like the pieces of a jigsaw puzzle. On this map, the relative motions of some of the major tectonic plates are shown with arrows.*

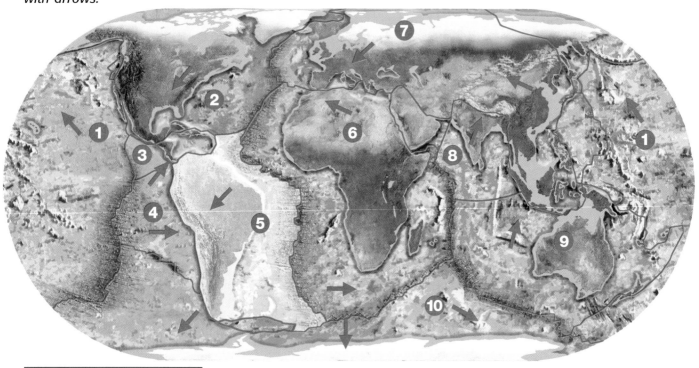

Major Tectonic Plates

1. Pacific plate
2. North American plate
3. Cocos plate
4. Nazca plate
5. South American plate
6. African plate
7. Eurasian plate
8. Indian plate
9. Australian plate
10. Antarctic plate

A Giant Jigsaw Puzzle Look at the world map above. All of the plates have names, some of which you may already be familiar with. Some of the major tectonic plates are listed in the key at left. Notice that each tectonic plate fits the other tectonic plates that surround it. The lithosphere is like a jigsaw puzzle, and the tectonic plates are like the pieces of a jigsaw puzzle.

You will also notice that not all tectonic plates are the same. Compare the size of the North American plate with that of the Cocos plate. But tectonic plates are different in other ways too. For example, the North American plate has an entire continent on it, while the Cocos plate only has oceanic crust. Like the North American plate, some tectonic plates include both continental *and* oceanic crust.

A Tectonic Plate Close-up What would a tectonic plate look like if you could lift it out of its place? **Figure 5** shows what the South American plate might look like if you could. Notice that this tectonic plate consists of both oceanic and continental crust, just like the North American plate.

The thickest part of this tectonic plate is on the South American continent, under the Andes mountain range. The thinnest part of the South American plate is at the Mid-Atlantic Ridge.

South American Plate

Andes mountain range

Oceanic crust

5

Continental crust

Mantle

Figure 5 *The South American plate is one of the many pieces of the spherical "jigsaw puzzle" we call the lithosphere.*

Tip of the Iceberg If you could look at a tectonic plate from the side, you would see that mountain ranges are like the tips of icebergs—there is much more material below the surface than above. Mountain ranges that occur in continental crust have very deep roots relative to their height. For example, the Rocky Mountains rise less than 5 km above sea level, but their roots go down to about 60 km *below* sea level.

But if continental crust is so much thicker than oceanic crust, why doesn't it sink down below the oceanic crust? Think back to the difference between continental and oceanic crust. Continental crust stands much higher than oceanic crust because it is both thicker and less dense. Both kinds of crust are less dense than the mantle and "float" on top of the asthenosphere, similar to the way ice floats on top of water.

QuickLab

Floating Mountains

1. Take a large **block** of wood and place it in a clear plastic **container.** The block of wood represents the mantle part of the lithosphere.

2. Fill the container with **water** at least 10 cm deep. The water represents the asthenosphere. Use a ruler to measure how far the top of the wood block sits above the surface of the water.

3. Now try loading the block of wood with several different **wooden objects,** each with a different weight. These objects represent different amounts of crustal material loaded onto the lithosphere during mountain building. Measure how far the block sinks under each different weight.

4. What can you conclude about how the tectonic plate reacts to increasing weight of crustal material?

5. What happens to a tectonic plate when the crustal material is removed?

TRY at HOME

Mapping the Earth's Interior

How do we know all these things about the deepest parts of the Earth, where no one has ever been? Scientists have never even drilled through the crust, which is only a thin skin on the surface of the Earth. So how do we know so much about the mantle and the core?

Would you be surprised to know that the answers come from earthquakes? When an earthquake occurs, vibrations called seismic waves are produced. *Seismic waves* are vibrations that travel through the Earth. Depending on the density and strength of material they pass through, seismic waves travel at different speeds. For example, a seismic wave traveling through solid rock will go faster than a seismic wave traveling through a liquid.

When an earthquake occurs, *seismographs* measure the difference in the arrival times of seismic waves and record them. Seismologists can then use these measurements to calculate the density and thickness of each physical layer of the Earth. **Figure 6** shows how one kind of seismic wave travels through the Earth.

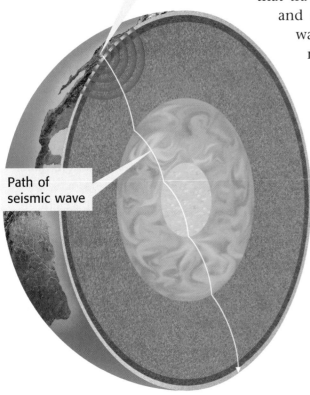

Earthquake

Path of seismic wave

Lithosphere 7–8 km/second

Asthenosphere 7–11 km/second

Mesosphere 11–13 km/second

Outer core 7–10 km/second

Inner core 11–12 km/second

Figure 6 *The speed of seismic waves depends on the density of the material they travel through. The denser the material, the faster seismic waves move.*

REVIEW

1. What is the difference between continental and oceanic crust?

2. How is the lithosphere different from the asthenosphere?

3. How do scientists know about the structure of the Earth's interior? Explain.

4. **Analyzing Relationships** Explain the difference between the crust and the lithosphere.

Restless Continents

Take a look at **Figure 7.** It shows how continents would fit together if you removed the Atlantic Ocean and moved the land together. Is it just coincidence that the coastlines fit together so well? Is it possible that the continents were actually together sometime in the past?

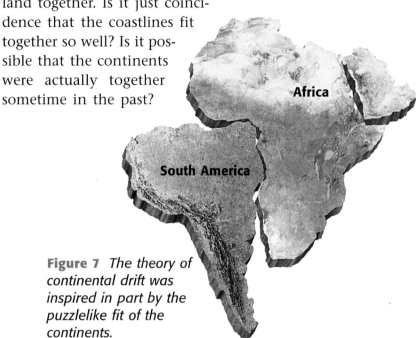

Figure 7 *The theory of continental drift was inspired in part by the puzzlelike fit of the continents.*

Wegener's Theory of Continental Drift

One scientist who looked at the pieces of this puzzle was Alfred Wegener (VEG e nuhr). In the early 1900s he wrote about his theory of *continental drift*. **Continental drift** is the theory that continents can drift apart from one another and have done so in the past. This theory seemed to explain a lot of puzzling observations, including the very good fit of some of the continents.

Continental drift also explained why fossils of the same plant and animal species are found on both sides of the Atlantic Ocean. Many of these ancient species could not have made it across the Atlantic Ocean. As you can see in **Figure 8,** without continental drift, this pattern of fossil findings would be hard to explain. In addition to fossils, similar types of rock and evidence of the same ancient climatic conditions were found on several continents.

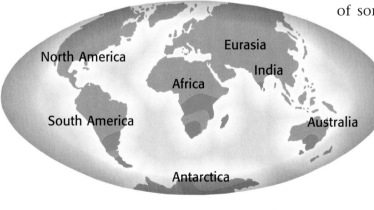

Mesosaurus

Glossopteris

Figure 8 *Fossils of* Mesosaurus, *a small, aquatic reptile, and* Glossopteris, *an ancient plant species, have been found on several continents.*

Continental drift also explained puzzling evidence left by ancient glaciers. Glaciers cut grooves in the ground that indicate the direction they traveled. When you look at the placement of today's continents, these glacial activities do not seem to be related. But when you bring all of these continental pieces back to their original arrangement, the glacial grooves match! Along with fossil evidence, glacial grooves supported Wegener's idea of continental drift.

The Breakup of Pangaea

Wegener studied many observations before establishing his theory of continental drift. He thought that all the separate continents of today were once joined in a single landmass that he called *Pangaea,* which is Greek for "all earth." As shown in **Figure 9,** almost all of Earth's landmasses were joined together in one huge continent 245 million years ago.

245 Million Years Ago Pangaea existed when some of the earliest dinosaurs were roaming the Earth. It was surrounded by a sea called *Panthalassa,* meaning "all sea."

Figure 9 *Over time, Earth's continents have changed shape and traveled great distances.*

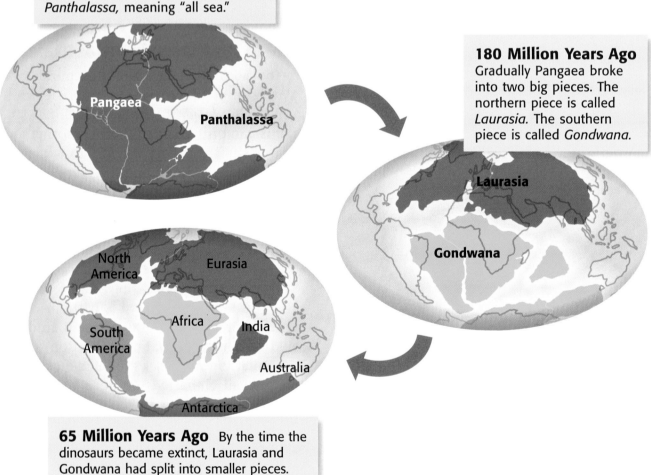

180 Million Years Ago Gradually Pangaea broke into two big pieces. The northern piece is called *Laurasia.* The southern piece is called *Gondwana.*

65 Million Years Ago By the time the dinosaurs became extinct, Laurasia and Gondwana had split into smaller pieces.

Sea-Floor Spreading

When Wegener put forth his theory of continental drift, many scientists would not accept his theory. What force of nature, they wondered, could move entire continents? In Wegener's day, no one could answer that question. It wasn't until many years later that new evidence provided some clues.

In **Figure 10** you will notice that there is a chain of submerged mountains running through the center of the Atlantic Ocean. The chain is called the Mid-Atlantic Ridge, part of a worldwide system of ocean ridges. Mid-ocean ridges are underwater mountain chains that run through Earth's ocean basins.

Mid-ocean ridges are places where sea-floor spreading takes place. **Sea-floor spreading** is the process by which new oceanic lithosphere is created as older materials are pulled away. As tectonic plates move away from each other, the sea floor spreads apart and magma rises to fill in the gap. Notice in **Figure 11** that the crust increases in age the farther it is from the mid-ocean ridge. This is because new crust continually forms from molten material at the ridge. The oldest crust in the Atlantic Ocean is found along the edges of the continents. It dates back to the time of the dinosaurs. The newest crust is in the center of the ocean. This crust has just formed!

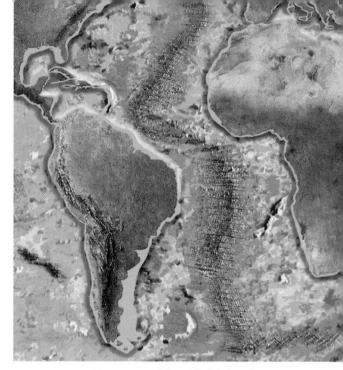

Figure 10 *The Mid-Atlantic Ridge is part of the longest mountain chain in the world.*

Figure 11 *Sea-floor spreading creates new oceanic lithosphere at mid-ocean ridges.*

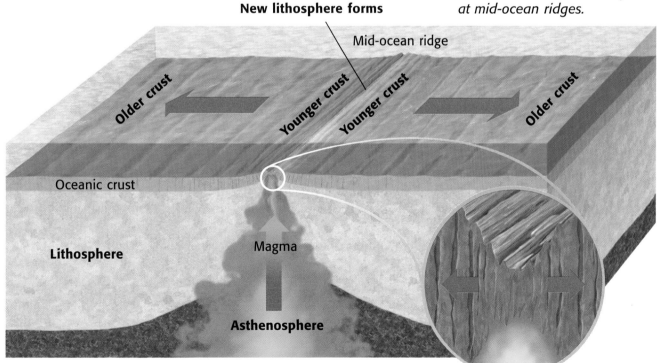

New lithosphere forms

Mid-ocean ridge

Older crust

Younger crust

Younger crust

Older crust

Oceanic crust

Lithosphere

Magma

Asthenosphere

All matter has the property of magnetism, though in most cases it is very weak compared with that of magnets. This explains why researchers have been able to levitate a frog—by creating a very strong magnetic field beneath it!

Magnetic Reversals

Some of the most important evidence of sea-floor spreading comes from magnetic reversals recorded in the ocean floor. Throughout Earth's history, the north and south magnetic poles have changed places many times. When Earth's magnetic poles change place, this is called a *magnetic reversal.*

The molten rock at the mid-ocean ridges contains tiny grains of magnetic minerals. These mineral grains act like compasses. They align with the magnetic field of the Earth. Once the molten rock cools, the record of these tiny compasses is literally set in stone. This record is then carried slowly away from the spreading center as sea-floor spreading occurs. As you can see in **Figure 12,** when the Earth's magnetic field reverses, a new band is started, and this time the magnetic mineral grains point in the opposite direction. The new rock records the direction of the Earth's magnetic field. This record of magnetic reversals was the final proof that sea-floor spreading does occur.

Figure 12 *Magnetic reversals in oceanic crust are shown here as bands of light and dark blue oceanic crust.*

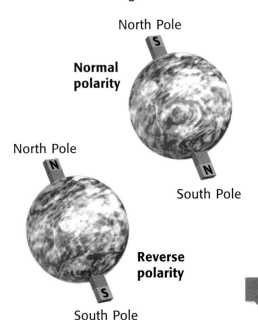

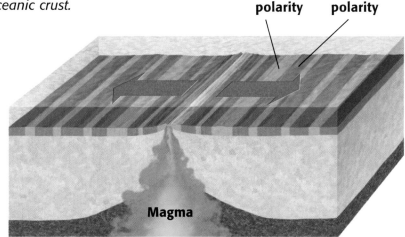

REVIEW

1. List three puzzling occurrences that the theory of continental drift helped to explain, and describe how it explained them.

2. Explain why Wegener's theory of continental drift was not accepted at first.

3. **Identifying Relationships** Explain how the processes of sea-floor spreading and magnetic reversal produce bands of oceanic crust that have different magnetic polarities.

North Pole
North Pole
Normal polarity
South Pole
Reverse polarity
South Pole

Normal polarity   **Reverse polarity**

Magma

The Theory of Plate Tectonics

The proof of sea-floor spreading supported Wegener's original idea that the continents move. But because both oceanic and continental crust appear to move, a new theory was devised to explain both continental drift and sea-floor spreading—the theory of *plate tectonics*. **Plate tectonics** is the theory that the Earth's lithosphere is divided into tectonic plates that move around on top of the asthenosphere.

Possible Causes of Tectonic Plate Motion

An incredible amount of energy is needed to move something as massive as a tectonic plate! We still don't know exactly why tectonic plates move as they do, but recently scientists have come up with some possible answers, as shown in **Figure 13.** Notice how all three are affected by heat and gravity.

Figure 13 Three Possible Driving Forces of Plate Tectonics

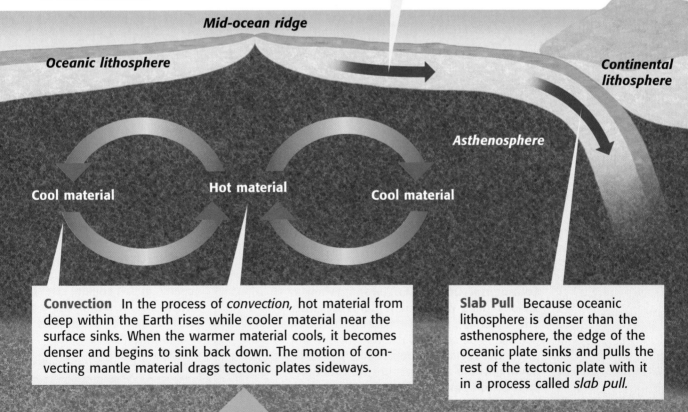

Ridge Push At mid-ocean ridges, the oceanic lithosphere is higher than it is where it sinks beneath continental lithosphere. *Ridge push* is the process by which an oceanic plate slides down the lithosphere-asthenosphere boundary.

Mid-ocean ridge

Oceanic lithosphere

Continental lithosphere

Asthenosphere

Cool material   Hot material   Cool material

Convection In the process of *convection*, hot material from deep within the Earth rises while cooler material near the surface sinks. When the warmer material cools, it becomes denser and begins to sink back down. The motion of convecting mantle material drags tectonic plates sideways.

Slab Pull Because oceanic lithosphere is denser than the asthenosphere, the edge of the oceanic plate sinks and pulls the rest of the tectonic plate with it in a process called *slab pull.*

Mesosphere

Heat

Tectonic Plate Boundaries

All tectonic plates have boundaries with other tectonic plates. These boundaries are divided into three main types depending on how the tectonic plates move relative to one another. Tectonic plates can collide, separate, or slide past each other. **Figure 14** shows some examples of tectonic plate boundaries.

Convergent Boundaries When two tectonic plates push into one another, the boundary where they meet is called a **convergent boundary.** What happens at a convergent boundary depends on what kind of crust—continental or oceanic—the leading edge of each tectonic plate has. As you can see below, there are three types of convergent boundaries—continental/continental, continental/oceanic, and oceanic/oceanic.

Figure 14 *This diagram shows five tectonic plate boundaries. Notice that there are three types of convergent boundaries.*

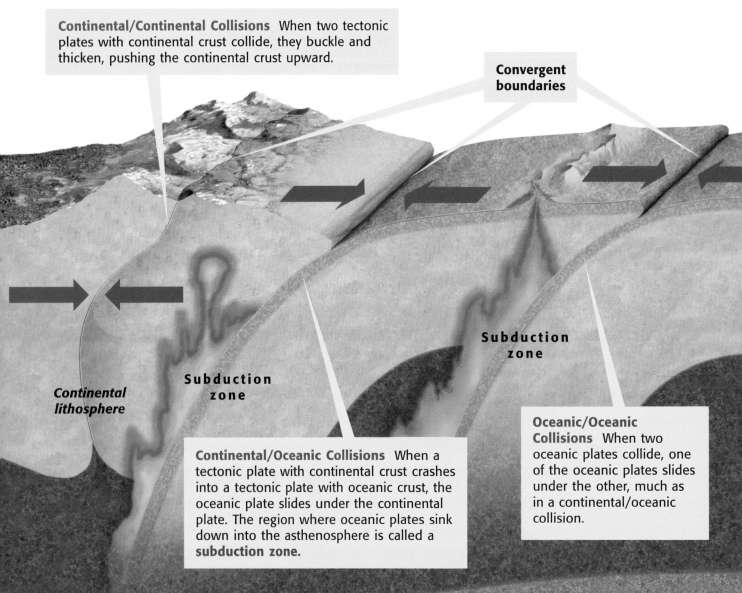

Continental/Continental Collisions When two tectonic plates with continental crust collide, they buckle and thicken, pushing the continental crust upward.

Convergent boundaries

Continental lithosphere

Subduction zone

Subduction zone

Continental/Oceanic Collisions When a tectonic plate with continental crust crashes into a tectonic plate with oceanic crust, the oceanic plate slides under the continental plate. The region where oceanic plates sink down into the asthenosphere is called a **subduction zone.**

Oceanic/Oceanic Collisions When two oceanic plates collide, one of the oceanic plates slides under the other, much as in a continental/oceanic collision.

Divergent Boundaries When two tectonic plates move away from one another, the boundary between them is called a **divergent boundary.** Remember sea-floor spreading? Divergent boundaries are where new oceanic lithosphere forms. The mid-ocean ridges that mark the spreading centers are the most common type of divergent boundary. However, divergent boundaries can also be found on continents.

Transform Boundaries When two tectonic plates slide past each other horizontally, the boundary between them is called a **transform boundary.** The San Andreas Fault, in California, is a good example of a transform boundary. This fault marks the place where the Pacific plate and the North American plate slide past each other.

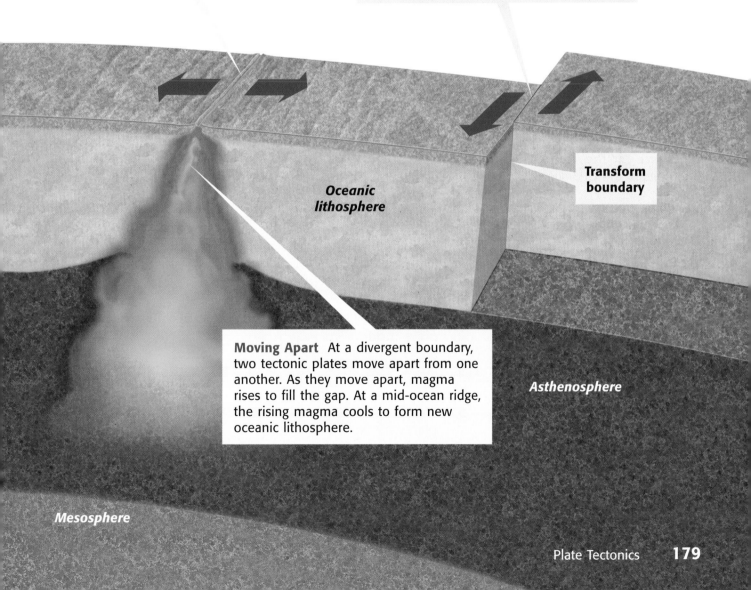

Divergent boundary

Sliding Past At a transform boundary, two tectonic plates slide past one another. Because tectonic plates are not smooth, they grind and jerk as they slide, producing earthquakes!

Transform boundary

Oceanic lithosphere

Asthenosphere

Moving Apart At a divergent boundary, two tectonic plates move apart from one another. As they move apart, magma rises to fill the gap. At a mid-ocean ridge, the rising magma cools to form new oceanic lithosphere.

Mesosphere

Tracking Tectonic Plate Motion

Just how fast do tectonic plates move? The answer to this question depends on many factors, such as the type of tectonic plate, the shape of the tectonic plate, and the way it interacts with the tectonic plates that surround it. Tectonic movements are generally so slow and gradual that you can't see or feel them—they are measured in centimeters per year.

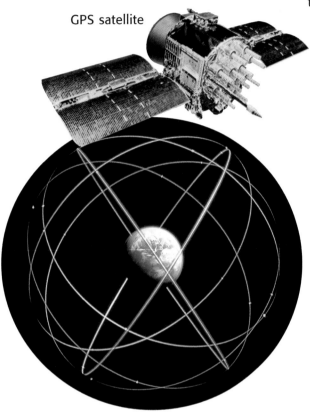

GPS satellite

One exception to this rule is the San Andreas Fault, in California. The Pacific plate and the North American plate do not slide past each other smoothly nor continuously. Instead, this movement happens in jerks and jolts. Sections of the fault remain stationary for years and then suddenly shift several meters, causing an earthquake. Large shifts that occur at the San Andreas fault can be measured right on the surface. Unfortunately for scientists, however, most movements of tectonic plates are very difficult to measure. So how do they do it?

Figure 15 *The image above shows the orbits of the GPS satellites.*

The Global Positioning System Scientists use a network of satellites called the *Global Positioning System* (GPS), shown in **Figure 15**, to measure the rate of tectonic plate movement. Radio signals are continuously beamed from satellites to GPS ground stations, which record the exact distance between the satellites and the ground station. Over time, these distances change slightly. By recording the time it takes for the GPS ground stations to move a given distance, scientists can measure the rate of motion of each tectonic plate.

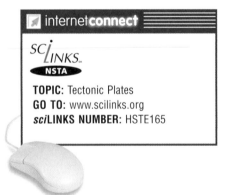

internetconnect

SCiLINKS.
NSTA

TOPIC: Tectonic Plates
GO TO: www.scilinks.org
*sci*LINKS NUMBER: HSTE165

REVIEW

1. List and describe three possible driving forces of tectonic plate motion.

2. How do the three types of convergent boundaries differ from one another?

3. Explain how scientists measure the rate at which tectonic plates move.

4. **Identifying Relationships** When convection takes place in the mantle, why does cooler material sink, while warmer material rises?

Deforming the Earth's Crust

What You'll Do

◆ Describe major types of folds.

◆ Explain how the three major types of faults differ.

◆ Name and describe the most common types of mountains.

◆ Explain how various types of mountains form.

Have you ever tried to bend something, only to have it break? Try this: take a long, uncooked piece of spaghetti, and bend it very slowly, and only a little. Now bend it again, but this time much farther and faster. What happened to it the second time? How can the same material bend at one time and break at another? The answer is that the *stress* you put on it was different. **Stress** is the amount of force per unit area that is put on a given material. The same principle works on the rocks in the Earth's crust. The conditions under which a rock is stressed determine its behavior.

Rocks Get Stressed

When rock changes its shape due to stress, this reaction is called *deformation*. In the example above, you saw the spaghetti deform in two different ways—by bending and by breaking. **Figure 16** illustrates this concept. The same thing happens in rock layers. Rock layers can bend when stress is placed on them. But when more stress is placed on them, they can break. Rocks can deform due to the forces of plate tectonics.

The type of stress that occurs when an object is squeezed, as when two tectonic plates collide, is called **compression.** Compression can have some spectacular results. The Rocky Mountains and the Cascade Range are two examples of compression at a convergent plate boundary.

Another form of stress is *tension.* **Tension** is stress that occurs when forces act to stretch an object. As you might guess, tension occurs at divergent plate boundaries, when two tectonic plates pull away from each other. In the following pages you will learn how these two tectonic forces—compression and tension—bend and break rock to form some of the common landforms you already know.

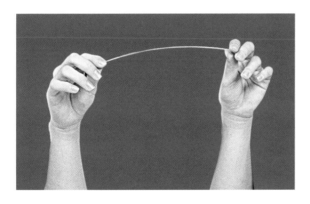

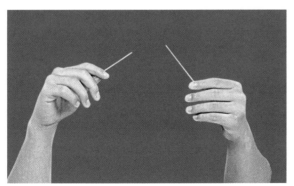

Figure 16 *With a small amount of stress, uncooked spaghetti bends. Additional stress causes it to break.*

Folding

Folding occurs when rock layers bend due to stress in the Earth's crust. We assume that all sedimentary rock layers started out as horizontal layers. So when you see a fold, you know that deformation has taken place. Depending on how the rock layers deform, different types of folds are made. **Figure 17** shows the two most common types—*anticlines* and *synclines.*

Another type of fold is a *monocline.* In a monocline, rock layers are folded so that both ends of the fold are still horizontal. Imagine taking a stack of paper and laying it on a table top. Think of all the sheets of paper as different rock layers. Now put a book under one end of the stack. You can see that both ends of the sheets are still horizontal, but all the sheets are bent in the middle.

Folds can be large or small. Take a look at **Figure 18.** The largest folds are measured in kilometers. They can make up the entire side of a mountain. Other folds are still obvious but much smaller. Note the size of the pocket knife in the smaller photo. Now look at the smallest folds. You would measure these folds in centimeters.

Undeformed Rock Layers

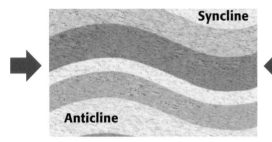

Syncline

Anticline

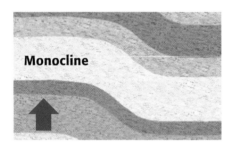

Monocline

Figure 17 *When tectonic forces put stress on rock layers, they can cause the layers to bend and fold.* Anticlines *and* synclines *form when horizontal stress acts on rock.* Monoclines *form when vertical stress acts on rock.*

Figure 18 *The larger photo at right shows mountain-sized folds in the Rocky Mountains. The smaller photo shows a rock with much smaller folds.*

Faulting

While some rock layers bend and fold when stress is applied, other rock layers break. The surface along which rocks break and slide past each other is called a **fault.** The blocks of crust on each side of the fault are called *fault blocks.*

If a fault is not vertical, it is useful to distinguish between its two sides—the *hanging wall* and the *footwall.* **Figure 19** shows the difference between a hanging wall and a footwall. Depending on how the hanging wall and foot-wall move relative to each other, one of two main types of faults can form.

Normal Faults A *normal fault* is shown in **Figure 20.** The movement of a **normal fault** causes the hanging wall to move down relative to the footwall. Normal faults usually occur when tectonic forces cause tension that pulls rocks apart.

Reverse Faults A *reverse fault* is shown in **Figure 21.** The movement of a **reverse fault** causes the hanging wall to move up relative to the footwall—the "reverse" of a normal fault. Reverse faults usually happen when tectonic forces cause compression that pushes rocks together.

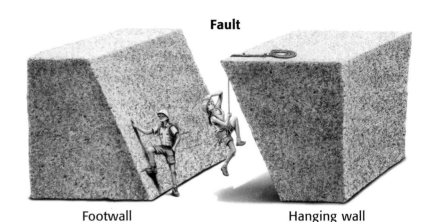

Fault

Footwall   Hanging wall

Figure 19 *The position of a fault block determines whether it is a hanging wall or a footwall.*

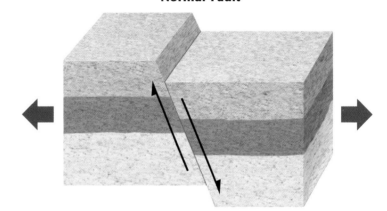

Normal Fault

Figure 20 *When rocks are pulled apart due to tension, normal faults often result.*

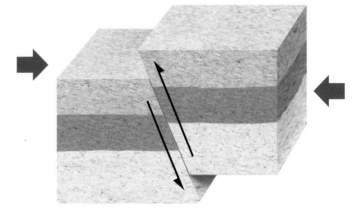

Reverse Fault

Figure 21 *When rocks are pushed together by compression, reverse faults often result.*

✔ Self-Check

How is folding different from faulting? *(See page 726 to check your answer.)*

Plate Tectonics   **183**

Figure 22 *The photo at left is a normal fault. The photo at right is a reverse fault.*

Telling the Difference It's easy to tell the difference between a normal fault and a reverse fault in diagrams with arrows. But what about the faults in **Figure 22?** You can certainly see the faults, but which one is a normal fault, and which one is a reverse fault? In the top left photo, one side has obviously moved relative to the other. You can tell this is a normal fault by looking at the sequence of sedimentary rock layers. You can see by the relative positions of the two dark layers that the hanging wall has moved down relative to the footwall.

Strike-slip Faults A third major type of fault is called a *strike-slip fault.* **Strike-slip faults** occur when opposing forces cause rock to break and move horizontally. If you were standing on one side of a strike-slip fault looking across the fault when it moved, the ground on the other side would appear to move to your left or right.

Tectonics and Natural Gas

Natural gas is used in many homes and factories as a source of energy. Some companies explore for sources of natural gas just as other companies explore for oil and coal. Like oil, natural gas travels upward through rock layers until it hits a layer through which it cannot travel and becomes trapped. Imagine that you are searching for pockets of trapped natural gas. Would you expect to find these pockets associated with anticlines, synclines, or faults? Explain your answer in your ScienceLog. Include drawings to help in your explanation.

Plate Tectonics and Mountain Building

You have just learned about several ways the Earth's crust changes due to the forces of plate tectonics. When tectonic plates collide, land features that start out as small folds and faults can eventually become great mountain ranges. The reason mountains exist is that tectonic plates are continually moving around and bumping into one another. As you can see in **Figure 23,** most major mountain ranges form at the edges of tectonic plates.

When tectonic plates undergo compression or tension, they can form mountains in several different ways. Let's take a look at three of the most common types of mountains—*folded mountains, fault-block mountains,* and *volcanic mountains.*

Folded Mountains *Folded mountains* form when rock layers are squeezed together and pushed upward. If you take a pile of paper on a table top and push on opposite edges of the pile, you will see how a folded mountain forms. You saw how these layers crunched together in Figure 17. **Figure 24** shows an example of a folded mountain range that formed at a convergent boundary.

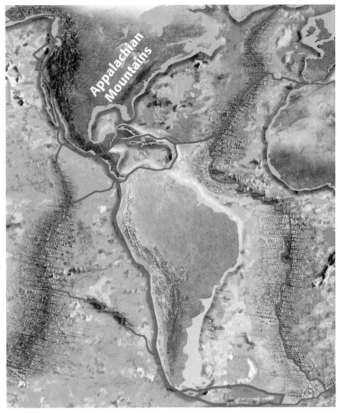

Figure 23 *Most of the world's major mountain ranges form at tectonic plate boundaries. Notice that the Appalachian Mountains, however, are located in the middle of the North American plate.*

Figure 24 *Once as mighty as the Himalayas, the Appalachians have been worn down by hundreds of millions of years of weathering and erosion.*

Did you know that plate tectonics is responsible for creating not only mountains but some of the lowest places on Earth as well? It's true. When one tectonic plate is subducted beneath another, a deep valley called a *trench* forms at the boundary. The Mariana Trench is the deepest point in the oceans— 11,033 m below sea level!

Formation of the Appalachian Mountains

Look back at Figure 23. The Appalachians are in the middle of the North American plate. How can this be? Shouldn't they be at the edge of a tectonic plate? Follow along in this diagram to find the answer.

1 About 500 million years ago, the landmasses that would become North America and Africa were on a collision course.

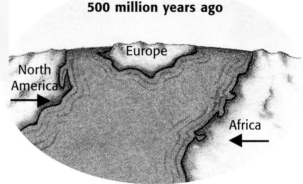

500 million years ago

2 About 390 million years ago, these tectonic plates collided, and the crust between them buckled and folded, forming the Appalachian Mountains.

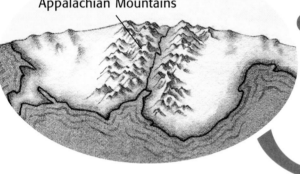

390 million years ago

Appalachian Mountains

3 About 208 million years ago, North America and Africa began to break apart, and a mid-ocean ridge formed between them. By 65 million years ago, a huge amount of new oceanic lithosphere had formed between the two tectonic plates. Because of this, the Appalachian Mountains were no longer at a tectonic plate boundary at all.

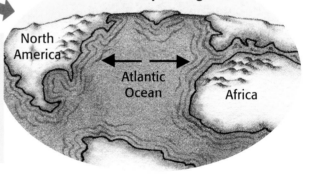

65 million years ago

Figure 25 *When the crust is subjected to tension, the rock can break along a series of normal faults, resulting in fault-block mountains.*

Fault-block Mountains Where tectonic forces put enough tension on the Earth's crust, a large number of normal faults can result. *Fault-block mountains* form when this faulting causes large blocks of the Earth's crust to drop down relative to other blocks. **Figure 25** shows one way this can happen.

Figure 26 *The Tetons formed as a result of tectonic forces that stretched the Earth's crust, causing it to break in a series of normal faults. Compare this photo with the illustration in Figure 25.*

When sedimentary rock layers are tilted up by faulting, they can produce mountains with sharp, jagged peaks. As you can see in **Figure 26,** the Tetons, in western Wyoming, are a spectacular example of this type of mountain.

Volcanic Mountains   Most of the world's major volcanic mountains are located at convergent boundaries. *Volcanic mountains* form when molten rock erupts onto the Earth's surface. Unlike folded and fault-block mountains, volcanic mountains form from new material being added to the Earth's surface. Most volcanic mountains tend to form over the type of convergent boundaries that include subduction zones. There are so many volcanic mountains around the rim of the Pacific Ocean that early explorers named it the *Ring of Fire.*

REVIEW

1. What is the difference between an anticline and a syncline?

2. What is the difference between a normal fault and a reverse fault?

3. Name and describe the type of tectonic stress that forms folded mountains.

4. Name and describe the type of tectonic stress that forms fault-block mountains.

5. **Making Predictions**   If a fault occurs in an area where rock layers have been folded, which type of fault is it likely to be? Why?

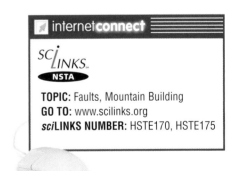

internet**connect**

*SC*LINKS.
NSTA

TOPIC: Faults, Mountain Building
GO TO: www.scilinks.org
*sci*LINKS NUMBER: HSTE170, HSTE175

Chapter Highlights

Vocabulary

crust *(p. 166)*

mantle *(p. 167)*

core *(p. 167)*

lithosphere *(p. 168)*

asthenosphere *(p. 168)*

mesosphere *(p. 169)*

outer core *(p. 169)*

inner core *(p. 169)*

tectonic plate *(p. 170)*

Section Notes

• The Earth is made of three basic compositional layers—the crust, the mantle, and the core.

• The Earth is made of five main structural layers—lithosphere, asthenosphere, mesosphere, outer core, and inner core.

• Tectonic plates are large pieces of the lithosphere that move around on the Earth's surface.

• Knowledge about the structure of the Earth comes from the study of seismic waves caused by earthquakes.

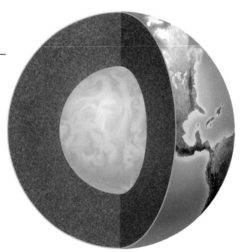

Vocabulary

continental drift *(p. 173)*

sea-floor spreading *(p. 175)*

Section Notes

• Wegener's theory of continental drift explained many puzzling facts, including the fit of the Atlantic coastlines of South America and Africa.

• Today's continents were originally joined together in the ancient continent Pangaea.

• Some of the most important evidence for sea-floor spreading comes from magnetic reversals recorded in the ocean floor.

☑ Skills Check

Math Concepts

MAKING MODELS Suppose you built a model of the Earth that had a radius of 100 cm (diameter of 200 cm). The radius of the real Earth is 6,378 km, and the thickness of its outer core is 2,200 km. What percentage of the Earth's radius is the outer core? How thick would the outer core be in your model?

$$\frac{2{,}200 \text{ km}}{6{,}378 \text{ km}} = 0.34 = 34\%$$

34% of 100 cm = 0.34 × 100 cm = 34 cm

Visual Understanding

SEA-FLOOR SPREADING This close-up view of a mid-ocean ridge shows how new oceanic lithosphere forms. As the two tectonic plates pull away from each other, magma fills in the cracks that open between them. When this magma solidifies, it becomes the newest part of the oceanic plate.

Vocabulary

plate tectonics *(p. 177)*

convergent boundary *(p. 178)*

subduction zone *(p. 178)*

divergent boundary *(p. 179)*

transform boundary *(p. 179)*

Section Notes

- The processes of ridge push, convection, and slab pull provide some possible driving forces for plate tectonics.

- Tectonic plate boundaries are classified as convergent, divergent, or transform.

- Data from satellite tracking indicate that some tectonic plates move an average of 3 cm a year.

Labs

Convection Connection *(p. 656)*

Vocabulary

stress *(p. 181)*

compression *(p. 181)*

tension *(p. 181)*

folding *(p. 182)*

fault *(p. 183)*

normal fault *(p. 183)*

reverse fault *(p. 183)*

strike-slip fault *(p. 184)*

Section Notes

- As tectonic plates move next to and into each other, a great amount of stress is placed on the rocks at the boundary.

- Folding occurs when rock layers bend due to stress.

- Faulting occurs when rock layers break due to stress and then move on either side of the break.

- Mountains are classified as either folded, fault-block, or volcanic, depending on how they form.

- Mountain building is caused by the movement of tectonic plates. Different types of movement cause different types of mountains.

Labs

Oh, the Pressure! *(p. 657)*

internet**connect**

GO TO: go.hrw.com

GO TO: www.scilinks.org

Visit the **HRW** Web site for a variety of learning tools related to this chapter. Just type in the keyword:

KEYWORD: HSTTEC

Visit the **National Science Teachers Association** on-line Web site for Internet resources related to this chapter. Just type in the *sci*LINKS number for more information about the topic:

TOPIC: Composition of the Earth	*sci*LINKS NUMBER: HSTE155
TOPIC: Structure of the Earth	*sci*LINKS NUMBER: HSTE160
TOPIC: Tectonic Plates	*sci*LINKS NUMBER: HSTE165
TOPIC: Faults	*sci*LINKS NUMBER: HSTE170
TOPIC: Mountain Building	*sci*LINKS NUMBER: HSTE175

Chapter Review

For each pair of terms, explain the difference in their meanings.

1. oceanic crust/continental crust

2. lithosphere/asthenosphere

3. convergent boundary/divergent boundary

4. folding/faulting

5. oceanic crust/oceanic lithosphere

6. normal fault/reverse fault

UNDERSTANDING CONCEPTS

Multiple Choice

7. The part of the Earth that is a liquid is the
   a. crust.
   b. mantle.
   c. outer core.
   d. inner core.

8. The part of the Earth on which the tectonic plates are able to move is the
   a. lithosphere.
   b. asthenosphere.
   c. mesosphere.
   d. subduction zone.

9. The ancient continent that contained all the landmasses is called
   a. Pangaea.
   b. Gondwana.
   c. Laurasia.
   d. Panthalassa.

10. The type of tectonic plate boundary involving a collision between two tectonic plates is
    a. divergent.
    b. transform.
    c. convergent.
    d. normal.

11. The type of tectonic plate boundary that sometimes has a subduction zone is
    a. divergent.
    b. transform.
    c. convergent.
    d. normal.

12. The San Andreas fault is an example of a
    a. divergent boundary.
    b. transform boundary.
    c. convergent boundary.
    d. normal boundary.

13. When a fold is shaped like an arch, with the fold in an upward direction, it is called a(n)
    a. monocline.
    b. anticline.
    c. syncline.
    d. decline.

14. The type of fault in which the hanging wall moves down relative to the footwall is called
    a. strike-slip.
    b. reverse.
    c. normal.
    d. fault-block.

15. The type of mountain involving huge sections of the Earth's crust being pushed up into anticlines and synclines is the
    a. folded mountain.
    b. fault-block mountain.
    c. volcanic mountain.
    d. strike-slip mountain.

16. Continental mountain ranges are usually associated with
    a. divergent boundaries.
    b. transform boundaries.
    c. convergent boundaries.
    d. normal boundaries.

17. Mid-ocean ridges are associated with
    a. divergent boundaries.
    b. transform boundaries.
    c. convergent boundaries.
    d. normal boundaries.

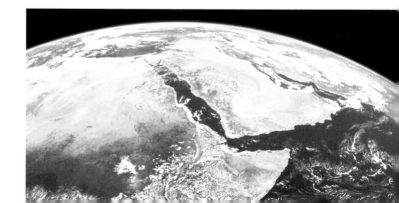

Short Answer

18. What is a tectonic plate?

19. What was the major problem with Wegener's theory of continental drift?

20. Why is there stress on the Earth's crust?

Concept Mapping

21. Use the following terms to create a concept map: sea-floor spreading, convergent boundary, divergent boundary, subduction zone, transform boundary, tectonic plates.

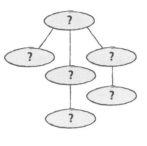

CRITICAL THINKING AND PROBLEM SOLVING

Write one or two sentences to answer each of the following questions:

22. Why is it necessary to think about the different layers of the Earth in terms of both their composition and their physical properties?

23. Folded mountains usually form at the edge of a tectonic plate. How can you explain old folded mountain ranges located in the middle of a tectonic plate?

24. New tectonic plate material continually forms at divergent boundaries. Tectonic plate material is also continually destroyed in subduction zones at convergent boundaries. Do you think the total amount of lithosphere formed on Earth is about equal to the amount destroyed? Why?

MATH IN SCIENCE

25. Assume that a very small oceanic plate is between a mid-ocean ridge to the west and a subduction zone to the east. At the ridge, the oceanic plate is growing at a rate of 5 km every million years. At the subduction zone, the oceanic plate is being destroyed at a rate of 10 km every million years. If the oceanic plate is 100 km across, in how many million years will the oceanic plate disappear?

INTERPRETING GRAPHICS

Imagine that you could travel to the center of the Earth. Use the diagram below to answer the questions that follow.

Composition	Structure
Crust (50 km)	Lithosphere (150 km)
Mantle (2,900 km)	Asthenosphere (250 km)
	Mesosphere (2,550 km)
Core (3,428 km)	Outer core (2,200 km)
	Inner core (1,228 km)

26. How far beneath Earth's surface would you have to go to find the liquid material in the Earth's core?

27. At what range of depth would you find mantle material but still be within the lithosphere?

Reading Check-up

Take a minute to review your answers to the Pre-Reading Questions found at the bottom of page 164. Have your answers changed? If necessary, revise your answers based on what you have learned since you began this chapter.

Science, Technology, and Society

Living on the Mid-Atlantic Ridge

Imagine living hundreds of kilometers from other people on an icy outcrop of volcanic rock surrounded by the cold North Atlantic Ocean. How would you stay warm? For the people of Iceland, this is an important question that affects their daily lives. Iceland is a volcanic island situated on the Mid-Atlantic Ridge, just south of the Arctic Circle. Sea-floor spreading produces active volcanoes, earthquakes, hot springs, and geysers that make life on this island seem a little unstable. However, the same volcanic force that threatens civilization provides the heat necessary for daily life. Icelanders use the geothermal energy supplied by their surroundings in ways that might surprise you.

▲ *The Blue Lagoon in Iceland is the result of producing energy from water power.*

Let's Go Geothermal!

Geothermal literally means "earth heat," *geo-* meaning "earth" and *therme* meaning "heat." Around the ninth century A.D., Iceland's earliest settlers took advantage of the Earth's heat by planting crops in naturally heated ground. This encouraged rapid plant growth and an early harvest of food. In 1928, Iceland built its first public geothermal utility project—a hole drilled into the Earth in order to pump water from a hot spring. After the oil crisis of the 1970s, geothermal-energy projects were built on a grand scale in Iceland. Today 85 percent of all houses in Iceland are heated by geothermal energy. Hot water from underground pools is pumped directly to houses, where it is routed through radiators to provide heating.

Geothermal water is also pumped to homes to provide hot tap water. This natural source meets all the hot-water needs for the city of Reykjavik, with a population of about 150,000 people!

There are still other uses for this hot water. For example, it is used to heat 120 public swimming pools. Picture yourself swimming outside in naturally hot water during the dead of winter! Greenhouses, where fruits and vegetables are grown, are also warmed by this water. Even fish farming on Iceland's exposed coastline wouldn't be possible without geothermal energy to adjust the water temperature. In other industries, geothermal energy is used to dry timber, wool, and seaweed.

Power Production

Although hydropower (producing energy from water power) is the principal source of electricity in Iceland, geothermal energy is also used. Water ranging in temperature from 300–700°C is pumped into a reservoir, where the water turns into steam that forces turbines to turn. The spinning motion of these turbines generates electricity. Power generation from geothermal sources is only about 5–15 percent efficient and results in a very large amount of water runoff. At the Svartsengi power plant, this water runoff has created a beautiful pool that swimmers call the Blue Lagoon.

Going Further

▶ Can you think of other abundant clean-energy resources? How could we harness such sources?

Continental Drift

When Alfred Wegener proposed his theory of continental drift in the early 1900s, many scientists laughed at the idea of continents plowing across the ocean. In fact, many people found his theory so ridiculous that Wegener, a university professor, had difficulty getting a job! Wegener's theory jolted the very foundation of geology.

Wegener's Theory

Wegener used geologic, fossil, and glacial evidence gathered on opposite sides of the Atlantic Ocean to support his theory of continental drift. For example, Wegener recognized geologic similarities between the Appalachian Mountains, in eastern North America, and the Scottish Highlands, as well as similarities between rock strata in South Africa and Brazil. He believed that these striking similarities could be explained only if these geologic features were once part of the same continent.

Wegener proposed that because they are less dense, continents float on top of the denser rock of the ocean floor. Although continental drift explained many of Wegener's observations, he could not find scientific evidence to develop a complete explanation of how continents move.

Alfred Wegener (1880–1930)

The Critics

Most scientists were skeptical of Wegener's theory and dismissed it as foolishness. Some critics held fast to old theories that giant land bridges could explain similarities among fossils in South America and Africa. Others argued that Wegener's theory could not account for the tremendous forces that would have been required to move continents such great distances. Wegener, however, believed that these forces could be the same forces responsible for earthquakes and volcanic eruptions.

The Evidence

During the 1950s and 1960s, discoveries of sea-floor spreading and magnetic reversal provided the evidence that Wegener's theory needed and led to the theory of plate tectonics. The theory of plate tectonics describes how the continents move. Today geologists recognize that continents are actually parts of moving tectonic plates that float on the asthenosphere, a layer of partially molten rock.

Like the accomplishments of so many scientists, Wegener's accomplishments went unrecognized until years after his death. The next time you hear a scientific theory that sounds far out, don't underestimate it. It may be proven true!

Also an Astronomer and Meteorologist

Wegener had a very diverse background in the sciences. He earned a Ph.D. in astronomy from the University of Berlin. But he was always very interested in geophysics and meteorology. His interest in geophysics led to his theory on continental drift. His interest in meteorology eventually led to his death. He froze to death in Greenland while returning from a rescue mission to bring food to meteorologists camped on a glacier.

On Your Own

▶ Photocopy a world map. Carefully cut out the continents from the map. Be sure to cut along the line where the land meets the water. Slide the continents together like a jigsaw puzzle. How does this relate to the tectonic plates and continental drift?

Earthquakes

Pre-Reading
Questions

1. What causes earthquakes?

2. Why are some earth-
   quakes stronger than
   others?

3. Why do some buildings
   remain standing during
   earthquakes while others
   fall down?

IF YOU BUILD IT, WILL IT STAND?

On September 21, 1999, the island of Taiwan was forever
changed. At 1:47 A.M., an earthquake struck, toppling buildings
and burying thousands of people in rubble. Why did this building collapse while those that surrounded it did not? The collapsed building was not built to be as strong as the other
buildings. In this chapter, you will learn about what causes earthquakes and what you can do to prepare for one. You will also
learn how buildings can be constructed to withstand the force
of an earthquake.

*Search and rescue dogs help
save lives after an earthquake.*

BEND, BREAK, OR SHAKE

If you were in a building during an earthquake, what would you want the building to be made of? To answer this question, you need to know how building materials react to stress.

Procedure

1. Gather a **small wooden stick,** a **wire clothes hanger,** and a **plastic clothes hanger.**

2. Draw a straight line on a **sheet of paper.** Use a **protractor** to measure and draw the following angles from the line: 20°, 45°, and 90°.

3. Put on your safety goggles. Using the angles that you drew as a guide, try bending each item 20° and then releasing it. What happens? Does it break? If it bends, does it return to its original shape? Write your observations in your ScienceLog.

4. Repeat step 3, but bend each item 45°. Repeat the test again, but bend each item 90°.

Analysis

5. How do the materials' responses to bending compare?

6. Where earthquakes happen, engineers use building materials that are flexible but do not break or stay bent. Which materials from this experiment would you want building materials to behave like? Explain your answer.

What Are Earthquakes?

Terms to Learn

seismology   seismic waves
fault   P waves
deformation   S waves
elastic rebound

What You'll Do

♦ Determine where earthquakes come from and what causes them.
♦ Identify different types of earthquakes.
♦ Describe how earthquakes travel through the Earth.

The word *earthquake* defines itself fairly well. But there is more to an earthquake than just ground shaking. In fact, there is a branch of Earth science devoted to earthquakes called seismology (siez MAHL uh jee). **Seismology** is the study of earthquakes. Earthquakes are complex, and they present many questions for *seismologists,* the scientists who study earthquakes.

Where Do Earthquakes Occur?

Most earthquakes take place near the edges of tectonic plates. *Tectonic plates* are giant masses of solid rock that make up the outermost part of the Earth. **Figure 1** shows the Earth's tectonic plates and the locations of recent major earthquakes recorded by scientists.

Tectonic plates move in different directions and at different speeds. Two plates can push toward each other or pull away from each other. They can also slip past each other like slow-moving trains traveling in opposite directions.

As a result of these movements, numerous features called faults exist in the Earth's crust. A **fault** is a break in the Earth's crust along which blocks of the crust slide relative to one another. Earthquakes occur along faults due to this sliding.

Faults occur in many places, but they are especially common near the edges of tectonic plates where they form the boundaries along which the plates move. This is why earthquakes are so common near tectonic plate boundaries.

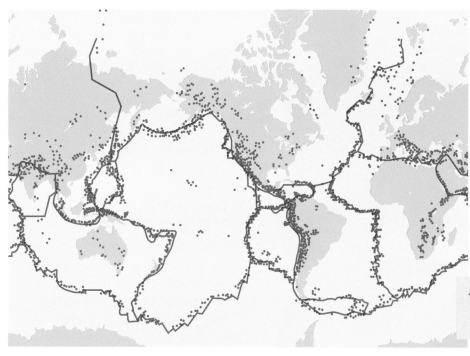

Figure 1 *The largest and most active earthquake zone lies along the plate boundaries surrounding the Pacific Ocean.*

— Plate boundary
• Recorded earthquake

What Causes Earthquakes?

As tectonic plates push, pull, or scrape against each other, stress builds up along faults near the plates' edges. In response to this stress, rock in the plates deforms. **Deformation** is the change in the shape of rock in response to stress. Rock along a fault deforms in mainly two ways—in a plastic manner, like a piece of molded clay, or in an elastic manner, like a rubber band. *Plastic deformation*, which is shown in **Figure 2,** does not lead to earthquakes.

Elastic deformation, however, does lead to earthquakes. While rock can stretch farther than steel without breaking, it will break at some point. Think of elastically deformed rock as a stretched rubber band. You can stretch a rubber band only so far before it breaks. When the rubber band breaks, it releases energy, and the broken pieces return to their unstretched shape.

Figure 2 *This photograph, taken in Hollister, California, shows how plastic deformation along the Calaveras Fault permanently bent a wall.*

Like the return of the broken rubber-band pieces to their unstretched shape, **elastic rebound** is the sudden return of elastically deformed rock to its original shape. Elastic rebound occurs when more stress is applied to rock than the rock can withstand. During elastic rebound, rock releases energy that causes an earthquake, as shown in **Figure 3.**

Figure 3 Elastic Rebound and Earthquakes

❶ The rock along the fault has no stress acting on it.

❸ When enough stress is applied, the rock slips along the fault and releases energy, which travels as seismic waves.

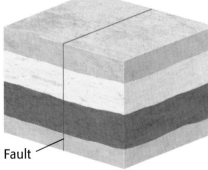

Fault

❷ Tectonic forces push rock on either side of the fault in opposite directions, but the rock is locked together and does not move. The rock deforms in an elastic manner.

Are All Earthquakes the Same?

Earthquakes differ in strength and in the depth at which they begin. These differences depend on the type of tectonic plate motion that produces the earthquake. Examine the chart and the diagram below to learn how earthquakes differ.

Plate motion	Prominent fault type	Earthquake characteristics
Transform	strike-slip fault	moderate, shallow
Convergent	reverse fault	strong, deep
Divergent	normal fault	weak, shallow

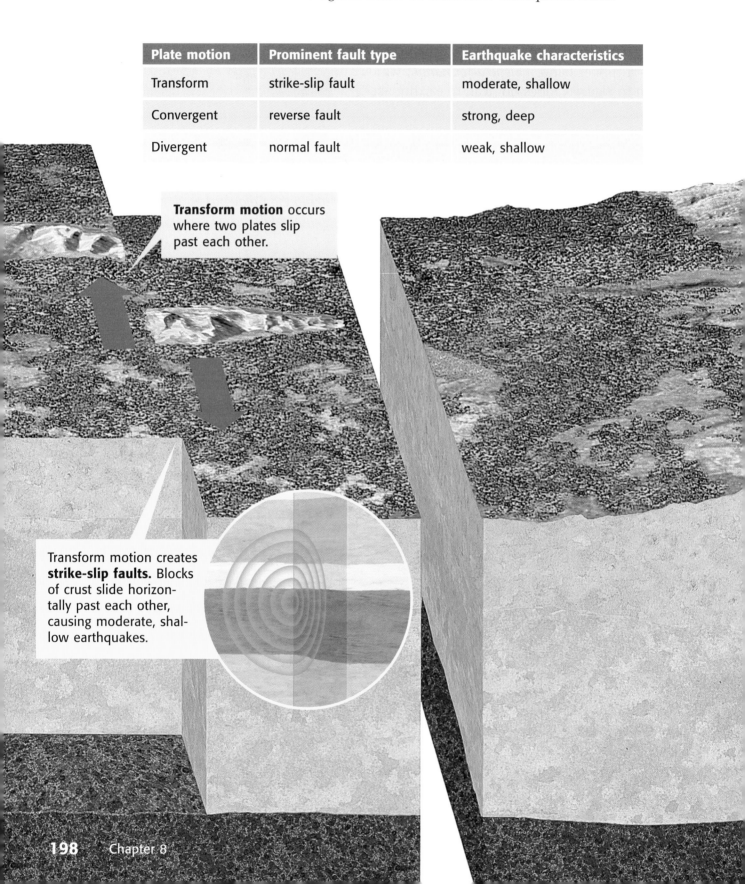

Transform motion occurs where two plates slip past each other.

Transform motion creates **strike-slip faults.** Blocks of crust slide horizontally past each other, causing moderate, shallow earthquakes.

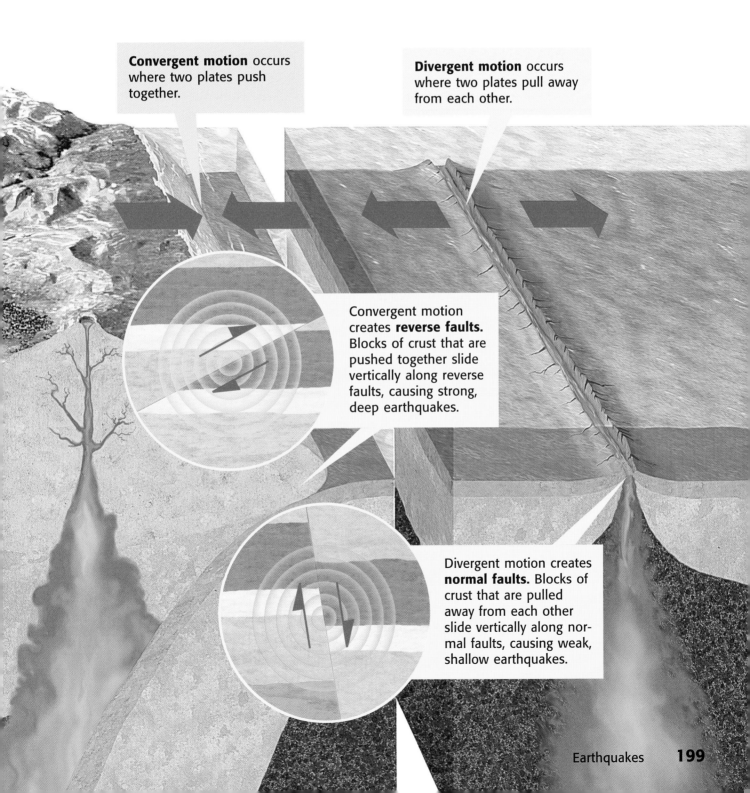

Convergent motion occurs where two plates push together.

Divergent motion occurs where two plates pull away from each other.

Convergent motion creates **reverse faults.** Blocks of crust that are pushed together slide vertically along reverse faults, causing strong, deep earthquakes.

Divergent motion creates **normal faults.** Blocks of crust that are pulled away from each other slide vertically along normal faults, causing weak, shallow earthquakes.

Physics
CONNECTION

All types of waves share basic features. Understanding one type, such as seismic waves, can help you understand many other types. Other types of waves include light waves, sound waves, and water waves.

How Do Earthquakes Travel?

Remember that rock releases energy when it springs back after being deformed. This energy travels in the form of seismic waves. **Seismic waves** are waves of energy that travel through the Earth. Seismic waves that travel through the Earth's interior are called *body waves*. There are two types of body waves: P waves and S waves. Seismic waves that travel along the Earth's surface are called *surface waves*. Different types of seismic waves travel at different speeds and move the materials that they travel through differently.

P Is for Primary If you squeeze an elastic material into a smaller volume or stretch it into a larger volume, the pressure inside the material changes. When you suddenly stop squeezing or stretching the material, it springs briefly back and forth before returning to its original shape. This is how P waves (pressure waves) affect rock, as shown in **Figure 4. P waves,** which travel through solids, liquids, and gases, are the fastest seismic waves. Because they are the fastest seismic waves and because they can move through all parts of the Earth, P waves always travel ahead of other seismic waves. Because P waves are always the first seismic waves to be detected, they are also called *primary* waves.

S Is for Secondary Rock can also be deformed from side to side. When the rock springs back to its original position after being deformed, S waves are created. **S waves,** or shear waves, are the second-fastest seismic wave. S waves shear rock back and forth, as shown in **Figure 5.** *Shearing* stretches parts of rock sideways from other parts.

Direction of wave travel

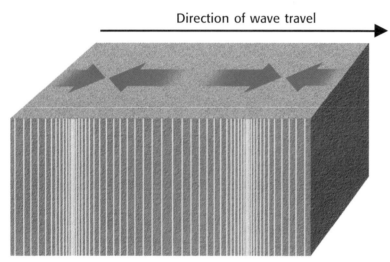

Figure 4 *P waves move rock back and forth between a squeezed position and a stretched position as they travel through it.*

Direction of wave travel

Figure 5 *S waves shear rock back and forth as they travel through it.*

Unlike P waves, S waves cannot travel through parts of the Earth that are completely liquid. Also, S waves are slower than P waves and always arrive second; thus, they are also called *secondary* waves.

Surface Waves Surface waves move the ground up and down in circles as the waves travel along the surface. This is shown in **Figure 6.** Many people have reported feeling like they were on a roller coaster during an earthquake. This feeling comes from surface waves passing along the Earth's surface. Surface waves travel more slowly than body waves but are more destructive. Most damage during an earthquake comes from surface waves, which can literally shake the ground out from under a building.

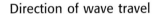
Direction of wave travel

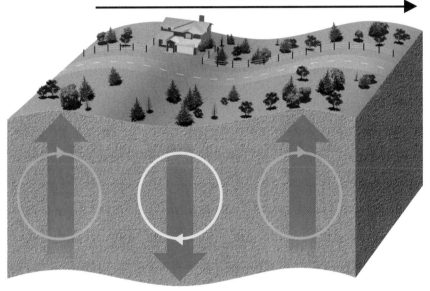

Figure 6 *Surface waves move the ground much like ocean waves move water particles.*

QuickLab

Modeling Seismic Waves

1. Stretch a **spring toy** lengthwise on a **table.**

2. Hold one end of the spring while a partner holds the other end. Push your end toward your partner's end, and observe what happens.

3. Repeat step 2, but this time shake the spring from side to side.

4. Which type of seismic wave is represented in step 2? in step 3?

TRY at HOME

REVIEW

1. Where do earthquakes occur?

2. What directly causes earthquakes?

3. Arrange the types of earthquakes caused by the three plate-motion types from weakest to strongest.

4. **Analyzing Relationships** Why are surface waves more destructive to buildings than P waves or S waves?

internetconnect

SCiLINKS
NSTA

TOPIC: What Is an Earthquake?
GO TO: www.scilinks.org
sciLINKS NUMBER: HSTE180

Earthquake Measurement

After an earthquake occurs, seismologists try to find out when and where it started. Earthquake-sensing devices enable seismologists to record and measure seismic waves. These measurements show how far the seismic waves traveled. The measurements also show how much the ground moved. Seismologists use this information to pinpoint where the earthquake started and to find out how strong the earthquake was.

Locating Earthquakes

How do seismologists know when and where earthquakes begin? They depend on earthquake-sensing instruments called seismographs. **Seismographs** are instruments located at or near the surface of the Earth that record seismic waves. When the waves reach a seismograph, the seismograph creates a seismogram, such as the one in **Figure 7**. A **seismogram** is a tracing of earthquake motion created by a seismograph.

When Did It Happen? Seismologists use seismograms to calculate when an earthquake started. An earthquake starts when rock slips suddenly enough along a fault to create seismic waves. Seismologists find an earthquake's start time by comparing seismograms and noting the difference in arrival times of P waves and S waves.

Where Did It Happen? Seismologists also use seismograms to find an earthquake's epicenter. An **epicenter** is the point on the Earth's surface directly above an earthquake's starting point. A **focus** is the point inside the Earth where an earthquake begins. **Figure 8** shows the relationship between an earthquake's epicenter and its focus.

Figure 7 *The line in a seismogram traces the movement of the ground as it shakes. The more the ground moves, the farther back and forth the line traces.*

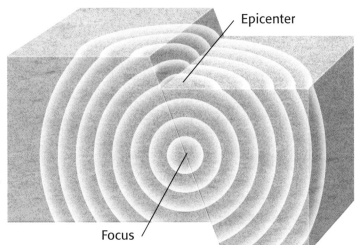

Epicenter

Focus

Figure 8 *An earthquake's epicenter is on the Earth's surface directly above the earthquake's focus.*

Putting It All Together Perhaps the most common method by which seismologists find an earthquake's epicenter is the *S-P-time method*. When using the S-P-time method, seismologists begin by collecting several seismograms of the same earthquake from different locations. Seismologists then place the seismograms on a time-distance graph so the first P waves line up with the P-wave curve and the first S waves line up with the S-wave curve. This is shown in **Figure 9.**

After the seismograms are placed on the graph, seismologists can see how far away from each station the earthquake was by reading the distance axis. After seismologists find out the distances, they can find the earthquake's epicenter as shown below.

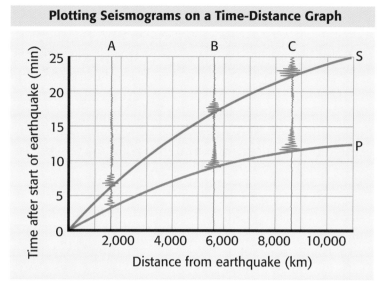

Plotting Seismograms on a Time-Distance Graph

Figure 9 *Seismologists subtract a wave's travel time (read from the vertical axis) from the time that the wave was recorded. This indicates when the earthquake started. The distance of the stations from the epicenter is read from the horizontal axis.*

Finding an Earthquake's Epicenter

❶ A circle is drawn around a seismograph station. The radius of the circle equals the distance from the seismograph to the epicenter. (This distance is taken from the time-distance graph.)

❷ When a second circle is drawn around another seismograph station, it overlaps the first circle in two spots. One of these spots is the earthquake's epicenter.

❸ When a third circle is drawn around a third seismograph station, all three circles intersect in only one spot. This spot is the earthquake's epicenter.

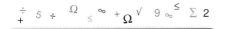

Moving Up the Scale

If the amount of energy released by an earthquake with a magnitude of 2.0 on the Richter scale is *n*, what are the amounts of energy released by earthquakes with the following magnitudes in terms of *n*: 3.0, 4.0, 5.0, and 6.0? (Hint: The energy released by an earthquake with a magnitude of 3.0 is 31.7*n*.)

Measuring Earthquake Strength

"How strong was the earthquake?" is a common question asked of seismologists. This is not an easy question to answer. But it is an important question for public officials, safety organizations, and businesses as well as seismologists. Fortunately, seismograms can be used not only to determine an earthquake's epicenter and its start time but also to find out an earthquake's strength.

The Richter Scale The *Richter scale* is commonly used to measure earthquake strength. It is named after Charles Richter, an American seismologist who developed the scale in the 1930s. A modified version of the Richter scale is shown below.

Modified Richter Scale	
Magnitude	**Estimated effects**
2.0	can be detected only by seismograph
3.0	can be felt at epicenter
4.0	felt by most in area
5.0	causes damage at epicenter
6.0	causes widespread damage
7.0	causes great, widespread damage

Earthquake Energy There is a pattern in the Richter scale relating an earthquake's magnitude and the amount of energy released by the earthquake. Each time the magnitude increases by 1 unit, the amount of energy released becomes 31.7 times larger. For example, an earthquake with a magnitude of 5.0 on the Richter scale will release 31.7 times as much energy as an earthquake with a magnitude of 4.0 on the Richter scale.

internet connect

SC*i*LINKS
NSTA

TOPIC: Earthquake Measurement
GO TO: www.scilinks.org
*sci*LINKS NUMBER: HSTE185

REVIEW

1. What is the difference between a seismogram and a seismograph?

2. How many seismograph stations are needed to use the S-P-time method? Why?

3. **Doing Calculations** If the amount of energy released by an earthquake with a magnitude of 7.0 on the Richter scale is *x*, what is the amount of energy released by an earthquake with a magnitude of 6.0 in terms of *x*?

Earthquakes and Society

Earthquakes are a fascinating part of Earth science, but they are very dangerous. Seismologists have had some success in predicting earthquakes, but simply being aware of earthquakes is not enough. It is important for people in earthquake-prone areas to be prepared.

Earthquake Hazard

Earthquake hazard measures how prone an area is to experiencing earthquakes in the future. An area's earthquake-hazard level is determined by past and present seismic activity. Look carefully at the map in **Figure 10.** As you can see, some areas of the United States have a higher earthquake-hazard level than others. This is because some areas have more seismic activity than others. The West Coast, for example, has a very high earthquake-hazard level because it has a lot of seismic activity. Areas such as the Gulf Coast or the Midwest have much lower earthquake-hazard levels because they do not have as much seismic activity.

Can you find the area where you live on the map? What level or levels of earthquake hazard are shown for your area? Look at the hazard levels in nearby areas. How do their hazard levels compare with your area's hazard level? What could explain the earthquake-hazard levels in your area and nearby areas?

Figure 10 *This is an earthquake-hazard map of the continental United States. It shows various levels of earthquake hazard for different areas of the country.*

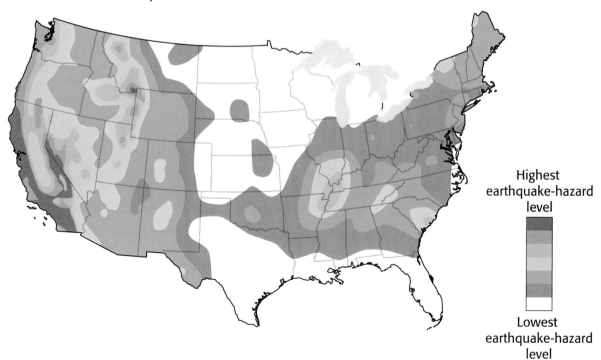

Highest
earthquake-hazard
level

Lowest
earthquake-hazard
level

Self-Check

According to the chart below, about how many earthquakes with a magnitude between 6.0 and 6.9 occur annually?

(See page 726 to check your answer.)

Earthquake Forecasting

Predicting when and where earthquakes will occur and how strong they will be is a difficult task. However, by closely monitoring active faults and other areas of seismic activity, seismologists have discovered some patterns in earthquakes that allow them to make some broad predictions.

Strength and Frequency As you learned earlier, earthquakes vary in strength. And you can probably guess that earthquakes don't occur on a set schedule. But what you may not know is that the strength of earthquakes is related to how often they occur. The chart in **Figure 11** provides more detail on this relationship.

Figure 11 *Generally, with each step down in earthquake magnitude, the number of earthquakes per year is about 10 times greater.*

Worldwide Earthquake Frequency (Based on Observations Since 1900)		
Descriptor	**Magnitude**	**Average occurring annually**
Great	8.0 and higher	1
Major	7.0–7.9	18
Strong	6.0–6.9	120
Moderate	5.0–5.9	800
Light	4.0–4.9	about 6,200
Minor	3.0–3.9	about 49,000
Very minor	2.0–2.9	about 365,000

This relationship between earthquake strength and frequency is also observed on a local scale. For example, each year approximately 10 earthquakes occur in the Puget Sound area of Washington with a magnitude of 4 on the Richter scale. Over this same time period, approximately 10 times as many earthquakes with a magnitude of 3 occur in this area. Scientists use these statistics to make predictions about the strength, location, and frequency of future earthquakes.

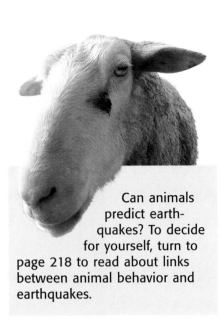

Can animals predict earthquakes? To decide for yourself, turn to page 218 to read about links between animal behavior and earthquakes.

The Gap Hypothesis Another method of predicting an earthquake's strength, location, and frequency is based on the gap hypothesis. The **gap hypothesis** states that sections of active faults that have had relatively few earthquakes are likely to be the sites of strong earthquakes in the future. The areas along a fault where relatively few earthquakes have occurred are called **seismic gaps. Figure 12** below shows an example of a seismic gap.

Figure 12 This diagram shows a cross section of the San Andreas Fault. Note how the seismic gap was filled by the 1989 earthquake and its aftershocks, which are weaker earthquakes that follow a stronger earthquake.

- Earthquakes prior to 1989 earthquake
- 1989 earthquake and aftershocks

San Francisco

San Jose

Santa Cruz

Seismic gap

Filled seismic gap

Before 1989 Earthquake

After 1989 Earthquake

The gap hypothesis helped seismologists forecast the approximate time, strength, and location of the 1989 Loma Prieta earthquake in the San Francisco Bay area. The seismic gap that they identified is illustrated in Figure 12. In 1988, seismologists predicted that over the next 30 years there was a 30 percent chance that an earthquake with a magnitude of at least 6.5 would fill this seismic gap. Were they correct? The Loma Prieta earthquake, which filled in the seismic gap in 1989, measured 7.1 on the Richter scale. That's very close, considering how complicated the forecasting of earthquakes is.

Figure 13 An earthquake shook the ground floor out from under the second story of this apartment building, which then collapsed.

Earthquakes and Buildings

Much like a judo master knocks the feet out from under his or her opponent, earthquakes shake the ground out from under buildings and bridges. Once the center of gravity of a structure has been displaced far enough off the structure's supporting base, most structures simply collapse.

Figure 13 shows what can happen to buildings during an earthquake. These buildings were not designed or constructed to withstand the forces of an earthquake.

Research a tall building to find out how its structure is reinforced. Would any of the building's reinforcements safeguard it against earthquakes? Has an earthquake occurred in the building's area since the building was constructed? If so, how well did the building withstand the shaking?

TRY at HOME

Earthquake Resistant Buildings People have learned a lot from building failure during earthquakes. Architects and engineers use the newest technology to design and construct buildings and bridges to better withstand earthquakes. Study this diagram carefully to learn about some of this modern technology.

The **mass damper** is a weight placed in the roof of a building. Motion sensors detect building movement during an earthquake and send messages to a computer. The computer then signals controls in the roof to shift the mass damper to counteract the building's movement.

Steel **cross-braces** are placed between floors. These braces counteract pressure that pushes and pulls at the side of a building during an earthquake.

The **active tendon system** works much like the mass damper system in the roof. Sensors notify a computer that the building is moving. Then the computer activates devices to shift a large weight to counteract the movement.

Flexible pipes help prevent water and gas lines from breaking. Engineers design the pipes with flexible joints so the pipes are better able to twist and bend without breaking during an earthquake.

Base isolators act as shock absorbers during an earthquake. They are made of layers of rubber and steel wrapped around a lead core. Base isolators absorb seismic waves, preventing them from traveling through the building.

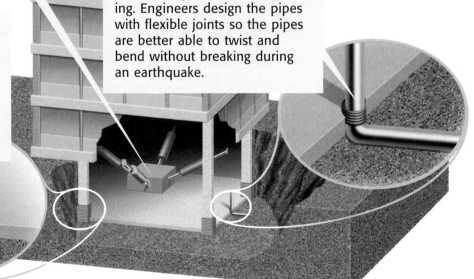

Are You Prepared for an Earthquake?

If you live in an earthquake-prone area or ever plan to visit one, there are many things you can do to protect yourself and your property from earthquakes. Plan ahead so you will know what to do before, during, and after an earthquake. Stick to your plan as closely as possible.

Before the Shaking Starts The first thing you should do is safeguard your house against earthquakes. For example, put heavier objects on lower shelves so they do not fall on anyone during the earthquake. You can also talk to adults about having your home reinforced. Make a plan with others (your family, neighbors, or friends) to meet somewhere after the earthquake is over. This way someone will know you are safe. During the earthquake, waterlines, power lines, and roadways may be damaged. Therefore, you should store nonperishable food, water, a fire extinguisher, a flashlight with batteries, and a first-aid kit in a place you can access after the earthquake.

When the Shaking Starts The best thing to do if you are indoors is to crouch or lie face down under a table or desk in the center of a room, as shown in **Figure 15.** If you are outside, lie face down away from buildings, power lines, and trees, and cover your head with your hands. If you are in a car on an open road, you should stop the car and remain inside.

Figure 14 *Simple precautions can greatly reduce the chance of injury during an earthquake.*

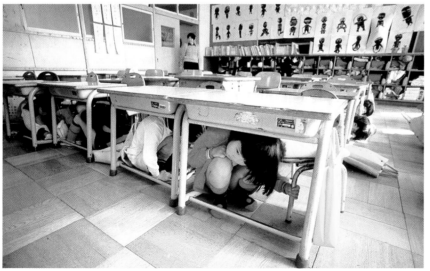

Figure 15 *These students are participating in an earthquake drill.*

Turn to page 660 to build your own earthquake-safe building.

After the Shaking Stops Being in an earthquake is a startling experience. Afterward, you should not be surprised to find yourself and others puzzled about what happened. You should try to calm down, get your bearings, and remove yourself from immediate danger, such as downed power lines, broken glass, and fire hazards. Be aware that there may be aftershocks. Recall your earthquake plan, and follow it through.

REVIEW

1. How is an area's earthquake hazard determined?

2. Which earthquake forecast predicts a more precise location—a forecast based on the relationship between strength and frequency or a forecast based on the gap hypothesis?

3. Describe two ways that buildings are reinforced against earthquakes.

4. Name four items that you should store in case of an earthquake.

5. **Using Graphics** Would the street shown in the photo at left be a safe place during an earthquake? Why or why not?

Earthquake Safety Plan

You are at home reading the evening news. On the front page you read a report from the local seismology station. Scientists predict an earthquake in your area sometime in the near future. You realize that you are not prepared.

Make a detailed outline of how you would prepare yourself and your home for an earthquake. Then write a list of safety procedures to follow during an earthquake. When you are done, exchange your work with a classmate. How do your plans differ from your classmate's? How might you work together to improve your earthquake safety plans?

Earthquake Discoveries Near and Far

Terms to Learn

Moho
shadow zone

What You'll Do

- ◆ Describe how seismic studies reveal Earth's interior.
- ◆ Summarize seismic discoveries on other cosmic bodies.

The study of earthquakes has led to many important discoveries about the Earth's interior. Seismologists learn about the Earth's interior by observing how seismic waves travel through the Earth. Likewise, seismic waves on other cosmic bodies allow seismologists to study the interiors of those bodies.

Discoveries in Earth's Interior

Have you ever noticed how light bends in water? If you poke part of a pencil into water and look at it from a certain angle, the pencil looks bent. This is because the light waves that bounce off the pencil bend as they pass through the water's surface toward your eye. Seismic waves bend in much the same way as they travel through rock. Seismologists have learned a lot about the Earth's interior by studying how seismic waves bend.

P wave

S wave

The **Moho** is a place within the Earth where the speed of seismic waves increases sharply. It marks the boundary between the Earth's crust and mantle.

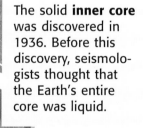

The solid **inner core** was discovered in 1936. Before this discovery, seismologists thought that the Earth's entire core was liquid.

The **shadow zone** is an area on the Earth's surface where no direct seismic waves from a particular earthquake can be detected. This discovery suggested that the Earth has a liquid core.

Quakes and Shakes on Other Cosmic Bodies

Seismologists have taken what they have learned from earthquakes and applied it to studies of other cosmic bodies, such as planets, moons, and stars. They have been able to learn about the interiors of these cosmic bodies by studying how seismic waves behave within them. The first and perhaps most successful seismic test on another cosmic body was on Earth's moon.

The Moon In July 1969, humans set foot on the moon for the first time. They brought with them a seismograph. Not knowing if the moon was seismically active, they left nothing to chance—they purposely crashed their landing vehicle back into the moon's surface after they left to create artificial seismic waves. What happened after that left seismologists astonished.

If the lander had crashed into the Earth, the equivalent seismograms would have lasted 20–30 seconds at most. The surface of the moon, however, vibrated for more than an hour and a half! At first scientists thought the equipment was not working properly. But the seismograph recorded similar signals produced by meteoroid impacts and "moonquakes" long after the astronauts had left the moon. **Figure 16** shows the nature of these seismic events, which were observed remotely from Earth.

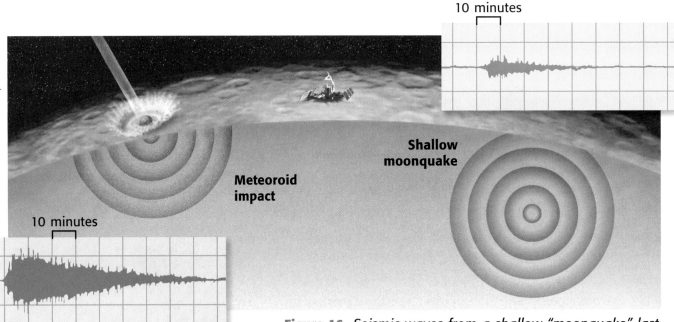

Figure 16 *Seismic waves from a shallow "moonquake" last 50 minutes. Seismic waves from a meteoroid impact last an hour and a half. Similar disturbances on Earth last less than a minute.*

Mars In 1976, a space probe called *Viking 1* allowed seismologists to learn about seismic activity on Mars. The probe, which was controlled remotely from Earth, landed on Mars and conducted several experiments. A seismograph was placed on top of the spacecraft to measure seismic waves on Mars. However, as soon as the craft landed, *Viking 1*'s seismograph began to shake. Scientists immediately discovered that Mars is a very windy planet and that the seismograph was working mainly as a wind gauge!

Although the wind on Mars interfered with the seismograph, the seismograph recorded seismograms for months. During that time, only one possible "marsquake" shook the seismograph harder than the wind did.

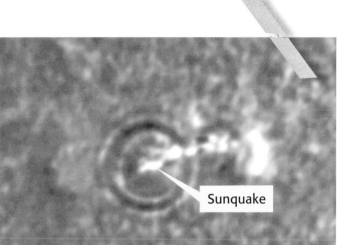

The Sun Seismologists have also studied seismic waves on the sun. Because humans cannot directly access the sun, scientists study it remotely by using a satellite called *SOHO*. Information gathered by *SOHO* has shown that solar flares produce seismic waves. *Solar flares* are powerful magnetic disturbances in the sun. The seismic waves that result cause "sunquakes," which are similar to earthquakes but are generally much stronger. For example, a moderate sunquake, shown in **Figure 17** beneath an image of *SOHO*, released more than 1 million times as much energy as the Great Hanshin earthquake mentioned at the beginning of this chapter!

Figure 17 SOHO *detects "sunquakes" that dwarf the greatest earthquakes in history.*

REVIEW

1. What observation of seismic-wave travel led to the discovery of the Moho?

2. Briefly describe one discovery seismologists have made about each of the following cosmic bodies: the moon, Mars, and the sun.

3. **Interpreting Graphics** Take another look at the figure on the first page of Section 4. Why don't S waves enter the Earth's outer core?

internet connect

SCiLINKS
NSTA

TOPIC: Earthquake Discoveries Near and Far
GO TO: www.scilinks.org
*sci*LINKS **NUMBER:** HSTE195

Chapter Highlights

SECTION 1

Vocabulary

seismology (p. 196)

fault (p. 196)

deformation (p. 197)

elastic rebound (p. 197)

seismic waves (p. 200)

P waves (p. 200)

S waves (p. 200)

Section Notes

- Earthquakes mainly occur along faults near the edges of tectonic plates.

- Elastic rebound is the direct cause of earthquakes.

- Earthquakes differ depending on what type of plate motion causes them.

- Seismic waves are classified as body waves or surface waves.

- Body waves travel through the Earth's interior, while surface waves travel along the surface.

- There are two types of body waves: P waves and S waves.

SECTION 2

Vocabulary

seismograph (p. 202)

seismogram (p. 202)

epicenter (p. 202)

focus (p. 202)

Section Notes

- Seismographs detect seismic waves and record them as seismograms.

- An earthquake's focus is the underground location where seismic waves begin. The earthquake's epicenter is on the surface directly above the focus.

- Seismologists use the S-P-time method to find an earthquake's epicenter.

- Seismologists use the Richter scale to measure an earthquake's strength.

Labs

Earthquake Waves (p. 662)

☑ Skills Check

Math Concepts

EARTHQUAKE STRENGTH The energy released by an earthquake increases by a factor of 31.7 with each increase in magnitude. The energy released decreases by a factor of 31.7 with each decrease in magnitude. All you have to do is multiply or divide.

If magnitude 4 releases energy y, then:

- magnitude 5 releases energy $31.7y$

- magnitude 3 releases energy $\dfrac{y}{31.7}$

Visual Understanding

TIME-DISTANCE GRAPH Note on the time-distance graph in Figure 9 that the difference in arrival times between P waves and S waves increases with distance from the epicenter.

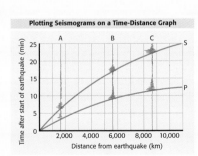

Plotting Seismograms on a Time-Distance Graph

SECTION 3

Vocabulary

gap hypothesis *(p. 207)*

seismic gap *(p. 207)*

Section Notes

- Earthquake hazard measures how prone an area is to experiencing earthquakes in the future.

- Some earthquake predictions are based on the relationship between earthquake strength and earthquake frequency. As earthquake frequency decreases, earthquake strength increases.

- Predictions based on the gap hypothesis target seismically inactive areas along faults for strong earthquakes in the future.

- An earthquake usually collapses a structure by displacing the structure's center of gravity off the structure's supporting base.

- Buildings and bridges can be reinforced to minimize earthquake damage.

- People in earthquake-prone areas should plan ahead for earthquakes.

Labs

Quake Challenge *(p. 660)*

SECTION 4

Vocabulary

Moho *(p. 211)*

shadow zone *(p. 211)*

Section Notes

- The Moho, shadow zone, and inner core are features discovered on and inside Earth by observing seismic waves.

- Seismology has been used to study other cosmic bodies.

- Seismic waves last much longer on the moon than they do on Earth.

- Based on early seismic studies, Mars appears much less active seismically than the Earth.

- "Sunquakes" produce energy far greater than any earthquakes we know of.

---

internetconnect

GO TO: go.hrw.com

Visit the **HRW** Web site for a variety of learning tools related to this chapter. Just type in the keyword:

KEYWORD: HSTEQK

GO TO: www.scilinks.org

Visit the **National Science Teachers Association** on-line Web site for Internet resources related to this chapter. Just type in the *sci*LINKS number for more information about the topic:

TOPIC: What Is an Earthquake?   *sci*LINKS NUMBER: HSTE180

TOPIC: Earthquake Measurement   *sci*LINKS NUMBER: HSTE185

TOPIC: Earthquakes and Society   *sci*LINKS NUMBER: HSTE190

TOPIC: Earthquake Discoveries Near and Far   *sci*LINKS NUMBER: HSTE195

Chapter Review

USING VOCABULARY

To complete the following sentences, choose the correct term from each pair of terms listed below:

1. Energy is released as __?__ occurs. *(deformation* or *elastic rebound)*

2. __?__ cannot travel through parts of the Earth that are completely liquid. *(S waves* or *P waves)*

3. Seismic waves are recorded by a __?__. *(seismograph* or *seismogram)*

4. Seismologists use the S-P-time method to find an earthquake's __?__. *(shadow zone* or *epicenter)*

5. The __?__ is a place that marks a sharp increase in seismic wave speed. *(seismic gap* or *Moho)*

UNDERSTANDING CONCEPTS

Multiple Choice

6. When rock is __?__, energy builds up in it. Seismic waves occur as this energy is __?__.
   a. elastically deformed; released
   b. plastically deformed; released
   c. elastically deformed; increased
   d. plastically deformed; increased

7. The strongest earthquakes usually occur
   a. near divergent boundaries.
   b. near convergent boundaries.
   c. near transform boundaries.
   d. along normal faults.

8. The last seismic waves to arrive are
   a. P waves.
   b. S waves.
   c. surface waves.
   d. body waves.

9. If an earthquake begins while you are in a building, the safest thing to do first is
   a. get under the strongest table, chair, or other piece of furniture.
   b. run out into the street.
   c. crouch near a wall.
   d. call home.

10. Studying earthquake waves currently allows seismologists to do all of the following *except*
    a. determine when an earthquake started.
    b. learn about the Earth's interior.
    c. decrease an earthquake's strength.
    d. determine where an earthquake started.

11. If a planet has a liquid core, then S waves
    a. speed up as they travel through the core.
    b. maintain their speed as they travel through the core.
    c. change direction as they travel through the core.
    d. cannot pass through the core.

Short Answer

12. What is the relationship between the strength of earthquakes and earthquake frequency?

13. You learned earlier that if you are in a car during an earthquake and are out in the open, it is best to stay in the car. Briefly describe a situation in which you might want to leave a car during an earthquake.

14. How did seismologists determine that the outer core of the Earth is liquid?

Concept Mapping

15. Use the following terms to create a concept map: focus, epicenter, earthquake start time, seismic waves, P waves, S waves.

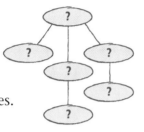

CRITICAL THINKING AND PROBLEM SOLVING

Write one or two sentences to answer the following questions:

16. How might the wall in Figure 2 appear if it had deformed elastically instead of plastically?

17. Why do strong earthquakes occur where there have not been many recent earthquakes? (Hint: Think about what gradually happens to rock before an earthquake occurs.)

18. What could be done to solve the wind problem with the seismograph on Mars? Explain how you would set up the seismograph.

MATH IN SCIENCE

19. Based on the relationship between earthquake magnitude and frequency, if 150 earthquakes with a magnitude of 2 occur in your area this year, about how many earthquakes with a magnitude of 4 should occur in your area this year?

INTERPRETING GRAPHICS

The graph below illustrates the relationship between earthquake magnitude and the height of the tracings on a seismogram. Charles Richter initially formed his magnitude scale by comparing the heights of seismogram readings for different earthquakes. Study the graph, and then answer the questions that follow.

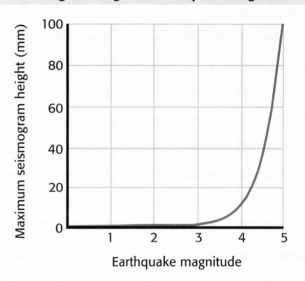

Seismogram Height Vs. Earthquake Magnitude

20. According to the graph, what would the magnitude of an earthquake be if its maximum seismograph height is 10 mm?

21. Look at the shape of the curve on the graph. What does this tell you about the relationship between seismogram heights and earthquake magnitudes? Explain.

Reading Check-up

Take a minute to review your answers to the Pre-Reading Questions found at the bottom of page 194. Have your answers changed? If necessary, revise your answers based on what you have learned since you began this chapter.

WEiRD SCIENCE

CAN ANIMALS PREDICT EARTHQUAKES?

It Could Happen to You!

One day you come home from visiting a friend for the weekend and learn that your dog Pepper is hiding under your bed. Your father explains that he has been trying to get Pepper out from under the bed for the last 6 hours. Just then your mother enters the room and says that she has found two snakes in the backyard—and that makes a total of five in 2 days! This is very odd because you usually don't find more than one each year.

All the animals seem to be acting very strange. Your goldfish is even hiding behind a rock. You wonder if there is some explanation.

What's Going On?

So what's your guess? What do you think is happening? Did you guess that an earthquake is about to occur? Well, if you did, you are probably right!

Publications from as far back as 1784 record unusual animal behavior prior to earthquakes. Some examples included zoo animals refusing to go into their shelters at night and domestic cattle seeking high ground. Other animals, like lizards, snakes, and small mammals, evacuate their underground burrows, and wild birds leave their usual habitats. All of these events occurred a few days, several hours, or a few minutes before the earthquakes happened.

Animals on Call?

Today the majority of scientists look to physical instruments in order to help them predict earthquakes. Yet the fact remains that none of the geophysical instruments we have allow scientists to predict exactly when an earthquake will occur. Could animals know the answer?

▼ *Goldfish or earthquake sensor?*

There are changes in the Earth's crust that occur prior to an earthquake, such as magnetic field changes, subsidence (sinking), tilting, and bulging of the surface. These things can be monitored by modern instruments. Many studies have shown that electromagnetic fields affect the behavior of living organisms. Is it possible that animals close to the epicenter of an earthquake are able to sense changes in their environment? Should we pay attention?

You Decide

▶ Currently, the United States government does not fund research that investigates whether animals can predict earthquakes. Have a debate with your classmates about whether the government should fund such research.

EYE ON THE ENVIRONMENT

What Causes Such Destruction?

At 5:04 P.M. on October 14, 1989, life in California's San Francisco Bay Area seemed as normal as ever. The third game of the World Series was underway in Candlestick Park, now called 3Com Park. While 62,000 fans filled the park, other people were rushing home from a day's work. By 5:05 P.M., however, things had changed drastically. The fact sheet of destruction looks like this:

Injuries:	3,757
Deaths:	68
Damaged homes:	23,408
Destroyed homes:	1,018
Damaged businesses:	3,530
Destroyed businesses:	366
Financial loss:	over $6 billion

The Culprit

The cause of such destruction was a 7.1 magnitude earthquake that lasted for 20 seconds. Its epicenter was 97 km south of San Francisco in an area called Loma Prieta. The earthquake was so strong that people in San Diego and western Nevada (740 km away) felt it too. Considering the earthquake's high magnitude and the fact that it occurred during rush hour, it is amazing that more people did not die. However, the damage to buildings was widespread—it covered an area of 7,770 km². And by October 1, 1990, there had been more than 7,000 aftershocks of this quake.

Take Heed

Engineers and seismologists had expected a major earthquake, so the amount of damage they saw from this earthquake was no surprise. But experts agree that if the earthquake were of a higher magnitude or centered closer to Oakland, San Jose, or San Francisco, the damage would have been much worse. They are concerned that people who live in these areas aren't paying attention to the warning this earthquake represents.

Many people have a false sense of security because their buildings withstood the quake with little or no damage. But engineers and seismologists agree that the only reason the buildings survived was because the ground motion in those areas was fairly low.

Tomorrow May Be Too Late

Many buildings that withstood this earthquake were poorly constructed and would not withstand another earthquake. Experts say there is a 50 percent chance that one or more 7.0 magnitude earthquakes will occur in the San Francisco Bay Area in the next 30 years. And the results of the next quake could be much more devastating if people don't reinforce their buildings before it's too late.

▲ *Notice the different levels of destruction for various buildings on the same street.*

On Your Own

▶ Research the engineering innovations for constructing bridges and buildings in areas with seismic activity. Share your information with the class.

CHAPTER 9

Volcanoes

Sections

Hot Lava, Quiet Eruption

Volcanic eruptions come in all sizes. In places like Hawaii, most eruptions are nonviolent. Lava flows in Hawaii are made of rock called basalt, which flows easily. Basaltic lava flows travel slowly but can reach a temperature of nearly 1,200°C! The lava flow shown here is slowly creeping across a road. As you can see, calm eruptions of lava can threaten property more than human life. In this chapter you will learn about nonexplosive eruptions, explosive eruptions, the formation of magma, and the ways that scientists are trying to predict volcanic eruptions.

This type of eruption is called a lava fountain.

Pre-Reading Questions

1. What causes a volcanic eruption?
2. What is lava, and how does it form?

ANTICIPATION

As you will see in this activity, volcanic eruptions are very difficult to predict.

Procedure

1. Place **10 mL of baking soda** in the center of a sheet of **bathroom tissue.** Fold the corners over the baking soda and crease the edges so that they stay in place. Place the tissue packet in the middle of a **large pan.**

2. Put **modeling clay** around the top edge of a **funnel.** Turn the funnel upside down over the tissue packet. Press down to make a tight seal.

3. Put your safety goggles on and add **50 mL of vinegar** and **several drops of liquid dish soap** to a 200 mL **beaker,** and stir.

4. Predict how much time will elapse before your volcano erupts.

5. Pour the liquid into the upturned funnel. Using a **stopwatch,** record the time you began to pour and the time your volcano erupts. How close was your prediction?

Analysis

6. How does your model represent the natural world?

7. What are some limitations of your model?

8. Based on the predictions of the entire class, what can you conclude about the accuracy of predicting volcanic eruptions?

volcano

lava

pyroclastic material

What You'll Do

◆ Distinguish between nonexplosive and explosive volcanic eruptions.

◆ Explain how the composition of magma determines the type of volcanic eruption that will occur.

◆ Classify the main types of lava and volcanic debris.

Volcanic Eruptions

Think about the force of the explosion produced by the first atomic bomb used in World War II. Now imagine an explosion 10,000 times stronger, and you get an idea of how powerful a volcanic eruption can be. As you may know, volcanic eruptions give rise to volcanoes. A **volcano** is a mountain that forms when molten rock, called *magma,* is forced to the Earth's surface.

Fortunately, few volcanoes give rise to explosive eruptions like that of Mount Pelée. Most eruptions are of a nonexplosive variety. You can compare these two types of eruptions by looking at the photographs on this and the next page.

Nonexplosive Eruptions

When people think of volcanic eruptions, they often imagine rivers of red-hot lava, called *lava flows.* Lava flows come from nonexplosive eruptions. **Lava** is magma that flows onto the Earth's surface. Relatively calm outpourings of lava, like the ones shown below, can release a huge amount of molten rock. Some of the largest mountains on Earth grew from repeated lava flows over hundreds of thousands of years.

In this nonexplosive ▶ eruption, a continuous stream of lava pours quietly from the crater of Kilauea, in Hawaii.

▲ *Sometimes nonexplosive eruptions can spray lava into the air. Lava fountains, such as this one, rarely exceed a few hundred meters in height.*

◀ *Lava can flow many kilometers before it finally cools and hardens. As you can see in this photograph, lava flows often pose a greater threat to property than to human life.*

Explosive Eruptions

Take a look at **Figure 1.** In an explosive volcanic eruption, clouds of hot debris and gases shoot out from the volcano, often at supersonic speeds. Instead of producing lava flows, molten rock is blown into millions of pieces that harden in the air. The dust-sized particles can circle the globe for years in the upper atmosphere, while larger pieces of debris fall closer to the volcano.

In addition to shooting molten rock into the air, an explosive eruption can blast millions of tons of solid rock from a volcano. In a matter of minutes, an explosive eruption can demolish rock formations that took thousands of years to accumulate. Thus, as shown in **Figure 2,** a volcano may actually shrink in size rather than grow from repeated eruptions.

Figure 1 *In what resembles a nuclear explosion, volcanic debris rockets skyward during an eruption of Mount Redoubt, in Alaska.*

Figure 2 *Within minutes, the 1980 eruption of Mount St. Helens, in Washington, blasted away a whole side of the mountain, flattening and scorching 600 km² of forest.*

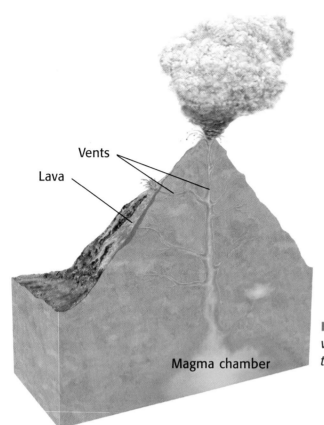

Vents

Lava

Magma chamber

Cross Section of a Volcano

Whether they produce explosive or nonexplosive eruptions, all volcanoes share the same basic features. **Figure 3** shows some of the features that you might see if you could look inside an erupting volcano. Deep underground, the driving force that creates volcanoes is hot liquid material known as magma. Magma rises through holes in the Earth's crust called *vents*. Vents can channel magma all the way up to the Earth's surface during an eruption.

Figure 3 *Volcanoes form around vents that release magma onto the Earth's surface.*

Magma

By comparing the composition of magma from different types of eruptions, scientists have made an important discovery—the composition of the magma determines whether a volcanic eruption is nonexplosive, explosive, or somewhere in between.

Water A volcano is more likely to erupt explosively if its magma has a high water content. The effect water has on magma is similar to the effect carbon dioxide gas has in a can of soda. When you shake the can up, the carbon dioxide that was dissolved in the soda is released, and because gases need much more room than liquids, a great amount of pressure builds up. When you open the can, soda comes shooting out. The same phenomenon occurs with explosive volcanic eruptions.

Silica Explosive eruptions are also caused by magma that contains a large percentage of silica (a basic building block of most minerals). Silica-rich magma has a thick, stiff consistency. It flows slowly and tends to harden in the volcano's vent. This plugs the vent, resulting in a buildup of pressure as magma pushes up from below. If enough pressure builds up, an explosive eruption results. Thick magma also prevents water vapor and other gases from easily escaping. Magma that contains a smaller percentage of silica has a thinner, runnier consistency. Gases escape this type of magma more easily, making it less likely that explosive pressure will build up.

Bubble, Bubble, Toil and Trouble

With a few simple items, you can easily discover how the consistency of a liquid affects the flow of gases.

1. Fill a **drinking cup** halfway with **water** and another cup halfway with **honey.**
2. Using a **straw,** blow into the water and observe the bubbles.
3. Take another straw and blow into the honey. What happens?
4. How does the honey behave differently from the water?
5. How do you think this difference relates to volcanic eruptions?

TRY at HOME

What Erupts from a Volcano?

Depending on how explosive a volcanic eruption is, magma erupts as either *lava* or *pyroclastic material*. **Pyroclastic material** consists of the rock fragments created by explosive volcanic eruptions. Nonexplosive eruptions produce mostly lava. Explosive eruptions produce mostly pyroclastic material. Over many years, a volcano may alternate between eruptions of lava and eruptions of pyroclastic material. Eruptions of lava and pyroclastic material may also occur as separate stages of a single eruption event.

Fire and ice! A phrase to describe volcanoes? That depends on where they are. Turn to page 241 to find out more.

Lava Like magma, lava ranges in consistency from thick to thin. *Blocky lava* is so thick in consistency that it barely creeps along the ground. Other types of lava, such as *pahoehoe* (pah HOY HOY), *aa* (AH ah), and *pillow lava,* are thinner in consistency and produce faster lava flows. These types of lava are shown in the photographs below.

Blocky lava *is cool, stiff* ▶ *lava that cannot travel far from the erupting vent. Blocky lava usually oozes from a volcano, forming jumbled heaps of sharp-edged chunks.*

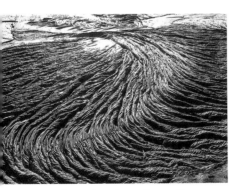

▲ **Pahoehoe** *lava flows slowly, like wax dripping from a candle, forming a glassy surface with rounded wrinkles.*

▲ **Aa** *is a Hawaiian word that refers to a type of lava that has a jagged surface. This slightly stiffer lava pours out quickly and forms a brittle crust. The crust is torn into jagged pieces as the molten lava underneath continues to move.*

▲ **Pillow lava** *forms when lava erupts underwater. As you can see here, it forms rounded lumps that are the size and shape of pillows.*

Pyroclastic Material Pyroclastic material is produced when magma explodes from a volcano and solidifies in the air. It is also produced when existing rock is shattered by powerful eruptions. It comes in a variety of sizes, from boulders the size of houses to particles so small they can remain suspended in the atmosphere for years. The photographs on this page show four major kinds of pyroclastic material: volcanic bombs, volcanic blocks, lapilli (luh PILL ee), and volcanic ash.

Volcanic blocks *are the largest pieces of pyroclastic material. They consist of solid rock blasted out of the volcano.*

Biology
C O N N E C T I O N

Volcanoes provide some of the most productive farmland in the world. It can take thousands of years for volcanic rock to break down into usable soil nutrients. On the other hand, the ash from a single explosive eruption can greatly increase the fertility of soil in only a few years and can keep the soil fertile for centuries.

Volcanic bombs *are large blobs of magma that harden in the air. The shape of the bomb shown here resulted from the magma's spinning through the air as it cooled.*

Lapilli, *which means "little stones" in Italian, are pebble-like bits of magma that became solid before they hit the ground.*

Volcanic ash *forms when the gases in stiff magma expand rapidly and the walls of the gas bubbles explode into tiny glasslike slivers.*

internetconnect

SC*LINKS*
NSTA

TOPIC: Volcanic Eruptions
GO TO: www.scilinks.org
*sci*LINKS NUMBER: HSTE205

REVIEW

1. Is a nonexplosive volcanic eruption more likely to produce lava or pyroclastic material? Explain.

2. If a volcano contained magma with small proportions of water and silica, would you predict a nonexplosive eruption or an explosive one? Why?

3. **Making Inferences** Pyroclastic material is classified primarily by the size of the particles. What is the basis for classifying lava?

Volcanoes' Effects on Earth

The effects of volcanic eruptions can be seen both on land and in the air. Heavier pyroclastic materials fall to the ground, causing great destruction, while ash and escaping gases affect global climatic patterns. Volcanoes also build mountains and plateaus that become lasting additions to the landscape.

An Explosive Impact

Because it is thrown high into the air, ash ejected during explosive volcanic eruptions can have widespread effects. The ash can block out the sun for days over thousands of square kilometers. Volcanic ash can blow down trees and buildings and can blanket nearby towns with a fine powder.

Flows and Fallout As shown in **Figure 4,** clouds of hot ash can flow rapidly downhill like an avalanche, choking and searing every living thing in their path. Sometimes large deposits of ash mix with rainwater or the water from melted glaciers during an eruption. With the consistency of wet cement, the mixture flows downhill, picking up boulders, trees, and buildings along the way. As volcanic ash falls to the ground, the effects can be devastating. Buildings may collapse under the weight of so much ash. Ash can also dam up river valleys, resulting in massive floods. And although ash is an effective plant fertilizer, too much ash can smother crops, causing food shortages and loss of livestock.

Figure 4 *During the 1991 eruption of Mount Pinatubo, in the Philippines, clouds of volcanic gases and ash sped downhill at up to 250 km/h.*

Climatic Changes In large-scale eruptions, volcanic ash, along with sulfur-rich gases, can reach the upper atmosphere. As the ash and gases spread around the globe, they can block out enough sunlight to cause the average global surface temperature to drop noticeably. The eruption of Mount Pinatubo in 1991 caused average global temperatures to drop by as much as 0.5°C. Although this may not seem like a large change in temperature, such a shift can disrupt climates all over the world. The lower average temperatures may last for several years, bringing wetter, milder summers and longer, harsher winters.

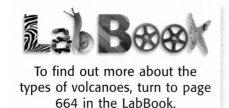

To find out more about the types of volcanoes, turn to page 664 in the LabBook.

Different Types of Volcanoes

The lava and pyroclastic material that erupt from volcanoes create a variety of landforms. Perhaps the best known of all volcanic landforms are the volcanoes themselves. Volcanoes result from the buildup of rock around a vent. Three basic types of volcanoes are illustrated in **Figure 5.**

Figure 5 Three Types of Volcanoes

Shield volcano

Cinder cone volcano

Composite volcano

Shield volcanoes are built out of layers of lava from repeated nonexplosive eruptions. Because the lava is very runny, it spreads out over a wide area. Over time, the layers of lava create a volcano with gently sloping sides. Although their sides are not very steep, shield volcanoes can be enormous. Hawaii's Mauna Kea, the shield volcano shown here, is the largest mountain on Earth. Measured from its base on the sea floor, Mauna Kea is taller than Mount Everest, the tallest mountain on land.

Cinder cone volcanoes are small volcanic cones made entirely of pyroclastic material from moderately explosive eruptions. The pyroclastic material forms steeper slopes with a narrower base than the lava flows of shield volcanoes, as you can see in this photo of the volcano Paricutín, in Mexico. Cinder cone volcanoes usually erupt for only a short time and often occur in clusters, commonly on the sides of shield and composite volcanoes. They erode quickly because the pyroclastic particles are not cemented together by lava.

Composite volcanoes, sometimes referred to as *stratovolcanoes,* are one of the most common types of volcanoes. They form by explosive eruptions of pyroclastic material followed by quieter outpourings of lava. The combination of both types of eruptions forms alternating layers of pyroclastic material and lava. Composite volcanoes, such as Japan's Mount Fuji, shown here, have broad bases and sides that get steeper toward the summit.

Craters and Calderas

At the top of the central vent in most volcanoes is a funnel-shaped pit called a **crater**. (Craters are also the circular pits made by meteorite impacts.) The photograph of the cinder cone on the previous page shows a well-defined crater. A crater's funnel shape results from explosions of material out of the vent as well as the collapse of material from the crater's rim back into the vent. A **caldera** forms when a magma chamber that supplies material to a volcano empties and its roof collapses. This causes the ground to sink, leaving a large, circular depression, as shown in **Figure 6.**

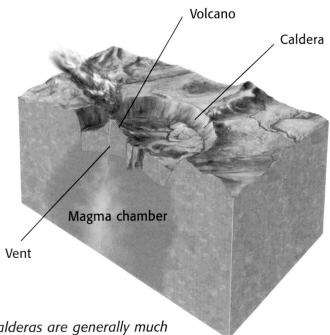

Figure 6 *Calderas are generally much larger than volcanic craters.*

Lava Plateaus

The most massive outpourings of lava do not come from individual volcanoes. Most of the lava on Earth's continents erupts from long cracks, or *fissures,* in the crust. In this non-explosive type of eruption, runny lava pours from a series of fissures and may spread evenly over thousands of square kilometers. The resulting landform is known as a *lava plateau.* The Columbia River Plateau, a lava plateau that formed about 15 million years ago, can be found in the northwestern United States.

REVIEW

1. Briefly explain why the ash from a volcanic eruption can be hazardous.

2. Why do cinder cone volcanoes have narrower bases and steeper sides than shield volcanoes?

3. **Comparing Concepts** Briefly describe the difference between a crater and a caldera.

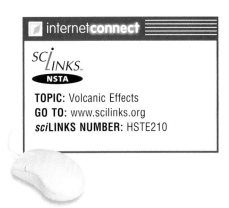

internet**connect**

*SCi*LINKS™
NSTA

TOPIC: Volcanic Effects
GO TO: www.scilinks.org
*sci*LINKS NUMBER: HSTE210

rift   hot spot

What You'll Do

◆ Describe the formation and movement of magma.

◆ Explain the relationship between volcanoes and plate tectonics.

◆ Summarize the methods scientists use to predict volcanic eruptions.

Reaction to Stress

1. Make a pliable "rock" by pouring 60 mL (¹/₄ cup) of **water** into a **plastic cup** and adding 150 mL of **cornstarch,** 15 mL (1 tbsp) at a time. Stir well after each addition.

2. Pour half of the cornstarch mixture into a **clear bowl.** Carefully observe how the "rock" flows. Be patient— this is a slow process!

3. Scrape the rest of the "rock" out of the cup with a **spoon.** Observe the behavior of the "rock" as you scrape.

4. What happened to the "rock" when you let it flow by itself? What happened when you put stress on the "rock"?

5. How is this pliable "rock" similar to the rock of the upper part of the mantle?

TRY at HOME

What Causes Volcanoes?

Scientists have learned a great deal over the years about what happens when a volcano erupts. Many of the results are dramatic and immediately visible. Unfortunately, understanding what causes a volcano to erupt in the first place is much more difficult. Scientists must rely on models based on rock samples and other data that provide insight into volcanic processes. Because it is so difficult to "see" what is going on deep inside the Earth, there are many uncertainties about why volcanoes form.

The Formation of Magma

You learned in the previous section that volcanoes form by the eruption of lava and pyroclastic material onto the Earth's surface. But the key to understanding why volcanoes erupt is understanding how magma forms. As you can see in **Figure 7,** volcanoes begin when magma collects in the deeper regions of the Earth's crust and in the uppermost layers of the mantle, the zone of intensely hot and pliable rock beneath the Earth's crust.

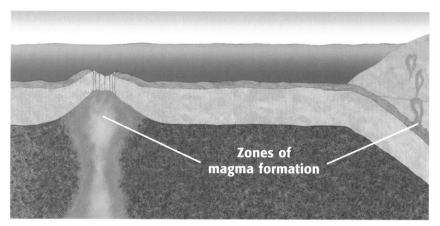

Zones of magma formation

Figure 7 *Magma forms below the Earth's surface in a region that includes the lower crust and part of the upper mantle.*

Pressure and Temperature Although hot and pliable, the rock of the mantle is considered a solid. But the temperature of the mantle is high enough to melt almost any rock, so why doesn't it melt? The answer has to do with pressure. The weight of the rock above the mantle exerts a tremendous amount of pressure. This pressure keeps the atoms of mantle rock tightly packed, preventing the rock from changing into a liquid state. An increase in pressure raises the melting point of most materials.

As you can see in **Figure 8,** rock melts and forms magma when the temperature of the rock increases or when the pressure on the rock decreases. Because the temperature of the mantle is relatively constant, a decrease in pressure is usually what causes magma to form.

Density   Once formed, the magma rises toward the surface of the Earth because it is less dense than the surrounding rock. Magma is commonly a mixture of liquid and solid mineral crystals and is therefore normally less dense than the completely solid rock that surrounds it. Like air bubbles that form on the bottom of a pan of boiling water, magma will rise toward the surface.

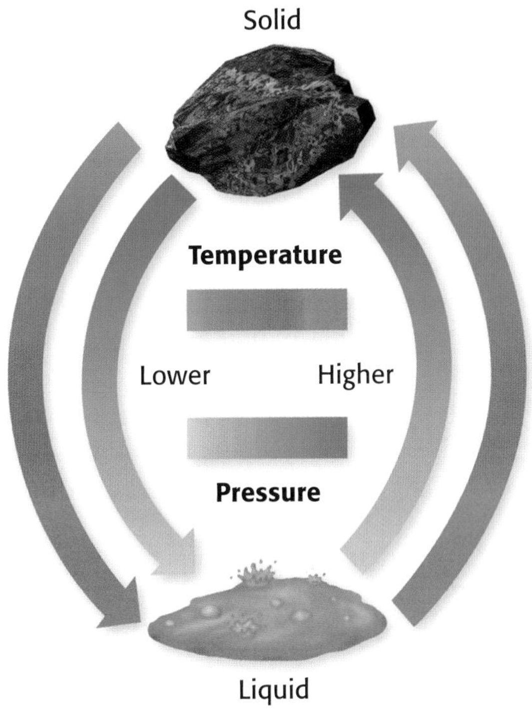

Solid

Temperature

Lower   Higher

Pressure

Liquid

Figure 8 *This diagram shows how both pressure and temperature affect the formation of magma within the mantle.*

✓ Self-Check

What two factors may cause solid rock to become magma? *(See page 726 to check your answer.)*

Where Volcanoes Form

The locations of volcanoes around the globe provide clues to how volcanoes form. The world map in **Figure 9** shows the location of the world's active volcanoes on land. It also shows tectonic plate boundaries. As you can see, a large number of the volcanoes lie directly on tectonic plate boundaries. In fact, the plate boundaries surrounding the Pacific Ocean have so many volcanoes that these boundaries together are called the *Ring of Fire.*

Why are most volcanoes on tectonic plate boundaries? These boundaries are where the plates either collide with one another or separate from one another. At these boundaries, it is easier for magma to travel upward through the crust. In other words, the boundaries are where the action is!

Ring of Fire

Figure 9 *Tectonic plate boundaries are likely places for volcanoes to form. The Ring of Fire contains nearly 75 percent of the world's active volcanoes on land.*

When Tectonic Plates Separate When two tectonic plates separate and move away from each other, a *divergent boundary* forms. As the tectonic plates separate, a deep crack, or **rift,** forms between the plates. Mantle material then rises to fill in the gap. Because the mantle material is now closer to the surface, the pressure on it decreases. This decrease in pressure causes the mantle rock to partially melt and become magma.

Because magma is less dense than the surrounding rock, it rises up through the rift. As the magma rises, it cools down, and the pressure on it decreases. So even though it becomes cooler as it rises, it remains molten because of the reduced pressure.

Magma continuously rises up through the rift between the separating plates and creates new crust. Although a few divergent boundaries exist on land, most are located on the ocean floor. There they produce long mountain chains called mid-ocean spreading centers, or *mid-ocean ridges*. **Figure 10** shows the process of forming such an underwater mountain range at a divergent boundary.

Figure 10 How Magma Forms at a Divergent Boundary

① *Mantle material rises to fill the space opened by separating tectonic plates. As the pressure decreases, the mantle begins to melt.*

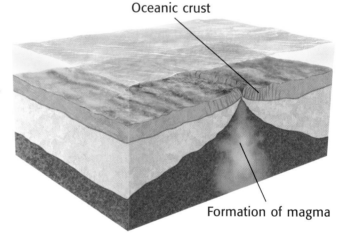

② *Because magma is less dense than the surrounding rock, it rises toward the surface, where it forms new crust on the ocean floor.*

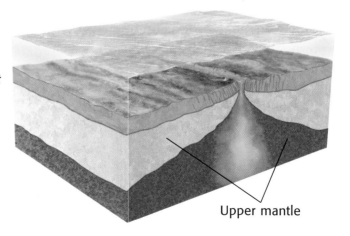

When Tectonic Plates Collide

If you slide two pieces of notebook paper into one another on a flat desktop, the papers will either buckle upward or one piece of paper will move under the other. This gives you an idea of what happens when tectonic plates collide. The place where two tectonic plates collide is called a *convergent boundary.*

Convergent boundaries are commonly located where oceanic plates collide with continental plates. The oceanic crust is denser and thinner and therefore moves underneath the continental crust. The movement of one tectonic plate under another is called *subduction,* shown in **Figure 11.**

As the descending oceanic crust scrapes past the continental crust, it sinks deeper into the mantle, getting hotter. As it does so, the pressure on the oceanic crust increases as well. The combination of increased heat and pressure causes the water contained in the oceanic crust to be released. The water then mixes with the mantle rock, which lowers the rock's melting point, causing it to melt.

Figure 11 How Magma Forms at a Convergent Boundary

① *As the oceanic plate moves downward, some of the rock melts and forms magma.*

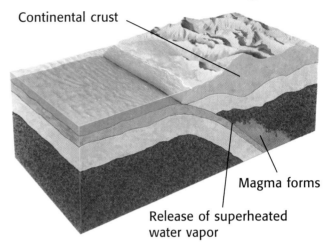

Continental crust

Magma forms

Release of superheated water vapor

② *When magma is less dense than the surrounding rock, it rises toward the surface.*

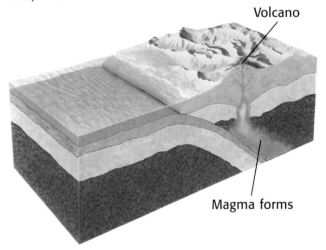

Volcano

Magma forms

Hot Spots

Not all magma develops along tectonic plate boundaries. For example, the Hawaiian Islands, some of the most well-known volcanoes on Earth, are nowhere near a plate boundary. The volcanoes of Hawaii and several other places on Earth are known as *hot spots.* **Hot spots** are places on the Earth's surface that are directly above columns of rising magma, called *mantle plumes.* Mantle plumes begin deep in the Earth, possibly at the boundary between the mantle and the core. Scientists are not sure what causes these plumes, but some think that a combination of heat conducted upward from the core and heat from radioactive elements keeps the plumes rising.

A hot spot often produces a long chain of volcanoes. This is because the mantle plume stays in the same spot, while the tectonic plate above moves over it. The Hawaiian Islands, for example, are riding on the Pacific plate, which is moving slowly to the northwest. **Figure 12** shows how a hot spot can form a chain of volcanic islands.

Figure 12 How a Hot Spot Forms Volcanoes

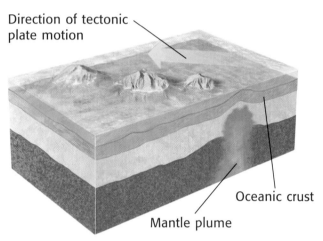

Direction of tectonic plate motion

Oceanic crust

Mantle plume

① *A plume of hot mantle rock flows slowly upward through the mantle.*

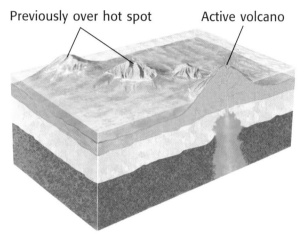

Previously over hot spot   Active volcano

② *As the tectonic plate moves slowly over the mantle plume, a chain of volcanic islands forms.*

Predicting Volcanic Eruptions

To help predict volcanic eruptions, scientists classify volcanoes based on their eruption histories and on how likely it is that they will erupt again. *Extinct* volcanoes are those that have not erupted in recorded history and probably never will again. *Dormant* volcanoes are those that are not currently erupting but have erupted at some time in recorded history. *Active* volcanoes are those that are in the process of erupting or that show signs of erupting in the very near future.

Figure 13 *Seismographs help scientists determine when magma is moving beneath a volcano.*

Measuring Small Quakes Most active volcanoes produce small earthquakes as the magma within them moves upward and causes the surrounding rock to shift. Just before an eruption, the number and intensity of the small earthquakes increase, and the occurrence of quakes may be continuous. These earthquakes are measured with a *seismograph,* as shown in **Figure 13.**

Measuring Slope Measurements of a volcano's slope also give scientists clues with which to predict eruptions. For example, bulges in the volcano's slope may form as magma pushes against the inside of the volcano. By attaching an instrument called a *tiltmeter* to the surface of the volcano, scientists can detect small changes in the angle of the slope.

Measuring Volcanic Gases The outflow of volcanic gases from a volcano can also help scientists predict eruptions. Some scientists think that the ratio of certain gases, especially that of sulfur dioxide (SO_2) to carbon dioxide (CO_2), is important in predicting eruptions. They know that when this ratio changes, it is an indication that things are changing in the magma chamber down below! As you can see in **Figure 14,** collecting this type of data is often dangerous.

Measuring Temperature from Orbit Some of the newest methods scientists are using to predict volcanic eruptions rely on satellite images. Many of these images record infrared radiation, which allows scientists to measure changes in temperature over time. They are taken from satellites orbiting more than 700 km above the Earth. By analyzing images taken at different times, scientists can determine if the site is getting hotter as magma pushes closer to the surface.

Figure 14 *As if getting this close to an active volcano is not dangerous enough, the gases that are being collected here are extremely poisonous.*

REVIEW

1. How does pressure determine whether the mantle is solid or liquid?

2. Describe a technology scientists use to predict volcanic eruptions.

3. **Interpreting Illustrations** Figure 9, shown earlier in this chapter, shows the locations of active volcanoes on land. Describe where on the map you would plot the location of underwater volcanoes and why. (Do not write in this book.)

internet connect

SCi *LINKS*
NSTA

TOPIC: What Causes Volcanoes?
GO TO: www.scilinks.org
*sci*LINKS NUMBER: HSTE215

Calling an Evacuation?

Although scientists have learned a lot about volcanoes, they cannot predict eruptions with total accuracy. Sometimes there are warning signs before an eruption, but often there are none. Imagine that you are the mayor of a town near a large volcano, and a geologist warns you that an eruption is probable. You realize that ordering an evacuation of your town could be an expensive embarrassment if the volcano doesn't erupt. But if you decide to keep quiet, people could be in serious danger if the volcano does erupt. Considering the social and economic consequences of your decision, your job is perhaps even more difficult. What would you do?

Chapter Highlights

Vocabulary

volcano (*p. 222*)

lava (*p. 222*)

pyroclastic material (*p. 225*)

Section Notes

- Volcanoes erupt both explosively and nonexplosively.

- The characteristics of a volcanic eruption are largely determined by the type of magma within the volcano.

- The amount of silica in magma determines whether it is thin and fluid or thick and stiff.

- Lava hardens into characteristic features that range from smooth to jagged, depending on how thick the lava is and how quickly it flows.

- Pyroclastic material, or volcanic debris, consists of solid pieces of the volcano as well as magma that solidifies as it travels through the air.

Vocabulary

shield volcano (*p. 228*)

cinder cone volcano (*p. 228*)

composite volcano (*p. 228*)

crater (*p. 229*)

caldera (*p. 229*)

Section Notes

- The effects of volcanic eruptions are felt both locally and around the world.

- Volcanic mountains can be classified according to their composition and overall shape.

- Craters are funnel-shaped pits that form around the central vent of a volcano. Calderas are large bowl-shaped depressions formed by a collapsed magma chamber.

☑ Skills Check

Math Concepts

CONVERTING TEMPERATURE SCALES So-called low-temperature magmas can be 1,100°C. Just how hot is such a magma? If you are used to measuring temperature in degrees Fahrenheit, you can use a simple formula to find out.

$$°F = \frac{9}{5}°C + 32$$

$$°F = \frac{9}{5}(1,100) + 32$$

$$°F = 1,980 + 32 = 2,012$$

$$2,012°F = 1,100°C$$

Visual Understanding

CALDERAS Calderas are caused by the release of massive amounts of magma from beneath the Earth's surface. When the volume of magma decreases, it no longer exerts pressure to hold the ground up. As a result, the ground sinks, forming a caldera.

- In the largest type of volcanic eruption, lava simply pours from long fissures in the Earth's crust to form lava plateaus.

Labs

Some Go "Pop," Some Do Not *(p. 664)*

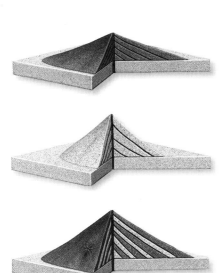

Vocabulary

rift *(p. 232)*

hot spot *(p. 233)*

Section Notes

- Volcanoes result from magma formed in the mantle.

- When pressure is reduced, some of the solid rock of the already hot mantle melts to form magma.

- Because it is less dense than the surrounding rock, magma rises to the Earth's surface. It either erupts as lava or solidifies in the crust.

- Most volcanic activity takes place along tectonic plate boundaries, where plates either separate or collide.

- Volcanoes also occur at hot spots. Chains of volcanic islands can form when tectonic plates move relative to the hot spot.

- Volcanic eruptions cannot be predicted with complete accuracy. But scientists now have several methods of forecasting future eruptions.

Labs

Volcano Verdict *(p. 666)*

---

internetconnect

GO TO: go.hrw.com

Visit the **HRW** Web site for a variety of learning tools related to this chapter. Just type in the keyword:

KEYWORD: HSTVOL

GO TO: www.scilinks.org

Visit the **National Science Teachers Association** on-line Web site for Internet resources related to this chapter. Just type in the *sci*LINKS number for more information about the topic:

TOPIC: Volcanic Eruptions	*sci*LINKS NUMBER: HSTE205
TOPIC: Volcanic Effects	*sci*LINKS NUMBER: HSTE210
TOPIC: What Causes Volcanoes?	*sci*LINKS NUMBER: HSTE215
TOPIC: The Ring of Fire	*sci*LINKS NUMBER: HSTE220

Chapter Review

For each pair of terms listed below, explain the difference in their meanings.

1. caldera/crater

2. lava/magma

3. lava/pyroclastic material

4. vent/rift

5. cinder cone volcano/shield volcano

Multiple Choice

6. The type of magma that often produces a violent eruption can be described as
   a. thin due to high silica content.
   b. thick due to high silica content.
   c. thin due to low silica content.
   d. thick due to low silica content.

7. When lava hardens quickly to form ropy formations, it is called
   a. aa lava.
   b. pahoehoe lava.
   c. pillow lava.
   d. blocky lava.

8. Volcanic dust and ash can remain in the atmosphere for months or years, causing
   a. decreased solar reflection and higher temperatures.
   b. increased solar reflection and lower temperatures.
   c. decreased solar reflection and lower temperatures.
   d. increased solar reflection and higher temperatures.

9. Mount St. Helens, in Washington, covered the city of Spokane with tons of ash. Its eruption would most likely be described as
   a. nonexplosive, producing lava.
   b. explosive, producing lava.
   c. nonexplosive, producing pyroclastic material.
   d. explosive, producing pyroclastic material.

10. Magma forms within the mantle most often as a result of
    a. high temperature and high pressure.
    b. high temperature and low pressure.
    c. low temperature and high pressure.
    d. low temperature and low pressure.

11. At divergent plate boundaries,
    a. heat from the Earth's core produces mantle plumes.
    b. oceanic plates sink, causing magma to form.
    c. tectonic plates move apart.
    d. hot spots produce volcanoes.

12. A theory that helps to explain the causes of both earthquakes and volcanoes is the theory of
    a. pyroclastics.
    b. plate tectonics.
    c. climatic fluctuation.
    d. mantle plumes.

Short Answer

13. Briefly describe two methods that scientists use to predict volcanic eruptions.

14. Describe how differences in magma affect volcanic eruptions.

15. Along what types of tectonic plate boundaries are volcanoes generally found? Why?

16. Describe the characteristics of the three types of volcanic mountains.

Concept Mapping

17. Use any of the terms from the vocabulary lists in Chapter Highlights to construct a concept map that illustrates the relationship between types of magma, the eruptions they produce, and the shapes of the volcanoes that result.

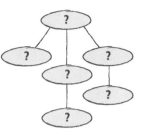

CRITICAL THINKING AND PROBLEM SOLVING

Write one or two sentences to answer the following questions:

18. Imagine that you are exploring a volcano that has been dormant for some time. You begin to keep notes on the types of volcanic debris you encounter as you walk. Your first notes describe volcanic ash, and later your notes describe lapilli. In what direction would you most likely be traveling—toward or away from the crater? Explain.

19. Loihi is a future Hawaiian island in the process of forming on the ocean floor. Considering how this island chain formed, tell where you think the new volcanic island will be located and why.

20. What do you think would happen to the Earth's climate if volcanic activity increased to 10 times its current level?

MATH IN SCIENCE

21. Midway Island is 1,935 km northwest of Hawaii. If the Pacific plate is moving to the northwest at 9 cm/yr, how long ago was Midway Island located over the hot spot that formed it?

INTERPRETING GRAPHICS

The following graph illustrates the average change in temperature above or below normal for a community over several years.

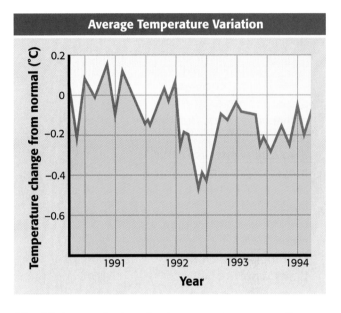

Average Temperature Variation

22. If the variation in temperature over the years was influenced by a major volcanic eruption, when did the eruption most likely take place? Explain.

23. If the temperature were plotted only in yearly intervals rather than several times per year, how might your interpretation be different?

Reading Check-up

Take a minute to review your answers to the Pre-Reading Questions found at the bottom of page 220. Have your answers changed? If necessary, revise your answers based on what you have learned since you began this chapter.

Science, Technology, and Society

Robot in the Hot Seat

Scientists have to be calm, cool, and collected to study active volcanoes. But the recently cooled magma in a volcanic crater isn't the most hospitable location for scientific study. What kind of daredevil would run the risk of creeping along a crater floor? A volcanologist like *Dante II,* that's who!

Hot Stuff

A volcano crater may seem empty after a volcano erupts, but it is in no way devoid of volcanic information. Gases hissing up through the crater floor give scientists clues about the molten rock underneath, which may help them understand how and why volcanoes erupt repeatedly. But these gases may be poisonous or scalding hot, and the crater's floor can crack or shift at any time. Over the years, dozens of scientists have been seriously injured or killed while trying to explore volcano craters. Obviously, volcanologists needed some help studying the steamy abyss.

Getting a Robot to Take the Heat

Enter *Dante II,* an eight-legged robot with cameras for eyes and computers for a brain. In 1994, led by a team of scientists from NASA, Carnegie Mellon University, and the Alaskan Volcano Observatory, *Dante II* embarked on its first mission. It climbed into a breach called Crater Peak on the side of Mount Spurr, an active volcano in Alaska. Anchored at the crater's rim by a strong cable, *Dante II* was

▲ *Dante II*

controlled partly by internal computers and partly by a team of scientists. The team communicated with the robot through a satellite link and Internet connections. *Dante II* moved very slowly, taking pictures and collecting scientific data. It was equipped with gas sensors that provided continuous readings of the crater gases. It performed the tasks human scientists could not, letting the humans keep their cool.

Mission Accomplished?

During its expedition, *Dante II* encountered large rocks, some of which were as big as the robot itself. In addition, while climbing out of the volcano, *Dante II* slipped and fell, damaging one of its legs. Eventually *Dante II* had to be rescued by helicopter because its support cable broke. Despite these obstacles, *Dante II* was able to gather valuable data from the volcano's crater.

Dante II's mission also met one of NASA's objectives: to prove that robots could be used successfully to explore extreme terrain, such as that found on planetary surfaces. *Dante II* paved the way for later robotic projects, such as the exploration of the surface of Mars by the *Sojourner* rover in 1997.

Write About It

▶ Write a proposal for a project in which a robot is used to explore a dangerous place. Don't forget to include what types of data the robot would be collecting.

Europa: Life on a Moon?

Smooth and brownish white, one of Jupiter's moons, Europa, has fascinated scientists and science-fiction writers for decades. More recently, scientists were excited by tantalizing images from the Galileo Europa Mission. Could it be that life is lurking (or sloshing) beneath Europa's surface?

An Active History

Slightly smaller than Earth's moon, Europa is the fourth largest of Jupiter's moons. It is unusual among other bodies in the solar system because of its extraordinarily smooth surface. The ridges and brownish channels that crisscross Europa's smooth surface may tell a unique story—the surface appears to be a slushy combination of ice and water. Some scientists think that the icy ridges and channels are ice floes left over from ancient volcanoes that erupted water! The water flowed over Europa's surface and froze, like lava flows and cools on Earth's surface.

A Slushy Situation

Scientists speculate that Europa's surface consists of thin tectonic plates of ice floating on a layer of slush or water. These plates, which would look like icy rafts floating in an ocean of slush, have been compared to giant glaciers floating in polar regions on Earth.

Where plates push together, the material of the plates may crumple, forming an icy ridge. Where plates pull apart, warmer liquid mixed with darker silicates may erupt toward the surface and freeze, forming the brownish icy channels that create Europa's cracked cue-ball appearance.

Life on Europa?

These discoveries have led scientists to consider an exciting possibility: Does Europa have an environment that could support primitive life-forms? In general, at least three things are necessary for life as we know it to develop—water, organic compounds (substances that contain carbon), and heat. Europa has water, and organic compounds are fairly common in the solar system. But is it hot enough? Europa's slushy nature suggests a warm interior. One theory is that the warmth is the result of Jupiter's strong gravitational pull on Europa. Another theory is that warmth is brought to Europa's surface by convection heating.

So does Europa truly satisfy the three requirements for life? The answer is still unknown, but the sloshing beneath Europa's surface has sure heightened some scientists' curiosity!

If You Were in Charge . . .

► If you were in charge of NASA's space-exploration program, would you send a spacecraft to look for life on Europa? (Remember that this would cost millions of dollars and would mean sacrificing other important projects!) Explain your answer.

◄ *Europa looks like a cracked cue ball.*

Reshaping the Land

In this unit, you will learn about the way the surface of the Earth changes. There is a constant struggle between the forces that build up Earth's land features and those that break them down. The mountains built by Earth's internal forces are torn down by the actions of weathering and erosion. This timeline shows some of the events that have occurred in this struggle as natural changes in the Earth's features continue to take place.

320
Million years ago

Vast swamps along the western edge of the Appalachian Mountains are buried by sediment and form the largest coal fields in the world.

➤ 280
Million years ago

The shallow inland sea that covered much of what is now the midwestern United States fills with sediment and disappears.

1880 ◄

Cleopatra's Needle, a granite obelisk, is moved from Egypt to New York City. Within the next 100 years, the weather and pollution severely damage the 3,000-year-old monument.

1930

Carlsbad Caverns National Park is established. It features the nation's deepest limestone cave and one of the largest underground chambers in the world.

➤ 1941

Mount Rushmore is completed—an example of purposeful human erosion.

140
Million years ago

The mouth of the Mississippi River is near present-day Cairo, Illinois.

Chicago

Cairo

65
Million years ago

Dinosaurs become extinct.

6
Million years ago

The Colorado River begins to carve the Grand Canyon, which today is roughly 2 km deep.

1775

The Battle of Bunker Hill, a victory for the Colonials, takes place on a drumlin, a tear-shaped mound of sediment that was formed by an ice-age glacier 10,000 years earlier.

12,000
Years ago

The Great Lakes form at the end of the last ice age.

1998

Hong Kong opens a new airport on an artificial island. Almost 150 million metric tons of rock and soil were deposited in the South China Sea to form the 3,000-acre island.

1987

An iceberg twice the size of Rhode Island breaks off the edge of Antarctica's continental glacier.

Pre-Reading
Questions

1. How do water and air
   cause rocks to crumble?

2. Why is soil one of our
   most important resources?

3. How are weathering and
   soil formation related?

NICE AND COZY

Badgers live throughout North America, Africa, Europe, Asia, and the Middle East. Although badgers are sometimes considered to be pests, they play an important ecological role. Badgers are known for their burrowing ability. They dig in the soil for food and build underground homes. As the badgers dig through the soil, they expose rock and soil to air and water. In this chapter, you will learn how animals like the badger and other natural processes contribute to weathering and soil formation.

WHAT'S THE DIFFERENCE?

In this chapter, you will learn about the processes and rates of weathering. Do this activity to learn about how the size and surface area of a material affect how quickly the substance breaks down.

Procedure

1. Fill **two small containers** about half full with **water.**

2. Add **one sugar cube** to one container.

3. Add 1 tsp of **granulated sugar** to the other container.

4. Using **two different spoons,** stir the water and sugar in each container at the same rate.

5. Using a **stopwatch,** measure how long it takes for the sugar to dissolve in each container.

Analysis

6. Did the sugar dissolve at the same rate in both containers? Explain why or why not.

7. Which do you think would wear away faster—a large rock or a small rock? Explain your answer.

What You'll Do

◆ Describe how ice, rivers, tree roots, and animals cause mechanical weathering.
◆ Describe how water, acids, and air cause chemical weathering of rocks.

Chemistry
C O N N E C T I O N

Almost all liquids contract when they freeze to form a solid—their volume decreases and their density increases. When these substances freeze, the frozen solid sinks. Just the opposite occurs to water when it freezes. Water expands and becomes less dense, which is why ice floats in water.

Weathering

Weathering is the breakdown of rock into smaller and smaller pieces. Rocks on Earth's surface are undergoing weathering all the time, either by mechanical means or by chemical means. You will learn the difference as you read on. You will also learn how these processes shape the surface of our planet.

Mechanical Weathering

If you were to crush one rock with another rock, you would be demonstrating one type of mechanical weathering. **Mechanical weathering** is simply the breakdown of rock into smaller pieces by physical means. Agents of mechanical weathering include ice, wind, water, gravity, plants, and even animals.

Ice As you know, water has the unusual property of expanding when it freezes. (This is just the opposite of most substances.) When water seeps into a crack in a rock during warm weather and then freezes during cold weather, it expands. And when it expands, it pushes against the sides of the crack, forcing it to open wider. This process is called _ice wedging_. **Figure 1** shows how ice wedging occurs over time.

Figure 1 _The granite at right has been broken down by repeated ice wedging, as shown in the illustration below._

Water · Ice · Water · Ice

Wind, Water, and Gravity When you write on a chalkboard, a process called *abrasion* takes place. As you scrape the piece of chalk against the chalkboard, some of the chalk rubs off to make a line on the board. As particles of chalk are worn off, the piece of chalk wears down and becomes more rounded at the tip. The same thing happens to rocks. In nature, **abrasion** is the action of rocks and sediment grinding against each other and wearing away exposed surfaces.

Abrasion can happen in many ways. For example, when rocks and pebbles roll along the bottom of swiftly flowing rivers, they bump into and scrape against each other. They eventually become river rocks, as shown in **Figure 2.**

Wind also causes abrasion. For example, when wind blows sand against exposed rock, the sand eventually wears away the rock's surface. **Figure 3** shows what this kind of sandblasting can do.

Abrasion also occurs when rocks fall on one another. **Figure 4** shows a rock slide. You can imagine the forces rocks exert on each other as they tumble down a mountainside. In fact, any time one rock hits another, abrasion takes place.

You can make your own "river rocks" in just a few shakes. See page 669 in your LabBook.

Figure 2 *These river rocks are rounded because they have been tumbled in the riverbed by fast-moving water for many years.*

Figure 3 *This rock has been shaped by blowing sand. Such rocks are called* ventifacts.

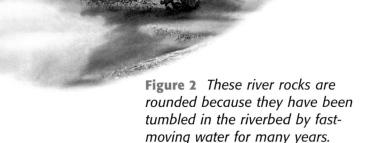

Figure 4 *Rocks grind against each other in a rock slide, creating smaller and smaller rock fragments.*

Figure 5 *Although they grow slowly, tree roots are strong enough to break solid rock.*

Plants You may not think of plants as being strong, but some plants can easily break rocks. Have you ever seen how tree roots can crack sidewalks and streets? Roots aren't fast, but they certainly are powerful! Plants often send their roots into existing cracks in rocks. As the plant gets bigger, the force of the expanding root becomes so strong that the crack is made larger. Eventually, the entire rock can split apart, as you can see in **Figure 5**.

Animals Believe it or not, earthworms cause a lot of weathering! They burrow through the soil and move soil particles around. This exposes fresh surfaces to continued weathering. Would you believe that some kinds of tropical worms move an estimated 100 metric tons of soil per acre every year? Almost any animal that burrows causes mechanical weathering. Ants, mice, coyotes, and rabbits all make their contribution. **Figure 6** shows some of these animals in action. The mixing and digging that animals do often contribute to another type of weathering, called *chemical weathering.* You will learn about this next.

Self-Check

Describe the property of water that causes ice wedging. *(See page 726 to check your answer.)*

Figure 6 *Animals that live in the soil cause a lot of weathering.*

Chemical Weathering

If you place a drop of strong acid on a rock, it will probably "eat away" a small part of the rock. This is an example of chemical weathering. **Chemical weathering** is the chemical breakdown of rocks and minerals into new substances. The most common agents of chemical weathering are water, weak acids, air, and soil. **Figure 7** shows the chemical weathering of granite.

Water If you drop a sugar cube into a glass of water, it will dissolve after a few minutes. If you drop a piece of chalk into a glass of water, it will also dissolve, only much slower than a sugar cube. Both cases are examples of chemical weathering. Even hard rock, like granite, is broken down by water; it just may take a few thousand years.

Acid Precipitation A car battery contains sulfuric acid, a very dangerous acid that should never touch your skin. A weaker form of sulfuric acid can be found in nature. In fact, precipitation such as rain and snow is naturally acidic and contains carbonic acid. Small amounts of sulfuric and nitric acids from natural sources, such as volcanoes, can make precipitation even more acidic. These acids can slowly break down rocks and other matter.

Precipitation that contains acids due to air pollution is called **acid precipitation.** Acid precipitation contains more acid than normal precipitation, so it can cause very rapid weathering of rock. Even the bronze statue shown in **Figure 8** is being chemically weathered by acid precipitation.

Figure 8 This statue is being damaged by acid precipitation.

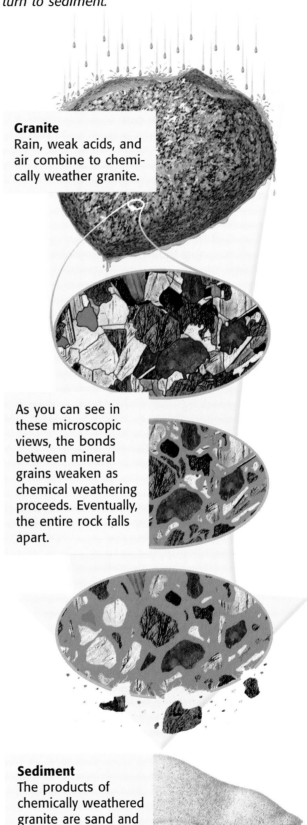

Figure 7 After thousands of years of chemical weathering, even hard rock, like granite, can turn to sediment.

Granite
Rain, weak acids, and air combine to chemically weather granite.

As you can see in these microscopic views, the bonds between mineral grains weaken as chemical weathering proceeds. Eventually, the entire rock falls apart.

Sediment
The products of chemically weathered granite are sand and clay.

Weathering and Soil Formation **249**

QuickLab

Acids React!

Have you ever heard someone refer to a certain food as being "acidic"? You consume acids in your food every day. For example, ketchup contains weak acids that can react with certain substances in a rather dramatic way. Try this:

1. Take a **penny** that has a dull appearance, rub **ketchup** on it for several minutes, and then rinse it off.

2. Where did all the grime go?

3. How is this similar to what happens to a rock when it is exposed to natural acids during weathering?

TRY at HOME

Acid precipitation starts with the burning of fossil fuels such as coal and oil. When these fuels are burned, they give off gases, including sulfur oxides, nitrogen oxides, and carbon oxides. When these compounds combine with water in the atmosphere, they can fall back to the ground in rain and snow. When the acidity is too high, acid precipitation can be harmful to vegetation and wildlife such as fish, amphibians, and insects.

Acid in Ground Water In certain places ground water contains weak acids, such as carbonic or sulfuric acid. When this ground water comes in contact with limestone, the limestone breaks down. Over a long period of time, this can have some spectacular results. Enormous caverns, like the one shown in **Figure 9,** can form as the limestone is eaten away. Limestone, you may remember, is made of calcite, which reacts strongly with acid.

Figure 9 At right is one of the many rooms of Mammoth Cave, a limestone cave system in Kentucky.

Acids in Living Things Another source of acids for weathering might surprise you. Take a look at **Figure 10.** Lichens produce organic acids that can slowly break down rock. If you have ever taken a walk in a park or forest, you have probably seen lichens growing on the sides of trees or rocks. Lichens can also grow in places where some of the hardiest plants cannot. Lichens can be found in deserts, in arctic areas, and in areas high above timberline, where even trees don't grow.

Figure 10 Lichens, which consist of fungi and algae living together, contribute to chemical weathering.

Air The car shown in **Figure 11** is undergoing chemical weathering due to the air. The oxygen in the air is reacting with the iron in the car, causing the car to rust. Water speeds up the process, but the iron would rust even if no water were present. This process also happens in certain types of rocks, particularly those containing iron, as you can see in **Figure 12**. Scientists call this process *oxidation*.

Oxidation is a chemical reaction in which an element, such as iron, combines with oxygen to form an oxide. (The chemical name for rust is *iron oxide*.) Oxidation is a common type of chemical weathering, and rust is probably the most familiar result of oxidation.

Activity

Imagine that you are a tin can—shiny, new, and clean. But something happens, and you don't make it to a recycling bin. Instead, you are left outside at the mercy of the elements. In light of what you have learned about physical and chemical weathering, write a story about what happens to you over a long period of time. What is your ultimate fate?

TRY at HOME

Figure 12 *The red color of the rock at Capitol Reef National Park is due to the oxidation of iron.*

Figure 11 *Rust is a result of chemical weathering.*

REVIEW

1. Describe three ways abrasion occurs in nature.

2. Describe the similarity between the ways tree roots and ice mechanically weather rock.

3. **Making Generalizations** Why does acid precipitation weather rocks faster than normal precipitation does?

internet connect

SCiLINKS
NSTA

TOPIC: Weathering
GO TO: www.scilinks.org
*sci*LINKS **NUMBER:** HSTE230

Rates of Weathering

Different types of rock weather at different rates. Some types of rock weather quickly, while other types weather slowly. The rate at which a rock weathers depends on many factors—climate, elevation, and, most important, what the rock is made of.

Terms to Learn

differential weathering

What You'll Do

◆ Explain how the composition of rock affects the rate of weathering.

◆ Describe how a rock's total surface area affects the rate at which it weathers.

◆ Describe how mechanical and chemical weathering work together to break down rocks and minerals.

◆ Describe how differences in elevation and climate affect the rate of weathering.

Differential Weathering

Hard rocks, such as granite, weather more slowly than softer rocks, such as limestone. This is because granite is made of minerals that are generally harder and more chemically stable than the minerals in limestone. **Differential weathering** is a process by which softer, less weather-resistant rocks wear away, leaving harder, more weather-resistant rocks behind.

Figure 13 shows a spectacular landform that has been shaped by differential weathering. Devils Tower, the core of an ancient volcano, was once a mass of molten rock deep within an active volcano. When the molten rock solidified, it was protected from weathering by the softer rock of the volcano. After thousands of years of weathering, the soft outer parts of the volcano have worn away, leaving the harder, more resistant rock of Devils Tower behind. Of course, not all landforms are this spectacular. But if you look closely, you can see the effects of differential weathering in almost any landscape.

Figure 13 *Devils Tower is a landform known as a* volcanic neck. *The illustration is an artist's conception of how the original volcano may have looked. The photo inset shows Devils Tower as it appears today.*

The Shape of Weathering

As you know, weathering takes place on the outside surface of rocks. So the more surface area that is exposed to weathering, the faster the rock will be worn down. A large rock has a large surface area, but it also has a large volume. Because of this, it will take a long time for a large rock to wear down.

If a big rock is broken into smaller rocks, weathering occurs much more quickly. This is because a smaller rock has more surface area relative to its volume. This means that more of a small rock is exposed to the weathering process. The cubes in **Figure 14** show how this principle works.

Figure 14 *As surface area increases, total volume stays the same. Each square in the background represents the face of a cube.*

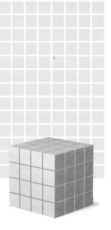

1 All cubes have both volume and surface area. The total surface area is equal to the sum of the areas of each of the six sides.

2 If you split the first cube into eight smaller cubes, you have the same amount of material (volume), but the surface area doubles.

3 If you split each of the eight cubes into eight smaller cubes, you have 64 cubes that together contain the same volume as the first cube. The total surface area, however, has doubled again!

÷ 5 ÷ Ω ≤ ∞ +Ω √ 9 ∞≤ Σ 2

MATH BREAK

The Power of 2

You can calculate the surface area of a square or rectangle by multiplying its width times its length ($w \times l$). For example, one side of a cube that measures 5 cm by 5 cm has a surface area of 25 cm^2. Now you try:

What is the surface area of one side of a cube that is 8 cm wide and 8 cm long? What is the surface area of the entire cube? (Hint: A cube has six equal sides.)

Weathering and Climate

Imagine that two people have the same kind of bicycle. The frames of both bikes are made of steel. One person lives in a hot, dry desert in New Mexico, and the other lives on the warm, humid coastline of Florida, as shown in **Figure 15.** Both bicycles are outside all the time. Which bike do you think will have more problems with rust?

Figure 15 *The climate in which this bike is located affects the rate at which it weathers, or rusts.*

If you think the Florida bike will have more rust problems, you are right! Rust is iron oxide, and oxidation occurs more quickly in warm, humid climates. This is true for bikes, rocks, or anything else that is affected by chemical weathering.

Weathering and Elevation

When a new mountain range forms, the rock is exposed to air and water. As a result, the mountain range gets slowly weathered down. Weathering occurs in the same way on mountains as it does everywhere else, but rocks at high elevations are exposed to more wind, rain, and ice than rocks at lower elevations.

Gravity also takes its toll. The steepness of mountain slopes strengthens the effects of mechanical and chemical weathering. Rainwater quickly runs off the sides of mountains, carrying sediment with it. This continual removal of sediment exposes fresh rock surfaces to the effects of weathering. When rocks fall away from the sides of mountains, new surfaces are exposed to weathering. As you have learned, the greater the surface area is, the faster weathering occurs. If new mountain ranges didn't keep forming, eventually there would be no mountains at all!

internetconnect

*sci*LINKS
NSTA

TOPIC: Rates of Weathering
GO TO: www.scilinks.org
*sci*LINKS **NUMBER:** HSTE233

REVIEW

1. How does surface area affect the rate of weathering?

2. How does climate affect the rate of weathering?

3. **Making Inferences** Does the rate at which a rock undergoes chemical weathering increase or stay the same when the rock becomes more mechanically weathered? Why?

From Bedrock to Soil

What You'll Do

◆ Define *soil.*
◆ Explain the difference between residual and transported soils.
◆ Describe the three soil horizons.
◆ Describe how various climates affect soil.

What is soil? The answer depends on who you ask. A farmer may have a different answer than an engineer. To a scientist, **soil** is a loose mixture of small mineral fragments and organic material. The layer of rock beneath soil is called **bedrock.**

Sources of Soil

Not all soils are the same. In fact, soils differ from one another in many ways. Because soils are made from weathered rock fragments, the type of soil that forms depends on the type of rock that weathers. For example, the soil that forms from granite will be different from the soil that forms from limestone. The rock that is the source of soil is called **parent rock.**

Figure 16 shows a layer of soil over bedrock. In this case, the bedrock is the parent rock because the soil above it formed from the bedrock below. Soil that remains above the bedrock from which it formed is called *residual soil.* Notice the trees growing in this soil. Plants and other organisms, plus chemical weathering from water, help break down the parent rock into soil.

After soil forms, it can be blown or washed away from its parent rock. Once the soil is deposited, it is called *transported soil.* **Figure 17** shows one way that soil is transported from one place to another. The movement of glaciers is also responsible for deposits of transported soil.

Living Things Also Add to Soil In addition to bits of rock, soils also contain very small particles of decayed plant and animal material called **humus** (HYU muhs). In other words, humus is the organic part of the soil. Humus contains nutrients necessary for plant growth. In general, soil that contains as much as 20–30 percent humus is considered to be very healthy soil for growing plants.

Figure 16 *Residual soil is soil that rests on top of its parent rock.*

Figure 17 *Transported soil may be moved long distances from its parent rock by rivers such as this one.*

255

Soil Layers

As you've already learned, much of the material in residual soil comes from the bedrock that lies below it. Because of the way it forms, soil often ends up in a series of layers, with humus-rich soil on top, sediment below that, and bedrock on the bottom. Geologists call these layers *horizons*. The word *horizon* tells you that the layers are horizontal. **Figure 18** shows what these horizons can look like. You can see these layers in some road cuts.

The top layer of soil is often called the **topsoil.** Topsoil contains more humus than the layers below it, so it is rich in the nutrients plants need in order to be healthy. This is why good topsoil is necessary for farming. Topsoil is in limited supply because it can take hundreds and even thousands of years to form.

Figure 18 *This is what the layers of soil might look like if you dug a hole down to bedrock.*

Horizon A This layer consists of the topsoil. Topsoil contains more humus than any other soil horizon.

Horizon B This layer is often called the *subsoil.* This is where clays and dissolved substances from horizon A collect. This layer contains less humus.

Horizon C This layer consists of partially weathered bedrock, which is usually the parent rock of the soil above.

Bedrock

As rainwater from the surface travels down through the horizons, it dissolves minerals, nutrients, and other substances from the soil above. This process is called **leaching.**

Soil and Climate

Soil types vary from place to place. As you know, this is partly due to differences in parent rocks. But it is also due to differences in climate. As you read on, you will see that climate can make big differences in the types of soil that develop around the world.

Tropical Climates   Take a look at **Figure 19.** In tropical climates the air is very humid and the land receives a large amount of rain. You might think that a lot of rain always leads to good soil for growing plants. But remember that as water moves through the soil, it leaches material from the topsoil downward. Heavy rains cause this downward movement to occur quickly and constantly. The result is that tropical topsoil is very thin.

The vegetation growing in the topsoil keeps heavy rains from eroding it away. The vegetation, in turn, depends on the thin topsoil because the subsoil will not support lush plant growth. Agricultural and mining practices that disrupt this fragile balance can expose the topsoil to erosion. Once the topsoil is gone, the original plants will not return, and the production of topsoil will stop.

Figure 19 *The soil in tropical rain forests supports some of the lushest vegetation on Earth. However, tropical topsoil is extremely thin.*

Desert Climates   While tropical climates get lots of rain, deserts get very little. Because of the lack of rain, deserts have very low rates of chemical weathering. When ground water trickles in from surrounding areas, some of it seeps upward. But as soon as the water gets close to the surface, it evaporates. This means that any materials that were dissolved in the water get left behind in the soil.

Often the chemicals left behind are various types of salts. The salts can sometimes get so concentrated that the soil becomes toxic, even to desert plants! This is one of the reasons for Death Valley's name. **Figure 20** shows the floor of Death Valley, in California.

Figure 20 *Very few plants can survive the harsh conditions of desert soils.*

Figure 21 *The rich soils in areas with a temperate climate support a vast farming industry.*

Temperate Climates Much of the continental United States has a temperate climate. An abundance of both mechanical and chemical weathering occurs in temperate climates. Temperate areas get enough rain to cause a high level of chemical weathering, but not so much that the nutrients are leached out. As a result, thick, fertile soils develop, as you can see in **Figure 21.**

Temperate soils are some of the most productive soils in the world. In fact, the midwestern part of the United States has earned the nickname "breadbasket" for the many crops the region's soil supports.

Arctic Climates You might not think that cold arctic climates are at all like desert climates. But many arctic areas have so little precipitation that they are actually cold deserts. As in the hot deserts, chemical weathering occurs very slowly, which means that soil formation also occurs slowly. This is why soil in arctic areas tends to be thin and is unable to support many plants, as shown in **Figure 22.**

Figure 22 *Arctic soils, such as the soil along Denali Highway, in Alaska, cannot support lush growth.*

internetconnect

SCi**LINKS**
NSTA

TOPIC: Soil and Climate
GO TO: www.scilinks.org
*sci***LINKS NUMBER:** HSTE235

REVIEW

1. What is the difference between residual and transported soils?

2. Which layer of soil is the most important for growing crops? Explain.

3. **Identifying Relationships** In which type of climate would leaching be more common—tropical or desert? Explain.

Soil Conservation

Terms to Learn

soil conservation
erosion

What You'll Do

◆ Describe three important benefits that soil provides.
◆ Describe three methods of preventing soil erosion.

If we do not take care of our soils, we can ruin them or even lose them altogether. Many people assume that if you simply plow a field and bury some seeds, plants will grow. They also assume that if you grew a crop last year, you can grow it again next year. These ideas might seem reasonable at first, but farmers and others involved with agriculture know better. Soil is a resource that must be conserved. **Soil conservation** consists of the various methods by which humans take care of the soil. Let's take a look at why soil is so important and worth conserving.

The Importance of Soil

Consider some of the benefits of soil. Soil provides minerals and other nutrients for plants. If the soil loses these nutrients, then plants will not be able to grow. Take a look at the plants shown in **Figure 23.** The plants on the bottom look unhealthy because they are not getting enough nutrients. Even though there is enough soil to support their roots, the soil is not providing them with the food they need. The plants on the top are healthy because the soil they live in is rich in nutrients.

Poor agricultural practices often cause rich soils to lose their nutrients. It is important to have healthy soil in order to have healthy plants. All animals get their energy from plants, either directly or indirectly.

Housing Soil also provides a place for animals to live. Earthworms, grubs, spiders, moles, and prairie dogs all live in soil. If the soil disappears, so do the homes of these animals. These animals are also important to the soil and to plant growth because they help break down plant and animal matter to make humus.

Figure 23 *Both photos above show the same crop. But the soil in the bottom photo is depleted of its nutrients.*

259

Figure 24 *When it rains, soil helps to store water that can later be used by plants and animals. When soil is removed or covered over, rainwater drains away.*

Storage Another benefit of soil is that it holds water, as shown in **Figure 24.** You might think of reservoirs, lakes, or even large tanks as places where water is stored. But soil is also extremely important in storing water. When water cannot sink into the ground, it quickly flows off somewhere else.

Now that we have looked at the importance of soil, let's look at some ways we can maintain soil.

Figure 25 *Some of the topsoil that was once in this field has eroded, and the subsoil that remains is less able to support plant growth.*

Preventing Soil Erosion

Erosion is the process by which wind and water transport soil and sediment from one location to another. When soil is left unprotected, it is subject to erosion. **Figure 25** shows a field that has been stripped of part of its topsoil because no plants were growing in it. So while plants need soil to grow, plants are needed to keep topsoil from being eroded by wind and water. Soil conservation practices, like those discussed on the next page, help ensure that the soil is preserved for generations to come.

Cover Crops Farmers can plant cover crops to prevent soil erosion. A *cover crop* is a crop that is planted between harvests to reduce soil erosion and to replace certain nutrients in the soil. Soybeans and clover are common cover crops.

Crop Rotation Fertile soil is soil that is rich in the nutrients that come from humus. If you grow the same crop year after year in the same field, certain nutrients become depleted. To slow this process down, crops can be changed from year to year. This practice, called *crop rotation,* is a common way to keep soils nutrient-rich.

Contour Plowing and Terracing How would you decide which direction to plow the rows in a field? If farmers plowed rows so that they ran up and down hills, what might happen during the first heavy rain? Hundreds of little river valleys would channel the rainwater down the hill, eroding the soil.

Take a look at the left-hand photo in **Figure 26.** Notice how the farmer has plowed across the slope of the hills instead of up and down the hills. This is called *contour plowing,* and it makes the rows act like a series of little dams instead of a series of little rivers. What if the hills are really steep? Farmers can use *terracing,* shown in the right-hand photo, to change one steep field into a series of smaller flat fields.

Nearly 4 billion metric tons of soil are washed or blown away from the United States every year. Worldwide, more than 70 billion metric tons of soil are lost each year to soil erosion!

Figure 26 *Contour plowing and terracing are effective methods of preventing soil erosion.*

REVIEW

1. Describe three essential benefits that soil provides.

2. How does crop rotation benefit soil?

3. List three methods of soil conservation, and describe how each helps to prevent the loss of soil.

4. **Applying Concepts** Why do all animals, even meat eaters, depend on soil to survive?

internet**connect**

SC*i*LINKS
NSTA

TOPIC: Soil Conservation
GO TO: www.scilinks.org
*sci*LINKS NUMBER: HSTE240

Chapter Highlights

Vocabulary

weathering *(p. 246)*

mechanical weathering *(p. 246)*

abrasion *(p. 247)*

chemical weathering *(p. 249)*

acid precipitation *(p. 249)*

oxidation *(p. 251)*

Section Notes

- Mechanical weathering is the breakdown of rock into smaller pieces by physical means.

- Ice wedging is a process by which water flows into cracks in rock and expands as it freezes, enlarging the cracks.

- The roots of plants can grow into cracks in rocks, and the roots can enlarge the cracks as they grow.

- Gravity, water, and wind are agents of abrasion in mechanical weathering.

- The activities of plants and animals can mechanically weather rock.

- Chemical weathering is the breakdown of rock into smaller pieces by chemical means.

- Water can dissolve some rocks and minerals.

- Sulfuric and nitric acids from pollution can cause chemical weathering.

- Natural acids found in air and water and produced by plants can cause chemical weathering.

- Oxidation can cause chemical weathering when oxygen combines with iron and other metallic elements.

Labs

Great Ice Escape *(p. 668)*

Rockin' Through Time *(p. 669)*

☑ Skills Check

Math Concepts

A CUBE'S TOTAL SURFACE AREA A cube has six sides—each is an identical square. To find the total surface area of a cube, first find the area of one of its sides. Then multiply the area of the square by 6 to find the total surface area of the cube. What is the total surface area of a cube that is 10 cm wide and 10 cm tall?

Area of a square = $l \times w$
Area of a cube = $6 (l \times w)$

$10 \text{ cm} \times 10 \text{ cm} = 100 \text{ cm}^2$
$6 \times 100 \text{ cm}^2 = 600 \text{ cm}^2$

Visual Understanding

DIFFERENTIAL WEATHERING When a volcano becomes extinct, molten rock solidifies beneath the surface, forming harder, more weather-resistant rock than the sides of the volcano are made of. Shown in Figure 13, Devils Tower is a dramatic example of differential weathering at work.

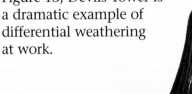

SECTION 2

Vocabulary

differential weathering (p. 252)

Section Notes

- The rate at which weathering occurs depends partly on the composition of the rock being weathered.

- The greater the surface area of a rock is, the faster the rate of weathering.

- Different climates promote different rates of weathering.

- Weathering usually occurs at a faster rate at higher elevations.

SECTION 3

Vocabulary

soil (p. 255)
bedrock (p. 255)
parent rock (p. 255)
humus (p. 255)
topsoil (p. 256)
leaching (p. 256)

Section Notes

- Soil is made up of loose, weathered material that can include organic material called humus.

- Residual soils rest on top of their parent rock, and transported soils collect in areas far from their parent rock.

- Soil usually consists of horizons, layers that are different from one another.

- Soil types vary, depending on the climate in which they form.

SECTION 4

Vocabulary

soil conservation (p. 259)
erosion (p. 260)

Section Notes

- Soils are important because they provide nutrients for plants, homes for animals, and storage for water.

- Soils need to be protected from nutrient depletion and erosion through the use of soil conservation methods.

Chapter Review

USING VOCABULARY

For each pair of terms, explain the difference in their meanings.

1. chemical weathering/mechanical weathering

2. oxidation/iron oxide

3. residual soil/transported soil

4. parent rock/bedrock

5. contour plowing/terracing

UNDERSTANDING CONCEPTS

Multiple Choice

6. Weathering by abrasion is usually caused by
   a. animals, plants, and wind.
   b. wind, water, and gravity.
   c. ice wedging, animals, and water.
   d. plants, gravity, and ice wedging.

7. Two acids found in acid precipitation are
   a. hydrochloric acid and sulfuric acid.
   b. nitric acid and hydrochloric acid.
   c. sulfuric acid and nitric acid.

8. Rust is produced by the oxidation of
   a. iron.   c. aluminum.
   b. tin.   d. manganese.

9. An acid normally involved in the formation of caves is
   a. nitric acid.
   b. hydrofluoric acid.
   c. hydrochloric acid.
   d. carbonic acid.

10. The soil horizon that contains humus is
    a. horizon A.   c. horizon C.
    b. horizon B.

11. The soil horizon that is made up of partially broken bedrock is
    a. horizon A.   c. horizon C.
    b. horizon B.

12. Tropical soils have the
    a. thickest horizon B.
    b. thickest horizon A.
    c. thinnest horizon A.
    d. thinnest horizon B.

13. The humus found in soils comes from
    a. parent rock.   c. bedrock.
    b. plants and   d. horizon B.
       animals.

14. Contour plowing means plowing
    a. up and down the slope of a hill.
    b. in steps along a hill.
    c. across the slope of a hill.
    d. in circles.

15. The main reason farmers use crop rotation is to slow down the process of
    a. soil removal by wind.
    b. soil removal by water.
    c. nutrient depletion.
    d. soil compaction.

Short Answer

16. Describe the two major types of weathering.

17. In what type of rock do caves usually form?

18. Why is Devils Tower higher than the surrounding area?

19. What can happen to soil when soil conservation is not practiced?

Concept Mapping

20. Use the following terms to create a concept map: weathering, chemical weathering, mechanical weathering, abrasion, ice wedging, oxidation, soil.

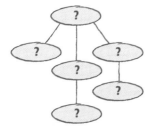

CRITICAL THINKING AND PROBLEM SOLVING

Write one or two sentences to answer the following questions:

21. Heat generally speeds up chemical reactions. But weathering, including chemical weathering, is usually slowest in hot, dry climates. Why is this?

22. How can too much rain deplete soil of its nutrients?

23. How does mechanical weathering speed up the effects of chemical weathering?

MATH IN SCIENCE

24. Imagine you are a geologist working in your natural laboratory—a mountainside. You are trying to find out the speed at which ice wedging occurs. You measure several cycles of freezing and thawing in a crack in a boulder. You discover that the crack gets deeper by about 1 mm per year. The boulder is 25 cm tall. Given this rate, how long will it take for ice wedging to split this boulder in half?

INTERPRETING GRAPHICS

The graph below shows how the density of water changes when temperature changes. The denser a substance is, the less volume it occupies. In other words, as most substances get colder, they contract and become more dense. But water is unlike most other substances—when it freezes, it expands and becomes less dense.

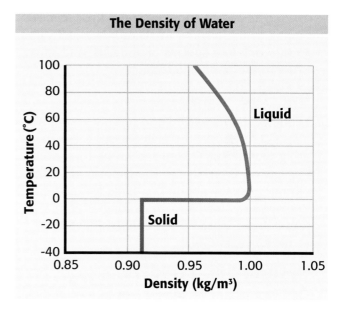

The Density of Water

25. Which will have the greater density, water at 40°C or water at −20°C?

26. How would the line in the graph look different if water behaved like most other liquids?

27. Which substance would be a more effective agent of mechanical weathering, water or some other liquid? Why?

Reading Check-up

Take a minute to review your answers to the Pre-Reading Questions found at the bottom of page 244. Have your answers changed? If necessary, revise your answers based on what you have learned since you began this chapter.

Worms of the Earth

How much do you know about earthworms? Did you know they have no eyes and no ears? And did you know they can be as small as 1 mm or as long as 3 m? Earthworms and their relatives belong to the phylum Annelida. There are almost 12,000 different species of annelids, and some of them are pretty interesting!

Big, Old Worms

The *Rhinodrilus* earthworm of South America is about 2 m long and weighs about 1 kg. That's a big worm! But Australia is home to a worm that grows even bigger. The Gippsland earthworm is usually about 1 m long, but some of these worms have grown as long as 3 m. And some Gippsland earthworms have lived to be 10 years old!

Natural Soil Builders

Earthworms are very important to forming soil. As they dig through the soil searching for food, the tunnels they create expose rocks and minerals to the effects of weathering. Over time, this makes new soil. And as the worms tunnel, they mix the soil, allowing air and water and smaller organisms to move deeper into the soil.

Worms have huge appetites. They eat organic matter and other materials in the soil. One earthworm can eat and digest about half its body weight each day! This would be like someone who weighs 50 kg eating more than 25 kg of food each day! And eating all that food means that earthworms leave behind a lot of waste. Earthworm wastes, called castings, are very high in nutrients and make excellent natural fertilizer. Castings enrich the soil and enhance plant growth.

Making More Soil

Worms build and fertilize the soil, and plants grow. Plants then help make more soil. As roots grow and seek out water and nutrients, they help break larger rock fragments into smaller ones. Have you ever seen a plant growing in a crack in the sidewalk? As the plant grows, its roots spread into tiny cracks in the sidewalk. These roots apply pressure to the cracks, and over time, the cracks get bigger.

The same process occurs in rocks in the soil and on mountainsides. No matter where this process occurs, as the cracks expand, more water runs into them and more weathering takes place. Slowly, new soil is made. Sooner or later, maybe after hundreds of years, worms will be burrowing through what remains of that sidewalk or mountainside.

On Your Own

▶ Using the Internet and the library, do some research about earthworms and their relatives. Learn more about *Rhinodrilus* and the Gippsland earthworm. Or find out about leeches, a relative of earthworms. Some people even think earthworms would make tasty burgers—what do you think of that idea?

▼ *Notice the rings on this night crawler. The name* annelida *comes from the Latin word* annellus, *which means "ring."*

EYE ON THE ENVIRONMENT

Losing Ground

▲ *In this example of sustainable farming, a new crop of soybeans grows up through the decaying remains of a corn crop.*

In the 1930s, massive dust storms in Oklahoma, Texas, Colorado, and New Mexico blew away the precious topsoil of many farms. Overplowing and a lack of rain caused this catastrophe—the Dust Bowl—that wreaked havoc on people's lives for 6 years. In the last 40 years, almost one-third of the world's topsoil has been lost to erosion. At the same time, the world's population has grown by 250,000 people per day. With more people to feed and less land to farm, some people are worried about having enough food to feed everyone.

Adding to the Problem

The topsoil on farmland is exposed to the full force of the weather. There are no trees to protect the loosely packed topsoil in a recently plowed field. Because of wind and water erosion, one hectare of farmland can lose more than 100,000 kg of soil in a year. Compare this loss to the mere 10–50 kg of soil lost in an average year by a forest densely packed with trees.

Tipping the Scales

In a healthy ecosystem, topsoil lost through erosion is replaced by other natural processes. These include the decomposition of organic matter by microorganisms and the breakdown of rocks by weathering. When a balance exists between the soil that is lost and the new soil that forms, the rate of topsoil loss is called sustainable. Currently, about 90 percent of the cropland in the United States is losing topsoil at a faster rate than is sustainable.

Sustainable Farming

The good news is that by changing their farming practices, many farmers have reduced the amount of soil lost from their fields. The critical step is to leave some plants growing in the ground. This protects the soil from the direct effects of wind and rain.

Many farmers have already switched to methods of sustainable farming. As the world's population continues to increase, more food will be needed. Because of this, preserving the topsoil that we have left will become more and more important.

On Your Own

▶ Find out what is meant by the term *desertification*. How does it relate to topsoil erosion?

CHAPTER 11

The Flow of Fresh Water

Pre-Reading
Questions

1. What role does water play in shaping the surface of the Earth?

2. What is the difference between erosion and deposition?

THE SOUND IS DEAFENING

You can hear the thundering roar of Iguaçu (EE gwah SOO) Falls for miles. The Iguaçu River travels more than 500 km across Brazil before it tumbles off the edge of a volcanic plateau in a series of 275 individual waterfalls separated by forested islands. Over the past 20,000 years, erosion has caused the falls to move 28 km upstream. Where will they be 20,000 years from now? In this chapter, you will learn how flowing water shapes Earth's surface.

STREAM WEAVERS

How do streams and river systems develop? Do the following activity to find out.

Procedure

1. Begin with a **bucket of sand** and enough **gravel** to fill the bottom of a **rectangular plastic washtub.**

2. Spread the gravel in a layer at the bottom of the washtub. Place 4–6 cm of sand on top of the gravel. Add more sand to one end of the washtub to form a slope.

3. Make a small hole in the bottom of a **paper cup.** Attach the cup to the inside of the tub with a **clothespin.** The cup should be placed at the end that has more sand. Fill the cup with water, and observe the **water** as it moves over the sand. Use a **magnifying lens** to observe features of the stream more closely.

4. Record your observations in your ScienceLog.

Analysis

5. At the start of your experiment, how did the moving water affect the sand?

6. As time passed, how did the moving water affect the sand?

7. Explain how this activity modeled the development of streams. In what ways was it accurate? How was it inaccurate?

The Flow of Fresh Water   **269**

Terms to Learn

erosion   divide
water cycle   channel
tributary   load
drainage basin

What You'll Do

◆ Illustrate the water cycle.
◆ Describe a drainage basin.
◆ Explain the major factors that affect the rate of stream erosion.
◆ Identify the stages of river development.

The Active River

You are probably familiar with the Grand Canyon, shown in **Figure 1.** But did you know that about 6 million years ago, the area now known as the Grand Canyon was nearly as flat as a pancake? The Colorado River cut down into the rock and formed the Grand Canyon over millions of years by washing billions of tons of soil and rock from its riverbed. This process is a type of *erosion*. **Erosion** is the removal and transport of surface material, such as rock and soil. Rivers are not the only agents of erosion. Wind, rain, ice, and snow can cause erosion as well.

Because of erosion caused by water, the Grand Canyon is now about 1.6 km deep and 446 km long. In this section, you will learn about stream development, river systems, and the different factors that affect the rate of stream erosion.

Figure 1 *The Grand Canyon is located in northwestern Arizona. It formed over millions of years as running water eroded rock and soil. In some places the canyon is 29 km wide.*

Water, Water Everywhere

Have you ever wondered how rivers keep flowing and where rivers get their water? The water cycle answers these and other questions. The **water cycle,** shown on the next page, is the continuous movement of water from water sources, such as lakes or oceans, into the air, onto land, into the ground, and back to the water sources.

The Water Cycle

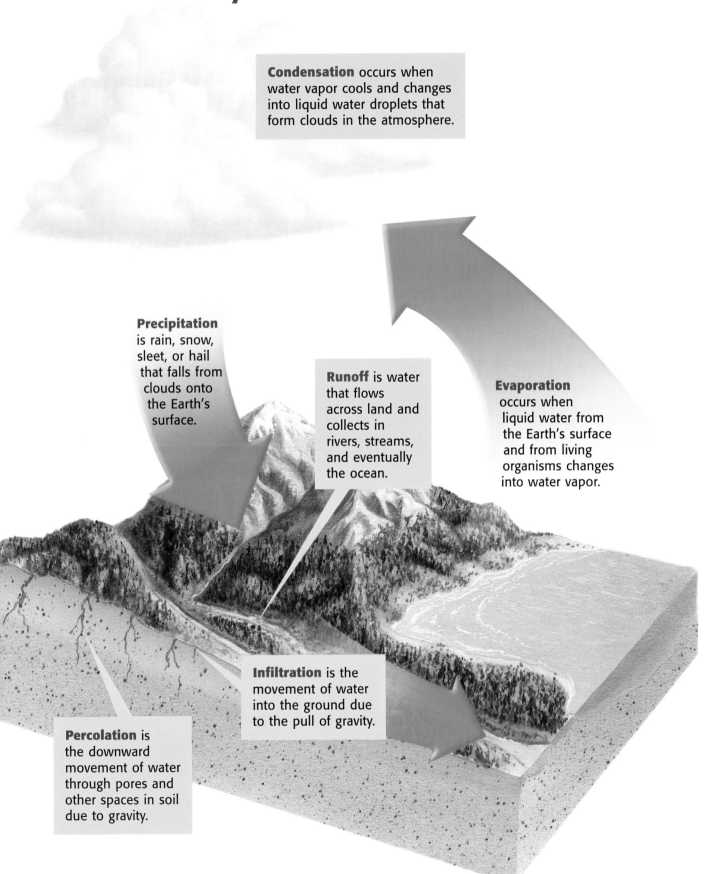

Condensation occurs when water vapor cools and changes into liquid water droplets that form clouds in the atmosphere.

Precipitation is rain, snow, sleet, or hail that falls from clouds onto the Earth's surface.

Runoff is water that flows across land and collects in rivers, streams, and eventually the ocean.

Evaporation occurs when liquid water from the Earth's surface and from living organisms changes into water vapor.

Infiltration is the movement of water into the ground due to the pull of gravity.

Percolation is the downward movement of water through pores and other spaces in soil due to gravity.

River Systems

Look at the pattern of lines on the palm of your hand. Notice how some of the smaller lines join together to form larger lines. Now imagine those lines are rivers and streams. The smaller lines would be the streams and tributaries and the larger lines would be rivers. **Tributaries** are smaller streams or rivers that flow into larger ones. Like the network of lines on the palm of your hand, streams and rivers make up a network on land. This network of streams and rivers is called a river system and it drains an area of its runoff.

Drainage Basins   River systems are divided into regions known as drainage basins. A **drainage basin,** or *watershed,* is the land drained by a river system, which includes the main river and all of its tributaries. The largest drainage basin in the United States is the Mississippi River basin. It has hundreds of tributaries that extend from the Rocky Mountains, in the West, to the Appalachian Mountains, in the East.

The map in **Figure 2** shows that the Mississippi River drainage basin covers more than one-third of the United States. Other major drainage basins in the United States are the Columbia, Rio Grande, and Colorado River basins.

Divides   Drainage basins are separated from each other by an area called a **divide.** A divide is generally an area of higher ground than the basins it separates. On the map below, you can see that the Continental Divide is a major divide in the United States. On which side do you live?

Continental Divide

Figure 2 *The Continental Divide runs through the Rocky Mountains. It separates the drainage basins that flow into the Atlantic Ocean and the Gulf of Mexico from those that flow into the Pacific Ocean.*

Stream Erosion

As a stream forms, it erodes soil and rock to create a channel. A **channel** is the path that a stream follows. At first, stream channels are small and steep. As more rock and soil are transported downstream, the channels become wider and deeper. When streams become longer, they are referred to as rivers. Have you ever wondered why some streams flow faster than others?

Gradient The stream shown in **Figure 3** is flowing down a steep mountain side. This stream has a high gradient. *Gradient* is the measure of the change in elevation over a certain distance. A high gradient gives a stream or river more energy to erode rock and soil. A river or stream with a low gradient, such as the one in **Figure 4,** has less energy for erosion.

Discharge The amount of water a stream or river carries in a given amount of time is called *discharge*. The discharge of a stream increases when a major storm occurs or when warm weather rapidly melts snow. As the stream's discharge increases, its erosive energy, speed, and load increase.

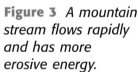

Calculating a Stream's Gradient

If a river starts at an elevation of 4,900 m and travels 450 km downstream to a lake that is at an elevation of 400 m, what is the stream's gradient?

Figure 3 *A mountain stream flows rapidly and has more erosive energy.*

Figure 4 *A river on a flat plain flows slowly and has less erosive energy.*

Load The materials carried in a stream's water are collectively called the stream's **load.** The size of the particles in the stream's load is affected by the stream's speed. Fast-moving streams can carry large particles. The load also affects the stream's rate of erosion. Rocks and pebbles bounce and scrape along the bottom and sides of the stream bed. The illustration below shows the three ways a stream can carry its load.

1 A stream can bounce large materials, such as pebbles and boulders, along the stream bed. These rocks are called the **bed load.**

2 A stream can carry small rocks and soil in suspension. These materials, called the **suspended load,** make the river look muddy.

3 Some material is carried in solution, meaning that the material is dissolved in the water. The **dissolved load** consists of dissolved materials, such as sodium and calcium.

✓ Self-Check

What would happen to a suspended load if the river slowed down? *(See page 726 to check your answer.)*

The Stages of a River

In the early 1900s, William Morris Davis developed a model that identified the stages of river development. According to this model, rivers evolve from a youthful stage to an old-age stage. Davis believed that all rivers erode in the same way and at the same rate. Today, however, scientists support a different model that considers the effects of a river's environment on stream development. For example, because different material erodes at different rates, one river may develop more quickly than another river. Many factors, including climate, gradient, and load, influence the development of a river. Although scientists no longer use Davis's model to explain river development, they still use many of his terms to describe a river. Remember, these terms do not tell the actual age of a river. Instead, they are used to describe the general characteristics of the river.

Youthful Rivers A youthful river, like the one shown in **Figure 5,** erodes its channel deeper rather than wider. The river flows quickly because of its steep gradient. Its sides and channel are steep and straight. The river tumbles over rocks in rapids and waterfalls. Youthful rivers have few tributaries.

Mature Rivers A mature river, as shown in **Figure 6,** erodes its channel wider rather than deeper. The gradient of a mature river is not as steep as that of a youthful river, and there are fewer falls and rapids. A mature river is fed by many tributaries, and because of its good drainage, it has more discharge than a younger river.

Figure 5 *This youthful river is located in Yellowstone National Park in Wyoming. The rapids and falls are located where the river flows over hard, resistant rock.*

Figure 6 *A mature river, such as this one in Peru, begins to curve back and forth. The bends in the river's channel are called* meanders.

Figure 7 *This old river is located in New Zealand.*

Old Rivers An old river has a low gradient and extremely low erosive power. Instead of widening and deepening its banks, the river deposits sediment in its channel and along its banks. Old rivers, like the one in **Figure 7,** are characterized by wide, flat *flood plains*, or valleys, and more meanders. Also, an older river has fewer tributaries than a mature river because the smaller tributaries have merged.

Rejuvenated Rivers Rejuvenated rivers occur where the land is raised by the Earth's tectonic forces. When land rises, the river's gradient becomes steeper. The increased gradient of a rejuvenated river allows the river to cut more deeply into the valley floor, as shown in **Figure 8.** Steplike *terraces* often form on both sides of a stream valley as a result of rejuvenation. Terraces are nearly flat portions of the landscape that end at a steep cliff.

Figure 8 *This rejuvenated river is located in Canyonlands National Park, Utah.*

internetconnect

*SCi*LINKS.
NSTA

TOPIC: Rivers and Streams
GO TO: www.scilinks.org
***sci*LINKS NUMBER:** HSTE260

REVIEW

1. How does the water cycle help to develop river systems?

2. Describe a drainage basin.

3. What are three factors that affect the rate of stream erosion?

4. **Summarizing Data** How do youthful, mature, and old rivers differ?

Terms to Learn

deposition   alluvial fan
alluvium   flood plain
delta

What You'll Do

◆ Describe the different types of stream deposits.
◆ Explain the relationship between rich agricultural regions and river flood plains.

Stream and River Deposits

You have learned that flowing rivers can pick up and move soil and rock. Sooner or later, this material must be deposited somewhere. **Deposition** is the process by which material is dropped, or settles. Imagine a mud puddle after a rainy day. If the water is not disturbed, the soil particles will eventually settle and the muddy water will become clear again. Deposition also forms and renews some of the world's most productive soils. People who live in the lower Mississippi River valley, for example, depend on the river to bring them new, fertile soil.

Deposition in Water

After rivers erode rock and soil, they deposit the rock and soil downstream. Rock and soil deposited by streams is called **alluvium.** Alluvium is dropped at places in a river where the speed of the current decreases. Take a look at **Figure 9** to see how this type of deposition occurs.

Figure 9 *This model illustrates erosion and deposition at a bend, or meander, of a river.*

a Erosion occurs on the outside bank where the water flows faster.

b Deposition occurs along the inside bank where the water flows slower.

Heavy minerals are sometimes deposited at places in a river where the current slows down. This kind of alluvium is called a *placer deposit*. Some placer deposits contain gold, as **Figure 10** shows. During the California gold rush, which began in 1849, many miners panned for gold in the placer deposits of rivers.

Designing a Delta The current also slows when a river empties into a large body of water, such as a lake or an ocean. Much of the river's load may be deposited where the river reaches the large body of water, forming a fan-shaped deposit called a **delta**. In **Figure 11** you can see an astronaut's view of the Nile Delta. A delta usually forms on a flat surface and consists mostly of mud. These mud deposits form new land, causing the coastline to grow.

Figure 10 *Miners rushed to California in the 1850s to find gold. They often found it in the bends of rivers in placer deposits.*

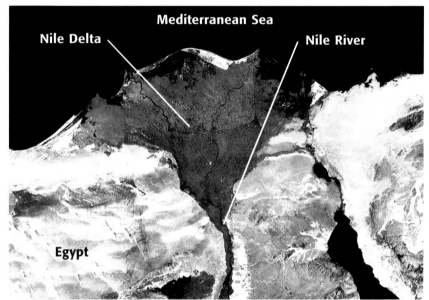

Figure 11 *Alluvium is dropped at the mouth of the Nile River, forming a delta.*

If you look back at the map of the Mississippi River drainage basin in Figure 2, you can see where the Mississippi River flows into the Gulf of Mexico. This is where the Mississippi Delta has formed. Each of the fine mud particles in the delta began its journey far upstream. Parts of Louisiana are made up of particles that were transported from as far away as Montana, Minnesota, Ohio, and Illinois.

Astronomy
CONNECTION

The remains of an ancient riverbed have been discovered on Mars. Satellite images show the deposits of stream channels, which indicate that liquid water once existed on the surface of this now dry and frozen planet.

✔ Self-Check

What is one factor that causes the current of a river to slow? *(See page 726 to check your answer.)*

Deposition on Land

When a fast-moving mountain stream flows onto a flat plain, the stream slows down. As the stream slows down, it deposits alluvium where the mountain meets the flat plain, forming an alluvial fan, such as the one shown in **Figure 12.** **Alluvial fans** are fan-shaped deposits that form on dry land.

During periods of high rainfall or rapid snowmelt, a sudden increase in the volume of water flowing into a stream can cause the stream to overflow its banks, flooding the surrounding land. This land is called a **flood plain.** When a stream floods, a layer of alluvium is deposited across the flood plain. Each flood adds another layer of alluvium.

Fatal Flooding Flood plains are very rich farming areas because periodic flooding brings new soil to the land. However, flooding can cause extensive property damage. Much farming activity takes place in the Mississippi River valley, a large flood plain with very rich soil. When the Mississippi River flooded in 1993, however, farms were abandoned and whole towns had to be evacuated. The flood was so huge that it caused damage in nine Midwestern states. **Figure 13** shows an area that was flooded just north of St. Louis, Missouri.

Figure 12 *An alluvial fan, such as this one from the Sierra Nevada, in California, forms when an eroding stream changes rapidly into a depositing stream.*

Figure 13 *The normal flow of the Mississippi River and Missouri River is shown in black. The area that was flooded when both rivers spilled over their banks in 1993 is shaded red.*

REVIEW

1. What happens to a river's flow that causes alluvium to be deposited?

2. How are alluvial fans and deltas similar? How are they different?

3. Explain why flood plains are good farming areas.

4. **Identifying Relationships** What factors increase the likelihood that alluvium will be deposited?

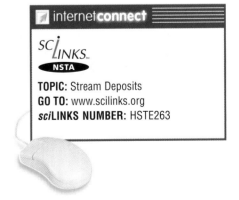

internetconnect

SC*LINKS*
NSTA

TOPIC: Stream Deposits
GO TO: www.scilinks.org
*sci***LINKS NUMBER:** HSTE263

Water Underground

Although we can see surface water in streams and lakes, there is a lot of water flowing underground that we cannot see. The water located within the rocks below the Earth's surface is called **ground water.** Ground water not only is an important resource but also plays an important role in erosion and deposition.

Terms to Learn

ground water
water table
aquifer
porosity

permeability
recharge zone
artesian spring

What You'll Do

◆ Identify and describe the location of a water table.
◆ Describe the characteristics of an aquifer.
◆ Explain how caves and sinkholes form as a result of erosion and deposition.

Location of Ground Water

Surface water seeps underground into the soil and rock. Earth scientists divide this underground area into two zones. The upper zone, called the *zone of aeration,* usually is not completely filled with water. The rock and soil that make up this zone are filled with water only immediately after a rain. Farther down, the water accumulates in an area called the *zone of saturation.* Here the spaces between the rock particles are filled with water.

These two zones meet at an underground boundary known as the **water table,** as shown in **Figure 14.** The water table rises during wet seasons and drops during dry seasons. In wet regions the water table can be just beneath the soil's surface or at the surface. But in deserts the water table may be hundreds of meters underground.

Figure 14 *The water table is the upper surface of the zone of saturation.*

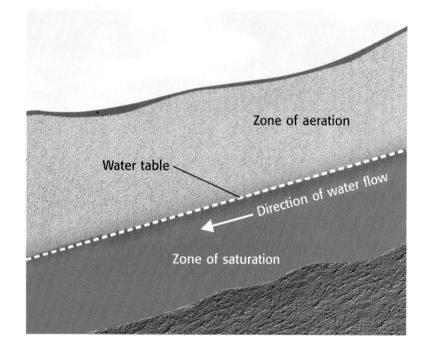

Zone of aeration

Water table

Direction of water flow

Zone of saturation

Aquifers

Some types of rock can hold large quantities of water, while other types can hold little or no water. A rock layer that stores and allows the flow of ground water is called an **aquifer.**

To qualify as an aquifer, a rock layer must be *porous,* or contain open spaces. A rock's **porosity** is the amount of open space between individual rock particles. The rock layer must also allow water to pass freely through it, from one pore to another. If the pores are connected, ground water can flow through the rock layer. A rock's ability to let water pass through it is called **permeability.** A rock that tends to stop the flow of water is impermeable.

Aquifer Geology and Geography The best aquifers are usually formed of sandstone, limestone, or layers of sand and gravel. Some aquifers cover large underground areas and are an important source of water for cities and agriculture. The map in **Figure 15** shows the location of aquifers in the United States.

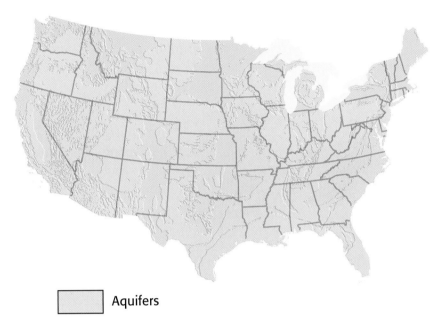

☐ Aquifers

Figure 15 **Aquifers in the Continental United States**

Recharge Zones Like rivers, aquifers are dependent on the water cycle to maintain a constant flow of water. The ground surface where water enters an aquifer is called the **recharge zone.** The size of the recharge zone varies depending on how permeable rock is at the surface. In an area that contains a permeable rock layer, the water can seep down into the aquifer. In areas where the aquifer is confined on top by an impermeable rock layer, the recharge zone is restricted to areas where there is a permeable rock layer.

Springs and Wells

Ground-water movement is determined by the slope of the water table. Just like surface water, ground water tends to move downslope, toward lower elevations. If the water table reaches the Earth's surface, water will flow out from the ground, forming a *spring*. Springs are an important source of drinking water. Lakes form in low areas, where the water table is higher than the Earth's surface.

Degree of Permeability

1. Obtain five **plastic-foam cups.**

2. Fill one cup halfway with **soil,** such as garden soil. Pack the soil.

3. Fill a second cup halfway with **sand.** Pack the sand.

4. Poke 5 to 7 holes in the bottom of each cup with a sharpened **pencil.**

5. Fill a third cup with **water.** Hold one of the remaining empty cups under the cup filled with soil. Pour the water into the top cup.

6. Allow the cup to drain for 45 seconds, and then put the cup aside (even if it is still draining). Put the cup filled with water aside.

7. Repeat steps 5 and 6 with the cup of sand. Compare the volumes of the two cups of water. The cup that allowed the most water to pass holds the more permeable sediment.

TRY at HOME

A mud pie the size of a house—where would you see something like that? Turn to page 294 to find out.

Artesian Springs A sloping layer of permeable rock sandwiched between two layers of impermeable rock is called an *artesian formation.* The permeable rock is an aquifer, and the top layer of the impermeable rock is called a *cap rock,* as shown in **Figure 16.** Artesian formations are the source of water for **artesian springs.** Artesian springs are springs that form where cracks occur naturally in the cap rock and the pressurized water in the aquifer flows through the cracks to the surface. Artesian springs are sometimes found in deserts, where they are often the only source of water.

Figure 16 *Artesian springs form when water from an aquifer flows through cracks in the cap rock of an artesian formation.*

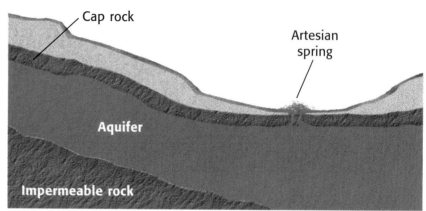

Wells A *well* is a human-made hole that is deeper than the level of the water table; therefore, wells fill with ground water, as shown in **Figure 17.** If a well is not deep enough, it will dry up when the water table falls below the bottom of the well. Also, if too many wells in an area remove ground water too rapidly, the water table will drop and all the wells will run dry.

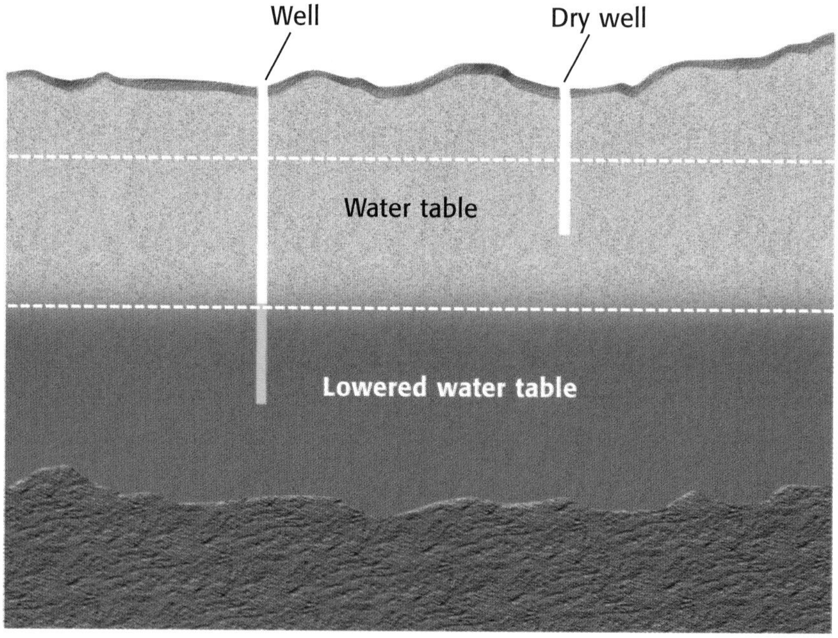

Figure 17 *A good well is drilled deep enough so that when the water table drops, the well still contains water.*

Self-Check

Why is it important that there is a layer of impermeable rock in an artesian formation? *(See page 726 to check your answer.)*

Underground Erosion and Deposition

Unlike a river, which erodes its banks when water moves over rock and soil, ground water erodes certain types of rock by dissolving the rock. Most of the world's caves formed over thousands of years as ground water dissolved limestone. Limestone, which is made of calcium carbonate, dissolves easily in water. As a result, caves form. Some caves reach spectacular proportions, such as the one in **Figure 18.**

Figure 18 *At Carlsbad Caverns, in New Mexico, underground passages and enormous "rooms" have been eroded below the surface of the Earth.*

Cave Formations While caves are formed by erosion, they also show signs of deposition. Water that drips from a crack in a cave's ceiling leaves behind deposits of calcium carbonate. These deposits of calcium carbonate are a type of limestone called *dripstone*. Water and dissolved limestone can drip downward into sharp, icicle-shaped dripstone features known as a stalactites. At the same time, water drops that fall to the cave's floor add to cone-shaped dripstone features known as stalagmites. If water drips long enough, the stalactites and stalagmites can reach each other and join, forming a dripstone column.

Environment
CONNECTION

Most bat species live in caves. These night-flying mammals navigate by sound and can reach speeds of 95 km/h. Today scientists know that bats play an extremely important role in the environment. Bats are great consumers of insects, and many bat species pollinate plants and distribute seeds.

Sinkholes When the water table is lower than the level of a cave, the cave is no longer supported by the water underneath. The roof of the cave can then collapse, leaving a circular depression called a *sinkhole.* Surface streams can "disappear" into sinkholes and then flow through underground caves. Sinkholes often form lakes in areas where the water table is high. Central Florida is covered with hundreds of round sinkhole lakes. **Figure 19** shows how underground caves can affect a landscape.

Figure 19 *This city block shows the effects of a sinkhole in Winter Park, Florida.*

internet**connect**

SC*LINKS*
NSTA

TOPIC: Water Underground
GO TO: www.scilinks.org
*sci***LINKS NUMBER:** HSTE265

REVIEW

1. What is the water table?

2. What is an aquifer?

3. What are some of the features formed by underground erosion and deposition?

4. **Analyzing Relationships** What is the relationship between the zone of aeration, the zone of saturation, and the water table?

Section 4

point-source pollution
nonpoint-source pollution
sewage treatment plant
septic tank

What You'll Do

- Describe the stages of treatment for water at a sewage treatment plant.
- Compare a septic system with a sewage treatment plant.
- Explain how ground water can be both a renewable and a nonrenewable resource.

Using Water Wisely

All living things need water to survive. But there is a limited amount of fresh water available on Earth. Only 3 percent of Earth's water is drinkable. And of the 3 percent that is drinkable, 75 percent is frozen in the polar icecaps. That's more than 100 times the volume of water found in the Earth's lakes and streams! This frozen water is not readily available for our use. Therefore, it is important that we use our water resources wisely.

Water Pollution

Surface water, such as rivers and lakes, and ground water are often polluted by waste from cities, factories, and farms. One type of pollution is called **point-source pollution** because it comes from one particular point, such as a sewer pipe or a factory drain. Fortunately, laws prohibit much of this type of pollution.

There is growing concern, however, about another type of pollution, called **nonpoint-source pollution.** This type of pollution, as shown in **Figure 20,** is much more difficult to control because it does not come from a single source. Most nonpoint-source pollution contaminates rivers and lakes by runoff. The main sources of nonpoint-source pollution are street gutters, fertilizers, eroded soils and silt from farming and logging, drainage from mines, and salts from irrigation.

As you know, ground water is an important source of fresh water. In fact, more than half of all household water in the United States comes from ground water. Farms use ground water for irrigation. Because ground water is supplied by water from the Earth's surface, ground water can become contaminated when surface water is polluted. And once polluted, ground water is very difficult to clean up.

Figure 20 *The runoff from this irrigation system could collect pesticides and other pollutants. The result would be nonpoint-source pollution.*

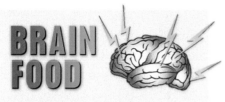
Cleaning Polluted Water

When you flush the toilet or watch water go down the shower drain, do you ever wonder where this water goes? If you live in a city or large town, the water flows through sewer pipes to a sewage treatment plant. **Sewage treatment plants** are factories that clean the waste materials out of water that comes from the sewer or drains. These plants help protect the environment from water pollution. They also protect us from diseases that are easily transmitted through dirty water.

Primary Treatment When water reaches a sewage treatment plant, it is cleaned in two different ways. First it goes through a series of steps known as *primary treatment*. In primary treatment, dirty water is passed through a large screen to catch solid objects, such as paper, rags, and bottle caps. The water is then placed in a large tank, where smaller particles can sink and be filtered out. These particles include things such as food, coffee grounds, and soil. Any floating oils and scum are skimmed off the surface.

Secondary Treatment At this point, the water is ready for *secondary treatment*. In secondary treatment, the water is sent to an aeration tank, where it is mixed with oxygen and bacteria. The bacteria feed on the wastes and use the oxygen. The water is then sent to another settling tank, where chlorine is added to disinfect the water. The water is finally released into a water source—a stream, a lake, or the ocean. **Figure 21** shows the major components of a sewage treatment plant.

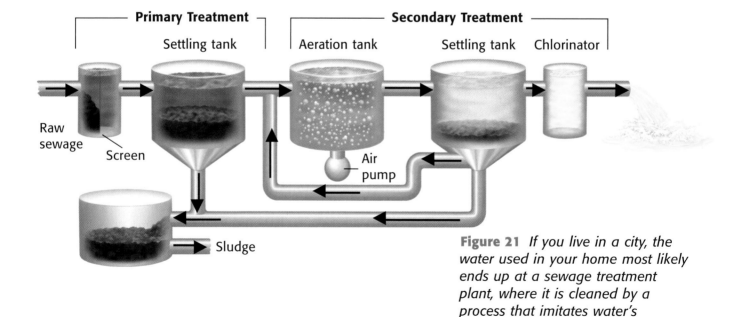

Figure 21 *If you live in a city, the water used in your home most likely ends up at a sewage treatment plant, where it is cleaned by a process that imitates water's natural cleaning cycle.*

Another Way to Clean Waste Water If you live in an area without a sewage treatment plant, your house probably has a septic tank, such as the one shown in **Figure 22**. A **septic tank** is a large underground tank that collects and cleans waste water from a household. Waste water flows from the house into the tank, where the solids sink to the bottom. Bacteria consume these wastes on the bottom of the tank. The water flows from the tank into a group of buried pipes. The buried pipes distribute the water, enabling it to soak into the ground. This group of pipes is called a *drain field*.

Get your hands dirty and learn about some of the methods used to clean up water. Check out page 672 of the LabBook.

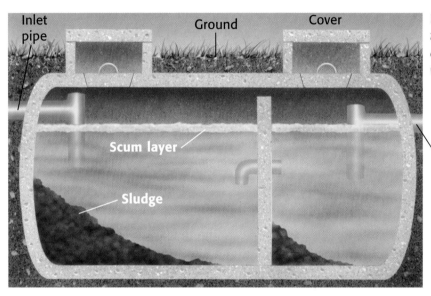

Inlet pipe · Ground · Cover

Scum layer

Sludge

Outlet pipe

Figure 22 *Most septic tanks must be cleaned out every few years in order to work properly.*

Where the Water Goes

The chart in **Figure 23** shows how an average household in the United States uses water. Notice that less than 8 percent of the water we use in our homes is used for drinking. The rest is used for flushing toilets, doing laundry, bathing, and watering lawns and plants.

Lawn watering, car washing, and pool maintenance—32%

Bathing, toilet flushing, and laundry—60%

Drinking, cooking, washing dishes, running a garbage disposal—8%

Figure 23 *The average household in the United States uses about 100 gal of water per day. This pie chart shows some common uses of this 100 gal.*

Activity

Study the chart at left and determine where the majority of water is used. Think of some ways that you can decrease the amount of water that you use in your home. Share your suggestions with your class.

TRY at HOME

Water in Industry The chart on the previous page shows how fresh water is used in homes. Even more water is required for industry, as shown in **Figure 24.** Water is used to cool power stations, to clean industrial products, to extract minerals, and to create power for factories. Many industries are trying to conserve water by reusing it in their production processes. In the United States, most of the water used in factories is recycled at least once. At least 90 percent of this water can be treated and returned to surface water.

Ground-water supplies also need to be monitored. Although ground water is considered to be a *renewable resource*, a resource that can be replenished, recycling ground water can be a lengthy process. When overused, ground water can sometimes be categorized as a *nonrenewable resource*, a substance that cannot be replaced once it is used. Ground water collects and moves slowly, and water taken from some aquifers might not be replenished for many years.

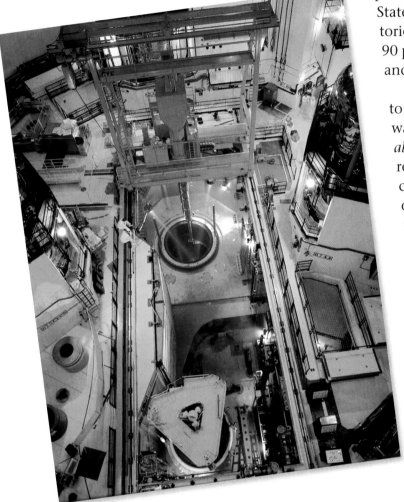

Figure 24 *The core of a nuclear reactor is cooled by water.*

APPLY

Wasting Water?

How much water do you use when you brush your teeth? Picture yourself at home brushing your teeth. Time how long it takes you to go through the procedure. In your ScienceLog, write down the steps you take, making sure to include how many times you turn on and turn off the faucet. During what percentage of the time spent brushing your teeth is the water running? How do you think you might be wasting water? What are some ways that you could conserve water while brushing your teeth?

Water in Agriculture The Ogallala aquifer is the largest known aquifer in North America. The map in **Figure 25** shows that the Ogallala aquifer runs beneath the ground through eight states, from South Dakota to Texas. For the last 100 years, the aquifer has been used heavily for farming. The Ogallala aquifer provides water for approximately one-fifth of the cropland in the United States. Recently, the water table in the aquifer has dropped so low that some scientists say that it would take at least 1,000 years to replenish the aquifer if it were no longer used.

The Ogallala aquifer can hold enough water to fill Lake Huron. At this time, however, the aquifer is being used 25 times as fast as it is being replenished.

Figure 25 *Because the Ogallala aquifer has been such a good source of ground water, it has become overused. The water table has dropped more than 30 m in some areas.*

Water resources are different from other resources. Because water is necessary for life, there is no alternative resource. Aquifers are often overused and therefore do not have time to replenish themselves. Like surface water, ground water must be conserved.

REVIEW

1. What is the difference between nonpoint-source and point-source pollution?

2. Summarize the process of water treatment in a sewage treatment plant.

3. What is the difference between a renewable resource and a nonrenewable resource?

4. **Summarizing Data** How does a septic tank work?

internetconnect

SCiLINKS
NSTA

TOPIC: Water Pollution and Conservation
GO TO: www.scilinks.org
*sci*LINKS **NUMBER:** HSTE270

Chapter Highlights

SECTION 1

Vocabulary

erosion *(p. 270)*
water cycle *(p. 270)*
tributary *(p. 272)*
drainage basin *(p. 272)*
divide *(p. 272)*
channel *(p. 273)*
load *(p. 274)*

Section Notes

- Erosion is the removal and transport of soil and rock.

- The water cycle is the continuous movement of water from water sources into the air, onto land, and back into water sources.

- A drainage basin, or watershed, includes a main river and all of its tributaries.

- The rate of stream erosion is affected by many factors, including the stream's gradient, discharge, speed, and load.

- Gradient is the change in elevation over distance.

- Discharge is the volume of water moved by a stream in a given amount of time.

- A stream's load is the material a stream can carry.

- Rivers can be described as youthful, mature, old, or rejuvenated.

Labs

Water Cycle—What Goes Up . . . *(p. 670)*

SECTION 2

Vocabulary

deposition *(p. 277)*
alluvium *(p. 277)*
delta *(p. 278)*
alluvial fan *(p. 279)*
flood plain *(p. 279)*

Section Notes

- Deposition occurs when eroded soil and rock are dropped.

- Alluvium is the material deposited by rivers and streams.

- Deltas are deposits of alluvium at a river's mouth.

- Alluvial fans are deposits of alluvium at the base of a mountain.

- Flood plains are rich farming areas because flooding brings new soils to the area.

☑ Skills Check

Math Concepts

A STREAM'S GRADIENT One factor that can affect the speed of a river is its gradient. The gradient is a measure of the change in elevation over a certain distance. You can use the following equation to calculate a stream's gradient:

$$\text{gradient} = \frac{\text{change in elevation}}{\text{distance}}$$

For example, consider a river that starts at an elevation of 5,500 m and travels 350 km downstream to a lake, which is at an elevation of 2,000 m. By using the formula above, you would find the stream's gradient to be 10 m/km.

$$10 \text{ m/km} = \frac{(5{,}500 \text{ m} - 2{,}000 \text{ m})}{350 \text{ km}}$$

Visual Understanding

A STREAM'S LOAD Look back at the diagram on page 274 to review the different types of loads a stream can carry.

A SEWAGE TREATMENT PLANT Study Figure 21 on page 286 to review the two processes used to clean water in a sewage treatment plant.

Vocabulary

ground water *(p. 280)*

water table *(p. 280)*

aquifer *(p. 280)*

porosity *(p. 280)*

permeability *(p. 280)*

recharge zone *(p. 281)*

artesian spring *(p. 282)*

Section Notes

- Ground water is located below the Earth's surface.

- Ground water can dissolve rock, especially limestone.

- The zone of aeration and the zone of saturation meet at a boundary called the water table.

- An aquifer is a porous and permeable rock layer through which ground water flows.

- A sinkhole forms when the water table is lower than the roof of an underground cave.

Vocabulary

point-source pollution *(p. 285)*

nonpoint-source pollution *(p. 285)*

sewage treatment plant *(p. 286)*

septic tank *(p. 287)*

Section Notes

- Sewage is treated in sewage treatment plants and in septic tanks.

- In a sewage treatment plant, water is cleaned in two different ways—primary treatment and secondary treatment.

- While water is generally considered to be a renewable resource, when overused it can sometimes be categorized as a nonrenewable resource.

Labs

Clean Up Your Act *(p. 672)*

---

internet connect

GO TO: go.hrw.com

Visit the **HRW** Web site for a variety of learning tools related to this chapter. Just type in the keyword:

KEYWORD: HSTDEP

GO TO: www.scilinks.org

Visit the **National Science Teachers Association** on-line Web site for Internet resources related to this chapter. Just type in the *sci*LINKS number for more information about the topic:

TOPIC: The Grand Canyon	*sci*LINKS NUMBER: HSTE255
TOPIC: Rivers and Streams	*sci*LINKS NUMBER: HSTE260
TOPIC: Stream Deposits	*sci*LINKS NUMBER: HSTE263
TOPIC: Water Underground	*sci*LINKS NUMBER: HSTE265
TOPIC: Water Pollution and Conservation	*sci*LINKS NUMBER: HSTE270

Chapter Review

USING VOCABULARY

For each set of terms, identify the term that doesn't belong, and explain why.

1. tributary/river/water table

2. load/recharge zone/aquifer

3. delta/alluvial fan/divide

4. porosity/permeability/deposition

5. point-source pollution/nonpoint-source pollution/septic tank

6. primary treatment/secondary treatment/drainage basin

UNDERSTANDING CONCEPTS

Multiple Choice

7. Which of the following processes is not part of the water cycle?
   a. evaporation
   b. infiltration
   c. condensation
   d. deposition

8. Which type of stream load makes a river look muddy?
   a. bed load
   b. dissolved load
   c. suspended load
   d. gravelly load

9. What features are common in youthful river channels?
   a. meanders
   b. flood plains
   c. rapids
   d. sandbars

10. Which depositional feature is found at the coast?
    a. delta
    b. flood plain
    c. alluvial fan
    d. placer deposit

11. Caves are mainly a product of
    a. erosion by rivers.
    b. river deposition.
    c. water pollution.
    d. erosion by ground water.

12. The largest drainage basin in the United States is the
    a. Amazon.
    b. Columbia.
    c. Colorado.
    d. Mississippi.

13. An aquifer must be
    a. nonporous and nonpermeable.
    b. nonporous and permeable.
    c. porous and nonpermeable.
    d. porous and permeable.

14. Which of the following is a point source of water pollution?
    a. fertilizer from a farming area
    b. runoff from city streets
    c. a wastewater pipe
    d. leaking septic tanks

15. During primary treatment at a sewage treatment plant,
    a. water is sent to an aeration tank.
    b. water is mixed with bacteria and oxygen.
    c. dirty water is passed through a large screen.
    d. water is sent to a settling tank where chlorine is added.

Short Answer

16. What is the relationship between tributaries and rivers?

17. How are aquifers replenished?

18. Why are caves usually found in limestone-rich regions?

Concept Mapping

19. Use the following terms to create a concept map: zone of aeration, zone of saturation, water table, gravity, porosity, permeability.

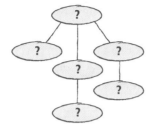

CRITICAL THINKING AND PROBLEM SOLVING

Write one or two sentences to answer the following questions:

20. What role does water play in erosion and deposition?

21. What are the features of a river channel that has a steep gradient?

22. Why is ground water hard to clean up?

23. Imagine you are hiking beside a mature stream. What would the stream be like?

24. How can water be considered both a renewable and a nonrenewable resource? Give an example of each case.

MATH IN SCIENCE

25. A sinkhole has formed in a town with a population of 5,000. The town is declared a disaster area, and $2 million is given to the town by the federal government. The local government uses 60 percent of the money for repairs to city property, and the rest is given to the townspeople.
    a. How much would each person receive?
    b. If there are 2,000 families in the town, how much would each family receive?
    c. Would each family receive enough money to help them rebuild a home? If not, how could the money be distributed more fairly?

INTERPRETING GRAPHICS

The hydrograph below illustrates river flow over a period of 1 year. The discharge readings are from the Yakima River, in Washington. The Yakima River flows eastward from the Cascade Mountains to the Columbia River.

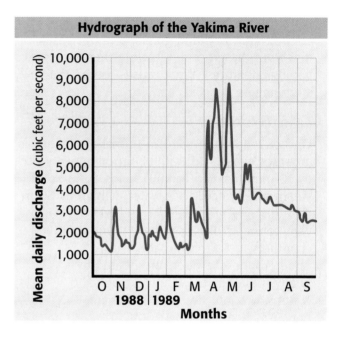

Hydrograph of the Yakima River

26. In which months is there the highest river discharge?

27. Why is there such a high river discharge during these months?

28. What might cause the peaks in river discharge between November and March?

Reading Check-up Take a minute to review your answers to the Pre-Reading Questions found at the bottom of page 268. Have your answers changed? If necessary, revise your answers based on what you have learned since you began this chapter.

WEIRD SCIENCE

BUBBLE, BOIL, & SQUIRT

In parts of Yellowstone National Park boiling water blasts into the sky, lakes of strange-colored mud boil and gurgle, and hot gases hiss from the ground. What are these strange geologic features? What causes them? The story begins deep in the Earth.

Old Geysers

One of Yellowstone's main tourist attractions is a *geyser* called Old Faithful. Erupting every 60 to 70 minutes, Old Faithful sends a plume of steam and scalding-hot water as high as 60 m into the air. A geyser is formed when a narrow vent connects one or more underground chambers to Earth's surface. These underground chambers are heated by nearly molten rock. As underground water flows into the vent and chambers, it is heated above 100°C. The superheated water quickly turns to steam and explodes first toward the surface and then into the air. And Old Faithful erupts right on schedule!

Nature's Hot Tub

A *hot spring* is a geyser without pressure. Its vents are wider than a geyser's, and they let the underground water cool a little and flow to the surface rather than erupt in a big fountain. To be called a hot spring, the water must be at least as warm as human body temperature (37°C). Some underground springs are several hundred degrees Celsius.

Flying Mud Pies

Mud pots form when steam or hot underground water trickles to the surface and chemically weathers and dissolves surface features, such as rocks. The mixture of dissolved rock and water creates a boiling, bubbling pool of sticky liquid clay. But don't get too close! Occasionally, the steam will rise quickly and forcefully enough to make the mud pot behave like a volcano. When it does, a mud pot can toss car-sized gobs of mud high into the air!

Some mud pots become *paint pots* when microorganisms or brightly colored minerals are mixed in. For instance, if there is a lot of iron in the mud, the paint pot will turn reddish brown or yellowish brown. Other minerals and bacteria can make the mud white or bluish in color. Some paint pots may even gurgle up blobs in several different colors.

▲ *Mud Pot in Yellowstone National Park*

What Do You Think?

▶ Some people believe that tapping geothermal energy sources such as geysers could harm the delicate ecology of those sources. Find out about the benefits and the risks of using geothermal energy. What is your opinion?

EYE ON THE ENVIRONMENT
Disaster Along the Delta

As the sun rises over the delta wetlands of the Mississippi River, fishermen test their skills. Long-legged birds step lightly through the marsh, hunting fish or frogs for breakfast. And hundreds of species of plants and animals start another day in this fragile ecosystem. But the delta ecosystem is in danger of being destroyed.

The threat comes from efforts to make the Mississippi more useful. Large portions of the river bottom were dredged to make the river deeper for ship traffic. Underwater channels were built to control flooding. What no one realized was that sediments that were once deposited to form new land now pass through the deep channels and flow out into the ocean.

Those river sediments replaced the land that was lost every year to erosion. Without the sediments, the river can't replace the land lost to erosion. And so the Mississippi River delta is disappearing. By 1995, more than half the wetlands were already gone, swept out to sea by waves along the Louisiana coast.

▲ *The Mississippi River flows from Minnesota through the Midwest to the Gulf of Mexico in the southern United States.*

Sedimental Journey

The Mississippi River journeys 3,766 km to empty 232 million metric tons of sediment into the Gulf of Mexico each year. The end of the Mississippi River delta forms the largest area of wetlands in North America. A *delta* forms when sediments settle at the mouth of a river. At the Mississippi River delta, the sediments build up and form new land along the Louisiana coastline. The area around the delta is called *wetlands.* It has fertile soil, which produces many crops, and a variety of habitats—marsh, freshwater, and saltwater—that support many species of plants and animals.

Taking Action to Preserve the Delta

Since the mid-1980s, local, state, and federal governments, along with Louisiana citizens and businesses, have been working together to monitor and restore the Mississippi River delta. Some projects to protect the delta include filling in canals that divert the sediments and even using old Christmas trees as fences to trap the sediments! With the continued efforts of scientists, government leaders, and concerned citizens, the Mississippi River delta stands a good chance of recovering.

Explore the Delta

▶ Find out more about the industries and organisms that depend on the Mississippi River delta for survival. What will happen to them if we don't take care of the ecosystem?

Agents of Erosion and Deposition

THE CRASHING SURF

On February 8, 1998, unusually large waves crashed against the cliffs along Broad Beach Road in Malibu, California. Eventually, the ocean-eroded cliffs buckled, causing a landslide. One house collapsed into the ocean, while two more dangled on the edge of the cliff. What made these waves stronger than usual? How can water cause this much damage? In this chapter, you will study how waves shape beaches and coastlines. You will also learn how wind, moving ice, and gravity sculpt the surface of our planet.

Pre-Reading Questions

1. What do waves and wind have in common?

2. How do waves, wind, and ice erode and deposit rock materials?

MAKING WAVES

Did you know that beaches and shorelines are shaped by crashing waves? See for yourself by creating some waves of your own.

Procedure

1. Make a beach by adding **sand** to one end of a **washtub.**

2. Fill the washtub with **water** to a depth of 5 cm.

3. In your ScienceLog, sketch the beach profile (side view), and label it "A."

4. Place a **block** at the end of the washtub opposite the beach. Move the block up and down very slowly to create small waves for 2 minutes. Sketch the new beach profile and label it "B."

5. Again place a block at the end of the washtub opposite the beach. Move the block up and down more rapidly to create large waves for 2 minutes. Sketch the new beach profile and label it "C."

Analysis

6. Compare the three beach profiles. What is happening to the beach?

7. How do small waves and large waves erode the beach differently?

8. What other factors might contribute to beach erosion?

Shoreline Erosion and Deposition

Terms to Learn

shoreline
beach
longshore current

What You'll Do

- ◆ Explain the connection between storms and wave erosion.
- ◆ Explain how waves break in shallow water.
- ◆ Describe how beaches form.
- ◆ Describe types of coastal landforms created by wave action.

What images pop into your head when you hear the word *beach*? You probably picture sand, blue ocean as far as the eye can see, balmy breezes, and waves. In this section you will learn how all those things relate to erosion and deposition along the shoreline. A **shoreline** is where land and a body of water meet. *Erosion,* as you may recall, is the breakdown and movement of materials. *Deposition* takes place when these materials are dropped. Waves can be powerful agents of erosion and deposition, as you will soon learn.

Wave Energy

Have you ever noticed the tiny ripples created by your breath when you blow on a cup of hot chocolate to cool it? Similarly, the wind moves over the ocean surface, producing ripples called *waves*. The size of a wave depends on how hard the wind is blowing and the length of time the wind blows. The harder and longer the wind blows, the bigger the wave is. Try it the next time you drink cocoa.

The wind that comes from severe winter storms and summer hurricanes generally produces the large waves that cause shoreline erosion. Waves may travel hundreds or even thousands of kilometers from a storm before reaching the shoreline. Some of the largest waves to reach the California coast are produced by storms as far away as Alaska and Australia. Thus, the California surfer in **Figure 1** can ride a wave produced by a storm on the other side of the Pacific Ocean.

Figure 1 *Waves produced by storms on the other side of the Pacific Ocean propel this surfer toward a California shore.*

Wave Trains On your imaginary visit to the beach, do you remember seeing just one wave? Of course not; waves don't move alone. They travel in groups called *wave trains*, as shown in **Figure 2.** As wave trains move away from their source, they travel through the ocean water without interruption. When they reach shallow water, they change form and begin to break. The ocean floor crowds the lower part of the wave, shortening the wave length and increasing the wave height. This results in taller, more closely spaced waves.

When the top of the wave becomes so tall that it cannot support itself, it begins to curl and break. These breaking waves are known as *surf*. Now you know how surfers got their name. The *wave period* is the time interval between breaking waves. Wave periods are usually 10 to 20 seconds long.

Figure 2 *Because waves travel in wave trains, they break at regular intervals.*

The Pounding Surf A tremendous amount of energy is released when waves break, as shown in **Figure 3.** A crashing wave can break solid rock or throw broken rocks back against the shore. The rushing water in breaking waves can easily wash into cracks in rock, helping to break off large boulders or fine grains of sand. The loose sand picked up by the waves polishes and wears down coastal rocks. Waves can also move sand and small rocks and deposit them in other locations, forming beaches.

MATH BREAK

Counting Waves

How many waves do you think reach a shoreline in a day if the wave period is 10 seconds?
(Hint: Calculate how many waves occur in a minute, in an hour, and in a day.)

Figure 3 *Breaking waves crash against the rocky shore, releasing their energy.*

✓ Self-Check

Would a large wave or a small wave have more erosive energy? Why? *(See page 726 to check your answer.)*

Wave Deposits

Waves carry an assortment of materials, including sand, rock fragments, and shells. Often this material is deposited on the shore. But as you will learn, this is not always the case.

Beaches You would probably recognize a beach if you saw one. But technically, a **beach** is any area of the shoreline made up of material deposited by waves. Some beach material arrives on the shoreline by way of rivers. Other beach material is eroded from areas located near the shoreline.

Not all beaches are the same. Compare the beaches shown in **Figure 4.** Notice that the colors and textures vary. This is because the type of material found on a beach depends on its source. Light-colored sand is the most common beach material. Much of this sand comes from the quartz in continental rock. But not all beaches are made of light-colored sand. For instance, on many tropical islands, beaches are made of fine white coral material, and some Florida beaches are made of tiny pieces of broken seashells. In Hawaii, there are black sand beaches made of eroded volcanic lava. In areas where stormy seas are common, beaches are made of pebbles and larger rocks.

Figure 4 *Beaches are made of different types of material deposited by waves.*

Wave Angle Makes a Difference The movement of sand along a beach depends on the angle at which the waves strike the shore. Most waves approach the beach at a slight angle and retreat in a direction more perpendicular to the shore. This moves the sand in a zigzag pattern along the beach, as you can see in **Figure 5.**

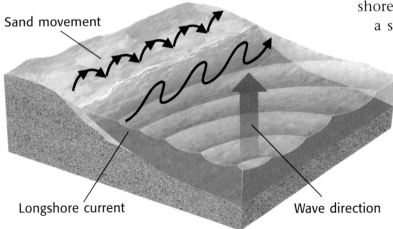

Figure 5 *When waves strike the shoreline at an angle, sand migrates along the beach in a zigzag path.*

Offshore Deposits Waves moving at an angle to the shoreline push water along the shore, creating longshore currents. A **longshore current** is a movement of water near and parallel to the shoreline. Sometimes waves erode material from the shoreline, and a longshore current transports and deposits it offshore, creating landforms in open water. Some of these landforms are shown in **Figure 6.**

Figure 6 Sandbars and barrier spits are types of offshore deposits.

A **sandbar** is an underwater or exposed ridge of sand, gravel, or shell material.

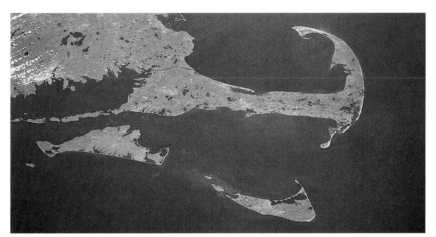

A **barrier spit,** like Cape Cod, Massachusetts, occurs when an exposed sandbar is connected to the shoreline.

Wave Erosion

Wave erosion produces a variety of features along a shoreline. *Sea cliffs,* like the ones in **Figure 7,** are formed when waves erode and undercut rock, producing steep slopes. Waves strike the base of the cliff, wearing away the soil and rock and making the cliff steeper. The rate at which the sea cliffs erode depends on the hardness of the rock and the energy delivered by the waves. Sea cliffs made of hard rock, such as granite, erode very slowly. Other sea cliffs, such as those made of soft sedimentary rock, erode rapidly, especially during storms.

Figure 7 *Ocean-view homes built on sedimentary rock are often threatened as cliffs erode.*

Shaping a Shoreline Much of the erosion responsible for landforms you might see along the shoreline takes place during storms. Large waves generated by storms release far more energy on the shoreline than do normal waves. This energy is so powerful that it is capable of removing huge chunks of rock. The following illustrations show some of the major landscape features that result from wave erosion.

Coastal Landforms Created by Wave Erosion

Sea stacks are offshore columns of resistant rock that were once connected to the mainland. In these instances, waves have eroded the mainland, leaving behind isolated columns of rock.

Sea arches form when wave action continues to erode a sea cave, cutting completely through the rock.

Sea caves form when waves cut large holes into fractured or weak rock along the base of sea cliffs. Sea caves are common in limestone cliffs, where the rock is usually quite soft.

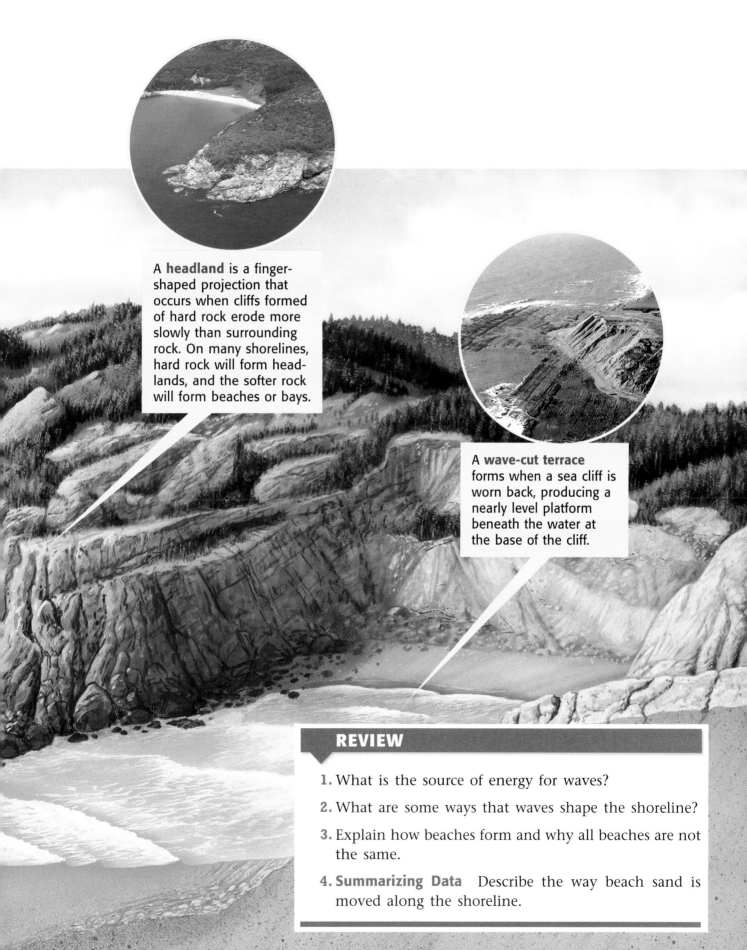

A **headland** is a finger-shaped projection that occurs when cliffs formed of hard rock erode more slowly than surrounding rock. On many shorelines, hard rock will form headlands, and the softer rock will form beaches or bays.

A **wave-cut terrace** forms when a sea cliff is worn back, producing a nearly level platform beneath the water at the base of the cliff.

REVIEW

1. What is the source of energy for waves?

2. What are some ways that waves shape the shoreline?

3. Explain how beaches form and why all beaches are not the same.

4. **Summarizing Data** Describe the way beach sand is moved along the shoreline.

Wind Erosion and Deposition

Terms to Learn

saltation   dune
deflation   loess
abrasion

What You'll Do

♦ Explain why areas with fine materials are more vulnerable to wind erosion.
♦ Describe how wind moves sand and finer materials.
♦ Describe the effects of wind erosion.
♦ Describe the difference between dunes and loess deposits.

Have you ever tried to track a moving rock? Sounds silly, but in California some rocks keep sneaking around. To find out more, turn to page 324.

Most of us at one time or another have been frustrated by a gusty wind that blew an important stack of papers all over the place. Remember how fast and far the papers traveled, and how it took forever to pick them up because every time you caught up with them they were on the move again? If you are familiar with this scene, then you already know how wind erosion works. Certain locations are more vulnerable to wind erosion than others. Areas with fine, loose rock material that have little protective plant cover can be significantly affected by the wind. Plant roots anchor sand and soil in place, reducing the amount of wind erosion. The landscapes most commonly shaped by wind processes are deserts and coastlines.

Process of Wind Erosion

Wind moves material in different ways. In areas where strong winds occur, material is moved by saltation. **Saltation** is the movement of sand-sized particles by a skipping and bouncing action in the direction the wind is blowing. As you can see in **Figure 8,** the wind causes the particles to bounce. When bouncing sand particles knock into one another, some particles bounce up in the air and fall forward, striking other sand particles. The impact may in turn cause these particles to roll forward or bounce up in the air.

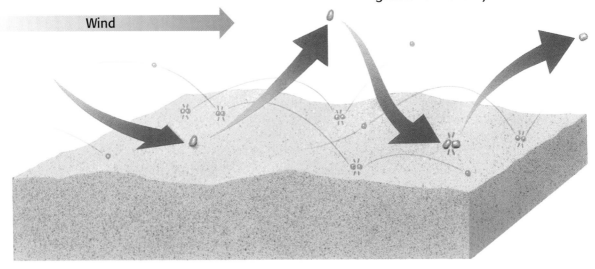

Figure 8 *The wind causes sand grains to move by saltation.*

Wind

Deflation The lifting and removal of fine sediment by wind is called **deflation.** During deflation, wind removes the top layer of fine sediment or soil, leaving behind rock fragments that are too heavy to be lifted by the wind. This hard, rocky surface, consisting of pebbles and small broken rocks, is known as *desert pavement*. An example is shown in **Figure 9.**

Figure 9 *Desert pavement, like that found in the Painted Desert, in Arizona, forms when wind removes all the fine materials.*

Have you ever blown on a layer of dust while cleaning off a dresser? If you have, you might have noticed that in addition to your face getting dirty, a little scooped-out depression formed in the dust. Similarly, where there is little vegetation, wind may scoop out depressions in the sand. These depressions, like the one shown in **Figure 10,** are known as *deflation hollows.*

Figure 10 *Wind erosion can cause deflation hollows to become hundreds of meters wide.*

✓ Self-Check

Why do deflation hollows form in areas where there is little vegetation? *(See page 726 to check your answer.)*

Describing the Dust Bowl

When a long period without rain, known as a *drought*, occurs, areas that are farmed or overgrazed can suffer extensive soil loss and dense dust storms. The removal of plants exposes the soil, making it more vulnerable to wind erosion.

During the 1930s, a section of the Great Plains suffered severe wind erosion and dust storms. This area became known as the *Dust Bowl*. The dust darkened the skies so much that street lights were left on during the day in Midwestern cities.

In areas where the conditions were even worse, people had to string ropes from their houses to their barns so they wouldn't get lost in the dense dust. The dust was so bad that people slept with damp cloths over their face to keep from choking. Describe the major erosional process that caused the Dust Bowl.

Abrasion The grinding and wearing down of rock surfaces by other rock or sand particles is called **abrasion.** Abrasion commonly occurs in areas where there are strong winds, loose sand, and soft rocks. The blowing of millions of sharp sand grains creates a sandblasting effect that helps to erode, smooth, and polish rocks.

Wind-Deposited Materials

Like a stack of papers blowing in the wind, all the material carried by the wind is eventually deposited downwind. The amount and size of particles the wind can carry depend on wind speed. The faster the wind blows, the more material and the heavier the particles it can carry. As wind speed slows, heavier particles are deposited first.

Dunes When the wind hits an obstacle, such as a plant or a rock, it slows down. As the wind slows, it deposits, or drops, the heavier material. As the material collects, it creates an additional obstacle. This obstacle causes even more material to be deposited, forming a mound. Eventually even the original obstacle becomes buried. The mounds of wind-deposited sand are called **dunes.** Dunes are common in deserts and along the shores of lakes and oceans.

Turn on a hair dryer—no, not to style your hair, but to find out how dunes migrate. Check out page 676 of the LabBook.

How Dunes Move Dunes tend to move in the direction of strong prevailing winds. Different wind conditions produce dunes in various shapes and sizes. A dune usually has a gently sloped side and a steeply sloped side, or *slip face,* as shown in **Figure 11.** In most cases, the gently sloped side faces the wind. The wind is constantly transporting material up this side of the dune. As sand moves over the crest, or peak, of the dune, it slides down the slip face, creating a steep slope.

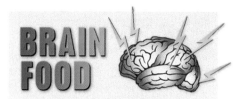

The largest sand dunes ever recorded were found in east-central Algeria in the Sahara. These dunes measured about 4.8 km long and 430 m high.

Figure 11 *Dunes migrate in the direction of the wind.*

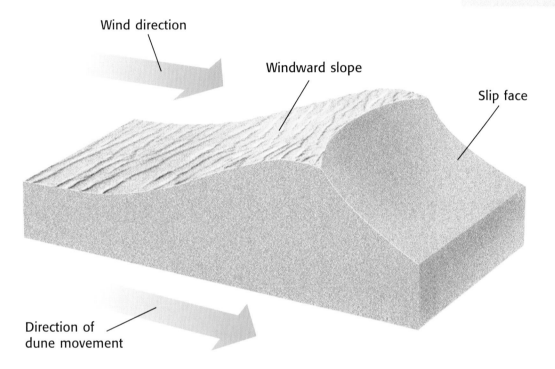

Wind direction

Windward slope

Slip face

Direction of dune movement

Disappearing Dunes and the Desert Tortoise

Dunes provide homes for hundreds of plant and animal species, including the desert tortoise. This tortoise, found in the Mojave and Sonoran Deserts of the southwestern United States, is able to live where ground temperatures are very hot. It escapes the heat by digging burrows in the sand dunes. The desert tortoise has a problem, though. Dune buggies and other motorized vehicles are destroying the dunes. Dunes are easily disturbed and are vulnerable to erosion. Motorized off-road vehicles break down dunes, destroying habitat of the tortoise as well as many other animal and plant species. For this reason, state and federal wildlife and land-management

agencies have taken an active role in helping protect the habitat of the desert tortoise and other sensitive desert species by making some areas off-limits to off-road vehicles.

Loess Wind can deposit material much finer than sand. Thick deposits of this windblown, fine-grained sediment are known as **loess** (LOH es). Loess feels much like the talcum powder you use after a shower.

Because wind carries fine-grained material much higher and farther than it carries sand, loess deposits are sometimes found far away from their source. Many loess deposits came from glacial sources during the last ice age.

Loess is present in much of the midwestern United States, along the eastern edge of the Mississippi Valley, and in eastern Oregon and Washington. Huge bluffs of loess are found in Mississippi, as shown in **Figure 12.**

Loess deposits can easily be prepared for growing crops and are responsible for the success of many of the grain-growing areas of the world.

Figure 12 *The thick loess deposits found in Mississippi contribute to the state's fertile soil.*

🖅 internet**connect**

SC*i*LINKS
NSTA

TOPIC: Wind Erosion
GO TO: www.scilinks.org
*sci*LINKS NUMBER: HSTE285

REVIEW

1. What areas have the greatest amount of wind erosion and deposition? Why?

2. Explain the process of saltation.

3. What is the difference between a dune and a loess deposit?

4. **Analyzing Relationships** Explain the relationship between deflation and dune movement.

Erosion and Deposition by Ice

Terms to Learn

glacier   glacial drift
iceberg   stratified drift
crevasse   till

What You'll Do

- Summarize why glaciers are important agents of erosion and deposition.
- Explain how ice in a glacier flows.
- Describe some of the landforms eroded by glaciers.
- Describe some of the landforms deposited by glaciers.

Can you imagine an ice cube the size of a football stadium? Well, glaciers can be even bigger than that. A **glacier** is an enormous mass of moving ice. Because glaciers are very heavy and have the ability to move across the Earth's surface, they are capable of eroding, moving, and depositing large amounts of rock materials. And while you will never see a glacier chilling a punch bowl, you might one day visit some of the spectacular landscapes carved by glacial activity.

Glaciers—Rivers of Ice

Glaciers form in areas so cold that snow stays on the ground year-round. Areas like these, where you can chill a can of juice by simply carrying it outside, are found at high elevations and in polar regions. Because the average temperature is freezing or near freezing, snow piles up year after year. Eventually, the weight of the snow on top causes the deep-packed snow to become ice crystals, forming a giant ice mass. These ice packs then become slow-moving "rivers of ice" as they are set in motion by the pull of gravity on their extraordinary mass.

Alpine Glaciers There are two main types of glaciers, *alpine* and *continental*. **Figure 13** shows an alpine glacier. As you can see, this type of glacier forms in mountainous areas. One common type of alpine glacier is a *valley glacier*. Valley glaciers form in valleys originally created by stream erosion. These glaciers flow slowly downhill, widening and straightening the valleys into broad U-shapes as they travel.

Figure 13 *Alpine glaciers start as snowfields in mountainous areas.*

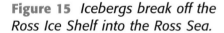

How far do you think the iceberg that struck the *Titanic* drifted before the two met that fateful night in 1912? Plot on a map of the North Atlantic Ocean the route of the *Titanic* from Southampton, England, to New York. Then plot a possible route of the drifting iceberg from Greenland to where the ship sank, just south of the Canadian island province of Newfoundland.

TRY at HOME

Continental Glaciers Not all glaciers are true "rivers of ice." In fact, some glaciers continue to get larger, spreading across entire continents. These glaciers, called continental glaciers, are huge continuous masses of ice. **Figure 14** shows the largest type of this glacier, a *continental ice sheet*. Ice sheets can cover millions of square kilometers with ice. The continent of Antarctica is almost completely covered by one of the largest ice sheets in the world, as you can see below. This ice sheet is approximately one and a half times the size of the United States. It is so thick—more than 4,000 m in places—that it buries everything but the highest mountain peaks.

Figure 14 *Antarctica contains approximately 91 percent of all the glacial ice on the planet.*

Ice Shelves An area where the ice is attached to the ice sheet but is resting on open water is called an *ice shelf*. The largest ice shelf is the Ross Ice Shelf, shown in **Figure 15,** which is attached to the ice sheet that covers Antarctica. This ice shelf covers an area of ocean about the size of Texas.

Figure 15 *Icebergs break off the Ross Ice Shelf into the Ross Sea.*

Icebergs Large pieces of ice that break off an ice shelf and drift into the ocean are called **icebergs.** The process by which an iceberg forms is called *calving.* Because most of an iceberg is below the surface of the water, it can be a hazard for ships that cannot see how far the iceberg extends. In the North Atlantic Ocean near Newfoundland, the *Titanic* struck an iceberg that calved off the Greenland ice sheet.

Glaciers on the Move When enough ice builds up on a slope, the ice begins to move downhill. The thickness of the ice and the steepness of the slope determine how fast a glacier will move. Thick glaciers move faster than thin glaciers, and the steeper the slope is, the faster the glacier will move. Glaciers move by two different methods. They move when the weight of the ice causes the ice at the bottom to melt. The water from the melted ice allows the glacier to move forward, like a partially melted ice cube moving across your kitchen counter. Glaciers also move when solid ice crystals within the glacier slip over each other, causing a slow forward motion. This process is similar to placing a deck of cards on a table and then tilting the table. The top cards will slide farther than the lower cards. Like the cards, the upper part, or surface, of the glacier flows faster than the glacier's base.

Crevasses As a glacier flows forward, sometimes crevasses occur. A **crevasse** (kruh VAS), as shown in **Figure 16,** is a large crack that forms where the glacier picks up speed or flows over a high point. Crevasses form because the ice cannot stretch quickly, and it cracks. They can be dangerous for people who are traveling across glaciers because a bridge layer of snow can hide them from view.

> ### ✔ Self-Check
>
> How are ice crevasses related to glacier flow?
> *(See page 726 to check your answer.)*

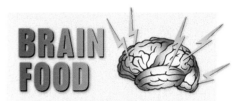

Speed of a Glacier
An alpine glacier is estimated to be moving forward at 5 m per day. Calculate how long it will take for the ice to reach a road and campground located 0.5 km from the front of the advancing glacier.

1 km = 1,000 m

Figure 16 *Crevasses can be dangerous for mountain climbers who must cross glaciers.*

Landforms Carved by Glaciers

Alpine glaciers and continental glaciers produce landscapes that are very different from one another. Alpine glaciers carve out rugged features in the mountain rocks through which they flow. Continental glaciers smooth the landscape by scraping and removing features that existed before the ice appeared, flattening even some of the highest mountains. **Figure 17** and **Figure 18** show the very different landscapes that each glacial type produces.

Figure 17
Continental glaciers smooth and flatten the landscape.

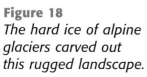

Figure 18
The hard ice of alpine glaciers carved out this rugged landscape.

Alpine glaciers carve out large amounts of rock material, creating spectacular landforms. These glaciers are responsible for landscapes such as the Rocky Mountains and the Alps. **Figure 19** shows the kind of landscape that is sculpted by alpine glacial erosion and revealed after the ice melts back.

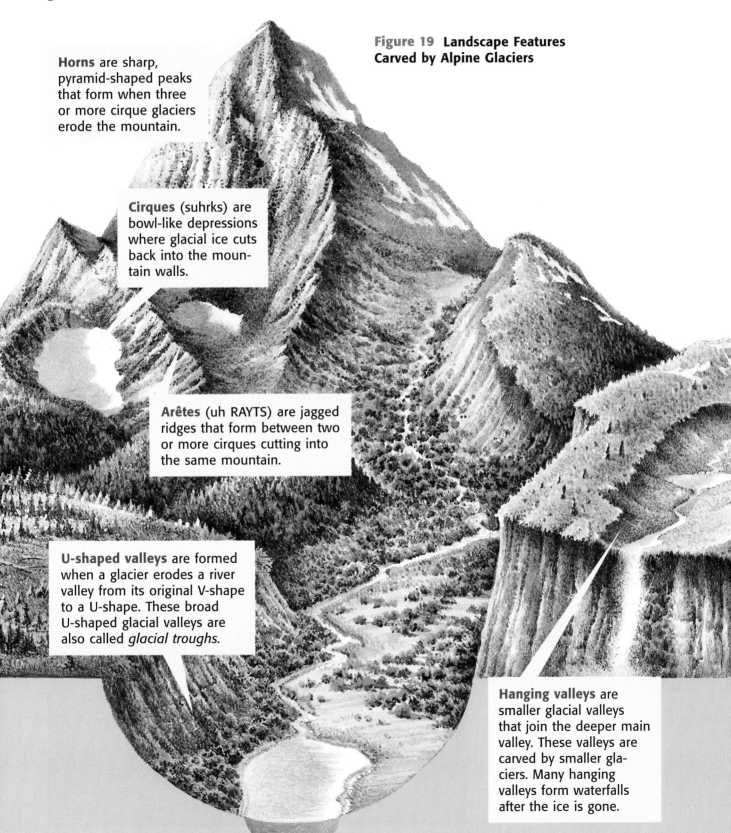

Figure 19 Landscape Features Carved by Alpine Glaciers

Horns are sharp, pyramid-shaped peaks that form when three or more cirque glaciers erode the mountain.

Cirques (suhrks) are bowl-like depressions where glacial ice cuts back into the mountain walls.

Arêtes (uh RAYTS) are jagged ridges that form between two or more cirques cutting into the same mountain.

U-shaped valleys are formed when a glacier erodes a river valley from its original V-shape to a U-shape. These broad U-shaped glacial valleys are also called *glacial troughs.*

Hanging valleys are smaller glacial valleys that join the deeper main valley. These valleys are carved by smaller glaciers. Many hanging valleys form waterfalls after the ice is gone.

Figure 20 *Striations, such as these seen in Central Park, in New York City, are evidence of glacial erosion.*

How did this glacier get into my classroom? To find out more about glaciers and erosion, turn to page 677 of the LabBook.

Striations While many of the erosional features created by glaciers are unique to alpine glaciers, alpine and continental glaciers share some common features. For example, when a glacier erodes the landscape, the glacier picks up rock material and carries it away. This debris is transported on the glacier's surface as well as beneath and within the glacier. Many times, rock material is frozen into the glacier's bottom. As the glacier moves, the rock pieces scrape and polish the surface rock. Larger rocks embedded in the glacier gouge out grooves in the surface rock. As you can see in **Figure 20,** these grooves, called *striations,* help scientists determine the direction of ice flow.

Types of Glacial Deposits

When a glacier melts, all the material it has been carrying is dropped. **Glacial drift** is the general term used to describe all material carried and deposited by glaciers. Glacial drift is divided into two main types, based on whether the material is sorted or unsorted.

Stratified Drift Rock material that has been sorted and deposited in layers by water flowing from the melted ice is called **stratified drift.** Many streams are created by the meltwater from the glacier. These streams carry an abundance of sorted material, which is deposited in front of the glacier in a broad area called an *outwash plain.* Sometimes a block of ice is left in the outwash plain when the glacier retreats. During the time it takes for the ice to melt, sediment builds up around the block of ice. After the ice has melted, a depression called a *kettle* is left. Kettles commonly fill with water, forming a lake or pond, as shown in **Figure 21.**

Figure 21 *Stratified drift is deposited on outwash plains in which kettle lakes are often found.*

Till Deposits The second type of glacial drift, **till,** is unsorted rock material that is deposited directly by the ice when it melts. *Unsorted* means that the till is made up of different sizes of rock material, ranging from large boulders to fine glacial silt. As a glacier flows, it carries different sizes of rock fragments. When the glacier melts, the unsorted material is deposited on the ground surface.

The most common till deposits are *moraines.* Moraines generally form ridges along the edges of glaciers. They are produced when glaciers carry material to the front of the ice and along the sides of the ice. As the ice melts, the sediment and rock it is carrying are dropped, forming the different types of moraines. The various types of moraines are shown in **Figure 22.**

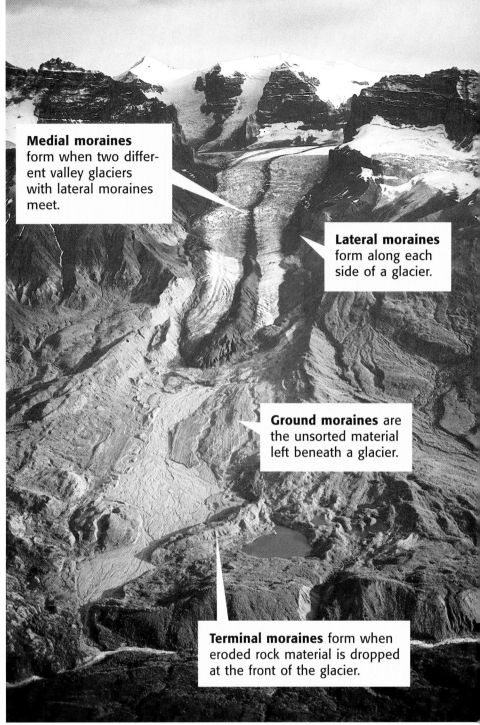

Medial moraines form when two different valley glaciers with lateral moraines meet.

Lateral moraines form along each side of a glacier.

Ground moraines are the unsorted material left beneath a glacier.

Terminal moraines form when eroded rock material is dropped at the front of the glacier.

Figure 22 *Moraines provide clues to where glaciers once were located.*

REVIEW

1. How does glaciation change the appearance of mountains?

2. Explain why continental glaciers smooth the landscape and alpine glaciers create a rugged landscape.

3. What do moraines indicate?

4. **Applying Concepts** How can a glacier deposit both sorted and unsorted material?

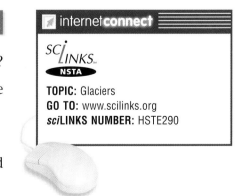

internetconnect

SC*i*LINKS.
NSTA

TOPIC: Glaciers
GO TO: www.scilinks.org
***sci*LINKS NUMBER:** HSTE290

Terms to Learn

mass movement   mudflow
rock fall   creep
landslide

What You'll Do

- ◆ Explain how slope is related to mass movement.
- ◆ State how gravity affects mass movement.
- ◆ Describe different types of mass movement.

Gravity's Effect on Erosion and Deposition

Waves, wind, and ice are all agents of erosion and deposition that you can see. And though you can't see it and might not be aware of it, gravity is also an agent of erosion and deposition constantly at work on the Earth's surface. Gravity not only influences the movement of water, such as waves, streams, and ice, but also causes rocks and soil to move downslope. **Mass movement** is the movement of any material, such as rock, soil, or snow, downslope. Mass movement is controlled by the force of gravity and can occur rapidly or slowly.

Angle of Repose

If dry sand is piled up, it will move downhill until the slope becomes stable. The *angle of repose* is the steepest angle, or slope, at which loose material will not slide downslope. This is demonstrated in **Figure 23.** The angle of repose is different for each type of surface material. Characteristics of the surface material, such as its size, weight, shape, and moisture level, determine at what angle the material will move downslope.

Figure 23 *If the slope on which material rests is less than the angle of repose, the material will stay in place. If the slope is greater than the angle of repose, the material will move downslope.*

Quick Lab

Angle of Repose

1. Pour a **container** of **dry sand** onto a lab table.

2. With a **protractor,** measure the slope of the sand, or the *angle of repose.*

3. Pour another beaker of sand on top of the first pile.

4. Measure the angle of repose again for the new pile.

5. Which pile is more likely to collapse? Why?

Rapid Mass Movement

The most destructive mass movements occur suddenly and rapidly. Rapid mass movement occurs when material, such as rock and soil, moves down-slope quickly. A rapid mass movement can be very dangerous, destroying everything in its path.

Rock Falls While driving along a mountain road, you might have noticed signs that warn of falling rock. A **rock fall** happens when a group of loose rocks falls down a steep slope, as seen in **Figure 24**. Steep slopes are sometimes created to make room for a road in mountainous areas. Loosened and exposed rocks above the road tend to fall as a result of gravity. The rocks in a rock fall can range in size from small fragments to large boulders.

Landslides Another type of rapid mass movement is a *landslide*. A **landslide** is the sudden and rapid movement of a large amount of material downslope. A *slump* is an example of one kind of landslide. Slumping occurs when a block of material moves downslope over a curved surface, as seen in **Figure 25.**

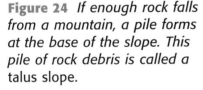
Figure 24 *If enough rock falls from a mountain, a pile forms at the base of the slope. This pile of rock debris is called a* talus slope.

Figure 25 *A slump is a type of landslide that occurs when a small block of land becomes detached and slides downhill.*

Mudflows A **mudflow** is a rapid movement of a large mass of mud. Mudflows, which are like giant moving mud pies, occur when a large amount of water mixes with soil and rock. The water causes the slippery mass of mud to flow rapidly downslope. Mudflows most commonly occur in mountainous regions when a long dry season is followed by heavy rains. As you can see in **Figure 26,** a mudflow can carry trees, houses, cars, and other objects that lie in its path.

Figure 26 *This photo shows one of the many mudflows that have occurred in California during rainy winters.*

Lahars The most dangerous mudflows occur as a result of volcanic eruptions. Mudflows of volcanic origin are called *lahars*. Lahars can move at speeds of more than 80 km/h and are as thick as concrete. In mountains with snowy peaks, a volcanic eruption can suddenly melt a great amount of ice, causing a massive and rapid lahar, as shown in **Figure 27.** The water from the ice liquefies the soil and volcanic ash, sending a hot mudflow downslope. Other lahars are caused by heavy rains on volcanic ash.

Figure 27 *This lahar overtook the city of Kyushu, in Japan.*

Slow Mass Movement

Sometimes you don't even notice mass movement occurring. While rapid mass movements are visible and dramatic, slow mass movements happen a little at a time. However, because slow mass movements occur more frequently, more material is moved collectively over time.

Creep Although most slopes appear to be stable, they are actually undergoing slow mass movement, as shown in **Figure 28.** The extremely slow movement of material downslope is called **creep.** Many factors contribute to creep. Water breaks up rock particles, allowing them to move freely. The roots of growing plants act as a wedge, forcing rocks and soil particles apart. Burrowing animals, such as gophers and groundhogs, loosen rock and soil particles.

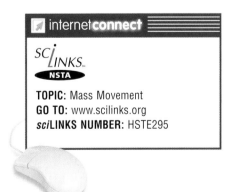

Figure 28 *Tilted fence posts and bent tree trunks are evidence that creep is occurring.*

REVIEW

1. In your own words, explain why slump occurs.

2. What factors increase the potential for mass movement?

3. How do slope and gravity affect mass movement?

4. **Analyzing Relationships** Some types of mass movement are considered dangerous to humans. Which types are most dangerous? Why?

internet connect

SCI*LINKS*
NSTA

TOPIC: Mass Movement
GO TO: www.scilinks.org
***sci*LINKS NUMBER:** HSTE295

Chapter Highlights

SECTION 1

Vocabulary

shoreline *(p. 298)*

beach *(p. 300)*

longshore current *(p. 301)*

Section Notes

• The wind from storms usually produces the large waves that cause shoreline erosion.

• Waves break when they enter shallow water, becoming surf.

• Beaches are made of any material deposited by waves.

• Sandbars and spits are depositional features caused by longshore currents.

• Sea cliffs, sea caves, sea arches, and sea stacks are coastal formations caused by wave erosion.

SECTION 2

Vocabulary

saltation *(p. 304)*

deflation *(p. 305)*

abrasion *(p. 306)*

dune *(p. 306)*

loess *(p. 308)*

Section Notes

• Wind is an important agent of erosion and deposition in deserts and along coastlines.

• Saltation is the process of the wind bouncing sand grains downwind along the ground.

• Deflation is the removal of materials by wind. If deflation removes all fine rock materials, a barren surface called desert pavement is formed.

• Abrasion is the grinding and wearing down of rock surfaces by other rock or sand particles.

• Dunes are formations caused by wind-deposited sand.

• Loess is wind-deposited silt, and it forms soil material good for farming.

Labs

Dune Movement *(p. 676)*

☑ Skills Check

Math Concepts

WAVE PERIOD Waves travel in intervals that are usually between 10 and 20 seconds apart. Use the following equation to calculate how many waves reach the shore in 1 minute:

$$\frac{\text{number of waves}}{\text{per minute}} = \frac{60 \text{ seconds}}{\text{waves period (seconds)}}$$

After you find out how many waves reach the shore in 1 minute, you can figure out how many waves occur in an hour or even a day. For example, consider a wave period of 15 seconds. Using the formula above, you find that 4 waves occur in 1 minute. To find out how many waves occur in 1 hour, multiply 4 by 60. To find out how many waves occur in 1 day, multiply 240 by 24.

$$\frac{\text{number of waves}}{\text{per day}} = \frac{60}{15} \times 60 \times 24 = 5{,}760$$

Visual Understanding

U-SHAPED VALLEYS AND MORE Look back at the illustration on page 313 to review the different types of landscape features carved by alpine glaciers.

Vocabulary

glacier *(p. 309)*

iceberg *(p. 310)*

crevasse *(p. 311)*

glacial drift *(p. 314)*

stratified drift *(p. 314)*

till *(p. 315)*

Section Notes

- Masses of moving ice are called glaciers.

- There are two main types of glaciers—alpine glaciers and continental glaciers.

- Glaciers move when the ice that comes into contact with the ground melts and when ice crystals slip over one another.

- Alpine glaciers produce rugged landscape features, such as cirques, arêtes, and horns.

- Continental glaciers smooth the landscape.

- There are two main types of glacial deposits—stratified drift and till.

- Some of the landforms deposited by glaciers include outwash plains and moraines.

Labs

Gliding Glaciers *(p. 677)*

Creating a Kettle *(p. 679)*

Vocabulary

mass movement *(p. 316)*

rock fall *(p. 317)*

landslide *(p. 317)*

mudflow *(p. 318)*

creep *(p. 319)*

Section Notes

- Mass movement is the movement of material downhill due to the force of gravity.

- The angle of repose is the steepest slope at which loose material will remain at rest.

- Rock falls, landslides, and mudflows are all types of rapid mass movement.

- Creep is a type of slow mass movement.

---

 internetconnect

GO TO: go.hrw.com

Visit the **HRW** Web site for a variety of learning tools related to this chapter. Just type in the keyword:

KEYWORD: HSTICE

SCi*LINKS* sm

N S T A

GO TO: www.scilinks.org

Visit the **National Science Teachers Association** on-line Web site for Internet resources related to this chapter. Just type in the *sci*LINKS number for more information about the topic:

TOPIC: Wave Erosion	*sci*LINKS NUMBER: HSTE280
TOPIC: Wind Erosion	*sci*LINKS NUMBER: HSTE285
TOPIC: Glaciers	*sci*LINKS NUMBER: HSTE290
TOPIC: Mass Movement	*sci*LINKS NUMBER: HSTE295
TOPIC: Wetlands	*sci*LINKS NUMBER: HSTE300

Chapter Review

Explain the difference between the words in the following pairs:

1. shoreline/longshore current

2. beaches/dunes

3. deflation/saltation

4. glacier/loess

5. stratified drift/till

6. mudflow/creep

UNDERSTANDING CONCEPTS

Multiple Choice

7. *Surf* refers to
   a. large storm waves in the open ocean.
   b. giant waves produced by hurricanes.
   c. breaking waves.
   d. small waves on a calm sea.

8. When waves cut completely through a headland, a ___?___ is formed.
   a. sea cave
   b. sea cliff
   c. sea stack
   d. sea arch

9. A narrow strip of sand that is formed by wave deposition and is connected to the shore is called a ___?___
   a. marine terrace.
   b. sandbar.
   c. spit.
   d. headland.

10. A wind-eroded depression is called a
    a. dune.
    b. desert pavement.
    c. deflation hollow.
    d. dust bowl.

11. Where is the world's largest ice sheet located?
    a. Greenland
    b. Canada
    c. Alaska
    d. Antarctica

12. The process of calving forms ___?___
    a. continental ice sheets.
    b. icebergs.
    c. U-shaped valleys.
    d. moraines.

13. What term describes all types of glacial deposits?
    a. drift
    b. loess
    c. till
    d. outwash

14. Which of the following is not a landform created by an alpine glacier?
    a. cirque
    b. deflation hollow
    c. horn
    d. arête

15. What is the term for a mass movement of volcanic origin?
    a. lahar
    b. slump
    c. creep
    d. rock fall

16. Which of the following is a slow mass movement?
    a. mudflow
    b. landslide
    c. creep
    d. rock fall

Short Answer

17. Why do waves break when they get near the shore?

18. What role do storms play in coastal erosion?

19. How do humans increase the erosion caused by dust storms?

20. In what direction do sand dunes move?

21. Why are glaciers such effective agents of erosion and deposition?

22. List some evidence for creep.

Concept Mapping

23. Use the following terms to create a concept map: deflation, dust storm, saltation, dune, loess.

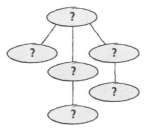

Write one or two sentences to answer the following questions:

24. What role does wind play in the processes of erosion and deposition?

25. What are the main differences between alpine glaciers and continental glaciers?

26. Describe the different types of moraines.

27. What kind of mass movement occurs continuously, day after day? Why can't you see it?

MATH IN SCIENCE

28. While standing on a beach, you can estimate a wave's speed in kilometers per hour. This is done by counting the seconds between each arriving wave crest to determine the wave period and then multiplying the wave period by 3.5. Calculate the speed of a wave with a 10-second period.

INTERPRETING GRAPHICS

The following graph illustrates coastal erosion and deposition occurring at an imaginary beach over a period of 8 years.

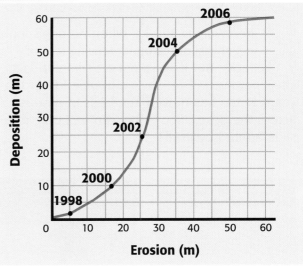

Erosion and Deposition (1998–2006)

29. What is happening to the beach over time?

30. In what year does the amount of erosion that has occurred along the shoreline equal the amount of deposition?

31. Based on the erosion and deposition data for 2000, what might happen to the beach in the years to follow?

Reading Check-up

Take a minute to review your answers to the Pre-Reading Questions found at the bottom of page 296. Have your answers changed? If necessary, revise your answers based on what you have learned since you began this chapter.

Science, Technology, and Society

Boulder Boogie

Karen weighs 320 kg. When no one's looking, she slides around, leaving lots of tracks. But Karen's not a person. In fact, she's not even alive—she's a boulder! Over the years, Karen has moved hundreds of meters across the desert floor. How can a 320 kg rock slide around by itself?

▲ *A mystery in Death Valley: What moved this rock across the desert floor?*

▲ *New technology is helping Paula Messina study the paths of the "dancing rocks."*

Slipping and Sliding

Karen is one of the mysterious dancing rocks of Death Valley. These rocks slide around—sometimes together, sometimes alone. There are nearly 200 of them, and they range in size from small to very large. No one has seen them move, but their trails show where they've been.

The rocks are scattered across a dry lake bed, called the Racetrack, in Death Valley, California. The Racetrack is very flat and has almost no plants or wildlife. Several times a year, powerful storms rip across the lake bed, bringing plenty of rain, wind, and sometimes snow. The Racetrack's clay surface becomes slippery, and that's apparently when the rocks dance.

Puzzles and Clues

What could push a 320 kg boulder hundreds of yards across the mud? With the help of technology, scientists like Paula Messina are finally getting some answers. Messina uses a global positioning system (GPS) receiver and a geographic information system (GIS) to study the rocks. Using GPS satellites, Messina is able to map the movements of the rocks. Her measurements are more accurate than ever before. This new device measures the locations within centimeters! A computer equipped with GIS software constructs maps that allow her to study how the rock movement relates to the terrain. Messina's investigations with this equipment have led her to conclude that wind is probably pushing the rocks.

But how does the wind push such massive rocks? Messina thinks the gaps in the mountains at one end of the valley funnel high-speed winds down onto the slippery clay surface, pushing the rocks along. And why do some rocks move while others nearby do not? This mystery will keep Messina returning to Death Valley for years.

Search and Find

▶ Go to the library or the Internet, and research the many uses for GPS devices. Make a list in your ScienceLog of all the uses for GPS devices you find.

EYE ON THE ENVIRONMENT

Beach Today, Gone Tomorrow

Beaches are fun, right? But what if you went to the coast and found that the road along the beach had washed away? It could happen. In fact, erosion is stripping away beaches from islands and coastlines around the world.

An Island's Beaches

The beaches of Anguilla, a small Caribbean island, are important to the social, economic, and environmental well-being of the island and its inhabitants. Anguilla's sandy shores protect coastal areas from wave action and provide habitats for coastal plants and animals. The shores also provide important recreational areas for tourists and local residents. When Hurricane Luis hit Anguilla in 1995, Barney Bay was completely stripped of sand. But Anguilla's erosion problems started long before Luis hit the island. Normal ocean wave action had already washed away some beaches.

Back in the United States

Louisiana provides a good example of coastal problems in the United States. Louisiana has 40 percent of the nation's coastal wetlands. As important as these wetlands are, parts of the Louisiana coast are disappearing at a rate of 65 to 90 km² per year. That's a football field every 15 minutes! At that rate of erosion, Louisiana's new coastline would be 48 km inland by the year 2040!

Save the Sand

The people of Louisiana and Anguilla have acted to stop the loss of their coastlines. But many of their solutions are only temporary. Waves, storms, and human activity continue to erode coastlines. What can be done about beach erosion?

Scientists know that beaches and wetlands come and go to a certain extent. Erosion is part of a natural cycle. Scientists must first determine how much erosion is normal for

▲ *This is what Barney Bay looked like in 1995 before and after Hurricane Luis.*

a particular area and how much is the result of human activities or some unusual process. The next step is to preserve or stabilize existing sand dunes, preserve coastal vegetation, and plant more shrubs, vines, grasses, and trees. The people of Louisiana and Anguilla have learned a lot from their problems and are taking many of these steps to slow further erosion. If steps are taken to protect valuable coastal areas, beaches will be there when you go on vacation.

Extending Your Knowledge

▶ What are barrier islands? How are they related to coastal erosion? On your own, find out more about barrier islands and why it is important to preserve them.

In this unit, you will learn about the Earth's oceans and the vast landscapes they cover. Together, the oceans form the largest single feature on the planet. In fact, they cover approximately 70 percent of the Earth's surface. Now that's a lot of water! Not only do the oceans serve as home for countless living organisms, but they also affect life on land. You will learn more about the oceans in this unit as well as in the timeline presented here. Take a deep breath, and dive in!

1872

The HMS *Challenger* begins its four-year voyage. Its discoveries lay the foundation for the science of oceanography.

1851

Herman Melville's novel *Moby-Dick* is published.

1977

Thermal vent communities of creatures that exist without sunlight are discovered on the ocean floor.

1978

Louise Brown, the first "test-tube baby," is born in England.

1986

Commercial whaling is officially banned by the International Whaling Commission, but some whaling continues.

1927

Charles Lindbergh completes the first nonstop solo airplane flight over the Atlantic Ocean.

1914

The Panama Canal is completed, linking the Atlantic Ocean with the Pacific Ocean.

1938

A coelacanth is discovered in the Indian Ocean near South Africa. Called a fossil fish, the coelacanth was thought to have been extinct for 60 million years.

1960

Jacques Piccard and Don Walsh dive to a record 10,910 m below sea level in their bathyscaph *Trieste.*

1943

Jacques Cousteau and Émile Gagnon invent the Aqualung, a breathing device that allows divers to freely explore the silent world of the oceans.

1990

The tunnel under the English Channel is completed, making train and auto travel between Great Britain and France possible.

1998

Ben Lecomte of Austin, Texas, successfully swims across the Atlantic Ocean from Massachusetts to France, a distance of 6,015 km. His record-breaking feat took 74 days.

Pre-Reading
Questions

1. How have Earth's oceans
   changed over time?

2. Name two ways to study
   the ocean without going
   under water.

3. Name two valuable
   resources that are taken
   from the ocean.

EXIT ONLY?

To study what life under water would be like, scientists sometimes live in underwater laboratories. How do these scientists enter and leave these labs? Believe it or not, the simplest way is through a hole in the lab's floor. You might think water would come in through the hole, but it doesn't. People inside the lab can breathe freely and can come and go through the hole at any time. How is this possible? Do the following activity to find out.

Procedure

1. Fill a **large bowl** about two-thirds full of **water.**

2. Turn a **clear plastic cup** upside down.

3. Slowly guide the cup straight down into the water. Be careful not to tip the cup.

4. Record your observations in your ScienceLog.

Analysis

5. How does the air inside the cup affect the water below the cup?

6. How do your findings relate to the hole in the bottom of the under-water research lab?

A NEW WORLD UNDER WATER

Seventy-one percent of the Earth's surface is covered by ocean water. However, large portions of the oceans, especially the deepest parts and the parts nearest the poles, remain completely unexplored. In the past several decades, new technologies have made underwater exploration possible, allowing scientists to gather important information about the Earth's greatest resource. In this chapter, you'll learn about the fascinating world under the water and the important part the oceans play in making our planet livable.

Earth's Oceans

Terms to Learn

salinity
thermocline
water cycle

What You'll Do

◆ Name the major divisions of the global ocean.
◆ Describe the history of Earth's oceans.
◆ Summarize the properties and other aspects of ocean water.
◆ Summarize the interaction between the ocean and the atmosphere.

Earth stands out from the other planets in our solar system primarily for one reason—71 percent of the Earth's surface is covered with water. Most of Earth's water is found in the global ocean, which is divided by the continents into four main oceans. This is shown in the figure below. The ocean is a unique body of water that plays many roles in regulating Earth's environment. Read on to learn more about one of our most important resources—the ocean.

Divisions of the Global Ocean

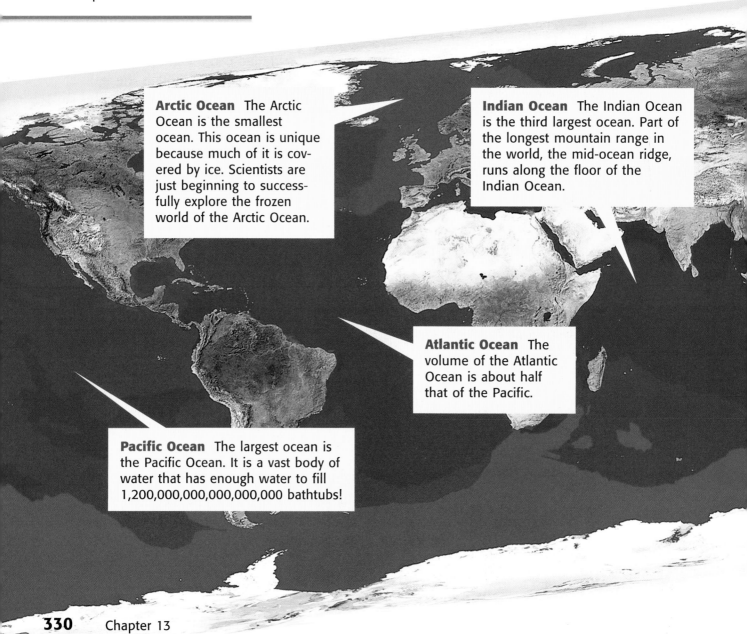

Arctic Ocean The Arctic Ocean is the smallest ocean. This ocean is unique because much of it is covered by ice. Scientists are just beginning to successfully explore the frozen world of the Arctic Ocean.

Indian Ocean The Indian Ocean is the third largest ocean. Part of the longest mountain range in the world, the mid-ocean ridge, runs along the floor of the Indian Ocean.

Atlantic Ocean The volume of the Atlantic Ocean is about half that of the Pacific.

Pacific Ocean The largest ocean is the Pacific Ocean. It is a vast body of water that has enough water to fill 1,200,000,000,000,000,000 bathtubs!

How Did the Oceans Form?

About four and a half billion years ago, the Earth was a very different place. There were no oceans. Volcanoes spewed lava, ash, and gases all over the planet, which was much hotter than it is today. The volcanic gases, including water vapor, began to form Earth's atmosphere. While the atmosphere developed, the Earth was cooling. Sometime before 4 billion years ago, the Earth cooled enough for water vapor to condense and fall as rain. The rain began filling the lower levels of Earth's surface, and the first oceans began to form.

Earth's oceans have changed a lot throughout history. Scientists who study oceans have learned much about the oceans' history, as shown in the diagram below.

Self-Check

Examine the diagram below. If North America and South America continue to drift westward and Asia continues to drift eastward, what will eventually happen? *(See page 726 to check your answer.)*

The Recent History of Earth's Oceans

About 245 million years ago, the continents were one giant landmass called *Pangaea* and the oceans were one giant water body called *Panthalassa*.

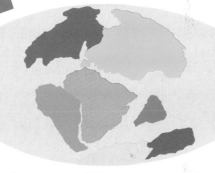

About 180 million years ago, the North Atlantic Ocean and the Indian Ocean began to form.

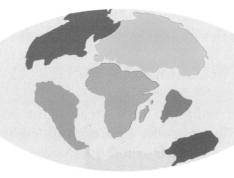

About 65 million years ago, the South Atlantic Ocean was much smaller than it is today.

Today the continents continue to move at a rate of 1–10 cm per year. While the Pacific Ocean is getting smaller, the other oceans are expanding.

Characteristics of Ocean Water

You know that ocean water is different from the water that flows from the faucet of your kitchen sink. For one thing, ocean water is not safe to drink. But there are other characteristics that make ocean water special.

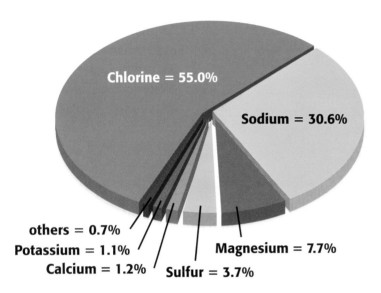

Figure 1 **Percentages of Dissolved Solids in Ocean Water** *This pie chart shows the relative amounts of the dissolved solids in ocean water.*

Chlorine = 55.0%
Sodium = 30.6%
others = 0.7%
Potassium = 1.1%
Calcium = 1.2%
Sulfur = 3.7%
Magnesium = 7.7%

Ocean Water Is Salty Have you ever swallowed a mouthful of water while swimming in the ocean? It sure had a nasty taste, didn't it? Most of the salt in the ocean is the same kind of salt that we sprinkle on our food. Scientists call this salt *sodium chloride.*

The ocean is so salty because salt has been added to it for billions of years. As rivers and streams flow toward the oceans, they dissolve various minerals on land. The running water carries these dissolved minerals to the ocean. At the same time, water is *evaporating* from the ocean, leaving the dissolved solids behind. The most abundant dissolved solid in the ocean is sodium chloride, a compound of the elements sodium (Na) and chlorine (Cl), as shown in **Figure 1.**

Chock-full of Solids If more water evaporates than enters the ocean, the ocean's salinity increases. **Salinity** is a measure of the amount of dissolved salts and other solids in a given amount of liquid. Salinity is usually measured as grams of dissolved solids per kilogram of water. Think of it this way: 1 kg (1,000 g) of ocean water contains 35 g of dissolved solids on average. Therefore, if you evaporated 1 kg of ocean water, about 35 g of solids would remain.

Factors That Affect Salinity Some areas of the ocean are saltier than others. Coastal water in areas with hotter, drier climates typically have a higher salinity than coastal water in cooler, more humid areas. This is because less fresh water runs into the ocean in drier areas and because heat increases the evaporation rate. Evaporation removes water but leaves salts and other dissolved solids behind. Also, coastal areas where major rivers run into the ocean have a relatively low salinity. In these areas, the rivers add to the ocean large volumes of fresh water, which contains fewer dissolved solids than sea water.

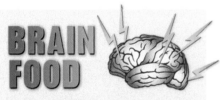

Did you know that there are about 9 million tons of gold dissolved in the ocean? Too bad the gold's concentration is only 0.000004 mg per kilogram of sea water. Mining the gold from the water would be difficult, and the cost of removing it would be greater than the gold's value.

Another factor that affects ocean salinity is water movement. Surface water in some areas of the ocean, such as bays, gulfs, and seas, circulates less than surface water in other parts. Areas in the open ocean that have no currents running through them can also be slow moving. **Figure 2** shows how salinity variations relate to many factors.

Temperature Zones The temperature of ocean water decreases as the depth of the water increases. However, this does not occur gradually from the ocean's surface to its bottom. Water in the ocean can be divided into three layers according to temperature. As you can see in the graph below, the water at the top is much warmer than the average temperature of the ocean.

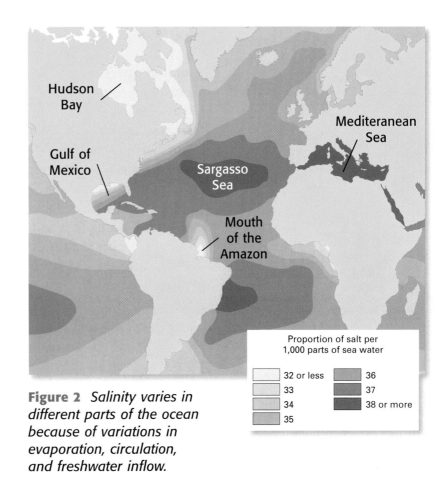

Figure 2 *Salinity varies in different parts of the ocean because of variations in evaporation, circulation, and freshwater inflow.*

Proportion of salt per 1,000 parts of sea water

32 or less	36
33	37
34	38 or more
35	

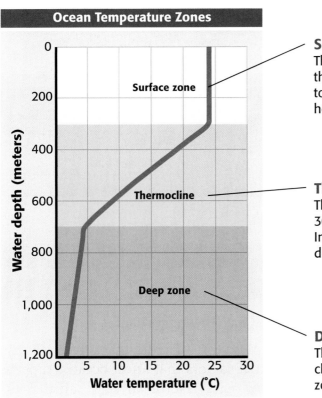

Ocean Temperature Zones

Surface zone
The surface zone is the warm, top layer of ocean water that extends to 300 m below sea level. Sunlight heats the top 100 m of the surface zone. Surface currents mix the heated water with cooler water below.

Thermocline
The **thermocline** is a layer of water extending from 300 m below sea level to about 700 m below sea level. In this zone, water temperature drops with increased depth faster than it does in the other two zones.

Deep zone
This bottom layer extends from the base of the thermocline to the bottom of the ocean. The temperature in this zone averages a chilling 2°C.

Surface Temperature Changes   Temperatures in the surface zone vary with latitude and the time of year. Surface temperatures range from 1°C near the poles to about 24°C near the equator. Areas of the ocean along the equator are warmer because they receive more sunlight per year than areas closer to the poles. However, the sun's rays in the Northern Hemisphere are more direct during the summer than during the winter. Therefore, the surface zone absorbs more thermal energy during the summer.

If you live near the coast, you may know firsthand how different a dip in the ocean feels in December than it feels in July. **Figure 3** shows how surface-zone temperatures vary depending on the time of year.

Figure 3 *These satellite images show that the surface temperatures in the northern Pacific Ocean change with the seasons.*

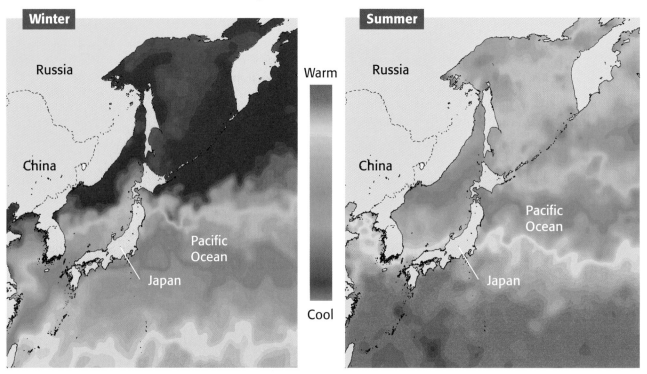

internetconnect

SciLINKS
NSTA

TOPIC: Exploring Earth's Oceans
GO TO: www.scilinks.org
*sci*LINKS NUMBER: HSTE305

REVIEW

1. Name the major divisions of the global ocean.

2. Explain how Earth's first oceans formed.

3. **Summarizing Data**   List three factors that affect salinity in the ocean and three factors that affect ocean temperatures. Explain how each factor affects salinity or temperature.

The Ocean and the Water Cycle

If you could sit on the moon and look down at Earth, what would you see? You would notice that Earth's surface is made up of three basic components—water, land, and air. All three are involved in an ongoing process called the water cycle, as shown below. The **water cycle** is a cycle that links all of Earth's solid, liquid, and gaseous water together. The ocean is an important part of the water cycle because nearly all of Earth's water is found in the ocean.

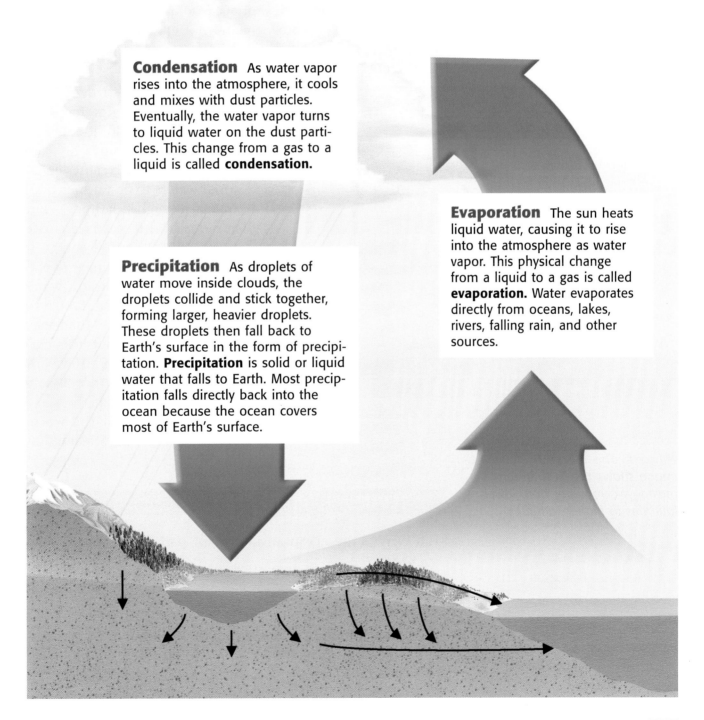

Condensation As water vapor rises into the atmosphere, it cools and mixes with dust particles. Eventually, the water vapor turns to liquid water on the dust particles. This change from a gas to a liquid is called **condensation.**

Precipitation As droplets of water move inside clouds, the droplets collide and stick together, forming larger, heavier droplets. These droplets then fall back to Earth's surface in the form of precipitation. **Precipitation** is solid or liquid water that falls to Earth. Most precipitation falls directly back into the ocean because the ocean covers most of Earth's surface.

Evaporation The sun heats liquid water, causing it to rise into the atmosphere as water vapor. This physical change from a liquid to a gas is called **evaporation.** Water evaporates directly from oceans, lakes, rivers, falling rain, and other sources.

A Global Thermostat

The ocean plays a vital role in maintaining conditions favorable for life on Earth. Perhaps the most important function of the ocean is to absorb and hold energy from sunlight. This function regulates temperatures in the atmosphere.

A Hot Exchange The ocean absorbs and releases thermal energy much more slowly than dry land does. If it were not for this function of the ocean, the average air temperature on Earth would vary from above 100°C during the day to below –100°C at night. This rapid exchange of energy between the atmosphere and the Earth's surface would cause violent weather patterns. Life as we know it could not exist with these unstable conditions.

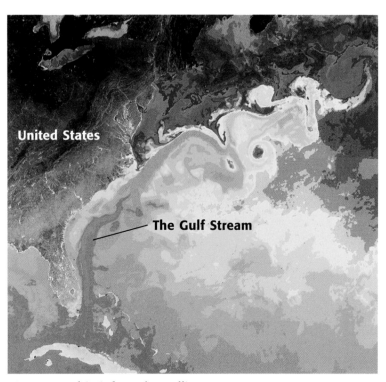

Figure 4 *This infrared satellite image shows the Gulf Stream moving warm water from lower latitudes to higher latitudes.*

Have Heat, Will Travel The ocean also regulates temperatures on a more local scale. At the equator, the sun's rays are more direct, which causes equatorial waters to be warmer than waters at higher latitudes. But currents in the oceans circulate water, as well as the energy it contains, as shown in **Figure 4.** This circulation of warm water causes some coastal lands to have warmer climates than they would have without the currents. The British Isles, for example, have a warmer climate than most regions at the same latitude because of the warm water of the Gulf Stream.

REVIEW

1. Why is the ocean an important part of the water cycle?

2. Between which two steps of the water cycle does the ocean fit?

3. **Making Inferences** Explain why St. Louis, Missouri, has colder winters and warmer summers than San Francisco, California, even though the two cities are at about the same latitude.

Section 2

Terms to Learn

continental shelf   mid-ocean ridge
continental slope   rift valley
continental rise   seamount
abyssal plain   ocean trench

What You'll Do

◆ Identify the two major regions of the ocean floor.
◆ Classify subdivisions and features of the two major regions of the ocean floor.
◆ Describe technologies for studying the ocean floor.

Science

CONNECTION

Turn to page 360 to meet the most famous underwater explorer who ever lived.

The Ocean Floor

What lies at the bottom of the ocean? How deep is the ocean? These are questions that were once unanswerable. But humans have learned a lot about the ocean floor, especially in the last few decades. Using state-of-the-art technology, scientists have discovered a wide variety of landforms on the ocean floor. Scientists have also determined accurate depths for almost the entire ocean floor.

Exploring the Ocean Floor

Some parts of the ocean are so deep that humans must use special underwater vessels to travel there. Perhaps the most familiar underwater vessel used by scientists to study the ocean floor is the minisub called *Alvin*. Scientists have used *Alvin* for many underwater missions, including searches for sunken ships, the recovery of a lost hydrogen bomb, and explorations of landforms on the sea floor.

Although the use of *Alvin* has enabled scientists to make some amazing discoveries, scientists are developing new vessels for ocean exploration, such as an underwater airplane called *Deep Flight*. This vessel, shown in **Figure 5**, moves through the water much like an airplane moves through the air. Future models of *Deep Flight* will be designed to transport pilots to the deepest part of the ocean.

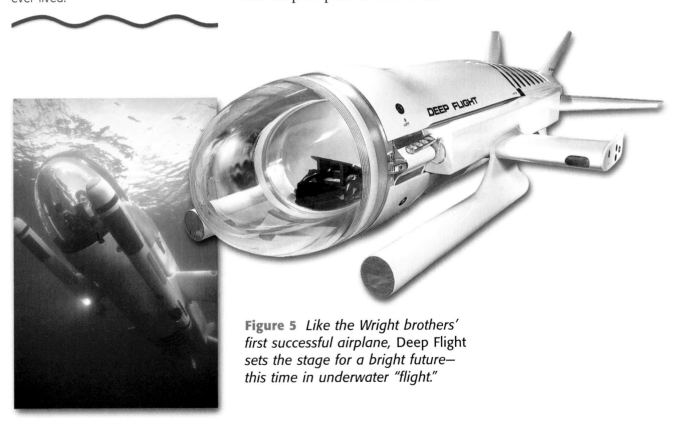

Figure 5 *Like the Wright brothers' first successful airplane,* Deep Flight *sets the stage for a bright future—this time in underwater "flight."*

Want to survey the ocean floor? Turn to page 680 in the LabBook to bring the ocean floor to your desktop.

Revealing the Ocean Floor

What if you were an explorer assigned to map uncharted areas on the planet? You might think there were not many uncharted areas left because most of the land had already been explored. But what about the bottom of the ocean? If you could travel to the bottom of the ocean in *Deep Flight,* you would see the world's largest mountain chain and canyons deeper than the Grand Canyon. And because it is under water, much of this area is unexplored.

As you began your descent into the underwater realm, you would notice two major regions—the *continental margin,* which is made of continental crust, and the *deep-ocean basin,* which is made of oceanic crust. It may help to imagine the ocean as a giant swimming pool; the continental margin is the shallow end and slope of the pool, and the deep-ocean basin is the deep end of the pool. **Figure 6** shows how these two regions are subdivided.

Figure 6 *The continental margin is subdivided into three depth zones, and the deep-ocean basin consists of one depth zone with several features.*

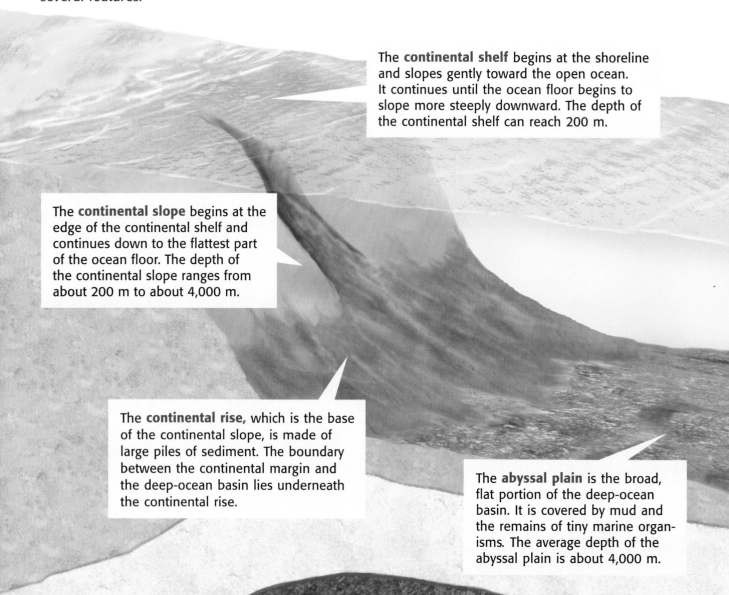

The **continental shelf** begins at the shoreline and slopes gently toward the open ocean. It continues until the ocean floor begins to slope more steeply downward. The depth of the continental shelf can reach 200 m.

The **continental slope** begins at the edge of the continental shelf and continues down to the flattest part of the ocean floor. The depth of the continental slope ranges from about 200 m to about 4,000 m.

The **continental rise**, which is the base of the continental slope, is made of large piles of sediment. The boundary between the continental margin and the deep-ocean basin lies underneath the continental rise.

The **abyssal plain** is the broad, flat portion of the deep-ocean basin. It is covered by mud and the remains of tiny marine organisms. The average depth of the abyssal plain is about 4,000 m.

Underwater Real Estate As you can see, the continental margin is subdivided into the continental shelf, the continental slope, and the continental rise based on depth and changes in slope. The deep-ocean basin consists of the abyssal plain, with features such as mid-ocean ridges, rift valleys, and ocean trenches that form near the boundaries of Earth's *tectonic plates*. On parts of the abyssal plain that are not near plate boundaries, thousands of seamounts are found on the ocean floor.

✔ Self-Check

How do the locations of rift valleys and ocean trenches differ? *(See page 726 to check your answer.)*

Activity

To get an idea of how deep parts of the ocean are, use an encyclopedia to find out how deep the Grand Canyon is. Compare this depth with that of the Mariana Trench, which is more than 11,000 m deep! Make a model of this difference using clay, or draw a graph of this difference to scale.

TRY at HOME

internet connect

SC*i*LINKS
NSTA

TOPIC: The Ocean Floor
GO TO: www.scilinks.com
*sci*LINKS NUMBER: HSTE310

Mid-ocean ridges are mountain chains formed where *tectonic plates* pull apart. This pulling motion creates cracks in the ocean floor called *rift zones.* As plates pull apart, magma rises to fill in the spaces. Heat from the magma causes the crust on either side of the rifts to expand, forming the ridges.

Seamounts are individual mountains of volcanic material. They form where magma pushes its way through or between tectonic plates. If a seamount builds up above sea level, it becomes a volcanic island.

As mountains build up, a **rift valley** forms between them in the rift zone.

Ocean trenches are seemingly bottomless cracks in the deep-ocean basin. Ocean trenches form where one oceanic plate is forced underneath a continental plate or another oceanic plate.

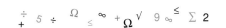

MATH BREAK

Depths of the Deep

The depths in a bathymetric profile are calculated using the following simple formula:

$$D = \frac{1}{2}t \times v$$

D is the depth of the ocean floor, t is the time it takes for the sound to reach the bottom and return to the surface, and v equals the speed of sound in water (1,500 m/s). Calculate D for the following three parts of the ocean floor:

1. a mid-ocean ridge ($t = 2$ s)
2. an ocean trench ($t = 14$ s)
3. an abyssal plain ($t = 5.3$ s)

Viewing the Ocean Floor from Above

In spite of the great success of underwater exploration, sending scientists into deep water is still risky. Fortunately, there are ways to survey the underwater realm from the surface and from high above in space. Read on to learn about two technologies—sonar and satellites—that enable scientists to study the ocean floor without going below the surface.

Seeing by Sonar *Sonar*, which stands for "sound navigation and ranging," is a technology based on the echo-ranging behavior of bats. Scientists use sonar to determine the ocean's depth by sending high-frequency sound pulses from a ship down into the ocean. The sound travels through the water, bounces off the ocean floor, and returns to the ship. The deeper the water is, the longer the round trip takes. Scientists then calculate the depth by multiplying half the travel time by the speed of sound in water (about 1,500 m/s). This process is shown in the illustration below.

1 To map a section of the ocean floor, scientists travel by ship across the ocean's surface, repeatedly sending sonar signals to the ocean floor.

2 The longer it takes for the sound to bounce off the ocean floor and return to the ship, the deeper the floor is in that spot.

3 Scientists plot sonar signals to make a *bathymetric profile,* which is basically a map of the ocean floor showing its depth variations.

Oceanography via Satellite In the 1970s, scientists began studying Earth from satellites in orbit around the Earth. In 1978, scientists launched the satellite *Seasat.* This satellite focused on the ocean, sending images back to Earth that allowed scientists to measure the direction and speed of ocean currents.

Geosat, once a top-secret military satellite, has been used to measure slight changes in the height of the ocean's surface. Different underwater features, such as mountains and trenches, affect the height of the water above them, thus reflecting the underwater topography of the ocean floor. Scientists measure the different heights of the ocean surface and use the measurements to make highly detailed maps of the ocean floor. As illustrated in **Figure 7,** oceanographers can make maps that cover a lot more territory by using satellites than by using ship-based sonar readings.

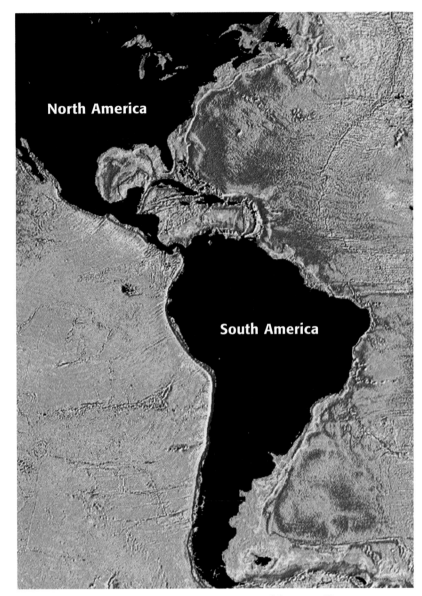

Figure 7 *The map above was generated by satellite measurements of different heights of the ocean surface.*

REVIEW

1. Name the two major regions of the ocean floor.

2. List the subdivisions of the continental margin.

3. List three technologies for studying the ocean floor, and explain how they are used.

4. **Interpreting Graphics** What part of the ocean floor would the bathymetric profile at right represent?

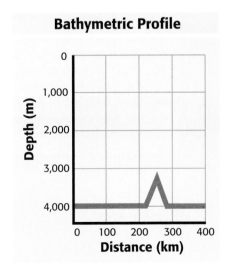

Life in the Ocean

Terms to Learn

plankton   benthic environment
nekton   pelagic environment
benthos

What You'll Do

◆ Identify and describe the three
  groups of marine organisms.
◆ Identify and describe the benthic
  and pelagic environments.
◆ Classify the zones of the benthic
  and pelagic environments.

The ocean contains a wide variety of life-forms, many of which
we know little about. Trying to study them can be quite a
challenge for scientists. To make things easier, scientists classify marine organisms into three main groups. Scientists also
divide the ocean into two main environments based on the
types of organisms that live in them. These two main environments are further subdivided into ecological zones based
on locations of different organisms.

The Three Groups of Marine Life

The three main groups of marine life are plankton, nekton,
and benthos. Marine organisms are placed into one of these
three groups according to where they live and how they move.
Carefully examine the figure below to understand the differences between these groups.

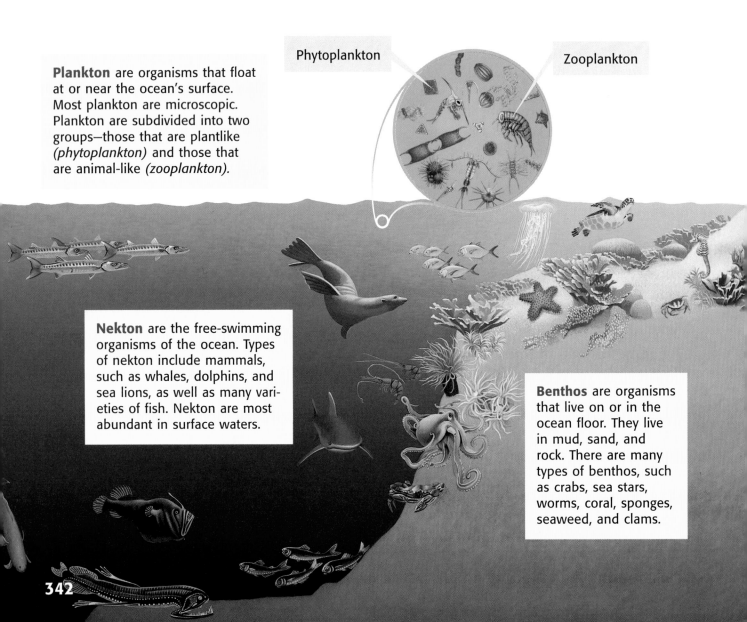

Phytoplankton

Zooplankton

Plankton are organisms that float
at or near the ocean's surface.
Most plankton are microscopic.
Plankton are subdivided into two
groups—those that are plantlike
(*phytoplankton*) and those that
are animal-like (*zooplankton).*

Nekton are the free-swimming
organisms of the ocean. Types
of nekton include mammals,
such as whales, dolphins, and
sea lions, as well as many varieties of fish. Nekton are most
abundant in surface waters.

Benthos are organisms
that live on or in the
ocean floor. They live
in mud, sand, and
rock. There are many
types of benthos, such
as crabs, sea stars,
worms, coral, sponges,
seaweed, and clams.

The Benthic Environment

In addition to being divided into zones based on depth, the ocean floor is divided into ecological zones based on where different types of benthos live. These zones are grouped into one major marine environment—the benthic environment. The **benthic environment,** or bottom environment, is the ocean floor and all the organisms that live on or in it.

Intertidal Zone The shallowest benthic zone, the *intertidal zone,* is located between the low-tide and high-tide limits. Twice a day, the intertidal zone transforms. As the tide flows in, the zone is covered with ocean water, and as the tide retreats, the intertidal zone is exposed to the air and sun.

Intertidal organisms must be able to live both underwater and on exposed land. Some organisms attach themselves to rocks and reefs to avoid being washed out to sea during low tide, as shown in **Figure 8.** Clams, oysters, barnacles, and crabs have tough shells that give them protection against strong waves during high tide and against harsh sunlight during low tide. Some animals can burrow in sand or between rocks. Plants such as seaweed have strong *holdfasts* (rootlike structures) that allow them to grow in this zone.

Sublittoral Zone The *sublittoral zone* begins where the intertidal zones ends, at the low-tide limit, and extends to the edge of the continental shelf. This benthic zone is more stable than the intertidal zone; the temperature, water pressure, and amount of sunlight remain fairly constant. Consequently, sublittoral organisms, such as corals, shown in **Figure 9,** do not have to cope with as much change as intertidal organisms. Although the sublittoral zone extends down 200 m below sea level, plants and most animals stay in the upper 100 m, where sunlight reaches the ocean floor.

Biology CONNECTION

Coral reefs, found in shallow marine waters, have the largest concentration of life in the ocean. Layers of skeletons from animals called *corals* form the reefs, which are the largest animal structures on Earth. Many other organisms live on, around, and even in coral reefs.

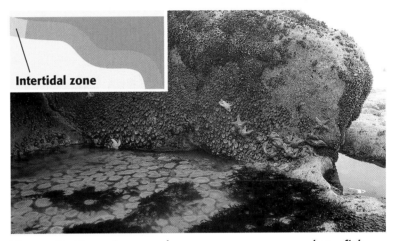

Figure 8 *Organisms such as sea anemones and starfish attach themselves to rocks and reefs. These organisms must be able to survive wet and dry conditions.*

Figure 9 *Corals, like many other types of organisms, can live in both the sublittoral zone and the intertidal zone. However, they are more common in the sublittoral zone.*

Figure 10 *Octopuses are one of the animals common to the bathyal zone.*

Figure 11 *Tube worms can tolerate higher temperatures than most other organisms. These animals survive in water as hot as 81°C.*

Figure 12 *These clams are one of the few types of organisms known to live in the hadal zone.*

Bathyal Zone The *bathyal zone* extends from the edge of the continental shelf to the abyssal plain. The depth of this zone ranges from 200 m to 4,000 m below sea level. Because of the lack of sunlight at these depths, plant life is scarce in this part of the benthic environment. Animals in this zone include sponges, *brachiopods,* sea stars, *echinoids,* and octopuses, such as the one shown in **Figure 10.**

Abyssal Zone No plants and very few animals live in the *abyssal zone,* which is on the abyssal plain. Among the abyssal animal types are crabs, sponges, worms, and sea cucumbers. Many of these organisms, such as the tube worms shown in **Figure 11,** live around hot-water vents called *black smokers.* The abyssal zone can reach 6,000 m in depth. Scientists know very little about this benthic zone because it is so deep and dark.

Hadal Zone The deepest benthic zone is the *hadal zone.* This zone consists of the floor of the ocean trenches and any organisms found there. Scientists know even less about the hadal zone than they do about the abyssal zone. So far, scientists have discovered a type of sponge, a few species of worms, and a type of clam, which is shown in **Figure 12.**

The Pelagic Environment

The **pelagic environment** is the entire volume of water in the ocean and the marine organisms that live above the ocean floor. There are two major zones in the pelagic environment—the *neritic zone* and the *oceanic zone*.

Neritic Zone The neritic zone includes the volume of water that covers the continental shelf. This warm, shallow zone contains the largest concentration of marine life. This is due to an abundance of sunlight and to the many benthos below the neritic zone that serve as a food supply. Fish, plankton, and marine mammals, such as the one in **Figure 13,** are just a few of the animal groups found here.

Oceanic Zone The oceanic zone includes the volume of water that covers the entire sea floor except for the continental shelf. In the deeper parts of the oceanic zone, the water temperature is colder and the pressure is much greater than in the neritic zone. Also, organisms are more spread out in the oceanic zone than in the neritic zone. While many of the same organisms that live in the neritic zone are found throughout the upper regions, some strange animals lurk in the darker depths, as shown in **Figure 14.** Other animals in the deeper parts of this zone include giant squids and some whale species.

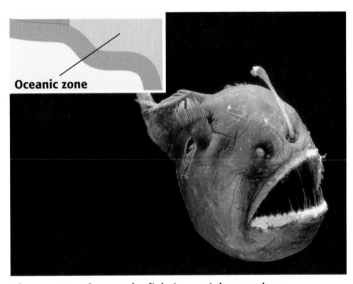

Figure 13 *Many marine mammals, such as this dolphin, live in the neritic zone.*

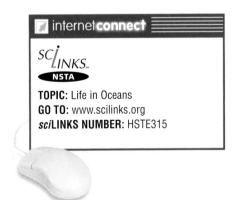

Figure 14 *The anglerfish is a tricky predator that uses a natural lure attached to its head to attract prey.*

REVIEW

1. List and briefly describe the three main groups of marine organisms.

2. Name the two ocean environments. List the zones of each environment.

3. **Making Predictions** How would the ocean's ecological zones change if sea level dropped 300 m?

internetconnect

SC*L*INKS
NSTA

TOPIC: Life in Oceans
GO TO: www.scilinks.org
*sci*LINKS NUMBER: HSTE315

Resources from the Ocean

The ocean offers a seemingly endless supply of resources. Food, raw materials, energy, and drinkable water are all harvested from the ocean. And there are probably undiscovered resources in unexplored regions of the ocean. As human populations have grown, however, the demand for these resources has increased while the availability has decreased.

Living Resources

People have been harvesting marine plants and animals for food for thousands of years. Many civilizations formed in coastal regions that were rich enough in marine life to support growing human populations. Read on to learn how humans harvest marine life today.

Fishing the Ocean Harvesting food from the ocean is a multi-billion-dollar industry. Of all the seafood taken from the ocean, fish are the most abundant. Almost 75 million tons of fish are harvested each year. With improved technology, such as sonar and drift nets, fishermen have become better at locating and taking fish from the ocean. **Figure 15** illustrates how drift nets are used. In recent years, many people have become concerned that we are overfishing the ocean—taking more fish than can be naturally replaced. Also, a few years ago, the public became aware that animals other than fish, especially dolphins and turtles, were accidentally being caught in drift nets. Today the fishing industry is making efforts to prevent overfishing and damage to other wildlife from drift nets.

Figure 15 *Drift nets are fishing nets that cover kilometers of ocean. Fishermen can harvest entire schools of fish in one drift net.*

Farming the Ocean As overfishing reduces fish populations and laws regulating fishing become stricter, it is becoming more difficult to supply our demand for fish. To compensate for this, many ocean fish, such as salmon and turbot, are being captively bred in fish farms. Fish farming requires several holding ponds, each containing fish at a certain level of development. **Figure 16** shows a holding pond in a fish farm. When the fish are old enough, they are harvested and packaged for shipping.

Figure 16 *Consuming fish raised in a fish farm helps reduce the number of fish harvested from the ocean.*

Savory Seaweed Fish are not the only seafood harvested in a farmlike setting. Shrimp, oysters, crabs, and mussels are raised in enclosed areas near the shore. Mussels and oysters are grown attached to ropes, as shown in **Figure 17.** Huge nets line the nursery area, preventing the animals from being eaten by their natural predators.

Many species of algae, commonly known as seaweed, are also harvested from the ocean. For example, kelp, a seaweed that grows as much as 33 cm a day, is harvested and used as a thickener in jellies, ice cream, and similar products. The next time you enjoy your favorite ice cream, remember that without seaweed, it would be a runny mess! Seaweed is rich in protein, and several species of seaweed are staples of the Japanese diet. For example, the rolled varieties of sushi, a Japanese dish, are wrapped in seaweed.

Figure 17 *In addition to fish, there are many other types of seafood, such as these mussels, that are raised in farms.*

Nonliving Resources

Humans harvest many types of nonliving resources from the ocean. These resources provide raw materials, drinkable water, and energy for our expanding population. Some resources are easily obtained, while others are rare or difficult to harvest.

Oil and Natural Gas Modern civilization continues to be very dependent on oil and natural gas as major sources of energy. Oil and natural gas are *nonrenewable resources,* which means that they are used up faster than they can be replenished naturally. Both oil and natural gas are found under layers of impermeable rock. Petroleum engineers must drill through this rock in order to reach the resources.

Searching for Oil How do petroleum engineers know where to drill for oil and natural gas? Ships with seismic equipment are used for this purpose. Special devices send powerful pulses of sound to the ocean floor. The pulses travel through the water and penetrate the rocks below. The pulses are then reflected back toward the ship, where they are recorded by electronic equipment and analyzed by a computer. The computer readings, such as the one in **Figure 18,** indicate how rock layers are arranged below the ocean floor. Petroleum geologists use these readings to locate a promising area to drill.

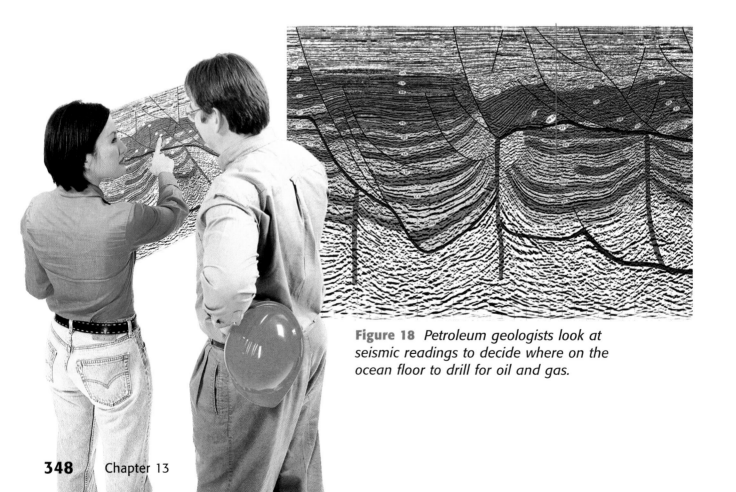

Figure 18 *Petroleum geologists look at seismic readings to decide where on the ocean floor to drill for oil and gas.*

Fresh Water and Desalination In some areas of the world where fresh water is limited, people desalinate ocean water. **Desalination** is the process of evaporating sea water so that the water and the salt separate. As the water cools and condenses, it is collected and processed for human use. But desalination is not as simple as it sounds, and it is very costly. Countries with an adequate amount of annual rainfall rely on the fresh water provided by precipitation and therefore do not need costly desalination plants. Some countries located in arid regions of the world must build desalination plants to provide an adequate supply of fresh water. Saudi Arabia, located in the desert region of the Middle East, has one of the largest desalination plants in the world.

Sea-Floor Minerals Mining companies are very interested in mineral nodules that are lying on the ocean floor. These nodules are made mostly of manganese, which can be used to make certain types of steel. They also contain iron, copper, nickel, and cobalt. Other nodules are made of phosphates, which are used in making fertilizer.

Nodules are formed from dissolved substances in sea water that stick to solid objects, such as pebbles. As more substances stick to the coated pebble, a nodule begins to grow. Manganese nodules range from the size of a marble to the size of a soccer ball. The photograph in **Figure 19** shows a number of nodules scattered across the ocean floor. It is believed that 15 percent of the ocean floor is covered with these nodules. However, they are located in the deeper parts of the ocean, and mining them is costly and difficult.

QuickLab

How Much Fresh Water Is There?

1. Fill a large **beaker** with 1,000 mL of **water.** This represents all the water on Earth.

2. Carefully pour 970 mL from the beaker into a **graduated cylinder.** This represents the amount of water in the ocean.

3. Pour another 20 mL from the beaker into a **second graduated cylinder.** This represents the amount of water frozen in icecaps and glaciers.

4. Pour another 5 mL into a **third graduated cylinder.** This represents nonconsumable water on land.

5. Take a look at the leftover water. This represents Earth's supply of fresh water.

Put freshwater problems on ice! Turn to page 361 to find out how.

Figure 19 *These manganese nodules could make you wealthy if you knew an affordable way to mine them.*

Figure 20 Using Tides to Generate Electricity

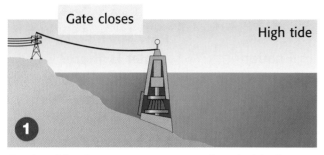

As the tide rises, water enters a bay behind a dam. The gate then closes at high tide.

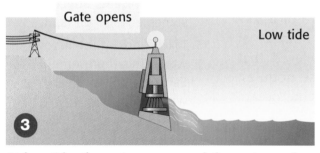

The gate remains closed as the tide lowers.

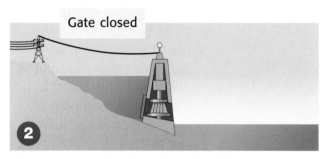

At low tide, the gate opens, and the water rushes through the dam, moving the turbines, which in turn create electricity.

Tidal Energy The ocean creates several types of energy resources simply because of its constant movement. The gravitational pull of the sun and moon causes the ocean to rise and fall as tides. *Tidal energy,* energy generated from the movement of tides, is an excellent alternative source of energy. If the water during high tide can be rushed through a narrow coastal passageway, the water's force can be powerful enough to generate electricity. **Figure 20** shows how this works. Tidal energy is a clean, inexpensive, and renewable resource once the dam is built. A *renewable resource* can be replenished, in time, after being used. Unfortunately, tidal energy is practical only in a few areas of the world, where the coastline has shallow, narrow channels. For example, the coastline at Cook Inlet, in Alaska, is perfect for generating tidal power.

Wave Energy Have you ever stood on the beach and watched as waves crashed onto the shore? This constant motion is an energy resource. Wave energy, like tidal energy, is a clean, renewable resource.

Recently, computer programs have been developed to analyze the energy of waves. Researchers have located certain areas of the world where wave energy can generate enough electricity to make it worthwhile to build power plants. Wave energy in the North Sea is strong enough to produce power for parts of Scotland and England.

internetconnect

SC*i*LINKS
NSTA

TOPIC: Ocean Resources
GO TO: www.scilinks.org
*sci*LINKS NUMBER: HSTE320

REVIEW

1. List two methods of harvesting the ocean's living resources.

2. Name four nonliving resources in the ocean.

3. **Interpreting Graphics** Take another look at Figure 20. As the tide is rising, will the gate be open or closed? How might this affect the turbines?

Ocean Pollution

Terms to Learn

nonpoint-source pollution

What You'll Do

◆ List different types of ocean pollution.
◆ Explain how to prevent or minimize different types of ocean pollution.
◆ Outline what is being done to control ocean pollution.

Humans have used the ocean for waste disposal for hundreds, if not thousands, of years. This has harmed the organisms that live in the oceans as well as animals that depend on marine organisms. People are also affected by polluted oceans. Fortunately, we are becoming more aware of ocean pollution, and we are learning from our mistakes.

Sources of Ocean Pollution

There are many sources of ocean pollution. Some of these sources are easily identified, but others are more difficult to pinpoint. Read on to find out where different types of ocean pollution come from and how they affect the ocean.

Trash Dumping People dump trash in many places, including the ocean. In the 1980s, scientists became alarmed by the kind of trash that was washing up on beaches. Bandages, vials of blood, and syringes (needles) were found among the waste. Some of the blood in the vials even contained the AIDS virus. The Environmental Protection Agency (EPA) began an investigation and discovered that hospitals in the United States produce an average of 3 million tons of medical waste each year. And where does some of this trash end up? You guessed it—in the ocean. Because of stricter laws, much of this medical waste is now buried in sanitary landfills. However, dumping trash in the deeper part of the ocean is still a common practice in many countries.

Figure 21 *This barge is headed out to the open ocean, where it will dump the trash it carries.*

Sludge Dumping By 1990, the United States alone had discharged 38 trillion liters of treated sludge into the waters along its coasts. What is sludge, and why is it so bad? To answer this question, we need to define *raw sewage*.

Raw sewage is all the liquid and solid wastes that are flushed down toilets and poured down drains. After collecting in sewer drains, raw sewage is sent through a treatment plant, where it undergoes a cleaning process that removes the solid waste. The solid waste is called *sludge*. In many areas, people dump sludge into the ocean several kilometers offshore, intending for it to settle to and stay on the ocean floor. Unfortunately, currents sometimes stir the sludge up and move it closer to shore. This can pollute beaches and kill marine life. Many countries have banned sludge dumping, but it continues to occur in many areas of the world.

Nonpoint-Source Pollution We usually think of water pollution as coming from large factories, but you may be surprised to know that most of the pollution comes from everyday citizens doing everyday things. This type of pollution, which is shown in **Figure 22,** is called **nonpoint-source pollution** because you cannot pinpoint its exact source. How does this pollution get into the ocean? All waste water and runoff eventually enter a body of water, usually a stream. Every stream leads to a river, and every river leads to the ocean.

Figure 22 *Nonpoint-source pollution contributes significantly to ocean pollution. What can you do to cut down on nonpoint-source pollution?*

Oil Spills Because oil is in such high demand across the world, large tankers must transport billions of barrels of it across the oceans. If not handled properly, these transports can quickly turn disastrous. In 1989, the supertanker *Exxon Valdez* struck a reef and spilled more than 260,000 barrels of crude oil. The effect of this accident on wildlife was catastrophic. Many animals died. Alaskans who made their living from fishing lost their businesses. Although many animals were saved, as shown in **Figure 23,** and the Exxon Oil Company spent $2.5 billion to try to clean up the mess, Alaska's wildlife and economy will continue to suffer for decades.

Today many oil companies are using new technology to safeguard against oil spills. Tankers are now being built with two hulls instead of one. This prevents oil from spilling into the ocean if the outside hull of the ship is damaged. **Figure 24** illustrates the design of a double-hulled tanker.

Figure 23 *Many oil-covered animals were rescued and cleaned after the* Exxon Valdez *spill.*

BRAIN FOOD

Within the first few weeks of the *Exxon Valdez* oil spill, more than half a million birds, including 109 endangered bald eagles, were covered with oil and drowned. Almost half the sea otters in the area also died either from drowning or from being poisoned by the oil.

Figure 24 *If the outside hull of a double-hulled tanker is punctured, the oil will still be contained within the inside hull.*

Saving Our Ocean Resources

Although humans have done much to harm the ocean's resources, we have also begun to do more to save them. From international treaties to volunteer cleanups, efforts to conserve the ocean's resources are making an impact around the world.

Nations Take Notice When ocean pollution reached an all-time high, many countries recognized the need to work together to solve the problem. In 1989, 64 countries ratified a treaty that prohibits the dumping of mercury, cadmium compounds, certain plastics, oil, and high-level radioactive wastes into the ocean. Many other international agreements restricting ocean pollution have been made, but enforcing them is often difficult.

In spite of efforts to protect the ocean, waste dumping and oil spills still occur, and contaminated organisms continue to wash ashore. Why are the laws not working as well as they should? Enforcing these laws takes money and human resources, and many agencies are lacking in both.

Action in the United States The United States, like many other countries, has taken additional measures to control local pollution. In 1972, Congress passed the Clean Water Act, which put the EPA in charge of issuing permits for any dumping of trash into the ocean. Later that year, a stricter law was passed. The U.S. Marine Protection, Research, and Sanctuaries Act prohibits the dumping of any material that would affect human health or welfare, the marine environment or ecosystems, or businesses that depend on the ocean.

Why worry about a few drops of oil? You might be surprised that a little goes a long way. Turn to page 682 in the LabBook to learn more.

Ocean Treaty

Get together with your classmates and divide yourselves into three groups: Nation A, Nation B, and Nation C. All three nations are located near the ocean, and all three nations share borders. Nation A has a very rich supply of oil, which it transports around the world. Nation B currently depends on nuclear energy and has many nuclear power plants near its shores. Nation B has no place on land to store radioactive waste from its nuclear power plants. Nation C sells nuclear technology to Nation B, buys oil from Nation A, and has the world's most diverse coastal ecosystem. The three nations must form a treaty to safeguard against ocean pollution without seriously harming any of their economies. Can you do it?

Figure 25 *The Adopt-a-Beach program in Texas has been a huge success.*

Citizens Take Charge   Citizens of many countries have demanded that their governments do more to solve the growing problem of ocean pollution. Because of public outcry, the United States now spends more than $130 million each year monitoring the oceans. United States citizens have also begun to take the matter into their own hands. In the early 1980s, citizens began organizing beach cleanups. One of the largest cleanups is the semiannual Adopt-a-Beach program, shown in **Figure 25,** that originated with the Texas Coastal Cleanup campaign. Millions of tons of trash have been gathered from the beaches, and people are being educated about the hazards of ocean dumping.

Though governments pass laws against ocean dumping, keeping the oceans clean is everyone's responsibility. The next time you and your family visit the beach, make sure the only items you leave behind on the sand are hermit crabs, shells, and maybe a few sand dollars.

REVIEW

1. List three types of ocean pollution. How can each of these types be prevented or minimized?

2. Which type of ocean pollution is most common?

3. **Summarizing Data**   List and describe three measures that governments have taken to control ocean pollution.

*internet***connect**

SC*i*LINKS
NSTA

TOPIC: Ocean Pollution
GO TO: www.scilinks.org
*sci***LINKS NUMBER:** HSTE323

Chapter Highlights

SECTION 1

Vocabulary

salinity *(p. 332)*

thermocline *(p. 333)*

water cycle *(p. 335)*

Section Notes

- The four oceans as we know them today formed within the last 300 million years.

- Salts have been added to the ocean for billions of years.

- The three temperature zones of ocean water are the surface zone, thermocline, and deep zone.

- The ocean plays the largest role in the water cycle.

- The ocean stabilizes Earth's conditions by absorbing and retaining thermal energy.

SECTION 2

Vocabulary

continental shelf *(p. 338)*

continental slope *(p. 338)*

continental rise *(p. 338)*

abyssal plain *(p. 338)*

mid-ocean ridge *(p. 339)*

rift valley *(p. 339)*

seamount *(p. 339)*

ocean trench *(p. 339)*

Section Notes

- The ocean floor is divided into zones based on depth and slope.

- The continental margin consists of the continental shelf, the continental slope, and the continental rise.

- The deep-ocean basin consists of the abyssal plain, with features such as mid-ocean ridges, rift valleys, seamounts, and ocean trenches.

- In addition to directly studying the ocean floor, scientists indirectly study the ocean floor using sonar and satellites.

Labs

Probing the Depths *(p. 680)*

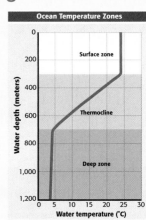

☑ Skills Check

Math Concepts

PERCENTAGES Percentages are a way of describing the parts within a whole. Percentages are expressed in hundredths. Take another look at Figure 1 on page 332. The pie chart shows the percentages of dissolved solids in ocean water. The amount of chlorine (Cl) dissolved in the ocean is 55 percent. This means that 55 of every 100 parts of dissolved solids in the ocean are chlorine.

Visual Understanding

TEMPERATURE ZONES Look back at the line graph on page 333 to review why the temperature of the ocean decreases with increasing depth.

Ocean Temperature Zones

Surface zone

Thermocline

Deep zone

Water depth (meters): 0, 200, 400, 600, 800, 1,000, 1,200

Water temperature (°C): 0, 5, 10, 15, 20, 25, 30

SECTION 3

Vocabulary

plankton *(p. 342)*

nekton *(p. 342)*

benthos *(p. 342)*

benthic environment *(p. 343)*

pelagic environment *(p. 345)*

Section Notes

- There are three main groups of marine life—plankton, nekton, and benthos.

- The two main ocean environments—the benthic and pelagic environments—are divided into ecological zones based on the locations of organisms that live in the environments.

SECTION 4

Vocabulary

desalination *(p. 349)*

Section Notes

- Humans depend on the ocean for living and non-living resources.

- Ocean farms raise fish and other marine life to help feed growing human populations.

- Nonliving ocean resources include oil and natural gas, fresh water, minerals, and tidal and wave energy.

SECTION 5

Vocabulary

nonpoint-source pollution *(p. 352)*

Section Notes

- Types of ocean pollution include trash dumping, sludge dumping, nonpoint-source pollution, and oil spills.

- Nonpoint-source pollution cannot be traced to specific points of origin.

- Efforts to save ocean resources include international treaties and volunteer cleanups.

Labs

Investigating an Oil Spill *(p. 682)*

---

 internetconnect

GO TO: go.hrw.com

Visit the **HRW** Web site for a variety of learning tools related to this chapter. Just type in the keyword:

KEYWORD: HSTOCE

 **GO TO:** www.scilinks.org

Visit the **National Science Teachers Association** on-line Web site for Internet resources related to this chapter. Just type in the *sci*LINKS number for more information about the topic:

Chapter Review

USING VOCABULARY

To complete the following sentences, choose the correct term from each pair of terms listed below:

1. The region of the ocean floor that is closest to the shoreline is the ___?___. *(continental shelf* or *continental slope)*

2. Below the surface layer of the ocean is a layer of water that gets colder with depth and extends to a depth of 700 m. This layer is called the ___?___. *(thermocline* or *benthic environment)*

3. ___?___ typically float at or near the ocean's surface. *(Plankton* or *Nekton)*

Correct the wrong terminology in each of the following sentences. A word bank is provided.

4. The water cycle is the process of evaporating sea water so that the water and salt separate.

5. Types of nekton include sea stars and clams.

Word bank:
nonpoint-source pollution, plankton, desalination, benthos

Explain the difference between the words in each of the following pairs:

6. ocean trench/rift valley

7. salinity/desalination

8. nekton/benthos

9. pelagic environment/benthic environment

UNDERSTANDING CONCEPTS

Multiple Choice

10. The largest ocean is the
    a. Indian Ocean.   c. Atlantic Ocean.
    b. Pacific Ocean.   d. Arctic Ocean.

11. One of the most abundant elements in the ocean is
    a. potassium.   c. chlorine.
    b. calcium.   d. magnesium.

12. Which of the following affects the ocean's salinity?
    a. fresh water added by rivers
    b. currents
    c. evaporation
    d. all of the above

13. Most precipitation falls
    a. on land.
    b. into lakes and rivers.
    c. into the ocean.
    d. in rain forests.

14. Which benthic zone has a depth range between 200 m and 4,000 m?
    a. bathyal zone   c. hadal zone
    b. abyssal zone   d. sublittoral zone

15. The ocean floor and all the organisms that live on it or in it is the
    a. benthic environment.
    b. pelagic environment.
    c. neritic zone.
    d. oceanic zone.

Short Answer

16. Why does coastal water in areas with hotter, drier climates typically have a higher salinity than coastal water in cooler, more humid areas?

17. What is the difference between the abyssal plain and the abyssal zone?

18. How do the continental shelf, the continental slope, the continental rise, and the continental margin relate to each other?

Concept Mapping

19. Use the following term to create a concept map: marine life, plankton, nekton, benthos, benthic environment, pelagic environment.

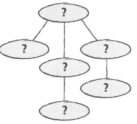

CRITICAL THINKING AND PROBLEM SOLVING

Write one or two sentences to answer the following questions:

20. Other than obtaining fresh water, what benefit comes from desalination?

21. Explain the difference between a bathymetric profile and a seismic reading.

MATH IN SCIENCE

22. Imagine that you are in the kelp-farming business and that your kelp grows 33 cm per day. You begin harvesting when your plants are 50 cm tall. During the first seven days of harvest, you cut 10 cm off the top of your kelp plants each day. How tall would your kelp plants be after the seventh day of harvesting?

INTERPRETING GRAPHICS

Examine the image below, and answer the questions that follow:

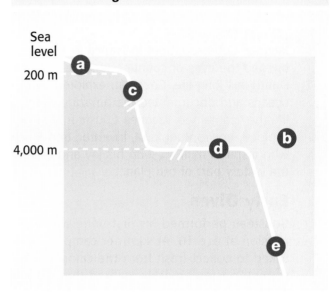

Ecological Zones of the Ocean

23. At which point *(a, b, c, d, or e)* would you most likely find an anglerfish?

24. At which point would you most likely find tube worms?

25. Which ecological zone is at point *c*? Which depth zone is at point *c*?

26. Name a type of organism you might find at point *e*.

Reading Check-up

Take a minute to review your answers to the Pre-Reading Questions found at the bottom of page 328. Have your answers changed? If necessary, revise your answers based on what you have learned since you began this chapter.

Exploring Ocean Life

Jacques Cousteau, born in France in 1910, opened the eyes of countless people to the sea. During his long life, Cousteau explored Earth's oceans and documented the amazing variety of life they contained. Jacques Cousteau was an explorer, environmentalist, inventor, and teacher who inspired millions with his joy and wonder at the watery part of our planet.

Early Dives

Cousteau performed his first underwater diving mission at age 10. At summer camp he was asked to collect trash from the camp's lake. The young Cousteau quickly realized that working underwater without goggles or breathing equipment was a tremendous challenge.

Cousteau had another early underwater experience when he visited Southeast Asia. He saw people diving into the water to catch fish with their bare hands. This fascinated Cousteau. Even at a young age, he was thinking about how to make equipment that would let a person breathe underwater.

▲ *Cousteau in front of the* Calypso II

Underwater Flight

As a young man, Cousteau and some friends developed the aqualung, a self-contained breathing system for underwater exploration. As someone who had often dreamed of flying, Cousteau was thrilled with his invention. After one of his first dives, Cousteau explained, "I experimented with all possible maneuvers— loops, somersaults, and barrel rolls. . . . Delivered from gravity and buoyancy, I flew around in space."

Using the aqualung and other underwater equipment he developed, Cousteau began making underwater films. In 1950, he bought a boat named *Calypso,* which became his home and floating laboratory. For the next 40 years, through his films and television series, Cousteau brought what he called "the silent world" of the oceans and seas to living rooms everywhere.

A Protector of Life

Cousteau was long an outspoken defender of the environment. "When I saw all this beauty under the sea, I fell in love with it. And finally, when I realized to what extent the oceans were threatened, I decided to campaign as vigorously as I could against everything that threatened what I loved."

Jacques Cousteau died in 1997 at age 87. Before his death, he dedicated the *Calypso II,* a new research vessel, to the children of the world.

Write About It

▶ Ocean pollution and overfishing are subjects of intense debate. Think about these issues, and discuss them with your classmates. Then write an essay in which you try to convince readers of your point of view.

EYE ON THE ENVIRONMENT

Putting Freshwater Problems on Ice

Imagine how different your life would be if you couldn't get fresh water. What would you drink? How would you clean things? The Earth has enough fresh water to supply 100 billion liters to each person, yet water shortages affect millions of people every day. So what's the problem?

The Ice-Water Planet

Three-quarters of Earth's fresh water is frozen in polar icecaps. Plenty of fresh water is there, but people can't use water that is frozen and thousands of kilometers away.

The ice sheet that covers Antarctica is thousands of meters thick and is almost twice the size of the United States. Hundreds of huge chunks break off its edges every year. These icebergs, which are made up entirely of frozen fresh water, float away into the sea and eventually melt. Water from 1 year's worth of these icebergs would be enough to supply all of southern California for more than a century. So why not use it?

Obvious but Not Easy

Transporting icebergs to areas that need fresh water is harder than it sounds. For one thing, many of the icebergs are huge. The largest ever recorded was about the size of Connecticut. Even small icebergs may be 2 km long and 1 km wide.

Researchers have considered many methods of transporting icebergs. Most of the ideas involve pushing or towing icebergs through the water. A few ideas involve attaching engines and propellers directly to the icebergs.

However, because icebergs are so large, it takes a long time to move them. And when an iceberg finally does get somewhere, a considerable amount of it has melted. To prevent melting, insulating materials could be wrapped around an iceberg.

▲ *Icebergs such as this one might provide water in the future.*

A Worthy Investment

Lakes and ground water still provide the cheapest fresh water in most areas. However, if there is no lake, river, or well water available, icebergs may then be a reasonable option to consider. Even though transporting icebergs is difficult, it may still be worthwhile to try. Irrigating 100 km² of desert with water from icebergs might cost as much as $1 million, but purifying enough sea water to irrigate that amount of desert could cost over $1 billion.

People in arid regions have spent considerable time on iceberg research. So far, no one has set up a program for harvesting icebergs. But someday water from icebergs may flow from our household faucets.

An Icy Investigation

▶ Float an ice cube in a bowl of cold water, and record the time it takes the cube to melt. Then try to insulate other ice cubes with different materials, such as cloth, plastic wrap, and aluminum foil. Which material works best? How could this material be used on real icebergs?

CHAPTER 14

The Movement of Ocean Water

AN OCEAN STREAM

The Gulf Stream current carries warm tropical water from the Caribbean Sea all the way to the North Atlantic Ocean. The climate in the British Isles, where the current ends, is controlled by the current's warm waters, which make the isles much warmer than other countries nearby. In this chapter, you will learn how currents like the Gulf Stream are formed. You also will learn about the other ways that ocean water moves and how these movements affect our lives.

Pre-Reading Questions

1. What factors control ocean currents?
2. What causes the ocean tides?

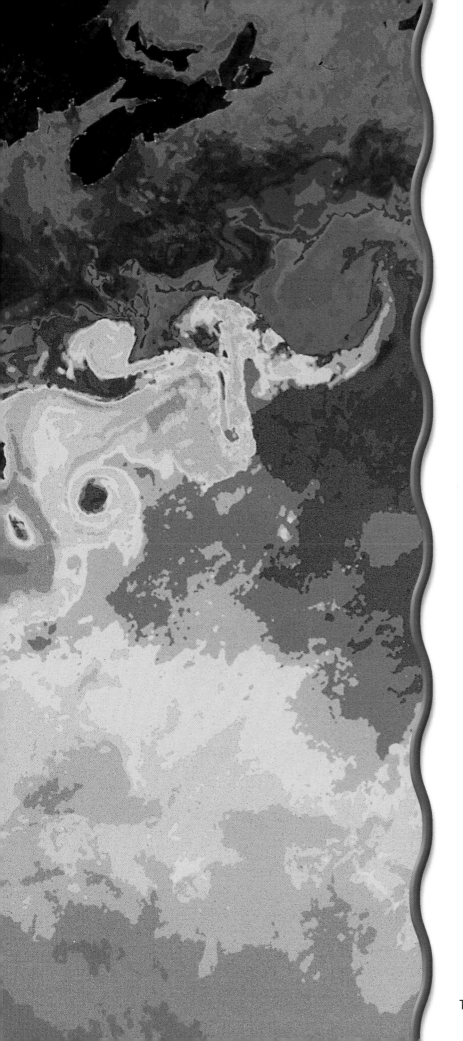

WHEN *WHIRLS* COLLIDE

Ocean currents in the Northern Hemisphere flow in a clockwise direction, while currents in the Southern Hemisphere flow in a counterclockwise direction. Sometimes, southern currents flow across the equator into the Northern Hemisphere and begin flowing clockwise. Do this activity to find out how currents flowing in opposite directions affect one another.

Procedure

1. Fill a large **tub** with **water** 5 cm deep.

2. Add **10 drops of red food coloring** to the water on one end of the tub.

3. Add **10 drops of blue food coloring** to the water at the other end of the tub.

4. Using a **pencil,** quickly stir the water at one end of the tub in a clockwise direction while your partner stirs the water at the other end in a counterclockwise direction. Stir both ends for about 5 seconds.

5. In your ScienceLog, draw what you see happening in the tub immediately after you stop stirring. (Both ends should still be swirling.)

Analysis

6. How did the blue water and the red water interact?

7. How does this activity relate to the ocean currents in the Northern and Southern Hemispheres?

The Movement of Ocean Water **363**

Terms to Learn

surface current   upwelling
Coriolis effect   El Niño
deep current

What You'll Do

◆ Describe surface currents, and list the three factors that control them.
◆ Describe deep currents.
◆ Illustrate the factors involved in deep-current movement.
◆ Explain how currents affect climate.

Currents

Imagine that you are stranded on a desert island. You stuff a distress message into a bottle and throw it into the ocean, hoping it will find its way to someone who will send help. Is there any way to predict where your bottle may land?

One Way to Explore Currents

In the 1940s, a Norwegian explorer named Thor Heyerdahl tried to answer similar questions that involved human migration across the ocean. Heyerdahl theorized that the inhabitants of Polynesia originally sailed from Peru on rafts powered only by the wind and ocean currents. Unable to convince scientists of his theory, he decided to prove it. In 1947, Heyerdahl and a crew of five people set sail from Peru on a raft, as shown in **Figure 1.**

Figure 1 *The handcrafted Kon-Tiki was made mainly from materials that would have been available to ancient Peruvians.*

On the 97th day of their expedition, Heyerdahl and his crew landed on an island in Polynesia. Currents had carried the raft westward more than 6,000 km across the South Pacific. This supported Heyerdahl's theory that ocean currents carried the ancient Peruvians across the Pacific to Polynesia. Now let's take a closer look at currents. For example, what determines the direction in which a current moves? What forces create a current? Read on to learn the answers to these and other questions about currents.

Surface Currents

Streamlike movements of water that occur at or near the surface of the ocean are called **surface currents.** Some surface currents are several thousand kilometers in length, traveling across entire oceans. The Gulf Stream, which is one of the longest surface currents, transports 25 times more water than all the rivers in the world. Surface currents are controlled by three factors: global winds, the Coriolis effect, and continental deflections. These three factors keep surface currents flowing in distinct patterns around the Earth.

Global Winds Have you ever blown gently on a cup of hot chocolate? You may have noticed ripples moving across the surface. These ripples are caused by a tiny surface current created by your breath. In much the same way, winds blowing across the Earth's surface create surface currents in the ocean. Surface currents can reach depths of several hundred meters and lengths of several thousand kilometers.

Different winds cause currents to flow in different directions. Near the equator, the winds blow ocean water east to west, but closer to the poles, ocean water is blown west to east, as shown in **Figure 2**. Merchant ships often use these currents to travel more quickly back and forth across the oceans.

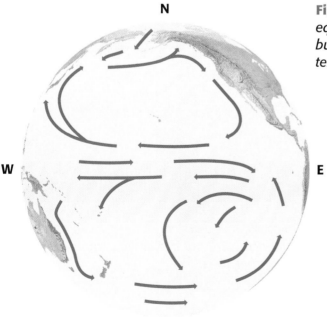

Figure 2 *Surface currents near the equator generally flow from east to west, but surface currents closer to the poles tend to flow from west to east.*

✔ Self-Check

Take another look at Figure 2. As Heyerdahl made his journey in 1947, from what direction would he have noticed the wind blowing? *(See page 726 to check your answer.)*

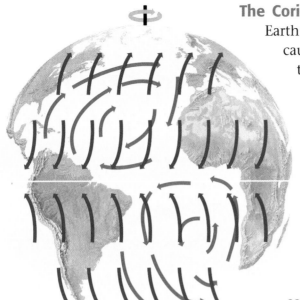

Figure 3 *The rotation of the Earth causes ocean currents (red arrows) and global winds (purple arrows) to move in opposite directions on either side of the equator.*

The Coriolis Effect Have you ever thought about how the Earth's rotation affects its surface? The Earth's rotation causes surface currents to move in curved paths rather than in straight lines. The curving of moving objects from a straight path due to the Earth's rotation is called the **Coriolis effect.** To understand the Coriolis effect, imagine trying to roll a ball straight across a turning merry-go-round. Because the merry-go-round is spinning, the path of the ball will curve before it reaches the other side. **Figure 3** shows that ocean currents in the Northern Hemisphere turn clockwise, while ocean currents in the Southern Hemisphere turn counterclockwise.

Continental Deflections If the Earth's surface were covered only with water, surface currents would travel freely across the globe in a very uniform pattern. However, we know that this is not the case—continents rise above sea level over roughly one-third of the Earth's surface. When surface currents meet continents, they *deflect,* or change direction. Notice in **Figure 4** how the Brazil Current deflects southward as it meets the east coast of South America.

Activity

Some people think the Coriolis effect can be seen in sinks; that is, water draining from sinks turns clockwise in the Northern Hemisphere and counterclockwise in the Southern Hemisphere. Is this true? Research this question at the library, on the Internet, and in your sinks and tubs at home.

TRY at HOME

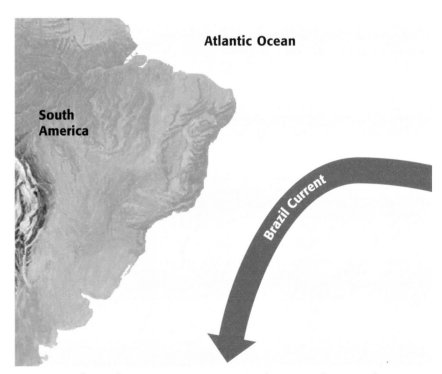

Figure 4 *If South America were not in the way, the Brazil Current would probably flow farther west.*

Taking Temperatures All three factors—global winds, the Coriolis effect, and continental deflections—work together to form a pattern of surface currents on Earth. But currents are also affected by the temperature of the water in which they arise. Warm-water currents begin near the equator and carry warm water to other parts of the ocean. Cold-water currents begin closer to the poles and carry cool water to other parts of the ocean. As you can see on the map in **Figure 5,** all the oceans are connected, and both warm-water and cold-water currents travel from one ocean to another.

Physics
CONNECTION

While winds are responsible for ocean currents, the sun is the initial energy source of the currents. Because the sun heats the Earth more in some places than in others, convection currents are formed, which cause winds to blow.

Figure 5 *This map shows Earth's surface currents. Warm-water currents are shown as red arrows, and cold-water currents are shown as blue arrows.*

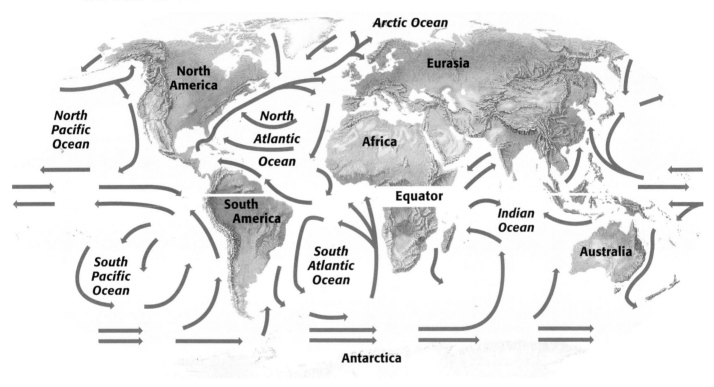

REVIEW

1. List the three factors that control surface currents.

2. Explain how the Earth's rotation affects the patterns of surface currents.

3. **Inferring Conclusions** If there were no land on Earth's surface, what would the pattern of surface currents look like? Explain.

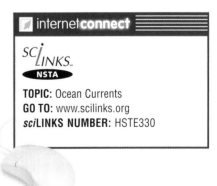

Deep Currents

Deep currents are streamlike movements of ocean water far below the surface. Unlike surface currents, deep currents are not directly controlled by wind or the Coriolis effect. Instead, they form in parts of the ocean where water density increases. *Density* is the ratio of the mass of a substance to its volume. Two main factors—temperature and salinity—combine to affect the density of ocean water, as shown below. As you can see, both decreasing the temperature of ocean water and increasing the water's salinity increase the water's density.

Turn to page 684 in the LabBook to demonstrate how temperature and salinity affect ocean water.

How Deep Currents Form

Decreasing Temperature In Earth's polar regions, cold air chills the water molecules at the ocean's surface, causing them to slow down and move closer together. This decreases the water's volume, making the water denser. The dense water sinks and eventually travels toward the equator as a deep current along the ocean floor.

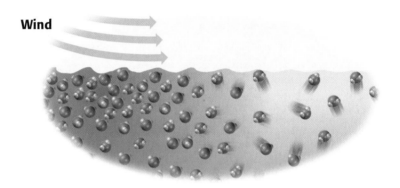

Wind

Increasing Salinity Through Freezing *Salinity* is a measure of the amount of dissolved solids in a liquid. If the ocean water freezes at the surface, ice will float on top of water because ice is less dense than liquid water. The dissolved solids are squeezed out of the ice and enter the liquid water below the ice, increasing the salinity. Because this water contains more dissolved solids, its density also increases.

Increasing Salinity Through Evaporation Another way salinity increases is through evaporation of surface water, which removes water but leaves solids behind. This is especially common in warm climates. Increasing salinity through freezing or evaporation causes water to become denser and sink to the ocean floor, becoming a deep current.

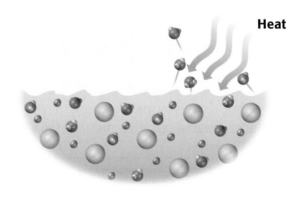

Heat

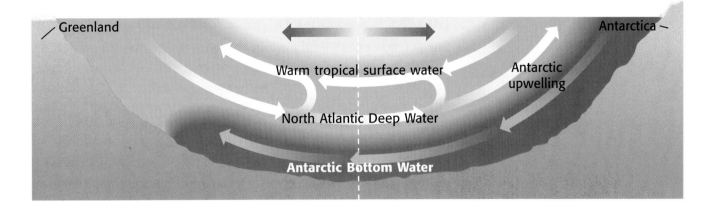

Greenland

Warm tropical surface water

Antarctic upwelling

Antarctica

North Atlantic Deep Water

Antarctic Bottom Water

Figure 6 *Less-dense water always flows on top of denser water, as shown in this cross section.*

Movement of Deep Currents The movement of deep currents as they travel along the ocean floor is very complex. Differences in temperature and salinity, and therefore in density, cause variations in deep currents. For example, the deepest current, the Antarctic Bottom Water, is denser than the North Atlantic Deep Water. Both currents spread out across the ocean floor as they flow toward the same equatorial region. But when the currents meet, the North Atlantic Deep Water actually flows on top of the denser Antarctic Bottom Water, as shown in **Figure 6.** The Antarctic Bottom Water is so dense that it moves incredibly slowly— it takes 750 years for water in this current to make it from Antarctica's coastal waters to the equator!

Currents Trading Places Now that you understand how deep currents form and how they move along the ocean floor, you can learn how they trade places with surface currents. To see how this works, study **Figure 7.**

Figure 7 *This cross section shows the movement of warm water and cold water between polar and equatorial regions.*

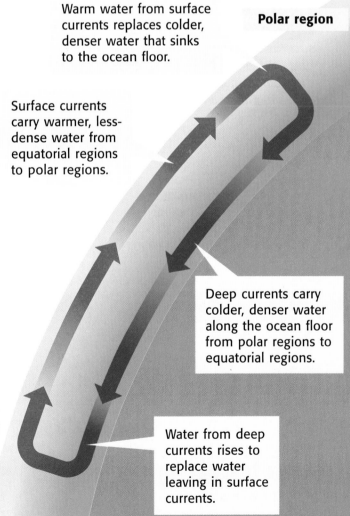

Warm water from surface currents replaces colder, denser water that sinks to the ocean floor.

Polar region

Surface currents carry warmer, less-dense water from equatorial regions to polar regions.

Deep currents carry colder, denser water along the ocean floor from polar regions to equatorial regions.

Water from deep currents rises to replace water leaving in surface currents.

Equatorial region

The Movement of Ocean Water **369**

Surface Currents and Climate

Surface currents greatly affect the climate in many parts of the world. Some surface currents warm or cool coastal areas year-round. Other surface currents sometimes change their circulation pattern. This causes changes in the atmosphere that disrupt the climate in many parts of the world.

Currents That Stabilize Climate Although surface currents are generally much warmer than deep currents, their temperatures do vary. Surface currents are classified as warm-water currents or cold-water currents. Look back at Figure 5 to see where each type is located. Because they are warm or cold, surface currents affect the climate of the land near the area where they flow. For example, warm-water currents create warmer climates in coastal areas that would otherwise be much cooler. Likewise, cold-water currents create cooler climates in coastal areas that would otherwise be much warmer. **Figure 8** shows how a warm-water current and a cold-water current affect coastal climates.

Figure 8 *Warm-water currents, such as the Gulf Stream (top), and cold-water currents, such as the California Current (bottom), can affect the climate of coastal regions.*

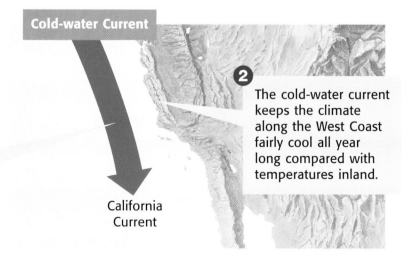

1 The Gulf Stream carries warm water from the Tropics to the North Atlantic Ocean.

2 The Gulf Stream flows to the British Isles. This creates a relatively mild climate for land at such a high latitude.

1 Cold water from the north is carried southward by the California Current, all the way to Mexico.

2 The cold-water current keeps the climate along the West Coast fairly cool all year long compared with temperatures inland.

Current Variations—El Niño The surface currents in the tropical region of the Pacific Ocean usually travel with the trade winds from east to west. This builds up warm water in the western Pacific and causes upwelling in the eastern Pacific. **Upwelling** is a process in which cold, nutrient-rich water from the deep ocean rises to the surface and replaces warm surface water. The warm water is blown out to sea by prevailing winds. But every 2 to 12 years, the South Pacific trade winds move less warm water to the western Pacific. As a result, surface water temperatures along the coast of South America rise. Gradually, this warming spreads westward. This periodic change in the location of warm and cool surface waters in the Pacific Ocean is called **El Niño.** El Niño not only affects surface waters but also changes the interaction between the ocean and the atmosphere, resulting in changes in global weather patterns.

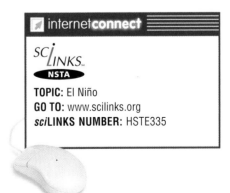
Effects of El Niño El Niño alters weather patterns enough to cause disasters, such as flash floods and mudslides in areas of the world that normally receive little rain. **Figure 9** shows homes destroyed by a mudslide in Southern California. While some regions flood, regions that usually get a lot of rain may experience droughts, which can lead to crop failures.

Figure 9 *This damage in Southern California was the result of excessive rain caused by El Niño in 1997.*

REVIEW

1. How do temperature and salinity relate to deep-current movement?

2. Why is the climate in Scotland relatively mild even though the country is located at a high latitude?

3. **Applying Concepts** Many marine organisms depend on upwelling to bring nutrients to the surface. How might an El Niño affect Peruvians' way of life?

Terms to Learn

crest	surf
trough	whitecap
wavelength	swells
wave height	tsunami
wave period	storm surge
breaker	

What You'll Do

◆ Identify wave components, and explain how they relate to wave movement.

◆ Describe how ocean waves form and how they move.

◆ Classify types of waves.

◆ Analyze types of dangerous waves.

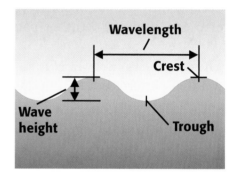

Waves

We all know what ocean waves look like. Even if you've never been to the seashore, you've most likely seen waves on television. But what are ocean waves? How do they form and move? Are all waves the same? And what do they do besides drop shells and sand dollars on the beach? Let us examine ocean waves so that we can answer these questions.

Anatomy of a Wave

Waves are made up of two main components—crests and troughs. A **crest** is the highest point of a wave, and a **trough** is the lowest point. Imagine a thrilling roller coaster designed with many rises and dips. The top of a rise on a roller-coaster track is similar to the crest of a wave, and the bottom of a dip in the track resembles the trough of a wave. The distance between two adjacent wave crests or wave troughs is a **wavelength.** The vertical distance between a wave's crest and its trough is a **wave height.**

Wave Formation and Movement

If you have watched ocean waves before, you may have noticed that water appears to move across the ocean's surface. However, this movement is only an illusion. Most waves form as wind blows across the water's surface, transferring energy to the water. As the energy moves through the water, so do the waves. But the water itself stays behind, rising and falling in circular movements. Notice in **Figure 10** that the floating bottle remains in the same spot as the waves travel from left to right. The circle of moving water that the bottle moves with has a diameter that is equal to the height of the waves that created it. Underneath this circle are smaller circles of moving water. The diameters of these circles get smaller with depth because wave energy decreases with depth. Wave energy only reaches to a certain depth. Below that depth, the water is not affected by wave energy.

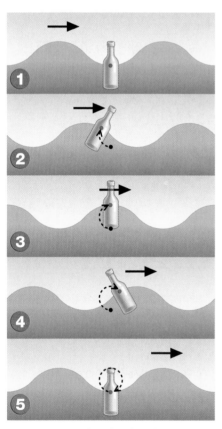

Figure 10 *Like the bottle in this figure, water remains in the same place as waves travel through it.*

Specifics of Wave Movement

Waves not only come in different sizes but also travel at different speeds. To calculate wave speed, scientists must know the wavelength and the wave period. **Wave period** is the time between the passage of two wave crests (or troughs) at a fixed point, as shown in **Figure 11.** Dividing wavelength by wave period gives you wave speed, as shown below.

$$\frac{\text{wavelength (m)}}{\text{wave period (s)}} = \text{wave speed (m/s)}$$

For any given wavelength, an increase in the wave period will decrease the wave speed, and a decrease in the wave period will increase the wave speed.

Figure 11 *The illustration below shows how the wave period is determined.*

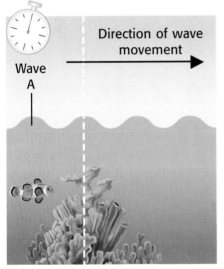

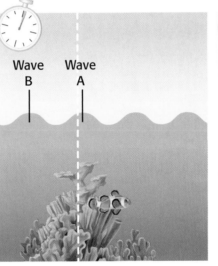

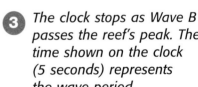

① *Notice that the waves are moving from left to right.*

② *The clock begins running as Wave A passes the reef's peak.*

③ *The clock stops as Wave B passes the reef's peak. The time shown on the clock (5 seconds) represents the wave period.*

Types of Waves

As you learned earlier in this section, wind forms most ocean waves. However, waves can form by other mechanisms. Underwater earthquakes and landslides as well as impacts by cosmic bodies can form different types of waves. The sizes of the different types of waves can vary, but most move the same way. Depending on their size and the angle at which they hit the shore, waves can generate a variety of near-shore events, some of which can be dangerous to humans.

Deep-Water Waves and Shallow-Water Waves Have you ever wondered why waves increase in height as they approach the shore? The answer has to do with the depth of the water. *Deep-water waves* are waves that move in water that is deeper than one-half of their wavelength. When the waves reach water that is shallower than one-half of their wavelength, they begin to interact with the ocean floor. These waves are called *shallow-water waves.* **Figure 12** shows how deep-water waves become shallow-water waves as they move toward the shore.

As deep-water waves become shallow-water waves, the water particles slow down and build up. This forces more water between wave crests and increases wave height. Gravity eventually pulls the high wave crests down, causing them to crash into the ocean floor as **breakers.** The area where waves first begin to tumble downward, or break, is called the *breaker zone.* Waves continue to break as they move from the breaker zone to the shore. The area between the breaker zone and the shore is called the **surf.**

Figure 12 *Deep-water waves become shallow-water waves when they reach depths of less than half of their wavelength.*

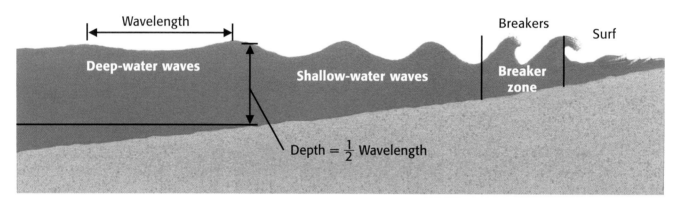

When waves crash on the beach head-on, the water they moved through flows back to the ocean underneath new incoming waves. This movement of water, which carries sand, rock particles, and plankton away from the shore, is called an *undertow.* **Figure 13** illustrates the back-and-forth movement of water at the shore.

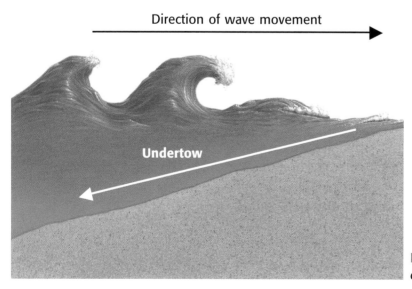

Figure 13 *Head-on waves create an undertow.*

When waves hit the shore at an angle, they cause water to move along the shore in a current called a *longshore current*. This process is shown in **Figure 14.** Longshore currents are responsible for most sediment transport in beach environments. This movement of sand and other sediment both tears down and builds up the coastline. Unfortunately, longshore currents also carry trash and other types of ocean pollution, spreading it along the shore.

Figure 14 *Longshore currents form where waves approach beaches at an angle.*

Open-Ocean Waves Sometimes waves called whitecaps form in the open ocean. **Whitecaps** are white, foaming waves with very steep crests that break in the open ocean before the waves get close to the shore. These waves usually form during stormy weather, and they are usually short-lived. Calmer winds form waves called swells. **Swells** are rolling waves that move in a steady procession across the ocean. Swells have longer wavelengths than whitecaps and can travel for thousands of kilometers. **Figure 15** shows how whitecaps and swells differ.

Figure 15 *Whitecaps, shown in the photo at left, break in the open ocean, while swells, shown in the photo at right, roll gently in the open ocean.*

Do the Wave

1. Tie one end of a thin piece of **rope** to a doorknob.

2. Tie a **ribbon** around the rope halfway between the doorknob and the other end of the rope.

3. Holding the rope at the untied end, quickly move the rope up and down, and observe the ribbon.

4. How does the movement of the rope and ribbon relate to the movement of water and deep-water waves?

5. Repeat step 3, but move the rope higher and lower this time.

6. How does this affect the waves in the rope?

TRY at HOME

Tsunamis Professional surfers often travel to Hawaii to catch some of the highest waves in the world. But even the best surfers would not be able to handle a tsunami. **Tsunamis** are waves that form when a large volume of ocean water is suddenly moved up or down. This movement can be caused by underwater earthquakes, volcanic eruptions, landslides, underwater explosions, or the impact of a meteorite or comet. The majority of tsunamis occur in the Pacific Ocean because of the greater number of earthquakes in that region. **Figure 16** shows how an earthquake can generate a tsunami.

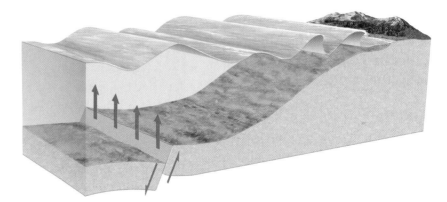

Figure 16 *An upward shift in the ocean floor creates an earthquake. The energy released by the earthquake pushes a large volume of water upward, creating a series of tsunamis.*

When tsunamis near continents, they slow down and their wavelengths shorten as they interact with the ocean floor. As tsunamis get closer together, their wave height increases. Tsunamis can reach more than 30 m in height as they slam into the coast, destroying just about everything in their path. The powerful undertow created by a tsunami can be as destructive as the tsunami itself. **Figure 17** shows a coastal community devastated by a tsunami.

Figure 17 *Imagine the strength of the tsunami that carried this boat so far inland!*

Timing a Tsunami

On May 22, 1960, an earth-quake off the coast of South America generated a tsunami that completely crossed the Pacific Ocean. Ten thousand kilometers away from the origin of the earthquake, the tsunami hit the city of Hilo on the coast of Hawaii, caus-ing extensive damage.

If the tsunami traveled at a speed of 188 m/s, how long after the earthquake occurred did the tsunami

reach Hilo? If the residents of Hilo heard about the earth-quake as soon as it hap-pened, do you think they had enough warning time?

What might be done to ensure that this amount of time would be sufficient warning for a tsunami?

Storm Surges

A **storm surge** is a local rise in sea level near the shore that is caused by strong winds from a storm, such as a hurricane. Winds form a storm surge by blowing water into a big pile under the storm. As the storm moves onto shore, so does the giant mass of water beneath it. Storm surges often disappear as quickly as they form, making them difficult to study. Storm surges contain a lot of energy and can reach about 8 m in height. This often makes them the most destructive part of hurricanes.

REVIEW

1. Explain how water moves as waves travel through it.

2. Where do deep-water waves become shallow-water waves?

3. Name five events that can cause a tsunami.

4. **Doing Calculations** Look again at Figure 11. If the wave speed is 0.8 m/s, what is the wavelength?

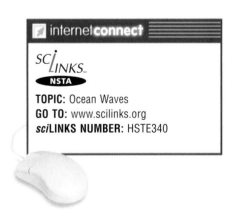

internet**connect**

SC*L*INKS.
NSTA

TOPIC: Ocean Waves
GO TO: www.scilinks.org
*sci***LINKS NUMBER:** HSTE340

Tides

You haved learned how winds and earthquakes can move ocean water. But there are less-obvious forces that continually move ocean water in regular patterns called tides. **Tides** are daily movements of ocean water that change the level of the ocean's surface. Tides are influenced by the sun and the moon, and they occur in a variety of cycles.

The Lure of the Moon

The phases of the moon and their relationship to the tides were first discovered more than 2,000 years ago by a Greek explorer named Pytheas. But Pytheas and other early investigators could not explain the relationship. A scientific explanation was not given until 1687, when Sir Isaac Newton's theories on the principle of gravitational pull were published. The gravity of the moon pulls on every particle of the Earth, but the pull is much more noticeable in liquids than in solids. This is because liquids move more easily. Even the liquid in an open soft drink is slightly pulled by the moon's gravity.

Gravitational forces from both the sun and the moon continuously pull on the Earth. Although the moon is much smaller than the sun, the moon's gravity is the dominant force behind Earth's tides.

High Tide and Low Tide How high tides get and how often they occur depend on the position of the moon as it revolves around the Earth. The moon's pull is strongest on the part of the Earth directly facing the moon. When that part happens to be a part of the ocean, the water there bulges toward the moon.

At the same time, water on the opposite side of the Earth bulges due to the motion of the Earth and the moon around each other. These bulges are called *high tides*. Notice in **Figure 18** how the position of the moon causes the water to bulge. Also notice that when high tides occur, water is drawn away from the area between the high tides, causing *low tides* to form.

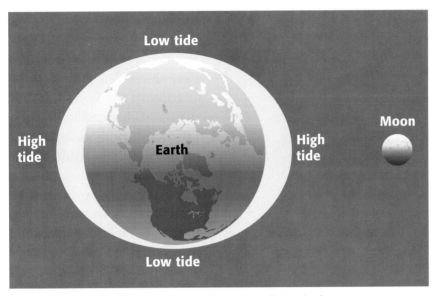

Figure 18 *High tide occurs on the part of Earth that is closest to the moon. At the same time, high tide also occurs on the opposite side of Earth.*

Timing the Tides The rotation of the Earth and the moon's revolution around the Earth determine when tides occur. If the Earth rotated at the same speed that the moon revolves around the Earth, tides would continuously occur at the same spots on Earth. But the moon revolves around the Earth much more slowly than the Earth rotates. **Figure 19** shows that it takes 24 hours and 50 minutes for a spot on Earth that is facing the moon to rotate so that it is facing the moon again.

Puzzled about why high tide also occurs on the side of the Earth opposite the moon? Turn to page 686 to see how you can find out for yourself.

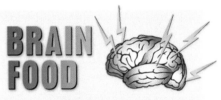

Even dry land has tides. For example, the land in Oklahoma moves up and down several centimeters throughout the day, corresponding with the tides. Tides on the solid part of Earth's surface are usually about one-third the size of ocean tides.

Tuesday, 11:00 A.M.

Wednesday, 11:50 A.M.

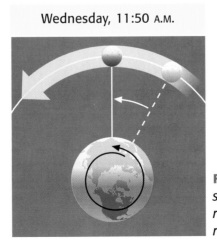

Figure 19 *Tides occur at different spots on Earth because the Earth rotates more quickly than the moon revolves around the Earth.*

The Movement of Ocean Water **379**

Tidal Variations

The sun also affects tides. The sun is much larger than the moon, but it is also much farther away. As a result, the sun's influence on tides is less powerful than the moon's influence. The combined forces of the sun and the moon on the Earth result in tidal ranges that vary based on the positions of all three bodies. A **tidal range** is the difference between levels of ocean water at high tide and low tide.

Figure 20 *During spring tides, the gravitational forces of the sun and moon pull on the Earth either from the same direction (left) or from opposite directions (right).*

Spring Tides When the sun, Earth, and moon are in alignment with one another, spring tides occur. **Spring tides** are tides with maximum daily tidal range that occur during the new and full moons. Spring tides occur every 14 days. The first time spring tides occur is when the moon is between the sun and Earth. The second time spring tides occur is when the moon and the sun are on opposite sides of the Earth. **Figure 20** shows the positions of the sun and moon during spring tides.

Neap Tides When the sun, Earth, and moon form a 90° angle, neap tides occur. **Neap tides** are tides with minimum daily tidal range that occur during the first and third quarters of the moon. Neap tides occur halfway between the occurrence of spring tides. When neap tides occur, the gravitational forces on the Earth by the sun and the moon work against each other. **Figure 21** shows the positions of the sun and moon during neap tides.

Figure 21 *During neap tides, the sun and moon are at right angles with respect to the Earth. This arrangement minimizes their gravitational effect on the Earth.*

Tides and Topography

Tides can be accurately predicted once the tidal range has been measured at a certain point over a period of time. This information can be useful for people who live near or visit the coast, as illustrated in **Figure 22.**

Figure 22 *It's a good thing the people on the beach (left) knew when high tide occurred (right). These photos show the Bay of Fundy, in New Brunswick, Canada. The Bay of Fundy has the greatest tidal range on Earth.*

In some coastal areas with narrow inlets, movements of water called tidal bores occur. A *tidal bore* is a body of water that rushes up through a narrow bay, estuary, or river channel during the rise of high tide, causing a very sudden tidal rise. Sometimes tidal bores form waves that rush up the inlets. Tidal bores occur in coastal areas of China, the British Isles, France, and Canada.

REVIEW

1. How does the position of the moon relate to the position of high tides?

2. Which tides have minimum tidal range? Which tides have maximum tidal range?

3. What causes tidal bores?

4. **Applying Concepts** How many days pass between minimum and maximum tidal range in any given area? Explain.

internet**connect**

*SC*L*INKS*
NSTA

TOPIC: The Tides
GO TO: www.scilinks.org
*sci*LINKS **NUMBER:** HSTE350

Chapter Highlights

SECTION 1

Vocabulary

surface current (*p. 365*)

Coriolis effect (*p. 366*)

deep current (*p. 368*)

upwelling (*p. 371*)

El Niño (*p. 371*)

Section Notes

- Currents are classified as surface currents and deep currents.

- Surface currents are controlled by three factors: global winds, the Coriolis effect, and continental deflections.

- Surface currents, such as the Gulf Stream, can be several thousand kilometers in length.

- Deep currents form where the density of ocean water increases. Water density depends on temperature and salinity.

- Surface currents affect the climate of the land near which they flow.

Labs

Up from the Depths (*p. 684*)

SECTION 2

Vocabulary

crest (*p. 372*)

trough (*p. 372*)

wavelength (*p. 372*)

wave height (*p. 372*)

wave period (*p. 373*)

breaker (*p. 374*)

surf (*p. 374*)

whitecap (*p. 375*)

swells (*p. 375*)

tsunami (*p. 376*)

storm surge (*p. 377*)

Section Notes

- Waves are made up of two main components—crests and troughs.

- Waves are usually created by the transfer of the wind's energy across the surface of the ocean.

☑ Skills Check

Math Concepts

TWO OUT OF THREE The wave equation on page 373 has three variables. If you know two of these variables, you can figure out the third. Take a look at the examples below.

1. wave speed = 0.6 m/s, wave period = 10 s
   $$\text{wavelength} = \text{wave speed} \times \text{wave period} = 6 \text{ m}$$

2. wave speed = 0.6 m/s, wavelength = 6 m
   $$\text{wave period} = \frac{\text{wavelength}}{\text{wave speed}} = 10 \text{ s}$$

Visual Understanding

BREAKING WAVES Before shallow-water waves break, their wave height increases and their wavelength decreases. Look at Figure 12 on page 374 again. Notice that the waves are taller and that their crests are closer together near the breaker zone.

- Waves travel through water near the water's surface, while the water itself rises and falls in circular movements.

- Waves travel in the direction the wind blows. If the wind blows over a long distance, the wavelength becomes very large and the waves travel quickly.

- Wind-generated waves are classified as deep-water and shallow-water waves.

- Tsunamis are dangerous waves that can be very destructive to coastal communities.

Vocabulary

tides *(p. 378)*

tidal range *(p. 380)*

spring tides *(p. 380)*

neap tides *(p. 380)*

Section Notes

- Tides are caused by the gravitational forces of the moon and sun tugging on the Earth.

- The moon's gravity is the main force behind tides.

- The relative positions of the sun and moon with respect to Earth cause different tidal ranges.

- Maximum tidal range occurs during spring tides.

- Minimum tidal range occurs during neap tides.

- Tidal bores occur as high tide rises in narrow coastal inlets.

Labs

Turning the Tides *(p. 686)*

---

internetconnect

GO TO: go.hrw.com

Visit the **HRW** Web site for a variety of learning tools related to this chapter. Just type in the keyword:

KEYWORD: HSTH2O

GO TO: www.scilinks.org

Visit the **National Science Teachers Association** on-line Web site for Internet resources related to this chapter. Just type in the *sci*LINKS number for more information about the topic:

TOPIC: Ocean Currents	*sci*LINKS NUMBER: HSTE330
TOPIC: El Niño	*sci*LINKS NUMBER: HSTE335
TOPIC: Ocean Waves	*sci*LINKS NUMBER: HSTE340
TOPIC: Tsunamis	*sci*LINKS NUMBER: HSTE345
TOPIC: The Tides	*sci*LINKS NUMBER: HSTE350

Chapter Review

USING VOCABULARY

For each pair of terms, explain the difference in their meaning.

1. wavelength/wave height

2. whitecap/swell

3. tsunami/storm surge

4. spring tide/neap tide

Replace the incorrect term in each of the following sentences with the correct term provided in the word bank below:

5. Deep currents are directly controlled by wind.

6. The Coriolis effect reduces upwelling along the coast of South America.

7. Neap tides occur when the moon is between the Earth and the sun.

8. A tidal bore is the difference between levels of ocean water at high tide and low tide.

Word bank: breakers, spring tides, tsunamis, surface currents, tidal range, El Niño.

UNDERSTANDING CONCEPTS

Multiple Choice

9. Surface currents are formed by
   a. the moon's gravity.
   b. the sun's gravity.
   c. wind.
   d. increased water density.

10. Deep currents form when
    a. cold air decreases water density.
    b. warm air increases water density.
    c. the ocean surface freezes and solids from the water underneath are removed.
    d. salinity increases.

11. When waves come near the shore,
    a. they speed up.
    b. they maintain their speed.
    c. their wavelength increases.
    d. their wave height increases.

12. Longshore currents transport sediment
    a. out to the open ocean.
    b. along the shore.
    c. during low tide only.
    d. during high tide only.

13. Whitecaps break
    a. in the surf.
    b. in the breaker zone.
    c. in the open ocean.
    d. as their wavelength increases.

14. Tidal range is greatest during
    a. spring tide.
    b. neap tide.
    c. a tidal bore.
    d. the day only.

15. Explain the relationship between upwelling and El Niño.

16. Explain what happens when the North Atlantic Deep Water meets the Antarctic Bottom Water.

17. Describe the relative positions of the Earth, the moon, and the sun during neap tide. Where do high tide and low tide occur during this time?

18. Explain the difference between the breaker zone and the surf.

Concept Mapping

19. Use the following terms to create a concept map: wind, deep currents, sun's gravity, types of ocean-water movement, surface currents, tides, increasing water density, waves, moon's gravity.

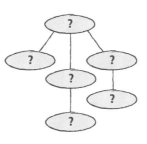

CRITICAL THINKING AND PROBLEM SOLVING

Write one or two sentences to answer the following questions:

20. What would happen to surface currents if the Earth reversed its rotation? Be specific.

21. How would you explain a bottle moving across the water in the same direction the waves are traveling?

22. You and a friend are planning a fishing trip to the ocean. Your friend tells you that the fish bite more in his secret fishing spot during low tide. If low tide occurred at the spot at 7 A.M. today and you are going to fish there in one week, at what time will low tide occur in that spot?

MATH IN SCIENCE

23. If a barrier island that is 1 km wide and 10 km long loses 1.5 m of its width per year to erosion by longshore current, how long will it take for the island to lose one-fourth of its width?

INTERPRETING GRAPHICS

Study the diagram below, and answer the questions that follow.

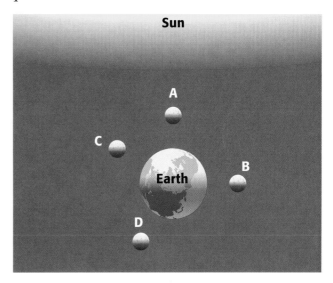

24. At which position (A, B, C, or D) would the moon be during a neap tide?

25. At which position (A, B, C, or D) would the moon be during a spring tide?

26. Would tidal range be greater with the moon at position C or position D? Why?

Reading Check-up

Take a minute to review your answers to the Pre-Reading Questions found at the bottom of page 362. Have your answers changed? If necessary, revise your answers based on what you have learned since you began this chapter.

CAREERS

SEISMOLOGIST

As a seismologist, **Hiroo Kanamori** studies how earthquakes occur and tries to reduce their impact on our society. He also analyzes the effects of earthquakes on oceans and how earthquakes cause tsunamis (tsoo NAH mes). He has discovered that even weak earthquakes can create tsunamis.

*B*ecause most tsunamis are caused by underwater earthquakes, scientists can monitor earthquakes to predict when and where a tsunami will hit land. But the predictions are not always accurate. Very weak earthquakes should not create powerful tsunamis, yet they do. Kanamori calls these special events *tsunami earthquakes,* and he has learned how to predict the size of the resulting tsunamis.

A tsunami can be more dangerous than an earthquake. When people feel the tremors created when the plates slide, they don't always realize that a large tsunami may be on the way. Because of this, people don't expect a tsunami and don't leave the area.

Measuring Tsunami Earthquakes

As tectonic plates grind against each other, they send out seismic waves. These waves travel through the earth's crust and can be recorded by a sensitive machine. But when the plates grind very slowly, only long period seismic waves are recorded. When Kanamori sees a long period wave, he knows that a tsunami will form.

"The speed of the average tsunami is about 800 km/h, which is much slower than the speed of the long period waves at 15,000 km/h. So these special seismic waves arrive at distant recording stations much earlier than a tsunami," explains Kanamori. This important fact lets scientists like Kanamori warn people in the tsunami's path so they can leave the area.

An Interesting Career

Kanamori finds his work very rewarding. "It is always good to see how what we learned in the classroom can solve our real-life problems," he explains. "We can see how physics and mathematics work to explain seemingly complex natural events, such as earthquakes, volcanoes, and tsunamis."

A Challenge

▶ The depth of an ocean influences how fast a tsunami travels. To investigate, fill a 0.5 m long tub with 5 cm of water. Tap the tub. How long does it take for the wave to go back and forth? Add more water, and tap it again. Did the wave move faster or slower?

▶ *Monster waves are well-known in many communities along the Pacific coast.*

Health

Red Tides

Imagine going to the beach only to find that the ocean water has turned red and fish are floating belly up all over the place. This is not an imaginary scene. It really happens. What could cause such widespread damage to the ocean? Single-cell algae, that's what!

Blooming Algae

When certain algae grow rapidly, they clump together on the ocean's surface in an algal bloom that changes the color of the water. People called these algal blooms red tides because the blooms often turned the water red or reddish-brown. They also believed that tidal conditions caused the blooms. Scientists now call these algae explosions harmful algal blooms (HABs) because HABs are not always red, and they are not directly related to tides. The blooms are harmful because certain species of algae produce toxins that can poison fish, shellfish, and people.

Scientists also have learned that the ocean's natural currents may carry HABs hundreds of miles along a coastline. For example, in 1987, the Gulf Stream off the Atlantic coast of Florida carried a toxic bloom up the coast to North Carolina.

Troublesome Toxins

Some people who ate tainted shellfish from the North Carolina coast in 1987 suffered from muscular aches, anxiety, sweating, dizziness, diarrhea, vomiting, and abdominal pain. Some algae toxins can even kill people who eat the tainted seafood. Another HAB occurred in 1987 in Nova Scotia, Canada. Four people died from

▲ *Harmful algal blooms are caused by algae like the one shown above right.*

eating contaminated shellfish, and another 150 people suffered from symptoms such as dizziness, headaches, seizures, short-term memory loss, and comas.

In the 1990s, Texas, Maryland, Alaska, and many other coastal states experienced HABs. However, the problem is not confined to North America. Throughout the 1990s, HABs caused health problems in South Africa, Argentina, India, New Zealand, and France.

No Signs to Read

Fish and shellfish are major sources of protein for people all over the world. Unfortunately, there are no outward signs when seafood is contaminated. The toxins don't change the flavor, and cooking the seafood doesn't eliminate the toxins. Sometimes a HAB rides into an area on an ocean current, causing fish to die and people to become ill before authorities are aware of the problem.

Fortunately, scientists all over the world are working on ways to monitor and even predict HABs. As a result, people eventually may be able to eat fish and shellfish without worrying about toxic algae.

Find Out More

▶ Some people think that human activities are causing more HABs than occurred in the past. Other people disagree. Find out more about this issue, and have a class debate about the role humans play in creating HABs.

Weather and Climate

In this unit, you will learn more about the ocean of air in which we live. You will learn about the atmosphere and how it affects conditions on the Earth's surface. The constantly changing weather is always a good topic for conversation. It is also the subject of the science of meteorology. Forecasting the weather is not an easy task. Climate, on the other hand, is much more predictable. This timeline shows some of the events that have occurred as scientists have tried to better understand weather and climate.

1281

A sudden typhoon destroys a fleet of Mongolian ships about to reach Japan. This "divine wind," or *kamikaze* in Japanese, saves the country from invasion and conquest.

1656

Saturn's rings are recognized as such. Galileo had seen them in 1612, but his telescope was not strong enough to make them out as rings.

1945

First atmospheric test of an atomic bomb takes place near Alamogordo, New Mexico.

1974

Chlorofluorocarbons (CFCs) are recognized as harmful to the ozone layer.

1982

Weather information becomes available 24 hours a day, 7 days a week on commercial television.

1714

Gabriel Fahrenheit builds the first mercury thermometer.

1749

Benjamin Franklin explains how updrafts of air are caused by the sun's heating of the local atmosphere.

1778

Karl Sheele and Antoine Lavoisier separately conclude that air is mostly made of nitrogen and oxygen.

1938

The cause of ice ages as a periodic result of the Earth's motion through space is determined by Yugoslav scientist Milutin Milankovitch.

1838

John James Audubon publishes *The Birds of America*.

1999

The first nonstop balloon trip around the world is successfully completed when Brian Jones and Bertrand Piccard land in Egypt.

1985

Scientists discover an ozone hole over Antarctica.

1986

The world's worst nuclear accident takes place at Chernobyl, Ukraine, spreading radiation through the atmosphere as far as the western United States.

The Atmosphere

Pre-Reading
Questions

1. What is air made of?
2. How is the atmosphere organized?
3. What is wind and how does it move?

FLOATING ON AIR

These skydivers might have checked their parachutes at least a half dozen times before they jumped. They probably also paid particular attention to the day's weather report. Skydivers should know what to expect from the atmosphere. The atmosphere can be unpredictable and dangerous, but it also provides us with the gases needed for our survival on Earth. In this chapter, you will learn about the Earth's atmosphere and how it affects your life.

START-UP
Activity

AIR—IT'S MASSIVE

In this activity, you will find out if air has mass.

Procedure

1. Use a **scale** to find the mass of a **ball,** such as a football or a basketball, with no air in it. Record the mass of the empty ball in your ScienceLog.

2. Pump up the ball with an **air pump.**

3. Use the scale to find the mass of the ball filled with air. Record the mass of the ball filled with air in your ScienceLog.

Analysis

4. Compare the mass of the empty ball with the mass of the ball filled with air. Did the mass of the ball change after you pumped it up?

5. Based on your results, does air have mass? Explain your answer.

Characteristics of the Atmosphere

Terms to Learn

atmosphere   stratosphere
air pressure   ozone
altitude   mesosphere
troposphere   thermosphere

What You'll Do

◆ Discuss the composition of the Earth's atmosphere.

◆ Explain why pressure changes with altitude.

◆ Explain how temperature changes with altitude.

◆ Describe the layers of the atmosphere.

If you were lost in the desert, you could survive for a few days without food and water. But you wouldn't last more than 5 minutes without the *atmosphere*. The **atmosphere** is a mixture of gases that surrounds the Earth. In addition to containing the oxygen we need to breathe, it protects us from the sun's harmful rays. But the atmosphere is always changing. Every breath we take, every tree we plant, and every motor vehicle we ride in affects the composition of our atmosphere. Later you will find out how the atmosphere is changing. But first you need to learn about the atmosphere's composition and structure.

Composition of the Atmosphere

Figure 1 shows the relative amounts of the gases that make up the atmosphere. Besides gases, the atmosphere also contains small amounts of solids and liquids. Tiny solid particles, such as dust, volcanic ash, sea salt, dirt, and smoke, are carried in the air. Next time you turn off the lights at night, shine a flashlight and you will see some of these tiny particles floating in the air. The most common liquid in the atmosphere is water. Liquid water is found as water droplets in clouds. Water vapor, which is also found in the atmosphere, is a gas and is not visible.

Figure 1 *Two gases—nitrogen and oxygen—make up 99 percent of the air we breathe.*

Nitrogen is the most abundant gas in the atmosphere. It is released into the atmosphere by volcanic eruptions and when dead plants and dead animals decay.

Oxygen, the second most common gas in the atmosphere, is produced by plant-like protists and plants.

The **remaining 1 percent** of the atmosphere is made up of argon, carbon dioxide, water vapor, and other gases.

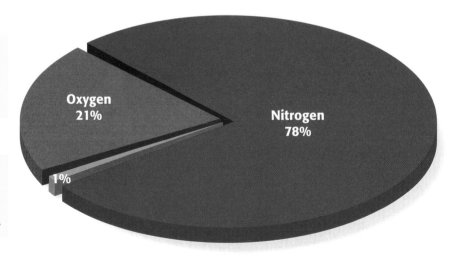

Oxygen 21%

1%

Nitrogen 78%

Atmospheric Pressure and Temperature

Have you ever been in an elevator in a tall building? If you have, you probably remember the "popping" in your ears as you went up or down. As you move up or down in an elevator, the air pressure outside your ears changes, while the air pressure inside your ears stays the same. **Air pressure** is the measure of the force with which the air molecules push on a surface. Your ears pop when the pressure inside and outside of your ears suddenly becomes equal. Air pressure changes throughout the atmosphere. Temperature and the kinds of gases present also change. Why do these changes occur? Read on to find out.

Pressure Think of air pressure as a human pyramid, as shown in **Figure 2.** The people at the bottom of the pyramid can feel all the weight and pressure of the people on top. The person on top doesn't feel any weight because there isn't anyone above. The atmosphere works in a similar way.

The Earth's atmosphere is held around the planet by gravity. Gravity pulls the gas molecules in the atmosphere toward the Earth's surface, giving them weight. This weight causes the air to push against the Earth's surface. As you move farther away from the Earth's surface, air pressure decreases because fewer gas molecules are pushing on you. **Altitude** is the height of an object above the Earth's surface. As altitude increases, air pressure decreases.

Figure 2 *Like the bottom row of the human pyramid, the lower atmosphere experiences greater pressure than the upper atmosphere.*

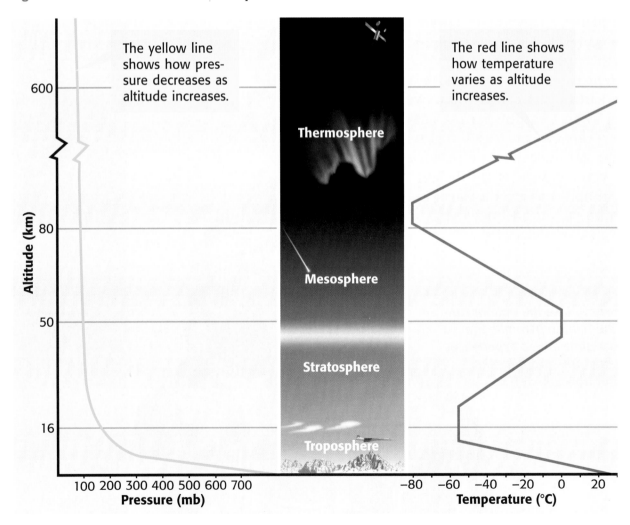

Self-Check

Does air become more or less dense as you climb a mountain? Why? *(See page 726 to check your answer.)*

Air Temperature Air temperature also changes as you increase altitude. As you pass through the atmosphere, air temperature changes between warmer and colder conditions. The temperature differences result mainly from the way solar energy is absorbed as it moves downward through the atmosphere. Some parts of the atmosphere are warmer because they contain gases that absorb solar energy. Other parts do not contain these gases and are therefore cooler.

Layers of the Atmosphere

Based on temperature changes, the Earth's atmosphere is divided into four layers—the troposphere, stratosphere, mesosphere, and thermosphere. **Figure 3** illustrates the four atmospheric layers, showing their altitude and temperature. As you can see, each layer has unique characteristics.

Figure 3 Profile of the Earth's Atmosphere

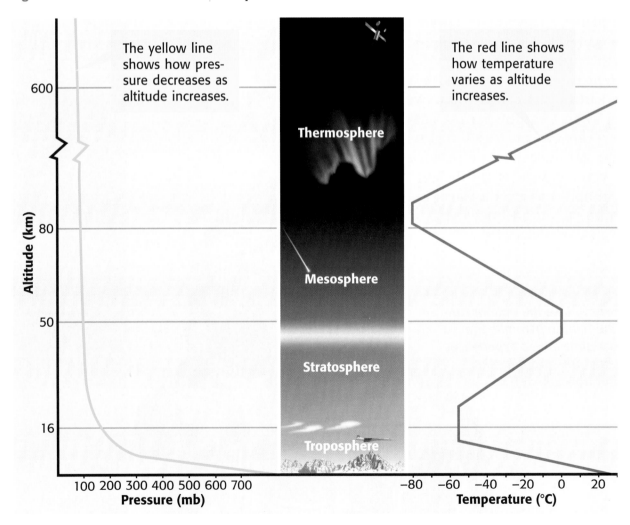

The yellow line shows how pressure decreases as altitude increases.

Thermosphere

Mesosphere

Stratosphere

Troposphere

The red line shows how temperature varies as altitude increases.

Altitude (km)

600

80

50

16

Pressure (mb)
100 200 300 400 500 600 700

Temperature (°C)
−80 −60 −40 −20 0 20

Troposphere The **troposphere,** which lies next to the Earth's surface, is the lowest layer of the atmosphere. The troposphere is also the densest atmospheric layer, containing almost 90 percent of the atmosphere's total mass. Almost all of Earth's carbon dioxide, water vapor, clouds, air pollution, weather, and life-forms are found in the troposphere. In fact, the troposphere is the layer in which you live. **Figure 4** shows the effects of altitude on temperature in the troposphere.

Stratosphere The atmospheric layer above the troposphere is called the **stratosphere.** In the stratosphere, the air is very thin and contains little moisture. The lower stratosphere is extremely cold, measuring about –60°C. In the stratosphere, the temperature rises with increasing altitude. This occurs because of ozone. **Ozone** is a molecule that is made up of three oxygen atoms, as shown in **Figure 5.** Almost all of the ozone in the atmosphere is contained in the *ozone layer* of the stratosphere. Ozone absorbs solar energy in the form of ultraviolet radiation, warming the air. By absorbing the ultraviolet radiation, the ozone layer also protects life at the Earth's surface.

Figure 4 *Snow can remain year-round on a mountain top. That is because as altitude increases, the atmosphere thins, losing its ability to absorb and transfer thermal energy.*

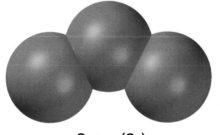

Oxygen gas (O₂)   **Ozone (O₃)**

Figure 5 *While ozone is made up of three oxygen atoms, the oxygen in the air you breathe is made up of two oxygen atoms.*

UV and SPFs

People protect themselves from the sun's damaging rays by applying sunblock. Exposure of unprotected skin to the sun's ultraviolet rays over a long period of time can cause skin cancer. The breakdown of the Earth's ozone layer is thinning the layer, which allows some harmful ultraviolet radiation to reach the Earth's surface. Sunblocks contain different ratings of SPFs, or skin protection factors. What do the SPF ratings mean?

Mesosphere Above the stratosphere is the mesosphere. The **mesosphere** is the coldest layer of the atmosphere. As in the troposphere, the temperature drops with increasing altitude. Temperatures can be as low as –93°C at the top of the mesosphere. Scientists have recently discovered large wind storms in the mesosphere with winds reaching speeds of more than 320 km/h.

Thermosphere The uppermost atmospheric layer is the **thermosphere.** Here temperature again increases with altitude because many of the gases are absorbing solar radiation. Temperatures in this layer can reach 1,700°C.

When you think of an area with high temperatures, you probably think of a place that is very hot. While the thermosphere has very high temperatures, it would not feel hot. Temperature and heat are not the same thing. Temperature is a measure of the average energy of particles in motion. A high temperature means that the particles are moving very fast. Heat, on the other hand, is the transfer of energy between objects at different temperatures. But in order to transfer energy, particles must touch one another. **Figure 6** illustrates how the density of particles affects the heating of the atmosphere.

Figure 6 *Temperatures in the thermosphere are higher than those in the troposphere, but the air particles are too far apart for energy to be transferred.*

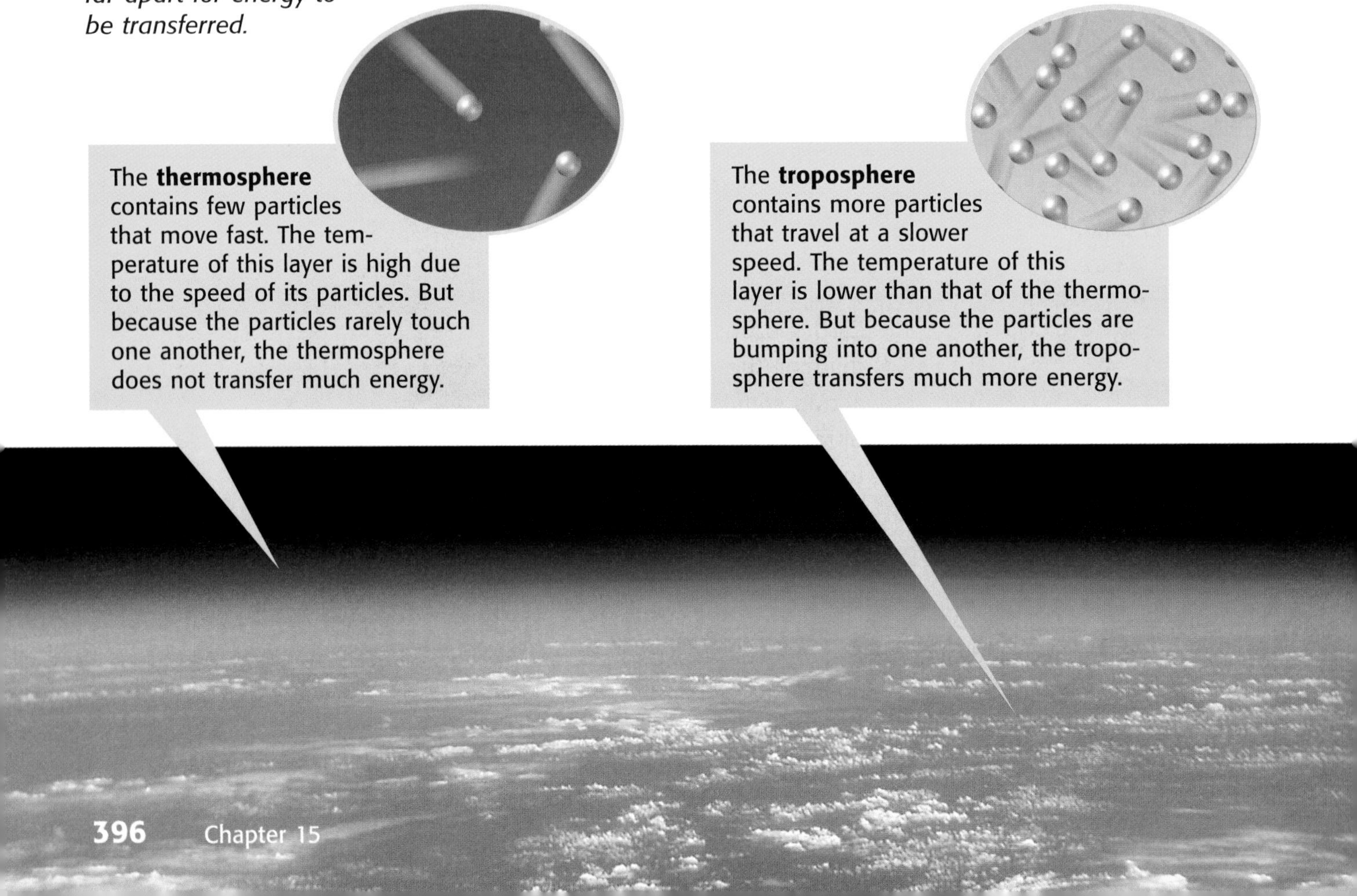

The **thermosphere** contains few particles that move fast. The temperature of this layer is high due to the speed of its particles. But because the particles rarely touch one another, the thermosphere does not transfer much energy.

The **troposphere** contains more particles that travel at a slower speed. The temperature of this layer is lower than that of the thermosphere. But because the particles are bumping into one another, the troposphere transfers much more energy.

Ionosphere In the upper mesosphere and the lower thermosphere, nitrogen and oxygen atoms absorb harmful solar energy, such as X rays and gamma rays. This absorption not only contributes to the thermosphere's high temperatures but also causes the gas particles to become electrically charged. Electrically charged particles are called ions; therefore, this part of the thermosphere is referred to as the *ionosphere*. Sometimes these ions radiate energy as light of different colors, as shown in **Figure 7.**

Figure 7 *Aurora borealis (northern lights) and aurora australis (southern lights) occur in the ionosphere.*

The ionosphere also reflects certain radio waves, such as AM radio waves. If you have ever listened to an AM radio station, you can be sure that the ionosphere had something to do with how clear it sounded. When conditions are right, an AM radio wave can travel around the world after being reflected off the ionosphere. These radio signals bounce off the ionosphere and are sent back to Earth.

REVIEW

1. Explain why pressure decreases but temperature varies as altitude increases.

2. What causes air pressure?

3. How can the thermosphere have high temperatures but not feel hot?

4. **Analyzing Relationships** Identify one characteristic of each layer of the atmosphere, and explain how that characteristic affects life on Earth.

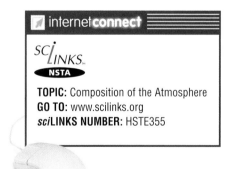

internetconnect

SC/*LINKS*
NSTA

TOPIC: Composition of the Atmosphere
GO TO: www.scilinks.org
*sci***LINKS NUMBER:** HSTE355

Heating of the Atmosphere

What You'll Do

◆ Describe what happens to radiation that reaches the Earth.

◆ Summarize the processes of radiation, conduction, and convection.

◆ Explain how the greenhouse effect could contribute to global warming.

Have you ever walked barefoot across a sidewalk on a sunny day? If so, your foot felt the warmth of the hot pavement. How did the sidewalk become so warm? The sidewalk was heated as it absorbed the sun's energy. The Earth's atmosphere is also heated in several ways by the transfer of energy from the sun. In this section you will find out what happens to the solar energy as it enters the Earth's atmosphere, how the energy is transferred through the atmosphere, and why it seems to be getting hotter every year.

Energy in the Atmosphere

The Earth receives energy from the sun by radiation. **Radiation** is the transfer of energy as electromagnetic waves. Although the sun releases a huge amount of energy, the Earth receives only about two-billionths of this energy. Yet even this small amount of energy has a very large impact on Earth. **Figure 8** shows what happens to all this energy once it enters the atmosphere.

When energy is absorbed by a surface, it heats that surface. For example, when you stand in the sun on a cool day, you can feel the sun's rays warming your body. Your skin

Figure 8 *The radiation absorbed by the land, water, and atmosphere is changed into thermal energy.*

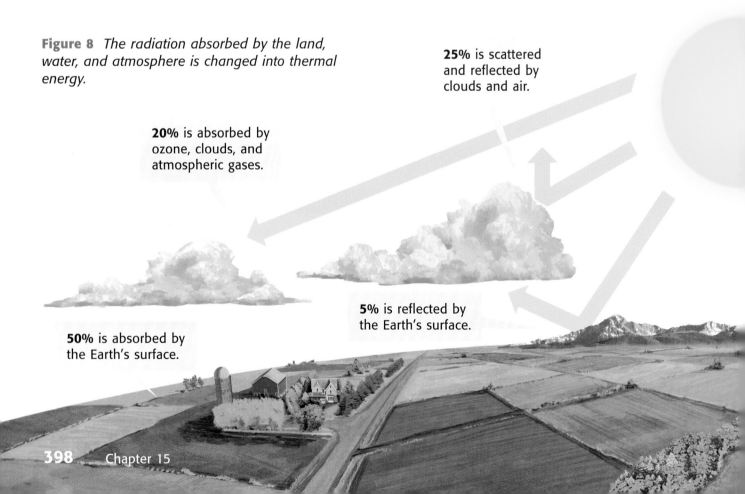

25% is scattered and reflected by clouds and air.

20% is absorbed by ozone, clouds, and atmospheric gases.

5% is reflected by the Earth's surface.

50% is absorbed by the Earth's surface.

absorbs the radiation, causing your skin's molecules to move faster. You feel this as an increase in temperature. The same thing happens when energy is absorbed by the Earth's surface. The energy from the Earth's surface can then be transferred to the atmosphere, which heats it.

Conduction **Conduction** is the transfer of thermal energy from one material to another by direct contact. Think back to the example about walking barefoot on a hot sidewalk. Conduction occurs when thermal energy is transferred from the sidewalk to your foot. Thermal energy always moves from warm to cold areas. Just as your foot is heated by the sidewalk, the air is heated by land and ocean surfaces. When air molecules come into direct contact with a warm surface, thermal energy is transferred to the atmosphere.

Convection Most thermal energy in the atmosphere moves by *convection.* **Convection** is the transfer of thermal energy by the circulation or movement of a liquid or gas. For instance, as air is heated, it becomes less dense and rises. Cool air is more dense and sinks. As the cool air sinks, it pushes the warm air up. The cool air is eventually heated by the ground and again begins to rise. This continual process of warm air rising and cool air sinking creates a circular movement of air, called a *convection current,* as shown in **Figure 9.**

If the Earth is continually absorbing solar energy and changing it to thermal energy, why doesn't the Earth get hotter and hotter? The reason is that much of this energy is lost to space. This is especially true on cloudless nights.

Figure 9 *There are three important processes responsible for heating the Earth and its atmosphere: radiation, conduction, and convection.*

a

Radiation moves energy through space in waves, heating the Earth's surface.

c

Convection currents are caused by the unequal heating of the atmosphere.

b

Near the Earth's surface, air is heated by **conduction.**

The Atmosphere **399**

The Greenhouse Effect

As you have already learned, 50 percent of the radiation that enters the Earth's atmosphere is absorbed by the Earth's surface. This energy is then reradiated to the Earth's atmosphere as thermal energy. Gases, such as carbon dioxide and water vapor, can stop this energy from escaping into space by absorbing it and then radiating it back to the Earth. As a result, the Earth's atmosphere stays warm. This is similar to how a blanket keeps you warm at night. The Earth's heating process, in which the gases in the atmosphere trap thermal energy, is known as the **greenhouse effect.** This term is used because the Earth's atmosphere works much like a greenhouse, as shown in **Figure 10.**

Figure 10 *The gases in the atmosphere act like a layer of glass. The gases allow solar energy to pass through. But some of the gases trap thermal energy.*

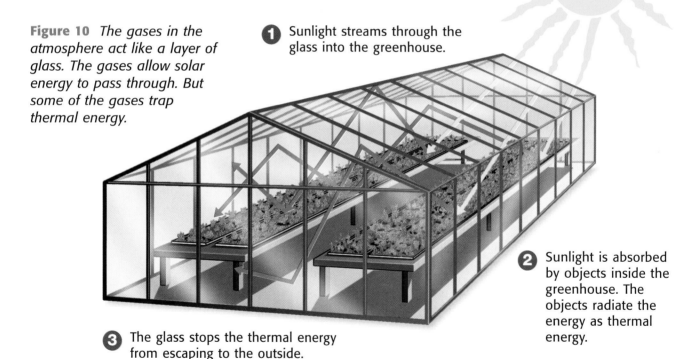

1 Sunlight streams through the glass into the greenhouse.

2 Sunlight is absorbed by objects inside the greenhouse. The objects radiate the energy as thermal energy.

3 The glass stops the thermal energy from escaping to the outside.

Global Warming Not every gas in the atmosphere traps thermal energy. Those that do trap this energy are called *greenhouse gases.* In recent decades, many scientists have become concerned that an increase of these gases, particularly carbon dioxide, may be causing an increase in the greenhouse effect. These scientists have hypothesized that a rise in carbon dioxide as a result of human activity has led to increased global temperatures. A rise in average global temperatures is called **global warming.** If there were an increase in the greenhouse effect, global warming would result.

The Radiation Balance For the Earth to remain livable, the amount of energy received from the sun and the amount of energy returned to space must be equal. As you saw in Figure 8, about 30 percent of the incoming energy is reflected back into space. Most of the 70 percent that is absorbed by the Earth and its atmosphere is also sent back into space. The balance between incoming energy and outgoing energy is known as the *radiation balance.* If greenhouse gases, such as carbon dioxide, continue to increase in the atmosphere, the radiation balance may be affected. Some of the energy that once escaped into space could be trapped. The Earth's temperatures would continue to rise, causing major changes in plant and animal communities.

Keeping the Earth Livable Some scientists argue that the Earth had warmer periods before humans ever walked the planet, so global warming may be a natural process. Nevertheless, many of the world's nations have signed a treaty to reduce activities that increase greenhouse gases in the atmosphere. Another step that is being taken to reduce high carbon dioxide levels in the atmosphere is the planting of millions of trees by volunteers, as shown in **Figure 11.**

Biology
CONNECTION

Did you know that if you lived in Florida, your fingernails and toenails would grow faster than if you lived in Minnesota? Studies by scientists at Oxford University, in England, showed that warm weather helps tissue growth, while cold weather slightly slows it.

Figure 11 *Plants take in harmful carbon dioxide and give off oxygen, which we need to breathe.*

REVIEW

1. Describe three things that can happen to energy when it reaches the Earth's atmosphere.

2. How is energy transferred through the atmosphere?

3. What is the greenhouse effect?

4. **Inferring Relationships** How does the process of convection rely on conduction?

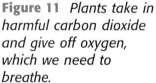

internet connect

SC*i*LINKS
NSTA

TOPIC: Energy in the Atmosphere
GO TO: www.scilinks.org
*sci*LINKS NUMBER: HSTE360

Terms to Learn

wind   westerlies
Coriolis effect   polar easterlies
trade winds   jet streams

What You'll Do

◆ Explain the relationship between air pressure and wind direction.
◆ Describe the global patterns of wind.
◆ Explain the causes of local wind patterns.

Atmospheric Pressure and Winds

Sometimes it cools you. Other times it scatters tidy piles of newly swept trash. Still other times it uproots trees and flattens buildings, as shown in **Figure 12**. **Wind** is moving air. In this section you will learn about air movement and about the similarities and differences between different kinds of winds.

Figure 12 In 1998, the winds from Hurricane Mitch reached speeds of 288 km/h, destroying entire towns in Honduras.

Why Air Moves

Wind is created by differences in air pressure. The greater the pressure difference is, the faster the wind moves. This difference in air pressure is generally caused by the unequal heating of the Earth. For example, the air at the equator is warmer and less dense. This warm, less-dense air rises. As it rises it creates an area of low pressure. At the poles, however, the air is colder and more dense. Colder, more-dense air is heavier and sinks. This cold, sinking air creates areas of high pressure. Pressure differences in the atmosphere at the equator and at the poles cause air to move. Because air moves from areas of high pressure to areas of low pressure, winds generally move from the poles to the equator, as shown in **Figure 13**.

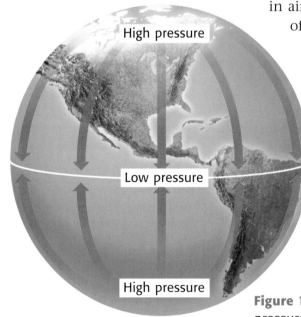

High pressure

Low pressure

High pressure

Figure 13 Surface winds blow from polar high-pressure areas to equatorial low-pressure areas.

Pressure Belts You may be imagining wind moving in one huge, circular pattern, from the poles to the equator. In fact, the pattern is much more complex. As warm air rises over the equator, it begins to cool. Eventually, it stops rising and moves toward the poles. At about 30° north and 30° south latitude, some of the cool air begins to sink. This cool, sinking air causes a high pressure belt near 30° north and 30° south latitude.

At the poles, cold air sinks. As this air moves away from the poles and along the Earth's surface, it begins to warm. As the air warms, the pressure drops, creating a low-pressure belt around 60° north and 60° south latitude. The circular patterns caused by the rising and sinking of air are called *convection cells,* as shown in **Figure 14.**

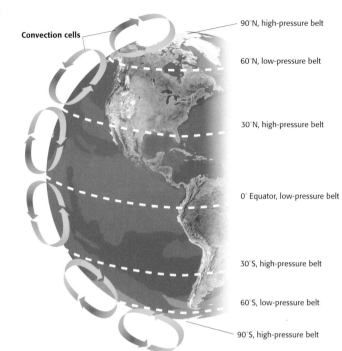

Figure 14 *The uneven heating of the Earth produces pressure belts. These belts occur at about every 30° of latitude.*

Coriolis Effect Winds don't blow directly north or south. The movement of wind is affected by the rotation of the Earth. The Earth's rotation causes wind to travel in a curved path rather than in a straight line. The curving of moving objects, such as wind, by the Earth's rotation is called the **Coriolis effect.** Because of the Coriolis effect, the winds in the Northern Hemisphere curve to the right, and those in the Southern Hemisphere curve to the left.

To better understand how the Coriolis effect works, imagine rolling a marble across a Lazy Susan while it is spinning. What you might observe is shown in **Figure 15.**

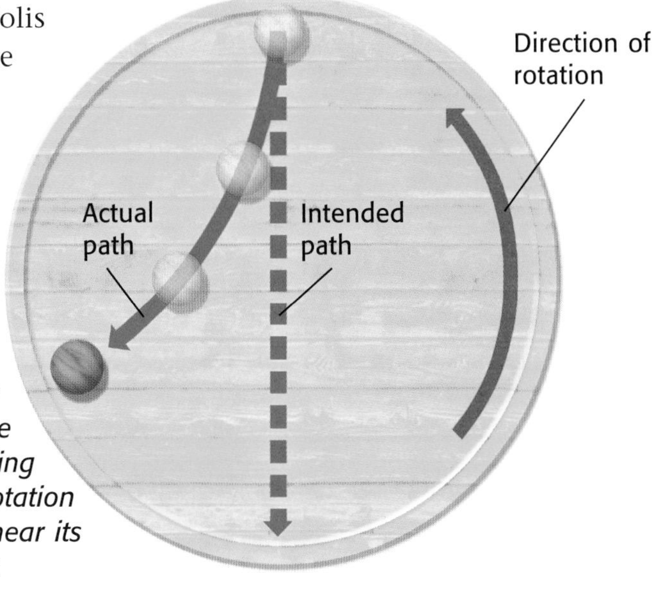

Figure 15 *Because of the Lazy Susan's rotation, the path of the marble curves instead of traveling in a straight line. The Earth's rotation affects objects traveling on or near its surface in much the same way.*

Full of "Hot Air"

1. Fill a **large clear-plastic container** with **cold water.**

2. Tie the end of a **string** around the neck of a **small bottle.**

3. Fill the small bottle with **hot water,** and add a few drops of **red food coloring** until the water has changed color.

4. Without tipping the small bottle, lower it into the plastic container until it rests on the bottom.

5. Observe what happens.

6. What process does this activity model? What do you think will happen if you fill the small bottle with cold water instead? Try it!

TRY at HOME

Types of Winds

There are two main types of winds: local winds and global winds. Both types are caused by the uneven heating of the Earth's surface and by pressure differences. *Local winds* generally move short distances and can blow from any direction. *Global winds* are part of a pattern of air circulation that moves across the Earth. These winds travel longer distances than local winds, and they each travel in a specific direction. **Figure 16** shows the location and movement of major global wind systems. First let's review the different types of global winds, and later in this section we will discuss local winds.

Trade Winds In both hemispheres, the winds that blow from 30° latitude to the equator are called **trade winds.** The Coriolis effect causes the trade winds to curve, as shown in Figure 16. Early traders used the trade winds to sail from Europe to the Americas. This is how they became known as "trade winds."

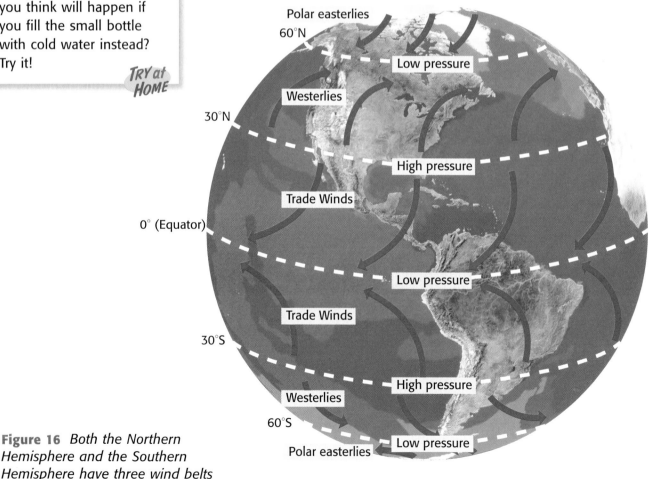

Figure 16 *Both the Northern Hemisphere and the Southern Hemisphere have three wind belts as a result of pressure differences.*

404   Chapter 15

The Doldrums and Horse Latitudes The trade winds of the Northern and Southern Hemispheres meet in an area of low pressure around the equator called the *doldrums*. In the doldrums there is very little wind because of the warm rising air. *Doldrums* comes from an Old English word meaning "foolish." Sailors were considered foolish if they got their ship stuck in these areas of little wind.

At about 30° north and 30° south latitude, sinking air creates an area of high pressure. This area is called the *horse latitudes*. Here the winds are weak. Legend has it that the name horse latitudes was given to these areas when sailing ships carried horses from Europe to the Americas. When the ships were stuck in this area due to lack of wind, horses were sometimes thrown overboard to save drinking water for the sailors.

Westerlies The **westerlies** are wind belts found in both the Northern and Southern Hemispheres between 30° and 60° latitude. The westerlies flow toward the poles in the opposite direction of the trade winds. The westerlies helped early traders return to Europe. Sailing ships, like the one in **Figure 17,** were designed to best use the wind to move the ship forward.

Environment
C O N N E C T I O N

Humans have been using wind energy for thousands of years. Today wind energy is being tapped to produce electricity at wind farms. Wind farms are made up of hundreds of wind turbines that look like giant airplane propellers attached to towers. Together these wind turbines can produce enough electricity for an entire town.

Figure 17 *This ship is a replica of Columbus's Santa Maria. If it had not sunk, the Santa Maria would have used the westerlies to return to Europe.*

Polar Easterlies The **polar easterlies** are wind belts that extend from the poles to 60° latitude in both hemispheres. The polar easterlies are formed from cold, sinking air moving from the poles toward 60° north and 60° south latitude.

To find out how to build a device that measures wind speed, turn to page 690 of the LabBook.

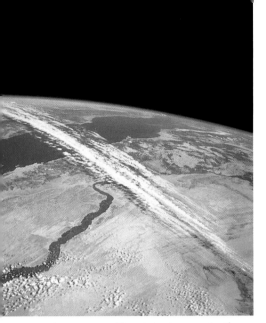

Figure 18 *The jet stream is the white stripe moving diagonally above the Earth.*

Jet Streams The **jet streams** are narrow belts of high-speed winds that blow in the upper troposphere and lower stratosphere, as shown in **Figure 18.** These winds often change speed and can reach maximum speeds of 500 km/h. Unlike other global winds, the jet streams do not follow regular paths around the Earth.

Knowing the position of the jet stream is important to both meteorologists and airline pilots. Because the jet stream controls the movement of storms, meteorologists can track a storm if they know the location of the jet stream. By flying in the direction of the jet stream, pilots can save time and fuel.

Local Winds Local winds are influenced by the geography of an area. An area's geography, such as a shoreline or a mountain, sometimes produces temperature differences that cause local winds like land and sea breezes, as shown in **Figure 19.** During the day, land heats up faster than water. The land heats the air above it. At night, land cools faster than water, cooling the air above the land.

Figure 19 **Sea and Land Breezes**

Warm air

As warm air rises, it creates an area of low pressure over the land.

The cool air moves toward the land, producing a *sea breeze.*

Cool air

Air over the water is cooler and creates an area of high pressure.

Cool air

Air over land is cooler and creates an area of high pressure.

The cool air moves toward the water, producing a *land breeze.*

Warm air

Air over the water is warmer and creates an area of low pressure.

Mountain and valley breezes are another example of local winds caused by an area's geography. Campers in mountain areas may feel a warm afternoon change into a cold night soon after the sun sets. The illustrations in **Figure 20** show you why.

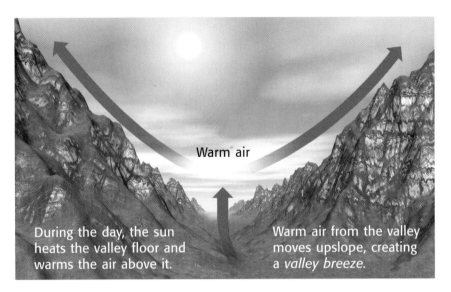

During the day, the sun heats the valley floor and warms the air above it.

Warm air

Warm air from the valley moves upslope, creating a *valley breeze.*

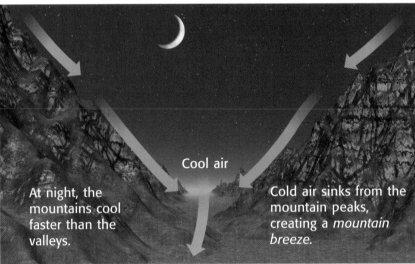

At night, the mountains cool faster than the valleys.

Cool air

Cold air sinks from the mountain peaks, creating a *mountain breeze.*

MATH BREAK

Calculating Groundspeed
An airplane has an airspeed of 500 km/h and is moving into a 150 km/h head wind due to the jet stream. What is the actual groundspeed of the plane? Over a 3-hour flight, how far would the plane actually travel? (Hint: To calculate actual ground-speed, subtract head-wind speed from airspeed.)

Figure 20 *During the day, a gentle breeze blows up the slopes. At night, cold air flows downslope and settles in the valley.*

REVIEW

1. How does the Coriolis effect affect wind movement?

2. What causes winds?

3. Compare and contrast global winds and local winds.

4. **Applying Concepts** Suppose you are vacationing at the beach. It is daytime and you want to go swimming in the ocean. You know the beach is near your hotel, but you don't know what direction it is in. How might the local wind help you find the ocean?

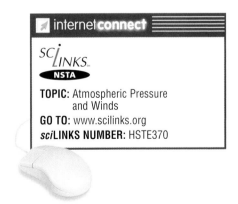

internet connect

SciLINKS
NSTA

TOPIC: Atmospheric Pressure and Winds
GO TO: www.scilinks.org
*sci*LINKS NUMBER: HSTE370

The Air We Breathe

Terms to Learn

primary pollutants
secondary pollutants
acid precipitation

What You'll Do

◆ Describe the major types of air pollution.
◆ Name the major causes of air pollution.
◆ Explain how air pollution can affect human health.
◆ Explain how air pollution can be reduced.

Air pollution, as shown in **Figure 21,** is not a new problem. By the middle of the 1700s, many of the world's large cities suffered from poor air quality. Most of the pollutants were released from factories and homes that burned coal for energy. Even 2,000 years ago, the Romans were complaining about the bad air in their cities. At that time the air was thick with the smoke from fires and the smell of open sewers. So you see, cities have always been troubled with air pollution. In this section you will learn about the different types of air pollution, their sources, and what the world is doing to reduce them.

Figure 21 *The air pollution in Mexico City is sometimes so dangerous that some people wear surgical masks when they go outside.*

Air Quality

Even "clean" air is not perfectly clean. It contains many pollutants from natural sources. These pollutants include dust, sea salt, volcanic gases and ash, smoke from forest fires, pollen, swamp gas, and many other materials. In fact, natural sources produce a greater amount of pollutants than humans do. But we have adapted to many of these natural pollutants.

Most of the air pollution mentioned in the news is a result of human activities. Pollutants caused by human activities can be solids, liquids, or gases. Human-caused air pollution, such as that shown in Figure 21, is most common in cities. As more people move to cities, urban air pollution increases.

Types of Air Pollution

Air pollutants are generally described as either *primary pollutants* or *secondary pollutants*. **Primary pollutants** are pollutants that are put directly into the air by human or natural activity. **Figure 22** shows some examples of primary air pollutants.

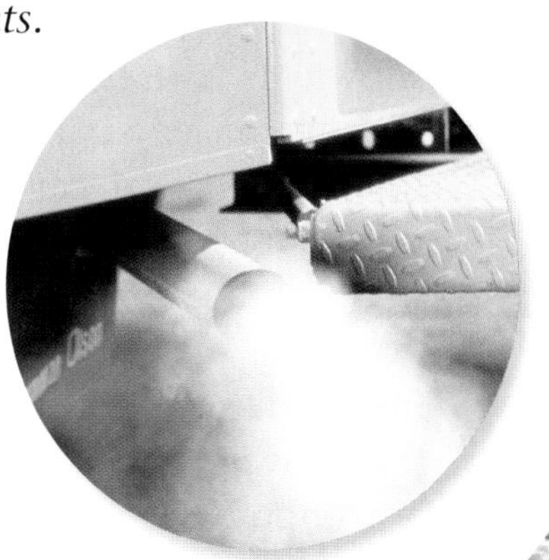

Figure 22 *Exhaust from vehicles, ash from volcanic eruptions, and soot from smoke are all examples of primary pollutants.*

Secondary pollutants are pollutants that form from chemical reactions that occur when primary pollutants come in contact with other primary pollutants or with naturally occurring substances, such as water vapor. Many secondary pollutants are formed when a primary pollutant reacts with sunlight. Ozone and smog are examples of secondary pollutants. As you read at the beginning of this chapter, ozone is a gas in the stratosphere that is helpful and absorbs harmful rays from the sun. Near the ground, however, ozone is a dangerous pollutant that affects the health of all organisms. Ozone and smog are produced when sunlight reacts with automobile exhaust, as illustrated in **Figure 23.**

Figure 23 *Many large cities suffer from smog, especially those with a sunny climate and millions of automobiles.*

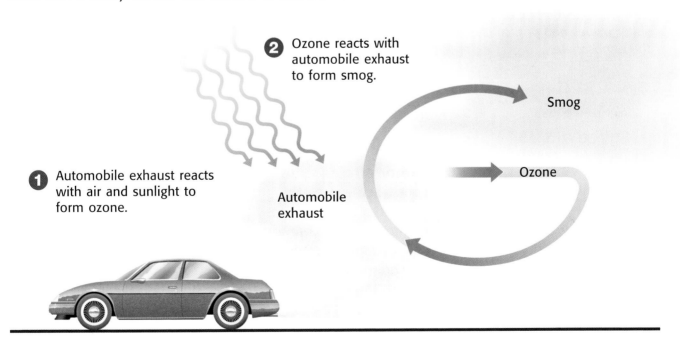

2 Ozone reacts with automobile exhaust to form smog.

Smog

1 Automobile exhaust reacts with air and sunlight to form ozone.

Automobile exhaust

Ozone

Sources of Human-Caused Air Pollution

Human-caused air pollution comes from a variety of sources. The major source of air pollution today is transportation, as shown in **Figure 24.** Cars contribute about 60 percent of the human-caused air pollution in the United States. The oxides that come from car exhaust, such as nitrogen oxide, contribute to smog and acid rain. *Oxides* are chemical compounds that contain oxygen and other elements.

Industrial Air Pollution Many industrial plants and electric power plants burn fossil fuels to get their energy. But burning fossil fuels causes large amounts of oxides to be released into the air, as shown in **Figure 25.** In fact, the burning of fossil fuels in industrial and electric power plants is responsible for 96 percent of the sulfur oxides released into the atmosphere.

Some industries also produce chemicals that form poisonous fumes. The chemicals used by oil refineries, chemical manufacturing plants, dry-cleaning businesses, furniture refinishers, and auto-body shops can add poisonous fumes to the air.

Figure 24 *Seventy percent of the carbon monoxide in the United States is produced by fuel-burning vehicles.*

Figure 25 *This power plant burns coal to get its energy and releases sulfur oxides and particulates into the atmosphere.*

Indoor Air Pollution Air pollution is not limited to the outdoors. Sometimes the air inside a home or building is even worse than the air outside. The air inside a building can be polluted by the compounds found in household cleaners and cooking smoke. The compounds in new carpets, paints, and building materials can also add to indoor air pollution, especially if the windows and doors are tightly sealed to keep energy bills low.

The Air Pollution Problem

Air pollution is both a local and global concern. As you have already learned, local air pollution, such as smog, generally affects large cities. Air pollution becomes a global concern when local pollution moves away from its source. Winds can move pollutants from one place to another, sometimes reducing the amount of pollution in the source area but increasing it in another place. For example, the prevailing winds carry air pollution created in the midwestern United States hundreds of miles to Canada. One such form of this pollution is acid precipitation.

Figure 26 *Acid precipitation can kill living things, such as fish and trees, by making their environment too acidic to live in.*

Acid Precipitation Precipitation that contains acids from air pollution is called **acid precipitation.** When fossil fuels are burned, they release oxides of sulfur and nitrogen into the atmosphere. When these oxides combine with water droplets in the atmosphere, they form sulfuric acid and nitric acid, which fall as precipitation. Acid precipitation has many negative effects on the environment, as shown in **Figure 26.**

The Ozone Hole Other global concerns brought about by air pollution include the warming of our planet and the ozone hole in the stratosphere. In the 1970s, scientists determined that some chemicals released into the atmosphere react with ozone in the ozone layer. The reaction results in a breakdown of ozone into oxygen, which does not block the sun's harmful ultraviolet rays. The loss of ozone creates an ozone hole, which allows more ultraviolet rays to reach the Earth's surface. **Figure 27** shows a satellite image of the ozone hole.

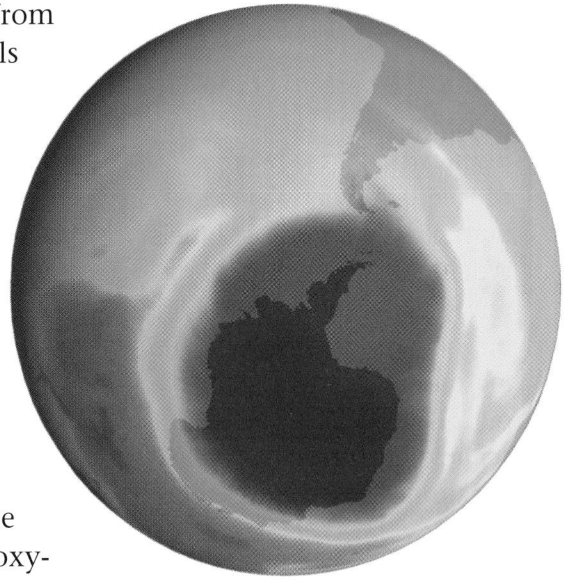

Figure 27 *This satellite image, taken in 1998, shows that the ozone hole, the dark blue area, is still growing.*

Effects on Human Health You step outside and notice a smoky haze. When you take a deep breath, your throat tingles and you begin to cough. Air pollution like this affects many cities around the world. For example, on March 17, 1992, in Mexico City, all children under the age of 14 were prohibited from going to school because of extremely high levels of air pollution. This is an extreme case, but daily exposure to small amounts of air pollution can cause serious health problems. Children, elderly people, and people with allergies, lung problems, and heart problems are especially vulnerable to the effects of air pollution. **Figure 28** illustrates some of the effects that air pollution has on the human body.

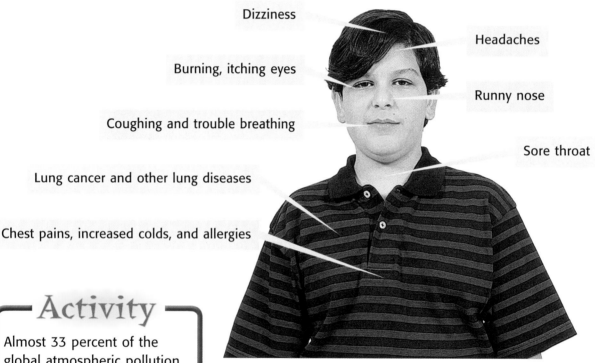

Dizziness

Headaches

Burning, itching eyes

Runny nose

Coughing and trouble breathing

Sore throat

Lung cancer and other lung diseases

Chest pains, increased colds, and allergies

Figure 28 *The Environmental Protection Agency blames air pollution for at least 2,000 new cases of cancer each year.*

Cleaning Up Our Act

Is all this talk about bad air making you a little choked up? Don't worry, help is on the way! In the United States, progress has been made in cleaning up the air. One reason for this progress is the Clean Air Act, which was passed by Congress in 1970. The Clean Air Act is a law that gives the Environmental Protection Agency (EPA) the authority to control the amount of air pollutants that can be released from any source, such as cars and factories. The EPA also checks air quality. If air quality worsens, the EPA can set stricter standards. What are car manufacturers and factories doing to improve air quality? Read on to find out.

Activity

Almost 33 percent of the global atmospheric pollution from carbon dioxide is caused by power plants that burn coal or other fossil fuels. We rely on these sources of power for a better way of life, but our use of them is polluting our air and worsening our quality of life. Use your school library or the Internet to find out about some other sources of electric power. What special problems does each source of energy bring with it?

TRY at HOME

Controlling Air Pollution from Vehicles The EPA has required car manufacturers to meet a certain standard for the exhaust that comes out of the tailpipe on cars. New cars now have devices that remove most of the pollutants from the car's exhaust as it exits the tailpipe. Car manufacturers are also making cars that run on fuels other than gasoline. Some of these cars run on hydrogen and natural gas, while others run on batteries powered by solar energy. The car shown in **Figure 29** is electric.

Are electric cars the cure for air pollution? Turn to page 419 and decide for yourself.

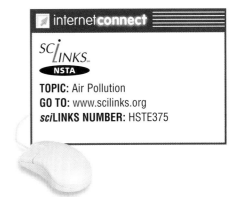

Figure 29 *Instead of having to refuel at a gas station, an electric car is plugged in to a recharging outlet.*

Controlling Air Pollution from Industry The Clean Air Act requires many industries to use scrubbers. A scrubber is a device that attaches to smokestacks to remove some of the more harmful pollutants before they are released into the air. One such scrubber is used in coal-burning power plants in the United States to remove ash and other particles from the smokestacks. Scrubbers prevent 22 million metric tons of ash from being released into the air each year.

Although we have a long way to go, we're taking steps in the right direction to keep the air clean for future generations.

REVIEW

1. How can the air inside a building be more polluted than the air outside?

2. Why might it be difficult to establish a direct link between air pollution and health problems?

3. How has the Clean Air Act helped to reduce air pollution?

4. **Applying Concepts** How is the water cycle affected by air pollution?

internet**connect**

SC*LINKS*
NSTA

TOPIC: Air Pollution
GO TO: www.scilinks.org
*sci*LINKS **NUMBER:** HSTE375

Chapter Highlights

Vocabulary

atmosphere *(p. 392)*

air pressure *(p. 393)*

altitude *(p. 393)*

troposphere *(p. 395)*

stratosphere *(p. 395)*

ozone *(p. 395)*

mesosphere *(p. 396)*

thermosphere *(p. 396)*

Section Notes

- The atmosphere is a mixture of gases.

- Nitrogen and oxygen are the two most abundant atmospheric gases.

- Throughout the atmosphere, there are changes in air pressure, temperature, and gases.

- Air pressure decreases as altitude increases.

- Temperature differences in the atmosphere are a result of the way solar energy is absorbed as it moves downward through the atmosphere.

- The troposphere is the lowest and densest layer of the atmosphere. All weather occurs in the troposphere.

- The stratosphere contains the ozone layer, which protects us from harmful radiation.

- The mesosphere is the coldest layer of the atmosphere.

- The uppermost atmospheric layer is the thermosphere.

Labs

Under Pressure! *(p. 692)*

Vocabulary

radiation *(p. 398)*

conduction *(p. 399)*

convection *(p. 399)*

greenhouse effect *(p. 400)*

global warming *(p. 400)*

Section Notes

- The Earth receives energy from the sun by radiation.

- Energy that reaches the Earth's surface is absorbed, reflected, or reradiated.

- Energy is transferred through the atmosphere by conduction and convection.

- The greenhouse effect is caused by gases in the atmosphere that trap thermal energy reflected off and radiated from the Earth's surface.

Labs

Boiling Over! *(p. 688)*

☑ Skills Check

Math Concepts

FLYING AGAINST THE JET STREAM The groundspeed of an airplane can be affected by the jet stream. The jet stream can push an airplane toward its final destination or slow it down. To find the groundspeed of an airplane, you either add or subtract the wind speed, depending on whether the airplane is moving with or against the jet stream. For example, if an airplane is traveling at an airspeed of 400 km/h and is moving with a 100 km/h jet stream, you would add the jet stream speed to the airspeed of the airplane to calculate the groundspeed.

$$400 \text{ km/h} + 100 \text{ km/h} = 500 \text{ km/h}$$

To calculate the groundspeed of an airplane traveling at 400 km/h that is moving into a 100 km/h jet stream, you would subtract the jet-stream speed from the airspeed of the airplane.

$$400 \text{ km/h} - 100 \text{ km/h} = 300 \text{ km/h}$$

Visual Understanding

GLOBAL WINDS Study Figure 16 on page 404 to review the global wind belts that result from air pressure differences.

Vocabulary

wind *(p. 402)*

Coriolis effect *(p. 403)*

trade winds *(p. 404)*

westerlies *(p. 405)*

polar easterlies *(p. 405)*

jet streams *(p. 406)*

Section Notes

- At the Earth's surface, winds blow from areas of high pressure to areas of low pressure.

- Pressure belts exist approximately every 30° of latitude.

- The Coriolis effect makes wind curve as it moves across the Earth's surface.

- Global winds are part of a pattern of air circulation across the Earth and include the trade winds, the westerlies, and the polar easterlies.

- Local winds move short distances, can blow in any direction, and are influenced by geography.

Labs

Go Fly a Bike! *(p. 690)*

Vocabulary

primary pollutants *(p. 409)*

secondary pollutants *(p. 409)*

acid precipitation *(p. 411)*

Section Notes

- Air pollutants are generally classified as primary or secondary pollutants.

- Human-caused pollution comes from a variety of sources, including factories, cars, and homes.

- Air pollution can heighten problems associated with allergies, lung problems, and heart problems.

- The Clean Air Act has reduced air pollution by controlling the amount of pollutants that can be released from cars and factories.

---

internetconnect

GO TO: go.hrw.com

Visit the **HRW** Web site for a variety of learning tools related to this chapter. Just type in the keyword:

KEYWORD: HSTATM

GO TO: www.scilinks.org

Visit the **National Science Teachers Association** on-line Web site for Internet resources related to this chapter. Just type in the *sci*LINKS number for more information about the topic:

TOPIC: Composition of the Atmosphere   *sci*LINKS NUMBER: HSTE355

TOPIC: Energy in the Atmosphere   *sci*LINKS NUMBER: HSTE360

TOPIC: The Greenhouse Effect   *sci*LINKS NUMBER: HSTE365

TOPIC: Atmospheric Pressure and Winds   *sci*LINKS NUMBER: HSTE370

TOPIC: Air Pollution   *sci*LINKS NUMBER: HSTE375

Chapter Review

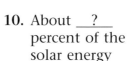

USING VOCABULARY

Explain the difference between the following sets of words:

1. air pressure/altitude

2. troposphere/thermosphere

3. greenhouse effect/global warming

4. convection/conduction

5. global wind/local wind

6. primary pollutant/secondary pollutant

UNDERSTANDING CONCEPTS

Multiple Choice

7. What is the most abundant gas in the air that we breathe?
   a. oxygen   c. hydrogen
   b. nitrogen   d. carbon dioxide

8. The major source of oxygen for the Earth's atmosphere is
   a. sea water.   c. plants.
   b. the sun.   d. animals.

9. The bottom layer of the atmosphere, where almost all weather occurs, is the
   a. stratosphere.
   b. troposphere.
   c. thermosphere.
   d. mesosphere.

10. About ___?___ percent of the solar energy that reaches the outer atmosphere is absorbed at the Earth's surface.
    a. 20
    b. 30
    c. 50
    d. 70

11. The ozone layer is located in the
    a. stratosphere.
    b. troposphere.
    c. thermosphere.
    d. mesosphere.

12. How does most thermal energy in the atmosphere move?
    a. conduction
    b. convection
    c. advection
    d. radiation

13. The balance between incoming and outgoing energy is called ___?___.
    a. convection
    b. conduction
    c. greenhouse effect
    d. radiation balance

14. Most of the United States is located in which prevailing wind belt?
    a. westerlies
    b. northeast trade winds
    c. southeast trade winds
    d. doldrums

15. Which of the following is not a primary pollutant?
    a. car exhaust
    b. acid precipitation
    c. smoke from a factory
    d. fumes from burning plastic

16. The Clean Air Act
  a. controls the amount of air pollutants that can be released from most sources.
  b. requires cars to run on fuels other than gasoline.
  c. requires many industries to use scrubbers.
  d. (a) and (c) only

Short Answer

17. Why does the atmosphere become less dense as altitude increases?

18. Explain why air rises when it is heated.

19. What causes temperature changes in the atmosphere?

20. What are secondary pollutants, and how are they formed? Give an example.

Concept Mapping

21. Use the following terms to create a concept map: altitude, air pressure, temperature, atmosphere.

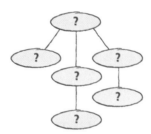

CRITICAL THINKING AND PROBLEM SOLVING

Write one or two sentences to answer the following questions:

22. What is the relationship between the greenhouse effect and global warming?

23. How do you think the Coriolis effect would change if the Earth were to rotate twice as fast? Explain.

24. Without the atmosphere, the Earth's surface would be very different. What are several ways that the atmosphere affects the Earth?

MATH IN SCIENCE

25. Wind speed is measured in miles per hour and in knots. One mile (statute mile or land mile) is 5,280 ft. One nautical mile (or sea mile) is 6,076 ft. Speed in nautical miles is measured in knots. Calculate the wind speed in knots if the wind is blowing at 25 mi/h.

INTERPRETING GRAPHICS

Use the wind-chill chart to answer the questions below.

Wind-Chill Chart

Wind Speed		Actual thermometer reading (°F)				
		40	30	20	10	0
Knots	mph	Equivalent temperature (°F)				
Calm		40	30	20	10	0
4	5	37	27	16	6	−5
9	10	28	16	4	−9	−21
13	15	22	9	−5	−18	−36
17	20	18	4	−10	−25	−39
22	25	16	0	−15	−29	−44
26	30	13	−2	−18	−33	−48
30	35	11	−4	−20	−35	−49

26. If the wind speed is 20 mi/h and the temperature is 40°F, how cold will the air seem?

27. If the wind speed is 30 mi/h and the temperature is 20°F, how cold will the air seem?

Reading Check-up

Take a minute to review your answers to the Pre-Reading Questions found at the bottom of page 390. Have your answers changed? If necessary, revise your answers based on what you have learned since you began this chapter.

Health

Particles in the Air

Take a deep breath. You have probably just inhaled thousands of tiny specks of dust, pollen, and other particles. These particles, called particulates, are harmless under normal conditions. But if concentrations of particulates get too high or if they consist of harmful materials, they are considered to be a type of air pollution.

Because many particulates are very small, our bodies' natural filters, such as nasal hairs and mucous membranes, cannot filter all of them out. When inhaled, particulates can cause irritation in the lungs. Over time, this irritation can lead to diseases such as bronchitis, asthma, and emphysema. The danger increases as the level of particulates in the air increases.

▲ *When the ash from Mount St. Helens settled from the air, it created scenes like this one.*

Where There's Smoke . . .

Unfortunately, dust and pollen are not the only forms of particulates. Many of the particulates in the air come from the burning of various materials. For example, when wood is burned, it releases particles of smoke, soot, and ash into the air. Some of these are so small that they can float in the air for days. The burning of fuels such as coal, oil, and gasoline also creates particulates. The particulates from these sources can be very dangerous in high concentrations. That's why particulate concentrations are one measure of air quality. Large concentrations of particulates are visible in the air. Along with other pollutants, particulates are

what make polluted air look brown or yellowish brown. But don't be fooled—even air that appears clean can be polluted.

Eruptions of Particulates

Volcanoes can be the source of incredible amounts of particulates. For example, when Mount St. Helens erupted in 1980, it launched thousands of tons of ash into the surrounding air. The air was so thick with ash that the area became as dark as night. For several hours, the ash completely blocked the light from the sun. When the ash finally settled from the air, it covered the surrounding landscape like a thick blanket of snow. This layer of ash killed plants and livestock for several kilometers around the volcano.

One theory to explain the extinction of dinosaurs is that a gargantuan meteorite hit the Earth with such velocity that the resulting impact created enough dust to block out the sun for years. During this dark period, plants were unable to grow and therefore could not support the normal food chains. Consequently, the dinosaurs died out.

Do Filters Really Filter?

▶ Since the burning of most substances creates particulates, there must be particulates in cigarette smoke. Do some research to find out if the filters on cigarettes are effective at preventing particulates from entering the smoker's body. Your findings may surprise you!

A Cure for Air Pollution?

Automobile emissions are responsible for at least half of all urban air pollution and a quarter of all carbon dioxide released into the atmosphere. Therefore, the production of a car that emits no polluting gases in its exhaust is a significant accomplishment. The only such vehicle currently available is the electric car. Electric cars are powered by batteries, so they do not produce exhaust gases. Supporters believe that switching to electric cars will reduce air pollution in this country. But critics believe that taxpayers will pay an unfair share for this switch and that the reduction in pollution won't be as great as promised.

▲ *Will a switch to electric cars such as this one reduce air pollution?*

Electric Cars Will Reduce Air Pollution

Even the cleanest and most modern cars emit pollutants into the air. Supporters of a switch to electric cars believe the switch will reduce pollution in congested cities. But some critics suggest that a switch to electric cars will simply move the source of pollution from a car's tailpipe to the power plant's smokestack. This is because most electricity is generated by burning coal.

In California, electric cars would have the greatest impact. Here most electricity is produced by burning natural gas, which releases less air pollution than burning coal.

Nuclear plants and dams release no pollutants in the air when they generate electricity. Solar power and wind power are also emission-free ways to generate electricity. Supporters argue that a switch to electric cars will reduce air pollution immediately and that a further reduction will occur when power plants convert to these cleaner sources of energy.

Electric Cars Won't Solve the Problem

Electric cars are inconvenient because the batteries have to be recharged so often. The batteries also have to be replaced every 2 to 3 years. The nation's landfills are already crowded with conventional car batteries, which contain acid and metals that may pollute ground water. A switch to electric cars would aggravate this pollution problem because the batteries have to be replaced so often.

Also, electric cars will likely replace the cleanest cars on the road, not the dirtiest. A new car may emit only one-tenth of the pollution emitted by an older model. If an older car's pollution-control equipment does not work properly, it may emit 100 times more pollution than a new car. But people who drive older, poorly maintained cars probably won't be able to afford expensive electric cars. Therefore, the worst offenders will stay on the road, continuing to pollute the air.

Analyze the Issue

▶ Do you think electric cars are the best solution to the air pollution problem? Why or why not? What are some alternative solutions for reducing air pollution?

Understanding Weather

Pre-Reading Questions

1. Name some different kinds of clouds. How are they different?
2. What causes weather?

TWISTING TERROR

North America experiences an average of 700 tornadoes per year—more tornadoes than any other continent. Most of these tornadoes hit an area in the central United States called Tornado Alley. Tornado Alley has more tornadoes than any other area because its flatness and location on the Earth's surface make it possible for warm air masses and cold air masses to collide. In this chapter, you will learn about what causes weather and how weather can suddenly turn violent.

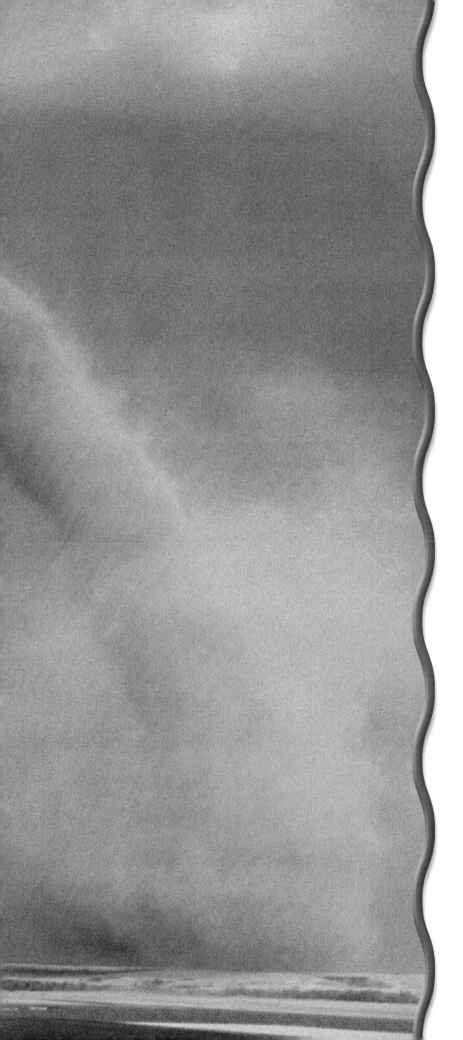

START-UP Activity

A MEETING OF THE MASSES

In this activity, you will model what happens when two air masses with different temperature characteristics meet.

Procedure

1. Fill a **beaker** with **500 mL of cooking oil.** Fill another **beaker** with **500 mL of water.** The cooking oil represents a less dense warm air mass. The water represents a denser cold air mass.

2. Predict what would happen if you tried to mix the two liquids together. Record your prediction in your ScienceLog.

3. Pour the contents of each beaker into a **clear, plastic rectangular container** at the same time from opposite ends of the container.

4. Observe what happens when the oil and water meet. Record your observations in your ScienceLog.

Analysis

5. What happens when the different liquids meet?

6. Does the prediction you made in step 2 match your results?

7. Based on your results, hypothesize what would happen if a cold air mass met a warm air mass. Record your hypothesis in your ScienceLog.

Terms to Learn

weather   condensation
water cycle   dew point
humidity   cloud
relative humidity   precipitation

What You'll Do

- Explain how water moves through the water cycle.
- Define *relative humidity*.
- Explain what the dew point is and its relation to condensation.
- Describe the three major cloud forms.
- Describe the four major types of precipitation.

Water in the Air

There might not be a pot of gold at the end of a rainbow, but rainbows hold another secret that you might not be aware of. Rainbows are evidence that the air contains water. Water droplets break up sunlight into the different colors that you can see in a rainbow. Water can exist in the air as a solid, liquid, or gas. Ice, a solid, is found in clouds as snowflakes. Liquid water exists in clouds as water droplets. And water in gaseous form exists in the air as water vapor. Water in the air affects the weather. **Weather** is the condition of the atmosphere at a particular time and place. In this section you will learn how water affects the weather.

The Water Cycle

Water in liquid, solid, and gaseous states is constantly being recycled through the water cycle. The **water cycle** is the continuous movement of water from water sources, such as lakes and oceans, into the air, onto and over land, into the ground, and back to the water sources. Look at **Figure 1** below to see how water moves through the water cycle.

Figure 1 *In the water cycle, water is returned to the Earth's surface through precipitation.*

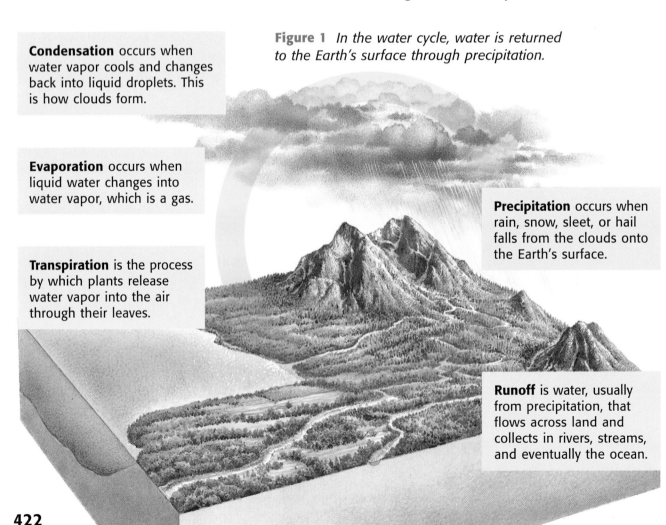

Condensation occurs when water vapor cools and changes back into liquid droplets. This is how clouds form.

Evaporation occurs when liquid water changes into water vapor, which is a gas.

Transpiration is the process by which plants release water vapor into the air through their leaves.

Precipitation occurs when rain, snow, sleet, or hail falls from the clouds onto the Earth's surface.

Runoff is water, usually from precipitation, that flows across land and collects in rivers, streams, and eventually the ocean.

Humidity

Have you ever spent a long time styling your hair before school and had a bad hair day anyway? You walked outside and—wham—your straight hair became limp, or your curly hair became frizzy. Most bad hair days can be blamed on humidity. **Humidity** is the amount of water vapor or moisture in the air. And it is the moisture in the air that makes your hair go crazy, as shown in **Figure 2**.

As water evaporates, the humidity of the air increases. But air's ability to hold water vapor depends on air temperature. As temperature increases, the air's ability to hold water also increases. **Figure 3** shows the relationship between air temperature and air's ability to hold water.

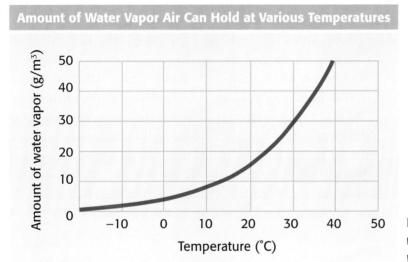

Figure 2 *When there is more water in the air, your hair absorbs moisture and becomes longer.*

Figure 3 *This graph shows that warmer air can hold more water vapor than cooler air.*

Relative Humidity   **Relative humidity** is the amount of moisture the air contains compared with the maximum amount it can hold at a particular temperature. Relative humidity is given as a percentage. When air holds all the water it can at a given temperature, the air is said to be *saturated*. Saturated air has a relative humidity of 100 percent. But how do you find the relative humidity of air that is not saturated? If you know the maximum amount of water vapor air can hold at a particular temperature and you know how much water vapor the air is actually holding, you can calculate the relative humidity.

Suppose that 1 m³ of air at a certain temperature can hold 24 g of water vapor. However, you know that the air actually contains 18 g of water vapor. You can calculate the relative humidity using the following formula:

$$\frac{\text{(present) } 18 \text{ g/m}^3}{\text{(saturated) } 24 \text{ g/m}^3} \times 100 = \text{(relative humidity) } 75\%$$

MATH BREAK

Relating Relative Humidity
Assume that a sample of air 1 m³ at 25°C, contains 11 g of water vapor. Calculate the relative humidity of the air using the value for saturated air shown in Figure 3.

Self-Check

How does humidity relate to the water cycle? *(Turn to page 726 to check your answer.)*

Water Vapor Versus Temperature If the temperature stays the same, relative humidity changes as water vapor enters or leaves the air. The more water vapor that is in the air at a particular temperature, the higher the relative humidity is. Relative humidity is also affected by changes in temperature. If the amount of water vapor in the air stays the same, the relative humidity decreases as the temperature rises and increases as the temperature drops.

Measuring Relative Humidity A *psychrometer* (sie KRAHM uht uhr) is an instrument used to measure relative humidity. It consists of two thermometers. One thermometer is called a wet-bulb thermometer. The bulb of this thermometer is covered with a damp cloth. The other thermometer is a dry-bulb thermometer. The dry-bulb thermometer measures air temperature.

As air passes over the wet-bulb thermometer, the water in the cloth begins to evaporate. As the water evaporates from the cloth, energy is transferred away from the wet-bulb and the thermometer begins to cool. If there is less humidity in the air, the water will evaporate more quickly and the temperature of the wet-bulb thermometer will drop. If the humidity is high, only a small amount of water will evaporate from the wet-bulb thermometer and there will be little change in temperature.

Follow the Numbers

Relative Humidity (in percentage)								
Dry-bulb reading (°C)	Difference between wet-bulb reading and dry-bulb reading (°C)							
	1	2	3	4	5	6	7	8
0	81	64	46	29	13			
2	84	68	52	37	22	7		
4	85	71	57	43	29	16		
6	86	73	60	48	35	24	11	
8	87	75	63	51	40	29	19	8
10	88	77	66	55	44	34	24	15
12	89	78	68	58	48	39	29	21
14	90	79	70	60	51	42	34	26
16	90	81	71	63	54	46	38	30
18	91	82	73	65	57	49	41	34
20	91	83	74	66	59	51	44	37

Relative humidity can be determined using a table such as this one. Locate the column that shows the difference between the wet-bulb and dry-bulb readings. Then locate the row that lists the temperature reading on the dry-bulb thermometer. The value where the column and row intersect is the relative humidity.

The difference in temperature readings between the wet-bulb and dry-bulb thermometers indicates the amount of water vapor in the air. A larger difference between the two readings indicates that there is less water vapor in the air and thus lower humidity.

The Process of Condensation

You have probably seen water droplets form on the outside of a glass of ice water, as shown in **Figure 4**. Did you ever wonder where those water droplets came from? The water came from the surrounding air, and droplets formed because of condensation. **Condensation** is the process by which a gas, such as water vapor, becomes a liquid. Before condensation can occur, the air must be saturated; it must have a relative humidity of 100 percent. Condensation occurs when saturated air cools further.

Figure 4 *Condensation occurred when the air next to the glass cooled to below its dew point.*

Dew Point Air can become saturated when water vapor is added to the air through evaporation or transpiration. Air can also become saturated, as in the case of the glass of ice water, when it cools to its dew point. The **dew point** is the temperature to which air must cool to be completely saturated. The ice in the glass of water causes the air surrounding the glass to cool to its dew point.

Before it can condense, water vapor must also have a surface to condense on. On the glass of ice water, water vapor condenses on the sides of the glass. Another example you may already be familiar with is water vapor condensing on grass, forming small water droplets called *dew*.

REVIEW

1. What is the difference between humidity and relative humidity?

2. What are two ways that air can become saturated with water vapor?

3. What does a relative humidity of 75 percent mean?

4. How does the water cycle contribute to condensation?

5. **Analyzing Relationships** What happens to relative humidity as the air temperature drops below the dew point?

Quick Lab

Out of Thin Air

1. Take a **plastic container,** such as a jar or drinking glass, and fill it almost to the top with room-temperature **water.**

2. Observe the outside of the can or container. Record your observations.

3. Add one or two **ice cubes,** and watch the outside of the container for any changes.

4. What happened to the outside of the container?

5. What is the liquid?

6. Where did the liquid come from? Why?

TRY at HOME

Clouds

Some look like cotton balls, some look like locks of hair, and others look like blankets of gray blocking out the sun. But what *are* clouds and how do they form? And why are there so many different-looking clouds? A **cloud** is a collection of millions of tiny water droplets or ice crystals. Clouds form as warm air rises and cools. As the rising air cools, it becomes saturated. At saturation the water vapor changes to a liquid or a solid depending on the air temperature. At higher temperatures, water vapor condenses on small particles, such as dust, smoke, and salt, suspended in the air as tiny water droplets. At temperatures below freezing, water vapor changes directly to a solid, forming ice crystals.

Cumulus

Figure 5 *Cumulus clouds look like piles of cotton balls.*

Cumulus Clouds Puffy, white clouds that tend to have flat bottoms, as shown in **Figure 5,** are called *cumulus clouds*. Cumulus clouds form when warm air rises. These clouds generally indicate fair weather. However, when these clouds get larger they produce thunderstorms. A cumulus cloud that produces thunderstorms is called a *cumulonimbus cloud*. When *-nimbus* or *nimbo-* is part of a cloud's name, it means that precipitation might fall from the cloud.

Stratus Clouds Clouds that form in layers, as shown in **Figure 6,** are called *stratus clouds*. Stratus clouds cover large areas of the sky, often blocking out the sun. These clouds are caused by a gentle lifting of a large body of air into the atmosphere. *Nimbostratus clouds* are dark stratus clouds that usually produce light to heavy, continuous rain. When water vapor condenses near the ground, it forms a stratus cloud called *fog*.

Stratus

Figure 6 *Although stratus clouds are not as tall as cumulus clouds, they cover more area.*

Cirrus Clouds As you can see in **Figure 7,** *cirrus* (SIR uhs) *clouds* are thin, feathery, white clouds found at high altitudes. Cirrus clouds form when the wind is strong. Cirrus clouds may indicate approaching bad weather if they thicken and lower in altitude.

Clouds are also classified by the altitude at which they form. The illustration in **Figure 8** shows the three altitude groups used to categorize clouds.

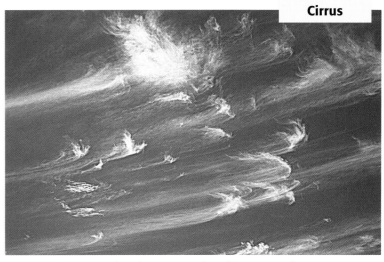

Cirrus

Figure 7 *Cirrus clouds are made of ice crystals.*

Figure 8 **Cloud Types Based on Form and Altitude**

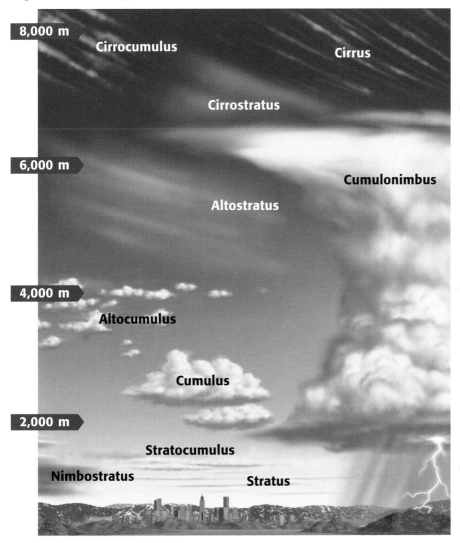

8,000 m
Cirrocumulus
Cirrus
Cirrostratus

6,000 m
Cumulonimbus
Altostratus

4,000 m
Altocumulus
Cumulus

2,000 m
Stratocumulus
Nimbostratus
Stratus

High Clouds
Because of the cold temperatures at high altitude, high clouds are made up of ice crystals. The prefix *cirro-* is used to describe high clouds.

Middle Clouds
Middle clouds can be made up of both water droplets and ice crystals. The prefix *alto-* is used to describe middle clouds.

Low Clouds
Low clouds are made up of water droplets. The prefix *strato-* is commonly used to describe these types of clouds.

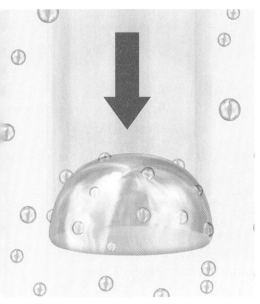

Figure 9 *Cloud droplets get larger by colliding and joining with other droplets. When the water droplets become too heavy, they fall as precipitation.*

Precipitation

Water vapor that condenses to form clouds can eventually fall to the ground as precipitation. **Precipitation** is water, in solid or liquid form, that falls from the air to the Earth. There are four major forms of precipitation—rain, snow, sleet, and hail.

Rain, the most common form of precipitation, is liquid water that falls from the clouds to Earth. A cloud produces rain when its water droplets become large enough to fall. A cloud droplet begins as a water droplet smaller than the period at the end of this sentence. Before a cloud droplet falls as precipitation, it must increase in size to about 100 times its normal diameter. **Figure 9** illustrates how a water droplet increases in size until it is finally large enough to fall as precipitation.

Snow and Sleet The most common form of solid precipitation is *snow.* Snow forms when temperatures are so cold that water vapor changes directly to a solid. Snow can fall as individual ice crystals or combine to form snowflakes, like the one shown in **Figure 10.**

Sleet, also called freezing rain, forms when rain falls through a layer of freezing air. The rain freezes, producing falling ice. Sometimes rain does not freeze until it hits a surface near the ground. When this happens, the rain changes into a layer of ice called *glaze,* as shown in **Figure 11.**

Figure 10 *Snowflakes are six-sided ice crytals that range in size from several millimeters to several centimeters.*

Figure 11 *Glaze ice forms as rain freezes on surfaces near the ground.*

Hail Solid precipitation that falls as balls or lumps of ice is called *hail*. Hail usually forms in cumulonimbus clouds. Updrafts of air in the clouds carry raindrops to high altitudes in the cloud, where they freeze. As the frozen raindrops fall, they collide and combine with water droplets. Another updraft of air can send the hail up again high into the cloud. Here the water drops collected by the hail freeze, forming another layer of frozen ice. If the upward movement of air is strong enough, the hail can accumulate many layers of ice. Eventually, the hail becomes too heavy and falls to the Earth's surface, as shown in **Figure 12.** Hail is usually associated with warm weather and most often occurs during the spring and summer months.

Figure 12 *The impact of large hailstones can damage property and crops.*

Measuring Precipitation A *rain gauge* is an instrument used to measure the amount of rainfall. A rain gauge typically consists of a funnel and a cylinder, as shown in **Figure 13.** Rain falls into the funnel and collects in the cylinder. Markings on the cylinder indicate how much rain has fallen.

Snow is measured by both depth and water content. The depth of snow is measured using a measuring stick. The snow's water content is determined by melting the snow and measuring the amount of water.

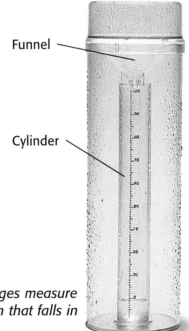

Funnel

Cylinder

Figure 13 *Rain gauges measure only the precipitation that falls in a particular place.*

REVIEW

1. How do clouds form?

2. Why are some clouds formed from water droplets, while others are made up of ice crystals?

3. Describe how rain forms.

4. **Applying Concepts** How can rain and hail fall from the same cumulonimbus cloud?

internet**connect**

SC*i*INKS.
NSTA

TOPIC: Collecting Weather Data
GO TO: www.scilinks.org
*sci*LINKS NUMBER: HSTE380

Air Masses and Fronts

Terms to Learn

air mass
front

What You'll Do

◆ Explain how air masses are characterized.
◆ Describe the four major types of air masses that influence weather in the United States.
◆ Describe the four major types of fronts.
◆ Relate fronts to weather changes.

Have you ever wondered how the weather can change so fast? One day the sun is shining and you are wearing shorts, and the next day it is so cold you need a coat. Changes in weather are caused by the movement and interaction of air masses. An **air mass** is a large body of air that has similar temperature and moisture throughout. In this section you will learn about air masses and how their interaction influences the weather.

Air Masses

An air mass gets its moisture and temperature characteristics from the area over which it forms. These areas are called *source regions*. For example, an air mass that develops over the Gulf of Mexico is warm and wet because this area is warm and has a lot of water that evaporates into the air. There are many types of air masses, each associated with a particular source region. The characteristics of these air masses are represented on maps with a two-letter symbol, as shown in **Figure 14.** The first letter indicates the moisture characteristics of the air mass, and the second symbol represents the temperature characteristics of the air mass.

Figure 14 *This map shows the source regions for air masses that influence weather in North America.*

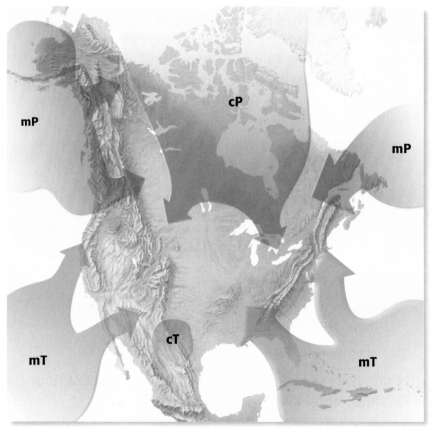

maritime (m)–forms over water; wet

continental (c)–forms over land; dry

polar (P)–forms over the polar regions; cold

tropical (T)–develops over the Tropics; warm

Cold Air Masses Most of the cold winter weather in the United States is influenced by three polar air masses. A continental polar air mass develops over land in northern Canada. In the winter, this air brings extremely cold weather to the United States, as shown in **Figure 15.** In the summer, it generally brings cool, dry weather.

A maritime polar air mass that forms over the North Pacific Ocean mostly affects the Pacific Coast. This air mass is very wet, but not as cold as the air mass that develops over Canada. In the winter, this air mass brings rain and snow to the Pacific Coast. In the summer, it brings cool, foggy weather.

A maritime polar air mass that forms over the North Atlantic Ocean usually affects New England and eastern Canada. In the winter, it produces cold, cloudy weather with precipitation. In the summer, the air mass brings cool weather with fog.

Figure 15 *A cP air mass generally moves southeastward across Canada and into the northern United States.*

Warm Air Masses Four warm air masses influence the weather in the United States. A maritime tropical air mass that develops over warm areas in the North Pacific Ocean is lower in moisture content and weaker than the maritime polar air mass. As a result, southern California receives less precipitation than the rest of California.

Other maritime tropical air masses develop over the warm waters of the Gulf of Mexico and the North Atlantic Ocean. These air masses move north across the East Coast and into the Midwest. In the summer, they bring hot and humid weather, thunderstorms, and hurricanes, as shown in **Figure 16.** In the winter, they bring mild, often cloudy weather.

Figure 16 *People in Texas experience the many thunderstorms brought by mT air masses from the Gulf of Mexico.*

A continental tropical air mass forms over the deserts of northern Mexico and the southwestern United States. This air mass influences weather in the United States only during the summer. It generally moves northeastward, bringing clear, dry, and very hot weather.

Fronts

Air masses with different characteristics, such as temperature and humidity, do not usually mix. So when two different air masses meet, a boundary forms between them. This boundary is called a **front.** Weather at a front is usually cloudy and stormy. The four different types of fronts—cold fronts, warm fronts, occluded fronts, and stationary fronts—are illustrated on these two pages. Fronts are usually associated with weather in the middle latitudes, where there are both cold and warm air masses. Fronts do not occur in the Tropics because only warm air masses exist there.

Cold Front

A cold air mass meets and displaces a warm air mass. Because the moving cold air is more dense, it moves under the less-dense warm air, pushing it up.

Cold fronts can move fast, producing thunderstorms, heavy rain, or snow. Cooler weather usually follows a cold front because the warm air is pushed away from the Earth's surface.

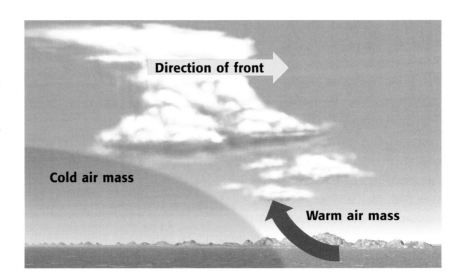

Warm Front

A warm air mass meets and overrides a cold air mass. The warm, less-dense air moves over the cold, denser air. The warm air gradually replaces the cold air.

Warm fronts generally bring drizzly precipitation. After the front passes, weather conditions are clear and warm.

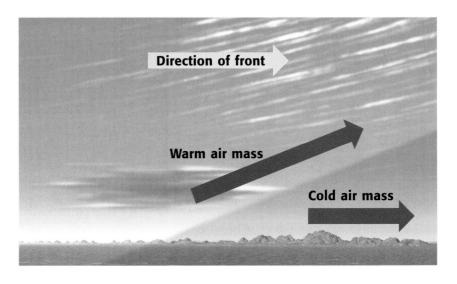

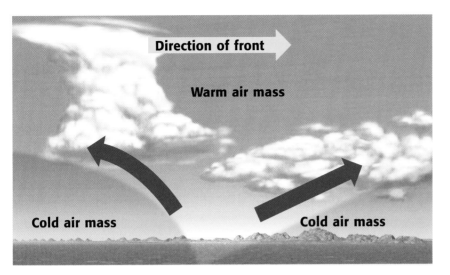

Direction of front

Warm air mass

Cold air mass   Cold air mass

Occluded Front

A faster-moving cold air mass overtakes a slower-moving warm air mass and forces the warm air up. The cold air mass then continues advancing until it meets a cold air mass that is warmer. The cold air mass then forces this air mass to rise.

An occluded front has cool temperatures and large amounts of precipitation.

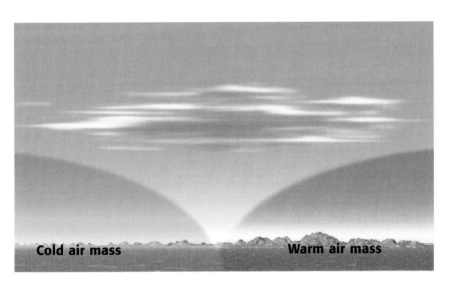

Cold air mass   Warm air mass

Stationary Front

A cold air mass meets a warm air mass and little horizontal movement occurs.

The weather associated with a stationary front is similar to that produced by a warm front.

REVIEW

1. What are the characteristics that define air masses?

2. What are the major air masses that influence the weather in the United States?

3. What are fronts, and what causes them?

4. What kind of front forms when a cold air mass displaces a warm air mass?

5. **Analyzing Relationships** Explain why the Pacific Coast has cool, wet winters and warm, dry summers.

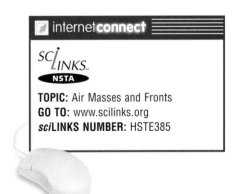

internet**connect**

SC*L*INKS.
NSTA

TOPIC: Air Masses and Fronts
GO TO: www.scilinks.org
*sci*LINKS NUMBER: HSTE385

What You'll Do

◆ Explain what lightning is.
◆ Describe the formation of thunderstorms, tornadoes, and hurricanes.
◆ Describe the characteristics of thunderstorms, tornadoes, and hurricanes.

Severe Weather

Weather in the mid-latitudes can change from day to day. These changes result from the continual shifting of air masses. Sometimes a series of storms will develop along a front and bring severe weather. *Severe weather* is weather that can cause property damage and even death. Examples of severe weather include thunderstorms, tornadoes, and hurricanes. In this section you will learn about the different types of severe weather and how each type forms.

Thunderstorms

Thunderstorms, as shown in **Figure 17,** are small, intense weather systems that produce strong winds, heavy rain, lightning, and thunder. As you learned in the previous section, thunderstorms can occur along cold fronts. But that's not the only place they develop. There are only two atmospheric conditions required to produce thunderstorms: the air near the Earth's surface must be warm and moist, and the atmosphere must be unstable. The atmosphere is unstable when the surrounding air is colder than the rising air mass. As long as the air surrounding the rising air mass is colder, the air mass will continue to rise.

Thunderstorms occur when warm, moist air rises rapidly in an unstable atmosphere. When the warm air reaches its dew point, the water vapor in the air condenses, forming cumulus clouds. If the atmosphere is extremely unstable, the warm air will continue to rise, causing the cloud to grow into a dark, cumulonimbus cloud. These clouds can reach heights of more than 15 km.

Figure 17 *A typical thunderstorm produces approximately 470 million liters of water and enough electricity to provide power to the entire United States for 20 minutes.*

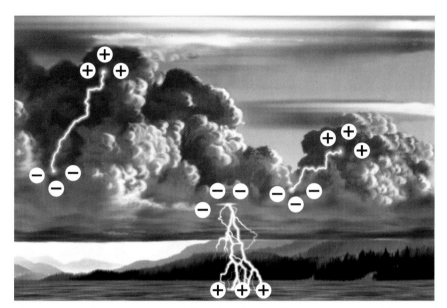

Figure 18 *The upper part of a cloud usually carries a positive electrical charge, while the lower part of the cloud carries mainly negative charges.*

Lightning Thunderstorms are very active electrically. **Lightning** is a large electrical discharge that occurs between two oppositely charged surfaces, as shown in **Figure 18.** Have you ever touched someone after scuffing your feet on the carpet and received a mild shock? If so, you have experienced how lightning forms. While walking around, friction between the floor and your shoes builds up an electrical charge in your body. When you touch someone else, the charge is released.

When lightning strikes, energy is released. This energy is transferred to the air and causes the air to expand rapidly and send out sound waves. **Thunder** is the sound that results from the rapid expansion of air along the lightning strike.

Severe Thunderstorms Severe thunderstorms produce one or more of the following conditions—high winds, hail, flash floods, and tornadoes. Hailstorms damage crops, dent the metal on cars, and break windows. Sudden flash flooding due to heavy rains causes millions of dollars in property damage annually and is the biggest cause of weather-related deaths.

Lightning, which occurs with all thunderstorms, is responsible for thousands of forest fires each year in the United States. Lightning also kills or injures hundreds of people a year in the United States.

Figure 19 *Lightning often strikes the highest object in an area.*

Tornadoes

Tornadoes are produced in only 1 percent of all thunderstorms. A **tornado** is a small, rotating column of air that has high wind speeds and low central pressure and that touches the ground. A tornado starts out as a funnel cloud that pokes through the bottom of a cumulonimbus cloud and hangs in the air. It is called a tornado when it makes contact with the Earth's surface. **Figure 20** shows the development of a tornado.

Figure 20 How a Tornado Forms

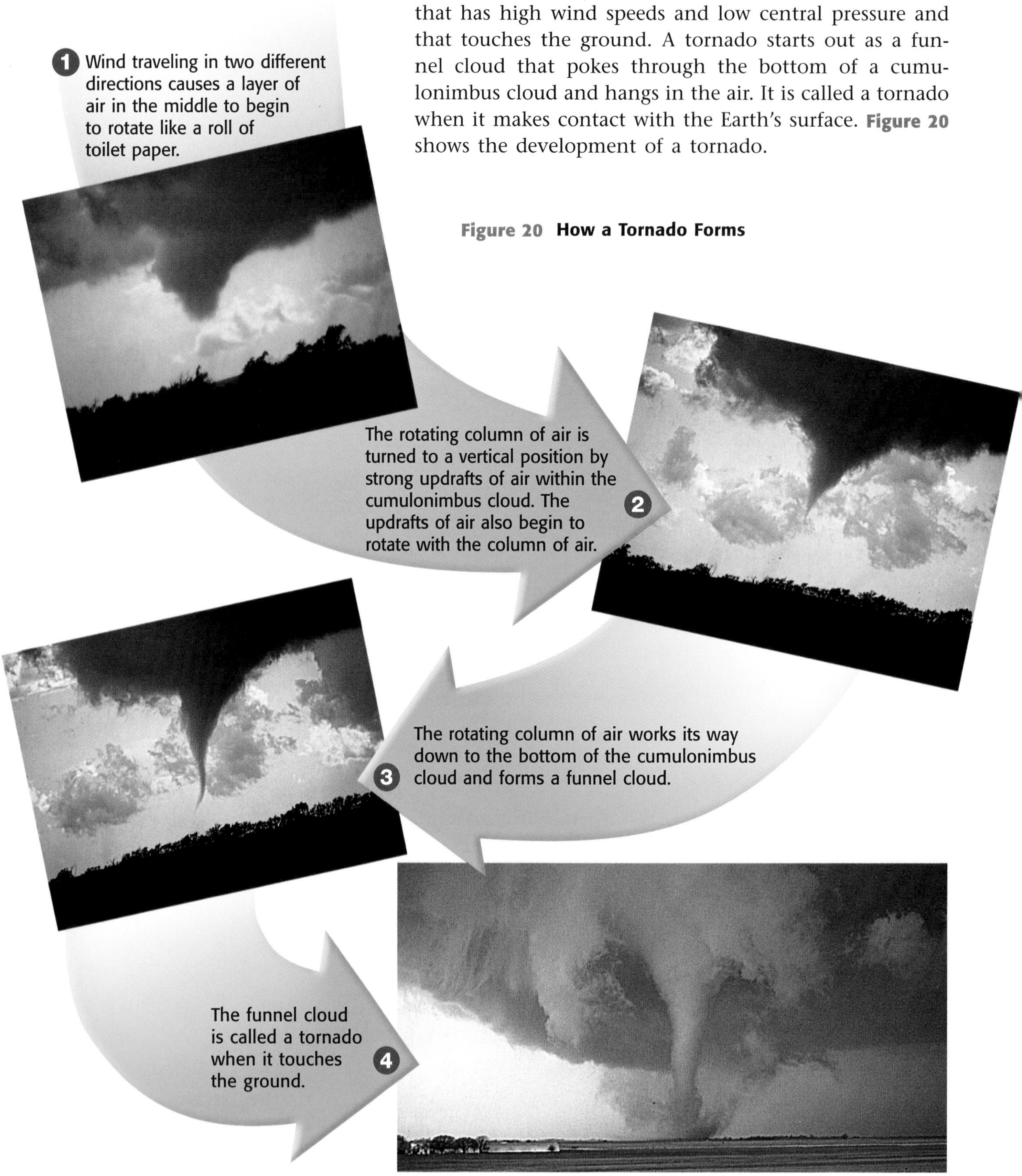

1 Wind traveling in two different directions causes a layer of air in the middle to begin to rotate like a roll of toilet paper.

2 The rotating column of air is turned to a vertical position by strong updrafts of air within the cumulonimbus cloud. The updrafts of air also begin to rotate with the column of air.

3 The rotating column of air works its way down to the bottom of the cumulonimbus cloud and forms a funnel cloud.

4 The funnel cloud is called a tornado when it touches the ground.

Twists of Terror About 75 percent of the world's tornadoes occur in the United States. The majority of these tornadoes happen in the spring and early summer when cold, dry air from Canada collides with warm, moist air from the Tropics. The length of a tornado's path of destruction can vary, but it is usually about 8 km long and 10–60 m wide. Although most tornadoes last only a few minutes, they can cause a lot of damage. This is due to their strong spinning winds. The average tornado has wind speeds between 120 and 180 km/h, but

Figure 21 The tornado that hit Kissimmee, Florida, in 1998 had wind speeds of up to 416 km/h.

rarer, more violent tornadoes can have spinning winds up to 500 km/h. The winds of tornadoes have been known to uproot trees and destroy buildings, as shown in **Figure 21.** Tornadoes are capable of picking up heavy objects, such as mobile homes and cars, and hurling them through the air.

Hurricanes

A **hurricane,** as shown in **Figure 22,** is a large, rotating tropical weather system with wind speeds of at least 119 km/h. Hurricanes are the most powerful storms on Earth. Hurricanes have different names in other parts of the world. In the western Pacific Ocean, they are called *typhoons.* Hurricanes that form over the Indian Ocean are called *cyclones.*

Hurricanes generally form in the area between 5° and 20° north and south latitude over warm, tropical oceans. At higher latitudes, the water is too cold for hurricanes to form. Hurricanes vary in size from 160 km to 1,500 km in diameter, and they can travel for thousands of miles.

Did you know that fish have been known to fall from the sky? Some scientists think the phenomenon of raining fish is caused by waterspouts. A waterspout is a tornado that occurs over water.

Figure 22 Hurricane Fran Photographed from Space

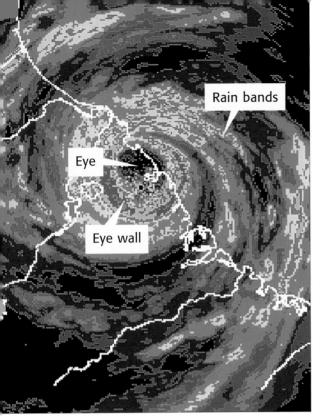

Rain bands

Eye

Eye wall

Figure 23 *The photo above gives you a bird's-eye view of a hurricane.*

Formation of a Hurricane

Formation of a Hurricane A hurricane begins as a group of thunderstorms moving over tropical ocean waters. Winds traveling in two different directions collide, causing the storm to rotate over an area of low pressure. Because of the Coriolis effect, the storm turns counterclockwise in the Northern Hemisphere and clockwise in the Southern Hemisphere.

Hurricanes get their energy from the condensation of water vapor. Once formed, the hurricane is fueled through contact with the warm ocean water. Moisture is added to the warm air by evaporation from the ocean. As the warm, moist air rises, the water vapor condenses, releasing large amounts of energy. The hurricane continues to grow as long as it is over its source of warm, moist air. When the hurricane moves into colder waters or over land, it begins to die because it has lost its source of energy. **Figure 23** and **Figure 24** show two views of a hurricane.

Figure 24 *The view below shows how a hurricane would look if you cut it in half and looked at it from the side. The arrows indicate the flow of air.*

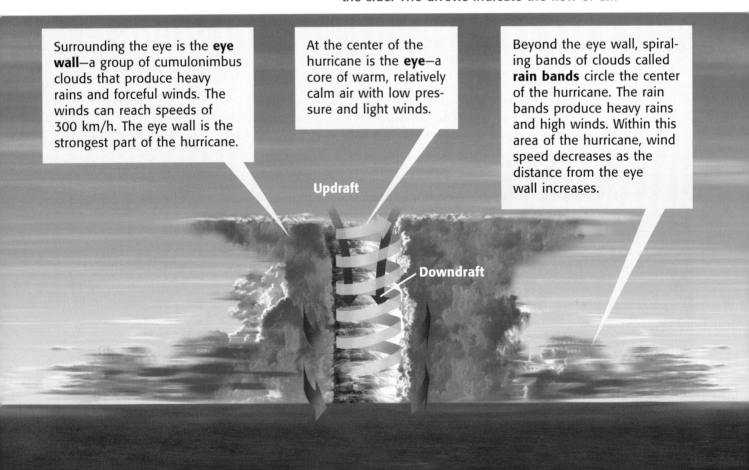

Surrounding the eye is the **eye wall**—a group of cumulonimbus clouds that produce heavy rains and forceful winds. The winds can reach speeds of 300 km/h. The eye wall is the strongest part of the hurricane.

At the center of the hurricane is the **eye**—a core of warm, relatively calm air with low pressure and light winds.

Beyond the eye wall, spiraling bands of clouds called **rain bands** circle the center of the hurricane. The rain bands produce heavy rains and high winds. Within this area of the hurricane, wind speed decreases as the distance from the eye wall increases.

Updraft

Downdraft

Damage Caused by Hurricanes Hurricanes can cause a lot of damage when they move near or onto land. The speed of the steady winds of most hurricanes ranges from 120 km/h to 150 km/h, and they can reach speeds as high as 300 km/h. Hurricane winds can knock down trees and telephone poles and can damage and destroy buildings and homes.

While high winds cause a great deal of damage, most hurricane damage is caused by flooding associated with heavy rains and storm surges. A *storm surge* is a wall of water that builds up over the ocean due to the heavy winds and low atmospheric pressure. The wall of water gets bigger and bigger as it nears the shore, reaching its greatest height when it crashes onto the shore. Depending on the hurricane's strength, a storm surge can be 1 m to 8 m high and 65 km–160 km long. Flooding causes tremendous damage to property and lives when a storm surge moves onto shore, as shown in **Figure 25.**

Astronomy
CONNECTION

The weather on Jupiter is more exciting than that on Earth. Wind speeds reach up to 540 km/h. Storms last for decades, and one—the Great Red Spot of Jupiter—has been swirling around since it was first discovered, in 1664. The Great Red Spot has a diameter of more than one and a half times that of the Earth. It is like a hurricane that has lasted more than 300 years.

Figure 25 *In 1998, the flooding associated with Hurricane Mitch devastated Central America. Whole villages were swept away by the flood waters and mudslides. Thousands of people were killed, and damages were estimated to be more than $5 billion.*

REVIEW

1. What is lightning?

2. Describe how tornadoes develop. What is the difference between a funnel cloud and a tornado?

3. Why do hurricanes form only over certain areas?

4. **Inferring Relationships** What happens to a hurricane as it moves over land? Why?

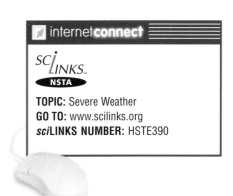

internet**connect**

SC**LINKS**
NSTA

TOPIC: Severe Weather
GO TO: www.scilinks.org
*sci*LINKS NUMBER: HSTE390

Forecasting the Weather

What You'll Do

◆ Describe the different types of instruments used to take weather measurements.

◆ Explain how to interpret a weather map.

◆ Explain why weather maps are useful.

Have you ever left your house in the morning wearing a short-sleeved shirt, only to need a sweater in the afternoon? At some time in your life, you have been caught off guard by the weather. Weather affects how you dress and your daily plans, so it is important that you get accurate weather forecasts. A *weather forecast* is a prediction of weather conditions over the next 3 to 5 days. Meteorologists observe and collect data on current weather conditions in order to provide reliable predictions. In this section you will learn about some of the methods used to collect weather data and how those data are displayed.

Weather Forecasting Technology

In order for meteorologists to accurately forecast the weather, they need to measure various atmospheric conditions, such as air pressure, humidity, precipitation, temperature, wind speed, and wind direction. Meteorologists use special instruments to collect data on weather conditions both near and far above the Earth's surface. You have already learned about two tools that meteorologists use near the Earth's surface—psychrometers, which are used to measure relative humidity, and rain gauges, which are used to measure precipitation. Read on to learn about other methods meteorologists use to collect data.

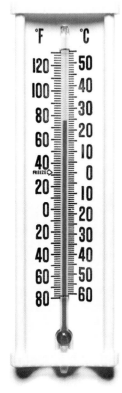

Figure 26 *A liquid thermometer is usually filled with alcohol that is colored red, or mercury, which is silver.*

Measuring Air Temperature A **thermometer** is a tool used to measure air temperature. A common type of thermometer uses a liquid sealed in a narrow glass tube, as shown in **Figure 26.** When air temperature increases, the liquid expands and moves up the glass tube. As air temperature decreases, the liquid shrinks and moves down the tube.

Air temperature is measured in both degrees Celsius and degrees Fahrenheit. In the United States, television weather forecasters generally report air temperature in degrees Fahrenheit.

Measuring Air Pressure A **barometer** is an instrument used to measure air pressure. The mercurial barometer provides the most accurate method of measuring air pressure. A mercurial barometer consists of a glass tube sealed at one end that is placed in a container full of mercury. The air pressure pushes on the mercury inside the container, causing the mercury to move up the glass tube. The greater the air pressure is, the higher the mercury will rise.

Measuring Wind Direction Wind direction can be measured using a **windsock** or a **wind vane.** A windsock, as shown in **Figure 27,** is a cone-shaped cloth bag open at both ends. The wind enters through the wide end and leaves through the narrow end. Therefore, the wide end points into the wind.

A wind vane is shaped like an arrow with a large tail and is attached to a pole. The wind pushes the tail of the wind vane, spinning it on the pole until the arrow points into the wind.

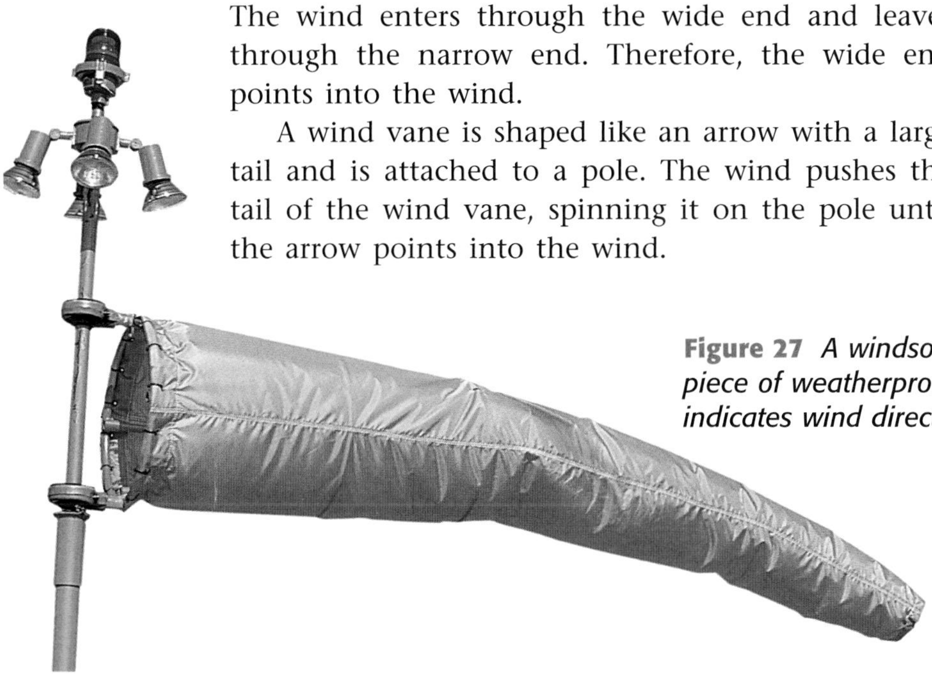

Figure 27 A windsock is a cone-shaped piece of weatherproof material that indicates wind direction.

Measuring Wind Speed Wind speed is measured by a device called an **anemometer.** An anemometer, as shown in **Figure 28,** consists of three or four cups connected by spokes to a pole. The wind pushes on the hollow sides of the cups, causing them to rotate on the pole. The motion sends a weak electrical current that is measured and displayed on a dial.

Measuring Weather in the Upper Atmosphere You have learned how weather conditions are recorded near the Earth's surface. But in order for meteorologists to better understand weather patterns, they must collect data from higher altitudes. Studying weather at higher altitudes requires the use of more-sophisticated equipment.

Figure 28 The faster the wind speed is, the faster the cups of the anemometer spin.

Figure 29 *Weather balloons carry radio transmitters that send measurements to stations on the ground.*

Eyes in the Sky Weather balloons carry electronic equipment that can measure weather conditions as high as 30 km above the Earth's surface. Weather balloons, such as the one in **Figure 29,** carry equipment that measures temperature, air pressure, and relative humidity.

Radar is used to find the location, movement, and intensity of precipitation. It can also detect what form of precipitation a weather system is carrying. You might be familiar with a type of radar called Doppler radar. **Figure 30** shows how Doppler radar is used to track precipitation.

Figure 30 *Using Doppler radar, meteorologists can predict a tornado up to 20 minutes before it touches the ground.*

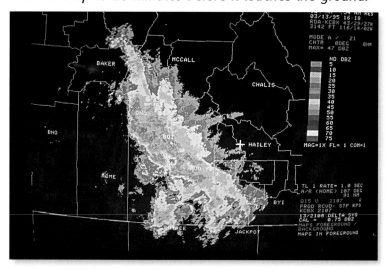

Weather satellites orbiting the Earth provide the images of the swirling clouds you can see on television weather reports. Satellites can measure wind speeds, humidity, and the temperatures at various altitudes.

Weather Maps

As you have learned, meteorologists base their forecasts on information gathered from many sources. In the United States, the National Weather Service (NWS) and the National Oceanic and Atmospheric Administration (NOAA) collect and analyze weather data. The NWS produces weather maps based on information gathered from about 1,000 weather stations across the United States. On these maps, each station is represented by a station model. A *station model,* as shown in **Figure 31,** is a small circle, which shows the location of the weather station, with a set of symbols and numbers surrounding it, which represent the weather data.

Activity

Throughout history, people have predicted approaching weather by interpreting natural signs. Animals and plants are usually more sensitive to changes in the atmosphere, such as air pressure, humidity, and temperature, than humans. To find out more about natural signs, research this topic at the library or on the Internet. Try searching using key words and phrases such as "weather and animals" or "weather and plants." Write a short paper on your findings to share with the class.

TRY at HOME

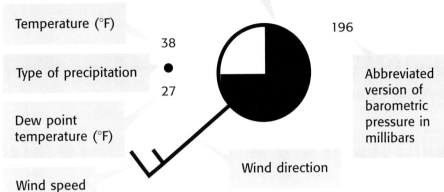

Temperature (°F)

Amount of cloud cover

Type of precipitation

Dew point temperature (°F)

Wind speed

38

27

196

Abbreviated version of barometric pressure in millibars

Wind direction

Figure 31 *Weather conditions at a station are represented by symbols.*

Under Pressure

Weather maps also include lines called isobars. Isobars are similar to contour lines on a topographical map, except **isobars** are lines that connect points of equal air pressure rather than equal elevation. Isobar lines that form closed circles represent areas of high or low pressure. These areas are usually marked on a map with a capital *H* or *L*. Fronts are also labeled on weather maps. Weather maps, like the one shown in **Figure 32,** provide useful information for making accurate weather forecasts.

Figure 32 *Can you identify the different fronts on the weather map?*

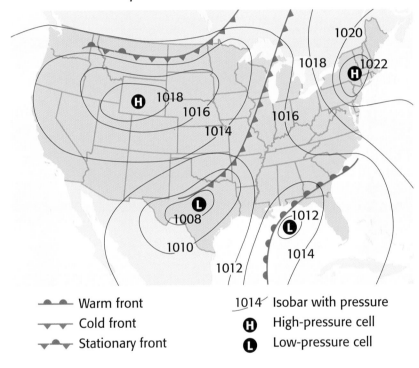

🔺🔺 Warm front
🔻🔻 Cold front
🔺🔻 Stationary front

1014 Isobar with pressure
Ⓗ High-pressure cell
Ⓛ Low-pressure cell

REVIEW

1. What are three methods meteorologists use to collect weather data?

2. What are weather maps based on?

3. What does a station model represent?

4. **Inferring Conclusions** Why would a meteorologist compare a new weather map with one 24 hours old?

internet**connect**

SC*L*INKS
NSTA

TOPIC: Forcasting the Weather
GO TO: www.scilinks.org
*sci*LINKS NUMBER: HSTE395

Chapter Highlights

SECTION 1

Vocabulary

weather *(p. 422)*

water cycle *(p. 422)*

humidity *(p. 423)*

relative humidity *(p. 423)*

condensation *(p. 425)*

dew point *(p. 425)*

cloud *(p. 426)*

precipitation *(p. 428)*

Section Notes

- Water is continuously moving and changing state as it moves through the water cycle.

- Humidity is the amount of water vapor or moisture in the air. Relative humidity is the amount of moisture the air contains compared with the maximum amount it can hold at a particular temperature.

- Water droplets form because of condensation.

- Dew point is the temperature to which air must cool to be saturated.

- Condensation occurs when the air next to a surface cools to below its dew point.

- Clouds are formed from condensation on dust and other particles above the ground.

- There are three major cloud forms—cumulus, stratus, and cirrus.

- There are four major forms of precipitation—rain, snow, sleet, and hail.

Labs

Let It Snow! *(p. 697)*

SECTION 2

Vocabulary

air mass *(p. 430)*

front *(p. 432)*

Section Notes

- Air masses form over source regions. An air mass has similar temperature and moisture content throughout.

- Four major types of air masses influence weather in the United States—maritime polar, maritime tropical, continental polar, continental tropical.

- A front is a boundary between contrasting air masses.

- There are four types of fronts—cold fronts, warm fronts, occluded fronts, and stationary fronts.

- Specific types of weather are associated with each front.

☑ Skills Check

Math Concepts

RELATIVE HUMIDITY Relative humidity is the amount of moisture the air is holding compared with the amount it can hold at a particular temperature. The relative humidity of air that is holding all the water it can at a given temperature is 100 percent, meaning it is saturated. You can calculate relative humidity with the following equation:

$$\frac{(present)\ g/m^3}{(saturated)\ g/m^3} \times 100 = relative\ humidity$$

Visual Understanding

HURRICANE HORSEPOWER Hurricanes are the most powerful storms on Earth. A cross-sectional view helps you identify the different parts of a hurricane. The diagram on page 438 shows a side view of a hurricane.

SECTION 3

Vocabulary

thunderstorm *(p. 434)*

lightning *(p. 435)*

thunder *(p. 435)*

tornado *(p. 436)*

hurricane *(p. 437)*

Section Notes

• Severe weather is weather that can cause property damage and even death.

• Thunderstorms are small, intense storm systems that produce lightning, thunder, strong winds, and heavy rain.

• Lightning is a large electrical discharge that occurs between two oppositely charged surfaces.

• Thunder is the sound that results from the expansion of air along a lightning strike.

• A tornado is a rotating funnel cloud that touches the ground.

• Hurricanes are large, rotating, tropical weather systems that form over the tropical oceans.

SECTION 4

Vocabulary

thermometer *(p. 440)*

barometer *(p. 441)*

windsock *(p. 441)*

wind vane *(p. 441)*

anemometer *(p. 441)*

isobars *(p. 443)*

Section Notes

• Weather balloons, radar, and weather satellites take weather measurements at high altitudes.

• Meteorologists present weather data gathered from stations as station models on weather maps.

Labs

Watching the Weather *(p. 694)*

Gone with the Wind *(p. 698)*

Chapter Review

USING VOCABULARY

Explain the difference between the following sets of words:

1. relative humidity/dew point

2. condensation/precipitation

3. air mass/front

4. lightning/thunder

5. tornado/hurricane

6. barometer/anemometer

UNDERSTANDING CONCEPTS

Multiple Choice

7. The process of liquid water changing to gas is called
   a. precipitation.
   b. condensation.
   c. evaporation.
   d. water vapor.

8. What is the relative humidity of air at its dew-point temperature?
   a. 0 percent
   b. 50 percent
   c. 75 percent
   d. 100 percent

9. Which of the following is not a type of condensation?
   a. fog
   b. cloud
   c. snow
   d. dew

10. High clouds made of ice crystals are called __?__ clouds.
    a. stratus
    b. cumulus
    c. nimbostratus
    d. cirrus

11. Large thunderhead clouds that produce precipitation are called __?__ clouds.
    a. nimbostratus
    b. cumulonimbus
    c. cumulus
    d. stratus

12. Strong updrafts within a thunderhead can produce
    a. snow.
    b. rain.
    c. sleet.
    d. hail.

13. A maritime tropical air mass contains
    a. warm, wet air.
    b. cold, moist air.
    c. warm, dry air.
    d. cold, dry air.

14. A front that forms when a warm air mass is trapped between cold air masses and forced to rise is called a(n)
    a. stationary front.
    b. warm front.
    c. occluded front.
    d. cold front.

15. A severe storm that forms as a rapidly rotating funnel cloud is called a
    a. hurricane.
    b. tornado.
    c. typhoon.
    d. thunderstorm.

16. The lines on a weather map connecting points of equal atmospheric pressure are called
    a. contour lines.
    b. highs.
    c. isobars.
    d. lows.

Short Answer

17. Explain the relationship between condensation and the dew point.

18. Describe the conditions along a stationary front.

19. What are the characteristics of an air mass that forms over the Gulf of Mexico?

20. Explain how a hurricane develops.

Concept Mapping

21. Use the following terms to create a concept map: evaporation, relative humidity, water vapor, dew, psychrometer, clouds, fog.

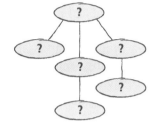

CRITICAL THINKING AND PROBLEM SOLVING

Write one or two sentences to answer the following questions:

22. If both the air temperature and the amount of water vapor in the air change, is it possible for the relative humidity to stay the same? Explain.

23. What can you assume about the amount of water vapor in the air if there is no difference between the wet- and dry-bulb readings of a psychrometer?

24. List the major similarities and differences between hurricanes and tornadoes.

MATH IN SCIENCE

You always see lightning before you hear thunder. That's because light travels at about 300,000,000 m/s, while sound travels only 330 m/s. One way you can determine how close you are to the thunderstorm is by counting how many seconds there are between the lightning and thunder. Usually, it takes thunder about 3 seconds to cover 1 km. Answer the following questions based on this estimate.

25. If you hear thunder 12 seconds after you see the flash of lightning, how far away is the thunderstorm?

26. If you hear thunder 36 seconds after you see the flash of lightning, how far away is the thunderstorm?

INTERPRETING GRAPHICS

Use the weather map below to answer the questions that follow.

27. Where are thunderstorms most likely to occur? Explain your answer.

28. What are the weather conditions like in Tulsa, Oklahoma? Explain your answer.

Reading Check-up

Take a minute to review your answers to the Pre-Reading Questions found at the bottom of page 420. Have your answers changed? If necessary, revise your answers based on what you have learned since you began this chapter.

CAREERS

METEOROLOGIST

Predicting floods, observing a tornado develop inside a storm, watching the growth of a hurricane, and issuing flood warnings are all in a day's work for **Cristy Mitchell.** As a meteorologist for the National Weather Service, Mitchell spends each working day observing the powerful forces of nature.

In addition to using computers, Mitchell also uses radar and satellite imagery to show regional and national weather. Meteorologists also use computerized models of the world's atmosphere to help forecast the weather.

Find Out for Yourself

▶ Use the library or the Internet to find information about hurricanes, tornadoes, or thunderstorms. How do meteorologists define these storms? What trends in air pressure, temperature, and humidity do meteorologists use to forecast storms?

When asked what made her job interesting, Mitchell replied, "There's nothing like the adrenaline rush you get when you see a tornado coming! I would say that witnessing the powerful forces of nature is what really makes my job interesting."

Meteorology is the study of natural forces in Earth's atmosphere. Perhaps the most familiar field of meteorology is weather forecasting. However, meteorology is also used in air-pollution control, agricultural planning, and air and sea transportation, and criminal and civil investigations. Meteorologists also study trends in Earth's climate, such as global warming and ozone depletion.

Collecting the Data

Meteorologists collect data on air pressure, temperature, humidity, and wind velocity. By applying what they know about the physical properties of the atmosphere and analyzing the mathematical relationships in the data, they are able to forecast the weather.

Meteorologists use a variety of tools, such as computers and satellites, to collect the data they need to make accurate weather forecasts. Mitchell explained, "The computer is an invaluable tool for me. Through it, I receive maps and detailed information, including temperature, wind speed, air pressure, lightning activity, and general sky conditions for a specific region."

▲ *This photograph of Hurricane Elena was taken from the space shuttle* Discovery *in September 1985.*

Science Fiction

"All Summer in a Day"

by Ray Bradbury

It is raining, just like it has been for 7 long years. That is 2,555 days of nonstop rain. For the men, women, and children who came to build a civilization on Venus, constant rain is a fact of life. But there is one special day—a day when it stops raining and the sun shines gloriously. This day comes about only once every 7 years. And today is that day!

At school the students have been looking forward to this day for weeks. In one class they've read about how the sun is like a lemon, and how hot it is. They've written stories and poems about what it might be like to see the sun.

And now that the day has finally arrived, all of the children in that class are peering through the window, searching for the sun. The children are 9 years old, and all of them but Margot have lived on Venus all their lives. None of them remember the day 7 years ago when the rain stopped. They only recall stories about the sunshine, and now they just can't wait to see it for themselves!

But Margot is different. She longs to see the sun even more than the others. The reason makes the other kids jealous. And jealous kids can be cruel. . . .

What happens to Margot? Find out for yourself by reading Ray Bradbury's "All Summer in a Day" in the *Holt Anthology of Science Fiction.*

Climate

Pre-Reading Questions

1. What is the difference between weather and climate?

2. List ways in which human influences such as pollution and technology can affect climate.

A HOT NEW HOME

Snow macaques normally live in cold pine forests in the mountains of Japan. However, in 1972, a group of these monkeys was relocated to a ranch in southern Texas. The monkeys were forced to adapt to a radically different climate and environment, which meant learning how to live with higher temperatures, different plants, and different animals. In this chapter, you will learn about the factors that affect climate and about the different environments found in each climate.

WHAT'S YOUR ANGLE?

Because the Earth is round, the sun's solar rays strike the Earth's surface at different angles. Try this activity to find out how the amount of solar energy received at the equator differs from the amount received at the poles.

Procedure

1. Plug in a **lamp,** and position it 30 cm from a **globe.**

2. Point the lamp so that the light shines directly on the globe's equator.

3. Using **adhesive putty,** attach a **thermometer** to the globe's equator in a vertical position. Attach **another thermometer** to the globe's north pole so that the tip points toward the lamp.

4. Record the temperature reading of each thermometer in your ScienceLog.

5. Turn on the lamp, and let the light shine on the globe for 3 minutes.

6. When the time is up, turn off the lamp, and record the temperature reading of each thermometer again.

Analysis

7. Was there a difference between the final temperature at the globe's north pole and that at the globe's equator? If so, what was it?

What Is Climate?

You have just received a call from a friend who is coming to visit you tomorrow. He is wondering what clothing to bring and wants to know about the current weather in your area. You step outside, check to see if there are rain clouds in the sky, and note the temperature. But what if your friend asked you about the climate in your area? What is the difference between weather and climate?

The main difference between weather and climate has to do with time. **Weather** is the condition of the atmosphere at a particular time and place. Weather conditions vary from day to day. **Climate,** on the other hand, is the average weather conditions in an area over a long period of time. Climate is determined by two main factors, temperature and precipitation. Study the map in **Figure 1,** and see if you can describe the climate in northern Africa.

Figure 1 *How does the climate in northern Africa differ from the climate where you live?*

As you can see in **Figure 2,** if you were to take a trip around the world, or even across the United States, you would experience different climates. For example, if you visited the Texas coast in the summer, you would find it hot and humid. But if you visited interior Alaska during the summer, it would probably be much cooler and less humid. Why are the climates so different? The answer is complicated. It includes factors such as latitude, wind patterns, geography, and ocean currents.

Figure 2 *Summer in Texas is different from summer in Alaska.*

Latitude

Think of the last time you looked at a globe. Do you recall the thin horizontal lines that circle the globe? These horizontal lines are called lines of latitude. **Latitude** is the distance north or south, measured in degrees, from the equator. In general, the temperature of an area depends on its latitude. The higher the latitude is, the colder the climate is. For example, one of the coldest places on Earth, the North Pole, is at 90° north of the equator. On the other hand, the equator, which has a latitude of 0°, is hot.

It's Hot! It's Not! Why are there such temperature differences at different latitudes? The answer has to do with solar energy. Solar energy heats the Earth. Latitude determines the amount of solar energy a particular area receives. You can see how this works in **Figure 3.** Notice that the sun's rays hit the area around the equator directly, at nearly a 90° angle. At this angle, a small area of the Earth's surface receives more direct solar energy, resulting in high temperatures. Near the poles, however, the sun's rays strike the surface at a lesser angle than at the equator. This lesser angle spreads the same amount of solar energy over a larger area, resulting in lower temperatures.

Figure 3 *The sun's rays strike the Earth's surface at different angles because the surface is curved.*

Seasons and Latitude In most places in the United States, the year consists of four seasons. Winter is probably cooler than summer where you live. But there are places in the world that do not have such seasonal changes. For example, areas near the equator have approximately the same temperatures and same amount of daylight year-round. **Figure 4** shows how latitude determines the seasons.

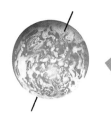

March 21

June 21

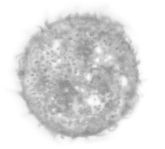

December 21

September 22

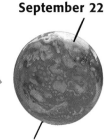

Figure 4 *The Earth is tilted on its axis at a 23.5° angle. This tilt affects how much solar energy an area receives as the Earth moves around the sun.*

 Self-Check

During what months does Australia have summer? *(See page 726 to check your answer.)*

Prevailing Winds

Prevailing winds are winds that blow mainly from one direction. These winds influence an area's moisture and temperature. Before you learn how the prevailing winds affect climate, take a look at **Figure 5** to learn about some of the basic properties of air.

Figure 5 *Because warm air is less dense, it tends to rise. Cooler, denser air tends to sink.*

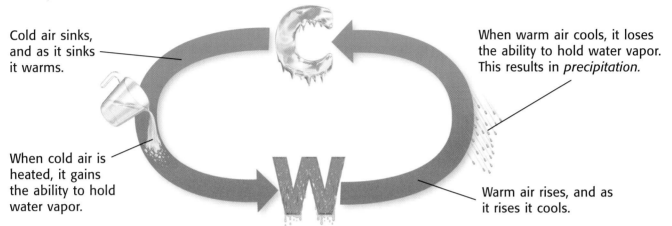

Cold air sinks, and as it sinks it warms.

When cold air is heated, it gains the ability to hold water vapor.

When warm air cools, it loses the ability to hold water vapor. This results in *precipitation.*

Warm air rises, and as it rises it cools.

Prevailing winds affect the amount of precipitation that a region receives. If the prevailing winds form from warm air, they will carry moisture. If the prevailing winds form from cold air, they will probably be dry.

The amount of moisture in prevailing winds is also affected by whether the winds blow across land or across a large body of water. Winds that travel across large bodies of water absorb moisture. Winds that travel across land tend to be dry. Even if a region borders the ocean, the area might be dry if the prevailing winds blow across the land, as shown in **Figure 6.**

Figure 6 *The Sahara Desert, in northern Africa, is extremely dry because of the dry prevailing winds that blow across the continent.*

QuickLab

A Cool Breeze

1. Hold a **thermometer** next to the top edge of a **cup of water** containing **two ice cubes.** Read the temperature next to the cup.

2. Have your lab partner fan the surface of the cup with a **paper fan.** Read the temperature again. Has the temperature changed? Why? Record your answer in your ScienceLog.

TRY at HOME

Geography

Mountains can influence an area's climate by affecting both temperature and precipitation. For example, Kilimanjaro, the tallest mountain in Africa, has snow-covered peaks year-round, even though it is only about 3° (320 km) south of the equator. Temperatures on Kilimanjaro and in other mountainous areas are affected by elevation. **Elevation** is the height of surface landforms above sea level. As the elevation increases, the atmosphere becomes less dense. When the atmosphere is less dense, its ability to absorb and hold thermal energy is reduced and temperatures are therefore lower.

Mountains also affect the climate of nearby areas by influencing the distribution of precipitation. **Figure 7** shows how the climates on two sides of a mountain can be very different.

Activity

Using a physical map, locate the mountain ranges in the United States. Does climate vary from one side of a mountain range to the other? If so, what does this tell you about the climatic conditions on either side of the mountain? From what direction are the prevailing winds blowing?

TRY at HOME

Figure 7 *Mountains block the prevailing winds from blowing across a continent, changing the amount of moisture the wind carries.*

The Wet Side

Mountains force air to rise. The air cools as it rises, releasing moisture as snow or rain. The land on the windward side of the mountain is usually green and lush due to the wind losing its moisture.

The Dry Side

After dry air crosses the mountain, the air begins to sink, warming and absorbing moisture as it sinks. The dry conditions created by the sinking, warm air usually produce a desert. This side of the mountain is in a *rain shadow*.

Ocean Currents

Because of water's ability to absorb and release thermal energy, the circulation of ocean surface currents has an enormous effect on an area's climate. **Surface currents,** which can be either warm or cold, are streamlike movements of water that occur at or near the surface of the ocean. **Figure 8** shows the pattern of the major warm and cold ocean surface currents.

Current Events As surface currents move, they carry warm or cool water to different locations. The surface temperature of the water affects the temperature of the air above it. Warm currents heat the surrounding air and cause warmer temperatures, while cool currents cool the surrounding air and cause cooler temperatures. For example, the Gulf Stream current carries warm water northward off the east coast of North America past Iceland, an island country located just below the Arctic Circle. The warm water from the Gulf Stream heats the surrounding air, creating warmer temperatures in southern Iceland. Iceland experiences milder temperatures than Greenland, its neighboring country, where the climate is not influenced by the Gulf Stream.

Science CONNECTION

What is El Niño? Can it affect our health? Turn to page 476 to find out.

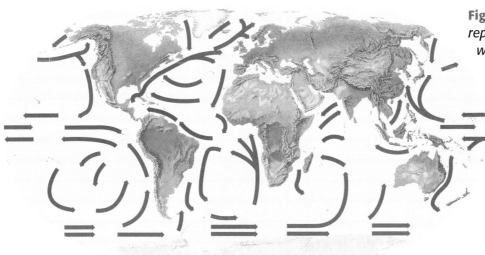

Figure 8 *The red arrows represent the movement of warm surface currents. The blue arrows represent the movement of cold surface currents.*

REVIEW

1. What is the difference between weather and climate?

2. How do mountains affect climate?

3. Describe how air temperature is affected by ocean surface currents.

4. **Analyzing Relationships** How would seasons be different if the Earth did not tilt on its axis?

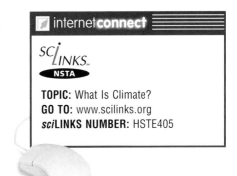

internet connect

SCiLINKS
NSTA

TOPIC: What Is Climate?
GO TO: www.scilinks.org
*sci*LINKS NUMBER: HSTE405

Climates of the World

Section 2

Terms to Learn

biome
tropical zone
temperate zone
deciduous
evergreens
polar zone
microclimate

What You'll Do

◆ Locate and describe the three major climate zones.
◆ Describe the different biomes found in each climate zone.

Have you ever wondered why the types of plants and animals in one part of the world are different from those found in another part? One reason involves climate. Plants and animals that have adapted to one climate may not be able to live in another climate. For instance, frogs do not live in Antarctica.

The three major climate zones of Earth—tropical, temperate, and polar—are illustrated in **Figure 9.** Each zone has a temperature range that relates to its latitude. However, in each of these zones there are several types of climates due to differences in the geography and the amount of precipitation. Because of the various climates in each zone, there are different biomes. A **biome** is a large region characterized by a specific type of climate and the plants and animals that live there.

Figure 10 shows the distribution of the Earth's land biomes. In this section we will review each of the three major climate zones and the biomes that are found in each zone.

Figure 9   Climate Zones of the Earth

Figure 10   The Earth's Land Biomes

- Tundra
- Taiga
- Temperate forest
- Tropical rain forest
- Temperate grassland
- Tropical savanna
- Temperate desert
- Tropical desert
- Chaparral
- Mountains

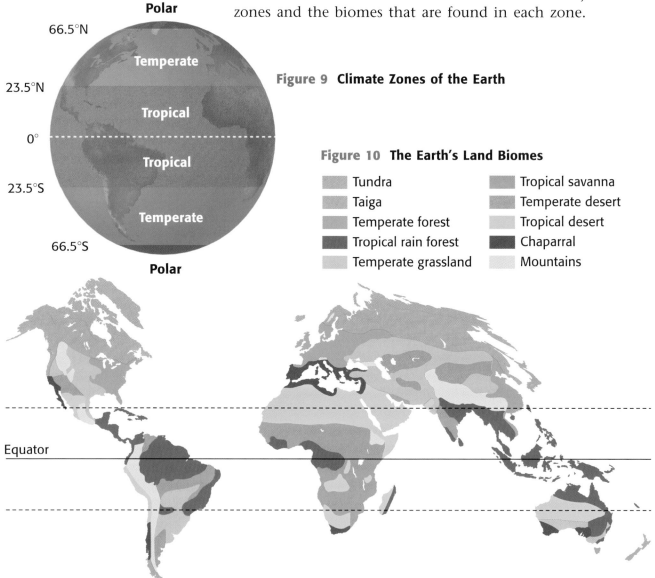

The Tropical Zone

The **tropical zone,** or the *Tropics,* is the warm zone located around the equator, as shown in **Figure 11.** This zone extends from the tropic of Cancer to the tropic of Capricorn. As you have learned, latitudes in this zone receive the most solar radiation. Temperatures are therefore usually hot, except at high elevations. Within the tropical zone there are three types of biomes—tropical rain forest, tropical desert, and tropical savanna. **Figure 12** shows the distribution of these biomes.

Figure 11 The Earth's Tropical Zone

23.5°N

0°

23.5°S

Figure 12 Biomes of the Tropical Zone

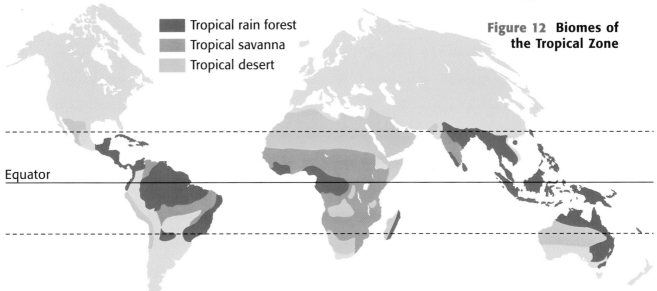

Tropical rain forest
Tropical savanna
Tropical desert

Equator

Tropical Rain Forest Tropical rain forests are always warm and wet. Because they are located near the equator, they receive strong sunlight year-round, causing little difference between seasons.

Tropical rain forests contain the greatest number of plant and animal species of any biome. But in spite of the lush vegetation, shown in **Figure 13,** the soil in rain forests is poor. The rapid decay of plants and animals returns nutrients to the soil, but these nutrients are quickly absorbed and used by the plants. The nutrients that are not immediately used by the plants are washed away by the heavy rains, leaving soil that is thin and nutrient poor.

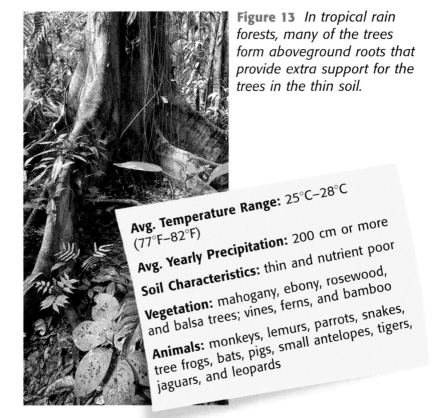

Figure 13 *In tropical rain forests, many of the trees form aboveground roots that provide extra support for the trees in the thin soil.*

Avg. Temperature Range: 25°C–28°C (77°F–82°F)

Avg. Yearly Precipitation: 200 cm or more

Soil Characteristics: thin and nutrient poor

Vegetation: mahogany, ebony, rosewood, and balsa trees; vines, ferns, and bamboo

Animals: monkeys, lemurs, parrots, snakes, tree frogs, bats, pigs, small antelopes, tigers, jaguars, and leopards

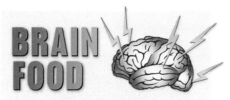
Tropical Deserts A desert is an area that receives less than 25 cm of rainfall per year. Because of this low yearly rainfall, deserts are the driest places on Earth. Desert plants, shown in **Figure 14,** are adapted to survive in a place with little water.

Deserts can be divided into hot deserts and cold deserts. The majority of hot deserts, such as the Sahara, in Africa, are tropical deserts. Hot deserts are caused by cool sinking air masses. Daily temperatures in tropical deserts vary from very hot daytime temperatures (50°C) to cool nighttime temperatures (20°C). Winters in hot deserts are usually mild. Because of the dryness, the soil is poor in organic matter, which fertilizes the soil. The dryness makes it hard to break down dead organic matter.

Avg. Temperature Range: 16°C–50°C (61°F–120°F)

Avg. Yearly Precipitation: 0–25 cm

Soil Characteristics: poor in organic matter

Vegetation: succulents (cactus and euphorbia), shrubs, thorny trees

Animals: kangaroo rats, lizards, scorpions, snakes, birds, bats, toads

Biology
C O N N E C T I O N

Some desert animals, such as the spadefoot toad, survive the scorching summer heat by burying themselves in the ground and sleeping through the dry season.

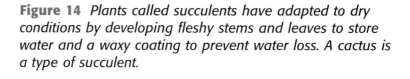

Figure 14 *Plants called succulents have adapted to dry conditions by developing fleshy stems and leaves to store water and a waxy coating to prevent water loss. A cactus is a type of succulent.*

Self-Check

If desert soil is so nutrient rich, why are deserts not suitable for agriculture? *(See page 726 to check your answer.)*

Tropical Savannas Tropical savannas, sometimes referred to as grasslands, are dominated by tall grasses, with trees scattered here and there. **Figure 15** is a photo of an African savanna. The climate is usually very warm, with a dry season that lasts four to eight months followed by short periods of rain. Savanna soils are generally nutrient poor, but grass fires, which are common during the dry season, leave the soils nutrient enriched.

Many plants have adapted to fire and use it to reproduce. Grasses sprout from their roots after the upper part of the plant is burned. The seeds of some plant species require fire in order to grow. For example, some species need fire to break open the seed's outer skin. Only after this skin is broken can the seed grow. Other species drop their seeds at the end of fire season. The heat from the fire triggers the plants to drop their seeds into the newly enriched soil.

Avg. Temperature Range: 27°C–32°C (80°F–90°F)

Avg. Yearly Precipitation: 100 cm

Soil Characteristics: generally nutrient poor

Vegetation: tall grasses (3–5 m), trees, thorny shrubs

Animals: gazelles, rhinoceroses, giraffes, lions, hyenas, ostriches, crocodiles, elephants

Figure 15 *The grass of a tropical savanna is 3–5 m tall, much taller than that of a temperate grassland.*

REVIEW

1. What are the soil characteristics of a tropical rain forest?

2. In what way has savanna vegetation adapted to fire?

3. **Summarizing Data** How do each of the tropical biomes differ?

internet**connect**

SC*i*LINKS.
NSTA

TOPIC: Climates of the World
GO TO: www.scilinks.org
*sci*LINKS NUMBER: HSTE410

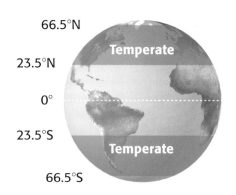

66.5°N

23.5°N

0°

23.5°S

66.5°S

Temperate

Temperate

Figure 16 The Earth's Temperate Zones

The Temperate Zone

The **temperate zone,** as shown in **Figure 16,** is the climate zone between the Tropics and the polar zone. Temperatures in the temperate zone tend to be moderate. The continental United States is in the temperate zone, which includes the following four biomes: temperate forest, temperate grassland, chaparral, and temperate desert. **Figure 17** shows the distribution of the biomes found in the temperate zone.

Figure 17 Biomes of the Temperate Zone

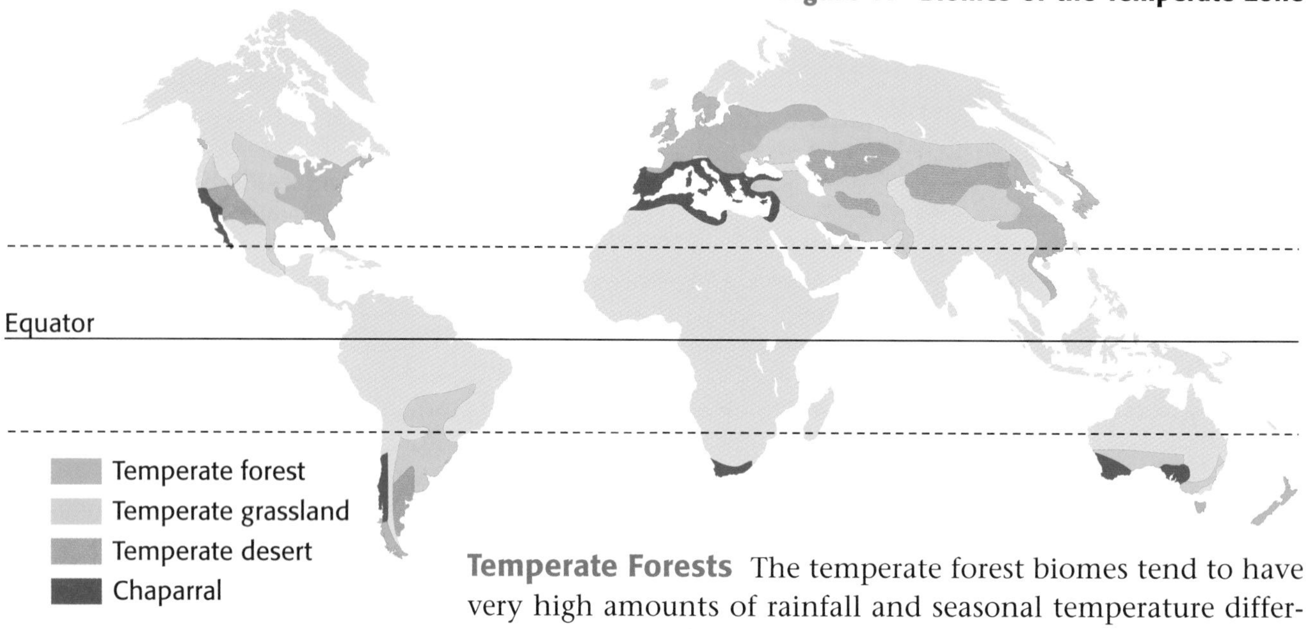

Equator

	Temperate forest
	Temperate grassland
	Temperate desert
	Chaparral

Temperate Forests The temperate forest biomes tend to have very high amounts of rainfall and seasonal temperature differences. Because of these distinct seasonal changes, summers are usually warm and winters are usually cold. The largest temperate forests are deciduous, such as the one shown in **Figure 18. Deciduous** trees are trees that lose their leaves when the weather becomes cold. These trees tend to be broad-leaved. The soils in deciduous forests are usually quite fertile because of the high organic content contributed by decaying leaves that drop every winter.

Another type of temperate forest is the evergreen forest. **Evergreens** are trees that keep their leaves year-round. Evergreens can be either broad-leaved trees or needle-leaved trees, such as pine trees. Mixed forests of broad-leaved and needle-leaved trees can be found in humid climates, such as Florida, where winter temperatures rarely fall below freezing.

Figure 18 *Deciduous trees have leaves that change color and drop when temperatures become cold.*

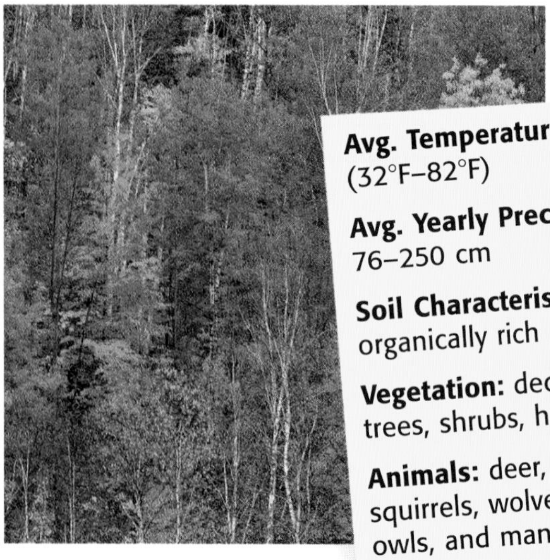

Avg. Temperature Range: 0°C–28°C (32°F–82°F)

Avg. Yearly Precipitation: 76–250 cm

Soil Characteristics: very fertile, organically rich

Vegetation: deciduous and evergreen trees, shrubs, herbs

Animals: deer, bears, boars, badgers, squirrels, wolves, wild cats, red foxes, owls, and many other birds

Temperate Grasslands Temperate grasslands, such as those shown in **Figure 19,** occur in regions that receive too little rainfall for trees to grow. This biome has warm summers and cold winters. The temperate grasslands are known by many local names—the *prairies* of North America, the *steppes* of Eurasia, the *veldt* of Africa, and the *pampas* of South America. Grasses are the most common type of vegetation found in this biome. Because grasslands have the most fertile soils of all biomes, much of the temperate grassland has been plowed to make room for croplands.

Avg. Temperature Range: -6°C–26°C (21°F–78°F)

Avg. Yearly Precipitation: 38–76 cm

Soil Characteristics: most fertile soils of all biomes

Vegetation: grasses

Animals: large grazing animals, including the bison of North America, the kangaroo of Australia, and the antelope of Africa

Figure 19 *The world's grasslands once covered about 42 percent of Earth's total land surface. Today they occupy only about 12 percent of the Earth's surface.*

Chaparrals Chaparral regions, as shown in **Figure 20,** have cool, wet winters and hot, dry summers. The vegetation is mainly evergreen shrubs, which are short, woody plants with thick, waxy leaves. The waxy leaves are adaptations that help prevent water loss in dry conditions. These shrubs grow in rocky, nutrient-poor soil. Like tropical-savanna vegetation, chaparral vegetation has adapted to fire. In fact, some plants, such as chamise, can grow back from their roots after a fire.

Figure 20 *Some plant species found in chaparral produce substances that help them catch on fire. These species require fire to reproduce.*

Avg. Temperature Range: 11°C–26°C (51°F–78°F)

Avg. Yearly Precipitation: 48–56 cm

Soil Characteristics: rocky, nutrient-poor soils

Vegetation: evergreen shrubs, scrubby trees, herbs

Animals: ground squirrels, deer, elk, mountain lions, coyotes, wolves

Temperate Deserts The temperate desert biomes, like the one shown in **Figure 21,** tend to be cold deserts. Like all deserts, cold deserts receive less than 25 cm of rainfall annually. Temperate deserts can be very hot in the daytime, but—unlike hot deserts—they tend to be very cold at night.

Avg. Temperature Range:
1°C–50°C (34°F–120°F)

Avg. Yearly Precipitation:
0–25 cm

Soil Characteristics: poor in organic matter

Vegetation: succulents (cactus), shrubs, thorny trees

Animals: kangaroo rats, lizards, scorpions, snakes, birds, bats, toads

Figure 21 *The Great Basin Desert is in the rain shadow of the Sierra Nevada.*

The temperatures sometimes drop below freezing. This large change in temperature between day and night is caused by low humidity and cloudless skies. These conditions allow for a large amount of energy to reach, and thus heat, the Earth's surface during the day. However, these same characteristics allow the energy to escape at night, causing temperatures to drop. You probably rarely think of snow and deserts together, but temperate deserts often receive light snow during the winter.

Temperate deserts are dry because they are generally located inland, far away from a moisture source, or are located on the rain-shadow side of a mountain range.

The Polar Zone

The **polar zone** includes the northernmost and southernmost climate zones, as shown in **Figure 22.** Polar climates have the coldest average temperatures. The temperatures in the winter stay below freezing, and the temperatures during the summer months remain chilly. **Figure 23,** on the next page, shows the distribution of the biomes found in the polar zone.

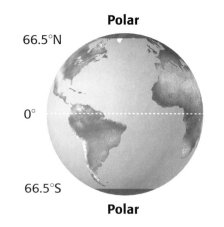

Polar

66.5°N

0°

66.5°S

Polar

Figure 22 The Earth's Polar Zones

Figure 23 Biomes of the Polar Zone

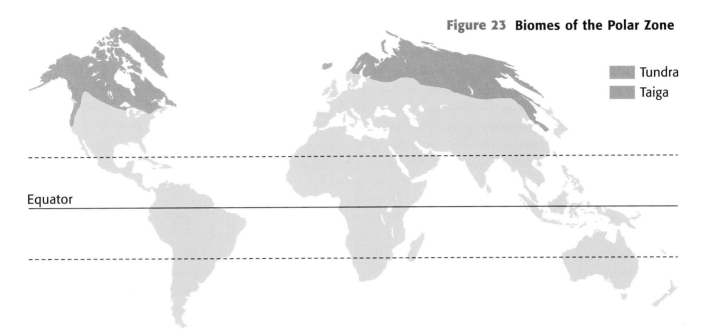

Tundra

Taiga

Equator

Tundra Next to deserts, the tundra, as shown in **Figure 24,** is the driest place on Earth. This biome has long, cold winters with almost 24 hours of night and short, cool summers with almost 24 hours of daylight. In the summer, only the top meter of soil thaws. Underneath the thawed soil lies a permanently frozen layer of soil, called *permafrost*. This frozen layer prevents the water in the thawed soil from draining. Because of the poor drainage, the upper soil layer is muddy and is therefore an excellent breeding ground for insects, such as mosquitoes. Many birds migrate to the tundra during the summer to feed on the insects.

Environment
C O N N E C T I O N

Subfreezing climates contain almost no decomposing bacteria. The well-preserved body of John Torrington, a member of an expedition that explored the Northwest Passage in Canada in the 1840s, was uncovered in 1984, appearing much as it did when he died, more than 140 years earlier.

Avg. Temperature Range: −27°C–5°C (−17°F–41°F)

Avg. Yearly Precipitation: 0–25 cm

Soil Characteristics: frozen

Vegetation: mosses, lichens, sedges, and dwarf trees

Animals: rabbits, lemmings, reindeer, caribou, musk oxen, wolves, foxes, birds, and polar bears

Figure 24 *In the tundra, mosses and lichens cover rocks. Dwarf trees grow close to the ground to protect themselves from strong winds and to absorb energy from the Earth's sunlit surface.*

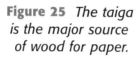

Avg. Temperature Range: -10°C–15°C (14°F–59°F)

Avg. Yearly Precipitation: 40–61 cm

Soil Characteristics: acidic soil

Vegetation: mosses, lichens, conifers

Animals: birds, rabbits, moose, elk, wolves, lynxes, and bears

Figure 25 *The taiga is the major source of wood for paper.*

Taiga (Northern Coniferous Forest)

Just south of the tundra lies the taiga biome. The taiga, as shown in **Figure 25,** has long, cold winters and short, warm summers. Like the tundra, the soil during the winter is frozen. The majority of the trees are evergreen needle-leaved trees called *conifers,* such as pine, spruce, and fir trees. The needles and bendable branches allow these trees to shed heavy snow before they can be damaged. Conifer needles contain acidic substances. When the needles die and fall to the soil, they make the soil acidic. Most plants cannot grow in acidic soil, and therefore the forest floor is bare except for some mosses and lichens.

Microclimates

You have learned the types of biomes that are found in each climate zone. But the climate and the biome of a particular place can also be influenced by local conditions. **Microclimates** are small regions with unique climatic characteristics. For example, elevation can affect an area's climate and therefore its biome. Tundra and taiga biomes exist in the Tropics on high mountains. How is this possible? Remember that as the elevation increases, the atmosphere loses its ability to absorb and hold thermal energy. This results in lower temperatures.

Cities are also microclimates. In a city, temperatures can be 1°C to 2°C warmer than the surrounding rural areas. This is because buildings and pavement made of dark materials absorb solar radiation instead of reflecting it. There is also less vegetation to take in the sun's rays. This absorption of the sun's rays by buildings and pavement heats the surrounding air and causes temperatures to rise.

Physics CONNECTION

Roof temperatures can get so hot that you can fry an egg on them! In a study of roofs on a sunny day when the air temperature was 13°C, scientists recorded roof temperatures ranging from 18°C to 61°C depending on color and material of the roof.

To find out more about microclimates, turn to page 701 of the LabBook.

REVIEW

1. Describe how tropical deserts and temperate deserts differ.

2. List and describe the three major climate zones.

3. **Inferring Conclusions** Rank each biome according to how suitable it would be for growing crops. Explain your reasoning.

Terms to Learn

ice age
global warming
greenhouse effect

What You'll Do

◆ Describe how the Earth's climate has changed over time.

◆ Summarize the different theories that attempt to explain why the Earth's climate has changed.

◆ Explain the greenhouse effect and its role in global warming.

Changes in Climate

As you know, the weather constantly changes—sometimes several times in one day. Saturday, your morning baseball game was canceled because of rain, but by that afternoon the sun was shining. Now think about the climate where you live. You probably haven't noticed a change in climate, because climates change slowly. What causes climates to change? Until recently, climatic changes were connected only to natural causes. However, studies indicate that human activities may have an influence on climatic change. In this section, you will learn how natural and human factors may influence climatic change.

Ice Ages

The geologic record indicates that the Earth's climate has been much colder than it is today. In fact, much of the Earth was covered by sheets of ice during certain periods. An **ice age** is a period during which ice collects in high latitudes and moves toward lower latitudes. Scientists have found evidence of many major ice ages throughout the Earth's geologic history. The most recent ice age began about 2 million years ago.

Glacial Periods During an ice age, there are periods of cold and periods of warmth. These periods are called glacial and interglacial periods. During *glacial periods,* the enormous sheets of ice advance, getting bigger and covering a larger area as shown in **Figure 26.** Because a large amount of ocean water is frozen during glacial periods, sea level drops.

Figure 26 *During the last glacial period, which ended 10,000 years ago, the Great Lakes were covered by an enormous block of ice that was 1.5 km high.*

Interglacial Periods Warmer times that occur between glacial periods are called *interglacial periods*. During an interglacial period, the ice begins to melt and the sea level rises again. The last interglacial period began 10,000 years ago and is still occurring. Why do these periods occur? Will the Earth have another glacial period in the future? These questions have been debated by scientists for the past 200 years.

Motions of the Earth There are many theories about the causes of ice ages. Each theory attempts to explain the gradual cooling that leads to the development of enormous ice sheets that periodically cover large areas of the Earth's surface. The *Milankovitch theory* explains why an ice age isn't just one long cold spell but instead alternates between cold and warm periods. Milutin Milankovitch, a Yugoslavian scientist, proposed that changes in the Earth's orbit and in the tilt of the Earth's axis cause ice ages, as illustrated in **Figure 27.**

Figure 27 *According to the Milankovitch theory, the amount of solar radiation the Earth receives varies due to three kinds of changes in the Earth's orbit.*

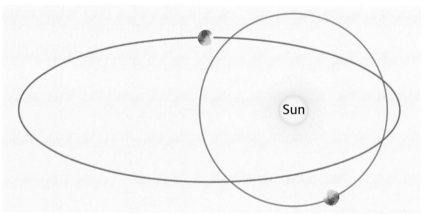

❶ Over a period of 100,000 years, the Earth's orbit slowly changes from a more circular shape to a more elliptical shape. When the orbit is more elliptical, the contrast between seasons is greater in one hemisphere and less in the other hemisphere. When the orbit is more circular, there is not as much seasonal change.

❷ Over a period of 41,000 years, the tilt of the Earth's axis varies between 21.8° and 24.4°. When the tilt is at 24.4°, the poles receive more solar energy.

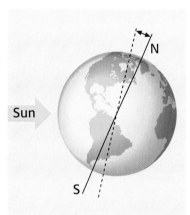

❸ The Earth's axis traces a complete circle every 26,000 years. The circular motion of the Earth's axis determines the time of year that the Earth is closest to the sun.

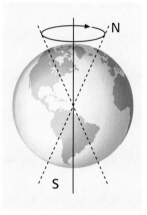

✓ **Self-Check**

How do you think the Earth's elliptical orbit affects the amount of solar radiation that reaches the surface? *(See page 726 to check your answer.)*

Volcanic Eruptions There are many natural factors that can affect global climate. Catastrophic events, such as volcanic eruptions, can influence climate. Volcanic eruptions send large amounts of dust, ash, and smoke into the atmosphere. Once in the atmosphere, the dust, smoke, and ash particles act as a shield, blocking out so much of the sun's rays that the Earth cools. **Figure 28** shows how dust particles from a volcanic eruption block the sun.

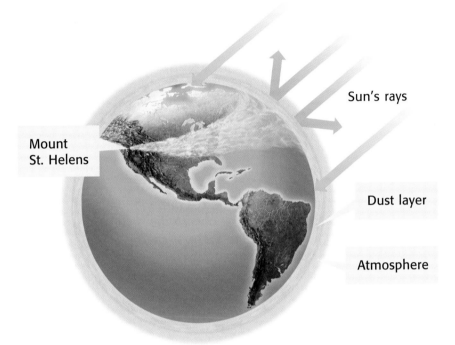

Sun's rays

Mount St. Helens

Dust layer

Atmosphere

Figure 28 *Volcanic eruptions, such as the one that occurred at Mount St. Helens, shown above, produce dust that reflects sunlight, as shown at left.*

Plate Tectonics The Earth's climate is further influenced by plate tectonics and continental drift. One theory proposes that ice ages occur when the continents are positioned closer to the polar regions. For example, approximately 250 million years ago, all the continents were connected near the South Pole in one giant landmass called Pangaea, as shown in **Figure 29.** During this time, ice covered a large area of the Earth's surface. As Pangaea broke apart, the continents moved toward the equator, and the ice age ended. During the last ice age, many large landmasses were positioned in the polar zones. Antarctica, northern North America, Europe, and Asia all were covered with large sheets of ice.

Pangaea

Figure 29 *Much of Pangaea—the part that is now Africa, South America, India, Antarctica, Australia, and Saudi Arabia—was covered by continental ice sheets.*

The Ride to School

Find out how much carbon dioxide is released into the atmosphere each month from the car or bus that transports you to school.

1. Figure out the distance from your home to school.

2. From this figure, calculate how many kilometers you travel to and from school, in a car or bus, per month.

3. Divide this number by 20. This represents approximately how many gallons of gas are used during your trips to school.

4. If burning 1 gal of gasoline produces 9 kg of carbon dioxide, how much carbon dioxide is released?

Global Warming

Is the Earth really experiencing global warming? **Global warming** is a rise in average global temperatures that can result from an increase in the greenhouse effect. To understand how global warming works, you must first learn about the greenhouse effect.

Greenhouse Effect The **greenhouse effect** is the Earth's natural heating process, in which gases in the atmosphere trap thermal energy. The Earth's atmosphere performs the same function as the glass windows in a car. Think about the car illustrated in **Figure 30.** It's a hot summer day, and you are about to get inside the car. You immediately notice that it feels hotter inside the car than outside. Then you sit down and—ouch!—you burn yourself on the seat.

Figure 30 *Sunlight streams into the car through the clear glass windows. The seats absorb the radiant energy and change it into thermal energy. The energy is then trapped in the car.*

Window to the World Greenhouse gases allow sunlight to pass through the atmosphere. It is absorbed by the Earth's surface and reradiated as thermal energy. Many scientists hypothesize that the rise in global temperatures is due to an increase of carbon dioxide, a greenhouse gas, as a result of human activity. Most evidence indicates that the increase in carbon dioxide is caused by the burning of fossil fuels that releases carbon dioxide into the atmosphere.

Another factor that may add to global warming is deforestation. *Deforestation* is the process of clearing forests, as shown in **Figure 31.** In many countries around the world, forests are being burned to clear land for agriculture. All types of burning release carbon dioxide into the atmosphere, thereby increasing the greenhouse effect. Plants use carbon dioxide to make food. As plants are removed from the Earth, the carbon dioxide that would have been used by the plants builds up in the atmosphere.

Figure 31 *Clearing land by burning leads to increased levels of carbon dioxide in the atmosphere.*

Consequences of Global Warming Many scientists think that if the average global temperature continues to rise, some regions of the world might experience flooding. Warmer temperatures could cause the icecaps to melt, raising the sea level and flooding low-lying areas, such as the coasts.

Areas that receive little rainfall, such as deserts, might receive even less due to increased evaporation. Scientists predict that the Midwest, an agricultural area, could experience warmer, drier conditions. A change in climate such as this could harm crops. But farther north, such as in Canada, weather conditions for farming would improve.

Reducing Pollution

A city just received a warning from the Environmental Protection Agency for exceeding the automobile fuel emissions standards. If you were the city manager, what suggestions would you make to reduce the amount of automobile emissions?

REVIEW

1. How has the Earth's climate changed over time? What might have caused these changes?

2. Explain how the greenhouse effect warms the Earth.

3. What are two ways that humans contribute to the increase in carbon dioxide levels in the atmosphere?

4. **Analyzing Relationships** How will the warming of the Earth affect agriculture in different parts of the world?

internet**connect**

SC*i*LINKS
NSTA

TOPIC: Changes in Climate
GO TO: www.scilinks.org
*sci*LINKS NUMBER: HSTE415

Chapter Highlights

Vocabulary

weather *(p. 452)*

climate *(p. 452)*

latitude *(p. 453)*

prevailing winds *(p. 455)*

elevation *(p. 456)*

surface currents *(p. 457)*

Section Notes

• Weather is the condition of the atmosphere at a particular time and place. Climate is the average weather conditions in a certain area over a long period of time.

• Climate is determined by temperature and precipitation.

• Climate is controlled by factors such as latitude, elevation, wind patterns, local geography, and ocean surface currents.

• The amount of solar energy an area receives is determined by the area's latitude.

• The seasons are a result of the tilt of the Earth's axis and its path around the sun.

• The amount of moisture carried by prevailing winds affects the amount of precipitation that falls.

• As elevation increases, temperature decreases.

• Mountains affect the distribution of precipitation. The dry side of the mountain is called the rain shadow.

• As ocean surface currents move across the Earth, they redistribute warm and cool water. The temperature of the surface water affects the air temperature.

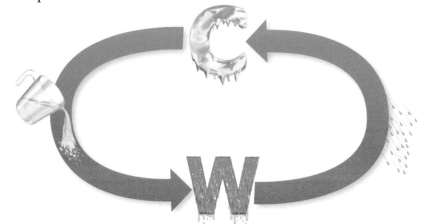

☑ Skills Check

Visual Understanding

THE SEASONS Seasons are determined by latitude. The diagram on page 454 shows how the tilt of the Earth affects how much solar energy an area receives as the Earth moves around the sun.

THE RAIN SHADOW The illustration on page 456 shows how the climates on two sides of a mountain can be very different. A mountain can affect the climate of areas nearby by influencing the amount of precipitation these areas receive.

LAND BIOMES OF THE EARTH Look back at Figure 10 on page 458 to review the distribution of the Earth's Land Biomes.

SECTION 2

Vocabulary

biome *(p. 458)*

tropical zone *(p. 459)*

temperate zone *(p. 462)*

deciduous *(p. 462)*

evergreens *(p. 462)*

polar zone *(p. 464)*

microclimate *(p. 466)*

Section Notes

- The Earth is divided into three climate zones according to latitude—the tropical zone, the temperate zone, and the polar zone.

- The tropical zone is the zone around the equator. The tropical rain forest, tropical desert, and tropical savanna are in this zone.

- The temperate zone is the zone between the tropical zone and the polar zone. The temperate forest, temperate grassland, chaparral, and temperate desert are in this zone.

- The polar zones are the northernmost and southernmost zones. The taiga and tundra are in this zone.

Labs

For the Birds *(p. 701)*

Biome Business *(p. 704)*

SECTION 3

Vocabulary

ice age *(p. 467)*

global warming *(p. 470)*

greenhouse effect *(p. 470)*

Section Notes

- Explanations for the occurrence of ice ages include changes in the Earth's orbit, volcanic eruptions, and plate tectonics and continental drift.

- Some scientists believe that global warming is occurring as a result of an increase in carbon dioxide from human activity.

- If global warming continues, it could drastically change climates, causing either floods or drought.

Labs

Global Impact *(p. 700)*

---

internet connect

GO TO: go.hrw.com

Visit the **HRW** Web site for a variety of learning tools related to this chapter. Just type in the keyword:

KEYWORD: HSTCLM

GO TO: www.scilinks.org

Visit the **National Science Teachers Association** on-line Web site for Internet resources related to this chapter. Just type in the *sci***LINKS** number for more information about the topic:

TOPIC: What Is Climate?   *sci***LINKS NUMBER:** HSTE405
TOPIC: Climates of the World   *sci***LINKS NUMBER:** HSTE410
TOPIC: Changes in Climate   *sci***LINKS NUMBER:** HSTE415
TOPIC: Modeling Earth's Climate *sci***LINKS NUMBER:** HSTE420

Chapter Review

USING VOCABULARY

To complete the following sentences, choose the correct term from each pair of terms listed below.

1. __?__ is the condition of the atmosphere in a certain area over a long period of time. *(Weather* or *Climate)*

2. __?__ is the distance north and south from the equator measured in degrees. *(Longitude* or *Latitude)*

3. Savannas are grasslands located in the __?__ zone between 23.5° north latitude and 23.5° south latitude. *(temperate* or *tropical)*

4. Trees that lose their leaves are found in a(n)__?__ forest. *(deciduous* or *evergreen)*

5. Frozen land in the polar zone is most often found in a __?__. *(taiga* or *tundra)*

6. A rise in global temperatures due to an increase in carbon dioxide is called __?__. *(global warming* or *the greenhouse effect)*

UNDERSTANDING CONCEPTS

Multiple Choice

7. The tilt of Earth as it orbits the sun causes
   a. global warming.
   b. different seasons.
   c. a rain shadow.
   d. the greenhouse effect.

8. What factor affects the prevailing winds as they blow across a continent, producing different climates?
   a. latitude
   b. mountains
   c. forests
   d. glaciers

9. What factor determines the amount of solar energy an area receives?
   a. latitude
   b. wind patterns
   c. mountains
   d. ocean currents

10. What climate zone has the coldest average temperature?
    a. tropical
    b. polar
    c. temperate
    d. tundra

11. What biome is not located in the tropical zone?
    a. rain forest
    b. savanna
    c. chaparral
    d. desert

12. What biome contains the greatest number of plant and animal species?
    a. rain forest
    b. temperate forest
    c. grassland
    d. tundra

13. Which of the following is not a theory for the cause of ice ages?
    a. the Milankovitch theory
    b. volcanic eruptions
    c. plate tectonics
    d. the greenhouse effect

14. Which of the following is thought to contribute to global warming?
    a. wind patterns
    b. deforestation
    c. ocean surface currents
    d. microclimates

Short Answer

15. Why do higher latitudes receive less solar radiation than lower latitudes?

16. How does wind influence precipitation patterns?

17. Give an example of a microclimate. What causes the unique temperature and precipitation characteristics of this area?

18. How have desert plants and animals adapted to this biome?

19. How are tundra and deserts similar?

Concept Mapping

20. Use the following terms to create a concept map: climate, global warming, deforestation, greenhouse effect, flooding.

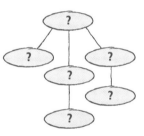

25. If the air temperature near the shore of a lake measures 24°C, and if the temperature increases by 0.05°C every 10 m traveled away from the lake, what would the air temperature be 1 km from the lake?

The following illustration shows the Earth's orbit around the sun.

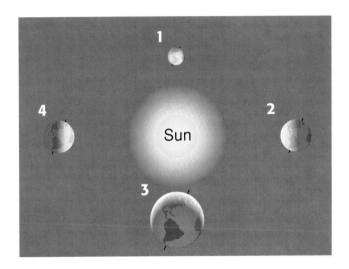

26. At what position, **1**, **2**, **3**, or **4**, is it spring in the Southern Hemisphere?

27. At what position does the South Pole receive almost 24 hours of daylight?

28. Explain what is happening in each climate zone in both the Northern Hemisphere and Southern Hemisphere at position **4**.

CRITICAL THINKING AND PROBLEM SOLVING

Write one or two sentences to answer the following questions:

21. Explain how ocean surface currents are responsible for milder climates.

22. In your own words, explain how a change in the Earth's orbit can affect the Earth's climates as proposed by Milutin Milankovitch.

23. Explain why the climate differs drastically on each side of the Rocky Mountains.

24. What are some steps you and your family can take to reduce the amount of carbon dioxide that is released into the atmosphere?

Reading Check-up

Take a minute to review your answers to the Pre-Reading Questions found at the bottom of page 450. Have your answers changed? If necessary, revise your answers based on what you have learned since you began this chapter.

Blame "The Child"

El Niño, which is Spanish for "the child," is the name of a weather event that occurs in the Pacific Ocean. Every 2 to 12 years, the interaction between the ocean surface and atmospheric winds creates El Niño. This event influences weather patterns in many regions of the world.

Difficult Breathing

For Indonesia and Malaysia, El Niño meant droughts and forest fires in 1998. Thousands of people in these countries suffered from respiratory ailments from breathing the smoke caused by these fires. Heavy rains in San Francisco created extremely high mold-spore counts. These spores cause problems for people with allergies. The spore count in February in San Francisco is usually between 0 and 100. In 1998, the count was often higher than 8,000!

Rodent Invasion

In areas where El Niño creates heavy rains, the result is lush vegetation. This lush vegetation provides even more food and shelter for rodents. As the rodent population increases, so does the threat of the diseases they spread. In states like Arizona, Colorado, and New Mexico, this means there is a greater chance among humans of contracting hantaviral pulmonary syndrome (HPS).

HPS is carried by deer mice and remains in their urine and feces. People are infected when they inhale dust contaminated with mouse feces or urine. Once infected, a person experiences flulike symptoms that can sometimes lead to fatal kidney or lung disease.

More Rodents and Insects

Heavy rains near Los Angeles might encourage a rodent-population explosion in the mountains east of the city. If so, there could be an increase in the number of rodents infected with bubonic plague. More infected rodents means more infected fleas, which carry bubonic plague to humans.

Ticks and mosquitoes could also increase in number. These insects can spread disease too. For example, ticks can carry Lyme disease, ehrlichiosis, babesiosis, and Rocky Mountain spotted fever. Mosquitoes can spread malaria, dengue fever, encephalitis, and Rift Valley fever.

◀ *If this flea carries bubonic plague bacteria, just one bite can infect a person.*

What About Camping?

Because all of these diseases can be fatal to humans, people must take precautions. Camping in the great outdoors increases the risk of infection. Campers should steer clear of rodents and their burrows. Don't forget to dust family pets with flea powder, and don't let them roam free. Try to remember that an ounce of prevention is worth a pound of cure.

Find Out More

▶ How do you think El Niño affects the fish and mammals that live in the ocean? Write your answer in your ScienceLog, and then do some research to see if you are correct.

Science, Technology, and Society

Some Say Fire, Some Say Ice . . .

The Earth's climate has undergone many drastic changes. For example, 6,000 years ago in the part of North Africa that is now a desert, hippos, crocodiles, and early Stone Age people shared shallow lakes that covered the area. Grasslands stretched as far as the eye could see.

Scientists have known for many years that Earth's climate has changed. What they didn't know was why. Using supercomputers and complex computer programs, scientists may now be able to explain why North Africa's lakes and grasslands became a desert. And that information may be useful for predicting future heat waves and ice ages.

Climate Models

Scientists who study Earth's atmosphere have developed climate models to try to imitate Earth's climate. A climate model is like a very complicated recipe with thousands of ingredients. These models do not make exact predictions about future climates, but they do estimate what might happen.

What ingredients are included in a climate model? One important ingredient is the level of greenhouse gases (especially carbon dioxide) in the atmosphere. Land and ocean water temperatures from around the globe are other ingredients. So is information about clouds, cloud cover, snow, and ice cover. And in more recent models, scientists have included information about ocean currents.

A Challenge to Scientists

Earth's atmosphere-ocean climate system is extremely complex. One challenge for scientists is to understand all the system's parts. Another is to understand how those parts work together. But understanding Earth's climate system is critical. An accurate climate model should help scientists predict heat waves, floods, and droughts.

Even the best available climate models must be improved. The more information scientists can include in a climate model, the more accurate the results. Today data are available from more locations, and scientists need more-powerful computers to process all the data.

As more-powerful computers are developed to handle all the data in a climate model, scientists' understanding of Earth's climate changes will improve. This knowledge should help scientists better predict the impact human activities have on global climate. And these models could help scientists prevent some of the worst effects of climate change, such as global warming or another ice age.

▲ *This meteorologist is using a high-powered supercomputer to do climate modeling.*

A Challenge for You

▶ Earth's oceans are a major part of the climate model. Find out some of the ways oceans affect climate. Do you think human activities are changing the oceans?

UNIT 7

Astronomy

In this unit, you will learn about the oldest of the sciences. Long before science was called science, people looked up at the night sky and tried to understand the meaning of the twinkling lights above. Early astronomers charted the stars and built calendars based on the movement of the moon and planets. Now the International Space Station is being built to further our exploration of the heavens. This timeline shows some of the events that have occurred throughout history as scientists have come to understand more about our planet's "neighborhood" in space.

1054

Chinese and Arabic astronomers record the appearance of a supernova—an exploding star. Strangely, no European observations of this event have ever been found.

1582

Ten days are dropped from October as the Julian calendar is replaced by the Gregorian calendar.

1977

Voyager 1 and *Voyager 2* are launched on missions to Jupiter, Saturn, and beyond. Now more than 10 trillion kilometers away from Earth, they are still sending back information about outer space.

1983

Sally Ride becomes the first American woman to travel in space.

DEC 31

1987

The year is shortened by one second to realign it with the Gregorian calendar.

1665
Using a prism, Isaac Newton discovers that white light is composed of different colors.

1898
H. G. Wells's book *The War of the Worlds* is published.

1924
An astronomer named Edwin Hubble confirms the existence of other galaxies.

1958
NASA, the National Aeronautics and Space Administration, is established to oversee the exploration of space.

1970
Apollo 13 is damaged shortly after leaving orbit. The spacecraft's three astronauts navigate around the moon in order to return safely to Earth.

1992
Astronomers discover the first planet outside the solar system.

1998
John Glenn becomes the oldest human in space. His second trip into space comes 36 years after he became the first American to orbit the Earth.

2003
America celebrates the 100th anniversary of the Wright brothers' historic flight at Kitty Hawk, North Carolina.

Observing the Sky

Pre-Reading
Questions

1. What are constellations?
2. How do astronomers
   observe objects they
   cannot see?

EYES TO THE SKY

This may look like an ordinary building to you, but inside
is something that will make you see stars, and it's painless!
In this building is the Harlan J. Smith Telescope (HJST).
You can find it in one of the darkest places in America.
The HJST is part of the McDonald Observatory located in
the Davis Mountains of West Texas. Since the late 1960s,
astronomers have used this telescope to view stars. In this
chapter, you will learn about the different types of stars
and how they evolve.

START-UP Activity

INDOOR STARGAZING

In this activity, you will measure an object's altitude using a simple instrument called an astrolabe (AS troh LAYB).

Procedure

1. Attach one end of a 12 cm long **piece of string** to the center of the straight edge of a **protractor** with tape. Attach a **paper clip** to the other end of the string.

2. Tape a **soda straw** lengthwise along the straight edge of the protractor. Your astrolabe is complete!

3. Hold the astrolabe in front of your face so you can look along the straw with one eye. The curve of the astrolabe should be pointed toward the floor.

4. Looking along the straw, use your astrolabe to sight one corner of the ceiling.

5. Pinch the string between your thumb and the protractor. Count the number of degrees between the string and the 90° marker on the protractor. This angle is the altitude of the corner. Record this measurement in your ScienceLog.

Analysis

6. How does this activity relate to observing objects in the sky? Explain how you would find the altitude of a star.

TRY at HOME

Section 1

Astronomy—The Original Science

Terms to Learn

astronomy	month
calendar	day
year	leap year

What You'll Do

- Identify the units of a calendar.
- Evaluate calendars from different ancient civilizations.
- Explain how our modern calendar developed.
- Summarize how astronomy began in ancient cultures and developed into a modern science.

Astronomy is the study of all physical objects beyond Earth. Before astronomy became a science, people in ancient cultures used the seasonal cycles of celestial objects to make calendars and organize their lives. Over time, some people began to observe the sky for less practical reasons—mainly to understand Earth's place in the universe. Today, astronomers all over the world are using new technologies to better understand the universe.

The Stars and Keeping Time

Most ancient cultures probably did not fully understand how celestial objects in our solar system move in relation to each other. However, they did learn the seasonal movements of these objects as they appeared in the Earth's sky and based their calendars on these cycles. People in ancient cultures gradually learned to depend on calendars to keep track of time. For example, by observing the yearly cycle of the sun's movement among the stars, early farmers learned the best times of year to plant and harvest various foods.

After learning the seasonal cycles of celestial objects many civilizations made calendars. One such calendar is shown in **Figure 1.** A **calendar** is a system for organizing time. Most calendars organize time within a single unit called a year. A **year** is the time required for the Earth to orbit the sun once. Within a year are smaller units of time called months. A **month** is roughly the amount of time required for the moon to orbit the Earth once. Within a month are even smaller units of time called days. A **day** is the time required for the Earth to rotate once on its axis.

Ancient Calendars Ancient cultures based their calendars on different observations of the sky. Examine **Figure 2** at the top of the next page to see how different cultures around the world used objects in the sky differently to keep track of time.

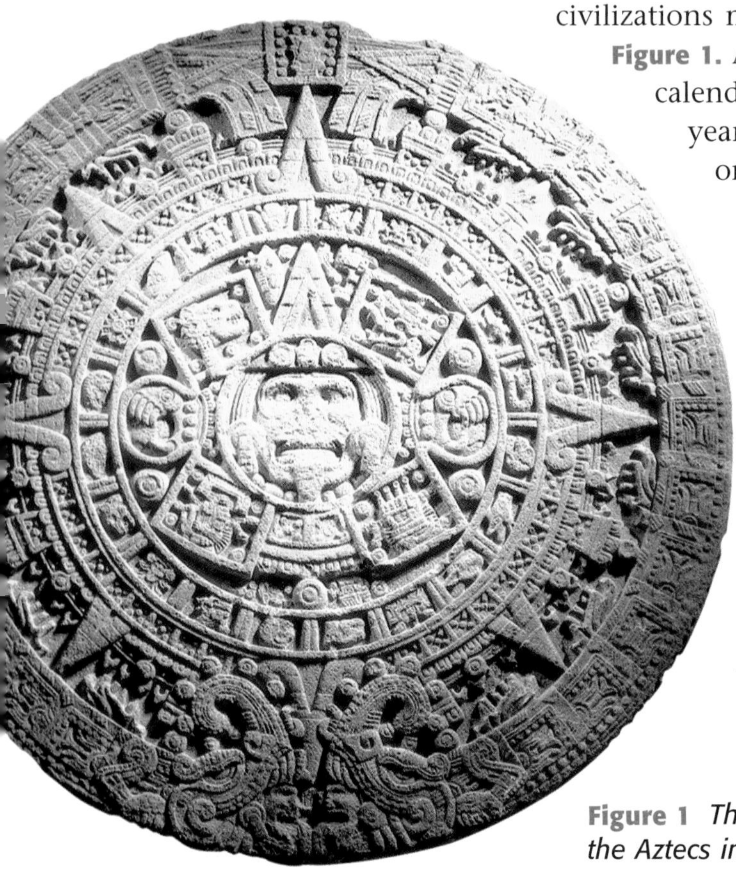

Figure 1 *This stone is a calendar used by the Aztecs in pre-colonial America.*

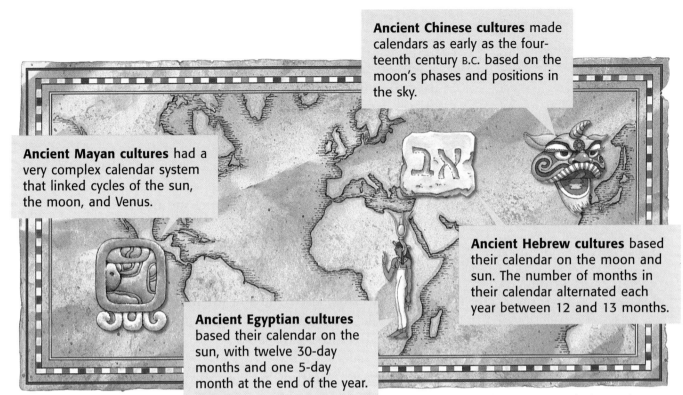

Ancient Chinese cultures made calendars as early as the fourteenth century B.C. based on the moon's phases and positions in the sky.

Ancient Mayan cultures had a very complex calendar system that linked cycles of the sun, the moon, and Venus.

Ancient Hebrew cultures based their calendar on the moon and sun. The number of months in their calendar alternated each year between 12 and 13 months.

Ancient Egyptian cultures based their calendar on the sun, with twelve 30-day months and one 5-day month at the end of the year.

Figure 2 *People in ancient cultures based their calendars on different kinds of celestial cycles.*

Toward a Modern Calendar The early Roman calendar had exactly 365 days in a year and 7 days in a week. The calendar worked well at first, but gradually the seasons shifted away from their original positions in the year.

It was then determined that there are actually about 365.25 days in a year. To correct this, Julius Caesar created the *Julian calendar.* He began by adding 90 days to the year 46 B.C., which put the seasons back to their original positions. He then added an extra day every 4 years to keep them from shifting again. A year in which an extra day is added to the calendar is called a **leap year.**

In the mid-1500s, people noticed that the Julian calendar was incorrect. Pope Gregory XIII presented this problem to a group of astronomers who determined that there are actually 365.242 days in a year. To solve the problem, a new calendar—the *Gregorian calendar*—was created. The Pope dropped 10 days from the year 1582 and restricted leap years to years that are divisible by 4 but not by 100 (except for years that are divisible by 400). This lowered the number of leap years that occur and made the average length of 1 year closer to 365.242 days. Today most countries use the Gregorian calendar, which scientists calculate will be accurate for another 3,000 years.

Julius Caesar and Pope Gregory XIII aren't the only ones who can decide when to have leap years—you can too! In fact, you can make your own calendar! Turn to page 706 in the LabBook to find out how.

Early Observers—The Beginnings of Astronomy

Scientists have found evidence for ancient astronomical activities all over the world. Some records are more complete than others. However, they all show that early humans recognized the cycles of celestial objects in the sky.

Nabta   The earliest record of astronomical observations is a 6,000 to 7,000-year-old group of stones near Nabta, in southern Egypt. Some of the stones are positioned such that they would have lined up with the sun during the summer solstice 6,000 years ago. The *summer solstice* occurs on the longest day of the year. Artifacts found at the site near Nabta suggest that it was created by African cattle herders. These people probably used the site for many purposes, including trade, social bonding, and ritual. **Figure 3** shows some of the stones at the site near Nabta.

Figure 3 *Some stones are still standing at the site near Nabta, in the Sahara Desert.*

Stonehenge   Another ancient site that was probably used to make observations of the sky is Stonehenge, near Salisbury, England. Stonehenge, shown in **Figure 4,** is a group of stones arranged primarily in circles. Some of the stones are aligned with the sunrise during the summer and winter solstices. People have offered many explanations for the purpose of Stonehenge as well as for who built and used it. Careful studies of the site reveal that it was built over a period of about 1,500 years, from about 3000 B.C. to about 1500 B.C. Most likely, Stonehenge was used as a place for ceremony and ritual. But the complete truth about Stonehenge is still a mystery.

Figure 4 *Although its creators have long since gone, Stonehenge continues to indicate the summer and winter solstices each year.*

The Babylonians   The ancient civilization of Babylon was the heart of a major empire located in present-day Iraq. From about 700 B.C. to about A.D. 50, the Babylonians precisely tracked the positions of planets and the moon. They became skilled at forecasting the movements of these celestial bodies, which enabled them to make an accurate calendar.

Ancient Chinese Cultures As early as 1000 B.C., ancient Chinese cultures could predict eclipses. *Eclipses* occur when the sun, the moon, and the Earth line up in space. The Chinese had also named 800 stars by 350 B.C. The Chinese skillfully tracked and predicted the same motions in the sky as the civilizations that influenced Western astronomy. The Chinese continued to improve their knowledge of the sky at the same time as many other civilizations, as shown in **Figure 5.**

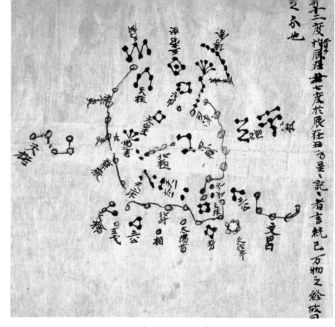

Figure 5 *This ancient Chinese manuscript is the world's oldest existing portable star map. It is more than 1,000 years old.*

The Ancient Greeks Like many other civilizations, the ancient Greeks learned to observe the sky to keep track of time. But the Greeks also took a giant leap forward in making astronomy a science. Greek philosophers tried to understand the place of Earth and humans in the universe. Their tools were logic and mathematics, especially geometry. One of the most famous Greek philosophers, Aristotle (ER is TAHT'L), successfully explained the phases of the moon and eclipses. He also correctly argued that the Earth is a sphere—an idea that was not very popular in his time.

Native Americans Archaeological records show that many of the pre-colonial civilizations in the Americas were skilled in observing the sky. Perhaps the most highly-skilled observers were the Maya, who flourished in the present-day Yucatan about 1,000 years ago. The Maya had complex systems of mathematics and astronomy. Many Mayan buildings, such as the one in **Figure 6,** are aligned with celestial bodies during certain astronomical events.

The Ancient Arabs After Greek, Roman, and early Christian civilizations weakened, the ancient Arabs inherited much of the Greeks' knowledge of astronomy. The Arabs continued to develop astronomy as a science while Europe fell into the Dark Ages. Today many stars have Arabic names. The Arabs also invented the astrolabe, algebra, and the number system that we use today.

Figure 6 *This Mayan building is the Caracol at Chichén Itzá, in the Yucatán. Many parts of the building align with Venus and the sun on certain days.*

The Who's Who of Early Astronomy

The science of astronomy has come a long way since the early days. The earliest astronomers had no history to learn from—almost everything they knew about the universe came from what they could discover with their own eyes and minds. Not surprisingly, most early astronomers thought that the universe consisted of the sun, moon, and planets, with all the stars occupying the edge of the universe. While they could not have known that our solar system is a very small part of a much larger universe, they had to start somewhere.

Ptolemy In A.D. 140, a Greek astronomer named Claudius Ptolemy (KLAW dee uhs TAHL uh mee) wrote a book that combined all the ancient knowledge of astronomy that he could find. Ptolemy expanded Aristotle's theories with careful mathematical calculations in what was called the *Ptolemaic theory.* As shown in **Figure 7,** Ptolemy thought that the Earth is at the center of the universe—with the sun and the other planets revolving around the Earth.

Even though it was incorrect, the Ptolemaic theory predicted the motions of the planets better than any known method at that time. For more than 1,500 years in Europe, the Ptolemaic theory was the most popular theory for the structure of the universe.

Figure 7 *According to the Ptolemaic theory, the Earth is at the center of the universe.*

Copernicus In 1543, a Polish astronomer named Nicolaus Copernicus (NIK uh LAY uhs koh PUHR ni kuhs) published a new theory that would eventually revolutionize astronomy. According to his theory, which is shown in **Figure 8,** the sun is at the center of the universe and the planets—including the Earth—orbit the sun. While Copernicus was correct about all the planets orbiting the sun, his theory did not immediately replace Ptolemy's theory.

Figure 8 *According to Copernicus's theory, the sun is at the center of the universe.*

Tycho Brahe Danish astronomer Tycho Brahe (TIE koh BRAW uh) used several large tools, such as the one shown in **Figure 9,** to observe the sky. Tycho favored an Earth-centered theory that was different from Ptolemy's. Tycho believed that the other planets revolve around the sun but that the sun and the moon revolve around the Earth. While Tycho's theory was not correct, he did record very precise observations of the planets and stars for several years.

Johannes Kepler After Tycho died, his assistant, Johannes Kepler, continued Tycho's work. Kepler did not agree with Tycho's theory, but he recognized how precise and valuable Tycho's data were. In 1609, after analyzing the data, Kepler announced some new laws of planetary motion. Kepler stated that all the planets revolve around the sun in elliptical orbits and that the sun is not in the exact center of the orbits.

Figure 9 *Tycho used the mural quadrant, which is a large quarter-circle on a wall, to measure the positions of stars and planets.*

Galileo Galilei In 1609, Galileo became the first person to use a telescope to observe celestial bodies. His telescope is shown in **Figure 10.** Galileo discovered four moons orbiting Jupiter, craters and mountains on the moon, sunspots on the sun, and phases of Venus. These discoveries showed that the planets are not just dots of light—they are physical bodies like the Earth. Galileo favored Copernicus's theory over Ptolemy's.

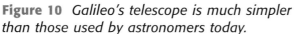

Figure 10 *Galileo's telescope is much simpler than those used by astronomers today.*

Isaac Newton Finally, in 1687 a scientist named Sir Isaac Newton explained *why* planets orbit the sun and why moons orbit planets. Newton explained that the force that keeps all of these objects in their orbit is the same one that holds us on the Earth—gravity. Newton's laws of motion and gravitation completed the work of Copernicus, Tycho, Kepler, and Galileo.

Self-Check

Name two astronomers who favored an Earth-centered universe and two astronomers who favored a sun-centered universe. *(See page 726 to check your answer.)*

Modern Astronomy

With Galileo's successful use of the telescope and Newton's discoveries about planetary motion, astronomy began to become the modern science that it is today. Gradually, people began to think of stars as more than dots of light at the edge of the universe.

From Fuzzy Patches to an Expanding Universe William Herschel, who discovered Uranus in 1781, used a telescope to study the stars in our galaxy. As he studied these stars, he found small, fuzzy patches in the sky. Herschel did not know what these patches were, but he did record their positions in a catalog.

The invention of photography in the 1800s allowed astronomers to make even better observations of the sky. In 1923, Edwin Hubble used photography to discover that some of the patches Herschel had found are actually other galaxies beyond our own. Before this discovery, scientists thought that the Milky Way galaxy was the entire universe! Hubble also discovered that the universe is expanding. In other words, distant objects in space are moving farther and farther away from each other.

Figure 11 *Today computers and telescopes are linked together. Computers not only control telescopes, but they also process the information gathered by the telescopes so that astronomers may better analyze it.*

Larger and Better Telescopes Today astronomers still gaze at the sky, trying to assign order to the universe. Larger and better telescopes on Earth and in space, supercomputers, spacecraft, and new models of the universe allow us to study objects both near and far. Many questions about the universe have been answered, but our studies continue to bring new questions to investigate.

REVIEW

1. Which ancient civilization's calendar gave rise to our modern calendar?

2. What advantage did Galileo have over the astronomers that went before him, and how did it help him?

3. **Analyzing Relationships** Is Copernicus's theory completely correct? Why or why not? How does his theory relate to what we know today about the sun's position in our solar system and in the universe?

Terms to Learn

constellation   celestial equator
altitude   ecliptic
right ascension   light-year
declination

What You'll Do

◆ Describe constellations and explain how astronomers use them.
◆ Explain how to measure altitude.
◆ Explain right ascension and declination.
◆ Evaluate the scale of the universe.

Mapping the Stars

Ancient cultures organized the sky by linking stars together in patterns. These patterns reflected the culture's beliefs and legends. Different civilizations often gave the stars names that indicated the stars' positions in their pattern. Today we can see the same star patterns that people in ancient cultures saw. Modern astronomers still use many of the names given to stars centuries ago.

Astronomers can now describe a star's location with precise numbers. These advances have led to a better understanding of just how far away stars are and how big the universe is.

Constellations

When people in ancient cultures linked stars in a section of the sky into a pattern, they named that section of the sky according to the pattern. **Constellations** are sections of the sky that contain recognizable star patterns. Many cultures organized the sky into constellations that honored their gods or reflected objects in their daily lives. Constellations helped people organize the sky and track the apparent motions of planets and stars.

In the Eye of the Beholder . . . Different civilizations had different names for the same constellations. For example, where the Greeks saw a hunter (Orion) in the northern sky, the Japanese saw a drum (*tsuzumi*), as shown in **Figure 12.** Today different cultures still interpret the sky differently.

Figure 12 *The drawing at left shows that the ancient Greeks saw Orion as a hunter. The drawing at right shows that the Japanese saw the same set of stars as a drum.*

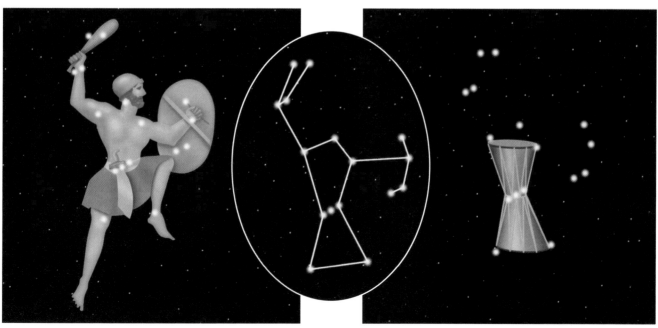

Self-Check

If a celestial object is said to be "in the constellation of Ursa Minor," does it have to be a part of the stick figure that makes up that constellation? Explain. *(See page 726 to check your answer.)*

Regions of the Sky When you think of constellations, you probably think of the stick figures made by connecting bright stars with imaginary lines. To an astronomer, however, a constellation is something more. As you can see in **Figure 13** below, a constellation is an entire region of the sky. Each constellation shares a border with its neighboring constellations. For example, in the same way that the state of Texas is a region of the United States, Ursa Major is a region of the sky. Every star or galaxy in the sky is located within a constellation. Modern astronomers divide the sky into 88 constellations. Around the world, astronomers use the same names for these constellations to make communication easier.

Figure 13 *This sky map shows some of the constellations in the Northern Hemisphere. Ursa Major is a region of the sky that includes all the stars that make up that constellation.*

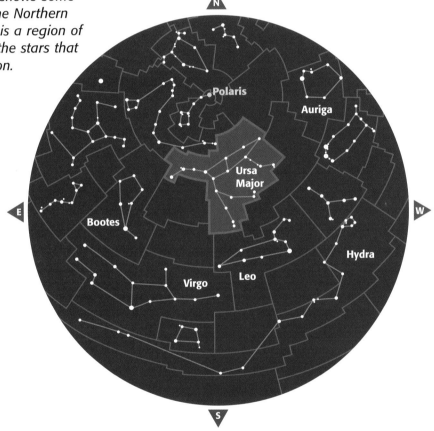

Quick Lab

Using a Sky Map

1. Hold your **textbook** over your head with the cover facing upward. Turn the book so that the direction at the bottom of the sky map is the same as the direction you are facing.

2. Notice the location of the constellations in relation to one another.

3. If you look up at the **sky** at night in the spring, you should see the stars positioned as they are on your map.

4. Why are *E* and *W* on sky maps the reverse of how they appear on land maps?

Seasonal Changes As we go around the sun each year, the constellations change from season to season. This is one reason that people in ancient cultures were able to keep track of the right time of year to plant and harvest their crops. Notice that the sky map in Figure 13 shows the night sky as seen from the Northern Hemisphere in the spring. This map would not be accurate for the other three seasons. Sky maps for summer, fall, and winter are in the Appendix of this book.

Finding Stars in the Night Sky

You can use what you learned in the Investigate to make your own observations of the sky. Have you ever tried to show another person a star or planet by pointing to it—only to have them miss what you were seeing? With just a few new references, as shown in **Figure 14,** you can tell them exactly where it is. **Figure 15** shows how you can use the astrolabe from the Investigate to make such measurements.

In astronomy, **altitude** is the angle between the object and the horizon.

The **zenith** is an imaginary point in the sky directly above an observer on Earth. The zenith always has an altitude of 90°.

90°

The **horizon** is the line where the sky and the Earth appear to meet.

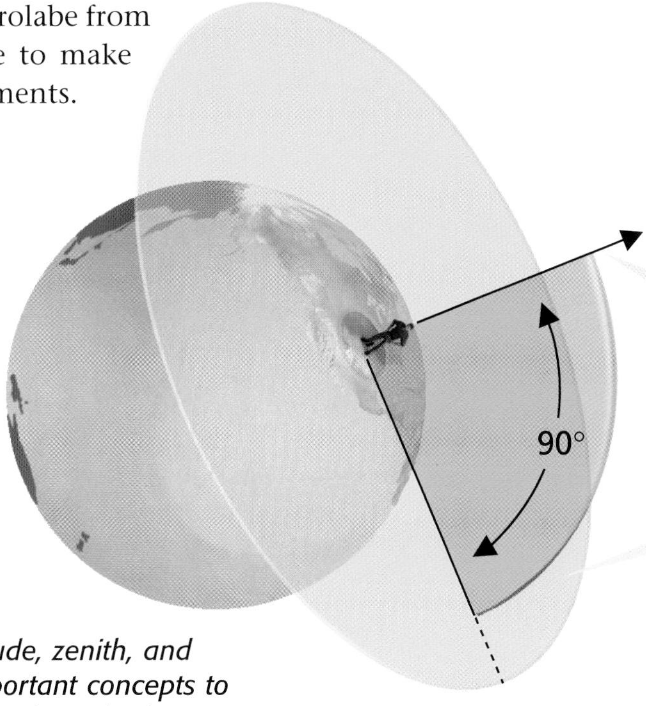

Figure 14 *Altitude, zenith, and horizon are important concepts to know when describing the locations of celestial objects.*

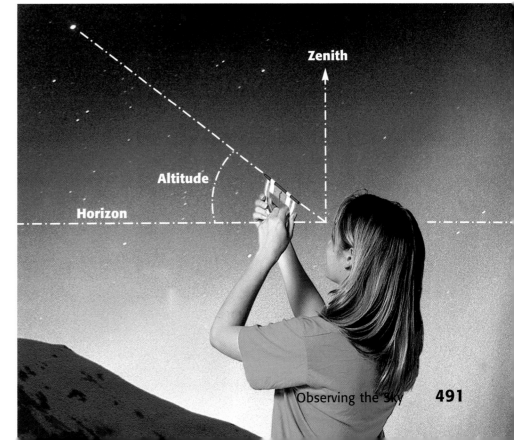

Figure 15 *With an astrolabe, you can measure the altitude of a star by measuring the angle between your horizon and the star. The altitude of any celestial object depends on where you are and when you look.*

Finding a star's altitude is one thing, but describing its position in a way that doesn't depend on where you are is another. To do this, astronomers have invented a reference system known as the *celestial sphere*. The celestial sphere surrounds the Earth and is what we look through when we observe the sky. Similar to the way we use latitude and longitude to plot positions on Earth, astronomers use right ascension (RA) and declination (dec) to plot positions in the sky. **Right ascension** is a measure of how far east an object is from the point at which the sun appears on the first day of spring. This point is called the *vernal equinox*. **Declination** is a measure of how far north or south an object is from the celestial equator.

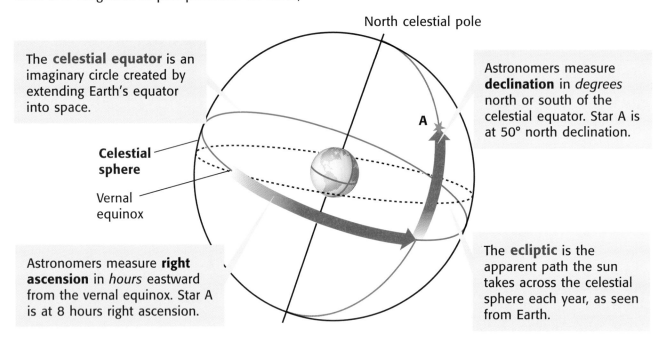

North celestial pole

The **celestial equator** is an imaginary circle created by extending Earth's equator into space.

Celestial sphere

Vernal equinox

Astronomers measure **right ascension** in *hours* eastward from the vernal equinox. Star A is at 8 hours right ascension.

Astronomers measure **declination** in *degrees* north or south of the celestial equator. Star A is at 50° north declination.

A

The **ecliptic** is the apparent path the sun takes across the celestial sphere each year, as seen from Earth.

Figure 16 *Time-lapse photography traces northern circumpolar stars, which never set below the horizon.*

Circumpolar Stars You see different stars in the sky depending on your location, the time of year, and the time of night. Why is this so? As **Figure 16** dramatically illustrates, the Earth rotates once on its axis each day. Because of this, most observers see some stars rise above and set below the horizon much like the sun does each day. Also, the combination of the Earth's motion around the sun and the tilt of Earth's axis causes different stars to be visible during different times of the year. Near the poles, however, stars are circumpolar. *Circumpolar stars* are stars that can be seen at all times of year and all times of night.

The Size and Scale of the Universe

Copernicus noticed that stars never shifted their relative position. If the stars were nearby, he reasoned, their position would appear to shift like the planets' positions do as the Earth travels around the sun. Based on this observation, Copernicus thought that the stars must be very far away from the planets.

Measuring Distance in Space Today we know that Copernicus was correct—the stars are very far away from Earth. In fact, stars are so distant that a new unit of length—the light-year—was created to measure their distance. A **light-year** is a unit of length equal to the distance that light travels through space in 1 year. One light-year is equal to about 9.46 trillion kilometers! **Figure 17** below illustrates how far away some stars that we see really are.

Even after astronomers figured out that stars were very distant, the nature of the universe was hard to understand. Some astronomers thought that our galaxy, the Milky Way, included every object in space. The other galaxies that astronomers found were thought by some to be fuzzy clouds within the Milky Way. In 1935, Edwin Hubble discovered that the Andromeda Galaxy, which is the closest major galaxy to our own, was past the edge of the Milky Way. This discovery confirmed the belief of many astronomers that the universe is much larger than was previously thought.

Physics CONNECTION

Have you ever noticed that when a driver in a passing car blows the horn, the horn's sound gets lower? This is called the *Doppler effect*. It works with both sound and light. As a light source moves away quickly, its light looks redder. This particular Doppler effect is called *red shift*. The farther apart two galaxies are moving, the faster the galaxies are moving apart. From the perspective of each galaxy, the other galaxy looks redder. Because all galaxies except our close neighbors are moving away, the universe must be expanding.

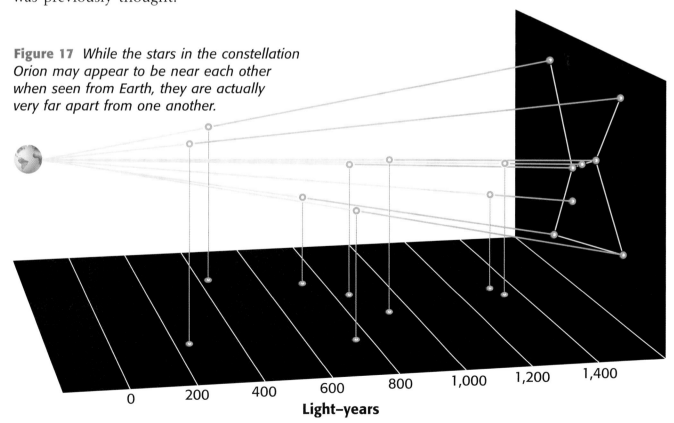

Figure 17 *While the stars in the constellation Orion may appear to be near each other when seen from Earth, they are actually very far apart from one another.*

0   200   400   600   800   1,000   1,200   1,400
Light–years

1 Let's start with something familiar, a baseball diamond. You are looking down on home plate from a distance of about 10 m.

Considering Scale in the Universe Today astronomers are studying the most distant objects yet detected in the universe. Every few months, newspapers announce new discoveries as astronomers probe deeper into space. Astronomers still argue about the size of the universe. The farthest objects we can observe are at least 10 billion light-years away.

When thinking about the universe and all the objects in it, it is important to think about scale. For example, stars appear to be very small in the night sky. But we know that most stars are a lot larger than the Earth. Examine the diagram on these two pages to better understand the scale of objects in the universe.

2 At 1,000 m away, home plate is hard to see, but now you can see the baseball stadium and the neighborhood it is located in.

3 Moving another 100 times farther away (100 km), you now see the city as a whole in relation to the countryside around it.

4 At 1,000,000 km away, you can see the Earth as a planet, with its companion, the moon.

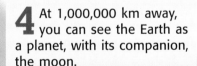

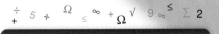

$$\div \; 5 \; \div \; \begin{matrix} \Omega \\ \leq \end{matrix} \; \infty \; + \Omega \; \sqrt{} \; 9 \; \infty \; \overset{\leq}{_\infty} \; \Sigma \; 2$$

MATH BREAK

Understanding Scale

From steps 1 to 2 and from steps 2 to 3 in the diagram at right, you increased your distance by a factor of 100. How many times farther away are you in step 4 than you were in step 3? How many times farther away in step 5 than you were in step 4?

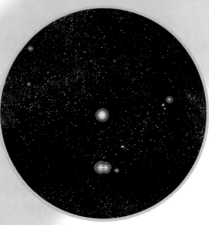

7 By the time we reach 10 light-years, the sun simply resembles any other star in space.

8 At 1 million light-years, our galaxy would look like the Andromeda galaxy shown here—an island of stars set in the blackness of space.

6 At 150 light-days, the solar system can be seen surrounded by a cloud of comets and other icy debris.

5 Moving 1,500,000,000 km away (83 light-minutes), we can look back at the sun and the inner planets.

9 When we reach 10 million light-years, our view shows us that the universe is crowded with galaxies, many like our own, and many strangely different.

REVIEW

1. How do constellations relate to patterns of stars? How are constellations like states?

2. How do astronomers plot a star's exact position?

3. **Analyzing Relationships** As shown in the diagram above, there are faraway objects that we can see only with telescopes. There are also objects in the universe that are too small for our unaided eyes to see. How do we detect these small objects?

internet connect

SCI LINKS
NSTA

TOPIC: Constellations
GO TO: www.scilinks.org
sciLINKS NUMBER: HSTE440

Telescopes—Then and Now

Terms to Learn

telescope
refracting telescope
reflecting telescope
electromagnetic spectrum

What You'll Do

◆ Compare and contrast refracting telescopes with reflecting telescopes.
◆ Explain why the atmosphere is an obstacle to astronomers and how they overcome the obstacle.
◆ List the types of electromagnetic radiation, other than visible light, that astronomers use to study space.

For professional astronomers and amateur stargazers, the telescope is the standard tool for observing the sky. A **telescope** is an instrument that collects *electromagnetic radiation* from the sky and concentrates it for better observation. You will learn more about electromagnetic radiation later in this section.

Optical Astronomy

An optical telescope collects visible light for closer observation. The simplest optical telescope is made with two lenses. One lens, called the *objective lens,* collects light and forms an image at the back of the telescope. The bigger the objective lens, the more light the telescope can gather. The second lens is located in the eyepiece of the telescope. This lens magnifies the image produced by the objective lens. Different eyepieces can be selected depending on the magnification desired.

Without a telescope, you can see about 6,000 stars in the night sky. With an optical telescope, you can see millions of stars and other objects. **Figure 18** shows how much more you can see with an optical telescope.

Figure 18 *The image at left shows a section of the sky as seen with the unaided eye. The image at right shows what the small clusters of stars in the left image look like when seen through a telescope.*

Refracting Telescopes Telescopes that use a set of lenses to gather and focus light are called **refracting telescopes.** The curved objective lens in a refracting telescope bends light that passes through it and focuses the light to be magnified by the eyepiece. **Figure 19** shows how refracting telescopes work. A refracting telescope's size is limited by the objective lens. If the curved lens is too large, the glass sags under its own weight, distorting images. This is why most professional astronomers use *reflecting telescopes*.

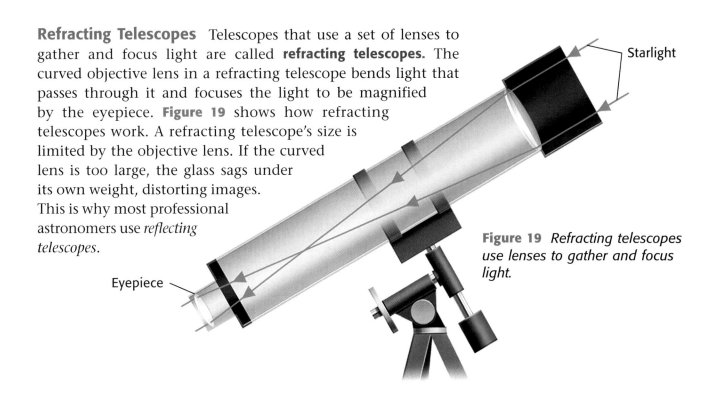

Starlight

Eyepiece

Figure 19 *Refracting telescopes use lenses to gather and focus light.*

Reflecting Telescopes Telescopes that use curved mirrors to gather and focus light are called **reflecting telescopes.** Light enters the telescope and is reflected from a large, curved mirror to a focal point above the mirror. As shown in **Figure 20,** reflecting telescopes use a second mirror in front of the focal point to reflect the light, in this case, through a hole in the side of the telescope. Here the light is collected for observation.

One advantage of reflecting telescopes over refracting telescopes is that mirrors can be made very large, which allows them to gather more light than lenses gather. Also, mirrors are polished on their curved side, preventing light from entering the glass. Therefore, any flaws in the glass do not affect the light. A third advantage is that mirrors reflect all colors of light to the same place, while lenses focus different colors of light at slightly different distances. Reflecting telescopes thus allow all colors of light from an object to be seen in focus at the same time.

Want to make your own telescope? Turn to page 710 in the LabBook to find out how to build and use a telescope.

Eyepiece

Starlight

Figure 20 *Reflecting telescopes use mirrors to gather and focus light.*

Very Large Reflecting Telescopes

In some very large reflecting telescopes, several mirrors work together to collect light and deliver it to the same focus. The Keck Telescopes, in Hawaii, shown in **Figure 21,** are twin telescopes that each have 36 hexagonal mirrors working together. Linking several mirrors allows more light to be collected and focused in one spot.

Figure 21 *The 36 hexagonal mirrors in each of the Keck Telescopes combine to form a light-reflecting surface that is 10 m across.*

Optical Telescopes and the Atmosphere The light gathered by telescopes on Earth is affected by the atmosphere. Earth's atmosphere causes starlight to shimmer and blur. Also, light pollution from large cities can make the sky look bright, which limits an observer's ability to view faint objects. Astronomers often place telescopes in dry areas to avoid water vapor in the air. Mountaintops are also good places to use a telescope because the air is thinner at higher elevations. The fact that air pollution and light pollution are generally lower on mountaintops also increases the visibility of stars.

Optical Telescopes in Space! To avoid interference by the atmosphere altogether, scientists have put telescopes in space. Although the mirror in the Hubble Space Telescope, shown below in **Figure 22,** is only 2.4 m across, the optical telescope produces images that are as good or better than any images produced by optical telescopes on Earth.

Figure 22 *The Hubble Space Telescope has provided clearer images of objects in deep space than any ground-based optical telescope.*

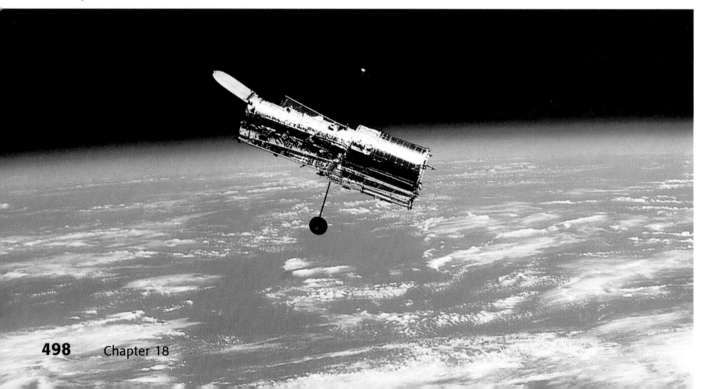

Non-Optical Astronomy

For thousands of years, humans have observed the universe with their eyes. But scientists eventually discovered that there are more forms of radiation than the kind we can see—*visible light*. In 1800, William Herschel discovered an invisible form of radiation called *infrared radiation*. We sense infrared radiation as heat.

In 1852, James Clerk Maxwell showed that visible light is a form of *electromagnetic radiation*. Each color of visible light represents a different wavelength of electromagnetic radiation. Visible light is just a small part of the electromagnetic spectrum, as shown in **Figure 23.** The **electromagnetic spectrum** is made of all of the wavelengths of electromagnetic radiation. Humans can see radiation only from blue light, which has a short wavelength, to red light, which has a longer wavelength. The rest of the electromagnetic spectrum is invisible to us!

Most electromagnetic radiation is blocked by the Earth's atmosphere. Think of the atmosphere as a screen that lets only certain wavelengths of radiation in. These wavelengths include infrared, visible light, some ultraviolet, and radio. All other wavelengths are blocked.

Activity

Artificial light at night is often needed for safety and security. But it also causes light pollution that interferes with stargazing. Do some research on this problem, and list some possible solutions. What compromises can be made so that people feel safe and stargazers can see objects in the night sky?

TRY at HOME

Figure 23 *Radio waves have the longest wavelengths and gamma rays have the shortest. Visible light is only a small band of the electromagnetic spectrum.*

Radio waves   Micro-waves   Infrared   Visible   Ultra-violet   X rays   Gamma rays

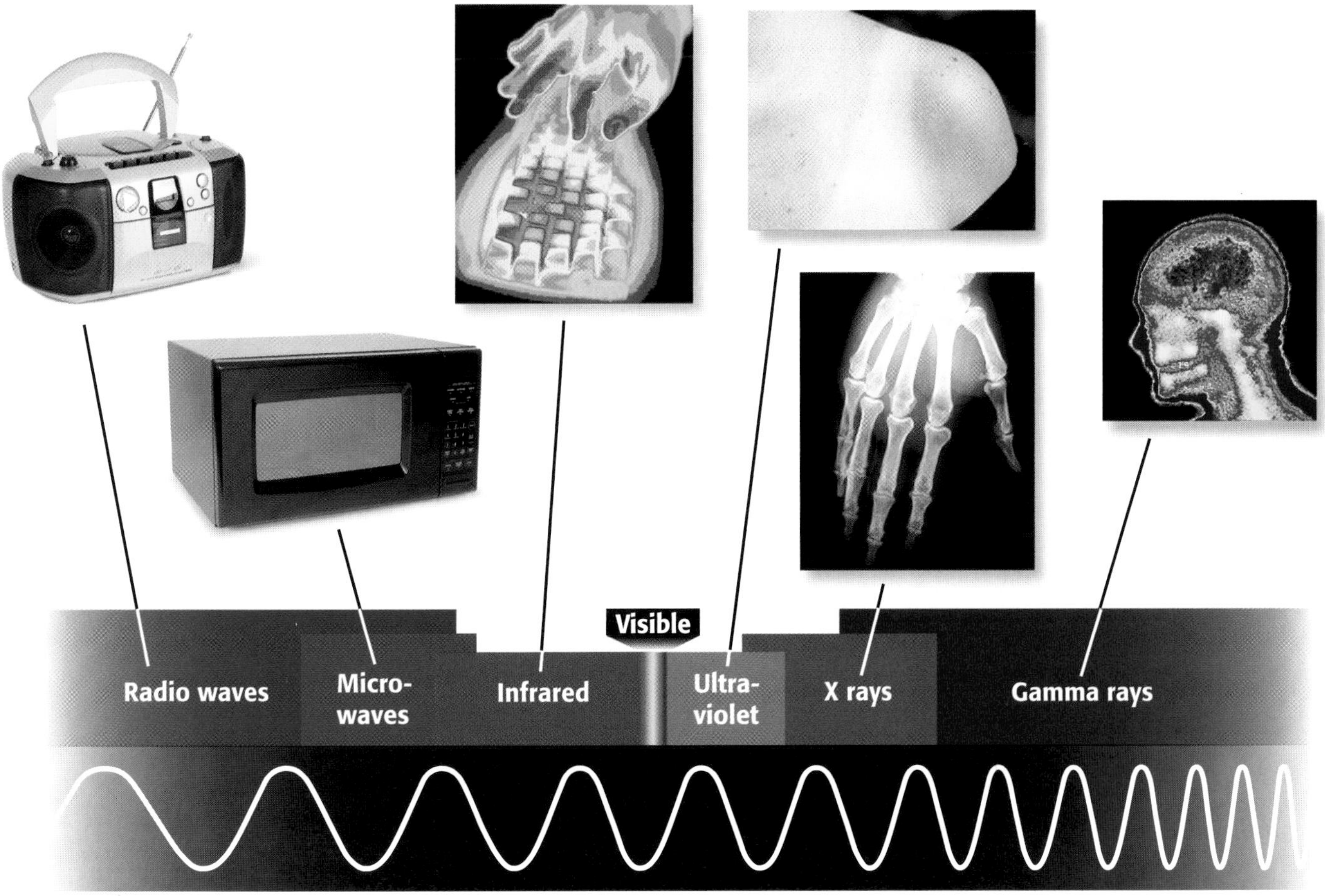

The Night Sky Through Different Eyes Astronomers are interested in all forms of electromagnetic radiation because different objects radiate at different wavelengths. For each type of radiation, a different type of telescope or detector is needed. For example, infrared telescopes have polished mirrors similar to those of reflecting telescopes, but the detectors are more sensitive to infrared waves than to visible light waves. As you can see in **Figure 24,** the universe looks much different when observed at other wavelengths.

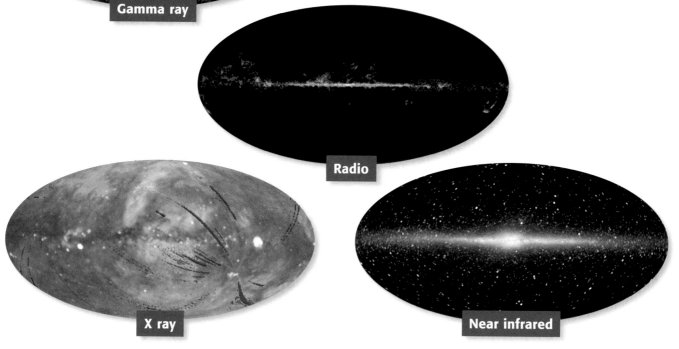

Figure 24 *Each image shows the night sky as it would appear if we could see other wavelengths of electromagnetic radiation. The "cloud" that goes across each picture is the Milky Way galaxy.*

Figure 25 *The Arecibo radio telescope is 305 m across. That is about the length of three football fields arranged end to end!*

Radio Telescopes Radio telescopes receive and focus radio waves. Radio telescopes have to be much larger than optical telescopes because radio wavelengths are about 1 million times longer than optical wavelengths. Also, very little radio radiation reaches Earth from objects in space. Radio telescopes must be very sensitive to detect these faint waves.

The surface of a radio telescope does not have to be as flawless as the lens of an optical telescope. In fact, the surface of a radio telescope does not even have to be completely solid. When it was first built, the Arecibo radio telescope, shown in **Figure 25,** was covered with chicken wire! To a radio wave, a surface made of chicken wire is solid because the wavelength is so much longer than the diameter of the holes.

Linking Radio Telescopes Together Astronomers can get clearer images of radio waves by using two or more radio telescopes at the same time. When radio telescopes are linked together, they work like a single giant telescope. For example, the Very Large Array (VLA), shown in **Figure 26,** consists of 27 separate telescopes that can be spread out 30 km. When the dishes are spread out to the maximum distance, they work as a single telescope that is 30 km across! The larger the area that linked telescopes cover, the more detailed the collected data are.

Figure 26 *The radio telescopes of the Very Large Array near Socorro, New Mexico, work together as one giant telescope.*

X-ray Vision Most electromagnetic waves are blocked by the Earth's atmosphere. To detect these blocked waves, scientists have put special telescopes in space. These telescopes include ultraviolet telescopes, infrared telescopes, gamma-ray telescopes, and X-ray telescopes. Each type of telescope is made to receive one type of radiation. For example, **Figure 27** shows a telescope that is designed to detect X rays.

Figure 27 *Launched in 1999, the Chandra X-ray Observatory is the most powerful X-ray telescope ever built.*

REVIEW

1. Name one way in which refracting telescopes and reflecting telescopes are similar and one way they are different.

2. Name two ways the atmosphere limits what astronomers can detect. What single method do astronomers use to solve both problems?

3. **Summarizing Data** Make two lists—one for electromagnetic wavelengths that commonly penetrate Earth's atmosphere and one for other wavelengths. Which wavelengths can astronomers detect from Earth? How do they detect each wavelength?

internetconnect

SC*i*LINKS
NSTA

TOPIC: Telescopes
GO TO: www.scilinks.org
*sci*LINKS NUMBER: HSTE445

Chapter Highlights

SECTION 1

Vocabulary

astronomy (*p. 482*)

calendar (*p. 482*)

year (*p. 482*)

month (*p. 482*)

day (*p. 482*)

leap year (*p. 483*)

Section Notes

- Calendars are based on movements of objects in the sky.

- Many ancient civilizations developed calendars.

- Our modern calendar developed from the Roman calendar.

- There is evidence all around the world for ancient astronomical observations.

- The Ptolemaic theory states that Earth is at the center of the universe, while Copernicus's theory states that the sun is at the center of the universe.

- Isaac Newton was the first scientist to explain why celestial objects move as they do.

- Galileo's use of the telescope brought the technology of astronomy to a new level.

Labs

Create a Calendar (*p. 706*)

SECTION 2

Vocabulary

constellation (*p. 489*)

altitude (*p. 491*)

right ascension (*p. 492*)

declination (*p. 492*)

celestial equator (*p. 492*)

ecliptic (*p. 492*)

light-year (*p. 493*)

Section Notes

- Astronomers divide the sky into 88 sections called *constellations.*

- Different constellations are visible from different locations, at different times of the year, and at different times of night.

- Star patterns appear as they do because of Earth's position in space. Most stars that appear close together are actually very far apart.

☑ Skills Check

Math Concepts

KEEPING IT SIMPLE Scientific notation is a way that scientists and others can use large numbers more easily. By using exponents, many place-holding zeros can be eliminated.

> For example:
> 1,000 can be written as 1×10^3, and
> 1,000,000 can be written as 1×10^6.

Notice that the exponent represents the number of zeros in each number. For more practice with scientific notation, turn to page 743 in the Appendix.

Visual Understanding

OPTICAL ILLUSION Constellations look like they do only because we see them from our location on Earth in patterns we recognize. Look back at Figure 17 on page 493. The constellation Orion would be unrecognizable if seen from the side.

- The north celestial pole, the celestial equator, the zenith, and the horizon are imaginary markers used to locate objects in the sky.

- Right ascension and declination, which are similar to latitude and longitude, give coordinates of objects in the sky.

- Astronomers measure the distance to most objects in the universe in light-years.

- The size and distance of celestial objects detected in the universe can be difficult to determine. Scale must always be considered.

Labs

The Sun's Yearly Trip Through the Zodiac *(p. 708)*

Vocabulary

telescope *(p. 496)*

refracting telescope *(p. 497)*

reflecting telescope *(p. 497)*

electromagnetic spectrum *(p. 499)*

Section Notes

- Telescopes collect and focus electromagnetic radiation.

- Humans can see only visible light. To detect other wavelengths of radiation, astronomers use special telescopes or detectors.

- Types of telescopes include optical, radio, ultraviolet, infrared, X-ray, and gamma-ray.

- Some telescopes are launched into space to avoid the blurring effects of Earth's atmosphere or to collect radiation that can't penetrate Earth's atmosphere.

- Telescopes are often linked together to function as one giant telescope.

Labs

Through the Looking Glass *(p. 710)*

Chapter Review

For each set of terms, explain the similarities and differences in their meanings.

1. reflecting telescope/refracting telescope

2. celestial equator/horizon

3. X rays/microwaves

4. right ascension/declination

5. leap year/light-year

Multiple Choice

6. The length of a day is based on
   a. the Earth orbiting the sun.
   b. the rotation of the Earth on its axis.
   c. the moon orbiting the Earth.
   d. the rotation of the moon on its axis.

7. Which of the following civilizations directly affected the development of our modern calendar?
   a. The Chinese
   b. The Maya
   c. The Romans
   d. The Polynesians

8. According to __?__, the Earth is at the center of the universe.
   a. the Ptolemaic theory
   b. Copernicus's theory
   c. Galileo's theory
   d. none of the above

9. The first scientist to successfully use a telescope to observe the night sky was
   a. Tycho.   c. Herschel.
   b. Galileo.   d. Kepler.

10. Astronomers divide the sky into
    a. galaxies.   c. zeniths.
    b. constellations.   d. phases.

11. The stars that you see in the sky depend on
    a. your latitude.
    b. the time of year.
    c. the time of night.
    d. All of the above

12. The altitude of an object in the sky is its angular distance
    a. above the horizon.
    b. from the north celestial pole.
    c. from the zenith.
    d. from the prime meridian.

13. Right ascension is a measure of how far east an object in the sky is from
    a. the observer.
    b. the vernal equinox.
    c. the moon.
    d. Venus.

14. Telescopes that work grounded on the Earth include all of the following except
    a. radio telescopes.
    b. refracting telescopes.
    c. X-ray telescopes.
    d. reflecting telescopes.

15. Which of the following is true about X-ray and radio radiation from objects in space?

a. Both types of radiation can be observed with the same telescope.

b. Separate telescopes are needed to observe each type of radiation, and both telescopes can be on Earth.

c. Separate telescopes are needed to observe each type of radiation, and both telescopes must be in space.

d. Separate telescopes are needed to observe each type of radiation, but only one of the telescopes must be in space.

Short Answer

Write one or two sentences to answer the following questions:

16. Explain how right ascension and declination are similar to latitude and longitude.

17. How does a reflecting telescope work?

Concept Mapping

18. Use the following terms to create a concept map: right ascension, declination, celestial sphere, degrees, hours, celestial equator, vernal equinox.

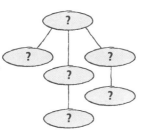

CRITICAL THINKING AND PROBLEM SOLVING

19. Why was it easier for people in ancient cultures to see celestial objects in the sky than it is for most people today?

20. Many forms of radiation do not penetrate Earth's atmosphere. While this limits astronomer's activities, how does it benefit humans in general?

MATH IN SCIENCE

21. How many kilometers away is an object whose distance is 8 light-years?

INTERPRETING GRAPHICS

Examine the sky map below, and answer the questions that follow. (Hint: The star Aldebaran is located at about 4 hours, 30 minutes right ascension, 16 degrees declination.)

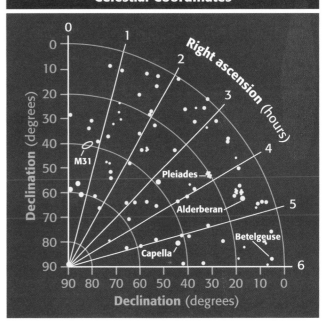

Celestial Coordinates

22. What object is located at 5 hr, 55 min right ascension and 7 degrees declination?

23. What are the celestial coordinates for the Andromeda galaxy (M31)? (Round off right ascension to the nearest half-hour.)

Reading Check-up

Take a minute to review your answers to the Pre-Reading Questions found at the bottom of page 480. Have your answers changed? If necessary, revise your answers based on what you have learned since you began this chapter.

Science, Technology, and Society

Planet or Star?

Humans have long wondered if there are inhabited planets in our galaxy or in far-off galaxies. For the first time, NASA's powerful Hubble Space Telescope has photographed what some astronomers believe is a young planet within our own galaxy. This gaseous object, called TMR-1C, is nearly 450 light-years from Earth. Is it really a planet, or is it a star?

Discovering Planets

Scientists have had trouble finding planets beyond our solar system because distant planets are often masked by the light of brighter stars. *Protoplanets,* planets in the process of forming, may be difficult to see because they are often surrounded by clouds of cosmic dust. As a planet revolves around a star, its gravity tugs on the star. This causes the star to move back and forth slightly. If the planet is massive enough, astronomers can see this movement as a "wobble" in the star's motion. Scientists use state-of-the-art technology to detect these minute changes in the star's velocity relative to Earth.

The picture of TMR-1C could be the first photographic evidence that planets exist outside our solar system. Astronomers discovered TMR-1C racing through space at 32,000 km/h in the constellation of Taurus. Scientists believe that TMR-1C was hurled into space by two stars that acted like a giant slingshot. The Hubble Space Telescope's camera used sensitive infrared light to penetrate through the cosmic clouds surrounding TMR-1C. Because TMR-1C is still hot from forming, it emits light, which is picked up by the telescope's camera.

The Birth of a Planet

Scientists believe that it takes millions of years for planets to form. Photographs of TMR-1C, however, have led some researchers to speculate that this process may be much quicker than was previously thought. The stars that ejected TMR-1C are only a few hundred thousand years old. Researchers have not determined for certain whether TMR-1C is a planet. If TMR-1C turns out to be older than these stars, it could not have been ejected from them. If that is the case, TMR-1C may prove to be a *brown dwarf* rather than a planet. Meanwhile, the research continues until scientists know for certain.

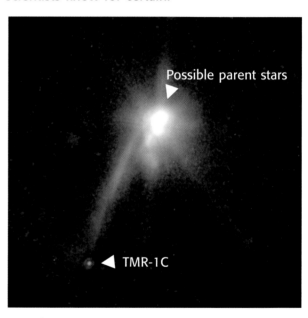

Possible parent stars

TMR-1C

▲ *TMR-1C is 209 billion km from possible parent stars.*

Think About It!

▶ So far, only a few of the many recently discovered planets may be habitable. One such planet, near the star 70 Virginis, is just the right distance from its star for the planet's water to be liquid rather than solid or gaseous. What other features would be necessary for this planet to sustain life as we know it on Earth?

EYE ON THE ENVIRONMENT

Eyes in the Sky

Have you ever gazed up at the sky on a crystal-clear night? What did you see? You probably noticed the moon and countless twinkling stars. It may surprise you to learn that some of those points of light are not stars at all. A few of them may be phonies.

Phony Stars Exposed

Some of the objects that we think are stars are really satellites circling Earth in low Earth orbit (LEO). The satellites in LEO specialize in observation. You might say that when we watch the sky, satellites are watching us as well. LEO is ideal for observation because of its proximity to Earth's surface.

In order to stay in orbit, satellites in LEO must travel very fast. Traveling at approximately 27,358 km/h, one of these satellites can circle the Earth in only 90 minutes! During these revolutions, some satellites gather weather information, while others might transmit phone calls or observe remote terrain. These "eyes in the sky" can even observe you taking a walk.

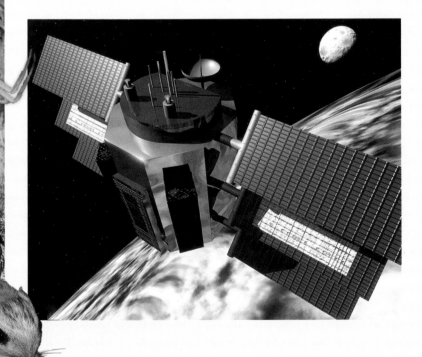

Space Junk Explosion

Like many things, satellites do not last forever. They eventually break down and may even explode into hundreds of pieces. Most of the time, these pieces continue to travel in LEO for many years. Some of these pieces are large enough to be catalogued by the United States Space Command. As of January 1, 2000, about 2,647 human-made satellites were recorded orbiting, along with 6,022 pieces of debris, or space junk. This debris poses no immediate threat to astronauts or space shuttles that travel through LEO, but there is the potential that one little piece of space junk could smash into an unwary space traveler with explosive results!

The Satellites Just Keep on Coming

We are dependent on satellites for many everyday tasks. Our ever-increasing quest for knowledge drives us to launch more satellites every year. In the booming satellite industry, there is fierce competition for a position in LEO. Many companies are willing to pay top dollar to ensure their position in space. With LEO quickly becoming a satellite highway, it may soon face a traffic jam.

Satellite Search

▶ Unlike stars, satellites in LEO move noticeably cross the sky. Research different types of satellites that orbit Earth. Look at the night sky, and try to spot some satellites. What kinds of satellites did you find? Present your observations to the class.

CHAPTER 19

Formation of the Solar System

Sections

Pre-Reading Questions

1. What keeps the planets in their orbits?
2. Why does the sun shine?
3. Why is the Earth round?

A STAR FACTORY

The Orion Nebula, a vast cloud of dust and gas 35 trillion miles across, is part of the familiar Orion constellation (*below*). Here, swirling clouds of dust and gas give birth to systems like our own solar system. In this chapter, you will learn about the formation of our sun and the planets that race around it.

STRANGE GRAVITY

If you drop a heavy object, will it fall faster than a lighter one? According to the law of gravity, the answer is no. In 1971, *Apollo 15* astronaut David Scott stood on the moon and dropped a feather and a hammer. Television audiences were amazed to see both objects strike the moon's surface at the same time. Now you can perform a version of this classic experiment in the classroom.

Procedure

1. Select **two pieces of identical notebook paper.** Crumple one piece of paper into a ball.

2. Place the flat piece of paper on top of a **book** and the paper ball on top of the flat piece of paper.

3. Hold the book waist high, and then drop it to the floor.

Analysis

4. Which piece of paper reached the bottom first? Did either piece of paper fall slower than the book? Explain your observations in your ScienceLog.

5. Now hold the crumpled paper in one hand and the flat piece of paper in the other. Drop both pieces of paper at the same time. What else affected the speed of the falling paper besides gravity? Record your observations in your ScienceLog, and share your ideas with your classmates.

TRY at HOME

A Solar System Is Born

Terms to Learn

solar system   orbit
nebula   revolution
solar nebula   period of revolution
planetesimal   ellipse
rotation   astronomical unit

What You'll Do

◆ Explain the basic process of planet formation.
◆ Compare the inner planets with the outer planets.
◆ Describe the difference between rotation and revolution.
◆ Describe the shape of the orbits of the planets, and explain what keeps them in their orbits.

You probably know that Earth is not the only planet orbiting the sun. In fact, it has eight fellow travelers in its cosmic neighborhood. Together these nine planets and the sun are part of the solar system. The **solar system** is composed of the sun (a star) and the planets and other bodies that travel around the sun. But how did our solar system come to be?

The Solar Nebula

All the ingredients for building planets are found in the vast, seemingly empty regions between the stars. But these regions are not really empty—they contain a mixture of gas and dust. The gas is mostly hydrogen and helium, while the dust is made up of tiny grains of elements such as carbon and iron. The dust and gas clump together in huge interstellar clouds called **nebulas** (or *nebulae*), which are so big that light takes many years to cross them! Nebulas, like the one shown in **Figure 1,** are cold and dark. Over time, light from nearby stars interacts with the dust and gas, forming many new chemicals. Eventually, complex molecules similar to those necessary for life form deep within the nebulas. These clouds are the first ingredients of a new planetary system.

Gravity Pulls Matter Together Because these clouds of dust and gas consist of matter, they have mass. *Mass,* which is a measure of the amount of matter in an object, is affected by the force of gravity. But because the matter in a nebula is so spread out, the attraction between the dust and gas particles is very small. If a nebula's density were great enough, then the attraction between the particles might be strong enough to pull everything together into the center of the cloud. But even large clouds don't necessarily collapse toward the center because there is another effect, or force, that pushes in the opposite direction of gravity. You'll soon find out what that force is.

Figure 1 *The Horsehead nebula is a cold, dark cloud of gas and dust as well as a possible site for future star formation.*

Pressure Pushes Matter Apart *Temperature* is a measure of how fast the particles in an object move around. If the gas molecules in a nebula move very slowly, the temperature is very low and the cloud is cold. If they move fast, the temperature is high and the cloud is warm. Because the cloud has a temperature that is above absolute zero, the gas molecules are moving. There is no particular structure in the cloud, and individual gas molecules can move in any direction. Sometimes they crash into each other. As shown in **Figure 2,** these collisions create a push, or *pressure,* away from the other gas particles. This pressure is what finally balances the gravity and keeps the cloud from collapsing.

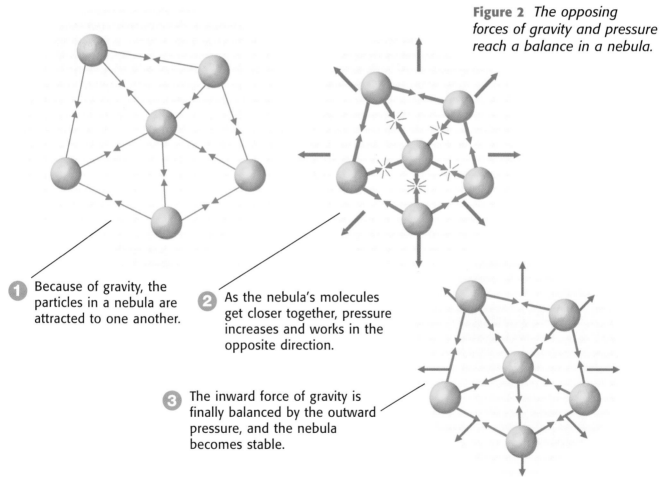

Figure 2 *The opposing forces of gravity and pressure reach a balance in a nebula.*

① Because of gravity, the particles in a nebula are attracted to one another.

② As the nebula's molecules get closer together, pressure increases and works in the opposite direction.

③ The inward force of gravity is finally balanced by the outward pressure, and the nebula becomes stable.

The Solar Nebula Forms Sometimes something happens to upset this balance. Two nebulas can crash into each other, for example, or a nearby star can explode, causing material from the star to crash into the cloud. These events compress small regions of the cloud so that gravity overcomes the pressure. Gravity then causes the cloud to collapse inward. At this point, the stage is set for the formation of a star and, as in the case of our sun, its planets. The **solar nebula** is the name of the nebula that formed into our own solar system.

Self-Check

What keeps a nebula from collapsing? *(See page 726 to check your answer.)*

From Planetesimals to Planets

Once the solar nebula started to collapse, things happened quickly, at least on a cosmic time scale. As the dark cloud collapsed, matter in the cloud got closer and closer together. This made the attraction between particles even stronger. The stronger attraction pulled the cloud together, and the gas and dust particles moved at a faster rate, increasing the temperature at the center of the cloud.

As things began to get crowded near the center of the solar nebula, particles of dust and gas in the cloud began to bump into other particles more often. Eventually much of the dust and gas began slowly rotating about the center of the cloud. The rotating solar nebula eventually flattened into a disk.

Planetesimals Sometimes bits of dust within the solar nebula stuck together when they collided, forming the tiny building blocks of the planets, called **planetesimals.** Within a few hundred thousand years, the planetesimals grew from microscopic sizes to boulder-sized, eventually measuring a kilometer across. The biggest planetesimals began to sweep up dust and debris in their paths, eventually forming planets.

Figure 3 **The Process of Solar System Formation**

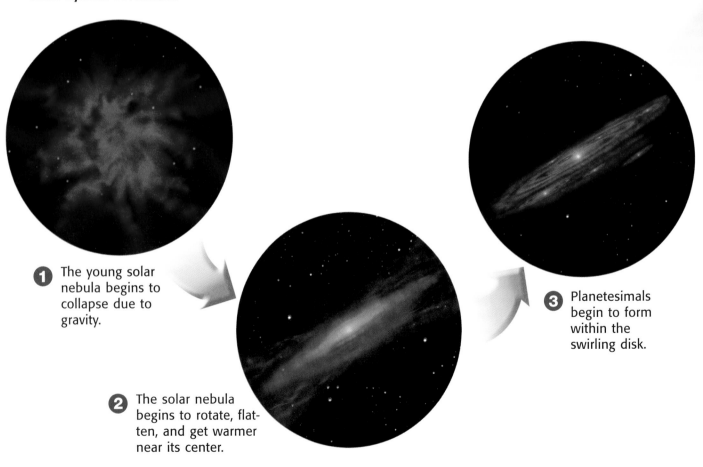

❶ The young solar nebula begins to collapse due to gravity.

❷ The solar nebula begins to rotate, flatten, and get warmer near its center.

❸ Planetesimals begin to form within the swirling disk.

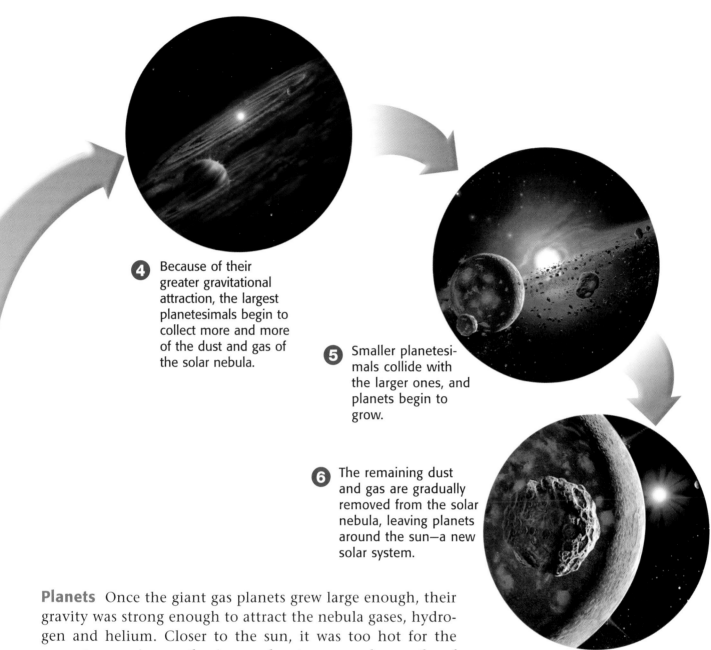

4 Because of their greater gravitational attraction, the largest planetesimals begin to collect more and more of the dust and gas of the solar nebula.

5 Smaller planetesimals collide with the larger ones, and planets begin to grow.

6 The remaining dust and gas are gradually removed from the solar nebula, leaving planets around the sun—a new solar system.

Planets Once the giant gas planets grew large enough, their gravity was strong enough to attract the nebula gases, hydrogen and helium. Closer to the sun, it was too hot for the gases to remain, so the inner planets are made mostly of rocky material.

Craters and Comets Collisions with smaller planetesimals became more violent as pieces of debris became larger, leaving many craters on the surface of the rocky planets. We see evidence of this today particularly on Mercury, Mars, and our moon.

In the final steps of planet formation, the remaining planetesimals crashed down on the planets or got thrown to the outer edge of the solar nebula by the gravity of the larger planets. Occasionally something, perhaps a passing star, sends them journeying toward the sun. If the planetesimal is icy, we see this visitor as a *comet*.

 Self-Check

Why are the giant gas planets so large? *(See page 726 to check your answer.)*

Birth of a Star

But what was happening at the middle of the solar nebula? The central part of the solar nebula contained so much mass and had become so hot that hydrogen fusion began. This created so much pressure at the center of the solar nebula that outward pressure balanced the inward force of gravity. At this point, the gas stopped collapsing. As the sun was born, the remaining gas and dust of the nebula were blown into deep space by a strong solar wind, and the new solar system was complete.

From the time the nebula first started to collapse, it took nearly 10 million years for the solar system to form. So how do we know that our ideas of star and planet formation are correct when nobody was around to watch it? Powerful telescopes, such as the Hubble Space Telescope, are now able to show us some of the fine details inside distant nebulas. One such nebula is shown in **Figure 4.** For the first time, scientists can see disks of dust around stars that are in the process of forming.

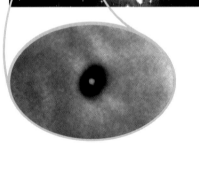

Figure 4 *The Orion nebula contains several "star nurseries"—disks of gas and dust where new stars form. The insets show newly-formed stars within some of these disks.*

internetconnect

SC*i*LINKS.
NSTA

TOPIC: The Planets
GO TO: www.scilinks.org
*sci*LINKS NUMBER: HSTE455

REVIEW

1. What two forces balance each other to keep a nebula of dust and gas from collapsing or flying apart?

2. Why does the composition of the giant gas planets differ from that of the rocky inner planets?

3. Explain why there is only one planet in each orbit around the sun.

4. **Making Inferences** Why do all the planets go around the sun in the same direction, and why do the planets all lie in a flat plane?

Planetary Motion

The solar system, which is now 4.6 billion years old, is not simply a collection of stationary planets and other bodies around the sun. Each one moves according to strict physical laws. The ways in which the Earth moves, for example, cause seasons and even day and night.

Rotation and Revolution How does the motion of the Earth cause day and night? The answer has to do with the Earth's spinning on its axis, or **rotation.** As the Earth rotates, only one-half of the Earth faces the sun at any given time. The half facing the sun is light (day), and the half facing away from the sun is dark (night).

In addition to rotating on its axis, the Earth also travels around the sun in a path called an **orbit.** This motion around the sun along its orbit is called **revolution.** The other planets in our solar system also revolve around the sun. The amount of time it takes for a single trip around the sun is called a **period of revolution.** The period for the Earth to revolve around the sun is 365 days. Mercury orbits the sun in 88 days.

All planets *revolve* around the sun in the same direction. If you could look down on the solar system from above the sun's north pole, you would see all the planets revolving in a counterclockwise direction. Not all planets *rotate* in the same direction, however. Venus, Uranus, and Pluto rotate backward compared with the rest of the planets.

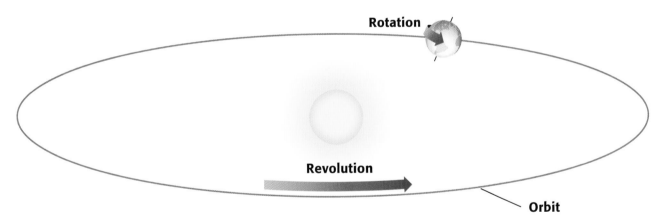

Figure 5 *A planet rotates on its own axis and revolves around the sun in a path called an orbit.*

Planetary Orbits But why do the planets continue to revolve around the sun? Does something hold them in their orbit? Why doesn't gravity pull the planets toward the sun? Or why don't they fly off into space? To answer these questions, we need to go back in time to look at the discoveries made by the scientists of the 1500s and 1600s.

Danish astronomer Tycho Brahe (TIE koh BRAW uh) carefully observed the positions of the planets for over a quarter of a century. When he died in 1601, his young assistant, Johannes Kepler, inherited all of his records. Kepler set out to understand the motions of the planets and to make a simple description of the solar system.

Kepler's First Law of Motion Kepler's first discovery, or *first law of motion,* came from his careful study of the movement of the planet Mars. He discovered that the planet did not move in a circle around the sun, but in an elongated circle called an *ellipse.* An **ellipse** is a closed curve in which the sum of the distances from the edge of the curve to two points (called *foci*) inside the ellipse is always the same, as shown in **Figure 6.**

Figure 6 Parts of an Ellipse

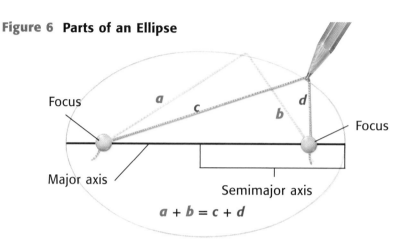

$$a + b = c + d$$

The maximum length of an ellipse is called its *major axis,* and half of this distance is the *semimajor axis,* which is usually used to give the size of an ellipse. The semimajor axis of Earth's orbit, for example, is 150 million kilometers. It represents the average distance between the Earth and the sun and is called one **astronomical unit,** or one AU.

Kepler's Formula

Kepler's third law can be expressed with the formula

$$P^2 = a^3$$

where P is the period of revolution and a is the semimajor axis of an orbiting body. For example, Mars's period is 1.88 years, and its semimajor axis is 1.523 AU. Therefore, $1.88^2 = 1.523^3 = 3.53$. If astronomers know either the period or the distance, they can figure the other one out.

Kepler's Second Law Kepler also discovered that the planets seem to move faster when they are close to the sun and slower when they are farther away. To illustrate this, imagine that a planet is attached to the sun by a string. The string will sweep out the same area in equal amounts of time. To keep the area of *A,* for example, equal to the area of *B,* the planet must move farther around its orbit in the same amount of time. This is Kepler's *second law of motion.*

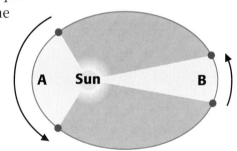

Kepler's Third Law Kepler's *third law of motion* compares the period of a planet's revolution with its semimajor axis. By doing some mathematical calculations, Kepler was able to demonstrate that by knowing a planet's period of revolution, the planet's distance from the sun can be calculated.

Newton's Law of Universal Gravitation

Kepler wondered what caused the planets closest to the sun to move faster than the planets farther away, but he never got an answer. It was Sir Isaac Newton who finally put the puzzle together. He did this with his ideas about *gravity*. Newton didn't understand *why* gravity worked or what caused it. Even today, modern scientists do not fully understand gravity. But Newton was able to combine the work of earlier scientists to explain *how* the force of attraction between matter works.

An Apple One Day Newton reasoned that small objects fall toward the Earth because the Earth and the objects are attracted to each other by the force of gravity. But because the Earth has so much more mass than a small object, say an apple, only the object appears to move.

Newton thus developed his *law of universal gravitation*, which states that the force of gravity depends on the product of the masses of the objects divided by the square of the distance between them. In other words, if two objects are moved twice as far apart, the gravitational attraction between them will decrease by a factor of $2 \times 2 = 4$, as shown in **Figure 7.** If the objects are moved 10 times as far apart, the gravitational attraction will decrease by a factor of $10 \times 10 = 100$.

Figure 7 *If two objects are moved twice as far apart, the gravitational attraction between them will be four times less.*

Newton's Law and Satellites

Space engineers that plan the paths of orbiting satellites must be able to calculate the height of the most appropriate orbit and the location of the satellite at each moment. To do this, they must take into account both Kepler's laws of motion and Newton's law of universal gravitation. Try this exercise: If the mass of the Earth were twice its actual mass, by how much would the gravity increase on a satellite in orbit around Earth? If the satellite were suddenly moved three times farther away, would Earth's gravitational pull on the satellite increase or decrease? By how much?

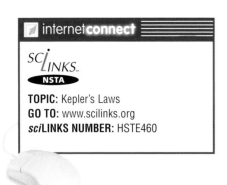

Activity

When the space shuttle is in orbit, we see the astronauts floating around as they work. Many people talk about this as a "zero-g" environment, meaning no gravity. Is this correct? Are shuttle astronauts affected by gravity? Do research to find out what happens when objects are in orbit around Earth.

TRY at HOME

Falling Down and Around How did Newton explain the orbit of the moon around the Earth? After all, according to gravity, the moon should come crashing into the Earth. And this is what the moon would do if it were not moving at a high velocity. In fact, if it were not for gravity, the moon would simply shoot off away from the Earth.

To understand this better, imagine twirling a ball on the end of a string. As long as you hold the string, the ball will orbit your hand. As soon as you let go of the string, the ball will fly off in a straight path. This same principle applies to the moon. But instead of a hand holding a string, gravity is keeping the moon from flying off in a straight path. **Figure 8** shows how this works. This same principle holds true for all bodies in orbit, including the Earth and other planets in our solar system.

Figure 8 *Gravity is actually causing the moon to fall toward the Earth, changing what would be a straight-line path. The resulting path is a curved orbit.*

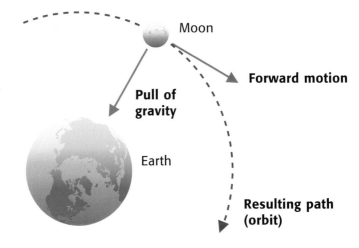

REVIEW

1. On what properties does the force of gravity between two objects depend?

2. Will a planet or comet be moving faster in its orbit when it is farther from or closer to the sun? Explain.

3. How does gravity keep a planet moving in an orbit around the sun?

4. **Applying Concepts** Suppose a certain planet had two moons, one of which was twice as far from the planet as the other. Which moon would complete one revolution of the planet first? Explain.

Section 2

The Sun: Our Very Own Star

Terms to Learn

corona
chromosphere
photosphere
convective zone
radiative zone
core
nuclear fusion
sunspot

What You'll Do

- Describe the basic structure and composition of the sun.
- Explain how the sun produces energy.
- Describe the surface activity of the sun, and name some of its effects on Earth.

There is nothing special about our sun, other than the fact that it is close enough to the Earth to give us light and warmth. Otherwise, the sun is similar to most of the other stars in our galaxy. It is basically a large ball of gas made mostly of hydrogen and helium held together by gravity. But let's take a closer look.

The Structure of the Sun

Although it may look like the sun has a solid surface, it does not. When we see a picture of the sun, we are really seeing through the sun's outer atmosphere, down to the point where the gas becomes so thick we cannot see through it anymore. As shown in **Figure 9,** the sun is composed of several layers.

Figure 9 Structure of the Sun and Its Atmosphere

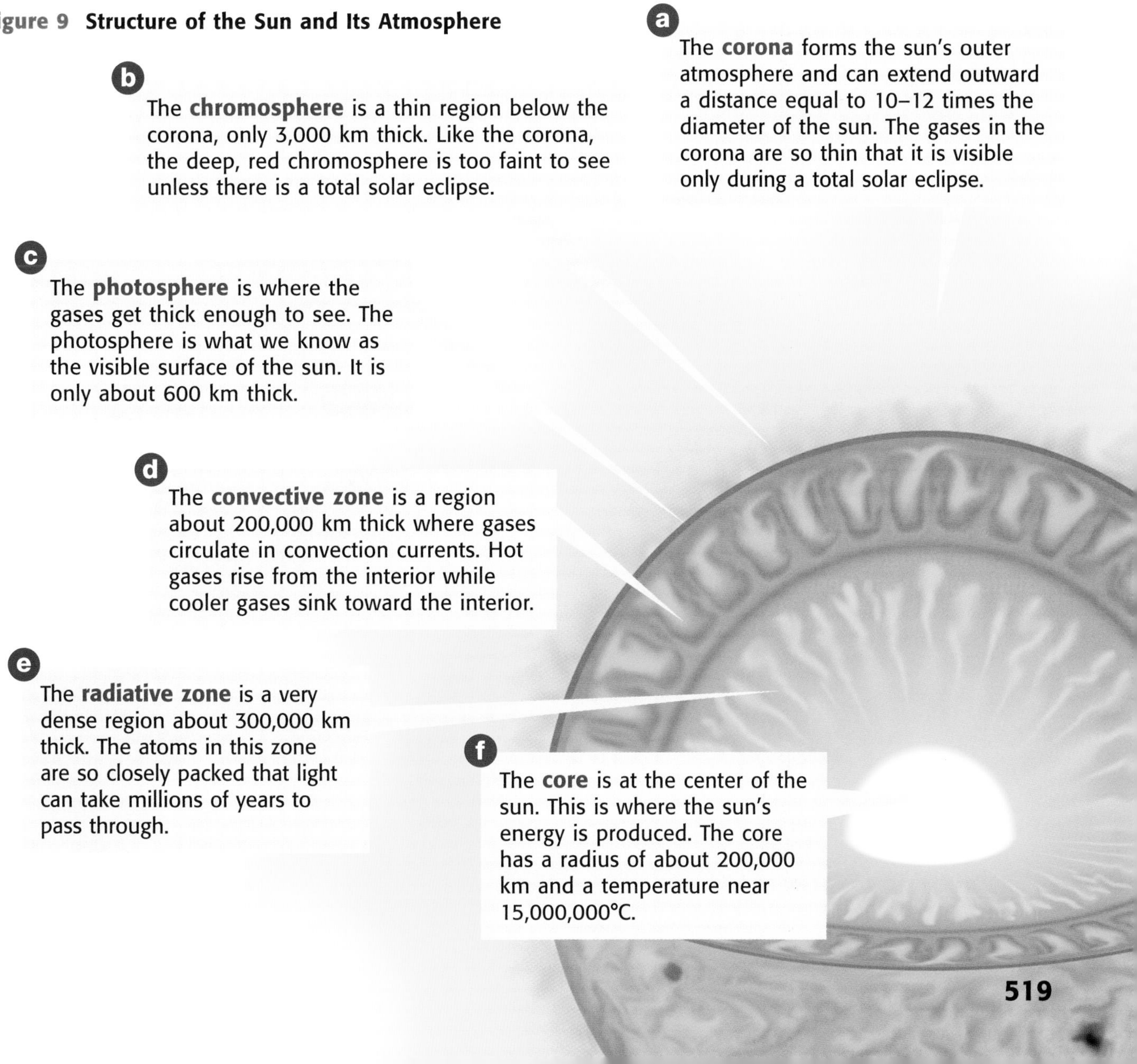
a
The **corona** forms the sun's outer atmosphere and can extend outward a distance equal to 10–12 times the diameter of the sun. The gases in the corona are so thin that it is visible only during a total solar eclipse.
b
The **chromosphere** is a thin region below the corona, only 3,000 km thick. Like the corona, the deep, red chromosphere is too faint to see unless there is a total solar eclipse.
c
The **photosphere** is where the gases get thick enough to see. The photosphere is what we know as the visible surface of the sun. It is only about 600 km thick.
d
The **convective zone** is a region about 200,000 km thick where gases circulate in convection currents. Hot gases rise from the interior while cooler gases sink toward the interior.
e
The **radiative zone** is a very dense region about 300,000 km thick. The atoms in this zone are so closely packed that light can take millions of years to pass through.
f
The **core** is at the center of the sun. This is where the sun's energy is produced. The core has a radius of about 200,000 km and a temperature near 15,000,000°C.

Energy Production in the Sun

The sun has been shining on the Earth for about 4.6 billion years. How can it stay hot for so long? And what makes it shine? Over the years, several theories have been proposed to answer these questions. Because the sun is so bright and hot, many people thought that it was burning fuel to create the energy. But the amount of energy that is released during burning would not be enough to power the sun. If the sun were simply burning, it would last for only 10,000 years.

Burning or Shrinking? It eventually became clear that burning wouldn't last long enough to keep the sun shining. Scientists began to think that the sun was slowly shrinking due to gravity and that perhaps this would release enough energy to heat the sun. While the release of gravitational energy is more powerful than burning, it is still not enough to power the sun. If all of the sun's gravitational energy were released, the sun would last for only 45 million years. We know that dinosaurs roamed the Earth more than 65 million years ago, so this couldn't be the explanation. Something even more powerful was needed.

Some type of burning fuel was first thought to be the source of the sun's energy.

Figure 10 *Ideas about the source of the sun's energy have changed over time.*

A shrinking sun was another explanation for solar energy.

The sun is difficult to study because it is far away from Earth. Just how far? You might be able to figure it out by turning to page 712 in the LabBook.

Nuclear Fusion At the beginning of the twentieth century, Albert Einstein demonstrated that matter and energy are interchangeable. Matter can be converted to energy according to his famous formula: $E = mc^2$, where E is energy, m is mass, and c is the speed of light. Because the speed of light is so large, even a small amount of matter can produce a large amount of energy. This idea paved the way for an understanding of a very powerful source of energy. **Nuclear fusion** is the process by which two or more nuclei with small masses (such as hydrogen) join together, or fuse, to form a larger, more massive nucleus (such as helium). During the process, energy is produced—a lot of it!

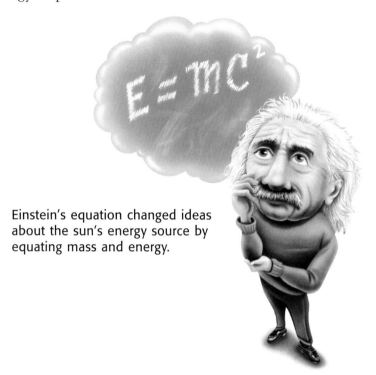

Einstein's equation changed ideas about the sun's energy source by equating mass and energy.

Biology CONNECTION

At the time Darwin introduced his theory of evolution, scientists thought that the sun was a few million years old at most. Some scientists argued that evolution—which takes place over billions of years—was therefore impossible because the sun could not have been shining that long. The nuclear fusion that fuels the sun, however, gives it a lifespan of at least 10 billion years!

Atomic Review

Let's do a little review. *Atoms* are the smallest particles of matter that keep their chemical identity. An atom consists of a *nucleus* surrounded by one or more *electrons,* which have a negative charge. A nucleus is made up of two types of particles—*protons,* with a positive charge, and *neutrons,* with no charge. The positively charged protons in the nucleus are balanced by an equal number of negatively charged electrons. The number of protons and electrons gives the atom its chemical identity. A helium atom, for example, has two protons and two electrons.

Helium

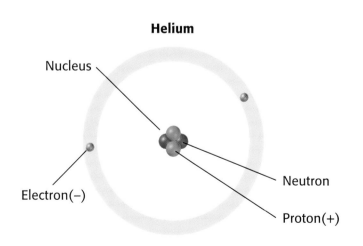

Nucleus

Electron(−)

Neutron

Proton(+)

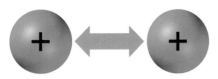

Figure 11 *Like charges repel, just like similar poles on a pair of magnets.*

Fusion in the Sun Under normal conditions, the nuclei of hydrogen atoms never get close enough to combine. This is because they are positively charged, and like charges repel each other, as shown in **Figure 11.** In the center of the sun, however, the temperature and pressure are very high because of the huge amount of matter within the core. This gives the hydrogen nuclei enough energy to overcome the repulsive force, allowing the conversion of hydrogen to helium, as shown in **Figure 12.**

Figure 12 Fusion of Hydrogen in the Sun

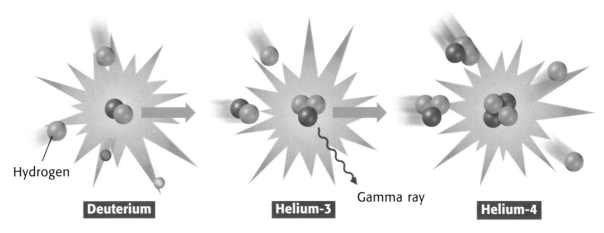

Hydrogen

Gamma ray

Deuterium　　　**Helium-3**　　　**Helium-4**

❶ Two hydrogen nuclei (protons) collide. One proton emits particles and energy, then becomes a neutron. The proton and neutron combine to produce a heavy form of hydrogen called *deuterium.*

❷ Deuterium combines with another hydrogen nucleus to form a variety of helium called helium-3. More energy is released, as well as gamma rays.

❸ Two helium-3 atoms then combine to form ordinary helium-4, releasing more energy and a pair of hydrogen nuclei.

The energy produced in the core of the sun takes millions of years to reach the sun's surface. In the radiative zone, the matter is so crowded that the light and energy keep getting blocked and sent off in different directions. Eventually the energy reaches the convective zone, where hot gases carry it up to the photosphere relatively quickly. From there the energy leaves the sun as light, taking only 8.3 minutes to reach Earth.

Activity on the Sun's Surface

The photosphere, or the visible surface of the sun, is a very dynamic place. As energy from the sun's interior reaches the surface, it causes the gas to boil and churn, a result of the rising and sinking of gases in the convective zone below.

The energy released during the nuclear fusion of 1 g of hydrogen is equal to about 100 tons of TNT! Each second, the sun converts about 5 million tons of matter into pure energy.

Sunspots The circulation of the gases within the sun, in addition to the sun's own rotation, produces magnetic fields that reach out into space. But these magnetic fields also tend to slow down the activity in the convective zone. This causes areas on the photosphere above to be slightly cooler than surrounding areas. These areas show up as sunspots. **Sunspots** are cooler, dark spots on the sun, as shown in **Figure 13.**

The number of sunspots and their location on the sun change in a regular cycle. Records of the number of sunspots have been kept ever since the invention of the telescope. In **Figure 14,** the sunspot cycle is shown, with the exception of the years 1645–1715, when sunspots were not observed.

Solar Flares The magnetic fields that cause sunspots also cause disturbances in the solar atmosphere. Giant storms on the surface of the sun, called *solar flares,* have temperatures of up to 5 million degrees Celsius. Solar flares send out huge streams of particles from the sun. These particles interact with the Earth's upper atmosphere, causing spectacular light shows called *auroras.* Solar flares can interrupt radio communications on Earth. They can also affect satellites in orbit. Scientists are trying to find ways to predict solar activity and give advanced warning of such events.

Figure 13 *Sunspots mark cooler areas on the sun's surface. They are related to changes in the magnetic properties of the sun.*

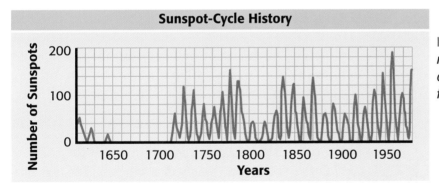

Sunspot-Cycle History

Figure 14 *This graph shows the number of sunspots that have occurred each year since Galileo's first observations, in 1610.*

REVIEW

1. According to modern understanding, what is the source of the sun's energy?

2. If nuclear fusion in the sun's core suddenly stopped today, would the sky be dark in the daytime tomorrow? Why?

3. **Interpreting Illustrations** In Figure 12, the nuclear fusion process ends up with one helium-4 nucleus and two free protons. What might happen to the two protons next?

Terms to Learn

crust   core
mantle

What You'll Do

◆ Describe the shape and structure of the Earth.
◆ Explain how the Earth got its layered structure and how this process affects the appearance of Earth's surface.
◆ Explain the development of Earth's atmosphere and the influence of early life on the atmosphere.
◆ Describe how the Earth's oceans and continents were formed.

The Earth Takes Shape

Investigating the early history of the Earth is not easy because no one was there to study it directly. Scientists develop ideas about what happened based on their knowledge of chemistry, biology, physics, geology, and other sciences. Astronomers are also gathering evidence from other stars where planets are forming to better understand how our own solar system formed.

The Solid Earth Takes Form

As scientists now understand it, the Earth formed from the accumulation of planetesimals. This would have taken place within the first 10 million years of the collapse of the solar nebula—the blink of an eye on the cosmic time scale!

The Effects of Gravity When a young planet is still small, it can have an irregular shape, like a potato. As more matter builds up on the young planet, the force of gravity increases and the material pushing toward the center of the planet gets heavier. When a rocky planet, such as Earth, reaches a diameter of about 350 km, pressure from all this material becomes greater than the strength of the rock. At this point, the planet starts to become spherical in shape as the rock in the center is crushed by gravity.

The Effects of Heat As planetesimals fell to Earth, the energy of their motion made the Earth warmer. A second source of energy for heating the Earth was radioactive material, which was present in the solar nebula. Radioactive material radiates energy, and as this energy collected within the Earth, it also heated the planet. Once the Earth reached a certain size, the interior could not cool off as fast as its temperature rose, and the rocky material inside began to melt. As you will see on the next page, the effects of heat and gravity contributed to the formation of the Earth's layers.

Figure 15 *The Earth has not always looked as inviting as it does today.*

✔ Self-Check

Why is the Earth spherical in shape, while most asteroids and comets are not? *(See page 726 to check your answer.)*

The Earth and Its Layers Have you ever dropped pebbles into water or tried mixing oil and vinegar together for a salad? What happens? The heavier material (either solid or liquid) sinks, and the lighter material floats to the top. This is because of gravity. The material with a higher density is more strongly attracted and falls to the bottom. The same thing happened in the young Earth. As its rocks melted, the heavy elements, such as nickel and iron, sank to the center of the Earth, forming what we call the *core*. Lighter materials floated to the surface. This process is illustrated in **Figure 16.**

Figure 16 Earth's Materials Separate into Layers

All materials in the early Earth are randomly mixed.

Rocks melt, and dense materials separate and sink.

Less-dense materials rise, and layers are formed.

Mixing It Up

Have you ever mixed oil and water and watched what happened? Try this.

1. Pour 50 mL of **water** into a 150 mL **beaker.**

2. Add 50 mL of **cooking oil** to the water. Stir vigorously.

3. Let the mixture stand undisturbed for a few minutes.

4. What happens to the oil and water?

5. How does this relate to the interior of the early Earth?

The Earth's Interior The Earth is divided into three distinct layers according to the composition of its materials. These layers are shown in **Figure 17.** Geologists map the interior of the Earth by measuring how sound waves pass through the planet during earthquakes and underground explosions.

Figure 17 *The interior of the Earth consists of three layers.*

1 The **crust** is the outermost layer of the Earth. It forms a thin skin over the entire planet, ranging from 5 km to 100 km thick.

2 The **mantle** lies below the crust, extending from about 100 km to about 2,900 km below the surface. The mantle contains denser rocks than the crust.

3 The **core**, at the center, contains the heaviest material (nickel and iron) and extends from the base of the mantle to the center of the Earth—almost 6,400 km below the surface.

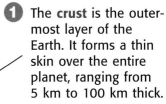

525

The Atmosphere Evolves

Other than the presence of life, one of the biggest differences between the Earth of today and the Earth of 4.6 billion years ago is the character of its atmosphere. Earth's atmosphere today is composed of 21 percent oxygen, 78 percent nitrogen, and about 1 percent argon (with tiny amounts of many other gases). But it has not always been this way. Read on to discover how the Earth's atmosphere has changed through time.

Earth's First Atmosphere Earth's early atmosphere was very different from the atmosphere of today. In the 1950s, laboratory experiments on the origins of life were based on the hypothesis that Earth's early atmosphere was largely made up of methane, ammonia, and water. And because the solar nebula was rich in hydrogen, many scientists thought that Earth's first atmosphere also contained a lot of hydrogen compounds.

New Evidence New evidence is changing the way we think about Earth's first atmosphere. For one thing, 85 percent of the Earth's matter probably came from material similar to *meteoroids*—planetesimals made of rock. The other 15 percent probably came from the outer solar system in the form of *comets*—planetesimals made of ice.

Volcanic Gases During the final stages of formation, the Earth was hit many times by planetesimals, and the surface was very hot, even molten in places, as illustrated in **Figure 18.** The ground would have been venting large amounts of gas released from the heated minerals. The composition of meteorites tells us that much of that gas would have been water vapor and carbon dioxide. These two gases are also commonly released during volcanic eruptions. Earth's first atmosphere was probably a steamy atmosphere made of water vapor and carbon dioxide.

Figure 18 *This is an artist's view of what Earth's surface may have looked like shortly after Earth's formation.*

The Role of Impacts Planetesimal impacts may have helped release gases from the Earth. In addition, they may have also helped to knock some of those gases back into space. Because planetesimals travel very fast, their impacts can speed up gas molecules in the atmosphere enough for them to overcome gravity and escape into space.

Heavier elements, such as iron, that were on the surface of the Earth also reacted chemically with water, giving off hydrogen—the lightest element. And because the early Earth was very warm, this hydrogen also had enough energy to escape.

Comets brought in a range of elements, such as carbon, hydrogen, oxygen, and nitrogen. They may also have brought water that eventually helped form the oceans, as shown in **Figure 19.**

Figure 19 *Comets may have brought some of the water that formed Earth's early oceans.*

Earth's Second Atmosphere After the Earth cooled off and the core formed, it became possible for the Earth's second atmosphere to take shape. This atmosphere formed from gases contributed by both volcanoes and comets. Volcanoes, like the one in **Figure 20,** produced large amounts of water vapor, along with chlorine, nitrogen, sulfur, and large amounts of carbon dioxide. This carbon dioxide kept the planet much warmer than it is today.

Figure 20 *As this volcano in Hawaii shows, a large amount of gas is released during an eruption.*

Environment
CONNECTION

Because carbon dioxide is a very good *greenhouse gas*—one that traps thermal energy—scientists have tried to estimate how much carbon dioxide the Earth must have had in its second atmosphere in order to keep it as warm as it was. For example, if all of the carbon dioxide that is now tied up in the rocks and minerals of the ocean floor were released, it would make an atmosphere of carbon dioxide 60 times as thick as our present atmosphere.

Earth's Current Atmosphere How did this early atmosphere change to become the atmosphere we know today? It happened with the help of solar ultraviolet (UV) radiation, the very thing that we worry about now for its cancer-causing ability. Solar UV light is dangerous because it has a lot of energy and can break molecules apart in the air or in your skin. Today we are shielded from most of the sun's ultraviolet rays by Earth's protective ozone layer. But Earth's early atmosphere had no ozone, and many molecules were broken apart in the atmosphere. The pieces were later washed out into shallow seas and tide pools by rain. Eventually a rich supply of these pieces of molecules collected in protected areas, forming a rich organic solution that is sometimes called a "primordial soup."

The Source of Oxygen Although there was no ozone, water offered protection from the effects of ultraviolet radiation. In these sheltered pools of water, complex molecules may have been able to form. Then, sometime between 4.6 and 3.9 billion years ago, life began on Earth. By 3.7 to 3.4 billion years ago, living organisms had evolved that were able to photosynthesize energy from sunlight and produce oxygen as a byproduct. These early life-forms are still around today, as shown in **Figure 21.**

Figure 21 *Fossilized algae (left) are among the earliest signs of life discovered. Today's stromatolites (right) are mats of microorganisms thought to be similar to the first life on Earth.*

Eventually, between 2.5 and 2.0 billion years ago, the amount of oxygen started to increase rapidly—reaching about 20 percent of the amount we have in the atmosphere today. As plants began to cover the land, oxygen levels increased because plants produce oxygen during photosynthesis. Therefore, it was the emergence of life that completely changed our atmosphere into the one we have today.

Oceans and Continents

It is hard to say exactly when the first oceans appeared on Earth, but they probably formed early, as soon as the Earth was cool enough for rain to fall and remain on the surface. We know that Earth's second atmosphere had plenty of water vapor. After millions of years of rainfall, water began to cover the Earth, and by 4 billion years ago, a giant global ocean covered the planet. For the first few hundred million years of the Earth's history, there were no continents.

So how and when did the continents appear? Continental crust material is very light compared with material in the mantle. The composition of the granite and other rocks making up the continents tells geologists that the rocks of the crust have melted and cooled many times in the past. Each time the rocks melted, the heavier elements sank, leaving the lighter ones to rise to the surface. This process is illustrated in **Figure 22.**

The Growth of Continents After a while, some of the rocks were light enough that they no longer sank, and they began to pile up on the surface. This was the beginning of the earliest continents. After gradually thickening, the continents slowly rose above the surface of the ocean. These scattered young continents didn't stay in the same place, however, because the slow convection in the mantle pushed them around. By around 2.5 billion years ago, continents really started to grow. By 1.5 billion years ago, the upper mantle had cooled and become denser and heavier, so it was easier for the colder parts of it to sink. Then the real continental action, or *plate tectonics,* began.

internet**connect**

SC*LINKS*
NSTA

TOPIC: The Layers of the Earth, The Oceans
GO TO: www.scilinks.org
*sci*LINKS **NUMBER:** HSTE470, HSTE475

Figure 22 *The slow convective motion in the Earth's mantle was the engine that caused mantle rock to rise and sink, forming the continents.*

Hot rocks, which are less dense, rose to the surface and melted, erupting through volcanoes.

Cooler materials, which are denser, sank because of gravity and became reheated. This started the process over again.

REVIEW

1. Why did the Earth separate into distinct layers?

2. How did the Earth's atmosphere change composition to become today's nitrogen and oxygen atmosphere?

3. Which are older, oceans or continents? Explain.

4. **Drawing Conclusions** If the Earth were not hot inside, would we have moving continents (plate tectonics)? Explain.

Chapter Highlights

Vocabulary

solar system *(p. 510)*

nebula *(p. 510)*

solar nebula *(p. 511)*

planetesimal *(p. 512)*

rotation *(p. 515)*

orbit *(p. 515)*

revolution *(p. 515)*

period of revolution *(p. 515)*

ellipse *(p. 516)*

astronomical unit *(p. 516)*

Section Notes

- The solar system formed out of a vast cloud of cold gas and dust called a nebula.

- Gravity and pressure were balanced, keeping the cloud unchanging until something upset the balance. Then the nebula began to collapse.

- Collapse of the solar nebula caused heating in the center. As material crowded closer together, planetesimals began to form.

- The central mass of the nebula became the sun. Planets formed from the surrounding disk of material.

- It took about 10 million years for the solar system to form, and it is now 4.6 billion years old.

- The orbit of one body around another has the shape of an ellipse.

- Planets move faster in their orbits when they are closer to the sun.

- The square of the period of revolution of the planet is equal to the cube of its semimajor axis.

- Gravity depends on the masses of the interacting objects and the square of the distance between them.

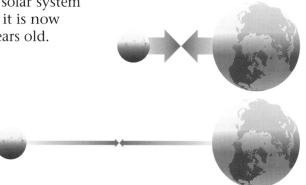

☑ Skills Check

Math Concepts

SQUARES AND CUBES Let's take another look at Kepler's third law of motion. Expanding the formula $P^2 = a^3$ to $P \times P = a \times a \times a$ may be an easier way to consider the calculation. The period of Venus, for example, is 0.61 years, and its semimajor axis is 0.72 AU. Thus,

$$P^2 = a^3$$
$$P \times P = a \times a \times a$$
$$0.61 \times 0.61 = 0.72 \times 0.72 \times 0.72$$
$$0.37 = 0.37$$

Visual Understanding

LIKE AN ONION The sun is formed of six different layers of gas. From the inside out, the layers are the core, radiative zone, convective zone, photosphere, chromosphere, and corona. Look back at Figure 9 on page 519 to review the characteristics of each layer.

SECTION 2

Vocabulary

corona *(p. 519)*

chromosphere *(p. 519)*

photosphere *(p. 519)*

convective zone *(p. 519)*

radiative zone *(p. 519)*

core *(p. 519)*

nuclear fusion *(p. 521)*

sunspot *(p. 523)*

Section Notes

- The sun is a gaseous sphere made primarily of hydrogen and helium.

- The sun produces energy in its core by a process called nuclear fusion.

- Magnetic changes within the sun cause sunspots and solar flares.

Labs

How Far Is the Sun? *(p. 712)*

SECTION 3

Vocabulary

crust *(p. 525)*

mantle *(p. 525)*

core *(p. 525)*

Section Notes

- The Earth is divided into three main layers—crust, mantle, and core.

- Materials with different densities separated because of melting inside Earth. Heavy elements sank to the center because of Earth's gravity.

- Earth's original atmosphere formed from the release of gases brought to Earth by meteorites and comets.

- Earth's second atmosphere arose from volcanic eruptions and impacts by comets. The composition was largely water and carbon dioxide.

- The presence of life dramatically changed Earth's atmosphere, adding free oxygen.

- Earth's oceans formed shortly after the Earth did, when it had cooled off enough for rain to fall.

- Continents formed when lighter materials gathered on the surface and rose above sea level.

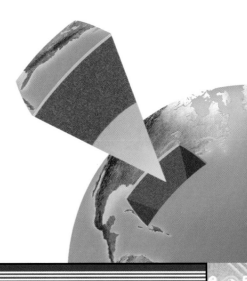

---

 internetconnect

 **SCILINKS**SM

N S T A

GO TO: go.hrw.com

GO TO: www.scilinks.org

Visit the **HRW** Web site for a variety of learning tools related to this chapter. Just type in the keyword:

KEYWORD: HSTSOL

Visit the **National Science Teachers Association** on-line Web site for Internet resources related to this chapter. Just type in the *sci*LINKS number for more information about the topic:

TOPIC:	The Planets	*sci*LINKS NUMBER:	HSTE455
TOPIC:	Kepler's Laws	*sci*LINKS NUMBER:	HSTE460
TOPIC:	The Sun	*sci*LINKS NUMBER:	HSTE465
TOPIC:	The Layers of the Earth	*sci*LINKS NUMBER:	HSTE470
TOPIC:	The Oceans	*sci*LINKS NUMBER:	HSTE475

Chapter Review

For each pair of terms, explain the difference in their meanings.

1. rotation/revolution

2. ellipse/circle

3. solar system/solar nebula

4. planetesimal/planet

5. temperature/pressure

6. photosphere/corona

To complete the following sentences, choose the correct term from each pair of terms below.

7. It takes millions of years for light energy to travel through the sun's ___?___.
   (*radiative zone* or *convective zone*)

8. ___?___ of the Earth causes night and day.
   (*Rotation* or *Revolution*)

9. Convection in Earth's mantle causes ___?___.
   (*plate tectonics* or *nuclear fusion*)

UNDERSTANDING CONCEPTS

Multiple Choice

10. Impacts in the early solar system
    a. brought new materials to the planets.
    b. released energy.
    c. dug craters.
    d. All of the above

11. Which type of planet will have a higher overall density?
    a. one that forms close to the sun
    b. one that forms far from the sun

12. Which process releases the most energy?
    a. nuclear fusion
    b. burning
    c. shrinking due to gravity

13. Which of the following planets has the shortest period of revolution?
    a. Pluto   c. Mercury
    b. Earth   d. Jupiter

14. Which gas in Earth's atmosphere tells us that there is life on Earth?
    a. hydrogen   c. carbon dioxide
    b. oxygen   d. nitrogen

15. Which layer of the Earth has the lowest density?
    a. the core
    b. the mantle
    c. the crust

16. What is the term for the speed of gas molecules?
    a. temperature   c. gravity
    b. pressure   d. force

17. Which of the following objects is least likely to have a spherical shape?
    a. a comet   c. the sun
    b. Venus   d. Jupiter

Short Answer

18. Why did the solar nebula begin to collapse to form the sun and planets if the forces of pressure and gravity were balanced?

19. How is the period of revolution related to the semimajor axis of an orbit? Draw an ellipse and label the semimajor axis.

20. How did our understanding of the sun's energy change over time?

Concept Mapping

21. Use the following terms to create a concept map: solar nebula, solar system, planetesimals, sun, photosphere, core, nuclear fusion, planets, Earth.

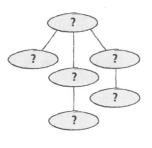

CRITICAL THINKING AND PROBLEM SOLVING

Write one or two sentences to answer the following questions:

22. Explain why nuclear fusion works inside the sun but not inside Jupiter, which is also made mostly of hydrogen and helium.

23. Why is it less expensive to launch an interplanetary spacecraft from the international space station in Earth's orbit than from Earth itself?

24. Soon after the formation of the universe, there was only hydrogen and helium. Heavier elements, such as carbon, oxygen, silicon, and all the matter that makes up the heavier minerals and rocks in the solar system, were made inside an earlier generation of stars. Do you think the first generation of stars had any planets like Earth, Venus, Mercury, and Mars? Explain.

MATH IN SCIENCE

25. Suppose astronomers discover a new planet orbiting our sun. The orbit has a semimajor axis of 2.52 AU. What is the planet's period of revolution?

26. If the planet in the previous question is twice as massive as the Earth but is the same size, how much would a person who weighs 100 lb on Earth weigh on this planet?

INTERPRETING GRAPHICS

Examine the illustration below, and answer the questions that follow.

27. Do you think this is a rocky, inner planet or a gas giant?

28. Did this planet form close to the sun or far from the sun? Explain.

29. Does this planet have an atmosphere? Why or why not?

Reading Check-up

Take a minute to review your answers to the Pre-Reading Questions found at the bottom of page 508. Have your answers changed? If necessary, revise your answers based on what you have learned since you began this chapter.

Science, Technology, and Society

Don't Look at the Sun!

You know you are not supposed to look at the sun, right? But how can we learn anything about the sun if we can't look at it? By using a solar telescope, of course! Where would you find one of these, you ask? Well, if you travel about 70 km southwest of Tucson, Arizona, you will arrive at Kitt Peak National Observatory, where you will find three of them. One telescope in particular has gone to great lengths to give astronomers extraordinary views of the sun!

Top Selection

In 1958, Kitt Peak was chosen from more than 150 mountain ranges to be the site for a national observatory. Located in the Sonoran Desert, Kitt Peak is a part of lands belonging to the Tohono O'odham nation. The McMath-Pierce Facility houses the three largest solar telescopes in the world. Astronomers come from around the globe to use these telescopes. The largest of the three, called the McMath-Pierce telescope, creates an image of the sun that is almost 1 m wide!

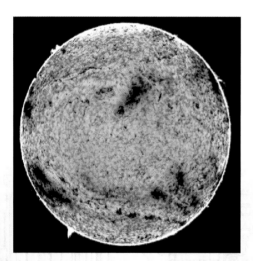

▲ *This is an image of the sun as viewed through the McMath-Pierce solar telescope.*

Too Hot to Handle

Have you ever caught a piece of paper on fire using only a magnifying glass and the rays from the sun? Sunlight that has been focused can produce a great amount of thermal energy—enough to start a fire. Now imagine a magnifying glass 1.6 m in diameter focusing the sun's rays. The resulting heat could melt metal. This is what would happen to a conventional telescope if it were pointed directly at the sun.

To avoid a meltdown, the McMath-Pierce solar telescope uses a mirror that produces a large image of the sun. This mirror directs the sun's rays down a diagonal shaft to another mirror 50 m underground. This mirror is adjustable to focus the sunlight. The sunlight is then directed to a third mirror, which directs the light to an observing room and instrument shaft.

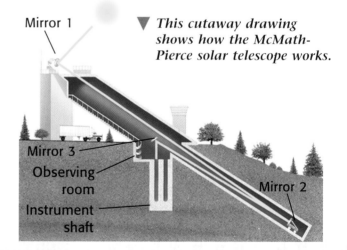

▼ *This cutaway drawing shows how the McMath-Pierce solar telescope works.*

Mirror 1

Mirror 3
Observing room
Instrument shaft

Mirror 2

Scope It Out

▶ Kitt Peak Observatory also has optical telescopes, which differ from solar telescopes. Do some research to find out how optical telescopes work and what the ones at Kitt Peak are used for.

Mirrors in Space

People who live in areas that do not get much sunshine are more prone to health problems such as depression and alcoholism. The people of Siberia, Russia, experience a shortage of sunshine during the winter, when the sun shines only 6 hours on certain days. Could there be a solution to this problem?

A Mirror From *Mir*

In February 1999, the crew of the space station *Mir* was scheduled to insert a large, umbrellalike mirror into orbit. The mirror was designed to reflect sunlight to Siberia. Once placed into orbit, however, problems arose and the crew was unable to unfold the mirror. Had things gone as planned, the beam of reflected sunlight was expected to be

▲ *The end of a winter day in Siberia*

5 to 10 times brighter than the light from the moon. If the first mirror had worked, this would have opened the door for Russia to build many more mirrors that are larger in diameter. These larger mirrors would have been launched into space to lengthen winter days, provide additional heat, and even reduce the amount of electricity used for lighting. The idea of placing mirrors in space, however, caused some serious concerns about the effects it could have.

Overcrowding

The first mirror was about 30 m in diameter. Because it was put in Low Earth Orbit (LEO), the light beam would have been obstructed by the Earth's horizon as the mirror made its orbit. As a result, it would have reflected light on a single area for only about 30 seconds. In order to shine light on Siberia on a large scale, hundreds of larger mirrors would have to be used. But using this many mirrors could result in collisions with satellites that share LEO.

Damage to Ecosystems

It is very difficult to determine what effects extra daylight would have on Siberian ecosystems. Many plants and animals have cycles for various biological functions, such as feeding, sleeping, moving, and reproducing. Extra light and increased temperatures could adversely affect these cycles. Birds might migrate so late that they wouldn't survive the trip across the colder climates because food would be scarce. Plants might sprout too soon and freeze. Arctic ice might melt and cause flooding.

Light Pollution

Astronomers may also be affected by orbiting mirrors. Already astronomers must plan their viewing times to avoid the passing of bright planets and satellites. More sunlight directed toward the Earth would increase light pollution and could make seeing into space more difficult. A string of several hundred mirrors shining light toward the Earth would likely cause additional light pollution in certain locations as the mirrors passed overhead.

What's the Current Status?

▶ Find out more about the Russian project and where it stands now. If you had to decide whether to pursue this project, what would you decide? Why?

Pre-Reading Questions

1. What are the differences between planets, moons, asteroids, comets, and meteoroids?

2. How can surface features tell us about a planet's history?

CLOSE NEIGHBORS IN SPACE

Can you identify the objects in this illustration? The planets and other objects of the solar system appear almost close enough to run into each other. From this perspective, you can easily observe the mysterious and beautiful differences between the planets—in terms of their visible properties. In this chapter, you will study the properties of planets, moons, comets, asteroids, and meteoroids—and learn about eclipses, the moon's phases, and measuring interplanetary distances.

MEASURING SPACE

Earth's distance from the sun is about 150 million kilometers, or 1 AU. *AU* stands for astronomical unit, which is the average distance between Earth and the sun. Do the following exercise to get a better idea of your solar neighborhood.

Procedure

1. Plant a **stake with a flag attached** at the goal line of a **football field**. This stake represents the sun. Then use the table to plant **9 more stakes with flags** representing the position of each planet.

Analysis

2. After you have positioned all the "planets," what do you notice about how the planets are spaced?

Interplanetary Distances		
Planet	**Distance from sun in AU**	**Scaled distance in yards**
Mercury	0.39	1.0
Venus	0.72	1.8
Earth	1.00	2.5
Mars	1.52	3.9
Jupiter	5.20	13.3
Saturn	9.58	24.4
Uranus	19.20	48.9
Neptune	30.05	76.6
Pluto	39.24	100

The Nine Planets

Terms to Learn

astronomical unit (AU)
terrestrial planets
prograde rotation
retrograde rotation
gas giants

What You'll Do

◆ List the names of the planets in the order they orbit the sun.

◆ Describe three ways in which the inner and outer planets are different from each other.

Ancient people knew about the existence of planets and could predict their motions. But it wasn't until the seventeenth century, when Galileo used the telescope to study planets and stars, that we began our first exploration of these alien worlds. Since the former Soviet Union launched *Sputnik 1*—the first artificial satellite—in 1957, over 150 successful missions have been launched to moons, planets, comets, and asteroids. **Figure 1** shows how far we have come since Galileo's time.

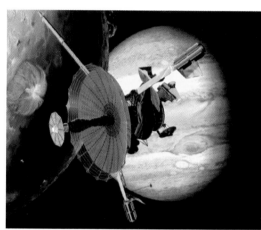

Figure 1 *Galileo Galilei (left) discovered Jupiter's four largest moons using the newly invented telescope in 1610. The Galileo spacecraft (right) arrived at Jupiter on December 7, 1995.*

Galileo Galilei

Measuring Interplanetary Distances

As you have seen, one way scientists measure distances in space is by using the astronomical unit. The **astronomical unit (AU)** is the average distance between the Earth and the sun. Another way to measure distances in space is by the distance light travels in a given amount of time. Light travels at about 300,000 km per second in space. This means that in 1 second, light travels a distance of 300,000 km—or about the distance you would cover if you traveled around Earth 7.5 times.

In 1 minute, light travels nearly 18,000,000 km! This distance is also called 1 *light-minute*. For example, it takes light from the sun 8.3 minutes to reach Earth, so the distance from the Earth to the sun is 8.3 light-minutes. Distances within the solar system can be measured in light-minutes and light-hours, but the distances between stars are measured in light-years!

Figure 2 *One astronomical unit equals about 8.3 light-minutes.*

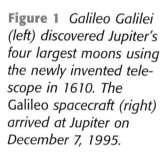

Sun

1 Light-minute

Earth

1 Astronomical unit

The Inner Planets

The solar system is divided into two groups of planets—the inner planets and the outer planets. As you learned from the Investigate, the inner planets are more closely spaced than the outer planets. Other differences between the inner and outer planets are their sizes and the materials of which they are made. The inner planets are called **terrestrial planets** because they are like Earth— small, dense, and rocky. The outer planets, except for icy Pluto, are much larger and are made mostly of gases.

Mercury—Closest to the Sun If you were to visit the planet Mercury, you would find a very strange world. For one thing, on Mercury you would weigh only 38 percent of what you weigh on Earth. The weight you experience on Earth is due to *surface gravity,* which is less on less massive planets. Also, a day on Mercury is almost 59 Earth days long! This is because Mercury spins on its axis much more slowly than Earth does. The spin of an object in space is called *rotation.* The amount of time it takes for an object to rotate once is called its *period of rotation.*

Another curious thing about Mercury is that its year is only 88 Earth days long. As you know, a year is the time it takes for a planet to go around the sun once. The motion of a body as it *orbits* another body in space is called *revolution.* The time it takes for an object to revolve around the sun once is called its *period of revolution.* Every 88 Earth days, or 1.5 Mercurian days, Mercury completes one revolution around the sun.

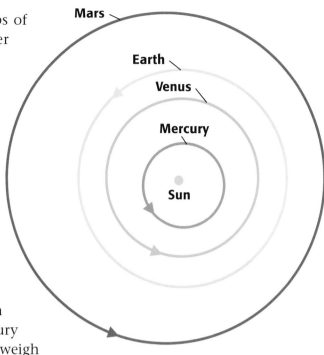

Figure 3 *The lines show orbits of the inner planets. The arrows indicate the direction of motion and the location of each planet on January 1, 2005.*

Figure 4 *This image of Mercury was taken by the* Mariner 10 *spacecraft on March 24, 1974, from a distance of 5,380,000 km.*

Mercury Statistics	
Distance from sun	**3.2** light-minutes
Period of rotation	**58** days, **16** hours
Period of revolution	**88** days
Diameter	**4,879** km
Density	**5.43** g/cm^3
Surface temperature	**−173** to **427**°C
Surface gravity	**38%** of Earth's

Figure 5 *This image of Venus was taken by* Mariner 10 *on February 5, 1974. The uppermost layer of clouds consists of sulfuric acid.*

Venus Statistics	
Distance from sun	**6.0** light-minutes
Period of rotation	**243** days, (R)*
Period of revolution	**224** days, **17** hours
Diameter	**12,104** km
Density	**5.24** g/cm^3
Surface temperature	**464°C**
Surface gravity	**91%** of Earth's

*R = retrograde rotation

Venus—Earth's Twin? In many ways Venus is more similar to Earth than is any other planet—they have about the same size, mass, and density. But in other ways Venus is very different from Earth. Unlike on Earth, on Venus the sun rises in the west and sets in the east. This is because Venus rotates in the opposite direction that Earth rotates. Earth is said to have **prograde rotation,** because when viewed from above its north pole, Earth appears to spin in a *counterclockwise* direction. If a planet spins in a *clockwise* direction, it is said to have **retrograde rotation.**

The Atmosphere of Venus At 90 times the pressure of Earth's atmosphere, the atmosphere of Venus is the densest of the terrestrial planets. It consists mostly of carbon dioxide, but it also contains some of the most corrosive acids known. The carbon dioxide in the atmosphere traps thermal energy from sunlight in a process known as the *greenhouse effect.* This is why the surface temperature is so high. With an average temperature of 464°C, Venus has the hottest surface of any planet in the solar system.

Mapping Venus's Surface Between 1990 and 1992, the *Magellan* spacecraft mapped the surface of Venus by using radar waves. The radar waves traveled through the clouds and bounced off the planet's surface. The radar image in **Figure 6** shows that, like Earth, Venus has an active surface.

Figure 6 *This false-color image of a volcano on the surface of Venus was made with radar data gathered by the* Magellan *spacecraft. Bright areas indicate massive lava flows.*

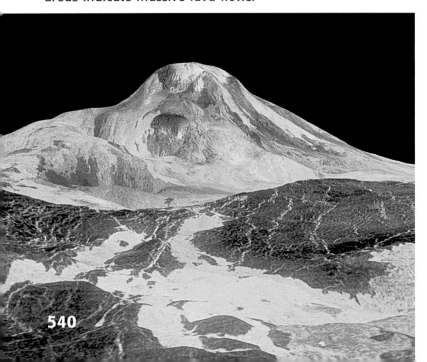

Earth—An Oasis in Space As viewed from space, Earth is like a sparkling blue oasis suspended in a black sea. Constantly changing weather patterns create the swirls of clouds that blanket the blue and brown sphere we call home. Why did Earth have such good fortune while its two nearest neighbors, Venus and Mars, are unsuitable for life as we know it?

Water on Earth Earth is fortunate enough to have formed at just the right distance from the sun. The temperatures are warm enough to prevent most of its water from freezing but cool enough to keep it from boiling away. Liquid water was the key to the development of life on Earth. Water provides a means for much of the chemistry that living things depend on for survival.

The Earth from Space You might think the only goal of space exploration is to make discoveries beyond Earth. But NASA has a program to study Earth using satellites—just as we study other planets. The goal of this project, called the Earth Science Enterprise, is to study the Earth as a system and to determine the effects humans have in changing the global environment. By studying Earth from space, we hope to understand how different parts of the global system—such as weather, climate, and pollution—interact.

Figure 7 *Earth is the only planet we know of that supports life.*

Figure 8 *This image of Earth was taken on December 7, 1972, by the crew of the* Apollo 17 *spacecraft while on their way to the moon.*

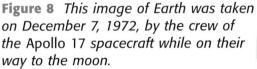

Earth Statistics	
Distance from sun	**8.3** light-minutes
Period of rotation	**23** hours, **56** minutes
Period of revolution	**365** days, **6** hours
Diameter	**12,756** km
Density	**5.52** g/cm^3
Surface temperature	**−13** to **37**°C
Surface gravity	**100%** of Earth's

Mars Statistics	
Distance from sun	**12.7** light-minutes
Period of rotation	**24** hours, **37** minutes
Period of revolution	**1** year, **322** days
Diameter	**6,794** km
Density	**3.93** g/cm^3
Surface temperature	**–123** to **37°C**
Surface gravity	**38%** of Earth's

Figure 9 *This* Viking *orbiter image shows the eastern hemisphere of Mars. The large circular feature in the center is the impact crater Schiaparelli, with a diameter of 450 km.*

Mars—The Red Planet Other than Earth, Mars is perhaps the most studied planet in the solar system. Much of our knowledge of Mars has come from information gathered by the *Viking 1* and *Viking 2* spacecraft that landed on Mars in 1976 and from the *Pathfinder* spacecraft that landed on Mars in 1997.

The Atmosphere of Mars Because of its thin atmosphere and its great distance from the sun, Mars is a cold planet. Mid-summer temperatures recorded by the *Pathfinder* lander ranged from –13°C to –77°C. The atmosphere of Mars is so thin that the air pressure at the planet's surface is roughly equal to the pressure 30 km above Earth's surface—about three times higher than most planes fly. The pressure is so low that any liquid water would quickly boil away. The only water you'll find on Mars is in the form of ice.

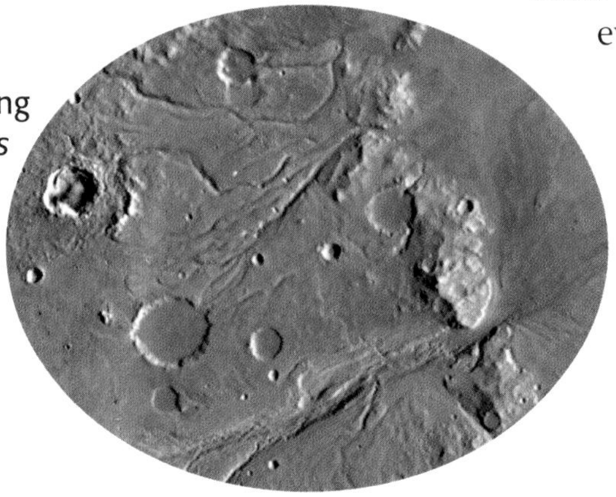

Figure 10 *This* Viking *orbiter image shows a drainage system on Mars formed by running water.*

Water on Mars Even though liquid water cannot exist on Mars's surface today, there is strong evidence that it did exist there in the past! **Figure 10** shows a region on Mars with features that look like dry river beds on Earth. This means that in the past Mars might have been a warmer place with a thicker atmosphere. Where is the water now?

Mars has two polar icecaps that contain both frozen water and frozen carbon dioxide, but this cannot account for all the water. Looking closely at the walls of some Martian craters, scientists have found that the debris surrounding the craters looks as if it were made by a mud flow rather than by the movement of dry material. Where does this suggest some of the "lost" Martian water went? Many scientists think it is frozen beneath the Martian soil.

Martian Volcanoes Mars has a rich volcanic history. Unlike on Earth, where volcanoes occur in many places, Mars has only two large volcanic systems. The largest, the Tharsis region, stretches 8,000 km across the planet. The largest mountain in the solar system, Olympus Mons, is an extinct shield volcano similar to Mauna Kea, on the island of Hawaii. Mars is not only smaller and cooler than Earth, but it also has a slightly different chemical composition. Those factors may have prevented the Martian crust from moving around as Earth's crust has, so the volcanoes kept building up in the same spots. Images and data sent back by probes like the *Sojourner* rover, shown in **Figure 11,** are helping to explain Mars's mysterious past.

Physics

C O N N E C T I O N

At sea level on Earth's surface, water boils at 100°C, but if you try to boil water on top of a high mountain, you will find that the boiling point is lower than 100°C. This is because the atmospheric pressure is less at high altitude. The atmospheric pressure on the surface of Mars is so low that liquid water can't exist at all!

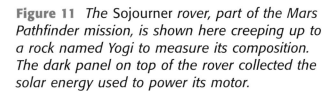

Figure 11 *The* Sojourner *rover, part of the Mars Pathfinder mission, is shown here creeping up to a rock named Yogi to measure its composition. The dark panel on top of the rover collected the solar energy used to power its motor.*

REVIEW

1. What three characteristics do the inner planets have in common?

2. List three differences and three similarities between Venus and Earth.

3. **Analyzing Relationships** Mercury is closest to the sun, yet Venus has a higher surface temperature. Explain why this is so.

The Outer Planets

The outer planets differ significantly in composition and size from the inner planets. All of the outer planets, except for Pluto, are gas giants. **Gas giants** are very large planets that don't have any known solid surfaces—their atmospheres blend smoothly into the denser layers of their interiors, very deep beneath the outer layers.

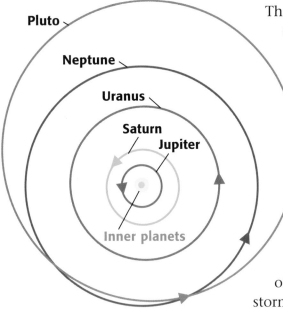

Figure 12 *This view of the solar system shows the orbits and positions of the outer planets on January 1, 2005.*

Figure 13 *This* Voyager 2 *image of Jupiter was taken at a distance of 28.4 million kilometers. Io, one of Jupiter's largest moons, can also be seen in this image.*

Jupiter—A Giant Among Giants Like the sun, Jupiter is made primarily of hydrogen and helium. The outer part of Jupiter's atmosphere is made of layered clouds of water, methane, and ammonia. The beautiful colors in **Figure 13** are probably due to trace amounts of organic compounds. Another striking feature of Jupiter is the Great Red Spot, which is a long-lasting storm system that has a diameter of about one and a half times that of Earth! At a depth of about 10,000 km, the pressure is high enough to change hydrogen gas into a liquid. Deeper still, the pressure changes the liquid hydrogen into a metallic liquid state. Unlike most planets, Jupiter radiates much more energy into space than it receives from the sun. This is because energy is continuously transported from Jupiter's interior to its outer atmospheric layers, where it is radiated into space.

NASA Missions to Jupiter There have been five NASA missions to Jupiter—two Pioneer missions, two Voyager missions, and the recent Galileo mission. The *Voyager 1* and *Voyager 2* spacecraft sent back images that revealed a thin faint ring around the planet, as well as the first detailed images of its moons. The *Galileo* spacecraft reached Jupiter in 1995 and released a probe that plunged into Jupiter's atmosphere. The probe sent back data on the atmosphere's composition, temperature, and pressure.

Jupiter Statistics	
Distance from sun	**43.3** light-minutes
Period of rotation	**9** hours, **56** minutes
Period of revolution	**11** years, **313** days
Diameter	**142,984** km
Density	**1.33** g/cm³
Temperature	**−153°C**
Gravity	**236%** of Earth's

Saturn Statistics	
Distance from sun	**1.3** light-hours
Period of rotation	**10** hours, **39** minutes
Period of revolution	**29** years, **155** days
Diameter	**120,536** km
Density	**0.69** g/cm^3
Temperature	**−185°C**
Gravity	**92%** of Earth's

Saturn—Still Forming Saturn, the second largest planet in the solar system, has roughly 764 times the volume of Earth and is 95 times more massive. Its overall composition, like Jupiter's, is mostly hydrogen and helium, with methane, ammonia, and ethane in the upper atmosphere. Saturn's interior is probably very similar to that of Jupiter. Like Jupiter, Saturn gives off a lot more energy than it receives from the sun. Scientists believe that, in Saturn's case, the extra energy is caused by helium raining out of the atmosphere and sinking to the core. In essence, Saturn is still forming!

The Rings of Saturn Although all of the gas giants have rings, Saturn's rings are the largest. Saturn's rings start near the top of Saturn's atmosphere and extend out 136,000 km, yet they are only a few hundred meters thick. The rings consist of icy particles that range in size from a few centimeters to several meters across. **Figure 15** shows a close-up view of Saturn's rings.

NASA Goes to Saturn Launched in 1997, the *Cassini* spacecraft is designed to study Saturn's rings, its moons, and its atmosphere. It will return more than 300,000 color images, beginning in 2004.

Figure 14 *This* Voyager 2 *image of Saturn was taken from 21 million kilometers away. The dot you see below the rings is the shadow of Tethys, one of Saturn's moons.*

Figure 15 *The different colors in this* Voyager 2 *image of Saturn's rings show differences in the chemical composition.*

Figure 16 *This image of Uranus was taken by* Voyager 2 *at a distance of 9.1 million kilometers.*

Uranus Statistics	
Distance from sun	**2.7** light-hours
Period of rotation	**17** hours, **14** minutes (R)*
Period of revolution	**83** years, **274** days
Diameter	**51,118** km
Density	**1.27** g/cm^3
Temperature	**−214**°C
Gravity	**89%** of Earth's

*R = retrograde rotation

Uranus—A Small Giant Uranus (YOOR uh nuhs) was discovered by the English amateur astronomer William Herschel in 1781. Viewed through a telescope, Uranus looks like a feature-less blue-green disk. The atmosphere is mainly hydrogen and methane gas, which absorbs the red part of sunlight very strongly. Uranus and Neptune are much smaller than Jupiter and Saturn, and yet they have similar densities. This suggests that they have lower percentages of light elements and more water in their interiors.

A Tilted Planet Uranus has about 63 times the volume of Earth and is nearly 15 times as massive. One especially unusual quality of Uranus is that it is tipped over on its side—the axis of rotation is tilted by almost 90° and lies almost in the plane of its orbit. **Figure 17** shows how far Uranus's axis is inclined. For part of a Uranus year, one pole points toward the sun while the other pole is in darkness. At the other end of Uranus's orbit the poles are reversed. Scientists suggest that early in its history, Uranus got hit by a massive object that tipped the planet over.

Figure 17 *Uranus's axis of rotation is tilted so that it is nearly parallel to the plane of Uranus's orbit. In contrast, the axes of most other planets are closer to being perpendicular to the plane of their orbits.*

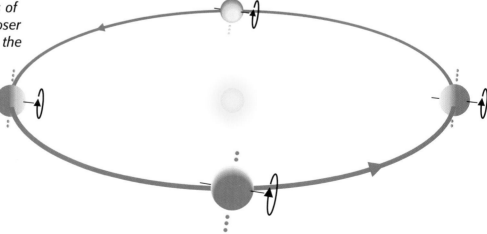

Surviving Space

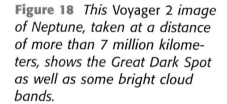

Neptune—The Blue World Irregularities in the orbit of Uranus suggested to early astronomers that there must be another planet beyond Uranus whose gravitational force causes Uranus to move off its predicted path. By using the predictions of the new planet's orbit, astronomers discovered the planet Neptune in 1846.

The Atmosphere of Neptune The *Voyager 2* spacecraft sent back images that gave us much new information about the nature of Neptune's atmosphere. Although the composition of Neptune's atmosphere is nearly the same as that of Uranus's atmosphere, Neptune's atmosphere contains belts of clouds that are much more visible. At the time of *Voyager 2*'s visit, Neptune had a Great Dark Spot, similar to the Great Red Spot on Jupiter. And like the interiors of Jupiter and Saturn, Neptune's interior releases energy to its outer layers. This helps the warm gases rise and the cool gases sink, setting up the wind patterns in the atmosphere that create the belts of clouds. *Voyager 2* images also revealed that Neptune has a set of very narrow rings.

Figure 18 *This* Voyager 2 *image of Neptune, taken at a distance of more than 7 million kilometers, shows the Great Dark Spot as well as some bright cloud bands.*

Neptune Statistics	
Distance from sun	**4.2** light-hours
Period of rotation	**16** hours, **7** minutes
Period of revolution	**163** years, **265** days
Diameter	**49,528** km
Density	**1.64** g/cm³
Temperature	**−225°C**
Gravity	**112%** of Earth's

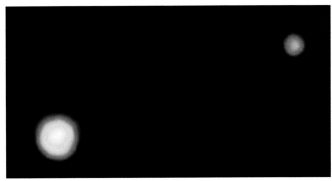

Pluto Statistics	
Distance from sun	**5.5** light-hours
Period of rotation	**6** days, **9** hours (R)*
Period of revolution	**248** years
Diameter	**2,390** km
Density	**2.05** g/cm³
Surface temperature	**−236°C**
Surface gravity	**6%** of Earth's

*R = retrograde rotation

Figure 19 *This Hubble Space Telescope image is one of the clearest ever taken of Pluto (left) and its moon, Charon.*

Figure 20 *An artist's view of the sun and Charon from Pluto shows just how little light and heat Pluto receives from the sun.*

Pluto—A Double Planet? Pluto is the farthest planet from the sun. It is also the smallest planet—less than half the size of Mercury. Another reason Pluto is unusual is that its moon, Charon (KER uhn), is more than half its size! In fact, Charon is the largest satellite relative to its planet in the solar system. **Figure 19** shows Pluto and Charon together.

From Earth, it is hard to separate the images of Pluto and Charon because they are so far away. **Figure 20** shows just how far away from the sun Pluto and Charon really are—from the surface of Pluto the sun appears to be only a very distant, bright star.

From calculations of Pluto's density, we know that it must be made of rock and ice. A very thin atmosphere of methane has been detected. While Pluto is covered by nitrogen ice, Charon is covered by water ice. Pluto is the only planet that has not been visited by a NASA mission, but plans are underway to finally visit this world and its moon in 2010.

REVIEW

1. How are the gas giants different from the terrestrial planets?

2. What is so unusual about Uranus's axis of rotation?

3. What conclusion can you draw about a planet's properties just by knowing how far it is from the sun?

4. **Applying Concepts** Why is the word *surface* not included in the statistics for the gas giants?

Moons

Terms to Learn

satellite
phases
eclipse

What You'll Do

◆ Describe the current theory for the origin of Earth's moon.
◆ Describe what causes the phases of Earth's moon.
◆ Explain the difference between a solar eclipse and a lunar eclipse.

Satellites are natural or artificial bodies that revolve around larger bodies like planets. Except for Mercury and Venus, all of the planets have natural satellites called *moons.*

Luna: The Moon of Earth

We know that Earth's moon—also called *Luna*—has a different overall composition from the Earth because its density is much less than Earth's. This tells us that the moon has a lower percentage of heavy elements than the Earth has. The composition of lunar rocks brought back by Apollo astronauts suggests that the composition of the moon is similar to that of the Earth's mantle.

The Surface of the Moon The explorations of the moon's surface by the Apollo astronauts have given us insights about other planets and moons of the solar system. For example, the lunar rocks brought back during the Apollo missions were found to be about 4.6 billion years old. Because these rocks have hardly changed since they formed, we know the solar system itself is about 4.6 billion years old.

In addition, we know that the surfaces of bodies that have no atmospheres preserve a record of almost all the impacts they have had with other objects. As shown in **Figure 22,** the moon's history is written on its face! Because we now know the age of the moon, we can count the number of impact craters on the moon and use that number to calculate the rate of cratering that has occurred since the birth of our solar system. By knowing the rate of cratering, scientists are able to use the number of craters on the surface of any body to estimate how old its surface is—without having to bring back rock samples!

Figure 21 Apollo 17 *astronaut Harrison Schmidt—the first geologist to walk on the moon—samples the lunar soil.*

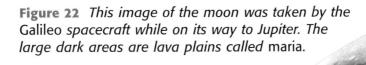

Figure 22 *This image of the moon was taken by the* Galileo *spacecraft while on its way to Jupiter. The large dark areas are lava plains called* maria.

Moon Statistics	
Period of rotation	**27** days, **8** hours
Period of revolution	**27** days, **8** hours
Diameter	**3,476** km
Density	**3.34** g/cm³
Surface temperature	**−170** to **134°**C
Surface gravity	**17%** of Earth's

Physics
C O N N E C T I O N

Did you know that the moon is falling? It's true. Because of gravity, every object in orbit around Earth is falling toward the planet. But the moon is also moving forward at the same time. The combination of the moon's forward motion and its falling motion results in the moon's curved orbit around Earth.

Lunar Origins Before rock samples from the Apollo missions confirmed the composition of the moon, there were three popular explanations for the formation of the moon: (1) it was a separate body captured by Earth's gravity, (2) it formed at the same time and from the same materials as the Earth, and (3) the newly formed Earth was spinning so fast that a piece flew off and became the moon. Each idea had problems. If the moon were captured by Earth's gravity, it would have a completely different composition from that of Earth, which is not the case. On the other hand, if the moon formed at the same time as the Earth or as a spin off of the Earth, the moon would have exactly the same composition as Earth, which it doesn't.

The current theory is that a large, Mars-sized object collided with Earth while the Earth was still forming. The collision was so violent that part of the Earth's mantle was blasted into orbit around Earth to form the moon. This theory is consistent with the composition of the lunar rocks brought back by the Apollo missions.

Formation of the Moon

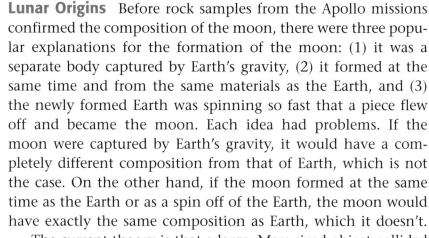

1 Impact
About 4.6 billion years ago, when Earth was still mostly molten, a large body collided with Earth. Scientists reason that the object must have been large enough to blast part of Earth's mantle into space, because the composition of the moon is similar to Earth's mantle.

2 Ejection
The resulting debris began to revolve around the Earth within a few hours of the impact. This debris consisted of mantle material from Earth and the impacting body as well as part of the iron core of the impacting body.

3 Formation
Soon after the giant impact, the clumps of material ejected into orbit around Earth began to join together to form the moon. Much later, as the moon cooled, additional impacts created deep basins and fractured the moon's surface. Lunar lava flowed from those cracks and flooded the basins to form the lunar maria we see today.

Phases of the Moon From Earth, one of the most noticeable aspects of the moon is its continually changing appearance. Within a month, its Earthward face changes from a fully lit circle to a thin crescent and then back to a circle. These different appearances of the moon result from its changing position with respect to the Earth and the sun. As the moon revolves around the Earth, the amount of sunlight on the side of the moon that faces the Earth changes. The different appearances of the moon due to its changing position are called **phases.** The phases of the moon are shown in **Figure 23.**

The moon's appearance changes every night. To find out how this occurs, turn to page 717 in your LabBook.

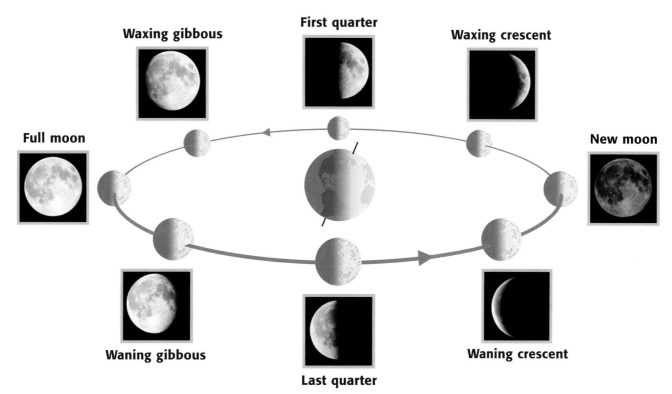

Figure 23 *The relative positions of the moon, sun, and Earth determine which phase the moon is in. The photo insets show how the moon looks from Earth at each phase.*

Waxing and Waning When the moon is *waxing*, it means that the sunlit fraction we can see from Earth is getting larger. When it is *waning*, the sunlit fraction is getting smaller. Notice in Figure 23 that even as the phases of the moon change, the total amount of sunlight the moon gets remains the same. Half the moon is always in sunlight, just as half the Earth is always in sunlight. But because the period of rotation for the moon is the same as its period of revolution, on Earth we always see the same side of the moon. If you lived on the far side of the moon, you would see the sun for half of each lunar day, but you would never see the Earth!

Eclipses An **eclipse** occurs when the shadow of one celestial body falls on another. A *lunar eclipse* happens when the Earth comes between the sun and the moon, and the shadow of the Earth falls on the moon. A *solar eclipse* happens when the moon comes between the Earth and the sun, and the shadow of the moon falls on part of Earth.

Solar Eclipses By a remarkable coincidence, the moon in the sky appears to be nearly the same size as the sun. So during a solar eclipse, the disk of the moon almost always covers the disk of the sun. However, because the moon's orbit is not completely circular, sometimes the moon is farther away from the Earth, and a thin ring of sunlight shows around the outer edge of the moon. This type of solar eclipse is called an *annular eclipse.* **Figure 24** illustrates the position of the Earth and the moon during a solar eclipse.

Solar eclipse

Figure 24 *Because the shadow of the moon on Earth is small, a solar eclipse can be viewed from only a few locations.*

NEVER look directly at the sun! You can permanently damage your eyes.

Figure 25 *This is an image of the sun's corona during the February 26, 1998, eclipse in the Caribbean. The solar corona is visible only when the entire disk of the sun is blocked by the moon.*

Lunar Eclipses As you can see in **Figure 26,** the view during a lunar eclipse is also spectacular. Earth's atmosphere acts like a lens and bends some of the sunlight into the Earth's shadow, and the interaction of the sunlight with the molecules in the atmosphere filters out the blue light. With the blue part of the light removed, most of the remaining light that illuminates the moon is red.

Lunar eclipse

Figure 26 *Because of atmospheric effects on Earth, the moon can have a reddish color during a lunar eclipse.*

Figure 27 *During a lunar eclipse, the moon passes within the Earth's shadow.*

The Moon's Orbit Is Tilted! From our discussion of the moon's phases, you might now be asking the question, "Why don't we see solar and lunar eclipses every month?" The answer is that the moon's orbit around the Earth is tilted—by about 5°—with respect to the orbit of the Earth around the sun. This tilt is enough to place the moon out of Earth's shadow for most full moons and the Earth out of the moon's shadow for most new moons.

REVIEW

1. What evidence suggests that Earth's moon formed from a giant impact?

2. Why do we always see the same side of the moon?

3. How are lunar eclipses different from solar eclipses?

4. **Analyzing Methods** How does knowing the age of a lunar rock help astronomers estimate the age of the surface of a planet like Mercury?

MATH BREAK

Orbits Within Orbits

The average distance between the Earth and the moon is about 384,400 km. As you have read, the average distance between the Earth and the sun is 1 AU, or about 150,000,000 km. Assume that the orbit of the Earth around the sun and the orbit of the moon around the Earth are perfectly circular. Using the distances given above, calculate the maximum and minimum distances between the moon and the sun.

The Moons of Other Planets

The moons of the other planets range in size from very small to as large as terrestrial planets. All of the gas giants have multiple moons, and scientists are still discovering new moons. Some moons have very elongated, or elliptical, orbits, and some even revolve around their planet backward! Many of the very small moons may be captured asteroids. As we are learning from recent space missions, moons can be some of the most bizarre and interesting places in the solar system!

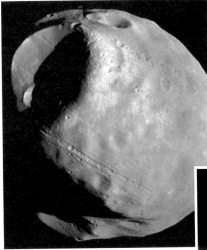

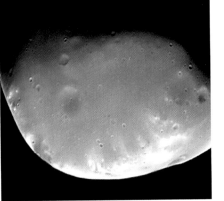

Figure 28 *Above is Mars's largest moon, Phobos, which is 28 km long. At right is the smaller moon, Deimos, which is 16 km long.*

The Moons of Mars Mars's two moons, Phobos and Deimos, are both small satellites that have irregular shapes. The two moons have very dark surfaces that reflect even less light than asphalt does. The surface materials are very similar to those found in asteroids, and scientists speculate that these two moons are probably captured asteroids.

The Moons of Jupiter Jupiter has dozens of known moons. The four largest—Ganymede, Callisto, Io, and Europa—were discovered in 1610 by Galileo and are known as the Galilean satellites. The largest moon, Ganymede, is even larger than the planet Mercury! Many of the smaller satellites are probably captured asteroids.

Moving outward from Jupiter, the first Galilean satellite is Io (IE oh), a truly bizarre world. Io is caught in a gravitational tug-of-war between Jupiter and Io's nearest neighbor, the moon Europa. This constant tugging stretches Io a little, causing it to heat up. Because of this, Io is the most volcanically active body in the solar system!

Recent pictures of the moon Europa support the idea that liquid water may lie beneath the moon's icy surface. This has many scientists wondering if life could have evolved in the subterranean oceans of Europa.

Figure 29 *At left is a* Galileo *image of Jupiter's innermost moon, Io. At right is a* Galileo *image of Jupiter's fourth largest moon, Europa.*

The Moons of Saturn Like Jupiter, Saturn also has dozens of moons. Most of these moons are small bodies made mostly of water ice with some rocky material. The largest satellite, Titan, was discovered in 1655 by Christiaan Huygens. In 1980, the *Voyager 1* spacecraft flew past Titan and discovered a hazy orange atmosphere, as shown in **Figure 30.** Titan's atmosphere is similar to what Earth's atmosphere may have been like before life began to evolve. In 1997, NASA launched the *Cassini* spacecraft to study Saturn and its moons, including Titan. By studying Titan, scientists hope to answer some of the questions about how life began on Earth.

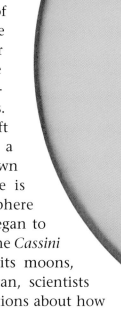

Figure 30 *Titan is one of only two moons that have a thick atmosphere. Titan's hazy orange atmosphere is made of nitrogen plus several other gases, such as methane.*

Self-Check

What is one major difference between Titan and the early Earth that would suggest that there probably isn't life on Titan? *(See page 726 to check your answer.)*

The Moons of Uranus Uranus has more than 20 moons. Like the moons of Saturn, the four largest moons are made of ice and rock and are heavily cratered. The little moon Miranda, shown in **Figure 31,** has some of the most unusual features in the solar system. Miranda's surface includes smooth, cratered plains as well as regions with grooves and cliffs up to 20 km high. Current ideas suggest that Miranda may have been hit and broken apart in the past but was able to come together again, leaving a patchwork surface.

Figure 31 *This* Voyager 2 *image shows Miranda, the most unusual moon of Uranus. Its patchwork terrain indicates that it has had a violent history.*

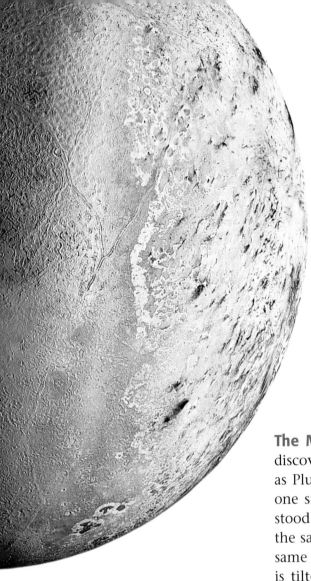

The Moons of Neptune Neptune has eight known moons, only one of which is large. This moon, Triton, revolves around the planet in a *retrograde,* or "backward," orbit, suggesting that it may have been captured by Neptune's gravity. Triton has a very thin atmosphere made mostly of nitrogen gas. The surface of Triton consists mainly of frozen nitrogen and methane. *Voyager 2* images revealed that it is geologically active. "Ice volcanoes," or geysers, were seen ejecting nitrogen gas high into the atmosphere. The other seven moons of Neptune are small, rocky worlds much like the smaller moons of Saturn and Jupiter.

Figure 32 *This* Voyager 2 *image shows Neptune's largest moon, Triton. The polar icecap currently facing the sun may have a slowly evaporating layer of nitrogen ice, adding to Triton's thin atmosphere.*

The Moon of Pluto Pluto's only known moon, Charon, was discovered in 1978. Charon's period of revolution is the same as Pluto's period of rotation—about 6.4 days. This means that one side of Pluto always faces Charon. In other words, if you stood on the surface of Pluto, Charon would always occupy the same place in the sky. Imagine Earth's moon staying in the same place every night! Because Charon's orbit around Pluto is tilted with respect to Pluto's orbit around the sun, as seen from Earth, Pluto is sometimes eclipsed by Charon. But don't hold your breath; this happens only once every 120 years!

REVIEW

1. What makes Io the most volcanically active body in the solar system?

2. Why is Saturn's moon Titan of so much interest to scientists studying the origins of life on Earth?

3. What two properties of Neptune's moon Triton make it unusual?

4. **Identifying Relationships** Charon always stays in the same place in Pluto's sky, but the moon always moves across Earth's sky. What causes this difference?

What You'll Do

◆ Explain why comets, asteroids, and meteoroids are important to the study of the formation of the solar system.

◆ Compare the different types of asteroids with the different types of meteoroids.

◆ Describe the risks to life on Earth from cosmic impacts.

Small Bodies in the Solar System

In addition to planets and moons, the solar system contains many other types of objects, including comets, asteroids, and meteoroids. As you will see, these objects play an important role in the study of the origins of the solar system.

Comets

A **comet** is a small body of ice, rock, and cosmic dust loosely packed together. Because of their composition, some scientists refer to comets as "dirty snowballs." Comets originate from the cold, outer solar system. Nothing much has happened to them since the birth of the solar system some 4.6 billion years ago. Because comets are probably the leftovers from the process of planet formation, each comet is a sample of the early solar system. Scientists want to learn more about comets in order to piece together the chemical and physical history of the solar system.

Comet Tails When a comet passes close enough to the sun, solar radiation heats the water ice so that the comet gives off gas and dust in the form of a long tail, as shown in **Figure 33.** Sometimes a comet has two tails—an *ion tail* and a *dust tail*. The ion tail consists of electrically charged particles called *ions*. The solid center of a comet is called its *nucleus*. Comet nuclei can range in size from less than half a kilometer to more than 100 km in diameter. **Figure 34** shows the different features of a comet when it passes close to the sun.

Figure 33 *Comet Hale-Bopp appeared in North American skies in the spring of 1997.*

Nucleus

Ion tail

Dust tail

Figure 34 *This image shows the physical features of a comet when it is close to the sun. The nucleus of a comet is hidden by brightly lit gases and dust.*

557

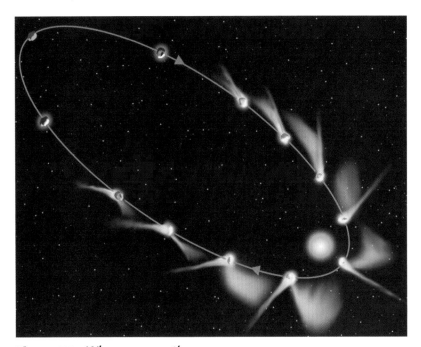

Figure 35 *When a comet's highly elliptical orbit carries it close to the sun, it can develop one or two tails. As shown here, the ion tail is blue and the dust tail is yellow.*

Comet Orbits   All orbits are *ellipses*—circles that are somewhat stretched out of shape. Whereas the orbits of most planets are nearly circular, comet orbits are highly elliptical—they are very elongated.

Notice in **Figure 35** that a comet's ion tail always points directly away from the sun. This is because the ion tail is blown away from the sun by the solar wind, which also consists of ions. The dust tail tends to follow the comet's orbit around the sun and does not always point away from the sun. When a comet is close to the sun its tail can extend millions of kilometers through space!

Comet Origins Where do comets come from? Many scientists think they may come from a spherical region, called the *Oort* (ohrt) *cloud,* that surrounds the solar system. When the gravity of a passing planet or star disturbs part of this cloud, comets can be pulled in toward the sun. Another recently discovered region where comets exist is called the *Kuiper* (KIE per) *belt,* which is the region outside the orbit of Neptune. These two regions where comets orbit are shown in **Figure 36.**

Figure 36 *The Kuiper belt is a disk-shaped region that extends outward from the orbit of Neptune. The Oort cloud is a spherical region far beyond the orbit of Pluto.*

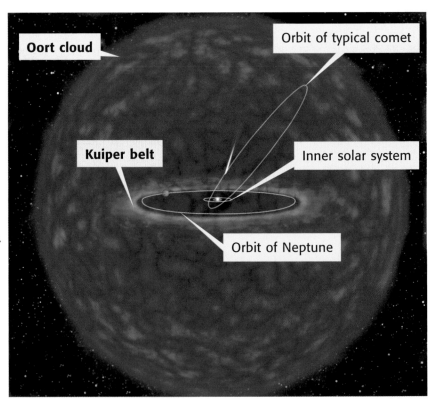

Oort cloud

Orbit of typical comet

Kuiper belt

Inner solar system

Orbit of Neptune

Asteroids

Asteroids are small, rocky bodies in orbit around the sun. They range in size from a few meters to more than 900 km in diameter. Asteroids have irregular shapes, although some of the larger ones are spherical. Most asteroids orbit the sun in a wide region between the orbits of Mars and Jupiter, called the **asteroid belt.** Like comets, asteroids are thought to be material left over from the formation of the solar system.

Types of Asteroids Asteroids can have a variety of compositions, depending on where they are located within the asteroid belt. In the outermost region of the asteroid belt, asteroids have dark reddish brown to black surfaces, which may indicate that they are rich in organic material. A little closer to the sun, asteroids have dark gray surfaces, indicating that they are rich in carbon. In the innermost part of the asteroid belt are light gray asteroids that have either a stony or metallic composition. **Figure 38** shows some examples of what some of the asteroids may look like.

Figure 37 *The asteroid Ida has a small companion asteroid that orbits it called Dactyl. Ida is about 52 km long.*

Figure 38 *The asteroid belt is a disk-shaped region located between the orbits of Mars and Jupiter.*

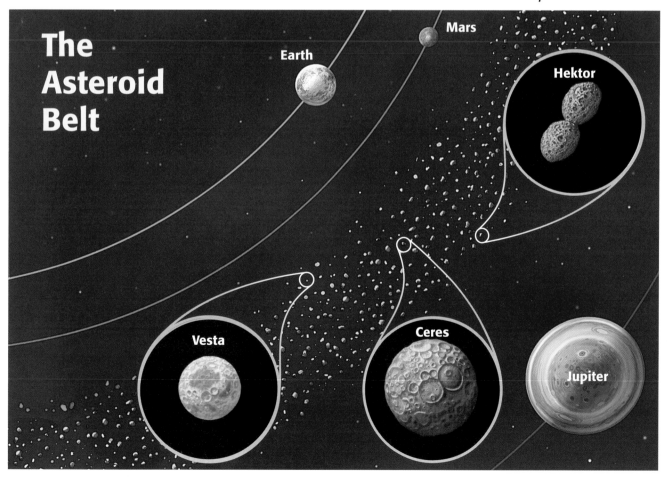

The Asteroid Belt

Mars
Earth
Hektor
Vesta
Ceres
Jupiter

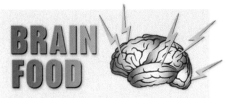

Figure 39 *Meteors are the streaks of light caused by meteoroids as they burn up in Earth's atmosphere.*

Meteoroids

A **meteoroid** is a small, rocky body orbiting the sun. Meteoroids are similar to asteroids, but they are much smaller. In fact, most meteoroids probably come from asteroids. If a meteoroid enters Earth's atmosphere and strikes the ground, it is then called a **meteorite.** When a meteoroid falls into Earth's atmosphere, it is usually traveling at such a high speed that its surface heats up and melts. As it burns up, the meteoroid glows red hot and gives off an enormous amount of light. From the ground, we see a spectacular streak of light, or a shooting star. The bright streak of light caused by a meteoroid or comet dust burning up in the atmosphere is called a **meteor.**

Meteor Showers Many of the meteors that we see come from very small (dust-sized to pebble-sized) rocks and can be seen on almost any night if you are far enough away from the city to avoid the glare of its lights. At certain times of the year, you can see large numbers of meteors, as shown in **Figure 39.** These events are called *meteor showers.* Meteor showers occur when Earth passes through the dusty debris left behind in the orbit of a comet.

Types of Meteorites Like their relatives the asteroids, meteorites have a variety of compositions. The three major types of meteorites—stony, metallic, and stony-iron—are shown in **Figure 40.** Many of the stony meteorites probably come from carbon-rich asteroids and may contain organic materials and water. Scientists use meteorites to study the early solar system. Like comets and asteroids, meteoroids are some of the building blocks of planets.

Figure 40 *There are three major types of meteorites.*

Stony meteorite
rocky material

Metallic meteorite
iron and nickel

Stony-iron meteorite
rocky material, iron, and nickel

The Role of Impacts in the Solar System

Planets and moons that have no atmosphere have many more impact craters than those that do have atmospheres. Look at **Figure 41.** The Earth's moon has many more impact craters than the Earth because it has no atmosphere or tectonic activity. Fewer objects land on Earth because Earth's atmosphere acts like a shield. Smaller bodies burn up before they ever reach the surface. On the moon, there is nothing to stop them! Also, most craters left on Earth have been erased due to weathering, erosion, and tectonic activity.

Figure 41 *The surface of the moon preserves a record of billions of years of cosmic impacts.*

Impacts on Earth Objects smaller than about 10 m across usually burn up in the atmosphere, causing a meteor. Larger objects are more likely to strike Earth's surface. In order to estimate the risk of cosmic impacts, we need to consider how often large impacts occur.

The number of large objects that could collide with Earth is relatively small. Scientists estimate that impacts powerful enough to cause a natural disaster might occur once every few thousand years. An impact large enough to cause a global catastrophe—such as the extinction of the dinosaurs—is estimated to occur once every 30 million to 50 million years on average.

REVIEW

1. Why is the study of comets, asteroids, and meteoroids important in understanding the formation of the solar system?

2. Why do a comet's two tails often point in different directions?

3. Describe one reason asteroids may become a natural resource in the future.

4. **Analyzing Viewpoints** Do you think the government should spend money on programs to search for asteroids and comets with Earth-crossing orbits? Discuss why.

internet connect

*SC*LINKS.
NSTA

TOPIC: Comets, Asteroids, and Meteoroids
GO TO: www.scilinks.org
*sci*LINKS NUMBER: HSTE500

Chapter Highlights

Vocabulary

astronomical unit (AU) *(p. 538)*

terrestrial planets *(p. 539)*

prograde rotation *(p. 540)*

retrograde rotation *(p. 540)*

gas giants *(p. 544)*

Section Notes

- The solar system has nine planets.

- Distances within the solar system can be expressed in astronomical units (AU) or in light-minutes.

- The inner four planets, called the terrestrial planets, are small and rocky.

- The outer planets, with the exception of Pluto, are gas giants.

- By learning about the properties of the planets, we get a better understanding of global processes on Earth.

Labs

Why Do They Wander? *(p. 714)*

Vocabulary

satellite *(p. 549)*

phases *(p. 551)*

eclipse *(p. 552)*

Section Notes

- Earth's moon probably formed from a giant impact on Earth.

- The moon's phases are caused by the moon's orbit around the Earth. At different times of the month, we view different amounts of sunlight on the moon because of the moon's position relative to the sun and the Earth.

- Lunar eclipses occur when the Earth's shadow falls on the moon.

☑ Skills Check

Math Concepts

INTERPLANETARY DISTANCES The distances between planets are so vast that scientists have invented new units of measurement to describe them. One of these units is the astronomical unit (AU). One AU is equal to the average distance between the Earth and the sun—about 150 million kilometers. If you wanted to get to the sun from the Earth in 10 hours, you would have to travel at a rate of 15,000,000 km/h!

$$\frac{150 \text{ million kilometers}}{15 \text{ million kilometers/hour}} = 10 \text{ hours}$$

Visual Understanding

AXIAL TILT A planet's axis of rotation is an imaginary line that runs through the center of the planet and comes out its north and south poles. The tilt of a planet's axis is the angle between the planet's axis and the plane of the planet's orbit around the sun.

- Solar eclipses occur when the moon is between the sun and the Earth, causing the moon's shadow to fall on the Earth.

- The plane of the moon's orbit around the Earth is tilted by 5° relative to the plane of the Earth's orbit around the sun.

Labs

Eclipses *(p. 716)*

Phases of the Moon *(p. 717)*

Vocabulary

comet *(p. 557)*

asteroid *(p. 559)*

asteroid belt *(p. 559)*

meteoroid *(p. 560)*

meteorite *(p. 560)*

meteor *(p. 560)*

Section Notes

- Comets are small bodies of water ice and cosmic dust left over from the formation of the solar system.

- When a comet is heated by the sun, the ices convert to gases that leave the nucleus and form an ion tail. Dust also comes off a comet to form a second kind of tail called a dust tail.

- All orbits are ellipses—circles that have been stretched out.

- Asteroids are small, rocky bodies that orbit the sun between the orbits of Mars and Jupiter.

- Meteoroids are small, rocky bodies that probably come from asteroids.

- Meteor showers occur when Earth passes through the dusty debris along a comet's orbit.

- Impacts that cause natural disasters occur once every few thousand years, but impacts large enough to cause global extinctions occur once every 30 million to 50 million years.

---

internetconnect

GO TO: go.hrw.com

Visit the **HRW** Web site for a variety of learning tools related to this chapter. Just type in the keyword:

KEYWORD: HSTFAM

GO TO: www.scilinks.org

Visit the **National Science Teachers Association** on-line Web site for Internet resources related to this chapter. Just type in the *sci*LINKS number for more information about the topic:

TOPIC:	sciLINKS NUMBER:
The Nine Planets	HSTE480
Studying Earth from Space	HSTE485
The Earth's Moon	HSTE490
The Moons of Other Planets	HSTE495
Comets, Asteroids, and Meteoroids	HSTE500

Chapter Review

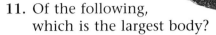

USING VOCABULARY

For each pair of terms, explain the difference in their meaning.

1. terrestrial planet/gas giant

2. asteroid/comet

3. meteor/meteorite

4. satellite/moon

5. Kuiper belt/Oort cloud

To complete the following sentences, choose the correct term from each pair of terms listed below:

6. The average distance between the sun and the Earth is 1 __?__ . *(light-minute* or *AU)*

7. A small rock in space is called a __?__ . *(meteor* or *meteoroid)*

8. The time it takes for the Earth to __?__ around the sun is one year. *(rotate* or *revolve)*

9. Most lunar craters are the result of __?__ . *(volcanoes* or *impacts)*

UNDERSTANDING CONCEPTS

Multiple Choice

10. When do annular eclipses occur?
    a. every solar eclipse
    b. when the moon is closest to the Earth
    c. only during full moon
    d. when the moon is farthest from the Earth

11. Of the following, which is the largest body?
    a. the moon
    b. Pluto
    c. Mercury
    d. Ganymede

12. Which is not true about impacts?
    a. They are very destructive.
    b. They can bring water to dry worlds.
    c. They only occurred as the solar system formed.
    d. They can help us do remote geology.

13. Which of these planets does not have any moons?
    a. Mercury
    b. Mars
    c. Uranus
    d. none of the above

14. What is the most current theory for the formation of Earth's moon?
    a. The moon formed from a collision between another body and the Earth.
    b. The moon was captured by the Earth.
    c. The moon formed at the same time as the Earth.
    d. The moon formed by spinning off from the Earth early in its history.

15. Liquid water cannot exist on the surface of Mars because
    a. the temperature is too hot.
    b. liquid water once existed there.
    c. the gravity of Mars is too weak.
    d. the atmospheric pressure is too low.

16. Which of the following planets is not a terrestrial planet?
    a. Mercury
    b. Mars
    c. Earth
    d. Pluto

17. All of the gas giants have ring systems.
    a. true
    b. false

18. A comet's ion tail consists of
    a. dust.
    b. electrically charged particles of gas.
    c. light rays.
    d. comet nuclei.

Short Answer

19. Do solar eclipses occur at the full moon or at the new moon? Explain why.

20. How do we know there are small meteoroids and dust in space?

21. Which planets have retrograde rotation?

Concept Mapping

22. Use the following terms to create a concept map: solar system, terrestrial planets, gas giants, moons, comets, asteroids, meteoroids.

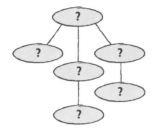

23. Even though we haven't yet retrieved any rock samples from Mercury's surface for radiometric dating, we know that the surface of Mercury is much older than that of Earth. How do we know this?

24. Where in the solar system might we search for life, and why?

25. Is the far side of the moon always dark? Explain your answer.

26. If we could somehow bring Europa as close to the sun as the Earth is, 1 AU, what do you think would happen?

MATH IN SCIENCE

27. Suppose you have an object that weighs 200 N (45 lbs.) on Earth. How much would that same object weigh on each of the other terrestrial planets?

INTERPRETING GRAPHICS

The graph below shows density versus mass for Earth, Uranus, and Neptune. Mass is given in Earth masses—the mass of Earth equals one. The relative volumes for the planets are shown by the size of each circle.

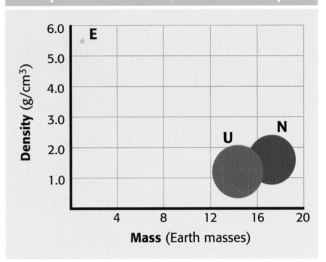

Density vs. Mass for Earth, Uranus, and Neptune

28. Which planet is denser, Uranus or Neptune? How can you tell?

29. You can see that although Earth has the smallest mass, it has the highest density. How can Earth be the densest of the three when Uranus and Neptune have so much more mass?

Reading Check-up

Take a minute to review your answers to the Pre-Reading Questions found at the bottom of page 536. Have your answers changed? If necessary, revise your answers based on what you have learned since you began this chapter.

Is Pluto Really a Planet?

We have all learned that Pluto is the planet farthest from the sun in our solar system. Since it was discovered in 1930, astronomers have grouped it with the outer planets. However, Pluto has not been a perfect fit in this group. Unlike the other outer planets, which are large and gaseous, Pluto is small and made of rock and ice. Pluto also has a very elliptical orbit that is unlike its neighboring planets. These and other factors once fueled a debate as to whether Pluto should be classified as a planet.

Kuiper Belt

In the early 1990s, astronomers discovered a belt of comets outside the orbit of Neptune. The belt was named the Kuiper Belt in honor of Gerard Kuiper, a Dutch-born American astronomer. So what does this belt have to do with Pluto? Given its proximity to Pluto, some astronomers thought Pluto might actually be a large comet that escaped the Kuiper Belt.

Comet?

Comets are basically dirty snowballs made of ice and cosmic dust. Pluto is about 30 percent ice and 70 percent rock. This is much more rock than is in a normal comet. Also, at 2,390 km in diameter, Pluto is much larger than a comet. For

◀ *A composite drawing of Pluto, Charon, Triton, and Halley's comet*

example, Halley's comet is only about 20 km in diameter. Even so, Pluto's orbit is very similar to that of a comet. Both have orbits that are very elliptical.

Escaped Moon?

Pluto and its moon, Charon, have much in common with Neptune's moon, Triton. All three have atmospheres made of nitrogen and methane, which suggests that they share a similar origin. And because Triton has a "backward" orbit compared with Neptune's other moons, it may have been captured by Neptune's gravity. Some astronomers thought Pluto might also have been captured by Neptune but broke free by some cataclysmic event.

New Category of Planet?

Some astronomers suggested that perhaps we should create a new subclass of planets, such as the ice planets, to add to the gas-giant and terrestrial classification we currently use. Pluto would be the only planet in this class, but scientists think we are likely to find others.

As there are more new discoveries, astronomers will likely continue to debate these issues. To date, however, Pluto is still officially considered a planet. This decision is firmly grounded by the fact that Pluto has been called a planet since its discovery.

You Decide

▶ Do some additional research about Pluto, the Kuiper Belt, and comets. What do you think Pluto should be called?

Science Fiction

"The Mad Moon"

by Stanley Weinbaum

The third largest satellite of Jupiter, called Io, can be a hard place to live. Although living comfortably is possible in the small cities at the polar regions, most of the moon is hot, humid, and jungle-like. There is also *blancha,* a kind of tropical fever that causes hallucinations, weakness, and vicious headaches. Without proper medication a person with *blancha* can go mad or even die.

Just 2 years ago, Grant Calthorpe was a wealthy hunter and famous sportsman. Then the gold market crashed, and he lost his entire fortune. What better way for an experienced hunter and explorer to get a fresh start than to set out for a little space travel? The opportunity to rekindle his fortune by gathering ferva leaves so that they can be converted into useful human medications lures Calthorpe to Io.

There he meets the loonies—creatures with balloon heads and silly grins atop *really* long necks. The three-legged parcat Oliver quickly becomes Calthorpe's pet and helps him cope with the loneliness and the slinkers. The slinkers, well, they would just as soon *not* have Calthorpe around at all, but they are pretty good at making even this famous outdoorsman wonder why he ever took this job.

In "The Mad Moon," you'll discover a dozen adventures with Grant Calthorpe as he struggles to stay alive—and sane. Read Stanley Weinbaum's story "The Mad Moon" in the *Holt Anthology of Science Fiction.* Enjoy your trip!

The Universe Beyond

Pre-Reading
Questions

1. Why do stars shine?
2. What is a galaxy?
3. How did the universe
   begin, and how will it
   end? or will it?

GALAXIES GALORE

If you had a telescope, what would you look for? In the 1920s, astronomer Edwin Hubble chose to look for galaxies much like the NGC 3031 galaxy shown here. Basically, a galaxy is a large group of stars. In 1995 the Hubble Space Telescope was used to develop the single image called the Hubble Deep Field shown below. The segment of sky in that image contains nearly 2,000 galaxies! In this chapter, you will learn about the different types of galaxies.

Hubble Deep Field image

EXPLORING GALAXIES IN THE UNIVERSE

Galaxies are large groupings of millions of stars. But not all galaxies are the same. In this activity, you will explore some of these differences.

Procedure

1. Look at the different galaxies in the Hubble Deep Field image on page 96. (The bright spot with spikes is a star that is much closer to Earth; you can ignore it.)

2. Can you find different types of galaxies? In your ScienceLog, make sketches of at least three different types. Make up a name that describes each type of galaxy.

3. In your ScienceLog, construct a chart to classify, compare, and describe the different characteristics you see in these galaxies.

Analysis

4. Why did you classify the galaxies the way you did?

5. Compare your types of galaxies with those of your classmates. Are there similarities?

Terms to Learn

spectrum
apparent magnitude
absolute magnitude
light-year
parallax

What You'll Do

◆ Describe how color indicates temperature.

◆ Compare absolute magnitude with apparent magnitude, and discuss how each measures brightness.

◆ Describe the difference between the apparent motion of stars and the real motion of stars.

Stars

Most stars look like faint dots of light in the night sky. But stars are actually huge, hot, brilliant balls of gas trillions of kilometers away from Earth. How do astronomers learn about stars when they are too far away to visit? They study starlight!

Color of Stars

Look closely at the flames on the candle and the Bunsen burner shown here. Which one has the hotter flame? How can you tell? Although artists may speak of *red* as a "hot" color, to a scientist, *red* is a "cool" color. The blue flame of the Bunsen burner is much hotter than the yellow flame of the candle. In the same way, the candle's yellow flame is hotter than the red glowing embers of a campfire.

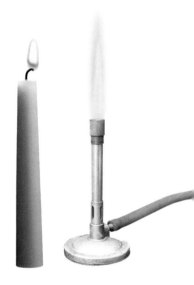

If you look carefully at the night sky, you might notice the different colors of some familiar stars. Betelgeuse (BET uhl jooz), which is red, and Rigel (RIE juhl), which is blue, are the stars that form two corners of the constellation Orion, shown in **Figure 1**. This constellation is easy to see in the evenings during the winter months. Because these two stars are different colors, we can infer that they have different temperatures.

Figure 1 Because Betelgeuse is red and Rigel is blue, astronomers know that Rigel is the hotter star.

Betelgeuse

Rigel

Composition of Stars

When you look at white light through a glass prism, you see a rainbow of colors called a **spectrum.** The spectrum consists of millions of colors, including the ones we recognize as red, orange, yellow, green, blue, indigo, and violet. A hot solid object, like the glowing wire inside a light bulb, gives off a *continuous spectrum*—one that shows all the colors. Astronomers use an instrument called a *spectrograph* to spread starlight out into its colors, just as you might use a prism to spread sunlight. Stars, however, don't have continuous spectra. Because they are not solid objects, stars give off spectra that are different from those of light bulbs.

Hot, Dense Gas Stars are made of various gases that are so dense that they act like a hot solid. For this reason, the "surface" of a star, or the part that we see, gives off a continuous spectrum. But the light we see passes through the star's "atmosphere," which is made of cooler gases than the star itself. A star therefore produces a spectrum with various lines in it. To understand what these lines are, let's look at something you might be more familiar with than stars.

Making an ID Many restaurants use neon signs to attract customers. The gas in a neon sign glows orange-red when an electric current flows through it. If we were to look at the sign with an astronomer's spectrograph, we would not see a continuous spectrum. Instead we would see *emission lines*. Emission lines are bright lines that are made when certain wavelengths of light are given off, or emitted, by hot gases. Only some colors in the spectrum show up, while all of the other colors are missing. Every tube of neon gas, for example, emits light with the same emission lines. Each element has its own unique set of emission lines. Emission lines are like fingerprints for the elements. You can see some of these "fingerprints" in **Figure 2.**

Physics CONNECTION

Police use spectrographs to "fingerprint" cars. Automobile manufacturers put trace elements in the paint of cars. Each make of car has its own special paint and therefore its own combination of trace elements. When a car is involved in a hit-and-run accident, the police can identify the make of the car by the paint that is left behind.

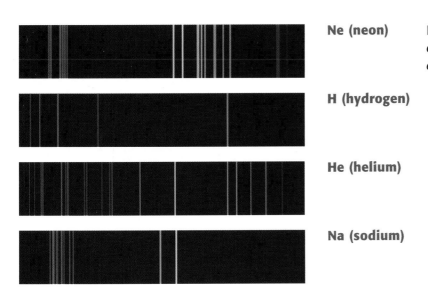

Ne (neon)

H (hydrogen)

He (helium)

Na (sodium)

Figure 2 *Neon gas produces its own characteristic pattern of emission lines, as do hydrogen, helium, and sodium.*

Trapping the Light The spectrum produced by a star is not continuous, nor is it made of bright lines similar to those of the elements you saw above. Because a star's atmosphere is cooler than the star itself, the gases in its atmosphere absorb some of the star's light. The cooler gases in a star's atmosphere remove certain colors of light from the continuous spectrum of the hot star. In fact, the colors that the atmosphere absorbs are the same colors it would emit if heated.

To learn more about the color and temperature of stars, turn to page 718 in the LabBook.

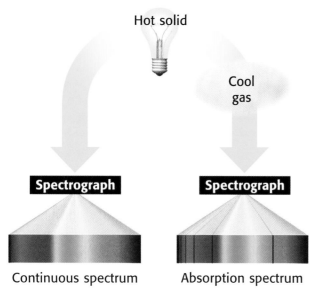

Hot solid

Cool gas

Spectrograph

Spectrograph

Continuous spectrum

Absorption spectrum

Figure 3 *An absorption spectrum (right) is produced when light passes through a cooler gas. Notice the dark lines in the spectrum.*

Biology
C O N N E C T I O N

Our eyes are not sensitive to colors when light levels are low. There are two types of light-sensitive cells inside the eye: rods and cones. Rods are good at distinguishing shades of light and dark as well as shape and movement. Cones are good for distinguishing colors. Cones, however, do not work well in low light. This is why it is hard to distinguish between star colors.

Cosmic Detective Work If light from a hot solid passes through a cooler gas, it produces an *absorption spectrum*—a continuous spectrum with dark lines where less light gets through. Take a look at **Figure 3.** Can you identify the element in the gas by comparing the position of the dark lines in its spectrum with the bright lines in Figure 2?

An astronomer's spectrum of a star shows an absorption spectrum. The pattern of lines shows some of the elements that are in the star's atmosphere. If a star were made of just one element, it would be simple to identify the element. But stars are a mixture of things, and all the different sets of lines for its elements appear together in a star's spectrum. Sorting out the patterns is often a puzzle.

Classifying Stars

In the 1800s, people started to collect the spectra of lots of stars and tried to classify them. At first, letters were assigned to each type of spectra. Stars with spectra that had very noticeable hydrogen patterns were classified as A type stars. Other stars were classified as B, and so on. Later, scientists realized that the stars were classified in the wrong order.

Differences in Temperature Stars are now classified by how hot they are. We see the temperature differences as colors. The original class O stars are blue—they are very hot, the hottest of all stars. If you arrange the letters in order of temperature, they are no longer in alphabetical order. The resulting order of star classes—OBAFGKM—is shown in the table on the next page.

If you see a certain pattern of absorption lines in a star, you know that a certain element or molecule is in the star or its atmosphere. But the absence of a pattern doesn't mean the element isn't there; the temperature might not be high enough or low enough to produce absorption lines.

Types of Stars				
Class	Color	Surface temperature (°C)	Elements detected	Examples of stars
O	blue	above 30,000	helium	10 Lacertae
B	blue-white	10,000–30,000	helium and hydrogen	Rigel, Spica
A	blue-white	7,500–10,000	hydrogen	Vega, Sirius
F	yellow-white	6,000–7,500	hydrogen and heavier elements	Canopus, Procyon
G	yellow	5,000–6,000	calcium and other metals	the sun, Capella
K	orange	3,500–5,000	calcium and molecules	Arcturus, Aldebaran
M	red	less than 3,500	molecules	Betelgeuse, Antares

Differences in Brightness With only their eyes to aid them, ancient astronomers also came up with a system to classify stars based on their brightness. They called the brightest stars in the sky *first magnitude* stars and the faintest stars *sixth magnitude* stars. But when they began to use telescopes, astronomers were able to see many stars that had previously been too faint to see. Rather than replace the old system of magnitudes, they added to it—positive numbers for dimmer stars and negative numbers for brighter stars. For example, with large telescopes, astronomers can see stars as dim as 29th magnitude. And the brightest star in the sky, Sirius, has a magnitude of –1.4.

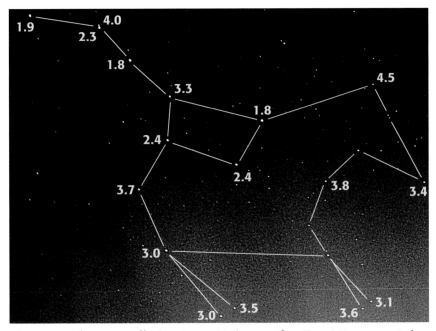

Figure 4 *The constellation Ursa Major, or the Great Bear, contains both bright and faint stars. Numbers indicate their relative brightness. What is the magnitude of the brightest star?*

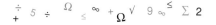

MATH BREAK

Starlight, Star Bright

Magnitude is used to indicate how bright one object is compared with another. Five magnitudes equal a factor of 100 times in brightness. The brightest blue stars, for example, have an absolute magnitude of –10. The sun is about +5. How much brighter is a blue star than the sun? Since each five magnitudes is a factor of 100 and the blue star and the sun are 15 magnitudes different, the blue star must be $100 \times 100 \times 100$ times brighter than the sun. This is 1,000,000 (one million) times!

How Bright Is That Star?

If you look at a row of street lights along a highway, like those shown in **Figure 5,** do they all look exactly the same? Does the light you are standing under look the same as a light several blocks away? Of course not! The nearest ones look bright, and the farthest ones look dim.

Figure 5 *You can estimate how far away each street light is by looking at its apparent brightness. Does this work with stars?*

Apparent Magnitude How bright a light looks, or appears, is called **apparent magnitude.** If you measure the brightness of a street light with a light meter, you will find that its brightness depends on the square of the distance between them. For example, a light that is 10 m away will appear four (2×2 or 2^2) times as bright as a light that is 20 m away. The same light will appear nine (3×3 or 3^2) times as bright as a light that is 30 m away.

Self-Check

If two identical stars are located the same distance away from Earth, what can you say about their apparent magnitudes? *(See page 726 to check your answer.)*

Environment

C O N N E C T I O N

And speaking of street lights . . . Someone looking at the night sky in a city would not see as many stars as someone looking at the sky in the country. Light pollution is a big problem for astronomers and backyard stargazers alike. Certain types of lighting can help reduce glare, but there will continue to be a conflict between lighting buildings at night and seeing the stars.

But unlike street lights, some stars are brighter than others because of their size or energy output, not their distance from Earth. So how can you tell the difference?

Absolute Magnitude Astronomers use a star's apparent magnitude (how bright it seems to be) and its distance from Earth to calculate its absolute magnitude. **Absolute magnitude** is the actual brightness of a star. In other words, if all stars could be placed the same distance away, their absolute magnitudes would be the same as their apparent magnitudes and the brighter stars would look brighter. The sun, for example, has an absolute magnitude of +4.8—pretty ordinary for a star. But because the sun is so close to Earth, its apparent magnitude is −26.8, making it the brightest object in the sky.

Distance to the Stars

Because they are so far away, astronomers use light-years to give the distances to the stars. A **light-year** is the distance that light travels in one year. Because the speed of light is about 300,000 km/s, it travels almost 9.5 trillion kilometers in one year. Obviously it would be easier to give the distance to the North Star as 431 light-years than 4,080,000,000,000,000 km. But how do astronomers measure a star's distance?

To get a clue, take a look at the QuickLab at right. Just as your thumb appeared to move, stars near the Earth seem to move compared with more-distant stars as Earth revolves around the sun, as shown in **Figure 6.** This apparent shift in position is called **parallax.** While this shift can be seen only through telescopes, using parallax and simple trigonometry (a type of math), astronomers can find the actual distance to stars that are close to Earth.

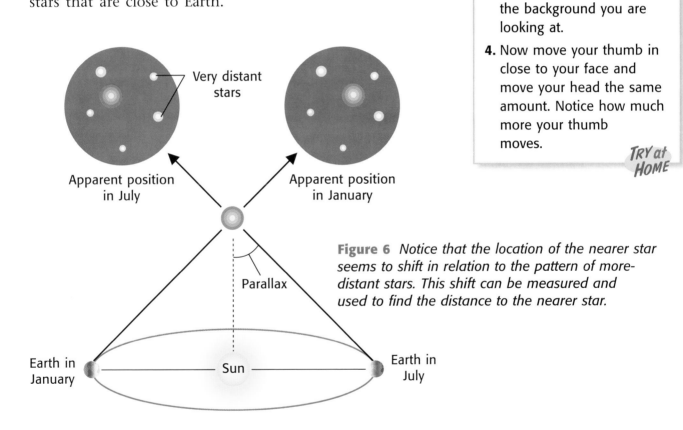

Figure 6 *Notice that the location of the nearer star seems to shift in relation to the pattern of more-distant stars. This shift can be measured and used to find the distance to the nearer star.*

Very distant stars

Apparent position in July

Apparent position in January

Parallax

Earth in January

Sun

Earth in July

Motions of Stars

As you know, the Earth rotates on its axis. As the Earth turns, different parts of its surface face the sun. This is why we have days and nights. The Earth also revolves around the sun. At different times of the year, you see different stars in the night sky. This is because the side of Earth that is away from the sun at night faces a different part of the universe.

To learn more about parallax, turn to page 720 in the LabBook.

Figure 7 *As Earth rotates on its axis, stars set in the western horizon.*

Apparent Motion Because of Earth's rotation, the sun appears to move across the sky. Likewise, if you look at the night sky long enough, the stars also appear to move. In fact, at night we can observe that the whole sky is rotating above us. As shown in **Figure 7,** the rest of the stars appear to rotate around Polaris, the North Star, which is directly above Earth's north pole. Because of Earth's rotation, all of the stars in the sky appear to make one complete circle around Polaris every 24 hours.

Actual Motion You now know that the apparent motion of the sun and stars in our sky is due to Earth's rotation. But each star is also really moving in space. Because stars are so distant, however, their real motion is hard to observe. If you could watch stars over thousands of years, their movement would be obvious. As shown in **Figure 8,** you would see that familiar star patterns slowly change their shapes.

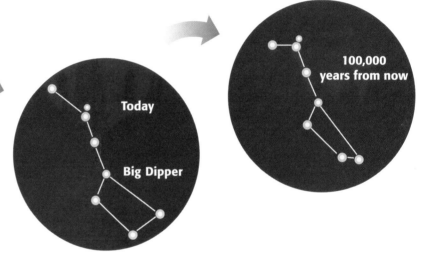

Figure 8 *Over time, the shapes of the constellations and other star groups change.*

REVIEW

1. Is a yellow star, such as the sun, hotter or cooler than an orange star? Explain.

2. Suppose you see two stars that have the same apparent magnitude. If one star is actually four times as far away as the other, how much brighter is the farther star?

3. **Interpreting Illustrations** Look back at Figure 7. How many hours passed between the first image and the second image? How can you tell?

The Life Cycle of Stars

Just like people, stars are born, grow old, and eventually die. But unlike people, stars exist for billions of years. They are born when clouds of gas and dust come together and become very hot and dense. As stars get older, they lose some of their material. Usually this is a gradual change, but sometimes it happens in a big explosion. Either way, when a star dies, much of its material returns to space. There some of it combines with more gas and dust to form new stars. How do scientists know these things about stars? Read on to find out.

The Diagram That Did It!

In 1911, a Danish astronomer named Ejnar Hertzsprung (IE nahr HUHRTZ sprung) compared the temperature and brightness of stars on a graph. Two years later, American astronomer Henry Norris Russell made some similar graphs. Although they used different data, these astronomers had similar results. The combination of their ideas is now called the *Hertzsprung-Russell,* or *H-R, diagram.* The **H-R diagram** is a graph showing the relationship between a star's surface temperature and its absolute magnitude. Russell's original diagram is shown in **Figure 9.**

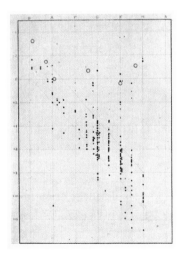

Figure 9 *Notice that a pattern begins to appear from the lower right to the upper left of the graph. Although it may not look like much, this graph began a revolution in astronomy.*

Over the years, the H-R diagram has become a tool for studying the nature of stars. It not only shows how stars are classified by temperature and brightness but also is a good way to illustrate how stars change over time. Turn the page to see a modern version of this diagram.

The H-R Diagram

Look closely at the diagram on these two pages. Temperature is given along the bottom of the diagram. Absolute magnitude, or brightness, is given along the left side. Hot (blue) stars are located on the left, and cool (red) stars are on the right. Bright stars are at the top, and faint stars are at the bottom. The brightest stars are a million times brighter than the sun. The faintest are 1/10,000 as bright as the sun. As you can see, there seems to be a band of stars going from the top left to the bottom right corner. This diagonal pattern of stars is called the **main sequence.** A star spends most of its lifetime as a main-sequence star and then changes into one of the other types of stars shown here.

Main-sequence
Stars in the main sequence form a band that runs along the middle of the H-R diagram. The sun is a main-sequence star. Stars similar to the sun are called *dwarfs.* The sun has been shining for about 5 billion years. Scientists think the sun is in midlife and that it will remain on the main sequence for another 5 billion years.

Absolute magnitude is measured upside down. That means the larger the number, the dimmer the star. At +5, the sun is not as bright as a −7 star.

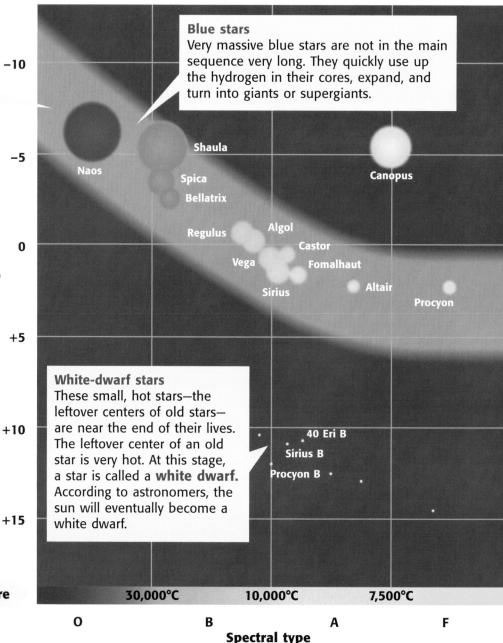

Blue stars
Very massive blue stars are not in the main sequence very long. They quickly use up the hydrogen in their cores, expand, and turn into giants or supergiants.

White-dwarf stars
These small, hot stars—the leftover centers of old stars—are near the end of their lives. The leftover center of an old star is very hot. At this stage, a star is called a **white dwarf.** According to astronomers, the sun will eventually become a white dwarf.

All stars begin as a ball of gas and dust in space as gravity pulls the gas and dust together into a sphere. As the sphere becomes denser, it gets hotter. When it is hot enough in the center, hydrogen turns into helium in a process called nuclear fusion and lots of energy is given off. A star is born!

Stars spend most of their lives on the main-sequence. Small-mass stars tend to be located at the lower right end of the main-sequence; more massive stars are found at the left end. As main-sequence stars age, they move up and to the right on the H-R diagram to become giants or supergiants. Such stars can then lose their atmospheres, leaving small cores behind, which end up in the lower left corner of the diagram as white dwarfs.

Giants and supergiants
When a star runs out of hydrogen in its core, the center of the star shrinks inward and the outer parts expand outward. In a star the size of our sun, the atmosphere will grow very large and cool. When this happens, the star becomes a **red giant.** If the star is very massive, it becomes a *supergiant.*

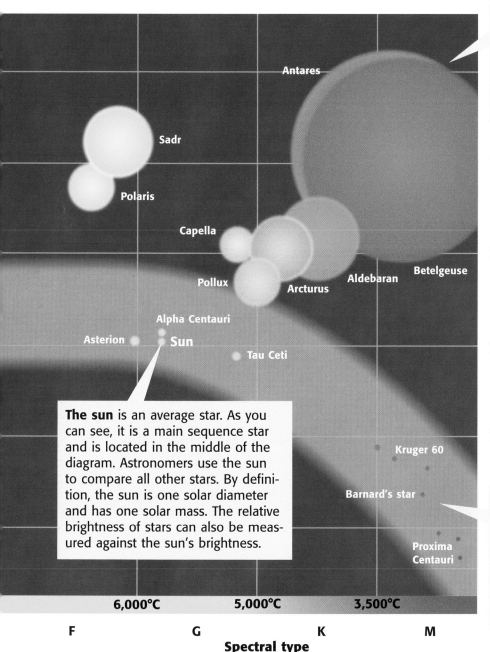

Antares

Sadr

Polaris

Capella

Pollux

Arcturus

Aldebaran

Betelgeuse

Alpha Centauri

Asterion

Sun

Tau Ceti

10,000

100

1

1/100

Relative brightness (compared with sun)

The sun is an average star. As you can see, it is a main sequence star and is located in the middle of the diagram. Astronomers use the sun to compare all other stars. By definition, the sun is one solar diameter and has one solar mass. The relative brightness of stars can also be measured against the sun's brightness.

Kruger 60

Barnard's star

Proxima Centauri

Red-dwarf stars
At the lower end of the main sequence are the red dwarf stars. Red dwarfs are low-mass stars. Low-mass stars remain on the main sequence a long time. The lowest mass stars may be some of the oldest stars in the galaxy.

6,000°C	5,000°C	3,500°C
F	G	K	M

Spectral type

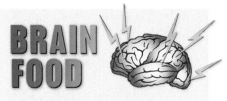
When Stars Get Old

While stars may stay on the main sequence for a long time, they don't stay there forever. Average stars, such as the sun, turn into red giants and then white dwarfs. But when massive stars get old, they may leave the main sequence in a more spectacular fashion. Stars much larger than the sun may explode with such violence that they turn into a variety of strange new objects. Let's take a look at some of these objects.

Supernovas Massive blue stars use up their hydrogen much faster than stars like the sun. This means they make a lot more energy, which makes them very hot and therefore blue! And compared with other stars, they don't last long. At the end of its life, a blue star may explode in a tremendous flash of light called a *supernova*. A **supernova** is basically the death of a large star by explosion. A supernova explosion is so powerful that it can be brighter than an entire galaxy for several days. Heavy elements, such as silver, gold, and lead, are formed by supernova explosions.

The ringed structure shown in **Figure 10** is the result of a supernova explosion that was first observed in February 1987. The star, located in a nearby galaxy, actually exploded before civilization began here on Earth, but it took 169,000 years for the light from the explosion to reach our planet!

Before (1984)

During (1987)

After (Hubble Space Telescope close-up, 1994)

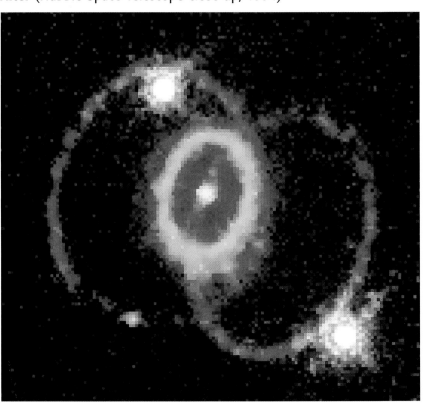

Figure 10 *Supernova 1987A was the first supernova visible to the unaided eye in 400 years. The first image shows what the original star must have looked like only a few hours before the explosion. Today its remains form a double ring of gas and dust, shown at right.*

Neutron Stars So what happens to a star that becomes a supernova? The leftover materials in the center of a super-nova are squeezed together to form a star of about two solar masses. But the star is only about 20 km in diameter. The particles inside the star become neutrons, so this star is called a **neutron star.** A neutron star is so dense that if you brought a teaspoon of it back to Earth, it would weigh nearly a billion metric tons!

Pulsars If a neutron star is spinning, it is called a **pulsar.** A pulsar sends out beams of radiation that also spin around very rapidly. These beams are much like the beams from a lighthouse. The beams are detected as rapid clicks or pulses by radio telescopes.

Black Holes Sometimes the leftovers of a supernova are so massive that they col-lapse to form a *black hole*. A **black hole** is an object with more than three solar masses squeezed into a ball only 10 km across—100 football fields long. A black hole's gravity is so strong that not even light can escape. That is why it is called a *black* hole. Contrary to some movie depictions, a black hole doesn't gobble up other stars. But if a star is nearby, some gas or dust from the star will spiral into the black hole, as shown in **Figure 11,** giving off X rays. It is by these X rays that astronomers can detect the existence of black holes.

Figure 11 *A black hole's gravity is so strong that it can pull in material from a nearby star, as shown in this artist's drawing.*

REVIEW

1. Are blue stars young or old? How can you tell?

2. In main-sequence stars, what is the relationship between brightness and temperature?

3. Arrange the following in order of their appearance in the life cycle of a star: white dwarf, red giant, main-sequence star. Explain your answer.

4. **Applying Concepts** Given that there are more low-mass stars than high-mass stars in the universe, do you think there are more white dwarfs or more black holes? Explain.

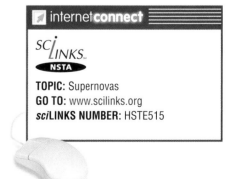

Galaxies

What You'll Do

◆ Identify the various types of galaxies from pictures.

◆ Describe the contents of galaxies.

◆ Explain why looking at distant galaxies reveals what early galaxies looked like.

Stars don't exist alone in space. They belong to larger groups that are held together by the attraction of gravity. The most common groupings are galaxies. **Galaxies** are large groupings of stars in space. Galaxies come in a variety of sizes and shapes. The largest galaxies contain more than a trillion stars. Some of the smaller ones have only a few million. Astronomers don't count the stars, of course; they estimate from the size and brightness of the galaxy how many sun-sized stars the galaxy might have.

Types of Galaxies

Look again at the Hubble Deep Field image at the beginning of this chapter. You'll notice many different types of *galaxies*. Edwin Hubble, the astronomer for whom the Hubble Space Telescope is named, began to classify galaxies in the 1920s, mostly by their shapes. We still use the galaxy names that Hubble originally assigned.

Figure 12 *The Milky Way galaxy is thought to be a spiral galaxy similar to the galaxy in Andromeda, shown here.*

Spiral Galaxies Spiral galaxies are what most people think of when you say *galaxy*. **Spiral galaxies** have a bulge at the center and very distinctive spiral arms. Hot blue stars in the spiral arms make the arms in spiral galaxies appear blue. The central region appears yellow because it contains cooler stars. **Figure 12** shows a spiral galaxy tilted, so you can see its pinwheel shape. Other spiral galaxies appear to be "edge-on." It is hard to tell what type of galaxy we are in because the gas, dust, and stars keep us from having a good view. It is like trying to figure out what pattern a marching band is making while you are in the band. Observing other galaxies and making measurements inside our galaxy lead astronomers to think that Earth is in a spiral galaxy.

Elliptical Galaxies About one-third of all galaxies are simply massive blobs of stars, as shown in **Figure 13.** Many look like spheres, while others are more elongated. Because we don't know how they are oriented, some of these galaxies could be cucumber shaped, with the round end facing us. These galaxies are called *elliptical galaxies.* **Elliptical galaxies** have very bright centers and very little dust and gas. Because there is so little gas, there are no new stars forming, and therefore elliptical galaxies contain only old stars. Some elliptical galaxies, like M87, at right, are huge and are therefore called *giant elliptical galaxies.* Others are much smaller and are called *dwarf elliptical galaxies.* There are probably lots of dwarf ellipticals, but because they are small and faint, they are very hard to detect.

Figure 13 *Unlike the Milky Way, the galaxy known as M87 has no spiral arms.*

Irregular Galaxies When Hubble first classified galaxies, he had a group of leftovers. He named them "irregulars." **Irregular galaxies** are galaxies that don't fit into any other class. As their name suggests, their shape is irregular. Many of these galaxies, such as the Large Magellanic Cloud, shown in **Figure 14,** are close companions of large spiral galaxies, whose gravity may be distorting the shape of their smaller neighbors.

Figure 14 *The Large Magellanic Cloud, an irregular galaxy, is located within our own galactic neighborhood.*

Activity

Now that you know the names Edwin Hubble gave to different shapes of galaxies, look at the names you gave the galaxies in the Hubble Deep Field activity at the beginning of this chapter. Rename your types with the Hubble names. Look for examples of spirals, ellipticals, and irregular galaxies.

TRY at HOME

Contents of Galaxies

Galaxies are composed of billions and billions of stars. But besides the stars and the planetary systems many of them probably have, there are larger features within galaxies that are made up of stars or the material of stars. Among these are gas clouds and star clusters.

Gas Clouds The Latin word for "cloud" is *nebula*. In space, **nebulas** (or *nebulae*) are giant clouds of gas and dust. Some types of nebulas glow by themselves, while others absorb light and hide stars. Still others reflect starlight, producing some amazing images. Some nebulas are regions where new stars form. **Figure 15** shows part of the Eagle nebula. Spiral galaxies generally contain nebulas, but elliptical galaxies don't.

Globular Clusters **Globular clusters** are groups of older stars. A globular cluster looks like a ball of stars, as shown in **Figure 16.** There may be 20,000 to 100,000 stars in an average globular cluster. Globular clusters are located in a spherical *halo* that surrounds spiral galaxies such as the Milky Way. Globular clusters are also common around giant elliptical galaxies.

Open Clusters **Open clusters** are groups of stars that are usually located along the spiral disk of a galaxy. Newly formed open clusters have many bright blue stars, as shown in **Figure 17.** There may be a few hundred to a few thousand stars in an open cluster.

Figure 15 *Part of a nebula in which stars are born is shown above. The finger-like shape to the left of the bright star is slightly wider than our solar system.*

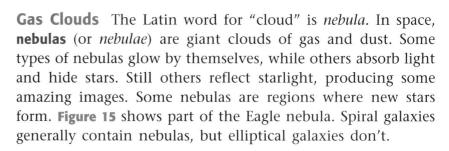

Figure 16 *With 5 to 10 million stars, Omega Centauri is the largest globular cluster in the Milky Way Galaxy.*

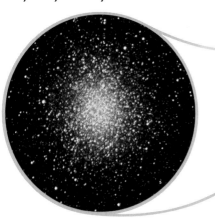

Figure 17 *The open cluster Pleiades is just visible without a telescope.*

Origin of Galaxies

How did galaxies form in the first place? To answer this question, astronomers must travel back in time, exploring the early universe through telescopes. Scientists investigate the early universe by observing objects that are extremely far away in space. Because it takes time for light to travel through space, looking through a telescope is like looking back in time. The farther out one looks, the further back in time one travels.

Looking at distant galaxies reveals what early galaxies looked like. This helps give scientists an idea of how galaxies evolve through time and perhaps what caused them to form in the first place. Scientists have already found some very strange looking objects in the early universe.

Quasars Among the most distant objects are **quasars,** which look like tiny points of light. But because they are very far away, they must be extremely bright for their size. Quasars are among the most powerful energy sources in the universe. They may be young galaxies with massive black holes at their centers. Some scientists think that what we see as quasars are galaxies in the process of forming. In **Figure 18,** you can see a quasar that is 6 billion light-years away. You are seeing it as it was 6 billion years ago—long before the Earth even existed!

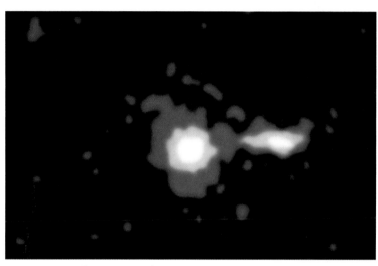

Figure 18 *The quasar known as PKS 0637-752 is as powerful as 10 trillion suns.*

REVIEW

1. Arrange these galaxies in order of decreasing size: spiral, giant elliptical, dwarf elliptical, irregular.

2. Describe the difference between an elliptical galaxy and a globular cluster.

3. **Analyzing Relationships** Suppose the quasar in Figure 18 suddenly underwent some dramatic change. How long would we have to wait to see this change? Explain.

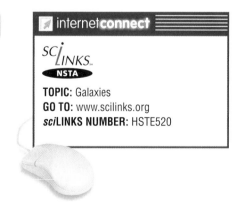

internet**connect**

SCI**LINKS**
NSTA

TOPIC: Galaxies
GO TO: www.scilinks.org
*sci*LINKS NUMBER: HSTE520

Terms to Learn

cosmology
big bang theory
cosmic background radiation

What You'll Do

◆ Describe the big bang theory.
◆ Explain evidence used to show support for the big bang theory.
◆ Explain how the expansion of the universe is explained by the big bang theory.

Formation of the Universe

So far you've learned about the contents of the universe. But what about its history? How did the universe begin? How might it end? Questions like these are a special part of astronomy called *cosmology*. **Cosmology** is the study of the origin and future of the universe. Like other scientific theories, theories about the beginning and end of the universe must be tested by observations or experiments.

The Big Bang Theory

One of the most important theories in cosmology is the big bang theory. The **big bang theory** states that the universe began with a tremendous explosion. According to the theory, 12 to 15 billion years ago, all the contents of the universe were gathered together under extreme pressure, temperature, and density in a very tiny spot. Then, for some reason, it rapidly expanded. In the early moments of the universe, some of the expanding energy turned into matter that eventually became the galaxies, as shown in **Figure 19.**

A Big Crunch?   As the galaxies move apart, they get older and eventually stop forming stars. What happens next depends on how much matter is contained in the universe. If there is enough matter, gravity will slow and eventually stop the expansion of the universe. The universe may even start collapsing to its original state, causing a "big crunch."

If there is not enough matter to stop the expansion, then as stars age and die, the universe will eventually become cold and dark. Recent observations suggest that there may not be enough matter to stop the universe from expanding forever, but the answer is still uncertain.

Figure 19 *The big bang caused the universe to expand in all directions.*

Supporting the Theory So how do we know if the big bang really happened? In 1964, two scientists, using the antenna shown in **Figure 20,** accidentally found radiation coming from all directions in space. One explanation for this radiation is that it is **cosmic background radiation** left over from the big bang.

Think about what happens when an oven door is left open after the oven has been used. Thermal energy is transferred throughout the kitchen and the oven cools. Eventually the room and the oven are the same temperature. According to the big bang theory, thermal energy from the original explosion was distributed in every direction as the universe expanded. This cosmic background radiation—corresponding to a temperture of $-270°C$—now fills all of space.

Figure 20 *Robert Wilson (left) and Arno Penzias (right) discovered the cosmic background radiation, giving a big boost to the big bang theory.*

Universal Expansion

Today, the big bang theory is widely accepted by astronomers. But where did the idea of a big bang come from? The answer is found in deep space. No matter what direction we look, galaxies are moving away from us, as shown in **Figure 21.** This observation may make it seem like our galaxy is the center of the universe, with all other galaxies moving away from our own. But this is not the case. Careful measurements have shown that all distant galaxies are moving away from all other galaxies.

With the discovery that the universe is expanding, scientists began to wonder what it would be like to watch the universe evolve backwards through time. In reverse, the universe would appear to be contracting, not expanding. All matter would eventually come together to a single point. Thinking about what would happen if all of the matter in the universe were squeezed into such a small space led scientists to the big bang theory.

Figure 21 *The big bang theory explains the expansion of the universe we observe as galaxies move outward in all directions.*

A Raisin-Bread Model

Imagine a loaf of raisin bread before it is baked. Inside the dough, each raisin is a certain distance from every other raisin. As the dough gets warm and rises, it expands and all of the raisins begin to move away from each other. No matter which raisin you observe, the other raisins are moving farther from it.

The universe itself is like the rising bread dough—it is expanding in all directions. And like the raisins, every distant galaxy is moving away from our galaxy as well as every other galaxy. In other words, there isn't any way to find the "center" of the universe.

How Old Is the Universe? One way scientists can measure the age of the universe is by measuring the distance to the farthest galaxies. Because light travels at a certain speed, the amount of time it takes light to travel this distance is a measure of the age of the universe. Another way to estimate the age of the universe is to calculate the ages of old, nearby stars. Because the universe must be at least as old as the oldest stars it contains, their ages provide a clue to the age of the universe. But according to these calculations, some stars are older than the universe itself! Astronomers continue to search for evidence that will solve this puzzle.

Graphing Expansion

Suppose you decide to make some raisin bread. You would form a lump of dough, as shown in the top image. The lower image represents dough that has been rising for 2 hours. Look at raisin **B** in the top image. Measure how far it is from each of the other raisins—**A, C, D, E, F,** and **G**—in millimeters. Now measure how far each raisin has moved away from **B** in the lower image. Make a graph of speed (in units of mm/h) versus original distance (in mm). Remember that speed equals distance divided by time. For example, if raisin **E** was originally 15 mm from raisin **B** and is now 30 mm away, it moved 15 mm in 2 hours. Its speed is therefore 7.5 mm/h. Repeat the procedure, starting with raisin **D**. Plot your results on the same graph, and compare the two results. What can you conclude from the information you graphed?

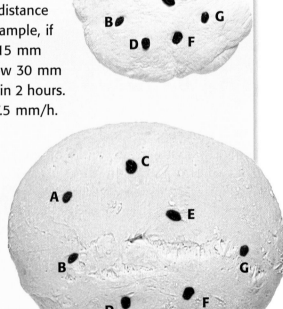

Structure of the Universe

The universe is an amazing place. From our home on planet Earth, it stretches out farther than we can see with our most sensitive instruments. It contains a variety of objects, some of which you have just learned about. But these objects are not simply scattered through the universe at random. The universe has a structure that is repeated over and over again.

A Cosmic Repetition You already know that the Earth is a planet. But planets are part of planetary systems. Our solar system is the one we are most familiar with, but recently planets have been detected in orbit around other stars. Scientists think that planetary systems are actually quite common in the universe. Stars are grouped in larger systems, ranging from star clusters to galaxies. Galaxies themselves are arranged in groups that are bound together by gravity. Even galaxy groups form galaxy clusters and superclusters, as shown in **Figure 22.**

Multiple Universes? Farther than the eye can see, the universe continues with this pattern, with great collections of galaxy clusters and vast empty regions of space in between. But is the universe itself alone? Some cosmologists think that our universe is only one of a great many other universes, perhaps similar to ours or perhaps not. At present, we cannot observe other universes. But someday, who knows? Maybe students in future classrooms will have much more to study!

Figure 22 *The Earth is only part of a vast system of matter.*

REVIEW

1. Name one observation that supports the big bang theory.

2. How does the big bang theory explain the observed expansion of the universe?

3. **Understanding Technology** Large telescopes gather more light than small telescopes gather. Why are large telescopes used to study very distant galaxies?

Chapter Highlights

SECTION 1

Vocabulary

spectrum *(p. 570)*
apparent magnitude *(p. 574)*
absolute magnitude *(p. 574)*
light-year *(p. 575)*
parallax *(p. 575)*

Section Notes

- The color of a star depends on its temperature. Hot stars are blue. Cool stars are red.

- The spectra of stars indicate their composition. Spectra are also used to classify stars.

- The magnitude of a star is a measure of its brightness.

- Apparent magnitude is how bright a star appears from Earth.

- Absolute magnitude is how bright a star actually is. Lower absolute magnitude numbers indicate brighter stars.

- Distance to nearby stars can be measured by their movement relative to stars farther away.

Labs

Red Hot, or Not? *(p. 718)*
I See the Light! *(p. 720)*

SECTION 2

Vocabulary

H-R diagram *(p. 577)*
main sequence *(p. 578)*
white dwarf *(p. 578)*
red giant *(p. 579)*
supernova *(p. 580)*
neutron star *(p. 581)*
pulsar *(p. 581)*
black hole *(p. 581)*

Section Notes

- New stars form from the material of old stars that have gone through their life cycles.

- The H-R diagram relates the temperature and brightness of a star. It also illustrates the life cycle of stars.

- Most stars are main-sequence stars. Red giants and white dwarfs are later stages in a star's life cycle.

- Massive stars become supernovas. Their cores turn into neutron stars or black holes.

☑ Skills Check

Math Concepts

SQUARING THE DIFFERENCE The difference in brightness (apparent magnitude) between a pair of similar stars depends on the difference in their distances from Earth. Compare a star that is 10 light-years away with a star that is 5 light-years away. One star is twice as close, so it is $2 \times 2 = 4$ times brighter than the other star. The star that is 5 light-years away is also 3^2, or 9, times brighter than one that is 15 light-years away.

Visual Understanding

READING BETWEEN THE LINES The composition of a star is determined by the absorption spectra it displays. Dark lines in the spectrum of a star indicate which elements are present. Look back at Figure 3 to review.

SECTION 3

Vocabulary

galaxy *(p. 582)*

spiral galaxy *(p. 582)*

elliptical galaxy *(p. 583)*

irregular galaxy *(p. 583)*

nebula *(p. 584)*

open cluster *(p. 584)*

globular cluster *(p. 584)*

quasar *(p. 585)*

Section Notes

- Edwin Hubble classified galaxies according to their shape. Major types include spiral, elliptical, and irregular galaxies.

- A nebula is a cloud of gas and dust. New stars are born in some nebulas.

- Open clusters are groups of stars located along the spiral disk of a galaxy. Globular star clusters are found in the halos of spiral galaxies and in elliptical galaxies.

- Because light travels at a certain speed, observing distant galaxies is like looking back in time. Scientists look at distant galaxies to learn what early galaxies looked like.

SECTION 4

Vocabulary

cosmology *(p. 586)*

big bang theory *(p. 586)*

cosmic background radiation *(p. 587)*

Section Notes

- The big bang theory states that the universe began with an explosion about 12 to 15 billion years ago.

- Cosmic background radiation fills the universe with radiation that is left over from the big bang. It is supporting evidence for the big bang theory.

- Observations show that the universe is expanding outward. There is no measurable center and no apparent edge.

- All matter in the universe is a part of larger systems, from planets to superclusters of galaxies.

---

internet**connect**

GO TO: go.hrw.com

Visit the **HRW** Web site for a variety of learning tools related to this chapter. Just type in the keyword:

KEYWORD: HSTUNV

GO TO: www.scilinks.org

Visit the **National Science Teachers Association** on-line Web site for Internet resources related to this chapter. Just type in the *sci*LINKS number for more information about the topic:

TOPIC: The Hubble Space Telescope	*sci*LINKS NUMBER: HSTE505
TOPIC: Stars	*sci*LINKS NUMBER: HSTE510
TOPIC: Supernovas	*sci*LINKS NUMBER: HSTE515
TOPIC: Galaxies	*sci*LINKS NUMBER: HSTE520
TOPIC: Structure of the Universe	*sci*LINKS NUMBER: HSTE525

Chapter Review

For each pair of terms, explain the difference in their meanings.

1. absolute magnitude/apparent magnitude

2. spectrum/parallax

3. main-sequence star/red giant

4. white dwarf/black hole

5. elliptical galaxy/spiral galaxy

6. big bang/cosmic background radiation

UNDERSTANDING CONCEPTS

Multiple Choice

7. The majority of stars in our galaxy are
   a. blue.
   b. white dwarfs.
   c. main-sequence stars.
   d. red giants.

8. Which would be seen as the brightest star in the following group?
   a. Alcyone—apparent magnitude of 3
   b. Alpheratz—apparent magnitude of 2
   c. Deneb—apparent magnitude of 1
   d. Rigel—apparent magnitude of 0

9. A cluster of stars forms in a nebula. There are red stars, blue stars, yellow stars, and white stars. Which stars are most like the sun?
   a. red   c. blue
   b. yellow   d. white

10. Individual stars are moving in space. How long will it take to see a noticeable difference without using a telescope?
    a. 24 hours   c. 100 years
    b. 1 year   d. 100,000 years

11. You visited an observatory and looked through the telescope. You saw a ball of stars through the telescope. What type of object did you see?
    a. a spiral galaxy
    b. an open cluster
    c. a globular cluster
    d. an irregular galaxy

12. In which part of a spiral galaxy do you expect to find nebulas?
    a. the spiral arms
    b. the central region
    c. the halo
    d. all parts of the galaxy

13. Which statement about the big bang theory is accurate?
    a. The universe will never end.
    b. New matter is being continuously created in the universe.
    c. The universe is filled with radiation coming from all directions in space.
    d. We can locate the center of the universe.

Short Answer

14. Describe how the apparent magnitude of a star varies with its distance from Earth.

15. Name six types of astronomical objects in the universe. Arrange them by size.

16. Which contains more stars on average, a globular cluster or an open cluster?

17. What does the big bang theory have to say about how the universe will end?

Concept Mapping

18. Use the following terms to create a concept map: black hole, neutron star, main-sequence star, red giant, nebula, white dwarf.

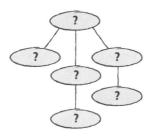

CRITICAL THINKING AND PROBLEM SOLVING

Write one or two sentences to answer the following questions:

19. If a certain star displayed a large parallax, what could you say about its distance from Earth?

20. Two M-type stars have the same apparent magnitude. Their spectra show that one is a red giant and the other is a red-dwarf star. Which one is farther from Earth? Explain your answer.

21. Look back at the H-R diagram in Section 2. Why do astronomers use absolute magnitudes to plot the stars? Why don't they use apparent magnitudes?

22. While looking at a galaxy through a nearby university's telescope, you notice that there are no blue stars present. What kind of galaxy is it most likely to be?

MATH IN SCIENCE

23. An astronomer observes two stars of about the same temperature and size. Alpha Centauri B is about 4 light-years away, and Sigma^2 Eridani A is about 16 light-years away. How much brighter does Alpha Centauri B appear?

INTERPRETING GRAPHICS

The following graph illustrates the Hubble law relating the distances of galaxies and their speed away from us.

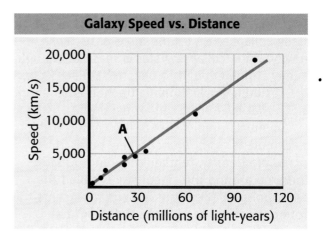

24. Look at the galaxy marked A in the graph. What is its speed and distance?

25. If a new galaxy with a speed of 15,000 km/s were found, at what distance would you expect it to be?

Reading Check-up

Take a minute to review your answers to the Pre-Reading Questions found at the bottom of page 568. Have your answers changed? If necessary, revise your answers based on what you have learned since you began this chapter.

WEIRD SCIENCE

HOLES WHERE STARS ONCE WERE

An invisible phantom lurks in outer space, ready to swallow up everything that comes near it. Once trapped in its grasp, matter is stretched, torn, and crushed into oblivion. Does this sound like a horror story? Guess again! Scientists call it a black hole.

Born of a Collapsing Star

As a star runs out of fuel, it cools and eventually collapses under the force of its own gravity. If the collapsing star is massive enough, it may shrink enough to become a black hole. The resulting gravitational attraction is so enormous that even light cannot escape!

Scientists predict that at the center of the black hole is a *singularity*, a tiny point of incredible density, temperature, and pressure. The area around the singularity is called the *event horizon*. The event horizon represents the boundary of the black hole. Anything that crosses the event horizon, including light, will eventually be pulled into the black hole. As matter comes near the event horizon, the matter begins to swirl in much the same way that water swirls down a drain.

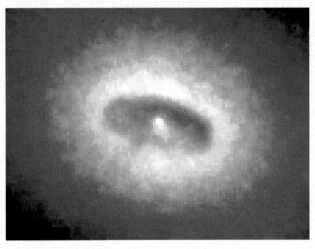

▲ *This photograph of M87 was taken by the Hubble Space Telescope.*

The Story of M87

For years, scientists had theorized about black holes but hadn't actually found one. Then in 1994, scientists found something strange at the core of a galaxy called M87. Scientists detected a disk-shaped cloud of gas with a diameter of 60 light-years, rotating at about 2 million kilometers per hour. When scientists realized that a mass more than 2 billion times that of the sun was crammed into a space no bigger than our solar system, they knew that something was pulling in the gases at the center of the galaxy.

Many astronomers think that black holes, such as the one in M87, lie at the heart of many galaxies. Some scientists suggest that there is a giant black hole at the center of our own Milky Way galaxy. But don't worry. The Earth is too far away to be caught.

Modeling a Black Hole

▶ Make a model to show how a black hole pulls in the matter surrounding it. Indicate the singularity and event horizon.

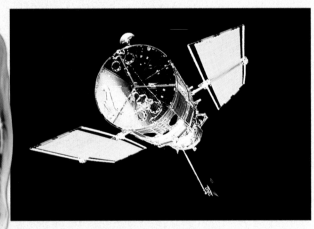

▲ *The Hubble Space Telescope*

CAREERS

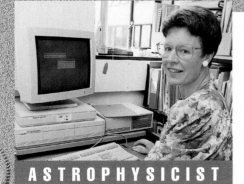

ASTROPHYSICIST

Jocelyn Bell-Burnell became fascinated with astronomy at an early age. As a research student at Cambridge University, Bell-Burnell discovered pulsars, celestial objects that emit radio waves at short and regular intervals. Today Bell-Burnell is a leading expert in the field of astrophysics and the study of stars. She is currently head of the physics department at the Open University, in Milton Keynes, England.

At Cambridge University in 1967, Bell-Burnell and her adviser, Antony Hewish, completed work on a gigantic radio telescope designed to pick up signals from quasars. Bell-Burnell's job was to operate the telescope and analyze the "chart paper" recordings of the telescope on a graph. Each day, the telescope recorded 29.2 m of chart paper! After a month of operating the telescope, Bell-Burnell noticed a few "bits of scruff" that she could not explain—they were very short, pulsating radio signals. The signals were only 6.3 mm long, and they occurred only once every 4 days. What Bell-Burnell had accidentally found was a needle in a cosmic haystack!

LGM 1

Bell-Burnell and Hewish struggled to find the source of this mysterious new signal. They double-checked the equipment and began eliminating all of the possible sources of the signal, such as satellites, television, and radar. Because they could not rule out that the signal was coming from aliens, Bell-Burnell and Hewish called it LGM 1. Can you guess why? LGM stood for "Little Green Men"!

The Answer: Neutron Stars

Shortly after finding the first signal, Bell-Burnell discovered yet another strange, pulsing signal within the vast quantity of chart paper. This signal was similar to the first, except that it came from the other side of the sky. To Bell-Burnell, this second signal was exciting because it meant that her first signal was not of local origin and that she had stumbled on a new and unknown signal from space! By January 1968, Bell-Burnell had discovered two more pulsating signals. In March of that year, her findings were published, to the amazement of the scientific community. The scientific press coined the term *pulsars*, from pulsating radio stars. Bell-Burnell and other scientists reached the conclusion that her "bits of scruff" were caused by rapidly spinning neutron stars!

Star Tracking

▶ Pick out a bright star in the sky, and keep a record of its position in relation to a reference point, such as a tree or building. Each night, record what time the star appears at this point in the sky. Do you notice a pattern?

▲ *An artist's depiction of a pulsar*

CHAPTER 22

Exploring Space

Sections

Pre-Reading Questions

1. What's the difference between a satellite and a space probe?

2. How has the space program benefited our daily lives?

3. How are humans preparing to live in space?

A SHUTTLE TO OUTER SPACE

The space shuttle was developed to take people into outer space. Because the shuttle can be reused, it lowers the cost of space launches by up to 90 percent. The lower cost of getting to outer space has opened a new era of space exploration in which space missions are more common. From these missions, scientists are able to gather important information that will eventually help humans adapt to living and working in space. In this chapter, you will see how technology and space exploration are connected and how they both impact us on Earth.

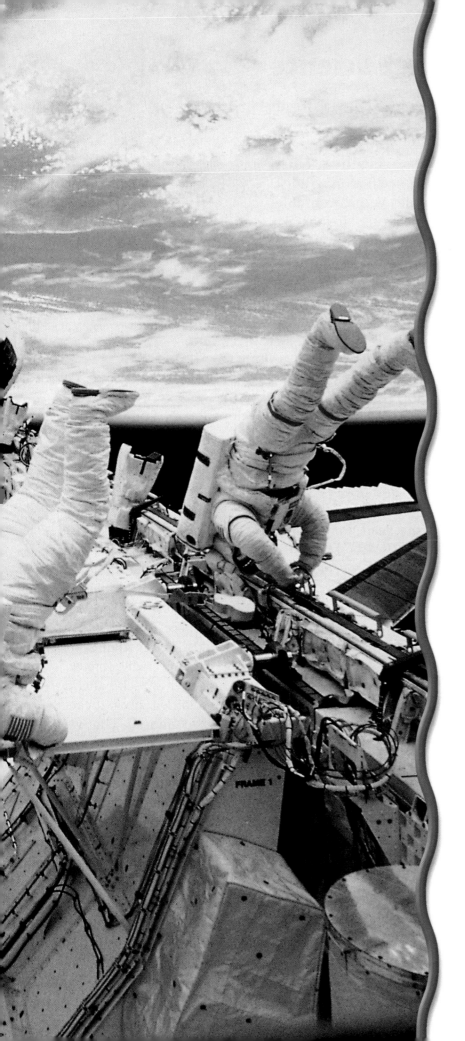

ROCKET FUN

Rockets are used to send people into space. Rockets work by forcing hot gas out one end of a tube. As this gas escapes in one direction, the rocket moves in the opposite direction. While you may have let a full balloon loose many times before, here you will use a balloon to learn about the principles of rocket propulsion.

Procedure

1. Thread a **string** through a **drinking straw,** and tie the string between two things that won't move, such as chairs. Make sure that the string is tight.

2. Blow into a large **balloon** until it is the size of a grapefruit. Hold the neck of the balloon closed.

3. **Tape** the balloon to the straw so that the opening of the balloon points toward one end of the string.

4. Move the balloon and straw to one end of the string, and then release the neck of the balloon. Record what happens in your ScienceLog.

5. Fill the balloon until it is almost twice the size it was in step 2, and repeat steps 3 and 4. Again record your observations.

Analysis

6. What happened during the second test that was different from the first? Can you figure out why?

Terms to Learn

rocket   orbital velocity
NASA   escape velocity
thrust

What You'll Do

- Outline the early development of rocket technology.
- Explain how a rocket works.
- Explain the difference between orbital velocity and escape velocity.

Rocket Science

How would you get to the moon? Before the invention of rockets, people could only dream of going into outer space. Science fiction writers, such as Jules Verne, were able to dress those dreams in scientific clothing by using what seemed like reasonable means of getting into space. For example, in a story he wrote in 1865, some of Verne's characters rode a capsule to the moon shot from a giant 900 ft long cannon.

But, as growing knowledge about the heavens was stimulating the imagination of writers and readers alike, an invention was slowly being developed that would become the key to exploring space. This was the rocket. A **rocket** is a machine that uses escaping gas to move.

The Beginning of Rocket Science

Around the year 1900, a Russian high school teacher named Konstantin Tsiolkovsky (KAHN stan teen TSEE uhl KAHV skee) began trying to understand the reasoning behind the motion of rockets. Tsiolkovsky's inspiration came from the fantastic, imaginative stories of Jules Verne. Tsiolkovsky believed that rockets were the key to space exploration. In his words, "The Earth is the cradle of mankind. But one does not have to live in the cradle forever." Tsiolkovsky is considered the father of rocket theory.

Although Tsiolkovsky explained how rockets work, he never built any rockets himself. That was left to American physicist Robert Goddard, who became known as the father of modern rocketry.

Modern Rocketry Gets a Boost Goddard, shown in **Figure 1,** conducted many rocket experiments in Massachusetts from 1915 to 1930. He then moved to New Mexico, where deserts provided enough room to conduct his tests safely. Between 1930 and 1941, Goddard tested more than 150 rocket engines, and by the time of World War II, his work was receiving much attention, most notably from the United States military.

Figure 1 *Robert Goddard tests one of his early rockets.*

From Rocket Bombs to Rocket Ships

During World War II, Germany developed the V-2 rocket, shown in **Figure 2,** and used it to bomb England. The design for the V-2 rocket came from Wernher von Braun, a young Ph.D. student whose research was being supported by the German military. In 1945, near the end of the war, von Braun and his entire research team surrendered to the advancing Americans. The United States thus gained 127 of the best German rocket scientists, and rocket research in the United States boomed in the 1950s.

The Birth of NASA The end of World War II marked the beginning of the Cold War—the arms race between the United States and the Soviet Union. The Soviet Union was made up of Russia and 15 other countries, forming a superpower that supported a military rivaling that of the United States.

On July 29, 1958, in response to the alarm Americans felt over a possible Soviet superiority in space, the National Aeronautics and Space Administration, or **NASA,** was formed. This organization combined all of the separate rocket-development teams in the United States. Their combined efforts led to the development of a series of rockets, including the Saturn V rocket and those used to launch the space shuttle, as shown in **Figure 3.**

Figure 2 *The V-2 rocket is the direct ancestor of all modern space vehicles.*

Figure 3 *Some of the space vehicles developed by NASA during its first 40 years are shown here to scale.*

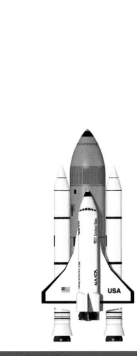

Mercury-Atlas	Delta	Titan IV	Saturn V	Space shuttle and boosters
1,400 kg payload	1,770 kg payload	18,000 kg payload	129,300 kg payload	29,500 kg payload
29 m tall	36 m tall	62 m tall	111 m tall	56 m tall

How Rockets Work

As you saw in the Investigate, rockets work on a simple physical principle. This principle, known as *Newton's third law of motion,* states that for every action there is an equal reaction in the opposite direction. For example, the air rushing backward from a balloon (the action) is paired with the forward motion of the balloon itself (the reaction).

In the case of rockets, however, the equality between the action and the reaction may not be obvious. This is because the mass of a rocket—which includes all of the fuel it carries—is much more than the mass of the hot gases as they come out of the exhaust nozzle. Because the hot gases are under extreme pressure, however, they exert a tremendous amount of force. The force that accelerates a rocket is called **thrust.** To learn more about how this works, look at **Figure 4.**

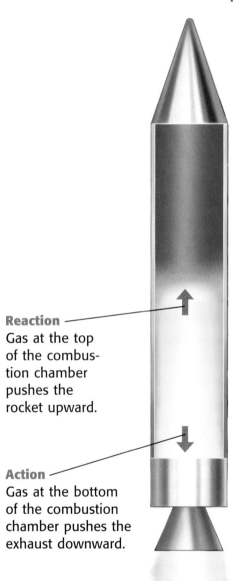

Reaction
Gas at the top of the combustion chamber pushes the rocket upward.

Action
Gas at the bottom of the combustion chamber pushes the exhaust downward.

Figure 4 *Rockets work according to Newton's third law of motion.*

Combustion All rockets have a combustion chamber in which hot gases are under very high pressure. As long as there is no opening for the gas to escape, the rocket remains at rest. In this state, the force that the gas exerts outward is the same as the force that the walls of the combustion chamber exert inward.

Pressure When the pressurized gas is released in only one direction—out the tail end of the rocket—the force of the hot gas against the top of the combustion chamber becomes greater than the opposing force of the air outside. As a result, the gas is forced out of the rocket nozzle.

Thrust If the force of the gas pushing against the top of the combustion chamber (thrust) becomes greater than the force of gravity holding the rocket down (the weight of the rocket), the rocket begins to move skyward.

How Fast Is Fast Enough? It is not enough for a rocket to have sufficient thrust to just move upward. It must have enough thrust to achieve *orbital velocity*. **Orbital velocity** is the speed and direction a rocket must have in order to orbit the Earth. The lowest possible speed a rocket may go and still orbit the Earth is about 8 km/s.

For Earth, all speeds less than about 8 km/s are *suborbital*. If the rocket goes any slower, it will fall back to Earth. If a rocket travels fast enough, however, it can attain *escape velocity*. **Escape velocity** is the speed and direction a rocket must travel in order to completely break away from a planet's gravitational pull. As you can see in **Figure 5,** the speed a rocket must attain to escape the Earth is about 11 km/s.

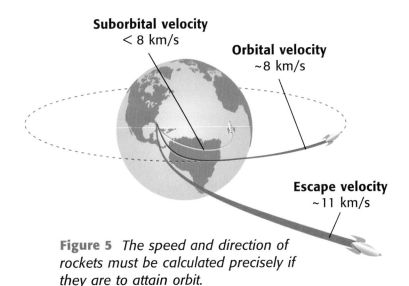

Suborbital velocity
< 8 km/s

Orbital velocity
~8 km/s

Escape velocity
~11 km/s

Figure 5 *The speed and direction of rockets must be calculated precisely if they are to attain orbit.*

You Need More Than Rocket Fuel . . . Rockets burn fuel to provide the thrust that propels them forward. But in order for something to burn, oxygen must be present. The earliest rocket fuel was gunpowder, which burns because oxygen is present in the atmosphere. Goddard was the first to use liquid fuel for rockets, which also burns in the presence of oxygen. But while oxygen is plentiful at the Earth's surface, in the upper atmosphere and in outer space, there is little or no oxygen. For this reason, rockets that go into outer space must carry enough oxygen with them to be able to burn their fuel. Otherwise the escaping gas would not create enough thrust to propel the rocket forward.

MATH BREAK

It's Just Rocket Science

As a burning gas (*g*) rushes out the back of a rocket (*r*), it provides thrust to move the rocket. The mass (*m*) and speed (*v*) of the gas and rocket are given by the following equation:

$$m_g \times v_g = m_r \times v_r$$

If the mass of a rocket is 100,000 kg, the speed of the gas leaving the rocket is 1,000 m/s, and the mass of the gas leaving the rocket is 1,000 kg, how fast will the rocket move?

REVIEW

1. What force must we overcome to reach outer space?

2. How does a rocket engine work?

3. What is the difference between orbital velocity and escape velocity?

4. **Making Inferences** How did World War II help us get into space exploration earlier than we otherwise would have?

internet connect

SC*i*LINKS
NSTA

TOPIC: Rocket Technology
GO TO: www.scilinks.org
*sci*LINKS NUMBER: HSTE530

Terms to Learn

artificial satellite
low Earth orbit
geosynchronous orbit

What You'll Do

◆ Describe how the launch of the first satellite started the space race.
◆ Explain why some orbits are better than others for communications satellites.
◆ Describe how the satellite program has given us a better understanding of the Earth as a global system.

Artificial Satellites

In 1955, President Dwight D. Eisenhower announced that the United States would launch an artificial satellite as part of America's contribution to international space science. An **artificial satellite** is any human-made object placed in orbit around a body in space, such as Earth. The Soviets were also working on a satellite program—and launched their satellite first!

The Space Race Begins

On October 4, 1957, a Soviet satellite became the first object to be placed in orbit around the Earth. *Sputnik 1,* shown in **Figure 6,** carried instruments to measure the properties of Earth's upper atmosphere. Less than a month later, the Soviets launched *Sputnik 2.* This satellite carried a dog named Laika.

Two months later, the U.S. Navy attempted to launch its own satellite by using a Vanguard rocket, which was originally intended for launching weather instruments into the atmosphere. To the embarrassment of the United States, the rocket rose only 1 m into the air and exploded.

The U.S. Takes a Close Second In the meantime, the U.S. Army was also busy modifying its military rockets to send a satellite into space, and on January 31, 1958, *Explorer 1,* the first United States satellite, was successfully launched. The space race was on!

Explorer 1, shown in **Figure 7,** carried scientific instruments to measure cosmic rays and small dust particles and to record temperatures of the upper atmosphere. *Explorer 1* discovered the Van Allen radiation belts around the Earth. These are regions in the Earth's magnetic field where charged particles from the sun have been trapped.

Figure 6 Sputnik 1 *was the first artificial satellite successfully placed in Earth orbit.*

Figure 7 *From left to right, NASA scientists William Pickering, James Van Allen, and Wernher von Braun show off a model of the first successfully launched American artificial satellite,* Explorer 1.

Into the Information Age

The first United States weather satellite, *Tiros 1,* was launched in April 1960 and gave meteorologists their first look at the Earth and its clouds from above. Weather satellites have given us an understanding of how storms develop and change by helping us study wind patterns and ocean currents. You now can see weather satellite images on your television at almost any time of the day or night or download them from the Internet.

Just a few months after *Tiros 1* began returning signals to Earth, the United States launched its first communications satellite, *Echo 1.* This satellite bounced signals from the ground to other areas on Earth, as shown in **Figure 8.** Within 3 years, sophisticated communications-satellite networks were sending TV signals from continent to continent.

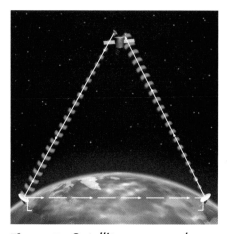

Figure 8 *Satellites can send signals beyond the curve of the Earth's surface, enabling communication around the world.*

Choose Your Orbit

All of the early satellites were placed in **low Earth orbit** (LEO), a few hundred kilometers above the Earth's surface. This location, while considered space, is still within the outermost part of Earth's atmosphere. A satellite in LEO travels around the Earth very quickly, which can place it out of contact much of the time.

Science fiction writer Arthur C. Clarke suggested a much higher orbit than LEO for weather and communications satellites. In this orbit, called a **geosynchronous orbit** (GEO), a satellite travels around the Earth at a speed that exactly matches the rotational speed of the Earth. This keeps the satellite positioned above the same spot on Earth at all times. Today there are many communications satellites in GEO. Ground stations are in continuous contact with these satellites, so your television program or phone call is not interrupted.

Self-Check

The space station being built by the United States and other countries is in LEO. What is one advantage of this location?
(See page 726 to check your answer.)

Anything GOES

The height above the Earth's surface for a geosynchronous orbit is 35,862 km. Today, a network of Geostationary Operational Environment Satellites (GOES) provides us with an international network of weather satellites. What would happen if a GOES satellite were placed in LEO rather than in GEO? How would that adversely affect the information the satellite was able to collect?

BRAIN FOOD

Not all satellites look down on Earth. Among the most important satellites to astronomers, for example, are the Hubble Space Telescope and the Chandra X-ray Observatory, both of which look out toward the stars.

Figure 9 *This image was taken in 1989 by a Soviet spy satellite in LEO about 220 km above the city of San Francisco. Can you identify any objects on the ground?*

Results of the Satellite Programs

Satellites gather information by *remote sensing.* Remote sensing is the gathering of images and data from high above the Earth's surface. The images and data help us investigate the Earth's surface by measuring the light and other forms of energy that reflect off Earth. Some satellites use radar, which bounces high-frequency radio waves off the surface of objects and measures the returned signal.

Military Satellites The United States military, which has a keen interest in satellites for defense and spying purposes, recognized that LEO was a perfect location for placing powerful telescopes that could be turned toward the Earth to photograph activities on the ground anywhere in the world.

The period from the late 1940s to the late 1980s is known as the Cold War. During that time, the United States and the former Soviet Union built up their military forces in order to ensure that neither nation became more powerful than the other. Both countries monitored each other using spy satellites. **Figure 9** shows an image of part of the United States taken by a Soviet spy satellite during the Cold War.

The military also launches satellites into GEO to aid in navigation and to serve as early warning systems against missiles launched toward the United States. Even though the Cold War is over, spy satellites continue to play an important role in the United States's military defense.

Eyes on the Environment

Satellites have given us a new vantage point for looking at the Earth. By getting above the Earth's atmosphere and looking down, we have been able to study the Earth in ways that were never before possible.

One of the most successful remote-sensing projects was the Landsat program, which began in 1972 and continues today. It has given us the longest continuous record of Earth's surface as seen from space. The newest Landsat satellite (number 7) was launched in 1999. It will gather images in several frequencies—from visible light that we can see to infrared. The Landsat program has produced millions of images that are being used to identify and track global and regional changes on Earth, as shown in **Figure 10.**

Remote sensing has allowed scientists to perform large-scale mapping, look at changes in patterns of vegetation growth, map the spread of urban development, help with mineral exploration, and study the effect of humans on the global environment.

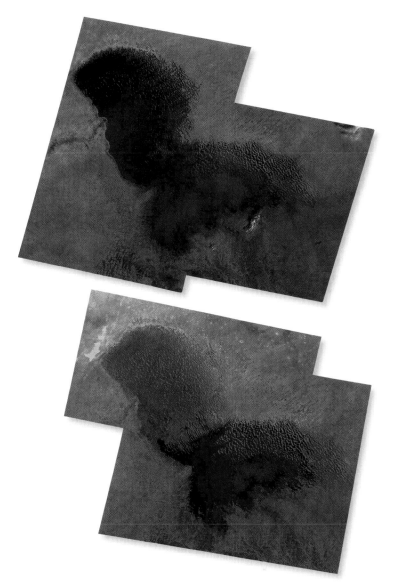

Figure 10 *These Landsat images of Lake Chad, Africa, show how environmental changes can be monitored from orbit. The top image was taken in 1973, and the bottom image was taken in 1987. Can you tell what changed?*

REVIEW

1. What types of satellites did the United States first place in orbit?

2. List two ways that satellites have benefited human society.

3. **Applying Concepts** The Hubble Space Telescope is located in LEO. Will the telescope move faster or slower around the Earth compared with a geosynchronous weather satellite? Explain.

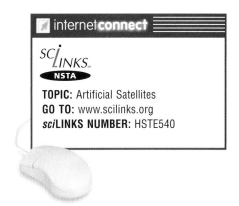

internet**connect**

SC*i*LINKS.
NSTA

TOPIC: Artificial Satellites
GO TO: www.scilinks.org
*sci*LINKS NUMBER: HSTE540

What You'll Do

◆ Describe some of the discoveries made by space probes.

◆ Explain how space-probe missions help us better understand the Earth.

◆ Describe how future space-probe missions will differ from the original missions to the planets.

Space Probes

The 1960s and early 1970s are known as the golden era of space exploration. The Soviets were the first to successfully launch a space probe. A **space probe** is a vehicle that carries scientific instruments to planets or other bodies in space. Unlike satellites, which stay in Earth orbit, space probes travel away from Earth. The early space probes gave us our first close encounters with the other planets and their moons.

Visits to Our Planetary Neighborhood

Because the Earth's moon and the inner planets of the solar system are so much closer to us than any other celestial bodies, they were the first to be targeted for exploration by the Soviet Union and the United States. Launched by the Soviets, *Luna 1* was the first space probe. In January of 1959, it flew past the moon. Two months later, an American space probe—*Pioneer 4*—accomplished the same feat. Follow along the next few pages to learn about space-probe missions since *Luna 1*.

The Moon

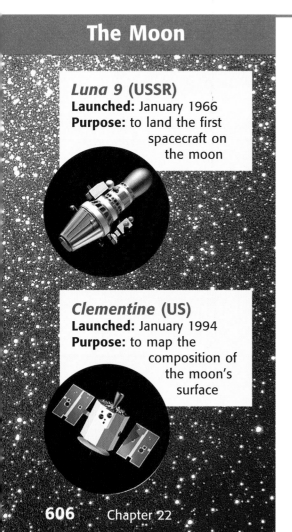

Luna 9 (USSR)
Launched: January 1966
Purpose: to land the first spacecraft on the moon

Clementine (US)
Launched: January 1994
Purpose: to map the composition of the moon's surface

The Luna 9 and Clementine Missions *Luna 9,* a Soviet probe, made the first soft landing on the moon's surface. During the next 10 years, there were more than 30 lunar missions made by the Soviet Union and the United States. Thousands of images of the moon's surface were taken.

In 1994, the probe *Clementine* discovered possible evidence of water at the south pole of the moon. The image below was taken by the *Clementine* space probe and shows the area surrounding the south pole of the moon. You can see that some of the craters at the pole are permanently in shadow. Elsewhere on the moon, sunlight would cause any ice to vaporize. Ice may have been left by comet impacts. If this frozen water exists, it will be very valuable to humans seeking to colonize the moon.

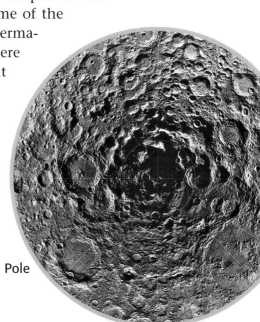

Lunar South Pole

The Venera 9 Mission The Soviet Union landed the first probe on Venus. The probe, called *Venera 9*, parachuted into Venus's atmosphere and transmitted the first images of the surface. *Venera 9* found that surface temperature and atmospheric pressure on Venus are much higher than on Earth. It also found that the chemistry of the surface rocks is similar to that of rocks on Earth. Perhaps most importantly, *Venera 9* and earlier missions showed us a planet with a severe greenhouse effect. Scientists study Venus's atmosphere to learn about how greenhouse gases released into Earth's atmosphere trap thermal energy.

The Magellan Mission In 1989, the United States launched the *Magellan* probe, which used radar to map 98 percent of the surface of Venus. The Magellan mission showed that, in many ways, the geology of Venus is similar to that of Earth. Venus has features that suggest some type of plate tectonics occurs, as it does on Earth. Venus also has volcanoes, some of which may have been active recently. The diagram at below left shows the *Magellan* probe using radar to penetrate the thick cloud layer. The radar data were then transmitted back to Earth, where computers were able to use the data to generate three-dimensional maps like the one at below right.

Venus

Venera 9 (USSR)
Launched: June 1975
Purpose: to record the surface conditions of Venus

Magellan (US)
Launched: May 1989
Purpose: to make a global map of the surface of Venus

Mars

The Viking Missions In 1975, the United States sent a pair of probes—*Viking 1* and *Viking 2*—to Mars. Because the surface of Mars is more like the Earth's surface than that of any other planet, one of the main goals of the Viking missions was to look for signs of life. The probes contained instruments designed to collect soil samples and test them for evidence of life. However, no hard evidence was found. The Viking missions did find evidence that Mars was once much warmer and wetter than it is now. The probes sent back images of dry water channels on the planet's surface. This discovery led scientists to ask even more questions about Mars. Why and when did the Martian climate change?

Viking 2 **(US)**
Launched: September 1975
Purpose: to search for life on the surface of Mars

Mars Pathfinder **(US)**
Launched: December 1996
Purpose: to use inexpensive technology to study the surface of Mars

The Mars Pathfinder Mission More than 20 years later, in 1997, the surface of Mars was visited again by a NASA space probe. The goal of the Mars Pathfinder mission was to show that Martian exploration is possible at a lower cost than that of the larger Viking mission. The *Mars Pathfinder* successfully landed on Mars and deployed the *Sojourner* rover, which traveled across the planetary surface for almost 3 months, collecting data and recording images of the Martian surface, as shown at left.

The Pioneer and Voyager Missions The *Pioneer 10* and *Pioneer 11* space probes were the first to visit the outer planets. Among other things, these probes sampled the *solar wind*—the flow of particles coming from the sun. The Pioneer probes also found that the dark belts on Jupiter are warmer than the light belts and that these dark belts provide deeper views into Jupiter's atmosphere. In June of 1983, *Pioneer 10* became the first space probe to travel past the orbit of Pluto, the outermost planet.

The Voyager space probes were the first to detect Jupiter's faint rings, and *Voyager 2* was the first space probe to fly by the four gas giant planets—Jupiter, Saturn, Uranus, and Neptune. The paths of the Pioneer and Voyager space probes are shown below. Today they are all near the edge of the solar system and are still sending back information.

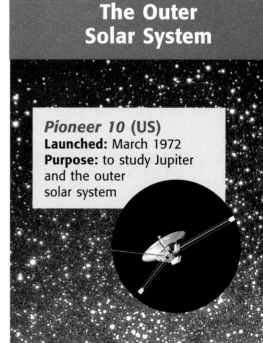

Pioneer 10 (US)
Launched: March 1972
Purpose: to study Jupiter and the outer solar system

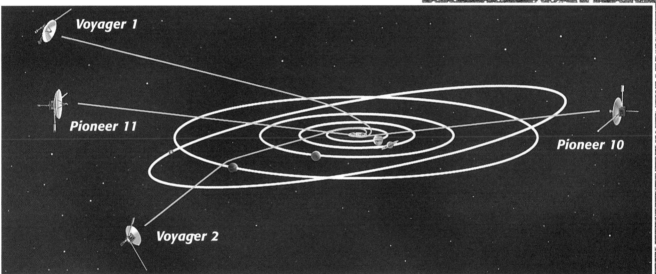

The Galileo Mission The *Galileo* space probe arrived at Jupiter in 1995. While *Galileo* itself began a long tour of Jupiter's moons, it sent a smaller probe into Jupiter's atmosphere to measure composition, density, temperature, and cloud structure. During its tour, *Galileo* gathered data that allowed scientists to study the geology of Jupiter's major moons and to examine Jupiter's magnetic properties more closely. The moons of Jupiter proved to be far more exciting than the earlier Pioneer and Voyager images had suggested. The *Galileo* probe discovered that two of Jupiter's moons have magnetic fields and that one of its moons, Europa, may have an ocean of liquid water lying under its icy surface.

Galileo (US)
Launched: October 1989
Purpose: to study Jupiter and its moons

Space Probes—A New Approach

NASA has a vision for missions that are "faster, cheaper, and better." The original space probes were very large, complex, and costly. Probes such as *Voyager 2* and *Galileo* took years to develop and carry out. One new program, called Discovery, seeks proposals for smaller science programs. The missions are supposed to bring faster results at much lower costs. The first six approved Discovery missions included sending small space probes to asteroids, another Mars landing, studies of the moon, the return of comet dust to Earth, collecting samples of the solar wind, and a tour of three comets.

Figure 11 Stardust *will visit a comet and collect samples of its dust tail.*

Stardust—Comet Detective

Launched in 1999, the *Stardust* space probe is a NASA Discovery mission and the first to focus only on a comet. As shown in **Figure 11,** it will arrive at the comet in 2004 and gather samples of the comet's dust tail, returning them to Earth in 2006. It will be the first time that material from beyond the orbit of the moon has been brought back to Earth. The comet dust should help scientists better understand the evolution of the sun and the planets.

***Deep Space 1*—The New Kid in Town** Another NASA project is the New Millennium program. Its purpose is to test new and risky technologies so that they can be used with confidence in the years to come. *Deep Space 1,* shown in **Figure 12,** undertook the first mission of this program. It is a space probe with an ion-propulsion system. Rather than burning chemical fuel, an ion rocket uses charged particles that exit the vehicle at high speed. An ion rocket still follows Newton's third law of motion, but it does so using a different source of propulsion.

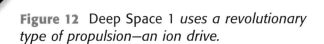

Figure 12 Deep Space 1 *uses a revolutionary type of propulsion—an ion drive.*

The Last of the Big Boys On October 15, 1997, the *Cassini* space probe was launched on a 7-year journey to Saturn. This is the last of the large old-style missions. The *Cassini* space probe will make a grand tour of Saturn's system of moons, much as *Galileo* toured Jupiter's system. As shown in **Figure 13,** a smaller probe, called the *Huygens probe,* will detach itself from *Cassini* and descend into the atmosphere of Saturn's moon Titan to study its chemistry.

Figure 13 *An artist's view of* Cassini *at Saturn, with* Huygens *falling toward Saturn's moon Titan.*

Future Missions Proposals for future missions include a first-ever space-probe visit to Pluto, an orbiter for Jupiter's moon Europa that will use radar to determine whether it has a liquid ocean, and a possible Mercury orbiter to survey the planet closest to the sun. These are just a few of the many exciting international missions planned for the future—opening up a new golden era of planetary exploration.

REVIEW

1. List three discoveries that have been made by space probes.

2. Which two planets best help us understand Earth's environment? Explain.

3. What are the advantages of the new Discovery program over the older space-probe missions?

4. **Inferring Conclusions** Why did we need space probes to discover water channels on Mars or ice on Europa?

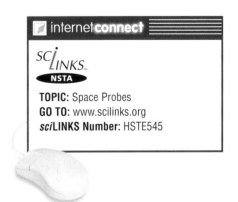

internet connect

SC*L*INKS
NSTA

TOPIC: Space Probes
GO TO: www.scilinks.org
*sci*LINKS **Number:** HSTE545

Living and Working in Space

Terms to Learn

space shuttle
space station

What You'll Do

- ◆ Summarize the benefits of the manned space program.
- ◆ Explain how large projects such as the Apollo program and the *International Space Station* developed.
- ◆ Identify future possibilities for human exploration of space.

Although sending human explorers into space was an early goal of the space program, it had to come in small steps. The first steps were to test the control of spacecraft with rocket-powered airplanes. Test flights in high-speed aircraft through the upper atmosphere became the beginnings of the Mercury program. The goal of the Mercury program was to put a man in orbit and to test his ability to function in space. Test flights began in 1959, but the dates for manned flight kept getting delayed because of unreliable rockets.

Human Space Exploration

On April 12, 1961, a Soviet cosmonaut named Yuri Gagarin became the first human to orbit the Earth. The United States didn't achieve its first suborbital flight until May 5, 1961, when Alan Shepard reached space but not orbit. Because the Soviets were first once again, they appeared to be winning the Cold War. As a result, many Americans began to consider the military advantages of a strong presence in space. On May 25, 1961, an announcement was made that would set the tone for American space policy for the next 10 years.

> *"I believe that this nation should commit itself to achieving the goal, before this decade is out, of landing a man on the moon and returning him safely to the Earth. No single space project in this period will be more impressive to mankind, or more important for the long-range exploration of space; and none will be so difficult or expensive to accomplish."*
>
> — *John F. Kennedy, President of the United States*

Figure 14 *In 1962, John Glenn flew aboard* Friendship 7, *the first NASA spacecraft to orbit the Earth.*

Many people were expecting the simple announcement of an accelerated space program, but Kennedy's proclamation took everyone by surprise—especially the leaders at NASA. Go to the moon? The United States had not even achieved Earth orbit yet! But the American people took the challenge seriously, and by February 1962, a new spaceport site in Florida was purchased, a manned space-center site was bought, and John Glenn, shown in **Figure 14,** was successfully launched into orbit around the Earth.

The Dream Comes True On July 20, 1969, the President's challenge was met. The *Apollo 11* landing module—the *Eagle,* shown in **Figure 15**—landed on the moon. Astronaut Neil Armstrong became the first human to set foot on a world other than Earth, forever changing the way we view ourselves and our planet.

Although the primary reason for the Apollo program was political (national pride), the Apollo missions also contributed to the advancement of science and technology. *Apollo 11* returned nearly 22 kg of moon rocks to Earth for study. Its crew also put devices on the moon to monitor moonquake activity and the solar wind. The results from these samples and studies completely changed our view of the solar system.

The Space Shuttle

The dream of human space flight and Kennedy's challenge were great for getting us into space, but they could not be the motivation for the continued political support of space exploration. The huge rockets required for launching spacecraft into orbit were just too expensive.

Early in the manned program, Wernher von Braun had suggested that a reusable space transportation system would be needed. Proposals for reusable launch vehicles were made in the 1950s and 1960s, but the Kennedy challenge overshadowed other efforts, and these ideas were not given serious attention. Finally in 1972, President Richard Nixon announced a space shuttle program to the American public, saying that this would be an economical way to get into space regularly. A **space shuttle** is a reusable vehicle that takes off like a rocket and lands like an airplane, as shown in **Figure 16.**

Figure 15 *Astronaut Neil Armstrong took this photo of Edwin "Buzz" Aldrin as he was about to become the second human being to step onto the moon.*

Figure 16 Columbia *was one of NASA's original shuttles.*

The first shuttle was launched on April 12, 1981, and was followed by two dozen successful missions until 1986, when tragedy struck. On January 28, 1986, the booster rocket on the space shuttle *Challenger* exploded just after takeoff, killing all seven of its astronauts. On board was Christa McAuliffe, who would have been the first teacher in space. All shuttle flights were suspended until this disaster could be explained. Finally in 1988, the space shuttle program resumed with the return of shuttle *Discovery* to space.

Commuter Shuttle? Currently efforts are underway to make space travel easier and cheaper. NASA is working to develop a space plane that will fly like a normal airplane through the atmosphere but will be equipped with rocket engines for use in the vacuum of space. Once in operation, space planes, such as the *X-33* shown in **Figure 17,** may lower the cost of getting material to LEO by 90 percent. Research is now being done on the next generation of space vehicles. New types of rockets and rocket fuels, as well as other means of sending vehicles into space, are being considered.

Figure 17 *Future space planes may provide inexpensive transportation not only between Earth and outer space but around the world.*

Biology

C O N N E C T I O N

When a human body stays in space for long periods of time without having to work against gravity, the bones lose mass and muscles become weaker. Long space-station missions, which can last for months, are very important in order to study whether humans can survive voyages to Mars and other planets. These missions will last for several years.

Space Stations—People Working in Space

On April 19, 1971, the Soviets became the first to successfully place a manned space station in low Earth orbit. A **space station** is a long-term orbiting platform from which other vehicles can be launched or scientific research can be carried out. In June of the same year, a crew of three Soviet cosmonauts entered *Salyut 1* to conduct a 23-day mission. By 1982, the Soviets had put up a total of seven space stations. Because of this experience, the Soviet Union became the world leader in space-station development and in the study of the effects of weightlessness on humans. Their discoveries will be important for future manned flights to other planets—journeys that will take years to complete.

A Home Away from Home *Skylab,* the United States's first space station, was a science and engineering lab that orbited the Earth in LEO at a height of 435 km. The lab, shown in **Figure 18,** was used to conduct a wide variety of scientific studies, including astronomy, biological experiments, and experiments in space manufacturing. Three different crews spent a total of 171 days on board *Skylab.*

All objects in LEO, including *Skylab,* eventually spiral toward Earth. Even at several hundred kilometers above the Earth, there is still a very small amount of atmosphere. The atmosphere slows down any object in orbit unless something periodically pushes the object in the opposite direction. *Skylab's* orbit began to decay in 1979. A space shuttle was supposed to return the lab to a higher orbit, but delays in the shuttle program prevented the rescue of *Skylab,* and it fell into the Indian Ocean.

Figure 18 Skylab, *in orbit above Earth, was lifted into space by a Saturn V rocket.*

From Russia with Peace In 1986, the Soviets began to launch the pieces for a much more ambitious space station called *Mir* (meaning "peace"). The Soviets, and later the Russians, used *Mir* to conduct astronomy experiments, provide biological and Earth orbital observations, and study manufacturing technologies in space. When completed, *Mir* had seven modules and measured 33 m long and 27 m wide.

Astronauts from the United States and other countries eventually became visitors to *Mir,* as shown in **Figure 19.** Almost continuously inhabited between 1987 and 1999, *Mir* became the inspiration to build the next generation of space station—the International Space Station.

Working in space requires the use of special tools, such as the space shuttle's robot arm. Turn to page 724 in the LabBook to extend your own reach.

Figure 19 Mir *provided an opportunity for American astronauts and Russian cosmonauts to live and work together in space.*

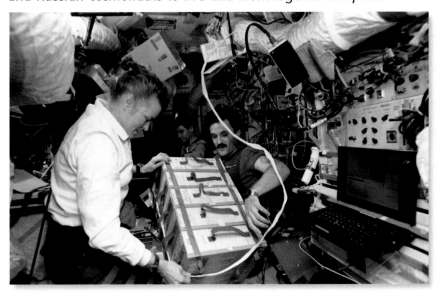

Science CONNECTION

Working together to live in space? To learn more about the latest station in orbit, turn to page 622.

Working together to live in space? To learn more about the latest station in orbit, turn to page 622.

BRAIN FOOD

It will take more than 40 shuttle flights and 6 years to lift into space the 400 tons of materials needed for the construction of the *International Space Station*.

The International Space Station

In 1993, a design for a new space station was proposed that called for international involvement and a collaboration between the newly formed Russian Republic and the United States. The new space station is called the *International Space Station (ISS)*. A drawing of the station when completed is shown in **Figure 20.**

The station is being assembled in LEO with materials brought up on the space shuttle or by Russian rockets. The United States is providing lab modules, the supporting truss, solar panels for power, living quarters, and a biomedical laboratory. The Russians are contributing a service module, docking modules, life support and research modules, and transportation to and from the station. Other components will come from Japan, Canada, and several European countries.

The *ISS* will provide many benefits—some of which we cannot even predict. What we do know is that it will be a good place to perform space-science experiments and perhaps to invent new technologies. Hopefully the *ISS* will also promote cooperation among countries and continue the pioneering spirit of the first astronauts and cosmonauts.

Figure 20 *This artist's view of the* International Space Station *shows what the station will look like once it is completed.*

The Moon, Mars, and Beyond

We may eventually need resources and living space beyond what Earth can provide. Space can provide abundant mineral resources. One interesting resource is a rare form of helium that can be found on the moon. Used as a fuel for nuclear reactors, it leaves no radioactive waste!

We have seen that there are also many scientific benefits to space exploration. For example, the far side of the moon can be 100 times darker than any observatory site on Earth. The moon also could be a wonderful place to locate factories that require a vacuum to process materials, as shown in **Figure 21.** A base in Earth orbit can produce materials that require low gravity. A colony or base on the moon or on Mars could be an important link to bringing space resources to Earth. The key will be to make these missions economically worthwhile.

Figure 21 *Humans may eventually colonize the moon for scientific, economic, and perhaps even recreational reasons.*

REVIEW

1. How was the race to explore our solar system influenced by the Cold War?

2. How did missions to the moon benefit space science?

3. How will space stations help in the exploration of space?

4. **Making Inferences** Why did the United States quit sending people to the moon after the Apollo program ended?

Chapter Highlights

Vocabulary

rocket *(p. 598)*

NASA *(p. 599)*

thrust *(p. 600)*

orbital velocity *(p. 601)*

escape velocity *(p. 601)*

Section Notes

- Two pioneers of rocketry were Konstantin Tsiolkovsky and Robert Goddard.

- Rockets work according to Newton's third law of motion—for every action there is an equal and opposite reaction.

- NASA was formed in 1958, combining rocket research from several programs. It was originally formed to compete with the Soviet Union's rocket program.

Labs

Water Rockets Save the Day!
(p. 722)

Vocabulary

artificial satellite *(p. 602)*

low Earth orbit *(p. 603)*

geosynchronous orbit *(p. 603)*

Section Notes

- The Soviet Union launched the first Earth-orbiting satellite in 1957. The first United States satellite went up in 1958.

- Low Earth orbits (LEOs) are located a few hundred kilometers above the Earth's surface. Satellites in geosynchronous orbits (GEOs) have an orbit period of 24 hours and remain over one spot.

- Satellite programs are used for weather observations, communications, mapping the Earth, and tracking ocean currents, crop growth, and urban development.

- One great legacy of the satellite program has been an increase in our awareness of the Earth's fragile environment.

☑ Skills Check

Math Concepts

THE ROCKET EQUATION Suppose the mass of a certain rocket is 1,000 kg and the mass of the gas leaving the rocket is 100 kg. If the speed that the gas leaves the rocket is 50 m/s, the rocket will move at a speed of 5 m/s. Rearranging the rocket equation:

$$m_g \times v_g = m_r \times v_r$$

$$\text{as} \quad v_r = m_g \times v_g/m_r$$

$$\text{gives} \quad v_r = \frac{100 \text{ kg} \times 50 \text{ m/s}}{1,000 \text{ kg}} = 5 \text{ m/s}$$

Visual Understanding

GLOBAL COMMUNICATION As you saw on page 603, satellites can relay television, radio, and telephone signals around the world. Because they remain in GEO, these satellites are always above the same spot on Earth, letting them relay our signals without interruption.

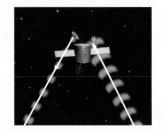

SECTION 3

Vocabulary

space probe *(p. 606)*

Section Notes

- Planetary exploration with space probes began with missions to the moon. The next targets of exploration were the inner planets: Venus, Mercury, and Mars.

- The United States has been the only country to explore the outer solar system, beginning with the Pioneer and Voyager missions.

- Space-probe science has given us information about how planets form and develop, helping us better understand our own planet Earth.

SECTION 4

Vocabulary

space shuttle *(p. 613)*
space station *(p. 614)*

Section Notes

- The great race to get a manned flight program underway and to reach the moon was politically motivated.

- The United States beat the Soviets to a manned moon landing with the Apollo moon flights in 1969.

- During the 1970s, the United States focused on developing the space shuttle. The Soviets focused on developing orbiting space stations.

- The United States, Russia, and 14 other international partners are currently developing the *International Space Station.*

- Because of scientific, economic, and even recreational reasons, humans may eventually live and work on other planets and moons.

Labs

Reach for the Stars *(p. 724)*

Chapter Review

USING VOCABULARY

For each pair of terms, explain the difference in their meaning:

1. geosynchronous orbit/low Earth orbit

2. space probe/space shuttle

3. artificial satellite/moon

To complete the following sentences, choose the correct term from each pair of terms listed below:

4. The force that accelerates a rocket is called ___?___. (*escape velocity* or *thrust*)

5. Rockets need to have ___?___ in order to burn their fuel. (*oxygen* or *nitrogen*)

UNDERSTANDING CONCEPTS

Multiple Choice

6. The father of modern rocketry is considered to be
   a. K. Tsiolkovsky.
   b. R. Goddard.
   c. W. von Braun.
   d. D. Eisenhower.

7. Rockets work according to Newton's
   a. first law of motion.
   b. second law of motion.
   c. third law of motion.
   d. law of universal gravitation.

8. The first artificial satellite to orbit the Earth was
   a. *Pioneer 4.*
   b. *Explorer 1.*
   c. *Voyager 2.*
   d. *Sputnik 1.*

9. Satellites are able to transfer TV signals across and between continents because satellites
   a. are located in LEOs.
   b. relay signals past the horizon.
   c. travel quickly around Earth.
   d. can be used during the day and night.

10. GEOs are better orbits for communications because satellites in GEO
   a. remain in position over one spot.
   b. are farther away from Earth's surface.
   c. do not revolve around the Earth.
   d. are only a few hundred kilometers high.

11. Which space probe discovered evidence of water at the moon's south pole?
   a. *Luna 9*
   b. *Viking 1*
   c. *Clementine*
   d. *Magellan*

12. When did humans first set foot on the moon?
   a. 1949   c. 1969
   b. 1959   d. 1979

13. Which one of these planets has not yet been visited by space probes?
   a. Mercury
   b. Neptune
   c. Mars
   d. Pluto

14. Of the following, which space probe is about to leave our solar system?
   a. *Galileo*
   b. *Magellan*
   c. *Mariner 10*
   d. *Pioneer 10*

15. Based on space-probe data, which of the following is the most likely place in our solar system to find liquid water?
   a. the moon
   b. Mars
   c. Europa
   d. Venus

Short Answer

16. Describe how Newton's third law of motion relates to the movement of rockets.

17. What is one disadvantage that objects in LEO have?

18. Why did the United States develop the space shuttle?

19. During which period were spy satellites first used?

Concept Mapping

20. Use the following terms to create a concept map: orbital velocity, thrust, LEO, artificial satellites, escape velocity, space probes, GEO, rockets.

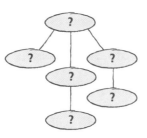

CRITICAL THINKING AND PROBLEM SOLVING

Write one or two sentences to answer the following questions:

21. What is the difference between speed and velocity?

22. Why must rockets that travel in outer space carry oxygen with them?

23. How will data from space probes help us understand the Earth's environment?

24. Why is it necessary for several nations to work together to create the *ISS*?

MATH IN SCIENCE

25. In order to escape Earth's gravity, a rocket must travel at least 11 km/s. This is pretty fast! If you could travel to the moon at this speed, how many hours would it take you to get there? (The moon is about 384,000 km away from Earth.) Round your answer to the nearest whole number.

INTERPRETING GRAPHICS

The map below was made using satellite data. It indicates the different amounts of chlorophyll in the ocean. Chlorophyll, in turn, identifies the presence of marine plankton. The blues and purples show the smallest amount of chlorophyll, and the reds and oranges show the most. Examine the map, and answer the questions that follow:

Chlorophyll Content

High ⟵⟶ Low

26. At which location, **A** or **B**, are more plankton concentrated?

27. What do you conclude about the conditions in which plankton prefer to live?

Reading Check-up

Take a minute to review your answers to the Pre-Reading Questions found at the bottom of page 596. Have your answers changed? If necessary, revise your answers based on what you have learned since you began this chapter.

International Space Station

On a June day in 1995, the space shuttle *Atlantis* docked at the Russian space station, *Mir,* and picked up three passengers. These passengers, one from the United States and two from Russia, had completed a 3-month stay at the space station. This mission was the first in a series of missions to develop construction techniques for assembling the *International Space Station.* These missions are considered to be phase one of the process.

An International Place in Space

Sixteen nations plan to build the *International Space Station (ISS)* by the year 2004. These nations are the United States, Russia, Canada, Brazil, Japan, Denmark, Germany, France, Italy, Belgium, the Netherlands, Switzerland, the United Kingdom, Spain, Norway, and Sweden.

The *ISS* will be made up of cylindrical rooms called *modules.* Each of these components will be built on the ground and then assembled 274 km above Earth. The current plan calls for more than 40 space flights to carry the parts of the space station into orbit. Once the *ISS* is completed, a seven-member crew will be able to live and work there.

Life Aboard

One of the strange things about living in space is the reduced effect of gravity known as *free fall.* Everything inside the space station that is not fastened down, including the astronauts, will float! The designers of the *ISS*'s habitation module have come up with some intriguing solutions to this problem. For example, each astronaut will sleep in a sack similar to a sleeping bag that is fastened to the module. The sack will keep the astronauts from floating around while they sleep. Astronauts will shower with a hand-held nozzle that squirts water onto their body. Afterward, the water droplets will be vacuumed up so that they won't float around. Other problems being studied include how to prepare and serve food, how to design an effective toilet, and how to dispose of waste.

Ready to Go

Phase two began with the actual construction of the *ISS* in orbit. In November and December of 1998, two modules, *Zarya* and *Unity,* were launched into orbit. In early 2000, a three-person crew began living on board—the first of many crews expected to inhabit the *International Space Station.*

Address the Gravity of a Situation

▶ Create a sketch for a device that will help the space-station crew cope with free fall. Pick a problem to solve such as brushing teeth, getting exercise, or washing hair.

▲ *Parts of the* International Space Station *are being assembled in space.*

Science Fiction

"Why I Left Harry's All-Night Hamburgers"

by Lawrence Watt-Evans

At 16, he needed a job. His dad was out of work and his family needed money. Right around the corner from his house was Harry's All-Night Hamburgers. With a little persistence, he talked Harry into giving him a job.

He worked from midnight to 7:30 A.M. so he could still go to school. He was the counterman, waiter, busboy, and janitor, all in one. Harry's was pretty quiet most nights, especially because the interstate was 8 mi away and nobody wanted to drive to Harry's. Most of the time, the customers were pretty normal.

There were some, though, who were unusual. For instance, one guy came in dressed for Arctic winter, even though it was April and it was 60°F outside. Then there were the folks who parked a very strange vehicle right out in the parking lot for anyone to see.

Pretty soon, the captivated waiter starts asking questions. What he learns startles and fascinates him. Soon he's thinking about leaving Harry's. Find out why by reading "Why I Left Harry's All-Night Hamburgers," by Lawrence Watt-Evans, in the *Holt Anthology of Science Fiction*.

Contents

Exploring, inventing, and investigating are essential to the study of science. However, these activities can also be dangerous. To make sure that your experiments and explorations are safe, you must be aware of a variety of safety guidelines.

You have probably heard of the saying, "It is better to be safe than sorry." This is particularly true in a science classroom where experiments and explorations are being performed. Being uninformed and careless can result in serious injuries. Don't take chances with your own safety or with anyone else's.

Following are important guidelines for staying safe in the science classroom. Your teacher may also have safety guidelines and tips that are specific to your classroom and laboratory. Take the time to be safe.

Safety Rules!

Start Out Right

Always get your teacher's permission before attempting any laboratory exploration. Read the procedures carefully, and pay particular attention to safety information and caution statements. If you are unsure about what a safety symbol means, look it up or ask your teacher. You cannot be too careful when it comes to safety. If an accident does occur, inform your teacher immediately, regardless of how minor you think the accident is.

Safety Symbols

All of the experiments and investigations in this book and their related worksheets include important safety symbols to alert you to particular safety concerns. Become familiar with these symbols so that when you see them, you will know what they mean and what to do. It is important that you read this entire safety section to learn about specific dangers in the laboratory.

If you are instructed to note the odor of a substance, wave the fumes toward your nose with your hand. Never put your nose close to the source.

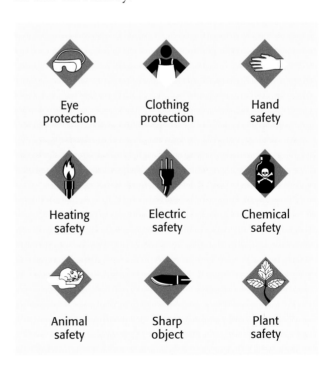

Eye protection

Clothing protection

Hand safety

Heating safety

Electric safety

Chemical safety

Animal safety

Sharp object

Plant safety

Eye Safety

Wear safety goggles when working around chemicals, acids, bases, or any type of flame or heating device. Wear safety goggles any time there is even the slightest chance that harm could come to your eyes. If any substance gets into your eyes, notify your teacher immediately, and flush your eyes with running water for at least 15 minutes. Treat any unknown chemical as if it were a dangerous chemical. Never look directly into the sun. Doing so could cause permanent blindness.

Avoid wearing contact lenses in a laboratory situation. Even if you are wearing safety goggles, chemicals can get between the contact lenses and your eyes. If your doctor requires that you wear contact lenses instead of glasses, wear eye-cup safety goggles in the lab.

Safety Equipment

Know the locations of the nearest fire alarms and any other safety equipment, such as fire blankets and eyewash fountains, as identified by your teacher, and know the procedures for using them.

Be extra careful when using any glassware. When adding a heavy object to a graduated cylinder, tilt the cylinder so the object slides slowly to the bottom.

Neatness

Keep your work area free of all unnecessary books and papers. Tie back long hair, and secure loose sleeves or other loose articles of clothing, such as ties and bows. Remove dangling jewelry. Don't wear open-toed shoes or sandals in the laboratory. Never eat, drink, or apply cosmetics in a laboratory setting. Food, drink, and cosmetics can easily become contaminated with dangerous materials.

Certain hair products (such as aerosol hair spray) are flammable and should not be worn while working near an open flame. Avoid wearing hair spray or hair gel on lab days.

Sharp/Pointed Objects

Use knives and other sharp instruments with extreme care. Never cut objects while holding them in your hands. Place objects on a suitable work surface for cutting.

Heat

Wear safety goggles when using a heating device or a flame. Whenever possible, use an electric hot plate as a heat source instead of an open flame. When heating materials in a test tube, always angle the test tube away from yourself and others. In order to avoid burns, wear heat-resistant gloves whenever instructed to do so.

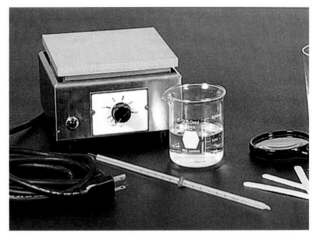

Electricity

Be careful with electrical cords. When using a microscope with a lamp, do not place the cord where it could trip someone. Do not let cords hang over a table edge in a way that could cause equipment to fall if the cord is accidentally pulled. Do not use equipment with damaged cords. Be sure your hands are dry and that the electrical equipment is in the "off" position before plugging it in. Turn off and unplug electrical equipment when you are finished.

Chemicals

Wear safety goggles when handling any potentially dangerous chemicals, acids, or bases. If a chemical is unknown, handle it as you would a dangerous chemical. Wear an apron and safety gloves when working with acids or bases or whenever you are told to do so. If a spill gets on your skin or clothing, rinse it off immediately with water for at least 5 minutes while calling to your teacher.

Never mix chemicals unless your teacher tells you to do so. Never taste, touch, or smell chemicals unless you are specifically directed to do so. Before working with a flammable liquid or gas, check for the presence of any source of flame, spark, or heat.

Animal Safety

Always obtain your teacher's permission before bringing any animal into the school building. Handle animals only as your teacher directs. Always treat animals carefully and with respect. Wash your hands thoroughly after handling any animal.

Plant Safety

Do not eat any part of a plant or plant seed used in the laboratory. Wash hands thoroughly after handling any part of a plant. When in nature, do not pick any wild plants unless your teacher instructs you to do so.

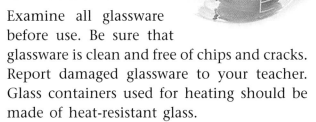

Glassware

Examine all glassware before use. Be sure that glassware is clean and free of chips and cracks. Report damaged glassware to your teacher. Glass containers used for heating should be made of heat-resistant glass.

MAKING MODELS

Using the Scientific Method

Geologists often use a technique called *core sampling* to learn what underground rock layers look like. This technique involves drilling several holes in the ground in different places and taking samples of the underground rock or soil. Geologists then compare the samples from each hole to construct a diagram that shows the bigger picture.

In this activity, you will model the process geologists use to diagram underground rock layers. You will first use modeling clay to form a rock-layer model. You will then exchange models with a classmate, take core samples, and draw a diagram of your classmate's layers.

Materials

- 3 colored pencils or markers
- nontransparent pan or box
- modeling clay in three colors
- 1/2 in. PVC pipe
- plastic knife

Ask a Question

1. Can unseen features be revealed by sampling parts of the whole?

Form a Hypothesis

2. Form a hypotheses on whether taking core samples from several locations will give a good indication of the entire hidden feature.

Test the Hypothesis

3. To test your hypothesis, you will take core samples from a model of underground rock layers, draw a diagram of the entire rock-layer sequence, and then compare your drawing with the actual model.

Build a Model
The model rock layers should be formed out of view of the classmates who will be taking the core samples.

4. Form a plan for your rock layers, and sketch the layers in your ScienceLog. Your sketch should include the three colors in several layers of varying thicknesses.

5. In the pan or box, mold the clay into the shape of the lowest layer in your sketch.

6. Repeat step 5 for each additional layer of clay. You now have a rock-layer model. Exchange models with a classmate.

Collect Data

7. Choose three places on the surface of the clay to drill holes. The holes should be far apart and in a straight line. (You do not need to remove the clay from the pan or box.)

8. Use the PVC pipe to "drill" a vertical hole in the clay at one of the chosen locations by slowly pushing the pipe through all the layers of clay. Slowly remove the pipe.

9. Remove the core sample from the pipe by gently pushing the clay out of the pipe with an unsharpened pencil.

10. Draw the core sample in your ScienceLog, and record your observations. Be sure to use a different color of pencil or marker for each layer.

11. Repeat steps 8–10 for the next two core samples. Make sure your drawings are side by side in your ScienceLog in the same order as the samples in the model.

Analyze the Results

12. Look at the pattern of rock layers in each of your core samples. Think about how the rock layers between the core samples might look. Then construct a diagram of the rock layers.

13. Complete your diagram by coloring the rest of the rock layers.

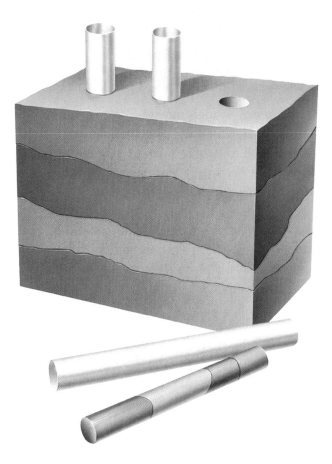

Draw Conclusions

14. Use the plastic knife to cut the clay model along a line connecting the three holes and remove one side of the model. The rock layers should now be visible.

15. How well does your rock-layer diagram match the model? Explain.

16. Is it necessary to revise your diagram from step 13? If so, how?

17. Do your conclusions support your hypothesis? Why or why not?

Going Further
What are two ways that the core-sampling method could be improved?

Using Scientific Methods

Round or Flat?

Eratosthenes thought he could measure the circumference of the Earth. He came up with the idea while reading that a deep vertical well in southern Egypt was entirely lit up by the sun at noon once each year. He realized that for this to happen, the sun must be directly over the well at that moment! But at the same moment, in a city just north of this well, a tall monument cast a shadow. Eratosthenes reasoned that the sun could not be directly over both the monument and the well at noon on the same day. In this experiment, you will test his idea and see for yourself how his experiment works.

Materials

- basketball
- 2 books or notebooks
- modeling clay
- 2 unsharpened pencils
- metric ruler
- meterstick
- masking tape
- flashlight or small lamp
- string, 10 cm long
- protractor
- tape measure
- calculator (optional)

Ask a Question

1. How could I use Eratosthenes' experiment to measure the size of the Earth?

Conduct an Experiment

2. Set the basketball on a table, and place a book or notebook on either side to hold the ball in place. The ball represents the Earth.

3. Use modeling clay to attach a pencil to the "equator" of the ball so that it sticks directly outward.

4. Attach the second pencil to the ball 5 cm above the first pencil. This second pencil should also stick directly outward, as shown on the next page.

5. Using a meterstick, mark a position 1 m away from the ball with masking tape. Label it "sun." Place the flashlight here.

6. When your teacher turns out the lights, turn on your flashlight, and point it so that the pencil on the equator does not cast a shadow. Ask a partner to hold the flashlight in this position. The second pencil should cast a shadow on the ball.

7. Tape one end of the string to the top of the second pencil. Hold the other end of the string against the ball at the far edge of the shadow. Make sure that the string is taut, but be careful not to pull the pencil over.

8. Use a protractor to measure the angle between the string and the pencil. Record this angle in your ScienceLog.

9. Use the following formula to calculate the *experimental circumference* of the ball:

$$\text{Circumference} = \frac{360° \times 5 \text{ cm}}{\text{angle between pencil and string}}$$

Record this circumference in your ScienceLog.

10. Wrap the tape measure around the ball's "equator" to measure the *actual circumference* of the ball. Record this circumference in your ScienceLog.

Analyze the Results

11. In your ScienceLog, compare the experimental circumference with the actual circumference.

12. What could have caused your experimental circumference to be different from the actual value?

13. What are some of the advantages and disadvantages of taking measurements this way?

Draw Conclusions

14. Was this an effective method for Eratosthenes to measure the Earth's circumference? Explain your answer.

Orient Yourself!

You have been invited to attend an orienteering event with your neighbors. In orienteering events, participants use maps and compasses to find their way along a course. There are several control points that each participant must reach. The object is to reach each control point and then the finish line. Orienteering events are often timed competitions. In order to find the fastest route through the course, the participants must read the map and use their compass correctly. Being the fastest runner does not necessarily guarantee finishing first. You also must choose the most direct route to follow.

Your neighbors participate in several orienteering events each year. They always come home raving about how much fun they had. You would like to join them, but you will need to learn how to use your compass first.

Materials

- magnetic compass
- course map
- ruler
- 2 colored pencils or markers

Procedure

1. Together as a class, go outside to the orienteering course your teacher has made.

2. Hold your compass flat in your hand. Turn the compass until the N is pointing straight in front of you. (The needle in your compass will always point north.) Turn your body until the needle lines up with the N on your compass. You are now facing north.

3. Regardless of which direction you want to face, you should always align the end of the needle with the N on your compass. If you are facing south, the needle will be pointing directly toward your body. When the N is aligned with the needle, the S will be directly in front of you, and you will be facing south.

4. Use your compass to face east. Align the needle with the N. Where is the E? Turn to face that direction. When the needle and the N are aligned and the E is directly in front of you, you are facing east.

5. In an orienteering competition, you will need to know how to determine which direction you are traveling. Now, face any direction you choose.

6. Do not move, but rotate the compass to align the needle on your compass with the N. What direction are you facing? You are probably not facing directly north, south, east, or west. If you are facing between north and west, you are facing northwest. If you are facing between north and east, you are facing northeast.

7. Find a partner or partners to follow the course your teacher has made. Get a copy of the course map from your teacher. It will show several control points. You must stop at each one. You will need to follow this map to find your way through the course. Find and stand at the starting point.

8. Face the next control point on your map. Rotate your compass to align the needle on your compass with the N. What direction are you facing?

9. Use the ruler to draw a line on your map between the two control points. Write the direction between the starting point and the next control point on your map.

10. Walk toward the control point. Keep your eyes on the horizon, not on your compass. You might need to go around obstacles such as a fence or building. Use the map to find the easiest way around.

11. Record the color or code word you find at the control point next to the control point symbol on your map.

12. Repeat steps 8–11 for each control point. Follow the points in order as they are labeled. For example, determine the direction from control point 1 to control point 2. Be sure to include the direction between the final control point and the starting point.

Analysis

13. The object of an orienteering competition is to arrive at the finish line first. The maps provided at these events do not instruct the participants to follow a specific path. In one form of orienteering, called "score orienteering," competitors may find the control points in any order. Look at your map. If this course were used for a score-orienteering competition, would you change your route? Explain.

14. If there is time, follow the map again. This time, use your own path to find the control points. Draw this path and the directions on your map in a different color. Do you believe this route was faster? Why?

Going Further
Do some research to find out about orienteering events in your area. The Internet and local newspapers may be good sources for the information. Are there any events that you would like to attend?

Topographic Tuber

Imagine that you live on top of a tall mountain and often look down on the lake below. Every summer, an island appears. You call it Sometimes Island because it goes away again during heavy fall rains. This summer you begin to wonder if you could make a topographic map of Sometimes Island. You don't have fancy equipment to make the map, but you have an idea. What if you place a meterstick with the 0 m mark at the water level in the summer? Then as the expected fall rains come, you could draw the island from above as the water rises. Would this idea really work?

Materials

- clear plastic storage container with transparent lid
- transparency marker
- metric ruler
- potato, cut in half
- water
- tracing paper

Ask a Question

1. How do I make a topographic map?

Conduct an Experiment

2. Place a mark at the storage container's base. Label this mark "0 cm" with a transparency marker.

3. Measure and mark 1 cm increments up the side of the container until you reach the top of the container. Label these marks "1 cm," "2 cm," "3 cm," and so on.

4. The scale for your map will be 1 cm = 10 m. Draw a line 2 cm long in the bottom right-hand corner of the lid. Place hash marks at 0 cm, 1 cm, and 2 cm. Label these marks "0 m," "10 m," and "20 m."

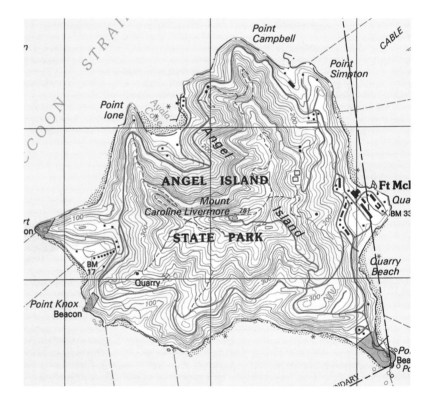

5. Place the potato flat side down in the center of the container.

6. Place the lid on the container, and seal it.

7. Viewing the potato from above, use the transparency marker to trace the outline of the potato where it rests on the bottom of the container. The floor of the container corresponds to the summer water level in the lake.

8. Label this contour 0 m. (For this activity, assume that the water level in the lake during the summer is the same as sea level.)

9. Pour water into the container until it reaches the line labeled "1 cm."

10. Again place the lid on the container, and seal it. Part of the potato will be sticking out above the water. Viewing the potato from above, trace the part of the potato that touches the top of the water.

11. Label the elevation of the contour line you drew in step 10. According to the scale, the elevation is 10 m.

12. Remove the lid. Carefully pour water into the container until it reaches the line labeled "2 cm."

13. Place the lid on the container, and seal it. Viewing the potato from above, trace the part of the potato that touches the top of the water at this level.

14. Use the scale to calculate the elevation of this line. Label the elevation on your drawing.

15. Repeat steps 12–14, adding 1 cm to the depth of the water each time. Stop when the potato is completely covered.

16. Remove the lid, and set it on a tabletop. Place tracing paper on top of the lid. Trace the contours from the lid onto the paper. Label the elevation of each contour line. Congratulations! You have just made a topographic map!

Analyze the Results

17. What is the contour interval of this topographic map?

18. By looking at the contour lines, how can you tell which parts of the potato are steeper?

19. What is the elevation of the highest point on your map?

Draw Conclusions

20. Do all topographic maps have a 0 m elevation contour line as a starting point? How would this affect a topographic map of Sometimes Island? Explain your answer.

21. Would this method of measuring elevation be an effective way to make a topographic map of an actual area on Earth's surface? Why or why not?

Going Further

Place all of the potatoes on a table or desk at the front of the room. Your teacher will mix up the potatoes as you trade topographic maps with another group. By reading the topographic map you just received, can you pick out the matching potato?

Mysterious Minerals

Imagine sitting on a rocky hilltop, gazing at the ground below you. You can see dozens of different types of rocks. How can scientists possibly identify the countless variations? It's a mystery!

In this activity you'll use your powers of observation and a few simple tests to determine the identities of rocks and minerals. Take a look at the Mineral Identification Key on the next page. That key will help you use clues to discover the identity of several minerals.

Materials

- several sample minerals
- glass microscope slides
- streak plate
- safety gloves
- iron filings

Procedure

1. In your ScienceLog, create a data chart like the one below.

2. Choose one mineral sample, and locate its column in your data chart.

3. Follow the Mineral Identification Key to find the identity of your sample. When you are finished, record the mineral's name and primary characteristics in the appropriate column in your data chart.
   Caution: Put on your gloves when scratching the glass slide.

4. Select another mineral sample, and repeat steps 3 and 4 until your data table is complete.

Analysis

5. Were some minerals easier to identify than others? Explain.

6. A streak test is a better indicator of a mineral's true color than visual observation. Why isn't a streak test used to help identify every mineral?

7. In your ScienceLog, summarize what you learned about the various characteristics of each mineral sample you identified.

Mineral Summary Chart						
Characteristics	1	2	3	4	5	6
Mineral name						
Luster						
Color						
Streak						
Hardness						
Cleavage						
Special properties						

Mineral Identification Key

1. **a.** If your mineral has a metallic luster, **GO TO STEP 2.**
   b. If your mineral has a nonmetallic luster, **GO TO STEP 3.**

2. **a.** If your mineral is black, **GO TO STEP 4.**
   b. If your mineral is yellow, it is **PYRITE.**
   c. If your mineral is silver, it is **GALENA.**

3. **a.** If your mineral is light in color, **GO TO STEP 5.**
   b. If your mineral is dark in color, **GO TO STEP 6.**

4. **a.** If your mineral leaves a red-brown line on the streak plate, it is **HEMATITE.**
   b. If your mineral leaves a black line on the streak plate, it is **MAGNETITE.** Test your sample for its magnetic properties by holding it near some iron filings.

5. **a.** If your mineral scratches the glass microscope slide, **GO TO STEP 7.**
   b. If your mineral does not scratch the glass microscope slide, **GO TO STEP 8.**

6. **a.** If your mineral scratches the glass slide, **GO TO STEP 9.**
   b. If your mineral does not scratch the glass slide, **GO TO STEP 10.**

7. **a.** If your mineral shows signs of cleavage, it is **ORTHOCLASE FELDSPAR.**
   b. If your mineral does not show signs of cleavage, it is **QUARTZ.**

8. **a.** If your mineral shows signs of cleavage, it is **MUSCOVITE.** Examine this sample for twin sheets.
   b. If your mineral does not show signs of cleavage, it is **GYPSUM.**

9. **a.** If your mineral shows signs of cleavage, it is **HORNBLENDE.**
   b. If your mineral does not show signs of cleavage, it is **GARNET.**

10. **a.** If your mineral shows signs of cleavage, it is **BIOTITE.** Examine your sample for twin sheets.
    b. If your mineral does not show signs of cleavage, it is **GRAPHITE.**

Going Further

Using your textbook and other reference books, research other methods of identifying different types of minerals. Based on your findings, create a new identification key. Give it to a friend along with a few sample minerals, and see if your friend can unravel the mystery!

Is It Fool's Gold?—A Dense Situation

Have you heard of fool's gold? Maybe you've seen a piece of it. This notorious mineral was often passed off as real gold. There are, however, simple tests you can do to keep from being tricked. Minerals can be identified by their properties. Some properties, such as color, vary between different samples of the same mineral. Other properties, such as density and specific gravity, remain consistent from one sample to another. In this activity, you will try to verify the identity of some mineral samples.

Materials

- spring scale
- ring stand
- pyrite sample
- galena sample
- balance
- string
- 400 mL beaker
- 400 mL of water

Ask a Question

1. How can I determine if an unknown mineral is not gold or silver?

Make Observations

2. Copy the data table below into your ScienceLog. Use it to record your observations.

Observation Chart		
Measurement	**Galena**	**Pyrite**
Mass in air (g)		
Weight in air (N)		
Beginning volume of water (mL)		
Final volume of water (mL)		
Volume of mineral (mL)		
Weight in water (N)		

DO NOT WRITE IN BOOK

3. Find the mass of each sample by laying the mineral on the balance. Record the mass of each in your data table.

4. Attach the spring scale to the ring stand.

5. Tie a string around the sample of galena, leaving a loop at the loose end. Suspend the galena from the spring scale, and find its weight in air. Do not remove the sample from the spring scale yet. Enter these data in your data table.

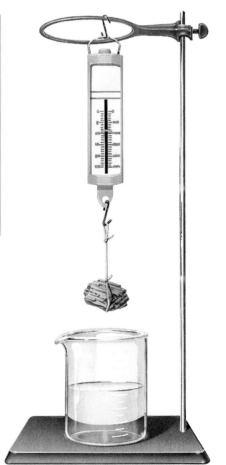

6. Fill a beaker halfway with water. Record the beginning volume of water in your data table.

7. Carefully lift the beaker around the galena until the mineral is completely submerged. Be careful not to splash any water out of the beaker! Be sure the mineral does not touch the beaker.

8. Record the new volume and weight in your data table.

9. Subtract the original volume of water from the new volume to find the amount of water displaced by the mineral. This is the volume of the mineral sample itself. Record this value in your data table.

10. Repeat steps 5–9 for the sample of pyrite.

Analyze the Results

11. Copy the data table below into your ScienceLog. **Note:** 1 mL = 1 cm³

12. Use the following equations to calculate the density and specific gravity of each mineral, and record your answers in your data table.

$$\text{Density} = \frac{\text{mass in air}}{\text{volume}}$$

$$\text{Specific gravity} = \frac{\text{weight in air}}{\text{weight in air} - \text{weight in water}}$$

Mineral	Density (g/cm³)	Specific gravity
Silver	10.5	10.5
Galena		
Pyrite		
Gold	19.3	19.3

DO NOT WRITE IN BOOK

Draw Conclusions

13. The density of pure gold is 19.3 g/cm³. How can you use this information to prove that your sample of pyrite is not gold?

14. The density of pure silver is 10.5 g/cm³. How can you use this information to prove that your sample of galena is not silver?

15. If you found a gold-colored nugget, how could you find out if the nugget was real gold or fool's gold?

Using Scientific Methods

Crystal Growth

Magma forms deep below the Earth's surface at depths of 25 to 160 km and at extremely high temperatures. Some magma reaches the surface and cools quickly. Other magma gets trapped in cracks or magma chambers beneath the surface and cools very slowly. When magma cools slowly, large, well-developed crystals form. On the other hand, when magma erupts onto the surface, thermal energy is lost rapidly to the air or water. There is not enough time for large crystals to grow. The size of the crystals found in igneous rocks gives geologists clues about where and how the crystals formed.

In this experiment, you will demonstrate how the rate of cooling affects the size of crystals in igneous rocks by cooling crystals of magnesium sulfate at two different rates.

Make a Prediction

1. Suppose you have two solutions that are identical in every way except for temperature. How will the temperature of a solution affect the size of the crystals and the rate at which they form?

Make Observations

2. Put on your gloves, apron, and goggles.

3. Fill the beaker halfway with tap water. Place the beaker on the hot plate, and let it begin to warm. The temperature of the water should be between 40°C and 50°C.
Caution: Make sure the hot plate is away from the edge of the lab table.

4. Examine two or three crystals of the magnesium sulfate with your magnifying lens. In your ScienceLog, describe the color, shape, luster, and other interesting features of the crystals.

5. Draw a sketch of the magnesium sulfate crystals in your ScienceLog.

Conduct an Experiment

6. Use the pointed laboratory scoop to fill the test tube about halfway with the magnesium sulfate. Add an equal amount of distilled water.

Materials

- heat-resistant gloves
- 400 mL beaker
- 200 mL of tap water
- hot plate
- Celsius thermometer
- magnesium sulfate ($MgSO_4$) (Epsom salts)
- magnifying lens
- pointed laboratory scoop
- medium test tube
- distilled water
- watch or clock
- aluminum foil
- test-tube tongs
- dark marker
- masking tape
- basalt
- pumice
- granite

7. Hold the test tube in one hand, and use one finger from your other hand to tap the test tube gently. Observe the solution mixing as you continue to tap the test tube.

8. Place the test tube in the beaker of hot water, and heat it for approximately 3 minutes.
Caution: Be sure to direct the opening of the test tube away from you and other students.

9. While the test tube is heating, shape your aluminum foil into two small boatlike containers by doubling the foil and turning up each edge.

10. If all the magnesium sulfate is not dissolved after 3 minutes, tap the test tube again, and heat it for 3 more minutes.
Caution: Use the test-tube tongs to handle the hot test tube.

11. With a marker and a piece of masking tape, label one of your aluminum boats "Sample 1," and place it on the hot plate. Turn the hot plate off.

12. Label the other aluminum boat "Sample 2," and place it on the lab table.

13. Using the test-tube tongs, remove the test tube from the beaker of water, and evenly distribute the contents to each of your foil boats. Carefully pour the hot water in the beaker down the drain. Do not move or disturb either of your foil boats.

Make Observations

14. Copy the table below into your ScienceLog. Using the magnifying lens, carefully observe the foil boats. Record the time it takes for the first crystals to appear.

Crystal-Formation Table			
Crystal formation	**Time**	**Size and appearance of crystals**	**Sketch of crystals**
Sample 1			
Sample 2			

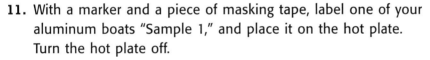

DO NOT WRITE IN BOOK

15. If crystals have not formed in the boats before class is over, carefully place the boats in a safe place. You may then record the time in days instead of in minutes.

16. When crystals have formed in both boats, use your magnifying lens to examine the crystals carefully.

Analyze the Results

17. Was your prediction correct? Explain.

18. Compare the size and shape of the crystals in Samples 1 and 2 with the size and shape of the crystals you examined in step 4. How long do you think the formation of the original crystals must have taken?

Draw Conclusions

19. Granite, basalt, and pumice are all igneous rocks. The most distinctive feature of each is the size of their crystals. Different igneous rocks form when magma cools at different rates. Examine a sample of each with your magnifying lens.

20. Copy the table below into your ScienceLog, and sketch each rock sample.

21. Use what you have learned in this activity to explain how each rock sample formed and how long it took for the crystals to form. Record your answers in your table.

Igneous Rock Observations			
	Granite	**Basalt**	**Pumice**
Sketch			
How did the rock sample form?			
Rate of cooling			

Going Further
Describe the size and shape of the crystals you would expect to find when a volcano erupts and sends material into the air and when magma oozes down the volcano's slope.

Let's Get Sedimental

How do we determine if sedimentary rock layers are undisturbed? The best way is to be sure that the top of the layer still points up. This activity will show you how to read rock features that say, in effect, "This side up." Then you can look for the signs at a real outcrop.

Procedure

1. Thoroughly mix the sand, gravel, and soil together, and fill the plastic container about one-third full of the mixture.

2. Add water until the container is two-thirds full. Twist the cap back onto the container, and shake the container vigorously until all of the sediment is mixed in the rapidly moving water.

3. Place the container on a tabletop. Using the scissors, carefully cut the top off the container a few centimeters above the water, as shown at right. This will promote evaporation.

4. Do not disturb the container. Allow the water to evaporate. (You may accelerate the process by carefully using the dropper pipet to siphon off some of the clear water after allowing the container to sit for at least 24 hours.)

5. Immediately after you set the bottle on the desk, describe what you see from above and through the sides of the bottle. Do this at least once each day. Record your observations in your ScienceLog.

6. After the sediment has dried and hardened, describe its surface in your ScienceLog.

7. Carefully lay the container on its side, and cut a strip of plastic out of the side to expose the sediments in the bottle. You may find it easier if you place pieces of clay on either side of the bottle to stabilize it.

Materials

- sand
- gravel
- soil (clay-rich, if available)
- 3 L mixing bowl
- plastic pickle jar or 3 L plastic soda bottle with a cap
- water
- scissors
- dropper pipet
- magnifying lens

8. Brush away the loose material from the sediment, and gently blow on the surface until it is clean. Examine the surface, and record your observations in your ScienceLog.

Analysis

9. Do you see anything through the side of the bottle that could help you determine if a sedimentary rock is undisturbed? Explain.

10. What structures do you see on the surface of the sediment that you would not expect to find at the bottom?

11. Explain how these features might be used to identify the top of the sedimentary bed in a real outcrop and to decide if the bed has been disturbed.

12. Did you see any structures on the side of the container that might indicate which direction is up?

13. After removing the side of the bottle, use the magnifying lens to examine the boundaries between the gravel, sand, and silt. What do you see? Do the size and type of sediment change quickly or gradually?

Going Further

Explain why the following statement is true: "If the top of a layer can't be found, finding the bottom of it works just as well."

Imagine that a layer was deposited directly above the layers in your container. Describe the bottom of this layer.

Metamorphic Mash

Metamorphism is a complex process that takes place deep within the Earth, where the temperature and pressure would turn a human into a crispy pancake. The effects of this extreme temperature and pressure are obvious in some metamorphic rocks. One of these effects is the reorganization of mineral grains within the rock. In this activity, you will investigate the process of metamorphism without being charred, flattened, or buried.

Materials

- modeling clay
- sequins or other small flat objects
- plastic knife
- small pieces of very stiff cardboard or plywood

Procedure

1. Flatten the clay into a layer about 1 cm thick. Sprinkle the surface with sequins.

2. Roll the corners of the clay toward the middle to form a neat ball.

3. Carefully use the plastic knife to cut the ball in half. In your ScienceLog, describe the position and location of the sequins inside the ball.

4. Put the ball back together, and use the sheets of cardboard or plywood to flatten the ball until it is about 2 cm thick.

5. Using the plastic knife, slice open the slab of clay in several places. In your ScienceLog, describe the position and location of the sequins in the slab.

Analysis

6. What physical process does flattening the ball represent?

7. Describe any changes in the position and location of the sequins that occurred as the clay ball was flattened into a slab.

8. How are the sequins oriented in relation to the force you put on the ball to flatten it?

9. Do you think the orientation of the mineral grains in a foliated metamorphic rock tells you anything about the rock? Defend your answer.

Going Further

Suppose you find a foliated metamorphic rock that has grains running in two distinct directions. Use what you have learned in this activity to offer a possible explanation for this observation.

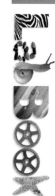

Using Scientific Methods

Make a Water Wheel

Lift Enterprises is planning to build a water wheel that will lift objects like a crane does. City planners feel that this would make very good use of the energy supplied by the river that flows through town. Development of the water wheel is in the early stages. The president of the company has asked you to modify the basic water-wheel design so that the final product will lift objects more quickly.

Ask a Question

1. What factors influence the rate at which a water wheel lifts a weight?

Form a Hypothesis

2. In your ScienceLog, change the question above into a statement giving your "best guess" as to what factors will have the greatest effect on your water wheel.

Build a Model

3. Measure and mark a 5 × 5 cm square on an index card. Cut the square out of the card.

4. Fold the square in half to form a triangle.

5. Measure and mark a line 8 cm from the bottom of the plastic jug. Use scissors to cut along this line. (Your teacher may need to use a safety razor to start this cut for you.) Keep both sections of the jug.

6. Use the permanent marker to trace four triangles onto the flat parts of the top section of the plastic jug. Use the paper triangle you made in step 4 as a template. Cut the triangles out of the plastic to form four fins.

7. Use a thumbtack to attach one corner of each plastic fin to the round edge of the cork, as shown at right. Make sure the fins are equally spaced around the cork.

8. Press a thumbtack into one of the flat sides of the cork. Jiggle the thumbtack to widen the hole in the cork, and then remove the thumbtack.

9. Repeat step 8 on the other side of the cork.

Materials

- index card
- metric ruler
- scissors
- safety razor (for teacher)
- large plastic milk jug
- permanent marker
- 5 thumbtacks
- cork
- glue
- 2 wooden skewers
- hole punch
- modeling clay
- transparent tape
- 20 cm of thread
- coin
- 2 L bottle filled with water
- watch or clock that indicates seconds

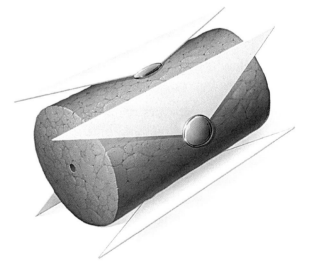

10. Place a drop of glue on the end of a skewer, and insert the skewer into one of the holes in the end of the cork. Insert the second skewer into the hole in the other end.

11. Use a hole punch to carefully punch two holes in the bottom section of the plastic jug. Punch each hole 1 cm from the top edge of the jug, directly across from one another.

12. Carefully push the skewers through the holes, and suspend the cork in the center of the jug.

13. Attach a small ball of clay to the end of each skewer. The clay balls should be the same size.

14. Tape one end of the thread to one skewer on the outside of the jug next to the clay ball. Wrap the thread around the clay ball three times. (As the water wheel turns, the thread should continue to wrap around the clay. The other ball of clay balances the weight and helps to keep the water wheel turning smoothly.)

15. Tape the free end of the thread to a coin. Wrap the thread around the coin once, and tape it again. You are now ready to test your hypothesis.

Test the Hypothesis

16. Slowly and carefully pour water from the 2 L bottle onto the fins so that the water wheel spins. What happens to the coin? Record your observations in your ScienceLog.

17. Lower the coin back to the starting position. Add more clay to the skewer to increase the diameter of the wheel. Repeat step 16. Did the coin rise faster or slower this time?

18. Lower the coin back to the starting position. Modify the shape of the clay, and repeat step 16. Does the shape of the clay affect how quickly the coin rises? Explain your answer.

19. What happens if you remove two of the fins from opposite sides? What happens if you add more fins? Modify your water wheel to find out.

20. Experiment with another fin shape. How does a different fin shape affect how quickly the coin rises?

Analyze the Results

21. What factors influence how quickly you can lift the coin?

Draw Conclusions

22. What recommendations would you make to Lift Enterprises to improve its water wheel?

Power of the Sun

The sun radiates energy in every direction. Like the sun, the energy radiated by a light bulb spreads out in all directions. But how much energy an object receives depends on how close that object is to the source. As you move farther from the source, the amount of energy you receive decreases. For example, if you measure the amount of energy that reaches you from a light and then move three times farther away, you will discover that nine times less energy will reach you at your second position. Energy from the sun travels as light energy. When light energy is absorbed by an object it is converted into thermal energy. *Power* is the rate at which one form of energy is converted to another, and it is measured in *watts.* Because power is related to distance, nearby objects can be used to measure the power of far-away objects. In this lab you will calculate the power of the sun using an ordinary 100-watt light bulb.

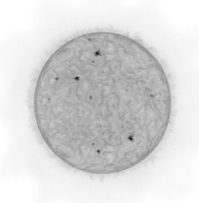

Materials

- protective gloves
- aluminum strip, 2 × 8 cm
- pencil
- black permanent marker
- Celsius thermometer
- mason jar, cap, and lid with hole in center
- modeling clay
- desk lamp with a 100 W bulb and removable shade
- metric ruler
- watch or clock that indicates seconds
- scientific calculator

Procedure

1. Gently shape the piece of aluminum around a pencil so that it holds on in the middle and has two wings, one on either side of the pencil.

2. Bend the wings outward so that they can catch as much sunlight as possible.

3. Use the marker to color both wings on one side of the aluminum strip black.

4. Remove the pencil and place the aluminum snugly around the thermometer near the bulb.
   Caution: Do not press too hard—you do not want to break the thermometer! Wear protective gloves when working with the thermometer and the aluminum.

5. Carefully slide the top of the thermometer through the hole in the lid. Place the lid on the jar so that the thermometer bulb is inside the jar, and screw down the cap.

6. Secure the thermometer to the jar lid by molding clay around the thermometer on the outside of the lid. The aluminum wings should be in the center of the jar.

7. Read the temperature on the thermometer. Record this as room temperature.

8. Place the jar on a windowsill in the sunlight. Turn the jar so that the black wings are angled toward the sun.

9. Watch the thermometer until the temperature reading stops rising. Record the temperature in your ScienceLog.

10. Remove the jar from direct sunlight, and allow it to return to room temperature.

11. Remove any shade or reflector from the lamp. Place the lamp at one end of a table.

12. Place the jar about 30 cm from the lamp. Turn the jar so that the wings are angled toward the lamp.

13. Turn on the lamp, and wait about 1 minute.

14. Move the jar a few centimeters toward the lamp until the temperature reading starts to rise. When the temperature stops rising, compare it with the reading you took in step 9.

15. Repeat step 14 until the temperature matches the temperature you recorded in step 9.

16. If the temperature reading rises too high, move the jar away from the lamp and allow it to cool. Once the reading has dropped to at least 5°C below the temperature you recorded in step 9, you may begin again at step 12.

17. When the temperature in the jar matches the temperature you recorded in step 9, record the distance between the center of the light bulb and the thermometer bulb in your ScienceLog.

Analysis

18. The thermometer measured the same amount of energy absorbed by the jar at the distance you measured to the lamp. In other words, your jar absorbed as much energy from the sun at a distance of 150 million kilometers as it did from the 100 W light bulb at the distance you recorded in step 17.

19. Use the following formula to calculate the power of the sun (be sure to show your work):

$$\frac{\text{power of the sun}}{(\text{distance to the sun})^2} = \frac{\text{power of the lamp}}{(\text{distance to the lamp})^2}$$

Hint: (distance)^2 means that you multiply the distance by itself. If you found that the lamp was 5 cm away from the jar, for example, the (distance)^2 would be 25.

Hint: Convert 150,000,000 km to 15,000,000,000,000 cm.

20. Review the discussion of scientific notation in the Math Refresher found in the Appendix at the back of this book. You will need to understand this technique for writing large numbers in order to compare your calculation with the actual figure. For practice, convert the distance to the sun given in step 19 to scientific notation.

15,000,000,000,000 cm = $1.5 \times 10^{\underline{?}}$ cm

21. The sun emits 3.7×10^{26} W of power. Compare your answer in step 19 with this value. Was this a good way to calculate the power of the sun? Explain.

How DO You Stack Up?

According to the *law of superposition,* in undisturbed sequences of sedimentary rock, the oldest layers are on the bottom. Geologists use this principle to determine the relative age of the rocks in a small area. Geologists can also use fossils in the rocks to date the rocks. When geologists find similar rock sequences and fossils in different areas, they can match parts of the sequences. Each new area they examine helps improve and expand our picture of the rock record. When enough areas around the world are examined, geologists then build a geologic column that shows a general history of the Earth and a relative age for each rock.

In this activity, you will model what geologists do by drawing stratigraphic sections for different rock outcrops. Then, along with your classmates, you will create a part of the geologic column, showing the geologic history of the area that contains all of the outcrops.

Materials

- metric ruler
- pencil
- colored pencils or crayons
- white paper
- scissors

Procedure

1. After your teacher assigns you to one of five groups, look at the illustration of the section for Outcrop 1 at right. Copy this section onto a blank piece of paper. Follow the specific instructions in steps 2–6 concerning rock color and texture and the contact between layers—bedding planes or unconformities. Use the Rock and Fossil Key on the next page to determine the color and texture of each layer.

2. Use a metric ruler and a pencil to draw a box 3 cm wide and 9 cm tall. With colored pencils, sketch a layer of conglomerate (A1) on the bottom of the box. It should reach from side to side and be 2 cm tall.

3. Use a black crayon or pencil to add B3 and C3 fossils to the conglomerate layer. The top of this layer is a bedding plane, so it should be a straight line.

4. Draw a 2 cm layer of sandstone (B1) with B3 fossils above the conglomerate layer. The top of the layer is an unconformity, so use a wavy line to represent the break in rock-layer sequence.

Section for Outcrop 1

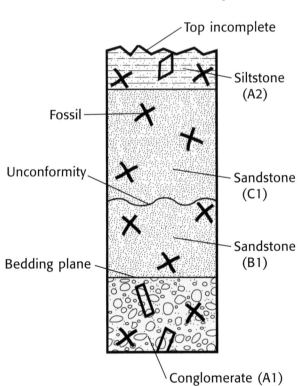

Top incomplete

Siltstone (A2)

Fossil

Unconformity

Sandstone (C1)

Sandstone (B1)

Bedding plane

Conglomerate (A1)

5. Add a 3 cm layer of another sandstone (C1) with B3 fossils. The top of this layer is another bedding plane.

6. Add a 1 cm layer of siltstone (A2) containing B3 and C4 fossils. The top of this layer is incomplete, so draw a jagged edge at the top. Write the outcrop number (1) at the top of the section.

Outcrop 1				
Layer	**Rock type**	**Fossils**	**Thickness**	**Upper contact**
top	siltstone (A2)	B3, C4	1 cm	incomplete
	sandstone (C1)	B3	3 cm	bedding plane
	sandstone (B1)	B3	2 cm	unconformity
bottom	conglomerate (A1)	B3, C3	2 cm	bedding plane

7. Compare the section you drew with the chart above. You will need to follow a similar chart to draw your own stratigraphic section. Be sure you understand how the section and chart for Outcrop 1 are related before you continue.

8. After your teacher assigns an outcrop to your group, find the chart on the following page that corresponds to your outcrop's section. As a group, use the chart to draw the section.

9. Sketch your section in a column that is 3 cm wide. The height of each rock layer is given in the chart for your section. Include the rock color, the rock type, and the types of fossils, as indicated in the chart and the Rock and Fossil Key at right. Pay close attention to the type of contact between the layers. (Assume that the bottom of the lowest layer is a bedding plane.)

10. When you finish your section, check to make sure it represents the information in the chart and key correctly. Write the outcrop number at the top of your section.

11. Make four more copies of your section, and pass them out to the other groups in your class. Ultimately, each group should have six sections, including the section for Outcrop 1.

Rock and Fossil Key			
	A	**B**	**C**
1			
2			
3			
4			
5			

Outcrop 2

Layer	Rock type	Fossils	Thickness	Upper contact
top	conglomerate (A1)	A4, B4, B5	4 cm	incomplete
	sandstone (B1)	A4	2 cm	bedding plane
	sandstone (C1)	A4	2 cm	bedding plane
bottom	limestone (A3)	A4, A5	3 cm	bedding plane

Outcrop 3

Layer	Rock type	Fossils	Thickness	Upper contact
top	shale (B2)	C5	4 cm	incomplete
	conglomerate (A1)	A4, B4, B5	6 cm	unconformity
bottom	sandstone (B1)	A4	2 cm	bedding plane

Outcrop 4

Layer	Rock type	Fossils	Thickness	Upper contact
top	conglomerate (A1)	A4, B4, B5	1 cm	incomplete
	sandstone (B1)	A4	1 cm	bedding plane
	limestone (A3)	A4, A5	1 cm	unconformity
.	shale (C2)	A4	6 cm	bedding plane
	shale (B2)	A4, C4	4 cm	bedding plane
bottom	siltstone (A2)	B3, C4	4 cm	bedding plane

Outcrop 5

Layer	Rock type	Fossils	Thickness	Upper contact
top	limestone (A3)	A4, A5	1 cm	incomplete
	shale (C2)	A4	4 cm	bedding plane
	siltstone (A2)	B3, C4	3 cm	unconformity
	sandstone (C1)	B3	4 cm	bedding plane
	sandstone (B1)	B3	2 cm	bedding plane
bottom	conglomerate (A1)	B3, C3	2 cm	bedding plane

Outcrop 6

Layer	Rock type	Fossils	Thickness	Upper contact
top	shale (B2)	C5	3 cm	incomplete
	siltstone (A2)	B5, C5	4 cm	bedding plane
	conglomerate (A1)	A4, B4, B5	8 cm	bedding plane
	sandstone (B1)	A4	2 cm	bedding plane
bottom	limestone (A3)	A4, A5	2 cm	unconformity

12. Cut the sections out of the paper. Don't cut off the outcrop numbers! In different sections, find layers that have the same rocks and contain the same fossils. Line the sections up next to each other by matching similar layers. Don't be surprised if layers don't look exactly the same. This happens in the real world, too.

13. If unconformities appear in any of the sections, there may be some rock layers missing. You may need to examine other sections to find out what fits between the layers above and below the unconformities. To leave space for these layers, cut the sections along the unconformities.

14. When you find layers that match, you should be able to do one of three things with the other sections—add rock layers to the bottom of your matched sections, add rock layers to the top of your matched sections, or slip missing rock layers between unconformities. Remember to determine whether any of the fossils are index fossils for certain layers.

15. After several tries, you should be able to create the part of the geologic column that corresponds to the area containing the six outcrops. The part of the column will show rock types and fossils for all the known layers in the area.

Analysis

16. How many layers are found in this part of the geologic column?

17. Which is the oldest layer in your column? Which rock layer is the youngest? Describe these layers in terms of rock type and the fossils they contain.

18. Which (if any) fossils can be used as index fossils for a single layer? Which layer or layers contain each of these fossils? Why are these fossils considered index fossils?

19. Fossils may also be used to distinguish similar layers from one another. Name two layers in your column that are distinguished only by the fossils they contain. Which fossil(s) identifies each layer?

20. List the fossils in your column from oldest to youngest. Label the oldest and youngest fossils.

21. Look at the unconformities in the sections for Outcrops 3 and 4. Which rock layers are partially or completely missing from each section? Explain how you know this.

Convection Connection

Some scientists think convection currents within the Earth's mantle are responsible for the movement of tectonic plates. Because these convection currents cannot be observed, scientists use models to simulate the process. In this activity, you will make your own model to simulate tectonic-plate movement.

Procedure

1. Place two hot plates side by side in the center of your lab table. Be sure they are away from the edge of the table.

2. Place the pan on top of the hot plates. Slide the wooden blocks under the pan to support the ends. Make sure the pan is level and secure.

3. Fill the pan with cold water. The water should be at least 4 cm deep. Turn on the hot plates, and put on your gloves.

4. After a minute or two, tiny bubbles will begin to rise in the water above the hot plates. Gently place two craft sticks on the water's surface.

5. Use the pencil to align the sticks parallel to the short ends of the pan. The sticks should be about 3 cm apart and near the center of the pan.

6. As soon as the sticks begin to move, place a drop of food coloring in the water at the center of the pan. Observe what happens to the food coloring.

7. With the help of a partner, hold one thermometer bulb just under the water at the center of the pan. Hold the other two thermometers just under the water near the ends of the pan. Record the temperatures.

8. When you are finished, turn off the hot plates. After the water has cooled, carefully empty the water into a sink.

Analysis

9. Based on your observations of the motion of the food coloring, how does the temperature of the water affect the direction the water moves?

10. How does the motion of the craft sticks relate to the motion of the water?

11. How does this model relate to plate tectonics and the movement of the continents?

Materials

- heat-resistant gloves
- 2 small hot plates
- rectangular aluminum pan
- wooden blocks
- cold water
- 2 craft sticks
- pencil
- metric ruler
- food coloring
- 3 thermometers

Oh, the Pressure!

When scientists want to understand natural processes, such as mountain formation, they often make models to help them. Models are useful in studying how rocks react to the forces of plate tectonics. In a short amount of time, a model can demonstrate geological processes that take millions of years. Do the following activity to find out how folding and faulting occur in the Earth's crust.

Materials

- modeling clay in 4 different colors
- 5 × 15 cm strip of poster board
- soup can or rolling pin
- newspaper
- colored pencils
- plastic knife
- 5 × 5 cm squares of poster board (2)

Ask a Question

1. How do synclines, anticlines, and faults form?

Conduct an Experiment

2. Use modeling clay of one color to form a long cylinder, and place the cylinder in the center of the glossy side of the poster-board strip.

3. Mold the clay to the strip. Try to make the clay layer the same thickness all along the strip; you can use the soup can or rolling pin to even it out. Pinch the sides of the clay so that it is the same width and length as the strip. Your strip should be at least 15 cm long and 5 cm wide.

4. Flip the strip over on the newspaper your teacher has placed across your desk. Carefully peel the strip from the modeling clay.

5. Repeat steps 2–4 with the other colors of modeling clay. Each member of your group should have a turn molding the clay. Each time you flip the strip over, stack the new clay layer on top of the previous one. When you are finished, you should have a block of clay made of four layers.

6. Lift the block of clay and hold it parallel to and just above the tabletop. Push gently on the block from opposite sides, as shown below.

7. Use the colored pencils to draw the results of step 6 in your ScienceLog. Use the terms *syncline* and *anticline* to label your diagram. Draw arrows to show the direction that each edge of the clay was pushed.

8. Repeat steps 2–5 to form a second block of clay.

9. Cut the second block of clay in two at a 45° angle as seen from the side of the block.

10. Press one poster-board square on the angled end of each of the block's two pieces. The poster board represents a fault. The two angled ends represent a hanging wall and a footwall. The model should resemble the one in the photograph above.

11. Keeping the angled edges together, lift the blocks and hold them parallel to and just above the tabletop. Push gently on the two blocks until they move. Record your observations in your Sciencelog.

12. Now hold the two pieces of the clay block in their original position, and slowly pull them apart, allowing the hanging wall to move downward. Record your observations.

Analyze the Results

13. What happened to the first block of clay in step 6? What kind of force did you apply to it?

14. What happened to the pieces of the second block of clay in step 11? What kind of force did you apply to them?

15. What happened to the pieces of the second block of clay in step 12? Describe the forces that acted on the block and how the pieces of the block reacted.

Draw Conclusions

16. Summarize how the forces you applied to the blocks of clay relate to the way tectonic forces affect rock layers. Be sure to use the terms *fold, fault, anticline, syncline, hanging wall, footwall, tension,* and *compression* in your summary.

Quake Challenge

In many parts of the world, it is important that buildings be built with earthquakes in mind. Each building must be designed so that the structure is protected during an earthquake. Architects have improved the design of buildings a lot since 1906, when an earthquake destroyed much of San Francisco. In this activity you will use marshmallows and toothpicks to build a structure that can withstand a simulated earthquake. In the process, you will discover some of the ways a building can be built to withstand an earthquake.

Materials

- 10 marshmallows
- 10 toothpicks
- square of gelatin, approximately 8 × 8 cm
- paper plate

Ask a Question

1. What features help a building withstand an earthquake? How can I use this information to build my structure?

Form a Hypothesis

2. Brainstorm with a classmate to design a structure that will resist the simulated earthquake. Sketch your design in your ScienceLog. Write two or three sentences to describe your design.

Test the Hypothesis

3. Follow your design to build a structure using the toothpicks and marshmallows.

4. Set your structure on a square of gelatin.

5. Shake the square of gelatin to test whether your building will remain standing during a quake. Do not pick up the gelatin.

6. If your first design does not work well, change it until you find a design that does. Try to determine why your building is falling so that you can improve your design each time.

7. Sketch your final design in your ScienceLog.

8. After you have tested your final design, place your structure on the gelatin square on your teacher's desk.

9. When every group has added a structure to the teacher's gelatin, your teacher will simulate an earthquake by shaking the gelatin. Watch to see which buildings withstand the most severe quake.

Analyze the Results

10. Which buildings were still standing after the final earthquake? What features made them more stable?

11. How would you change your design to make your structure more stable?

Communicate Results

12. This was a simple model of a real-life problem for architects. Based on this activity, what advice would you give to those who design buildings in earthquake-prone areas?

Earthquake Waves

The energy from an earthquake travels as seismic waves in all directions through the Earth. Seismologists can use the properties of certain types of seismic waves to find the epicenter of an earthquake.

P waves travel more quickly than S waves and are always detected first. The average speed of P waves in the Earth's crust is 6.1 km/s. The average speed of S waves in the Earth's crust is 4.1 km/s. The difference in arrival time between P waves and S waves is called *lag time.*

In this activity you will use the S-P-time method to determine the location of an earthquake's epicenter.

Materials

- calculator (optional)
- compass
- metric ruler

Procedure

1. The illustration below shows seismographic records made in three cities following an earthquake. These traces begin at the left and show the arrival of P waves at time zero. The second set of waves on each record represents the arrival of S waves.

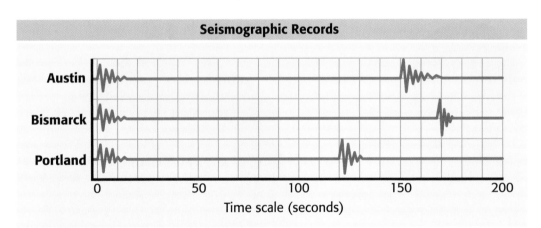

Seismographic Records

Austin

Bismarck

Portland

0　　　　　50　　　　　100　　　　　150　　　　　200

Time scale (seconds)

2. Copy the data table on the next page into your ScienceLog.

3. Use the time scale provided with the seismographic records to find the lag time between the P waves and the S waves for each city. Remember, the lag time is the time between the moment when the first P wave arrives and the moment when the first S wave arrives. Record this data in your table.

4. Use the following equation to calculate how long it takes each wave type to travel 100 km:

    100 km ÷ average speed of the wave = time

5. To find lag time for earthquake waves at 100 km, subtract the time it takes P waves to travel 100 km from the time it takes S waves to travel 100 km. Record the lag time in your ScienceLog.

6. Use the following formula to find the distance from each city to the epicenter:

$$\text{distance} = \frac{\text{measured lag time (s)} \times 100 \text{ km}}{\text{lag time for 100 km (s)}}$$

In your Data Table, record the distance from each city to the epicenter.

7. Trace the map below into your ScienceLog.

8. Use the scale to adjust your compass so that the radius of a circle with Austin at the center is equal to the distance between Austin and the epicenter of the earthquake.

Epicenter Data Table		
City	Lag time (seconds)	Distance to the epicenter (km)
Austin, TX		
Bismarck, ND		
Portland, OR		

DO NOT WRITE IN BOOK

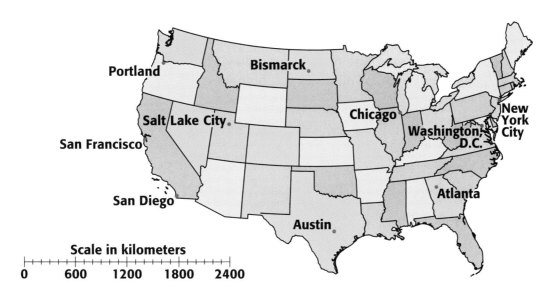

Scale in kilometers
0   600   1200   1800   2400

9. Put the point of your compass at Austin on your copy of the map, and draw a circle.

10. Repeat steps 8 and 9 for Bismarck and Portland. The epicenter of the earthquake is located near the point where the three circles meet.

Analysis

11. Which city is closest to the epicenter?

12. Why do seismologists need measurements from three different locations to find the epicenter of an earthquake?

Some Go "Pop," Some Do Not

Volcanic eruptions range from mild to violent. When volcanoes erupt, the materials left behind provide information to scientists studying the Earth's crust. Mild, or nonexplosive, eruptions produce thin, runny lava that is low in silica. During nonexplosive eruptions, lava simply flows down the side of the volcano. Explosive eruptions, on the other hand, do not produce much lava. Instead, the explosions hurl ash and debris into the air. The materials left behind are light in color and high in silica. These materials help geologists determine the composition of the crust underneath the volcanoes.

Materials

- graph paper
- metric ruler
- red, yellow, and orange colored pencils or markers

TRY at HOME

Procedure

1. Copy the map below onto graph paper. Take care to line the grid up properly.

2. Locate each volcano from the list on the next page by drawing a circle with a diameter of about 1 cm in the proper location on your copy of the map. Use the latitude and longitude grids to help you.

3. Review all the eruptions for each volcano. For each explosive eruption, color the circle red. For each quiet volcano, color the circle yellow. For volcanoes that have erupted in both ways, color the circle orange.

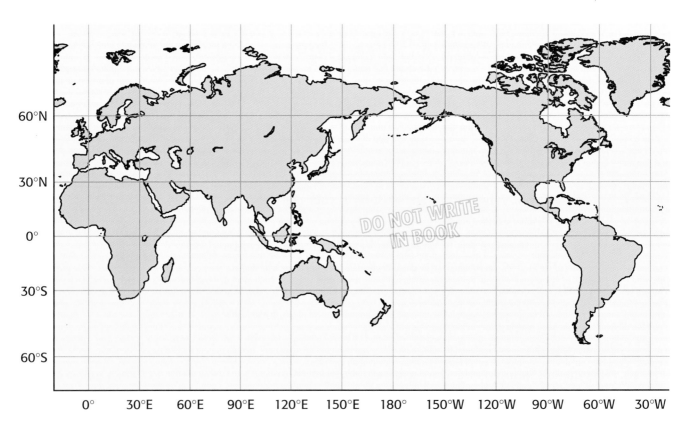

DO NOT WRITE IN BOOK

Volcanic Activity Chart

Volcano name	Location	Description
Mount St. Helens	46°N 122°W	An explosive eruption blew the top off the mountain. Light-colored ash covered thousands of square kilometers. Another eruption sent a lava flow down the southeast side of the mountain.
Kilauea	19°N 155°W	One small eruption sent a lava flow along 12 km of highway.
Rabaul caldera	4°S 152°E	Explosive eruptions have caused tsunamis and have left 1–2 m of ash on nearby buildings.
Popocatépetl	19°N 98°W	During one explosion, Mexico City closed the airport for 14 hours because huge columns of ash made it too difficult for pilots to see. Eruptions from this volcano have also caused damaging avalanches.
Soufriere Hills	16°N 62°W	Small eruptions have sent lava flows down the hills. Other explosive eruptions have sent large columns of ash into the air.
Long Valley caldera	37°N 119°W	Explosive eruptions have sent ash into the air.
Okmok	53°N 168°W	Recently, there have been slow lava flows from this volcano. Twenty-five hundred years ago, ash and debris exploded from the top of this volcano.
Pavlof	55°N 161°W	Eruption clouds have been sent 200 m above the summit. Eruptions have sent ash columns 10 km into the air. Occasionally, small eruptions have caused lava flows.
Fernandina	42°N 12°E	Eruptions have ejected large blocks of rock from this volcano.
Mount Pinatubo	15°N 120°E	Ash and debris from an explosive eruption destroyed homes, crops, and roads within 52,000 km² around the volcano.

Analysis

4. According to your map, where are volcanoes that always have nonexplosive eruptions located?

5. Where are volcanoes that always erupt explosively located?

6. Where are volcanoes that erupt in both ways located?

7. If volcanoes get their magma from the crust below them, what can you say about the silica content of Earth's crust under the oceans?

8. What is the composition of the crust under the continents? How do we know?

9. What is the source of materials for volcanoes that erupt in both ways? How do you know?

10. Do the locations of volcanoes that erupt in both ways make sense based on your answers to questions 7 and 8? Explain.

Going Further

Volcanoes are present on other planets. If a planet had only nonexplosive volcanoes on its surface, what would we be able to infer about the planet? If a planet had volcanoes that ranged from nonexplosive to explosive, what might that tell us about the planet?

Volcano Verdict

You will need to pair up with a partner for this exploration. You and your partner will act as geologists who work in a city located near a volcano. City officials are counting on you to predict when the volcano will erupt next. You and your partner have decided to use limewater as a gas-emissions tester. You will use this tester to measure the levels of carbon dioxide emitted from a simulated volcano. The more active the volcano is, the more carbon dioxide it releases.

Materials

- 1 L of limewater
- 9 oz clear plastic cup
- graduated cylinder
- 100 mL of water
- 140 mL of white vinegar
- 16 oz drink bottle
- modeling clay
- flexible drinking straw
- 15 mL of baking soda
- 2 sheets of bathroom tissue
- coin
- box or stand for plastic cup

Procedure

1. Put on your safety goggles, and carefully pour limewater into the plastic cup until the cup is three-fourths full. This is your gas-emissions tester.

2. Now build a model volcano. Begin by pouring 50 mL of water and 70 mL of vinegar into the drink bottle.

3. Form a plug of clay around the short end of the straw, as shown below. The clay plug must be large enough to cover the opening of the bottle. Be careful not to get the clay wet.

4. Sprinkle 5 mL of baking soda along the center of a single section of bathroom tissue. Then roll the tissue and twist the ends so that the baking soda can't fall out.

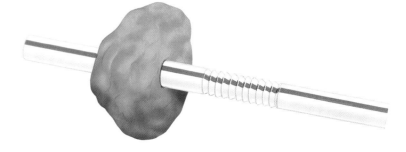

5. Drop the tissue into the drink bottle, and immediately put the short end of the straw inside the bottle, making a seal with the clay.

6. Put the other end of the straw into the limewater, as shown at right.

7. You have just taken your first measurement of gas levels from the volcano. Record your observations in your ScienceLog.

8. Imagine that it is several days later and you need to test the volcano again to collect more data. Before you continue, toss a coin. If it lands heads up, go to step 9a. If it lands tails up, go to step 9b. Write the step you take in your ScienceLog.

9a. Repeat steps 1–7. This time add 2 mL of baking soda to the vinegar and water. **Note:** You must use fresh water, vinegar, and limewater. Describe your observations in your ScienceLog. Go to step 10.

9b. Repeat steps 1–7. This time add 8 mL of baking soda to the vinegar and water. **Note:** You must use fresh water, vinegar, and limewater. Describe your observations in your ScienceLog. Go to step 10.

Analysis

10. How do you explain the difference in the appearance of the limewater from one trial to the next?

11. What do your measurements indicate about the activity in the volcano?

12. Based on your results, do you think it would be necessary to evacuate the city?

13. How would a geologist use a gas-emissions tester to forecast volcanic eruptions?

Using Scientific Methods

Great Ice Escape

Did you know that ice acts as a natural wrecking ball? Even rocks don't stand a chance against the power of ice. When water trapped in rock freezes, a process called *ice wedging* occurs. The water volume increases, and the rock cracks to "get out of the way." This expansion can fragment a rock into several pieces. In this exercise you will see how this natural wrecker works, and you will try to stop the great ice escape.

Ask a Question

1. If a plastic jar is filled with water, is there a way to prevent the jar from breaking when the water freezes?

Conduct an Experiment

2. Fill three identical jars to overflowing with water, and close two of them securely.

3. Measure the height of the water in the unsealed container. Record the height in your ScienceLog.

4. Tightly wrap one of the closed jars with tape, string, or other items to reinforce the jar. These items must be removable. The unwrapped, sealed jar will serve as your control.

5. Place all three jars in resealable sandwich bags, and leave them in the freezer overnight. (Make sure the open jar does not spill.)

6. Remove the jars from the freezer, and carefully remove the wrapping from the reinforced jar.

Make Observations

7. Did your reinforced jar crack? Why or why not?

8. What does each jar look like? Record your observations in your ScienceLog.

9. In your ScienceLog, record the height of the ice in the unsealed jar. How does the new height compare with the height you measured in step 3?

Analyze the Results

10. Do you think it is possible to stop the ice from breaking the sealed jars? Why or why not?

11. How could ice wedging affect soil formation?

Materials

- 3 small, identical hard-plastic jars with screw-on lids, such as spice containers

- water

- metric ruler

- tape, strings, rubber bands, and other items to bind or reinforce the jars

- 3 resealable sandwich bags

- freezer

Rockin' Through Time

MAKING MODELS

Wind, water, and gravity constantly change rocks. As wind and water rush over the rocks, the rocks may be worn smooth. As rocks bump against one another, their shapes change. The form of mechanical weathering that occurs as rocks collide and scrape together is called **abrasion.** In this activity, you will shake some pieces of limestone to model the effects of abrasion.

Materials

- poster board
- markers
- 24 pieces of limestone, all about the same size
- 3 L plastic wide-mouth bottle with lid
- tap water

Procedure

1. Copy the chart below onto a piece of poster board. Allow enough space to place rocks in each square.

2. Lay three of the limestone pieces on the poster board in the area marked "0 shakes." Be careful not to bump the poster board once you have added the rocks.

3. Place the remaining 21 rocks in the 3 L bottle. Then fill the bottle halfway with water. Close the lid securely.

4. Shake the bottle vigorously 100 times.

5. Remove three rocks from the bottle, and place them on the poster board in the area marked "100 shakes."

6. Repeat steps 4 and 5 six times until all of the rocks have been added to the board.

Rocks Table	
0 shakes	100 shakes
200 shakes	300 shakes
400 shakes	500 shakes
600 shakes	700 shakes

Analysis

7. Describe the surface of the rocks that you placed in the area marked "0 shakes." Are they smooth or rough?

8. How did the shapes of the rocks change as you performed this activity?

9. Why did the rocks change?

10. What did the water look like at the beginning of the activity?

11. How did the water change during the activity? Why did it change?

12. What would happen if you did this experiment with a much harder rock, like gneiss?

13. How do the results of this experiment compare with what happens in a river?

Water Cycle— What Goes Up . . .

Why does a bathroom mirror "fog up"? What happens when water "dries up"? Where does rain come from, and why doesn't it just "run out"? These questions relate to the major parts of the water cycle—condensation, evaporation, and precipitation. In this activity, you will make a model of the water cycle and watch water as it moves through the model.

Materials

- graduated cylinder
- 50 mL of tap water
- heat-resistant gloves
- beaker
- hot plate
- glass plate or watch glass
- tongs or forceps

Procedure

1. Use the graduated cylinder to pour 50 mL of water into the beaker. Note the water level in the beaker.

2. Put on your gloves, and place the beaker securely on the hot plate. Turn on the heat to medium, and bring the water to a boil.

3. While waiting for the water to boil, practice picking up and handling the glass plate or watch glass with the tongs. Hold the glass plate a few centimeters above the beaker, and tilt it so that the lowest edge of the glass is still above the beaker.

4. Observe the glass plate as the water in the beaker heats. In your ScienceLog, write down the changes you see in the beaker, in the air above the beaker, and on the glass plate held over the beaker. Write down any changes you see in the water.

5. Continue until you have observed steam rising off the water, the glass plate above the beaker becoming foggy, and water dripping from the glass plate.

6. Carefully set the glass plate on a counter or other safe surface as directed by your teacher.

7. Turn off the hot plate, and allow the beaker to cool. Move the hot beaker with gloves or tongs if directed to do so by your teacher.

8. Copy the illustration shown on the next page into your ScienceLog. On your sketch, draw and label the water cycle as it occurred in your model. Include arrows and labels for condensation, evaporation, and precipitation.

Analysis

9. Compare the water level in the beaker now with the water level at the beginning of the experiment. Was there a change? Explain why or why not.

10. If you had used a scale or balance to measure the mass of the water in the beaker before and after this activity, would the mass have changed? Why or why not?

11. How is your model similar to the Earth's water cycle? On your sketch of the illustration above, label where the processes shown in the model mimic the Earth's water cycle.

12. When you finished this experiment, the water in the beaker was still hot. What stores much of the energy in the Earth's water cycle?

Going Further

As rainwater runs over the land, the rainwater picks up minerals and salts. Do these minerals and salts evaporate, condense, and precipitate as part of the water cycle? Where do they go?

If the average global temperature on Earth gets warmer, how would you expect sea levels to change, and why? What if the average global temperature cools?

Clean Up Your Act

When you wash dishes, the family car, the bathroom sink, or your clothes, you wash them with water. But have you ever wondered how water gets clean? Two major methods of purifying water are filtration and evaporation. In this activity you will use both of these methods to test how well they remove pollutants from water. You will test detritus (decaying plant matter), soil, vinegar, and detergent. Your teacher may also ask you to test other pollutants.

Form a Hypothesis

1. Form a hypothesis about whether filtration and evaporation will clean each of the four pollutants from the water and how well they might do it. Then use the procedures below to test your hypothesis.

Part A: Filtration

Filtration is a common method of removing various pollutants from water. It requires very little energy—gravity pulls water down through the layers of filter material. See how well this energy-efficient method works to clean your sample of polluted water.

Conduct an Experiment

2. Put on your gloves and goggles. Use scissors to cut the bottom out of the empty soda bottle carefully.

3. Carefully punch four or five small holes through the plastic cap of the bottle using a small nail and hammer. Screw the plastic cap onto the bottle.

4. Turn the bottle upside down, and set its neck in a ring on a ring stand, as shown on the next page. Put a handful of gravel into the inverted bottle. Add a layer of activated charcoal, followed by thick layers of sand and gravel. Place a 400 mL beaker under the neck of the bottle.

5. Fill each of the large beakers with 1,000 mL of clean water. Set one beaker aside to serve as the control. Add three or four spoonfuls of each of the following pollutants to the other beaker: detritus, soil, household vinegar, and dishwashing detergent.

Materials

Part A
- scissors
- plastic 2 L soda bottle with cap
- hammer and small nail
- gravel
- activated charcoal
- sand

Part B
- Erlenmeyer flask
- one-hole rubber stopper with a glass tube
- 1.5 m of plastic tubing
- heat-resistant gloves
- hot plate
- sealable plastic sandwich bag
- ice

Parts A and B
- ring stand with ring
- 400 mL beaker
- 1,000 mL beakers (2)
- 2,000 mL of water
- detritus (grass and leaf clippings)
- soil
- household vinegar
- dishwashing detergent
- hand lens
- 2 plastic spoons
- pH test strips

Collect Data

6. Copy the table below into your Science-Log, and record your observations for each beaker in the columns labeled "Before cleaning."

7. Observe the color of the water in each beaker.

8. Use a hand lens to examine the water for visible particles.

9. Smell the water, and note any unusual odors.

10. Stir the water in each beaker rapidly with a plastic spoon, and check for suds. Use a different spoon for each sample.

11. Use a pH test strip to find the pH of the water.

12. Gently stir the clean water, and then pour half of it through the filtration device.

13. Observe the water in the collection beaker for color, particles, odors, suds, and pH. Be patient. It may take several minutes for the water to travel through the filtration device.

14. Record your observations in the appropriate "After filtration" column in your table.

15. Repeat steps 12–14 using the polluted water.

Results Table						
	Before cleaning (clean water)	Before cleaning (polluted water)	After filtration (clean water)	After filtration (polluted water)	After evaporation (clean water)	After evaporation (polluted water)
Color						
Particles						
Odor						
Suds						
pH						

DO NOT WRITE IN BOOK

Analyze the Results

16. How did the color of the polluted water change after the filtration? Did the color of the clean water change?

17. Did the filtration method remove all of the particles from the polluted water? Explain.

18. How much did the pH of the polluted water change? Did the pH of the clean water change? Was the final pH of the polluted water the same as the pH of the clean water before cleaning? Explain.

Part B: Evaporation

Cleaning water by evaporation is more expensive than cleaning water by filtration. Evaporation requires more energy, which can come from a variety of sources. In this activity, you will use an electric hot plate as the energy source. See how well this method works to clean your sample of polluted water.

Conduct an Experiment

19. Fill an Erlenmeyer flask with about 250 mL of the clean water, and insert the rubber stopper and glass tube into the flask.

20. Wearing goggles and gloves, connect about 1.5 m of plastic tubing to the glass tube.

21. Set the flask on the hot plate, and run the plastic tubing up and around the ring and down into a clean, empty 400 mL collection beaker.

22. Fill the sandwich bag with ice, seal the bag, and place the bag on the ring stand. Be sure the plastic bag and the tubing touch, as shown below.

23. Bring the water in the flask to a slow boil. As the water vapor passes by the bag of ice, the vapor will condense and drip into the collection beaker.

Collect Data

24. Observe the water in the collection beaker for color, particles, odor, suds, and pH. Record your observations in the appropriate "After evaporation" column in your data table.

25. Repeat steps 23–24 using the polluted water.

Analyze the Results

26. How did the color of the polluted water change after evaporation? Did the color of the clean water change after evaporation?

27. Did the evaporation method remove all of the particles from the polluted water? Explain.

28. How much did the pH of the polluted water change? Did the pH of the final clean water change? Was the final pH of the polluted water the same as the pH of the clean water before it was cleaned? Explain.

Draw Conclusions (Parts A and B)

29. Which method—filtration or evaporation—removed the most pollutants from the water? Explain your reasoning.

30. Describe any changes that occurred in the clean water during this experiment.

31. What do you think are the advantages and disadvantages of each method?

32. Explain how you think each material (sand, gravel, and charcoal) used in the filtration system helped clean the water.

33. List areas of the country where you think each method of purification would be the most and the least beneficial. Explain your reasoning.

Going Further

Do you think either purification method would remove oil from water? If time permits, repeat your experiment using several spoonfuls of cooking oil as the pollutant.

Filtration is only one step in the purification of water at water-treatment plants. Research other methods used to purify public water supplies.

Dune Movement

Wind moves the sand by a process called *saltation.* The sand skips and bounces along the ground in the direction the wind is blowing. As the sand is blown across the beach, the dunes change. In this activity, you will investigate the effect wind has on a model sand dune.

Materials

- marker
- metric ruler
- shallow cardboard box
- fine sand
- paper bag, large enough to hold half the box
- filter mask
- hair dryer
- watch or clock that indicates seconds

Procedure

1. Use the marker to draw and label vertical lines 5 cm apart along one side of the box.

2. Fill the box about halfway with sand. Brush the sand into a dune shape about 10 cm from the end of the box.

3. Use the lines you drew along the edge of the box to measure the location of the dune's peak to the nearest centimeter.

4. Slide the box into the paper bag until only about half the box is exposed, as shown below.

5. Put on your safety goggles and filter mask. Hold the hair dryer so that it is level with the peak of the dune and about 10–20 cm from the open end of the box.

6. Turn on the hair dryer at the lowest speed, and direct the air toward the model sand dune for 1 minute.

7. Record the new location of the model dune in your ScienceLog.

8. Repeat steps 5 and 6 three times. After each trial, measure and record the location of the dune's peak.

Analysis

9. How far did the dune move during each trial?

10. How far did the dune move overall?

11. How might the dune's movement be affected if you were to turn the hair dryer to the highest speed?

Going Further

Flatten the sand. Place a barrier, such as a rock, in the sand. Position the hair dryer level with the top of the sand's surface. How does the rock affect the dune's movement?

Gliding Glaciers

A glacier is large moving mass of ice. Glaciers are responsible for shaping many of the Earth's natural features. Glaciers are set in motion by the pull of gravity. As a glacier moves it changes the landscape, eroding the surface over which it passes.

Slip-Sliding Away

The material that is carried by a glacier erodes the Earth's surface, gouging out grooves called *striations*. Different materials have varying effects on the landscape. By creating a model glacier, you will demonstrate the effects of glacial erosion by various materials.

Procedure

1. Fill one margarine container with sand to a depth of 1 cm. Fill another margarine container with gravel to a depth of 1 cm. Leave the third container empty. Fill the containers with water.

2. Put the three containers in a freezer, and leave them overnight.

3. Retrieve the containers from the freezer, and remove the three ice blocks from the containers.

4. Use a rolling pin to flatten the modeling clay.

5. Hold the plain ice block firmly with a towel, and press as you move it along the length of the clay. Do this three times. In your ScienceLog, sketch the pattern the ice block makes in the clay.

6. Repeat steps 4 and 5 with the ice block that contains sand. Sketch the pattern this ice block makes in the clay.

7. Repeat steps 4 and 5 with the ice block that contains gravel. Sketch the pattern this ice block makes in the clay.

Materials

- 3 empty margarine containers
- sand
- gravel
- metric ruler
- water
- freezer
- rolling pin
- modeling clay
- small towel
- 3 bricks
- 3 pans
- 50 mL graduated cylinder
- timer

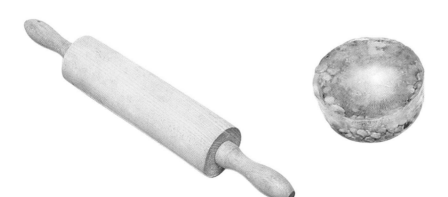

Analysis

8. Did any material from the clay become mixed with the material in the ice blocks? Explain.

9. Was any material deposited on the clay surface? Explain.

10. What glacial features are represented in your clay model?

11. Compare the patterns formed by the three model glaciers. Do the patterns look like features carved by alpine glaciers or by continental glaciers? Explain.

Going Further

Replace the clay with different materials, such as soft wood or sand. How does each ice block affect the different surface materials? What types of surfaces do the different materials represent?

Slippery When Wet

As the layers of ice build up and the glacier gets larger, the glacier will eventually begin to melt. The water from the melted ice allows the glacier to move forward. In this activity, you'll learn about the effect of pressure on the melting rate of a glacier.

Procedure

12. Place one ice block upside down in each pan.

13. Place one brick on top of one of the ice blocks. Place two bricks on top of another ice block. Leave the third ice block alone.

14. After 15 minutes, remove the bricks from the ice blocks.

15. Measure the amount of water that has melted from each ice block using the graduated cylinder.

16. Record your findings in your ScienceLog.

Analysis

17. Which ice block produced the most water?

18. What did the bricks represent?

19. What part of the ice block melted first? Explain.

20. How could you relate this investigation to the melting rate of glaciers? Explain.

Creating a Kettle

As glaciers recede, they leave huge amounts of rock material behind. Sometimes receding glaciers form moraines by depositing some of the rock material in ridges. At other times, glaciers leave chunks of ice that form depressions called *kettles.* These depressions may form ponds or lakes. In this activity, you will create your own kettle and discover how they are formed by glaciers.

Materials

- small tub
- sand
- 4–5 ice cubes of various sizes
- metric ruler

 TRY at HOME

Ask a Question

1. How are kettles formed?

Conduct an Experiment

2. Fill the tub three-quarters full with sand.

3. In your ScienceLog, describe the size and shape of the ice cubes.

4. Push the ice cubes to various depths in the sand.

5. Put the tub where it won't be disturbed overnight.

Make Observations

6. Look for the ice cubes the next day. Closely observe the sand around the area where you left each ice cube.

7. What happened to the ice cubes?

8. Use a metric ruler to measure the depth and diameter of the indentation left by the ice cubes.

Analyze the Results

9. How does this model relate to the size and shape of a natural kettle?

10. In what ways are your model kettles similar to real ones? How are they different?

Draw Conclusions

11. Based on your model, what can you conclude about the formation of kettles by receding glaciers?

Probing the Depths

In the 1870s, the crew of the ship the HMS *Challenger* used a wire and a weight to discover and map some of the deepest places in the world's oceans. Scientists tied a wire to a weight and dropped the weight overboard. When the weight reached the bottom of the ocean, they hauled the weight back up to the surface and measured the length of the wet wire. In this way, they were eventually able to map the ocean floor.

In this activity, you will model this traditional method of mapping by making a map of an ocean-floor model.

Materials

- modeling clay
- shoe box and lid
- scissors
- 8 unsharpened pencils
- metric ruler

Procedure

1. Use the clay to make a model ocean floor in the shoe box. Give the floor some mountains and valleys.

2. Cut eight holes in a line along the center of the lid. The holes should be just big enough to slide a pencil through. Close the box.

3. Exchange boxes with another student or group of students. Do not look into the box.

4. Copy the data table below into your ScienceLog. Also make a copy of the graph on the next page.

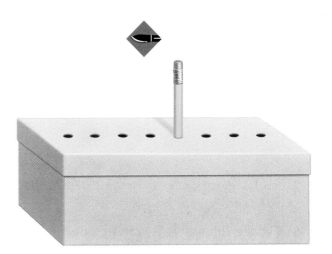

Ocean Depth Chart				
Hole position	Original length of probe	Amount of probe showing	Depth in centimeters	Depth in meters (cm × 200)
1				
2				
3				
4				
5				
6				
7				
8				

DO NOT WRITE IN BOOK

5. Measure the length of the probe (pencil) in centimeters. Record the length in your data table.

6. Gently insert the probe into the first hole position in the box until it touches the bottom. Do not force the probe down; this could affect your reading.

7. Making sure the probe is straight up and down, measure the length of probe showing above the lid. Record your data in the data table.

8. Use the following formula to calculate the depth in centimeters:

$$\text{original length of probe} - \text{amount of probe showing} = \text{depth in cm}$$

9. Use the scale 1 cm = 200 m to convert the depth in centimeters to meters to better represent real ocean depths. Add the data to your table.

10. Transfer the data to your graph for position 1.

11. Repeat steps 6–10 for the additional positions in the box.

12. After plotting all the points onto your graph, connect the points with a smooth curve.

13. Put a pencil in each of the holes in the shoe box. Compare the rise and fall of the set of pencils with your graph.

Analysis

14. What was the depth of your deepest point? your shallowest point?

15. Did your graph resemble the ocean-floor model, as shown by the pencils? If not, why not?

16. What difficulties might scientists have when measuring the real ocean floor? Do they ever get to "open the box"? Explain.

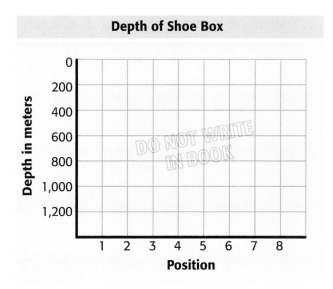

Depth of Shoe Box

DO NOT WRITE IN BOOK

Investigating an Oil Spill

Have you ever wondered why it is important to bring used motor oil to a recycling center rather than simply pouring it down the nearest drain or sewer? Or have you ever wondered why an oil spill of only a few thousand liters into an ocean containing many millions of liters of water can cause so much damage? The reason has to do with the fact that a little oil goes a long way.

Materials

- safety gloves
- large pan (at least 22 cm in diameter)
- water
- pipet
- 15 mL light machine oil
- metric ruler
- graduated cylinder
- calculator (optional)

Observing Oil and Water

You may have heard the expression "Oil and water don't mix." This is true—oil dropped on water will spread out thinly over the surface of the water. In this activity, you'll learn exactly how far oil can spread when it is in contact with water.

Procedure

1. Fill the pan two-thirds full with water. Be sure to wear your goggles and gloves.

2. Using the pipet, carefully add one drop of oil to the water in the middle of the pan.
   Caution: Machine oil is poisonous. Keep materials that have contacted oil out of your mouth and eyes.

3. Observe what happens to the drop of oil for the next few seconds. Record your observations in your ScienceLog.

4. Using a metric ruler, measure the diameter of the oil slick to the nearest centimeter.

5. Determine the area of the oil slick in square centimeters by using the formula for finding the area of a circle ($A = \pi r^2$). The radius (r) is equal to the diameter you measured in step 4 divided by 2. Multiply the radius by itself to get the square of the radius (r^2). Pi (π) is equal to 3.14.

   > **Example**
   > If your diameter is 10 cm,
   > $r = 5$ cm, $r^2 = 25$ cm^2, $\pi = 3.14$
   > $A = \pi r^2$
   > $A = 3.14 \times 25$ cm^2
   > $A = 78.5$ cm^2

6. Record your answers in your ScienceLog.

Analysis

7. What happened to the drop of oil when it came in contact with the water? Did this surprise you?

8. What total surface area was covered by the oil slick? (Be sure to show your calculations.)

9. What does this experiment tell you about the density of oil compared with the density of water? Explain.

Going Further

Can you devise a way to clean the oil from the water? Get permission from your teacher before testing your cleaning method.

Do you think oil behaves the same way in ocean water? Devise an experiment to test your hypothesis.

Finding the Number of Drops in a Liter

"It's only a few drops," you may think as you spill something toxic on the ground. But those drops eventually add up. Just how many drops does it take to make a difference? In this activity, you'll learn just what an impact a few drops can have.

Procedure

10. Using a clean pipet, count the number of water drops it takes to fill the graduated cylinder to 10 mL. Be sure to add the drops slowly so you get an accurate count.

11. Since there are 1,000 mL in a liter, multiply the number of drops in 10 mL by 100. This gives you the number of drops in a liter.

Analysis

12. How many drops of water from your pipet does it take to fill a 1 L container?

13. What would happen if someone spilled 4 L of oil into a lake?

Going Further

Find out how much oil supertankers contain. Can you imagine the size of an oil slick that would form if one of these tankers spilled its oil?

Up from the Depths

Every year, the water in certain parts of the ocean "turns over." This means that the water at the bottom rises to the top and the water at the top falls to the bottom. This yearly change brings fresh nutrients from the bottom of the ocean to the fish living near the surface. That makes it a great time for fishing! However, the water in some parts of the ocean never turns over. You will use this activity to find out why.

Some parts of the ocean are warmer at the bottom, and some are warmer at the top. Sometimes the saltiest water is at the bottom; sometimes it is not. You will investigate how these factors help determine whether the water will turn over.

Ask a Question

1. Why do some parts of the ocean turn over, while others do not?

Conduct an Experiment

2. Label the beakers 1 through 5. Fill beakers 1 through 4 with tap water.

3. Add a drop of blue food coloring to the water in beakers 1 and 2. Stir.

4. Place beaker 1 in the bucket of ice for 10 minutes.

5. Add a drop of red food coloring to the water in beakers 3 and 4. Stir.

6. Set beaker 3 on a hot plate turned to a low setting for 10 minutes.

7. Add one spoonful of salt to the water in beaker 4, and stir.

8. While beaker 1 is cooling and beaker 3 is heating, copy the data table on the next page into your ScienceLog.

Materials

- 400 mL beakers (5)
- tap water
- blue and red food coloring
- spoon
- bucket of ice
- watch or clock
- hot plate
- heat-resistant gloves
- 4 pieces of plastic wrap, approximately 30 × 20 cm
- salt

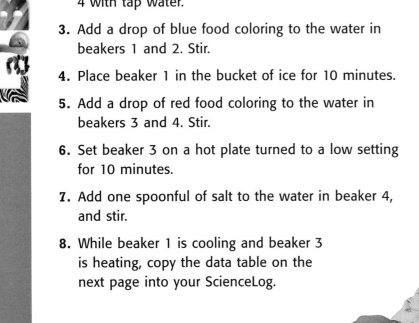

Observations Chart	
Mixture of water	**Observations**
Warm water placed above cold water	
Cold water placed above warm water	DO NOT WRITE IN BOOK
Salty water placed above fresh water	
Fresh water placed above salty water	

9. Pour half of the water in beaker 1 into beaker 5. Return beaker 1 to the bucket of ice.

10. Tuck a sheet of plastic wrap into beaker 5 so that the plastic rests on the surface of the water and lines the upper half of the beaker.

11. Put on your gloves. Slowly pour half of the water in beaker 3 into the plastic-lined upper half of beaker 5 to form two layers of water. Return beaker 3 to the hot plate, and remove your gloves.

12. Very carefully pull on one edge of the plastic wrap and remove it so that the warm, red water rests on the cold, blue water.
    Caution: The plastic wrap may be warm.

Make Observations

13. Wait about 5 minutes, and then observe the layers in beaker 5. Did one layer remain on top of the other? Was there any mixing or turning over? Record your observations in your data table.

14. Empty and rinse beaker 5 with clean tap water.

15. Repeat the procedure in steps 9–14, this time with warm, red water from beaker 3 on the bottom and cold, blue water from beaker 1 on top. (Use gloves when pouring warm water.)

16. Again repeat the procedure used in steps 9–14, this time with blue tap water from beaker 2 on the bottom and red, salty water from beaker 4 on top.

17. Repeat the procedure used in steps 9–14 a third time, this time with red, salty water from beaker 4 on the bottom and blue tap water from beaker 2 on top.

Analyze the Results

18. Compare the results of all four trials. Explain why the water turned over in some of the trials but not in all of them.

Draw Conclusions

19. What is the effect of temperature and salinity on the density of water?

20. What makes the temperature of ocean water decrease? What could make the salinity of ocean water increase?

21. What explanations can you give for the fact that some parts of the ocean turn over in the spring, while some do not?

Going Further
Suggest a method for setting up a model that tests the combined effects of temperature and salinity on the density of water. Consider using more than two water samples and dyes.

Turning the Tides

Daily tides are caused by two "bulges" on the ocean's surface—one on the side of the Earth facing the moon and the other on the opposite side. The bulge on the side facing the moon is caused by the moon's gravitational pull on the water. But the bulge on the opposite side is slightly more difficult to explain. Whereas the moon pulls the water on one side of the Earth, the combined rotation of the Earth and the moon "pushes" the water on the opposite side of the Earth. In this activity, you will model the motion of the Earth and the moon to investigate the tidal bulge on the side of Earth facing away from the moon.

Materials

- 2 disks of corrugated cardboard, one large and one small, with centers marked
- white glue
- piece of dowel, $1/4$ in. in diameter and 36 cm long
- 5 cm length of string
- stapler with staples
- 1×1 cm piece of cardboard
- sharp pencil

Procedure

1. Draw a line from the center of each disk along the folds in the cardboard to the edge of the disk. This line is the radius.

2. Place a drop of white glue on one end of the dowel. Lay the larger disk flat, and align the dowel with the line for the radius you drew in step 1. Insert about 2.5 cm of the dowel into the edge of the disk.

3. Add a drop of glue to the other end of the dowel, and push that end into the smaller disk, again along its radius. The setup should look like a large two-headed lollipop, as shown below. This is a model of the Earth-moon system.

4. Staple the string to the edge of the large disk on the side opposite the dowel. Staple the cardboard square to the other end of the string. This smaller piece of cardboard represents the Earth's oceans that face away from the moon.

5. Place the tip of the pencil at the center of the large disk, as shown in the figure on the next page, and spin the model. You may poke a small hole in the bottom of the disk with your pencil, but DO NOT poke all the way through the cardboard. Record your observations in your ScienceLog. **Caution:** Be sure you are at a safe distance from other people before spinning your model.

6. Now find your model's *center of mass.* This is the point at which the model can be balanced on the end of the pencil. **Hint:** It might be easier to find the center of mass using the eraser end. Then use the sharpened end of the pencil to balance the model. This balance point should be just inside the edge of the larger disk.

7. Place the pencil at the center of mass, and spin the model around the pencil. Again, you may wish to poke a small hole in the disk. Record your observations in your ScienceLog.

Analysis

8. What happened when you tried to spin the model around the center of the large disk? This model, called the Earth-centered model, represents the incorrect view that the moon orbits the center of the Earth.

9. What happened when you tried to spin the model around its center of mass? This point, called the *barycenter,* is the point around which both the Earth and the moon rotate.

10. In each case, what happened to the string and cardboard square when the model was spun?

11. Which model—the Earth-centered model or the barycentric model—explains why the Earth has a tidal bulge on the side opposite the moon? Explain.

Moon

Earth

Tidal bulges

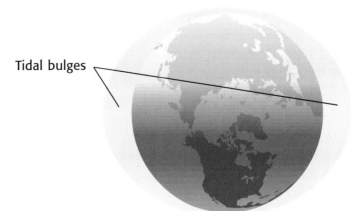

Boiling Over!

Safety Industries, Inc., would like to offer the public safer alternatives to the mercury thermometer. Many communities have complained that the glass thermometers are easy to break, and people are concerned about mercury poisoning. As a result, we would like your team of inventors to come up with a workable prototype that uses water instead of mercury. Safety Industries would like to offer a contract to the team that comes up with the best substitute for a mercury thermometer. In this activity, you will design and test your own water thermometer. Good luck!

Ask a Question

1. What conditions cause the liquid to rise in a thermometer? How can I use this information to build a thermometer?

Form a Hypothesis

2. Brainstorm with a classmate to design a thermometer that requires only water. Sketch your design in your ScienceLog. Write a one-sentence hypothesis that describes how your thermometer will work.

Test the Hypothesis

3. Follow your design to build a thermometer using only materials from the materials list. Like a mercury thermometer, your thermometer will need a bulb and a tube. However, the liquid in your thermometer will be water.

4. To test your design, place the aluminum pie pan on a hot plate. Carefully pour water into the pan until it is halfway full. Allow the water to heat.

5. Put on your gloves, and carefully place the "bulb" of your thermometer in the hot water. Observe the water level in the tube. Does it rise?

6. If the water level does not rise, adjust your design as necessary, and repeat steps 3–5. When the water level does rise, sketch your final design in your ScienceLog.

7. After you finalize your design, you must calibrate your thermometer with a laboratory thermometer by taping an index card to the thermometer tube so that the entire part of the tube protruding from the "bulb" of the thermometer touches the card.

Materials

- heat-resistant gloves
- aluminum pie pan
- hot plate
- water
- assorted containers, such as plastic bottles, soda cans, film canisters, medicine bottles, test tubes, balloons, and yogurt containers with lids
- assorted tubes, such as clear inflexible plastic straws or 5 mm diameter plastic tubing, 30 cm long
- modeling clay
- food coloring
- pitcher
- transparent tape
- index card
- Celsius thermometer
- a paper cone-shaped filter or funnel
- 2 large plastic-foam cups
- ice cubes
- metric ruler

8. Place the cone-shaped filter or funnel into the plastic-foam cup. Carefully pour hot water from the hot plate into the filter or funnel. Be sure that no water splashes or spills.

9. Place your own thermometer and a laboratory thermometer in the hot water. Mark the water level on the index card as it rises. Observe and record the temperature on the laboratory thermometer, and write this value on the card beside the mark.

10. Repeat steps 8–9 with warm water from the faucet.

11. Repeat steps 8–9 with ice water.

12. Divide the markings on the index card into equally sized increments, and write the corresponding temperatures on the index card.

Analyze the Results

13. How effective is your thermometer at measuring temperature?

14. Compare your thermometer design with other students' designs. How would you modify your design to make your thermometer measure temperature even better?

Draw Conclusions

15. Take a class vote to see which design should be chosen for a contract with Safety Industries. Why was this thermometer chosen? How did it differ from other designs in the class?

Go Fly a Bike!

Your friend Daniel just invented a bicycle that can fly! Trouble is, the bike can fly only when the wind speed is between 3 m/s and 10 m/s. If the wind is not blowing hard enough, the bike won't get enough lift to rise into the air, and if the wind is blowing too hard, the bike is difficult to control. Daniel needs to know if he can fly his bike today. Can you build a device that can estimate how fast the wind is blowing?

Materials

- scissors
- 5 small paper cups
- metric ruler
- hole punch
- 2 straight plastic straws
- colored marker
- small stapler
- thumbtack
- sharp pencil with an eraser
- modeling clay
- masking tape
- watch or clock that indicates seconds

Ask a Question

1. How can I construct a device to measure wind speed?

Construct an Anemometer

2. Cut off the rolled edges of all five paper cups. This will make them lighter, so that they can spin more easily.

3. Measure and place four equally spaced markings 1 cm below the rim of one of the paper cups.

4. Use the hole punch to punch a hole at each mark so that the cup has four equally spaced holes. Use the sharp pencil to carefully punch a hole in the center of the bottom of the cup.

5. Push a straw through two opposite holes in the side of the cup.

6. Repeat step 5 for the other two holes. The straws should form an X.

7. Measure 3 cm from the bottom of the remaining paper cups, and mark each spot with a dot.

8. At each dot, punch a hole in the paper cups with the hole punch.

9. Color the outside of one of the four cups.

10. Slide a cup on one of the straws by pushing the straw through the punched hole. Rotate the cup so that the bottom faces to the right.

11. Fold the end of the straw, and staple it to the inside of the cup directly across from the hole.

12. Repeat steps 10–11 for each of the remaining cups.

13. Push the tack through the intersection of the two straws.

14. Push the eraser end of a pencil through the bottom hole in the center cup. Push the tack as far as it will go into the end of the eraser.

15. Push the sharpened end of the pencil into some modeling clay to form a base. This will allow the device to stand up without being knocked over, as shown at right.

16. Blow into the cups so that they spin. Adjust the tack so that the cups can freely spin without wobbling or falling apart. Congratulations! You have just constructed an anemometer.

Conduct an Experiment

17. Find a suitable area outside to place the anemometer vertically on a surface away from objects that would obstruct the wind, such as buildings and trees.

18. Mark the surface at the base of the anemometer with masking tape. Label the tape "starting point."

19. Hold the colored cup over the starting point while your partner holds the watch.

20. Release the colored cup. At the same time, your partner should look at the watch or clock. As the cups spin, count the number of times the colored cup crosses the starting point in 10 seconds.

Analyze the Results

21. How many times did the colored cup cross the starting point in 10 seconds?

22. Divide your answer in step 21 by 10 to get the number of revolutions in 1 second.

23. Measure the diameter of your anemometer (the distance between the outside edges of two opposite cups) in centimeters. Multiply this number by 3.14 to get the circumference of the circle made by the cups of your anemometer.

24. Multiply your answer from step 23 by the number of revolutions per second (step 22). Divide that answer by 100 to get wind speed in meters per second.

25. Compare your results with those of your classmates. Did you get the same result? What could account for any slight differences in your results?

Draw Conclusions

26. Could Daniel fly his bicycle today? Why or why not?

Under Pressure!

You are planning a picnic with your friends, so you look in the newspaper for the weather forecast. The temperature this afternoon should be in the low 80s. This sounds quite comfortable! But you notice that the newspaper's forecast also includes the barometer reading. What does the reading tell you? In this activity, you will build your own barometer and discover what this instrument can tell you.

Materials

- balloon
- scissors
- large empty coffee can with 10 cm diameter
- masking tape or rubber band
- drinking straw
- transparent tape
- index card

Ask a Question

1. How can I construct a device that measures changes in atmospheric pressure?

Conduct an Experiment

2. Stretch and inflate the balloon. Let the air out. This will allow your barometer to be more sensitive to changes in atmospheric pressure.

3. Cut off the end of the balloon that you put in your mouth to inflate it. Stretch the balloon snugly over the mouth of the coffee can. Attach the balloon to the can with the tape or the rubber band.

4. Cut one end of the straw at an angle to form a pointer.

5. Place the straw with the pointer pointed away from the center of the stretched balloon so that 5 cm of the end of the straw hangs over the edge of the can, as shown on the next page. Tape the straw to the balloon.

6. Tape the index card to the can near the straw. Congratulations! You have just constructed a barometer!

7. Find a suitable area outside to place the barometer. Record the location of the straw for 3–4 days by marking it on the index card.

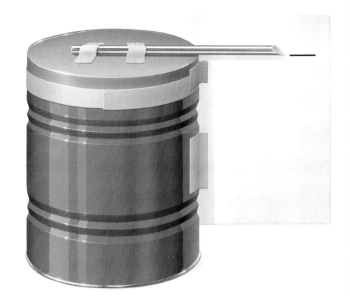

Analyze the Results

8. What factors affect how your barometer works? Explain your answer.

9. What does an upward movement of the straw indicate?

10. What does a downward movement of the straw indicate?

Draw Conclusions

11. Compare your results with the barometric pressures listed in your local newspaper. What kind of weather is associated with high pressure? What kind of weather is associated with low pressure?

Going Further

Now you can calibrate your barometer! Gather the weather section from your local newspaper for the same 3 or 4 days that you were testing your barometer. Find the barometer reading in the newspaper for each day, and record it beside that day's mark on your index card. Divide the markings on the index card into regular increments, and write the corresponding barometric pressures on the card.

Watching the Weather

Imagine that you own a private consulting firm that helps people plan for big occasions, such as weddings, parties, and celebrity events. One of your duties is making sure the weather doesn't put a damper on your clients' plans. In order to provide the best service possible, you have taken a crash course in reading weather maps. Will the celebrity golf match have to be delayed on account of rain? Will the wedding ceremony have to be moved inside so the blushing bride doesn't get soaked? It is your job to say "yea" or "nay."

Procedure *TRY at HOME*

1. Study the station model and legend shown on the next page. You will use the legend to interpret the weather map on the final page of this activity.

2. Weather data is represented on a weather map by a station model. A station model is a small circle that shows the location of the weather station along with a set of symbols and numbers around the circle that represent the data collected at the weather station. Study the table below.

Weather-Map Symbols		
Weather conditions	**Cloud cover**	**Wind speed (mph)**
•• Light rain	◯ No clouds	◎ Calm
∴ Moderate rain	◑ One-tenth or less	3–8
⁖ Heavy rain	◔ Two- to three-tenths	9–14
, Drizzle	◑ Broken	15–20
✳ ✳ Light snow	◖ Nine-tenths	21–25
✳∗✳ Moderate snow	● Overcast	32–37
℞ Thunderstorm	⊗ Sky obscured	44–48
∾ Freezing rain	**Special Symbols**	55–60
∞ Haze	▲▲▲▲ Cold front	66–71
≡ Fog	●●●● Warm front	
	H High pressure	
	L Low pressure	
	𝓢 Hurricane	

Wind speed is represented by whole and half tails.

A line indicates the direction the wind is coming from.

Air temperature

A symbol represents the current weather conditions. If there is no symbol, there is no precipitation.

Atmospheric pressure in millibars (mbar). This number has been shortened on the station model. To read the number properly you must follow a few simple rules.

- If the first number is greater than 5, place a 9 in front of the number and a decimal point between the last two digits.
- If the first number is less than or equal to 5, place a 10 in front of the number and a decimal point between the last two digits.

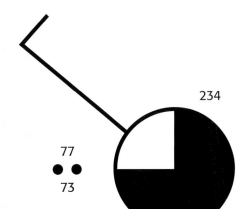

234

77

73

Dew point temperature

Shading indicates the cloud coverage.

Interpreting Station Models

The station model below is for Boston, Massachusetts. The current temperature in Boston is 42°F, and the dew point is 39°F. The barometric pressure is 1011.0 mbar. The sky is overcast, and there is a moderate rainfall. The wind is coming from the southwest at 15–20 mph.

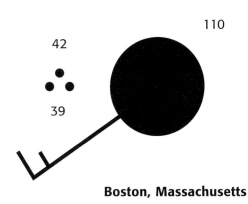

110

42

39

Boston, Massachusetts

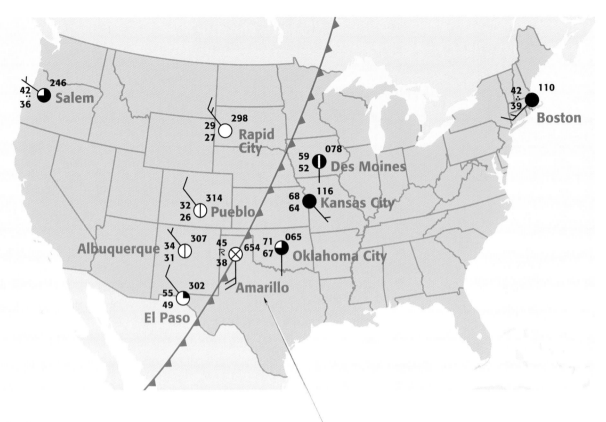

Analysis

3. Based on the weather for the entire United States, what time of year is it? Explain your answer.

4. Interpret the station model for Salem, Oregon. What is the temperature, dew point, cloud coverage, wind direction, wind speed, and atmospheric pressure? Is there any precipitation? If so, what kind?

5. What is happening to wind direction, temperature, and pressure as the cold front approaches? as it passes?

6. Interpret the station model for Amarillo, Texas.

Let It Snow!

While an inch of rain might be good for your garden, 7 or 8 cm could cause an unwelcome flood. But what about snow? How much snow is too much? A blizzard might drop 40 cm of snow overnight. Sure it's up to your knees, but how does this much snow compare with rain? This activity will help you find out.

Materials

- 150 mL of shaved ice
- 100 mL beaker
- metric ruler
- heat-resistant gloves
- hot plate
- graduated cylinder

Procedure

1. Pour 50 mL of shaved ice into your beaker. Do not pack the ice into the beaker. This ice will represent your snowfall.

2. Use the ruler to measure the height of the snow in the beaker.

3. Turn on the hot plate to a low setting. **Caution:** Wear heat-resistant gloves and goggles when working with the hot plate.

4. Place the beaker on the hot plate, and leave it there until all of the snow melts.

5. Pour the water into the graduated cylinder, and record the height and volume of the water in your ScienceLog.

6. Repeat steps 1–5 two more times.

Analysis

7. What was the difference in height before and after the snow melted in each of your three trials? What was the average difference?

8. Why did the volume change after the ice melted?

9. In this activity, what was the ratio of snow height to water height?

10. Use the ratio you found in step 9 to calculate how much water 50 cm of this snow would produce. Use the following equation to help.

$$\frac{\text{measured height of snow}}{\text{measured height of water}} = \frac{50 \text{ cm of snow}}{? \text{ cm of water}}$$

11. Why is it important to know the water content of a snowfall?

Going Further

Shaved ice isn't really snow. Research to find out how much water real snow would produce. Does every snowfall produce the same ratio of snow height to water depth?

Gone with the Wind

Pilots at the Fly Away Airport need your help—fast! Last night, lightning destroyed the orange windsock. This windsock helped pilots measure which direction the wind was blowing. But now the windsock is gone with the wind, and an incoming airplane needs to land. The pilot must know what direction the wind is blowing and is counting on you to make a device that can measure wind direction.

Materials

- paper plate
- drawing compass
- metric ruler
- protractor
- index card
- scissors
- stapler
- straight plastic straw
- sharpened pencil
- thumbtack or pushpin
- magnetic compass
- small rock

Ask a Question

1. How can I measure wind direction?

Conduct an Experiment

2. Find the center of the plate by tracing around its edge with a drawing compass. The pointed end of the compass should poke a small hole in the center of the plate.

3. Use a ruler to draw a line across the center of the plate.

4. Use a protractor to help you draw a second line through the center of the plate. This new line should be at a 90° angle to the line you drew in step 3.

5. Moving clockwise, label each line *N, E, S,* and *W.*

6. Use a protractor to help you draw two more lines through the center of the plate. These lines should be at a 45° angle to the lines you drew in steps 3 and 4.

7. Moving clockwise from *N,* label these new lines *NE, SE, SW,* and *NW.* The plate now resembles the face of a magnetic compass. This will be the base of your wind-direction indicator. It will help you read the direction of the wind at a glance.

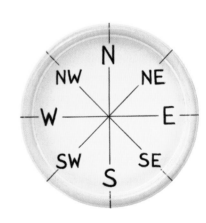

8. Measure and mark a 5 × 5 cm square on an index card. Cut the square out of the card. Fold the square in half to form a triangle.

9. Staple an open edge of the triangle to the straw so that one point of the triangle touches the end of the straw.

10. Hold the pencil at a 90° angle to the straw. The eraser should touch the balance point of the straw. Push a thumbtack or pushpin through the straw and into the eraser. The straw should spin without falling off.

11. Find a suitable area outside to measure the wind direction. The area should be clear of trees and buildings.

12. Press the sharpened end of the pencil through the center hole of the plate and into the ground. The labels on your paper plate should be facing the sky, as shown below.

13. Use a compass to find magnetic north. Rotate the plate so that the *N* on the plate points north. Place a small rock on top of the plate so that it does not turn.

14. Watch the straw as it rotates. The triangle will point in the direction the wind is blowing.

Analyze the Results

15. From what direction is the wind coming?

16. In what direction is the wind blowing?

Draw Conclusions

17. Would this be an effective way for pilots to measure wind direction? Why or why not?

18. What improvements would you suggest to Fly Away Airport to measure wind direction more accurately?

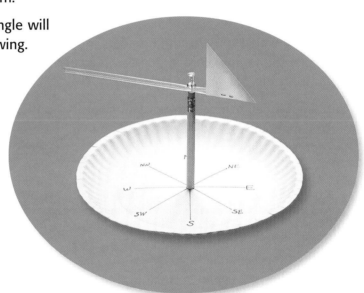

Going Further
Use this tool to measure and record wind direction for several days. What changes in wind direction occur as a front approaches? as a front passes?

Review magnetic declination in the chapter titled "Maps as Models of the Earth." How might magnetic declination affect your design for a tool to measure wind direction?

Global Impact

For years scientists have debated the topic of global warming. Is the temperature of the Earth actually getting warmer? Sample sizes are a very important factor in any scientific study. In this activity, you will examine a chart to determine if the data indicate any trends. Be sure to notice how much the trends seem to change as you analyze different sets of data.

Materials

- 4 colored pencils
- metric ruler

TRY at HOME

Procedure

1. Look at the chart below. It shows average global temperatures recorded over the last 100 years.

2. Draw a graph in your ScienceLog. Label the horizontal axis "Time," and mark the grid in 5-year intervals. Label the vertical axis "Temperature (°C)," with values ranging from 13°C to 15°C.

3. Starting with 1900, use the numbers in red to plot the temperature in 20-year intervals. Connect the dots with straight lines.

4. Using a ruler, estimate the overall slope of temperatures, and draw a red line to represent the slope.

5. Using different colors, plot the temperatures at 10-year intervals and 5-year intervals on the same graph. Connect each set of dots, and draw the average slope for each set.

Analysis

6. Examine your completed graph, and explain any trends you see in the graphed data. Was there an increase or a decrease in average temperature over the last 100 years?

7. What differences did you see in each set of graphed data? what similarities?

8. What conclusions can you draw from the data you graphed in this activity?

9. What would happen if your graph were plotted in 1-year intervals? Try it!

Average Global Temperatures											
Year	°C	Year	°C	Year	°C	Year	°C	Year	°C	Year	°C
1900	14.0	1917	13.6	1934	14.0	1951	14.0	1968	13.9	1985	14.1
1901	13.9	1918	13.6	1935	13.9	1952	14.0	1969	14.0	1986	14.2
1902	13.8	1919	13.8	1936	14.0	1953	14.1	1970	14.0	1987	14.3
1903	13.6	1920	13.8	1937	14.1	1954	13.9	1971	13.9	1988	14.4
1904	13.5	1921	13.9	1938	14.1	1955	13.9	1972	13.9	1989	14.2
1905	13.7	1922	13.9	1939	14.0	1956	13.8	1973	14.2	1990	14.5
1906	13.8	1923	13.8	1940	14.1	1957	14.1	1974	13.9	1991	14.4
1907	13.6	1924	13.8	1941	14.1	1958	14.1	1975	14.0	1992	14.1
1908	13.7	1925	13.8	1942	14.1	1959	14.0	1976	13.8	1993	14.2
1909	13.7	1926	14.1	1943	14.0	1960	14.0	1977	14.2	1994	14.3
1910	13.7	1927	14.0	1944	14.1	1961	14.1	1978	14.1	1995	14.5
1911	13.7	1928	14.0	1945	14.0	1962	14.0	1979	14.1	1996	14.4
1912	13.7	1929	13.8	1946	14.0	1963	14.0	1980	14.3	1997	14.4
1913	13.8	1930	13.9	1947	14.1	1964	13.7	1981	14.4	1998	14.5
1914	14.0	1931	14.0	1948	14.0	1965	13.8	1982	14.1	1999	
1915	14.0	1932	14.0	1949	13.9	1966	13.9	1983	14.3	2000	
1916	13.8	1933	13.9	1950	13.8	1967	14.0	1984	14.1	2001	

For the Birds

You and a partner have a new business building birdhouses. But your first clients have told you that birds do not want to live in the birdhouses you have made. The clients want their money back unless you can solve the problem. You need to come up with a solution right away!

You remember reading an article about microclimates in a science magazine. Cities often heat up because the pavement and buildings absorb so much solar radiation. Maybe the houses are too warm! How can the houses be kept cooler?

You decide to investigate the roofs; after all, changing the roofs would be a lot easier than building new houses. In order to help your clients and the birds, you decide to test different roof colors and materials to see how these variables affect a roof's ability to absorb the sun's rays.

One partner will test the color, and the other partner will test the materials. You will then share your results and make a recommendation together.

Materials

- 4 pieces of cardboard
- black, white, and light-blue tempera paint
- 4 Celsius thermometers
- watch or clock
- beige or tan wood
- beige or tan rubber

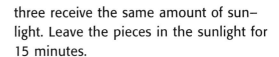

Part A: Color Test

Ask a Question

1. What color would be the best choice for the roof of a birdhouse?

Form a Hypothesis

2. In your ScienceLog, write down the color you think will keep a birdhouse coolest.

Test the Hypothesis

3. Paint one piece of cardboard black, another piece white, and a third light blue.

4. After the paint has dried, take the three pieces of cardboard outside, and place a thermometer on each piece.

5. In an area where there is no shade, place each piece at the same height so that all three receive the same amount of sunlight. Leave the pieces in the sunlight for 15 minutes.

6. Leave a fourth thermometer outside in the shade to measure the temperature of the air.

7. In your ScienceLog, record the reading of the thermometer on each piece of cardboard. Also record the outside temperature.

Analyze the Results

8. Did each of the three thermometers record the same temperature after 15 minutes? Explain.

9. Were the temperature readings on each of the three pieces of cardboard the same as the reading for the outside temperature? Explain.

Draw Conclusions

10. How do your observations compare with your hypothesis?

Part B: Material Test

Ask a Question

11. Which material would be the best choice for the roof of a birdhouse?

Form a Hypothesis

12. In your ScienceLog, write down the material you think will keep a birdhouse coolest.

Test the Hypothesis

13. Take the rubber, wood, and the fourth piece of cardboard outside, and place a thermometer on each.

14. In an area where there is no shade, place each material at the same height so that they all receive the same amount of sunlight. Leave the materials in the sunlight for 15 minutes.

15. Leave a fourth thermometer outside in the shade to measure the temperature of the air.

16. In your ScienceLog, record the temperature of each material. Also record the outside temperature.

Analyze the Results

17. Did each of the thermometers on the three materials record the same temperature after 15 minutes? Explain.

18. Were the temperature readings on the rubber, wood, and cardboard the same as the reading for the outside temperature? Explain.

Draw Conclusions

19. How do your observations compare with your hypothesis?

Sharing Information (Parts A and B)

Communicate Results

After you and your partner have finished your investigations, take a few minutes to share your results. Then work together to design a new roof.

20. Which material would you use to build the roofs for your birdhouses? Why?

21. Which color would you use to paint the new roofs? Why?

Going Further

Make three different-colored samples for each of the three materials. When you measure the temperatures for each sample, how do the colors compare for each material? Is the same color best for all three materials? How do your results compare with what you concluded in steps 20 and 21 of this activity? What's more important, color or material?

Biome Business

You have just been hired as an assistant to a world-famous botanist. Your duties include collecting vegetation samples to study the effects of human activity on different plant species. Unfortunately, you were hired at the last minute, and no one has explained tomorrow's plan to you. You have been provided with climatographs for three biomes. A *climatograph* is a graph that shows the temperature and precipitation patterns for an area for a year.

You can use the information provided in the graphs to determine the type of climate in each biome. You also have a general map of the biomes, but nothing is labeled. Using this information, you must figure out what the environment will be like so that you can prepare yourself.

In this activity you will use climatographs and maps to determine where you will be traveling. You can find the exact locations by tracing the general maps and matching them to Figure 10 in the Climate chapter. Good luck!

Procedure *TRY at HOME*

1. Look at each climatograph. The shaded areas show the average precipitation for the biome. The red line shows the average temperature.

2. Use the climatographs to determine the climate patterns for each biome. Compare the maps with the general map in Figure 10 to find the exact location of each region.

Analysis

3. Describe the precipitation patterns of each biome by answering the following questions:
   a. When does it rain the most in this biome?
   b. Do you think the biome is relatively dry, or do you think it rains a lot?

4. Describe the temperature patterns of each biome by answering the following questions:
   a. What are the warmest months of the year?
   b. Does the biome seem to have temperature cycles, like seasons, or is the temperature almost always the same?
   c. Do you think the biome is warm or cool? Explain.

5. Name each biome.

6. Where is each biome located?

Biome A

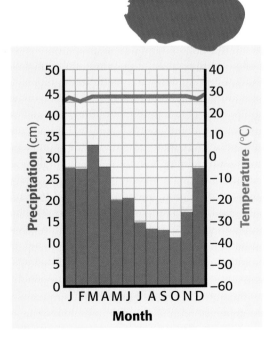

Biome B

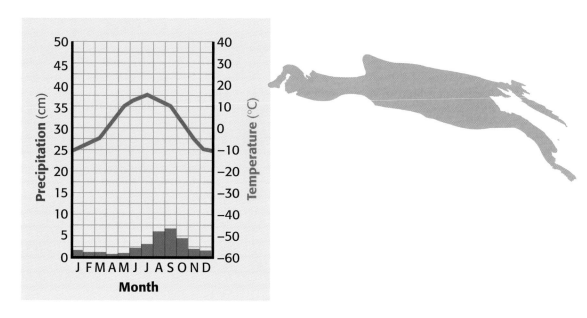

Biome C

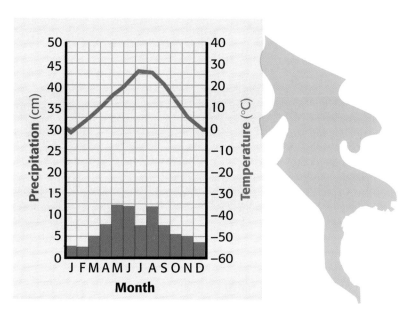

Going Further

In a cardboard box no bigger than a shoe box, build a model of one of the biomes that you investigated. Include things to represent the biome, such as the plants and animals that inhabit the area. Use magazines, photographs, colored pencils, plastic figurines, clay, or whatever you like. Be creative!

Create a Calendar

Imagine that you live in the first colony on Mars. You have been trying to follow the Earth calendar, but it just isn't working anymore. Mars takes almost 2 Earth years to revolve around the sun—almost 687 Earth days to be exact! That means that there are two seasons each Earth calendar year. One year, you get winter and spring, but the next year, you get only summer and fall! And Martian days are longer than Earth days. Mars takes 24.6 Earth hours to rotate on its axis. Even though they are similar, Earth days and Martian days just don't match. This won't do!

Several groups of Mars pioneers have been chosen to design a new calendar that will be based on the Martian year. The best design will be chosen as the Martian calendar. The winner will go down in history as the founder of the modern Martian calendar. Your calendar should include months, weeks, and days.

Materials

- poster board
- ruler
- colored pencils
- calculator (optional)
- marker

Ask a Question

1. How can I create a calendar for Mars that includes months, weeks, and days?

Conduct an Experiment

2. Use the following formulas to determine the number of Martian days there are in a Martian year:

$$\frac{687 \text{ Earth days}}{1 \text{ Martian year}} \times \frac{24 \text{ Earth hours}}{1 \text{ Earth day}} = \text{Earth hours per Martian year}$$

$$\text{Earth hours per Martian year} \times \frac{1 \text{ Martian day}}{24.6 \text{ Earth hours}} = \text{Martian days per Martian year}$$

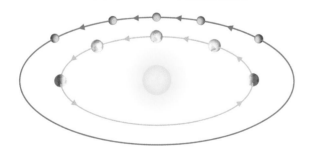

3. Decide how to divide your calendar into Martian months, weeks, and days. Will you have a leap day, a leap week, a leap month, or a leap year? How often will it occur?

4. Choose names for the months and days of your calendar. In your ScienceLog, explain why you chose each name. If you have time, explain how you would number the Martian years. For instance, would the first year correspond to a certain Earth year?

5. Follow your design to create your own calendar for Mars. Draw the calendar on your piece of poster board. Make sure it is brightly colored and easy to follow.

6. Present your calendar to the class. Explain how you chose your months, weeks, and days.

Analyze the Results

7. What advantages does your calendar design have? Are there any disadvantages to your design?

8. Which student or group created the most original calendar? Which design was the most useful? Explain.

9. What might you do to improve your calendar?

Draw Conclusions

10. Take a class vote to decide which design should be chosen as the new calendar for Mars. Why was this calendar chosen? How did it differ from other designs?

11. Why is it useful to have a calendar that matches the cycles of the planet you live on?

The Sun's Yearly Trip Through the Zodiac

During the course of a year, the sun appears to move through a circle of twelve constellations in the sky. The twelve constellations make up a "belt" in the sky called the *zodiac.* Each month, the sun appears to be in a different constellation. The ancient Babylonians developed a 12-month calendar based on the idea that the sun moved through this circle of constellations as it revolved around the Earth. They believed that the constellations of stars were fixed in position and that the sun and planets moved past the stars. Later, Copernicus developed a model of the solar system in which the Earth and the planets revolve around the sun. But how can Copernicus's model of the solar system be correct when the sun appears to move through the zodiac?

Materials

- 12 chairs
- 12 index cards
- roll of masking tape
- inflated ball
- large cardboard box

Ask a Question

1. If the sun is at the center of the solar system, why does it appear to move with respect to the stars in the sky?

Conduct an Experiment

2. Set the chairs in a large circle so that the backs of the chairs all face the center of the circle. Make sure that the chairs are equally spaced, like the numbers on the face of a clock.

3. Write the name of each constellation in the zodiac on the index cards. You should have one card for each constellation.

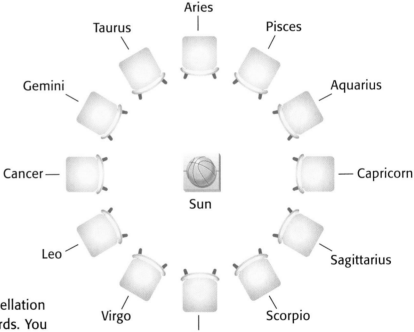

4. Stand inside the circle with the masking tape and the index cards. Moving counterclockwise, attach the cards to the backs of the chairs in the following order: Aries, Taurus, Gemini, Cancer, Leo, Virgo, Libra, Scorpio, Sagittarius, Capricorn, Aquarius, and Pisces.

5. Use masking tape to label the ball "Sun."

6. Place the large closed box in the center of the circle. Set the roll of masking tape flat on top of the box.

7. Place the ball on top of the roll of masking tape so that the ball stays in place.

8. Stand inside of the circle of chairs. You will represent the Earth. As you move around the ball, you will model the Earth's orbit around the sun. Notice that even though only the "Earth" is moving, as seen from the Earth, the sun appears to move through the entire zodiac!

9. Stand in front of the chair labeled "Aries." Look at the ball representing the sun. Then look past the ball to the chair at the opposite side of the circle. Where in the zodiac does the sun appear to be?

10. Move to the next chair on your right (counterclockwise). Where does the sun appear to be? Is it in the same constellation? Explain your answer.

11. Repeat step 10 until you have observed the position of the sun from each chair in the circle.

Analyze the Results

12. Did the sun appear to move through the 12 constellations, even though the Earth was orbiting around the sun? How can you explain this?

Draw Conclusions

13. How does Copernicus's model of the solar system explain the apparent movement of the sun through the constellations of the zodiac?

Through the Looking Glass

Have you ever looked toward the horizon or up into the sky and wished you could see farther? Think a telescope might help? Astronomers use huge telescopes to study the universe. You can build your very own telescope to get a glimpse of what astronomers see with their incredible equipment.

Materials

- masking tape
- 2 convex lenses, 3 cm in diameter
- desk lamp
- sheet of construction paper
- metric ruler
- cardboard wrapping-paper tube
- cardboard toilet-paper tube
- scissors
- modeling clay

Procedure

1. Use modeling clay to form a base to hold one of the lenses upright on your desktop. When the lights are turned off, your teacher will turn on a lamp at the front of the classroom. Rotate your lens so that the light from the lamp passes through it.

2. Hold the construction paper so that the light passing through the lens lands on the paper. Slowly move the paper closer to or farther from the lens until you see the sharpest image of the light on the paper. Hold the paper in this position.

3. With the metric ruler, measure the distance between the lens and the paper. Record this distance in your ScienceLog.

4. How far is the paper from the lens? This distance, called the *image distance,* is how far the paper has to be from the lens in order for the image to be in focus.

5. Repeat steps 1–4 with the other lens.

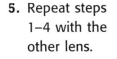

6. From one end of the long cardboard tube, measure and mark the image distance of the lens with the longer image distance. Place a mark 2 cm past this line toward the other end of the tube, and label the mark "cut."

7. From one end of the short cardboard tube, measure and mark the image distance of the lens with the shorter image distance. Place a mark 2 cm past this line toward the other end of the tube, and label the mark "cut."

8. Shorten the tubes by cutting along the marks labeled "cut."

9. Tape the lens with the longer image distance to one end of the longer tube. Tape the other lens to one end of the shorter tube. Slip one tube inside the other. Be sure the lenses are at each end of this new, longer tube.

10. Congratulations! You have just constructed a telescope! To use your telescope, look through the short tube (the eyepiece), and point the long end at various objects in the room. You can focus the telescope by adjusting its length. Are the images right side up, or upside down? Observe birds, insects, trees, or other outside objects.
Caution: Never look directly at the sun! This could cause permanent blindness.

Analysis

11. Which type of telescope did you just construct—a refracting telescope or a reflecting telescope? What makes it one type and not the other?

12. Would upside-down images negatively affect astronomers looking at stars through their telescopes? Explain your answer.

How Far Is the Sun?

It doesn't slice, it doesn't dice, but it can give you an idea of how big our universe is! You can build your very own stellar-distance measuring device from household items. Amaze your friends by figuring out how many metersticks can be placed between Earth and the sun.

Materials

- poster board
- scissors
- square of aluminum foil
- thumbtack
- masking tape
- index card
- meterstick
- metric ruler

Ask a Question

1. If it were possible, how many metersticks could I place between the sun and the Earth?

Conduct an Experiment

2. Measure and cut a 4 × 4 cm square from the middle of the poster board. Tape the foil square in the center of the poster board.

3. Carefully prick the foil with a thumbtack to form a tiny hole in the center. Congratulations—you have just constructed your very own stellar-distance measuring device!

4. Tape the device to a window facing the sun so that sunlight shines directly through the pinhole.
   Caution: Do not look directly into the sun.

5. Place one end of the meterstick against the window and beneath the foil square, and steady the meterstick with one hand.

6. With the other hand, hold the index card close to the pinhole. You should be able to see a circular image on the card. This is an image of the sun.

7. Move the card back until the image is large enough to measure. Be sure to keep the image on the card sharply focused. Reposition the meterstick so that it touches the bottom of the card.

8. Ask your partner to measure the diameter of the image on the card with the metric ruler. Record the diameter of the image in your ScienceLog.

9. Record the distance between the window and the index card by reading the point at which the card rests on the meterstick.

10. Calculate the distance between the Earth and the sun using the following formula:

$$\text{Distance between the sun and Earth} = \text{sun's diameter} \times \frac{\text{distance to the image}}{\text{image's diameter}}$$

1 cm = 10 mm
1 m = 100 cm
1 km = 1,000 m

Hint: The sun's diameter is 1,392,000,000 m.

Analyze the Results

11. According to your calculations, how far is the sun from the Earth? Don't forget to convert your measurements to meters.

Draw Conclusions

12. You could put 150 billion metersticks between the Earth and the sun. Compare this with your result in step 11. Do you think that this is a good way to measure the Earth's distance from the sun? Support your answer.

713

Using Scientific Methods

Why Do They Wander?

Before the discoveries of Nicholas Copernicus in the early 1500s, most people thought that the planets and the sun revolve around the Earth and that the Earth was the center of the solar system. But Copernicus observed that the sun is the center of the solar system and that all the planets, including Earth, revolve around the sun. He also explained a puzzling aspect of the movement of planets across the night sky.

If you watch a planet every night for several months, you'll notice that it appears to "wander" among the stars. While the stars remain in fixed positions relative to each other, the planets appear to move independently of the stars. First Mars travels to the left, then it goes back to the right a little, and finally it reverses direction and travels again to the left. No wonder the early Greeks called the planets wanderers!

In this lab you will make your own model of part of the solar system to find out how Copernicus's model of the solar system explained this zigzag motion of the planets.

Materials

- drawing compass
- white paper
- metric ruler
- colored pencils

Ask a Question

1. Why do the planets appear to move back and forth in the Earth's night sky?

Conduct an Experiment

2. Use the compass to draw a circle with a diameter of 9 cm on the paper. This circle will represent the orbit of the Earth around the sun. (Note: The orbits of the planets are actually slightly elliptical, but circles will work for this activity.)

3. Using the same center point, draw a circle with a diameter of 12 cm. This circle will represent the orbit of Mars.

4. Using a blue pencil, draw three parallel lines in a diagonal across one end of your paper, as shown at right. These lines will help you plot the path Mars appears to travel in Earth's night sky. Turn your paper so that the diagonal lines are at the top of the page.

5. Place 11 dots on your Earth orbit, as shown on the next page, and number them 1 through 11. These dots will represent Earth's position from month to month.

6. Now place 11 dots along the top of your Mars orbit, as shown below. Number the dots as shown. These dots will represent the position of Mars at the same time intervals. Notice that Mars travels slower than Earth.

7. Use a green line to connect the first dot on Earth's orbit to the first dot on Mars's orbit, and extend the line all the way to the first diagonal line at the top of your paper. Place a green dot where this green line meets the first blue diagonal line, and label the green dot *1*.

8. Now connect the second dot on Earth's orbit to the second dot on Mars's orbit, and extend the line all the way to the first diagonal at the top of your paper. Place a green dot where this line meets the first blue diagonal line, and label this dot *2*.

9. Continue drawing green lines from Earth's orbit through Mars's orbit and finally to the blue diagonal lines. Pay attention to the pattern of dots you are adding to the diagonal lines. When the direction of the dots changes, extend the green line to the next diagonal, and add the dots to that line instead.

10. When you are finished adding green lines, draw a red line to connect all the dots on the blue diagonal lines in the order you drew them.

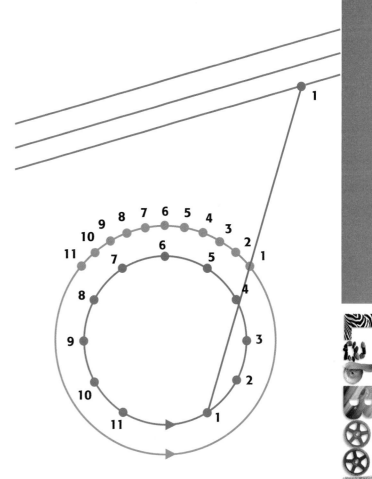

Analyze the Results

11. What do the green lines connecting points along Earth's orbit and Mars's orbit represent?

12. What does the red line connecting the dots along the diagonal lines look like? How can you explain this?

Draw Conclusions

13. What does this demonstration show about the motion of Mars?

14. Why do planets appear to move back and forth across the sky?

15. Were the Greeks justified in calling the planets wanderers? Explain.

Eclipses

As the Earth and the moon revolve around the sun, they both cast shadows into space. An eclipse occurs when one planetary body passes through the shadow of another. You can demonstrate how an eclipse occurs by using clay models of planetary bodies.

Materials

- modeling clay
- metric ruler
- sheet of notebook paper
- small flashlight

Procedure

1. Make two balls out of the modeling clay. One ball should have a diameter of about 4 cm and will represent the Earth. The other should have a diameter of about 1 cm and will represent the moon.

2. Place the two balls about 15 cm apart on the sheet of paper. (You may want to prop the smaller ball up on folded paper or on clay so that the centers of the two balls are at the same level.)

3. Hold the flashlight approximately 15 cm away from the large ball. The flashlight and the two balls should be in a straight line. Keep the flashlight at about the same level as the clay. When the whole class is ready, your teacher will turn off the lights.

4. Turn on your flashlight. Shine the light on the larger ball, and sketch your model in your ScienceLog. Include the beam of light in your drawing.

5. Move the flashlight to the opposite side of the paper. The flashlight should now be approximately 15 cm away from the smaller clay ball. Repeat step 4.

Analysis

6. What does the flashlight in your model represent?

7. As viewed from Earth, what event did your model represent in step 4?

8. As viewed from the moon, what event did your model represent in step 4?

9. As viewed from Earth, what event did your model represent in step 5?

10. As viewed from the moon, what event did your model represent in step 5?

11. According to your model, how often would solar and lunar eclipses occur? Is this accurate? Explain.

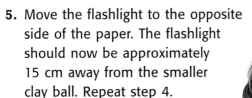

Phases of the Moon

It's easy to see when the moon is full. But you may have wondered exactly what happens when the moon appears as a crescent or when you cannot see the moon at all. Does the Earth cast its shadow on the moon? In this activity, you will discover how and why the moon appears as it does in each phase.

Materials

- globe
- light source
- plastic-foam ball

Procedure

1. Place your globe near the light source. Be sure that the north pole is tilted toward the light. Rotate the globe so that your state faces the light.

2. Using the ball as your model of the moon, move the moon between the Earth (the globe) and the sun (the light). The side of the moon that faces the Earth will be in darkness. Write your observations of this new-moon phase in your ScienceLog.

3. Continue to move the moon in its orbit around the Earth. When part of the moon is illuminated by the light, as viewed from Earth, the moon is in the crescent phase. Add your observations to your ScienceLog.

4. If you have time, you may draw your own moon-phase diagram.

Analysis

5. About 2 weeks after the new moon appears, the entire moon is visible in the sky. Move the ball to show this event.

6. What other phases can you add to your diagram? For example, when does the quarter moon appear?

7. Explain why the moon sometimes appears as a crescent to viewers on Earth.

Red Hot, or Not?

When you look at the night sky, some stars are brighter than others. Some are even different colors from what you might expect. For example, one star in the constellation Orion glows red; and Sirius, the brightest star in the sky, glows a bluish white. Astronomers use these colors to estimate the temperature of the stars. In this activity, you will experiment with a light bulb and some batteries to discover what the color of a glowing object reveals about the temperature of the object.

Materials

- electrical tape
- 2 conducting wires
- weak D cell
- flashlight bulb
- 2 fresh D cells

Procedure

1. Tape one end of a conducting wire to the positive pole of the weak D cell. Tape one end of the second conducting wire to the negative pole.

2. Touch the free end of each wire to the light bulb. Hold one of the wires against the bottom tip of the light bulb. Hold the second wire against the side of the metal portion of the bulb. The bulb should light.

3. In your ScienceLog, record the color of the filament in the light bulb. Carefully touch your hand to the bulb. Observe the temperature of the bulb. Record your observations in your ScienceLog.

4. Repeat steps 1–3 with one of the two fresh D cells.

5. Use the electrical tape to connect the two fresh D cells in a continuous circuit so that the positive pole of the first cell is connected to the negative pole of the second cell.

6. Repeat steps 1–3 with both fresh D cells in combination.

Analysis

7. How did the color of the filament change in the three trials? How did the temperature change?

8. What information does the color of a star provide?

9. What color are stars with relatively high surface temperatures? What color are stars with relatively low surface temperatures?

10. Arrange the following stars in order from highest to lowest surface temperature: Sirius is bluish white. Aldebaran is orange. Procyon is yellow-white. Capella is yellow. Betelgeuse (BET uhl jooz) is red.

I See the Light!

How do you find the distance to an object you can't reach? You can do it by measuring something you can reach, finding a few angles, and using mathematics. In this activity, you'll practice measuring the distances of objects here on Earth. When you get used to it, you can take your skills to the stars!

Procedure

1. Draw a line 4 cm away from the edge of one side of the piece of poster board. Fold the poster board along this line.

2. Tape the protractor to the poster board with its flat edge against the fold, as shown in the photo below.

3. Use a sharp pencil to carefully punch a hole through the poster board along its folded edge at the center of the protractor.

4. Thread the string through the hole, and tape one end to the underside of the poster board. The other end should be long enough to hang off the far end of the poster board.

5. Carefully punch a second hole in the smaller area of the poster board halfway between its short sides. The hole should be directly above the first hole and should be large enough for the pencil to fit through. This is the viewing hole of your new parallax device. This device will allow you to measure the distance of faraway objects.

6. Find a location outside that is at least 50 steps away from a tall, narrow object, such as the school's flagpole or a tall tree. (This object will represent background stars.) Set the meterstick on the ground with one of its long edges facing the flagpole.

7. Ask your partner, who represents a nearby star, to take 10 steps toward the flagpole, starting at the left end of the meterstick. You will be the observer. When you stand at the left end of the meterstick, which represents the location of the sun, your partner's nose should be lined up with the flag pole.

Materials

- 16 × 16 cm piece of poster board
- metric ruler
- protractor
- scissors
- sharp pencil
- 30 cm string
- transparent tape
- meterstick
- metric measuring tape
- scientific calculator

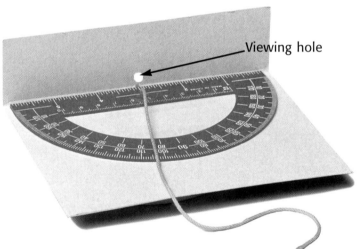

Viewing hole

8. Move to the other end of the meterstick, which represents the location of Earth. Does your partner appear to the left or right of the flagpole? Record your observations in your ScienceLog.

9. Hold the string so that it runs straight from the viewing hole to the 90° mark on the protractor. Using one eye, look through the viewing hole along the string and point the device at your partner's nose.

10. Holding the device still, slowly move your head until you can see the flagpole through the viewing hole. Move the string so that it lines up between your eye and the flagpole. Make sure the string is taut, and hold it tightly against the protractor.

11. Read and record the angle made by the string and the string's original position at 90° (count the number of degrees between 90° and the string's new position).

12. Use the measuring tape to find and record the distance from the left end of the meterstick to your partner's nose.

13. Now find a place outside that is at least 100 steps away from the flagpole. Set the meterstick on the ground as before, and repeat steps 7–12.

Analysis

14. The angle you recorded in step 11 is called the *parallax angle.* The distance from one end of the meterstick to the other is called the *baseline.* With this angle and the length of your baseline, you can calculate the distance to your partner.

15. To calculate the distance (d) to your partner, use the following equation:

$$d = b/\tan A$$

In this equation, A is the parallax angle and b is the length of the baseline (1 m). (Tan A means the tangent of angle A, which you will learn more about in high school math classes.)

16. To find d, enter 1 (the length of your baseline in meters) into the calculator, press the "divide" key, enter the value of A (the parallax angle you recorded), then press the "tan" key. Finally, press the "equals" key.

17. Record this result in your ScienceLog. It is the distance in meters between the left end of the meterstick and your partner. You may want to use a table like the one shown at right.

18. How close is this calculated distance to the distance you measured in step 12?

19. Repeat steps 15–17 using the angle you found when the flagpole was 100 steps away.

Conclusions

20. At which position, 50 steps or 100 steps from the flagpole, did your calculated distance better match the actual distance as measured in step 12?

21. What do you think would happen if you were even farther from the flagpole?

22. When astronomers use parallax, their "flagpole" is the very distant stars. How might this affect the accuracy of their parallax readings?

Distance by Parallax Versus Measuring Tape		
	At 50 steps	**At 100 steps**
Parallax angle		
Distance (calculated)	DO NOT WRITE IN BOOK	
Distance (measured)		

Using Scientific Methods

Water Rockets Save the Day!

Imagine that for the big Fourth of July celebration you and your friends had planned a full day of swimming, volleyball, and fireworks at the lake. You've just learned however, that the city passed a law that bans all fireworks within city limits. But you are not one to give up so easily on having fun. Last year at summer camp you learned how to build water rockets. And you kept the launcher in your garage all this time! With a little bit of creativity, you and your friends are going to celebrate with a splash!

Materials

- 2 L soda bottle with cap
- foam board
- modeling clay
- duct tape
- scissors
- water
- bucket, 5-gal
- rocket launcher
- watch or clock that indicates seconds

Ask a Question

1. How can I use water and a soda bottle to build a rocket?

Conduct an Experiment

2. Decide how you want your rocket to look. Draw a sketch in your ScienceLog.

3. Using only the materials listed, decide how to build your rocket. Describe your design in your ScienceLog. Keep in mind that you will need to leave the opening of your bottle clear. It will be placed over a rubber stopper on the rocket launcher.

4. Fins are often used to stabilize rockets. Do you want fins on your water rocket? Decide on the best shape for the fins, and then decide how many fins your rocket needs. Use the foam board to construct the fins.

5. Your rocket must be heavy enough to fly along a controlled pathway. Consider using clay in the body of your rocket to provide some additional weight and stability.

6. Pour water into your rocket until it is one-third to one-half full.

7. Your teacher will provide the launcher and assist you during blastoff. Attach your rocket to the launcher by placing its opening on the rubber stopper.

8. When the rocket is in place, clear the immediate area and begin pumping air into your rocket. Watch the pump gauge, and take note of how much pressure is needed for liftoff.
   Caution: Be sure to step back from the launch site. You should be several meters away from the bottle when you launch it.

9. Use the watch to time your rocket's flight. (How long was your rocket in the air?)

10. Make small changes in your rocket design that you think will improve the rocket's performance. Consider using different amounts of water and clay or experimenting with different fins. You may also want to compare your design with those of your classmates.

Analyze the Results

11. How did your rocket perform? If you used fins, do you think they helped your flight? Explain.

12. What do you think propelled your rocket? Use Newton's third law of motion to justify your answer.

13. How did the amount of water in your rocket affect the launch?

Draw Conclusions

14. What modifications made your rocket fly for the longest time? How did the design help the rockets fly so far?

15. Which group's rockets were the most stable? How did the design help the rockets fly straight?

16. How can you improve your design to make your rocket perform even better?

Newton's third law of motion: For every action there is an equal and opposite reaction.

Reach for the Stars

Have you ever thought about living and working in space? Well, in order for you to do so, you would have to learn to cope with the new environment and surroundings. At the same time astronauts are adjusting to the topsy-turvy conditions of space travel, they are also dealing with special tools used to repair and build space stations. In this activity, you will get the chance to model one tool that might help astronauts work in space.

Materials

- cardboard box
- scissors
- metric ruler
- hole punch
- 2 paper brads
- metal wire
- 2 jumbo paper clips
- plastic-foam ball

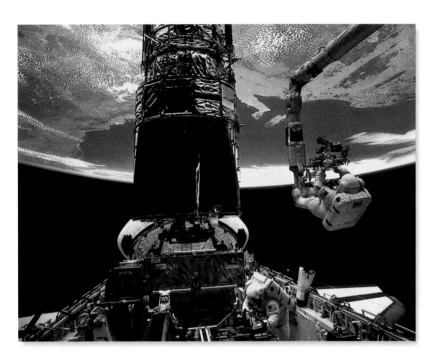

Ask a Question

1. How can I build a piece of equipment that models how astronauts work in space?

Conduct an Experiment

2. Cut three strips from the cardboard box. Each strip should be about 5 cm wide. The strips should be at least 20 cm long but not longer than 40 cm.

3. Punch holes near the center of each end of the three cardboard strips. The holes should be about 3 cm from the end of each strip.

4. Lay the strips end to end along your table. Slide the second strip toward the first strip so that a hole in the first strip lines up with a hole in the second strip. Slip a paper brad through the holes and bend its ends out to attach the cardboard strips.

5. Use another brad to attach the third cardboard strip to the free end of the second strip. Now you have your mechanical arm. The paper brads create joints where the cardboard strips meet.

6. Straighten the wire, and slide it through the hole in one end of your mechanical arm. Bend about 3 cm of the wire in a 90° angle so that it will not slide back out of the hole.

7. Now try to move the arm by holding the free ends of the cardboard and wire. The arm should bend and straighten at the joints. If it is difficult to move your mechanical arm, adjust the design. Consider loosening the brads, for example.

8. Now your mechanical arm needs a hand. Otherwise, it won't be able to pick things up! Straighten one paper clip, and slide it through the hole where you attached the wire in step 6. Bend one end of the paper clip to form a loop around the cardboard and the other end to form a hook. You will use this hook to pick things up.

9. Bend a second paper clip into a U-shape. Stick the straight end of this paper clip into the foam ball. Leave the ball on your desk.

10. Move your mechanical arm so that you can lift the foam ball. The paper-clip hook on the mechanical arm will have to catch the paper clip on the ball.

Analyze the Results

11. Did you have any trouble moving the mechanical arm in step 7? What adjustments did you make?

12. Did you have trouble picking up the foam ball? What might have made this easier?

Draw Conclusions

13. What improvements could you make to your mechanical arm that might make it easier to use?

14. How would a tool like this one help astronauts work in space?

Going Further

Adjust the design for your mechanical arm. Can you find a way to lift objects other than the foam ball? For example, can you lift heavier objects or objects that do not have a loop attached? How?

Research the tools that astronauts use on space stations and on the space shuttle. How do their tools help them work in the special conditions of space?

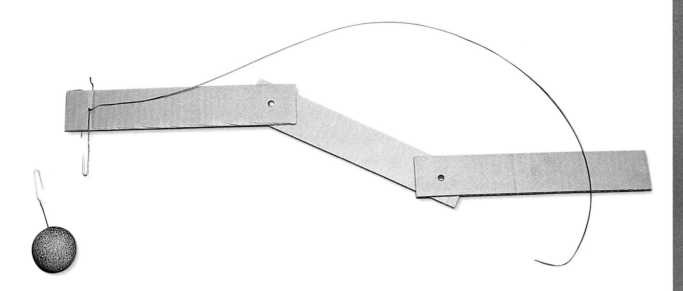

Self-Check Answers

Chapter 2—Maps as Models of the Earth

Page 36: The Earth rotates around the geographic poles.

Page 47: If the lines are close together, then the mapped area is steep. If the lines are far apart, the mapped area has a gradual slope or is flat.

Chapter 3—Minerals of the Earth's Crust

Page 69: These minerals form wherever salt water has evaporated.

Chapter 4—Rocks: Mineral Mixtures

Page 88: From fastest-cooled to slowest-cooled, the rocks in Figure 10 are: basalt, rhyolite, gabbro, and granite.

Page 96: A rock can come into contact with magma and also be subjected to pressure underground.

Chapter 5—Energy Resources

Page 123: Both devices harness energy from falling water.

Chapter 6—The Rock and Fossil Record

Page 148: Coprolites and tracks are trace fossils because they are evidence of animal activity rather than fossilized organisms.

Chapter 7—Plate Tectonics

Page 183: When folding occurs, sedimentary rock strata bend but do not break. When faulting occurs, sedimentary rock strata break along a fault, and the fault blocks on either side move relative to each other.

Chapter 8—Earthquakes

Page 199: Convergent motion creates reverse faults, while divergent motion creates normal faults. Convergent motion produces deep, strong earthquakes, while divergent motion produces shallow, weak earthquakes.

Chapter 9—Volcanoes

Page 231: Solid rock may become magma when pressure is released, when the temperature rises above its melting point, or when its composition changes.

Chapter 10—Weathering and Soil Formation

Page 248: Water expands as it freezes. This expansion exerts a force great enough to crack rock.

Chapter 11—The Flow of Fresh Water

Page 274: If a river slowed down, the suspended load would be deposited.

Page 278: Answers will vary. A river might slow where there is a bend, where the gradient decreases, or where the river empties into a large body of water.

Page 282: The impermeable rock layer in the aquifer traps the water in the permeable layer below. This creates the pressure needed to form an artesian spring.

Chapter 12—Agents of Erosion and Deposition

Page 299: A large wave has more erosive energy than a small wave because a large wave releases more energy when it breaks.

Page 305: Deflation hollows form in areas where there is little vegetation because there are no plant roots to anchor the sediment in place.

Page 311: When a moving glacier picks up speed or flows over a high point, a crevasse may form. This occurs because the ice cannot stretch quickly while it is moving, and it cracks.

Chapter 13—Exploring the Oceans

Page 331: If North America and South America continue to drift westward and Asia continues to drift eastward, the continents will eventually collide on the other side of the Earth.

Page 339: Rift valleys form where tectonic plates pull apart, and ocean trenches form where one oceanic plate is forced underneath a continental plate or another oceanic plate.

Chapter 14—The Movement of Ocean Water

Page 365: Because he was traveling from Peru to a Polynesian island to the west, Heyerdahl would have noticed the wind blowing from the east.

Chapter 15—The Atmosphere

Page 394: As you climb a mountain, the air becomes less dense because there are fewer air molecules. So even though cold air is generally more dense than warm air, it is less dense at higher elevations.

Chapter 16—Understanding Weather

Page 424: Evaporation occurs when liquid water changes into water vapor and returns to the air. Humidity is the amount of water vapor in the air.

Chapter 17—Climate

Page 454: Australia has summer during our winter months, December–February.

Page 460: Because of its dryness, desert soil is poor in organic matter, which fertilizes the soil. Without this natural fertilizer, crops would not be able to grow.

Page 468: The Earth's elliptical orbit causes seasonal differences. When the Earth's orbit is more elliptical, summers are hotter because the Earth is closer to the sun and receives more solar radiation. Winters are cooler because the Earth is farther from the sun and receives less solar radiation.

Chapter 18—Observing the Sky

Page 487: Ptolemy and Tycho Brahe thought that the universe was Earth-centered. Copernicus and Galileo thought the universe was sun-centered.

Page 490: No, the object is within the boundaries of the constellation.

Chapter 19—Formation of the Solar System

Page 511: The balance between pressure and gravity keeps a nebula from collapsing.

Page 513: The giant gas planets were massive enough for their gravity to attract hydrogen and helium.

Page 524: The Earth has enough mass that gravitational pressure crushed and melted rocks during its formation. The force of gravity pulled this material toward the center, forming a sphere. Asteroids are not massive enough for their interiors to be crushed or melted.

Chapter 20—A Family of Planets

Page 555: The surface of Titan is much colder than the surface of the Earth.

Chapter 21—The Universe Beyond

Page 574: The two stars would have the same apparent magnitude.

Chapter 22—Exploring Space

Page 603: It requires much less fuel to reach LEO.

CONTENTS

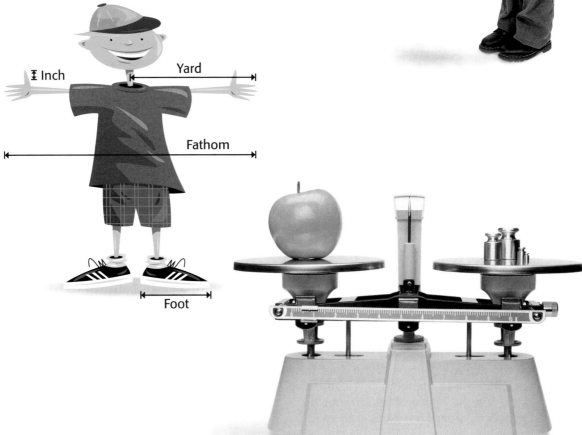

Inch

Yard

Fathom

Foot

Concept Mapping: A Way to Bring Ideas Together

What Is a Concept Map?

Have you ever tried to tell someone about a book or a chapter you've just read and found that you can remember only a few isolated words and ideas? Or maybe you've memorized facts for a test and then weeks later discovered you're not even sure what topics those facts covered.

In both cases, you may have understood the ideas or concepts by themselves but not in relation to one another. If you could somehow link the ideas together, you would probably understand them better and remember them longer. This is something a concept map can help you do. A concept map is a way to see how ideas or concepts fit together. It can help you see the "big picture."

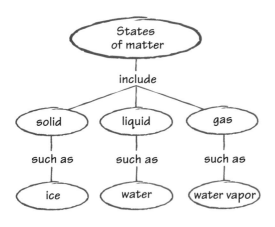

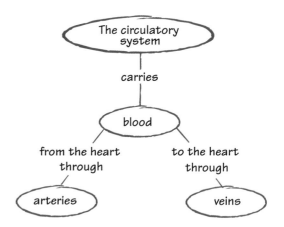

How to Make a Concept Map

① Make a list of the main ideas or concepts.

It might help to write each concept on its own slip of paper. This will make it easier to rearrange the concepts as many times as necessary to make sense of how the concepts are connected. After you've made a few concept maps this way, you can go directly from writing your list to actually making the map.

② Arrange the concepts in order from the most general to the most specific.

Put the most general concept at the top and circle it. Ask yourself, "How does this concept relate to the remaining concepts?" As you see the relationships, arrange the concepts in order from general to specific.

③ Connect the related concepts with lines.

④ On each line, write an action word or short phrase that shows how the concepts are related.

Look at the concept maps on this page, and then see if you can make one for the following terms:

plants, water, photosynthesis, carbon dioxide, sun's energy

One possible answer is provided at right, but don't look at it until you try the concept map yourself.

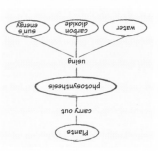

SI Measurement

The International System of Units, or SI, is the standard system of measurement used by many scientists. Using the same standards of measurement makes it easier for scientists to communicate with one another.

SI works by combining prefixes and base units. Each base unit can be used with different prefixes to define smaller and larger quantities. The table below lists common SI prefixes.

SI Prefixes

Prefix	Abbreviation	Factor	Example
kilo-	k	1,000	kilogram, 1 kg = 1,000 g
hecto-	h	100	hectoliter, 1 hL = 100 L
deka-	da	10	dekameter, 1 dam = 10 m
		1	meter, liter
deci-	d	0.1	decigram, 1 dg = 0.1 g
centi-	c	0.01	centimeter, 1 cm = 0.01 m
milli-	m	0.001	milliliter, 1 mL = 0.001 L
micro-	μ	0.000 001	micrometer, 1 μm = 0.000 001 m

SI Conversion Table

SI units	From SI to English	From English to SI
Length		
kilometer (km) = 1,000 m	1 km = 0.621 mi	1 mi = 1.609 km
meter (m) = 100 cm	1 m = 3.281 ft	1 ft = 0.305 m
centimeter (cm) = 0.01 m	1 cm = 0.394 in.	1 in. = 2.540 cm
millimeter (mm) = 0.001 m	1 mm = 0.039 in.	
micrometer (μm) = 0.000 001 m		
nanometer (nm) = 0.000 000 001 m		
Area		
square kilometer (km^2) = 100 hectares	1 km^2 = 0.386 mi^2	1 mi^2 = 2.590 km^2
hectare (ha) = 10,000 m^2	1 ha = 2.471 acres	1 acre = 0.405 ha
square meter (m^2) = 10,000 cm^2	1 m^2 = 10.765 ft^2	1 ft^2 = 0.093 m^2
square centimeter (cm^2) = 100 mm^2	1 cm^2 = 0.155 $in.^2$	1 $in.^2$ = 6.452 cm^2
Volume		
liter (L) = 1,000 mL = 1 dm^3	1 L = 1.057 fl qt	1 fl qt = 0.946 L
milliliter (mL) = 0.001 L = 1 cm^3	1 mL = 0.034 fl oz	1 fl oz = 29.575 mL
microliter (μL) = 0.000 001 L		
Mass		
kilogram (kg) = 1,000 g	1 kg = 2.205 lb	1 lb = 0.454 kg
gram (g) = 1,000 mg	1 g = 0.035 oz	1 oz = 28.349 g
milligram (mg) = 0.001 g		
microgram (μg) = 0.000 001 g		

Temperature Scales

Temperature can be expressed using three different scales: Fahrenheit, Celsius, and Kelvin. The SI unit for temperature is the kelvin (K).

Although 0 K is much colder than 0°C, a change of 1 K is equal to a change of 1°C.

Three Temperature Scales

	Fahrenheit	Celsius	Kelvin
Water boils	212°	100°	373
Body temperature	98.6°	37°	310
Room temperature	68°	20°	293
Water freezes	32°	0°	273

Temperature Conversions Table

To convert	Use this equation:	Example
Celsius to Fahrenheit °C ⟶ °F	$°F = \left(\dfrac{9}{5} \times °C\right) + 32$	Convert 45°C to °F. $°F = \left(\dfrac{9}{5} \times 45°C\right) + 32 = 113°F$
Fahrenheit to Celsius °F ⟶ °C	$°C = \dfrac{5}{9} \times (°F - 32)$	Convert 68°F to °C. $°C = \dfrac{5}{9} \times (68°F - 32) = 20°C$
Celsius to Kelvin °C ⟶ K	$K = °C + 273$	Convert 45°C to K. $K = 45°C + 273 = 318\ K$
Kelvin to Celsius K ⟶ °C	$°C = K - 273$	Convert 32 K to °C. $°C = 32\ K - 273 = -241°C$

Measuring Skills

Using a Graduated Cylinder

When using a graduated cylinder to measure volume, keep the following procedures in mind:

1 Make sure the cylinder is on a flat, level surface.

2 Move your head so that your eye is level with the surface of the liquid.

3 Read the mark closest to the liquid level. On glass graduated cylinders, read the mark closest to the center of the curve in the liquid's surface.

Using a Meterstick or Metric Ruler

When using a meterstick or metric ruler to measure length, keep the following procedures in mind:

1 Place the ruler firmly against the object you are measuring.

2 Align one edge of the object exactly with the zero end of the ruler.

3 Look at the other edge of the object to see which of the marks on the ruler is closest to that edge. **Note:** Each small slash between the centimeters represents a millimeter, which is one-tenth of a centimeter.

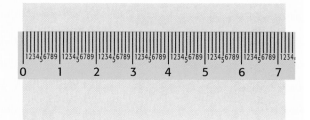

Using a Triple-Beam Balance

When using a triple-beam balance to measure mass, keep the following procedures in mind:

1 Make sure the balance is on a level surface.

2 Place all of the countermasses at zero. Adjust the balancing knob until the pointer rests at zero.

3 Place the object you wish to measure on the pan. **Caution:** Do not place hot objects or chemicals directly on the balance pan.

4 Move the largest countermass along the beam to the right until it is at the last notch that does not tip the balance. Follow the same procedure with the next-largest countermass. Then move the smallest countermass until the pointer rests at zero.

5 Add the readings from the three beams together to determine the mass of the object.

6 When determining the mass of crystals or powders, use a piece of filter paper. First find the mass of the paper. Then add the crystals or powder to the paper and re-measure. The actual mass of the crystals or powder is the total mass minus the mass of the paper. When finding the mass of liquids, first find the mass of the empty container. Then find the mass of the liquid and container together. The mass of the liquid is the total mass minus the mass of the container.

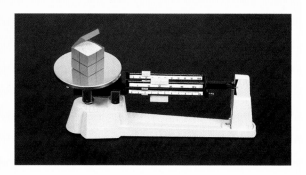

Scientific Method

The series of steps that scientists use to answer questions and solve problems is often called the **scientific method.** The scientific method is not a rigid procedure. Scientists may use all of the steps or just some of the steps of the scientific method. They may even repeat some of the steps. The goal of the scientific method is to come up with reliable answers and solutions.

Six Steps of the Scientific Method

Ask a Question

1 **Ask a Question** Good questions come from careful **observations.** You make observations by using your senses to gather information. Sometimes you may use instruments, such as microscopes and telescopes, to extend the range of your senses. As you observe the natural world, you will discover that you have many more questions than answers. These questions drive the scientific method.

Questions beginning with *what, why, how,* and *when* are very important in focusing an investigation, and they often lead to a hypothesis. (You will learn what a hypothesis is in the next step.) Here is an example of a question that could lead to further investigation.

Question: How does acid rain affect plant growth?

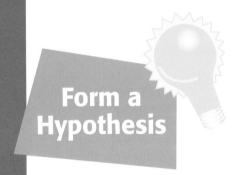

Form a Hypothesis

2 **Form a Hypothesis** After you come up with a question, you need to turn the question into a **hypothesis.** A hypothesis is a clear statement of what you expect the answer to your question to be. Your hypothesis will represent your best "educated guess" based on your observations and what you already know. A good hypothesis is testable. If observations and information cannot be gathered or if an experiment cannot be designed to test your hypothesis, it is untestable, and the investigation can go no further.

Here is a hypothesis that could be formed from the question, "How does acid rain affect plant growth?"

Hypothesis: Acid rain causes plants to grow more slowly.

Notice that the hypothesis provides some specifics that lead to methods of testing. The hypothesis can also lead to predictions. A **prediction** is what you think will be the outcome of your experiment or data collection. Predictions are usually stated in an "if . . . then" format. For example, **if** meat is kept at room temperature, **then** it will spoil faster than meat kept in the refrigerator. More than one prediction can be made for a single hypothesis. Here is a sample prediction for the hypothesis that acid rain causes plants to grow more slowly.

Prediction: If a plant is watered with only acid rain (which has a pH of 4), then the plant will grow at half its normal rate.

3 **Test the Hypothesis** After you have formed a hypothesis and made a prediction, you should test your hypothesis. There are different ways to do this. Perhaps the most familiar way is to conduct a **controlled experiment.** A controlled experiment tests only one factor at a time. A controlled experiment has a **control group** and one or more **experimental groups.** All the factors for the control and experimental groups are the same except for one factor, which is called the **variable.** By changing only one factor, you can see the results of just that one change.

Sometimes, the nature of an investigation makes a controlled experiment impossible. For example, dinosaurs have been extinct for millions of years, and the Earth's core is surrounded by thousands of meters of rock. It would be difficult, if not impossible, to conduct controlled experiments on such things. Under such circumstances, a hypothesis may be tested by making detailed observations. Taking measurements is one way of making observations.

4 **Analyze the Results** After you have completed your experiments, made your observations, and collected your data, you must analyze all the information you have gathered. Tables and graphs are often used in this step to organize the data.

5 **Draw Conclusions** Based on the analysis of your data, you should conclude whether or not your results support your hypothesis. If your hypothesis is supported, you (or others) might want to repeat the observations or experiments to verify your results. If your hypothesis is not supported by the data, you may have to check your procedure for errors. You may even have to reject your hypothesis and make a new one. If you cannot draw a conclusion from your results, you may have to try the investigation again or carry out further observations or experiments.

6 **Communicate Results** After any scientific investigation, you should report your results. By doing a written or oral report, you let others know what you have learned. They may want to repeat your investigation to see if they get the same results. Your report may even lead to another question, which in turn may lead to another investigation.

Test the Hypothesis

Analyze the Results

Draw Conclusions

Do they support your hypothesis?

No

Yes

Communicate Results

Scientific Method in Action

The scientific method is not a "straight line" of steps. It contains loops in which several steps may be repeated over and over again, while others may not be necessary. For example, sometimes scientists will find that testing one hypothesis raises new questions and new hypotheses to be tested. And sometimes, testing the hypothesis leads directly to a conclusion. Furthermore, the steps in the scientific method are not always used in the same order. Follow the steps in the diagram below, and see how many different directions the scientific method can take you.

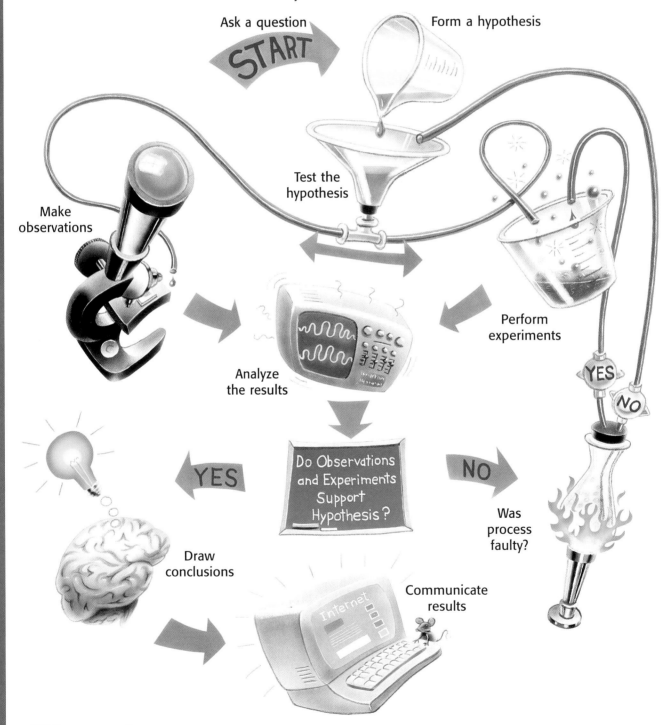

Ask a question

START

Form a hypothesis

Make observations

Test the hypothesis

Perform experiments

Analyze the results

YES

NO

YES

Do Observations and Experiments Support Hypothesis?

NO

Draw conclusions

Was process faulty?

Communicate results

Making Charts and Graphs

Circle Graphs

A circle graph, or pie chart, shows how each group of data relates to all of the data. Each part of the circle represents a category of the data. The entire circle represents all of the data. For example, a biologist studying a hardwood forest in Wisconsin found that there were five different types of trees. The data table at right summarizes the biologist's findings.

Wisconsin Hardwood Trees

Type of tree	Number found
Oak	600
Maple	750
Beech	300
Birch	1,200
Hickory	150
Total	3,000

How to Make a Circle Graph

1 In order to make a circle graph of this data, first find the percentage of each type of tree. To do this, divide the number of individual trees by the total number of trees and multiply by 100.

$$\frac{600 \text{ oak}}{3,000 \text{ trees}} \times 100 = 20\%$$

$$\frac{750 \text{ maple}}{3,000 \text{ trees}} \times 100 = 25\%$$

$$\frac{300 \text{ beech}}{3,000 \text{ trees}} \times 100 = 10\%$$

$$\frac{1,200 \text{ birch}}{3,000 \text{ trees}} \times 100 = 40\%$$

$$\frac{150 \text{ hickory}}{3,000 \text{ trees}} \times 100 = 5\%$$

2 Now determine the size of the pie shapes that make up the chart. Do this by multiplying each percentage by 360°. Remember that a circle contains 360°.

$20\% \times 360° = 72°$ $25\% \times 360° = 90°$
$10\% \times 360° = 36°$ $40\% \times 360° = 144°$
$5\% \times 360° = 18°$

3 Then check that the sum of the percentages is 100 and the sum of the degrees is 360.

$20\% + 25\% + 10\% + 40\% + 5\% = 100\%$
$72° + 90° + 36° + 144° + 18° = 360°$

4 Use a compass to draw a circle and mark its center.

5 Then use a protractor to draw angles of 72°, 90°, 36°, 144°, and 18° in the circle.

6 Finally, label each part of the graph, and choose an appropriate title.

A Community of Wisconsin Hardwood Trees

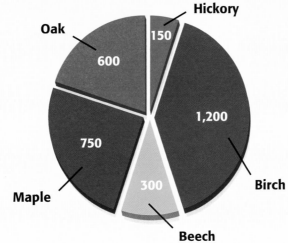

Line Graphs

Line graphs are most often used to demonstrate continuous change. For example, Mr. Smith's science class analyzed the population records for their hometown, Appleton, between 1900 and 2000. Examine the data at left.

Because the year and the population change, they are the *variables*. The population is determined by, or dependent on, the year. Therefore, the population is called the **dependent variable**, and the year is called the **independent variable**. Each set of data is called a **data pair**. To prepare a line graph, data pairs must first be organized in a table like the one at left.

Population of Appleton, 1900–2000	
Year	Population
1900	1,800
1920	2,500
1940	3,200
1960	3,900
1980	4,600
2000	5,300

How to Make a Line Graph

1 Place the independent variable along the horizontal (*x*) axis. Place the dependent variable along the vertical (*y*) axis.

2 Label the *x*-axis "Year" and the *y*-axis "Population." Look at your largest and smallest values for the population. Determine a scale for the *y*-axis that will provide enough space to show these values. You must use the same scale for the entire length of the axis. Find an appropriate scale for the *x*-axis too.

3 Choose reasonable starting points for each axis.

4 Plot the data pairs as accurately as possible.

5 Choose a title that accurately represents the data.

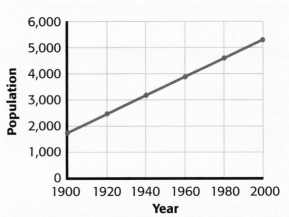

Population of Appleton, 1900–2000

How to Determine Slope

Slope is the ratio of the change in the *y*-axis to the change in the *x*-axis, or "rise over run."

1 Choose two points on the line graph. For example, the population of Appleton in 2000 was 5,300 people. Therefore, you can define point *a* as (2000, 5,300). In 1900, the population was 1,800 people. Define point *b* as (1900, 1,800).

2 Find the change in the *y*-axis.
(*y* at point *a*) − (*y* at point *b*)
5,300 people − 1,800 people = 3,500 people

3 Find the change in the *x*-axis.
(*x* at point *a*) − (*x* at point *b*)
2000 − 1900 = 100 years

4 Calculate the slope of the graph by dividing the change in *y* by the change in *x*.

$$\text{slope} = \frac{\text{change in } y}{\text{change in } x}$$

$$\text{slope} = \frac{3,500 \text{ people}}{100 \text{ years}}$$

$$\text{slope} = 35 \text{ people per year}$$

In this example, the population in Appleton increased by a fixed amount each year. The graph of this data is a straight line. Therefore, the relationship is **linear.** When the graph of a set of data is not a straight line, the relationship is **nonlinear.**

Using Algebra to Determine Slope

The equation in step 4 may also be arranged to be:

$$y = kx$$

where *y* represents the change in the *y*-axis, *k* represents the slope, and *x* represents the change in the *x*-axis.

$$\text{slope} = \frac{\text{change in } y}{\text{change in } x}$$

$$k = \frac{y}{x}$$

$$k \times x = \frac{y \times x}{x}$$

$$kx = y$$

Bar Graphs

Bar graphs are used to demonstrate change that is not continuous. These graphs can be used to indicate trends when the data are taken over a long period of time. A meteorologist gathered the precipitation records at right for Hartford, Connecticut, for April 1–15, 1996, and used a bar graph to represent the data.

Precipitation in Hartford, Connecticut April 1–15, 1996

Date	Precipitation (cm)	Date	Precipitation (cm)
April 1	0.5	April 9	0.25
April 2	1.25	April 10	0.0
April 3	0.0	April 11	1.0
April 4	0.0	April 12	0.0
April 5	0.0	April 13	0.25
April 6	0.0	April 14	0.0
April 7	0.0	April 15	6.50
April 8	1.75		

How to Make a Bar Graph

1. Use an appropriate scale and a reasonable starting point for each axis.
2. Label the axes, and plot the data.
3. Choose a title that accurately represents the data.

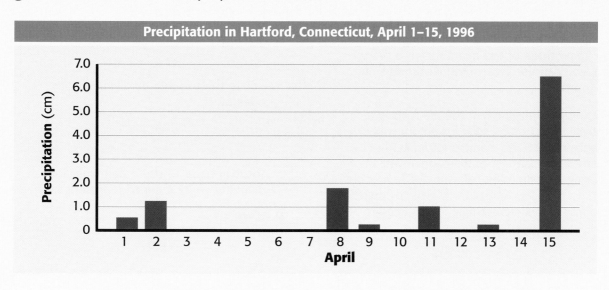

Precipitation in Hartford, Connecticut, April 1–15, 1996

Math Refresher

Science requires an understanding of many math concepts. The following pages will help you review some important math skills.

Averages

An **average,** or **mean,** simplifies a list of numbers into a single number that *approximates* their value.

Example: Find the average of the following set of numbers: 5, 4, 7, and 8.

Step 1: Find the sum.

$$5 + 4 + 7 + 8 = 24$$

Step 2: Divide the sum by the amount of numbers in your set. Because there are four numbers in this example, divide the sum by 4.

$$\frac{24}{4} = 6$$

The average, or mean, is **6.**

Ratios

A **ratio** is a comparison between numbers, and it is usually written as a fraction.

Example: Find the ratio of thermometers to students if you have 36 thermometers and 48 students in your class.

Step 1: Make the ratio.

$$\frac{36 \text{ thermometers}}{48 \text{ students}}$$

Step 2: Reduce the fraction to its simplest form.

$$\frac{36}{48} = \frac{36 \div 12}{48 \div 12} = \frac{3}{4}$$

The ratio of thermometers to students is **3 to 4,** or $\frac{3}{4}$. The ratio may also be written in the form 3:4.

Proportions

A **proportion** is an equation that states that two ratios are equal.

$$\frac{3}{1} = \frac{12}{4}$$

To solve a proportion, first multiply across the equal sign. This is called cross-multiplication. If you know three of the quantities in a proportion, you can use cross-multiplication to find the fourth.

Example: Imagine that you are making a scale model of the solar system for your science project. The diameter of Jupiter is 11.2 times the diameter of the Earth. If you are using a plastic-foam ball with a diameter of 2 cm to represent the Earth, what diameter does the ball representing Jupiter need to be?

$$\frac{11.2}{1} = \frac{x}{2 \text{ cm}}$$

Step 1: Cross-multiply.

$$\frac{11.2}{1} \diagdown\!\!\!\!\diagup \frac{x}{2}$$

$$11.2 \times 2 = x \times 1$$

Step 2: Multiply.

$$22.4 = x \times 1$$

Step 3: Isolate the variable by dividing both sides by 1.

$$x = \frac{22.4}{1}$$
$$x = 22.4 \text{ cm}$$

You will need to use a ball with a diameter of **22.4 cm** to represent Jupiter.

Percentages

A **percentage** is a ratio of a given number to 100.

> **Example:** What is 85 percent of 40?

Step 1: Rewrite the percentage by moving the decimal point two places to the left.

$$.85$$

Step 2: Multiply the decimal by the number you are calculating the percentage of.

$$0.85 \times 40 = 34$$

85 percent of 40 is **34.**

Decimals

To **add** or **subtract decimals,** line up the digits vertically so that the decimal points line up. Then add or subtract the columns from right to left, carrying or borrowing numbers as necessary.

> **Example:** Add the following numbers: 3.1415 and 2.96.

Step 1: Line up the digits vertically so that the decimal points line up.

$$
\begin{array}{r}
3.1415 \\
+\ 2.96 \\
\hline
\end{array}
$$

Step 2: Add the columns from right to left, carrying when necessary.

$$
\begin{array}{r}
{}^{1}\ {}^{1}\ \\
3.1415 \\
+\ 2.96 \\
\hline
6.1015
\end{array}
$$

The sum is **6.1015.**

Fractions

Numbers tell you how many; **fractions** tell you *how much of a whole.*

> **Example:** Your class has 24 plants. Your teacher instructs you to put 5 in a shady spot. What fraction does this represent?

Step 1: Write a fraction with the total number of parts in the whole as the denominator.

$$\frac{?}{24}$$

Step 2: Write the number of parts of the whole being represented as the numerator.

$$\frac{5}{24}$$

$\frac{\mathbf{5}}{\mathbf{24}}$ of the plants will be in the shade.

Reducing Fractions

It is usually best to express a fraction in simplest form. This is called *reducing* a fraction.

> **Example:** Reduce the fraction $\frac{30}{45}$ to its simplest form.

Step 1: Find the largest whole number that will divide evenly into both the numerator and denominator. This number is called the greatest common factor (GCF).

factors of the numerator 30: 1, 2, 3, 5, 6, 10, **15,** 30

factors of the denominator 45: 1, 3, 5, 9, **15,** 45

Step 2: Divide both the numerator and the denominator by the GCF, which in this case is 15.

$$\frac{30}{45} = \frac{30 \div 15}{45 \div 15} = \frac{2}{3}$$

$\frac{30}{45}$ reduced to its simplest form is $\frac{\mathbf{2}}{\mathbf{3}}$.

Adding and Subtracting Fractions

To **add** or **subtract fractions** that have the **same denominator,** simply add or subtract the numerators.

Examples:
$$\frac{3}{5} + \frac{1}{5} = ? \quad \text{and} \quad \frac{3}{4} - \frac{1}{4} = ?$$

Step 1: Add or subtract the numerators.
$$\frac{3}{5} + \frac{1}{5} = \frac{4}{} \quad \text{and} \quad \frac{3}{4} - \frac{1}{4} = \frac{2}{}$$

Step 2: Write the sum or difference over the denominator.
$$\frac{3}{5} + \frac{1}{5} = \frac{4}{5} \quad \text{and} \quad \frac{3}{4} - \frac{1}{4} = \frac{2}{4}$$

Step 3: If necessary, reduce the fraction to its simplest form.

$\frac{4}{5}$ cannot be reduced, and $\frac{2}{4} = \frac{1}{2}$.

To **add** or **subtract fractions** that have **different denominators,** first find the least common denominator (LCD).

Examples:
$$\frac{1}{2} + \frac{1}{6} = ? \quad \text{and} \quad \frac{3}{4} - \frac{2}{3} = ?$$

Step 1: Write the equivalent fractions with a common denominator.
$$\frac{3}{6} + \frac{1}{6} = ? \quad \text{and} \quad \frac{9}{12} - \frac{8}{12} = ?$$

Step 2: Add or subtract.
$$\frac{3}{6} + \frac{1}{6} = \frac{4}{6} \quad \text{and} \quad \frac{9}{12} - \frac{8}{12} = \frac{1}{12}$$

Step 3: If necessary, reduce the fraction to its simplest form.

$\frac{4}{6} = \frac{2}{3}$, and $\frac{1}{12}$ cannot be reduced.

Multiplying Fractions

To **multiply fractions,** multiply the numerators and the denominators together, and then reduce the fraction to its simplest form.

Example:
$$\frac{5}{9} \times \frac{7}{10} = ?$$

Step 1: Multiply the numerators and denominators.
$$\frac{5}{9} \times \frac{7}{10} = \frac{5 \times 7}{9 \times 10} = \frac{35}{90}$$

Step 2: Reduce.
$$\frac{35}{90} = \frac{35 \div 5}{90 \div 5} = \frac{7}{18}$$

Dividing Fractions

To **divide fractions,** first rewrite the divisor (the number you divide *by*) upside down. This is called the reciprocal of the divisor. Then you can multiply and reduce if necessary.

Example:
$$\frac{5}{8} \div \frac{3}{2} = ?$$

Step 1: Rewrite the divisor as its reciprocal.
$$\frac{3}{2} \rightarrow \frac{2}{3}$$

Step 2: Multiply.
$$\frac{5}{8} \times \frac{2}{3} = \frac{5 \times 2}{8 \times 3} = \frac{10}{24}$$

Step 3: Reduce.
$$\frac{10}{24} = \frac{10 \div 2}{24 \div 2} = \frac{5}{12}$$

Scientific Notation

Scientific notation is a short way of representing very large and very small numbers without writing all of the place-holding zeros.

    Example: Write 653,000,000 in scientific notation.

Step 1: Write the number without the place-holding zeros.

$$653$$

Step 2: Place the decimal point after the first digit.

$$6.53$$

Step 3: Find the exponent by counting the number of places that you moved the decimal point.

$$6.53000000$$

The decimal point was moved eight places to the left. Therefore, the exponent of 10 is positive 8. Remember, if the decimal point had moved to the right, the exponent would be negative.

Step 4: Write the number in scientific notation.

$$\mathbf{6.53 \times 10^8}$$

Area

Area is the number of square units needed to cover the surface of an object.

    Formulas:
    Area of a square = side × side
    Area of a rectangle = length × width
    Area of a triangle = $\frac{1}{2}$ × base × height

    Examples: Find the areas.

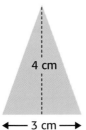

Triangle
Area = $\frac{1}{2}$ × base × height
Area = $\frac{1}{2}$ × 3 cm × 4 cm
Area = **6 cm²**

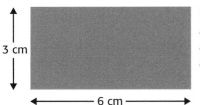

Rectangle
Area = length × width
Area = 6 cm × 3 cm
Area = **18 cm²**

Square
Area = side × side
Area = 3 cm × 3 cm
Area = **9 cm²**

Volume

Volume is the amount of space something occupies.

    Formulas:
    Volume of a cube =
    side × side × side

    Volume of a prism =
    area of base × height

    Examples:
    Find the volume
    of the solids.

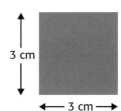

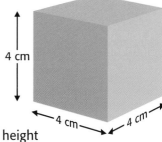

Cube
Volume = side × side × side
Volume = 4 cm × 4 cm × 4 cm
Volume = **64 cm³**

Prism
Volume = area of base × height
Volume = (area of triangle) × height
Volume = $\left(\frac{1}{2} \times 3 \text{ cm} \times 4 \text{ cm} \right) \times 5 \text{ cm}$
Volume = 6 cm² × 5 cm
Volume = **30 cm³**

Periodic Table of the Elements

Each square on the table includes an element's name, chemical symbol, atomic number, and atomic mass.

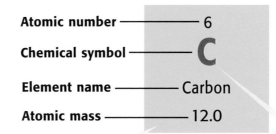

Atomic number ——— 6

Chemical symbol ——— C

Element name ——— Carbon

Atomic mass ——— 12.0

The background color indicates the type of element. Carbon is a nonmetal.

Background

Metals	
Metalloids	
Nonmetals	

The color of the chemical symbol indicates the physical state at room temperature. Carbon is a solid.

Chemical symbol

Solid	
Liquid	
Gas	

Period 1

| 1 |
| **H** |
| Hydrogen |
| 1.0 |

	Group 1	Group 2
Period 2	3 **Li** Lithium 6.9	4 **Be** Beryllium 9.0
Period 3	11 **Na** Sodium 23.0	12 **Mg** Magnesium 24.3

	Group 1	Group 2	Group 3	Group 4	Group 5	Group 6	Group 7	Group 8	Group 9
Period 4	19 **K** Potassium 39.1	20 **Ca** Calcium 40.1	21 **Sc** Scandium 45.0	22 **Ti** Titanium 47.9	23 **V** Vanadium 50.9	24 **Cr** Chromium 52.0	25 **Mn** Manganese 54.9	26 **Fe** Iron 55.8	27 **Co** Cobalt 58.9
Period 5	37 **Rb** Rubidium 85.5	38 **Sr** Strontium 87.6	39 **Y** Yttrium 88.9	40 **Zr** Zirconium 91.2	41 **Nb** Niobium 92.9	42 **Mo** Molybdenum 95.9	43 **Tc** Technetium (97.9)	44 **Ru** Ruthenium 101.1	45 **Rh** Rhodium 102.9
Period 6	55 **Cs** Cesium 132.9	56 **Ba** Barium 137.3	57 **La** Lanthanum 138.9	72 **Hf** Hafnium 178.5	73 **Ta** Tantalum 180.9	74 **W** Tungsten 183.8	75 **Re** Rhenium 186.2	76 **Os** Osmium 190.2	77 **Ir** Iridium 192.2
Period 7	87 **Fr** Francium (223.0)	88 **Ra** Radium (226.0)	89 **Ac** Actinium (227.0)	104 **Rf** Rutherfordium (261.1)	105 **Db** Dubnium (262.1)	106 **Sg** Seaborgium (263.1)	107 **Bh** Bohrium (262.1)	108 **Hs** Hassium (265)	109 **Mt** Meitnerium (266)

A row of elements is called a period.

A column of elements is called a group or family.

Lanthanides

| 58 **Ce** Cerium 140.1 | 59 **Pr** Praseodymium 140.9 | 60 **Nd** Neodymium 144.2 | 61 **Pm** Promethium (144.9) | 62 **Sm** Samarium 150.4 |

Actinides

| 90 **Th** Thorium 232.0 | 91 **Pa** Protactinium 231.0 | 92 **U** Uranium 238.0 | 93 **Np** Neptunium (237.0) | 94 **Pu** Plutonium 244.1 |

These elements are placed below the table to allow the table to be narrower.

TOPIC: Periodic Table
GO TO: go.hrw.com
KEYWORD: HN0 Periodic

Visit the HRW Web site to see the most
recent version of the periodic table.

Group 18

| 2 |
| **He** |
| Helium |
| 4.0 |

This zigzag line
reminds you where
the metals, nonmetals,
and metalloids are.

Group 13	Group 14	Group 15	Group 16	Group 17
5	6	7	8	9
B	**C**	**N**	**O**	**F**
Boron	Carbon	Nitrogen	Oxygen	Fluorine
10.8	12.0	14.0	16.0	19.0

| 10 |
| **Ne** |
| Neon |
| 20.2 |

13	14	15	16	17	18
Al	**Si**	**P**	**S**	**Cl**	**Ar**
Aluminum	Silicon	Phosphorus	Sulfur	Chlorine	Argon
27.0	28.1	31.0	32.1	35.5	39.9

Group 10	Group 11	Group 12						
28	29	30	31	32	33	34	35	36
Ni	**Cu**	**Zn**	**Ga**	**Ge**	**As**	**Se**	**Br**	**Kr**
Nickel	Copper	Zinc	Gallium	Germanium	Arsenic	Selenium	Bromine	Krypton
58.7	63.5	65.4	69.7	72.6	74.9	79.0	79.9	83.8
46	47	48	49	50	51	52	53	54
Pd	**Ag**	**Cd**	**In**	**Sn**	**Sb**	**Te**	**I**	**Xe**
Palladium	Silver	Cadmium	Indium	Tin	Antimony	Tellurium	Iodine	Xenon
106.4	107.9	112.4	114.8	118.7	121.8	127.6	126.9	131.3
78	79	80	81	82	83	84	85	86
Pt	**Au**	**Hg**	**Tl**	**Pb**	**Bi**	**Po**	**At**	**Rn**
Platinum	Gold	Mercury	Thallium	Lead	Bismuth	Polonium	Astatine	Radon
195.1	197.0	200.6	204.4	207.2	209.0	(209.0)	(210.0)	(222.0)
110	111	112						
Uun	**Uuu**	**Uub**						
Ununnilium	Unununium	Ununbium						
(271)	(272)	(277)						

The names and symbols of elements 110–112 are
temporary. They are based on the atomic number of
the element. The official name and symbol will be
approved by an international committee of scientists.

63	64	65	66	67	68	69	70	71
Eu	**Gd**	**Tb**	**Dy**	**Ho**	**Er**	**Tm**	**Yb**	**Lu**
Europium	Gadolinium	Terbium	Dysprosium	Holmium	Erbium	Thulium	Ytterbium	Lutetium
152.0	157.3	158.9	162.5	164.9	167.3	168.9	173.0	175.0
95	96	97	98	99	100	101	102	103
Am	**Cm**	**Bk**	**Cf**	**Es**	**Fm**	**Md**	**No**	**Lr**
Americium	Curium	Berkelium	Californium	Einsteinium	Fermium	Mendelevium	Nobelium	Lawrencium
(243.1)	(247.1)	(247.1)	(251.1)	(252.1)	(257.1)	(258.1)	(259.1)	(262.1)

A number in parentheses is the mass number
of the most stable isotope of that element.

Physical Science Refresher

Atoms and Elements

Every object in the universe is made up of particles of some kind of matter. **Matter** is anything that takes up space and has mass. All matter is made up of elements. An **element** is a substance that cannot be separated into simpler components by ordinary chemical means. This is because each element consists of only one kind of atom. An **atom** is the smallest unit of an element that has all of the properties of that element.

Atomic Structure

Atoms are made up of small particles called subatomic particles. The three major types of subatomic particles are **electrons, protons,** and **neutrons.** Electrons have a negative electric charge, protons have a positive charge, and neutrons have no electric charge. The protons and neutrons are packed close to one another to form the **nucleus.** The protons give the nucleus a positive charge. Electrons are most likely to be found in regions around the nucleus called **electron clouds.** The negatively charged electrons are attracted to the positively charged nucleus. An atom may have several energy levels in which electrons are located.

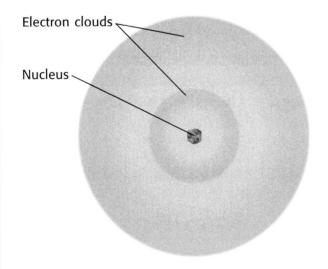

Electron clouds

Nucleus

Atomic Number

To help in the identification of elements, scientists have assigned an **atomic number** to each kind of atom. The atomic number is the number of protons in the atom. Atoms with the same number of protons are all the same kind of element. In an uncharged, or electrically neutral, atom there are an equal number of protons and electrons. Therefore, the atomic number equals the number of electrons in an uncharged atom. The number of neutrons, however, can vary for a given element. Atoms of the same element that have different numbers of neutrons are called **isotopes.**

Periodic Table of the Elements

In the periodic table, the elements are arranged from left to right in order of increasing atomic number. Each element in the table is in a separate box. An atom of each element has one more electron and one more proton than an atom of the element to its left. Each horizontal row of the table is called a **period.** Changes in chemical properties of elements across a period correspond to changes in the electron arrangements of their atoms. Each vertical column of the table, known as a **group,** lists elements with similar properties. The elements in a group have similar chemical properties because their atoms have the same number of electrons in their outer energy level. For example, the elements helium, neon, argon, krypton, xenon, and radon all have similar properties and are known as the noble gases.

APPENDIX

Molecules and Compounds

When two or more elements are joined chemically, the resulting substance is called a **compound.** A compound is a new substance with properties different from those of the elements that compose it. For example, water, H_2O, is a compound formed when hydrogen (H) and oxygen (O) combine. The smallest complete unit of a compound that has the properties of that compound is called a **molecule.** A chemical formula indicates the elements in a compound. It also indicates the relative number of atoms of each element present. The chemical formula for water is H_2O, which indicates that each water molecule consists of two atoms of hydrogen and one atom of oxygen. The subscript number is used after the symbol for an element to indicate how many atoms of that element are in a single molecule of the compound.

Acids, Bases, and pH

An ion is an atom or group of atoms that has an electric charge because it has lost or gained one or more electrons. When an acid, such as hydrochloric acid, HCl, is mixed with water, it separates into ions. An **acid** is a compound that produces hydrogen ions, H^+, in water. The hydrogen ions then combine with a water molecule to form a hydronium ion, H_3O^+. A **base,** on the other hand, is a substance that produces hydroxide ions, OH^-, in water.

To determine whether a solution is acidic or basic, scientists use pH. The **pH** is a measure of the hydronium ion concentration in a solution. The pH scale ranges from 0 to 14. The middle point, pH = 7, is neutral, neither acidic nor basic. Acids have a pH less than 7; bases have a pH greater than 7. The lower the number is, the more acidic the solution. The higher the number is, the more basic the solution.

Chemical Equations

A chemical reaction occurs when a chemical change takes place. (In a chemical change, new substances with new properties are formed.) A chemical equation is a useful way of describing a chemical reaction by means of chemical formulas. The equation indicates what substances react and what the products are. For example, when carbon and oxygen combine, they can form carbon dioxide. The equation for the reaction is as follows:

$$C + O_2 \rightarrow CO_2.$$

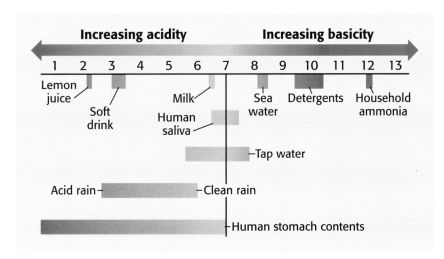

Physical Laws and Equations

Law of Conservation of Energy

The law of conservation of energy states that energy can be neither created nor destroyed.

The total amount of energy in a closed system is always the same. Energy can be changed from one form to another, but all the different forms of energy in a system always add up to the same total amount of energy, no matter how many energy conversions occur.

Law of Universal Gravitation

The law of universal gravitation states that all objects in the universe attract each other by a force called gravity. The size of the force depends on the masses of the objects and the distance between them.

The first part of the law explains why a bowling ball is much harder to lift than a table-tennis ball. Because the bowling ball has a much larger mass than the table-tennis ball, the amount of gravity between the Earth and the bowling ball is greater than the amount of gravity between the Earth and the table-tennis ball.

The second part of the law explains why a satellite can remain in orbit around the Earth. The satellite is carefully placed at a distance great enough to prevent the Earth's gravity from immediately pulling it down but small enough to prevent it from completely escaping the Earth's gravity and wandering off into space.

Newton's Laws of Motion

Newton's first law of motion states that an object at rest remains at rest and an object in motion remains in motion at constant speed and in a straight line unless acted on by an unbalanced force.

The first part of the law explains why a football will remain on a tee until it is kicked off or until a gust of wind blows it off.

The second part of the law explains why a bike's rider will continue moving forward after the bike tire runs into a crack in the sidewalk and the bike comes to an abrupt stop until gravity and the sidewalk stop the rider.

Newton's second law of motion states that the acceleration of an object depends on the mass of the object and the amount of force applied.

The first part of the law explains why the acceleration of a 4 kg bowling ball will be greater than the acceleration of a 6 kg bowling ball if the same force is applied to both.

The second part of the law explains why the acceleration of a bowling ball will be larger if a larger force is applied to it.

The relationship of acceleration (a) to mass (m) and force (F) can be expressed mathematically by the following equation:

$$\text{acceleration} = \frac{force}{mass} \quad \text{or} \quad a = \frac{F}{m}$$

This equation is often rearranged to the form:

$$\text{force} = \text{mass} \times \text{acceleration}$$
$$\text{or}$$
$$F = m \times a$$

Newton's third law of motion states that whenever one object exerts a force on a second object, the second object exerts an equal and opposite force on the first.

This law explains that a runner is able to move forward because of the equal and opposite force the ground exerts on the runner's foot after each step.

Useful Equations

Average speed

$$\text{Average speed} = \frac{\text{total distance}}{\text{total time}}$$

Example: A bicycle messenger traveled a distance of 136 km in 8 hours. What was the messenger's average speed?

$$\frac{136 \text{ km}}{8 \text{ h}} = 17 \text{ km/h}$$

The messenger's average speed was **17 km/h.**

Average acceleration

$$\frac{\text{Average}}{\text{acceleration}} = \frac{\text{final velocity} - \text{starting velocity}}{\text{time it takes to change velocity}}$$

Example: Calculate the average acceleration of an Olympic 100 m dash sprinter who reaches a velocity of 15 m/s south at the finish line. The race was in a straight line and lasted 10 s.

$$\frac{15 \text{ m/s} - 0 \text{ m/s}}{10 \text{ s}} = 1.5 \text{ m/s/s}$$

The sprinter's average acceleration is **1.5 m/s/s south.**

Net force

Forces in the Same Direction
When forces are in the same direction, add the forces together to determine the net force.

Example: Calculate the net force on a stalled car that is being pushed by two people. One person is pushing with a force of 13 N north-west and the other person is pushing with a force of 8 N in the same direction.

$$13 \text{ N} + 8 \text{ N} = 21 \text{ N}$$

The net force is **21 N northwest.**

Forces in Opposite Directions
When forces are in opposite directions, subtract the smaller force from the larger force to determine the net force.

Net force (cont'd)

Example: Calculate the net force on a rope that is being pulled on each end. One person is pulling on one end of the rope with a force of 12 N south. Another person is pulling on the opposite end of the rope with a force of 7 N north.

$$12 \text{ N} - 7 \text{ N} = 5 \text{ N}$$

The net force is **5 N south.**

Density

$$\text{Density} = \frac{\text{mass}}{\text{volume}}$$

Example: Calculate the density of a sponge with a mass of 10 g and a volume of 40 mL.

$$\frac{10 \text{ g}}{40 \text{ mL}} = 0.25 \text{ g/mL}$$

The density of the sponge is **0.25 g/mL.**

Pressure

Pressure is the force exerted over a given area. The SI unit for pressure is the pascal, which is abbreviated Pa.

$$\text{Pressure} = \frac{\text{force}}{\text{area}}$$

Example: Calculate the pressure of the air in a soccer ball if the air exerts a force of 10 N over an area of 0.5 m^2.

$$\text{Pressure} = \frac{10 \text{ N}}{0.5 \text{ m}^2} = 20 \text{ N/m}^2 = 20 \text{ Pa}$$

The pressure of the air inside of the soccer ball is **20 Pa.**

Concentration

$$\text{Concentration} = \frac{\text{mass of solute}}{\text{volume of solvent}}$$

Example: Calculate the concentration of a solution in which 10 g of sugar is dissolved in 125 mL of water.

$$\frac{10 \text{ g of sugar}}{125 \text{ mL of water}} = 0.08 \text{ g/mL}$$

The concentration of this solution is **0.08 g/mL.**

Properties of Common Minerals

Silicate Minerals

Mineral	Color	Luster	Streak	Hardness
Beryl	deep green, pink, white, bluish green, or light yellow	vitreous	none	7.5–8
Chlorite	green	vitreous to pearly	pale green	2–2.5
Garnet	green or red	vitreous	none	6.5–7.5
Hornblende	dark green, brown, or black	vitreous or silky	none	5–6
Muscovite	colorless, gray, or brown	vitreous or pearly	white	2–2.5
Olivine	olive green	vitreous	none	6.5–7
Orthoclase	colorless, white, pink, or other colors	vitreous to pearly	white or none	6
Plagioclase	blue gray to white	vitreous	white	6
Quartz	colorless or white; any color when not pure	vitreous or waxy	white or none	7

Nonsilicate Minerals

Native Elements

Mineral	Color	Luster	Streak	Hardness
Copper	copper-red	metallic	copper-red	2.5–3
Diamond	pale yellow or colorless	vitreous	none	10
Graphite	black to gray	submetallic	black	1–2

Carbonates

Mineral	Color	Luster	Streak	Hardness
Aragonite	colorless, white, or pale yellow	vitreous	white	3.5–4
Calcite	colorless or white to tan	vitreous	white	3

Halides

Mineral	Color	Luster	Streak	Hardness
Fluorite	light green, yellow, purple, bluish green, or other colors	vitreous	none	4
Halite	colorless or gray	vitreous	white	2.5–3

Oxides

Mineral	Color	Luster	Streak	Hardness
Hematite	reddish brown to black	metallic to earthy	red to red-brown	5.6–6.5
Magnetite	iron black	metallic	black	5–6

Sulfates

Mineral	Color	Luster	Streak	Hardness
Anhydrite	colorless, bluish, or violet	vitreous to pearly	white	3–3.5
Gypsum	white, pink, gray, or colorless	vitreous, pearly, or silky	white	1–2.5

Sulfides

Mineral	Color	Luster	Streak	Hardness
Galena	lead gray	metallic	lead gray to black	2.5
Pyrite	brassy yellow	metallic	greenish, brownish, or black	6–6.5

Density (g/cm³)	Cleavage, Fracture, Special Properties	Common Uses
2.6–2.8	1 cleavage direction; irregular fracture; some varieties fluoresce in ultraviolet light	gemstones, ore of the metal beryllium
2.6–3.3	1 cleavage direction; irregular fracture	
4.2	no cleavage; conchoidal to splintery fracture	gemstones, abrasives
3.2	2 cleavage directions; hackly to splintery fracture	
2.7–3	1 cleavage direction; irregular fracture	electrical insulation, wallpaper, fireproofing material, lubricant
3.2–3.3	no cleavage; conchoidal fracture	gemstones, casting
2.6	2 cleavage directions; irregular fracture	porcelain
2.6–2.7	2 cleavage directions; irregular fracture	ceramics
2.6	no cleavage; conchoidal fracture	gemstones, concrete, glass, porcelain, sandpaper, lenses
8.9	no cleavage; hackly fracture	wiring, brass, bronze, coins
3.5	4 cleavage directions; irregular to conchoidal fracture	gemstones, drilling
2.3	1 cleavage direction; irregular fracture	pencils, paints, lubricants, batteries
2.95	2 cleavage directions; irregular fracture; reacts with hydrochloric acid	minor source of barium
2.7	3 cleavage directions; irregular fracture; reacts with weak acid, double refraction	cements, soil conditioner, whitewash, construction materials
3.2	4 cleavage directions; irregular fracture; some varieties fluoresce or double refract	hydrochloric acid, steel, glass, fiberglass, pottery, enamel
2.2	3 cleavage directions; splintery to conchoidal fracture; salty taste	tanning hides, fertilizer, salting icy roads, food preservation
5.25	no cleavage; splintery fracture; magnetic when heated	iron ore for steel, gemstones, pigments
5.2	2 cleavage directions; splintery fracture; magnetic	iron ore
2.89–2.98	3 cleavage directions; conchoidal to splintery fracture	soil conditioner, sulfuric acid
2.2–2.4	3 cleavage directions; conchoidal to splintery fracture	plaster of Paris, wallboard, soil conditioner
7.4–7.6	3 cleavage directions; irregular fracture	batteries, paints
5	no cleavage; conchoidal to splintery fracture	dyes, inks, gemstones

Sky Maps

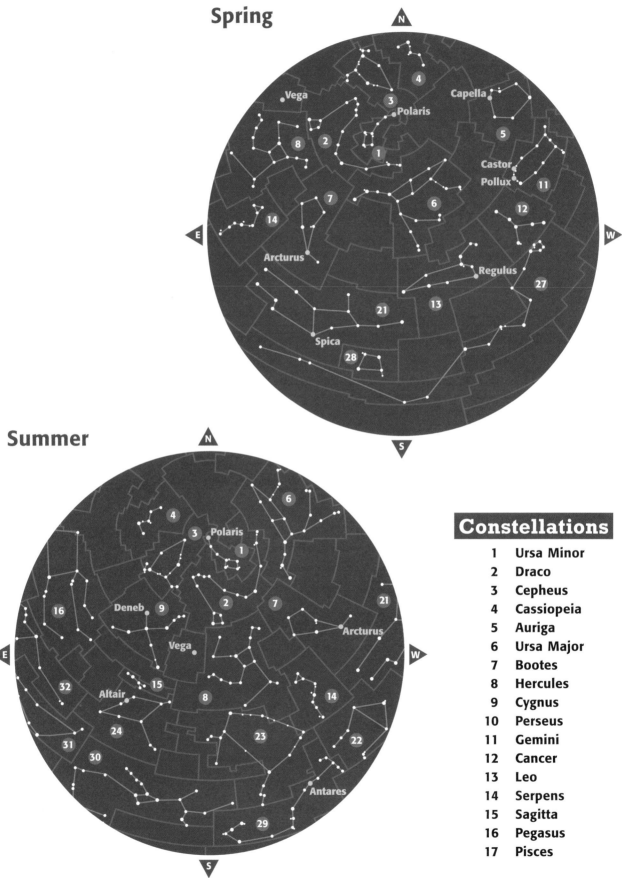

Spring

Summer

Constellations

1 Ursa Minor
2 Draco
3 Cepheus
4 Cassiopeia
5 Auriga
6 Ursa Major
7 Bootes
8 Hercules
9 Cygnus
10 Perseus
11 Gemini
12 Cancer
13 Leo
14 Serpens
15 Sagitta
16 Pegasus
17 Pisces

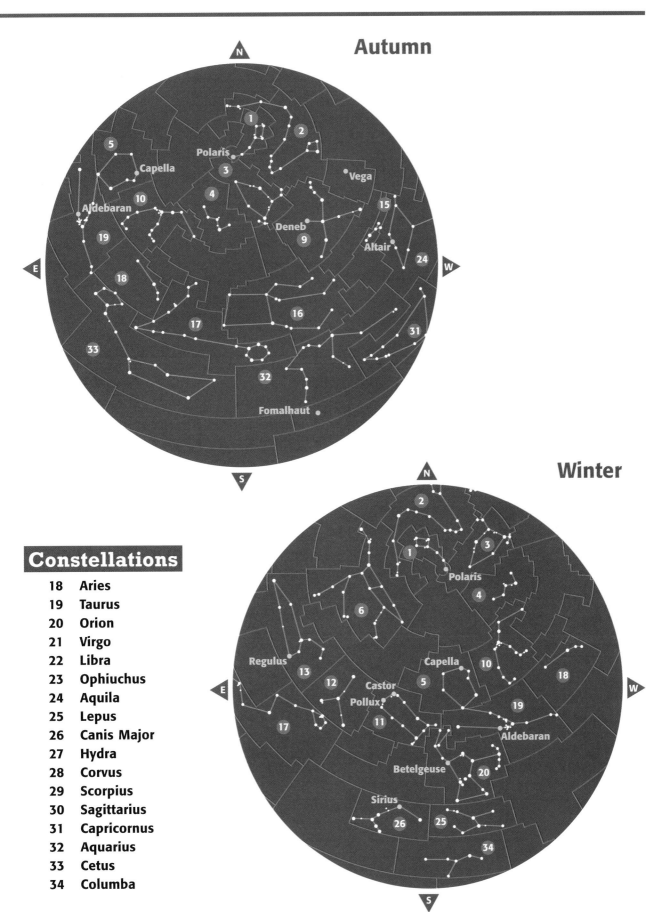

Autumn

N

Polaris

Capella

5

10

Aldebaran

19

18

E

33

17

32

Fomalhaut

1

2

3

4

Vega

15

Deneb

9

Altair

24

W

16

31

S

Winter

N

2

1

3

Polaris

4

6

Capella

10

18

W

Regulus

13

12

5

19

Castor

Pollux

11

Aldebaran

17

Betelgeuse

20

Sirius

26

25

34

E

S

Constellations

18 Aries
19 Taurus
20 Orion
21 Virgo
22 Libra
23 Ophiuchus
24 Aquila
25 Lepus
26 Canis Major
27 Hydra
28 Corvus
29 Scorpius
30 Sagittarius
31 Capricornus
32 Aquarius
33 Cetus
34 Columba

Glossary

A

abrasion the grinding and wearing down of rock surfaces by other rock or sand particles (247, 306)

absolute dating the process of establishing the age of an object, such as a fossil or rock layer, by determining the number of years it has existed (142)

absolute magnitude the actual brightness of a star (574)

abyssal (uh BIS uhl) **plain** the broad, flat portion of the deep-ocean basin (338)

acid precipitation precipitation that contains acids due to air pollution (116, 249, 411)

aerial photograph a photograph taken from the air (43)

air mass a large body of air that has similar temperature and moisture throughout (430)

air pressure the measure of the force with which air molecules push on a surface (393)

alluvial (uh LOO vee uhl) **fan** fan-shaped deposits of alluvium that form on dry land (279)

alluvium (uh LOO vee uhm) rock and soil deposited by streams (277)

altitude the height of an object above the Earth's surface (393); in astronomy, the angle between an object in the sky and the horizon (491)

anemometer (AN uh MAHM uht uhr) a device used to measure wind speed (441)

annular (AN yoo luhr) **eclipse** a solar eclipse during which the outer ring of the sun can be seen around the moon (552)

anticline a bowl-shaped fold in sedimentary rock layers (182)

apparent magnitude how bright a light appears to an observer (574)

aquifer (AHK wuh fuhr) a rock layer that stores and allows the flow of ground water (280)

arête (uh RAYT) a jagged ridge that forms between two or more cirques cutting into the same mountain (313)

artesian (ahr TEE zhuhn) **spring** a spring that forms where cracks occur naturally in the cap rock and the pressurized water in the aquifer flows through the cracks to the surface (282)

artificial satellite any human-made object placed in orbit around a body in space (602)

asteroid a small, rocky body that revolves around the sun (559)

asteroid belt the region of the solar system most asteroids occupy; roughly between the orbits of Mars and Jupiter (559)

asthenosphere (as THEN uh SFIR) the soft layer of the mantle on which pieces of the lithosphere move (168)

astronomical unit (AU) the average distance between the Earth and the sun, or approximately 150,000,000 km (516, 538)

astronomy the study of all physical objects beyond Earth (9, 482)

atmosphere a mixture of gases that surrounds a planet, such as Earth (392)

atom the smallest part of an element that has all of the properties of that element (61)

azimuthal (AZ i MYOOTH uhl) **projection** a map projection that is made by transferring the features of the globe onto a plane (42)

B

barometer an instrument used to measure air pressure (441)

beach an area of the shoreline made up of material deposited by waves (300)

bedrock the layer of rock beneath soil (255)

benthic environment the ocean floor and all the organisms that live on or in it; also known as the bottom environment (343)

benthos organisms that live on or in the ocean floor (342)

big bang theory the theory that states the universe began with a tremendous explosion (586)

biomass organic matter, such as plants, wood, and waste, that contains stored energy (124)

biome a large region characterized by a specific type of climate and the plants and animals that live there (458)

black hole an object with more than three solar masses squeezed into a ball only 10 km across whose gravity is so strong that not even light can escape (581)

breaker a heightened water wave that begins to tumble downward, or break, upon nearing the shore (374)

caldera (kahl DER uh) a circular depression that forms when a magma chamber empties and causes the ground above to sink (229)

calendar a system for organizing time; most calendars organize time within a single unit called a year (482)

cardinal directions north, south, east, and west (35)

cast an object created when sediment fills a mold and becomes rock (148)

catastrophism a principle that states that all geologic change occurs suddenly (135)

celestial equator imaginary circle created by extending Earth's equator into space (492)

channel the path a stream follows (273)

chemical weathering the chemical breakdown of rocks and minerals into new substances (249)

chromosphere (KROH muh SFIR) a thin region of the sun's atmosphere between the corona and the photosphere; too faint to see unless there is a total solar eclipse (519)

cinder cone volcano a small, steeply sloped volcano that forms from moderately explosive eruptions of pyroclastic material (228)

circumpolar stars stars that can be seen at all times of the year and all times of the night (492)

cirque (suhrk) a bowl-like depression where glacial ice cuts back into mountain walls (313)

cirrus (SIR uhs) **clouds** thin, feathery white clouds found at high altitudes (427)

cleavage (KLEEV ij) the tendency of a mineral to break along flat surfaces (65)

climate the average weather conditions in an area over a long period of time (452)

cloud a collection of millions of tiny water droplets or ice crystals (426)

coal a solid fossil fuel formed underground from buried, decomposed plant material (112)

comet a small body of ice, rock, and cosmic dust loosely packed together that gives off gas and dust in the form of a tail as it passes close to the sun (557)

composite volcano a volcano made of alternating layers of lava and pyroclastic material; also called *stratovolcano* (228)

composition the makeup of a rock; describes either the minerals or elements present in it (85)

compound a pure substance made of two or more elements that have been chemically joined, or bonded together (61)

compression the type of stress that occurs when an object is squeezed (181)

condensation the change of state from a gas to a liquid (335, 425)

conduction the transfer of thermal energy from one material to another by direct contact; conduction can also occur within a substance (399)

conic (KAHN ik) **projection** a map projection that is made by transferring the features of the globe onto a cone (42)

constellation a section of the sky that contains a recognizable star pattern (489)

continental drift the theory that continents can drift apart from one another and have done so in the past (173)

continental margin the portion of the Earth's surface beneath the ocean that is made of continental crust (338)

continental rise the base of the continental slope (338)

continental shelf the flattest part of the continental margin (338)

continental slope the steepest part of the continental margin (338)

contour interval the difference in elevation between one contour line and the next (47)

contour lines lines that connect points of equal elevation (46)

convection the transfer of thermal energy by the circulation or movement of a liquid or a gas (399)

convective zone a region of the sun where gases circulate in convection currents, bringing the sun's energy to the surface (519)

convergent boundary the boundary between two colliding tectonic plates (178)

coprolites (KAHP roh LIETS) preserved feces, or dung, from animals (148)

core the central, spherical part of the Earth below the mantle (167, 525); *also* the center of the sun where the sun's energy is produced (519)

Coriolis (KOHR ee OH lis) **effect** the curving of moving objects from a straight path due to the Earth's rotation (366, 403)

corona the sun's outer atmosphere, which can extend outward a distance equal to 10–12 times the diameter of the sun (519)

cosmic background radiation radiation left over from the big bang that fills all of space (587)

cosmology the study of the origin and future of the universe (586)

crater a funnel-shaped pit around the central vent of a volcano (229)

creep the extremely slow movement of material downslope (319)

crest the highest point of a wave (372)

crevasse (kruh VAS) a large crack that forms where a glacier picks up speed or flows over a high point (311)

crust the thin, outermost layer of the Earth, or the uppermost part of the lithosphere (166, 525)

crystal the solid, geometric form of a mineral produced by a repeating pattern of atoms (61)

cumulus (KYOO myoo luhs) **clouds** puffy, white clouds that tend to have flat bottoms (426)

D

day the time required for the Earth to rotate once on its axis (482)

deciduous (dee SIJ oo uhs) describes trees that lose their leaves when the weather becomes cold (462)

declination a measure of how far north or south an object is from the celestial equator (492)

deep current a streamlike movement of ocean water far below the surface (368)

deep-ocean basin the portion of the Earth's surface beneath the ocean that is made of oceanic crust (338)

deflation the lifting and removal of fine sediment by wind (305)

deformation the change in the shape of rock in response to stress (197)

delta a fan-shaped deposit of alluvium at the mouth of a stream, where the stream empties into a large body of water (278)

density the amount of matter in a given space; mass per unit volume (66)

deposition the process by which material is dropped or settles (277)

desalination the process of evaporating sea water so that the water and the salt separate (349)

dew point the temperature to which air must cool to be completely saturated (425)

differential weathering the process by which softer, less weather-resistant rocks wear away, leaving harder, more weather-resistant rocks behind (252)

discharge the amount of water a stream or river carries in a given amount of time (273)

divergent boundary the boundary between two tectonic plates that are moving away from each other (179)

divide an area of higher ground that separates drainage basins (272)

drainage basin the land drained by a river system, which includes the main river and all of its tributaries (272)

dune a mound of wind-deposited sand (306)

E

eclipse an event in which the shadow of one celestial body falls on another (552)

ecliptic the apparent path the sun takes across the celestial sphere (492)

ecosystem a community of organisms and their nonliving environment (10)

elastic rebound the sudden return of elastically deformed rock to its original shape (197)

electromagnetic spectrum all the wavelengths of electromagnetic radiation (499)

element a pure substance that cannot be separated or broken down into simpler substances by ordinary chemical means (60)

elevation the height of an object above sea level; the height of surface landforms above sea level (46, 456)

ellipse a closed curve in which the sum of the distances from the edge of the curve to two points inside the ellipse is always the same (516)

elliptical galaxy a spherical or elongated galaxy with a bright center and very little dust and gas (583)

El Niño periodic change in the location of warm and cool surface waters in the Pacific Ocean (371)

energy resource a natural resource that humans use to produce energy (111)

eon the largest division of geologic time (153)

epicenter the point on the Earth's surface directly above an earthquake's starting point (202)

epoch (EP uhk) the fourth-largest division of geologic time (153)

equator a circle halfway between the poles that divides the Earth into the Northern and Southern Hemispheres (37)

era the second-largest division of geologic time (153)

erosion the removal and transport of material by wind, water, or ice (260, 270)

escape velocity the speed and direction a rocket must travel in order to completely break away from a planet's gravitational pull (601)

evaporation the change of state from a liquid to a vapor (335)

evergreens trees that keep their leaves year-round (462)

extrusive (eks TROO siv) the type of igneous rock that forms when lava or pyroclastic material cools and solidifies on the Earth's surface (90)

F

fault a break in the Earth's crust along which blocks of the crust slide relative to one another due to tectonic forces (183, 196)

fault block a block of the Earth's crust on one side of a fault (183)

fault-block mountain a mountain that forms when faulting causes large blocks of the Earth's crust to drop down relative to other blocks (186)

felsic (FEL sik) describes relatively light-colored, light-weight igneous rocks that are rich in silicon, aluminum, sodium, and potassium (88)

flood plain an area along a river formed from sediments deposited by floods (279)

focus the point inside the Earth where an earthquake begins (202)

folded mountain a mountain that forms when rock layers are squeezed together and pushed upward (185)

folding the bending of rock layers due to stress in the Earth's crust (182)

foliated the texture of metamorphic rock in which the mineral grains are aligned like the pages of a book (98)

footwall the fault block that is below a fault (183)

fossil any naturally preserved evidence of life (146)

fossil fuel a nonrenewable energy resource that forms in the Earth's crust over millions of years from the buried remains of once-living organisms (111)

fracture the tendency of a mineral to break along curved or irregular surfaces (65)

front the boundary that forms between two different air masses (432)

G

galaxy a large grouping of stars in space (582)

gap hypothesis states that sections of active faults that have had relatively few earthquakes are likely to be the sites of strong earthquakes in the future (207)

gas giants the large, gaseous planets of the outer solar system (544)

gasohol a mixture of gasoline and alcohol that is burned as a fuel (124)

geologic column an ideal sequence of rock layers that contains all the known fossils and rock formations on Earth arranged from oldest to youngest (138)

geologic time scale a scale that divides Earth's 4.6-billion-year history into distinct intervals of time (152)

geology the study of the solid Earth (6)

geosynchronous orbit an orbit in which a satellite travels at a speed that matches the rotational speed of the Earth exactly, keeping the satellite positioned above the same spot on Earth at all times (603)

geothermal energy energy from within the Earth (125)

glacial drift all material carried and deposited by glaciers (314)

glacier an enormous mass of moving ice (309)

global warming a rise in average global temperatures (18, 400, 470)

globular cluster a group of older stars that looks like a ball of stars (584)

gradient a measure of the change in elevation over a certain distance (273)

greenhouse effect the natural heating process of a planet, such as the Earth, by which gases in the atmosphere trap thermal energy (400, 470, 540)

ground water water that is located within rocks below the Earth's surface (280)

H

half-life for a particular radioactive sample, the time it takes for one-half of the sample to decay (143)

hanging valley a small glacial valley that joins the deeper main valley (313)

hanging wall the fault block that is above a fault (183)

hardness the resistance of a mineral to being scratched (66)

horizon the line where the sky and the Earth appear to meet (491)

horn a sharp, pyramid-shaped peak that forms when three or more cirque glaciers erode a mountain (313)

hot spot a place on Earth's surface that is directly above a column of rising magma called a mantle plume (233)

H-R diagram Hertzsprung-Russell diagram; a graph that shows the relationship between a star's surface temperature and its absolute magnitude (577)

humidity the amount of water vapor or moisture in the air (423)

humus (HYU muhs) very small particles of decayed plant and animal material in soil (255)

hurricane a large, rotating tropical weather system with wind speeds of at least 119 km/h (437)

hydroelectric energy electricity produced by falling water (123)

hypothesis a possible explanation or answer to a question (14)

I

ice age a period during which ice collects in high latitudes and moves toward lower latitudes (467)

iceberg a large piece of ice that breaks off an ice shelf and drifts into the ocean (310)

ice wedging the mechanical weathering process in which water seeps into cracks in rock, freezes, then expands, opening the cracks even wider (246)

igneous rock rock that forms from the cooling of magma (84)

index contour a darker, heavier contour line that is usually every fifth line and is labeled by elevation (47)

index fossil a fossil of an organism that lived during a relatively short, well-defined time span; a fossil that is used to date the rock layers in which it is found (150)

inner core the solid, dense center of the Earth (169)

intrusive (in TROO siv) the type of igneous rock that forms when magma cools and solidifies beneath Earth's surface (89)

irregular galaxy a galaxy that does not fit into any other category; one with an irregular shape (583)

isobars lines that connect points of equal air pressure (443)

isotopes atoms of the same element that have the same number of protons but have different numbers of neutrons (142)

J

jet streams narrow belts of high-speed winds that blow in the upper troposphere and the lower stratosphere (406)

K

Kuiper (KIE per) **Belt** the region of the solar system outside the orbit of Neptune that is occupied by small, icy, cometlike bodies (558)

L

landslide a sudden and rapid movement of a large amount of material downslope (317)

latitude the distance north or south from the equator; measured in degrees (37, 453)

lava magma that flows onto the Earth's surface (84, 222)

leaching the process by which rainwater dissolves and carries away the minerals and nutrients in topsoil (256)

leap year a year in which an extra day is added to the calendar (483)

light-minute a unit of length equal to the distance light travels in space in 1 minute, or 18,000,000 km (538)

lightning the large electrical discharge that occurs between two oppositely charged surfaces (435)

light-year a unit of length equal to the distance that light travels through space in 1 year (493, 575)

lithosphere (LITH oh SFIR) the outermost, rigid layer of the Earth that consists of the crust and the rigid upper part of the mantle (168)

load the materials carried in a stream's water (274)

loess (LOH ES) thick deposits of windblown, fine-grained sediments (308)

longitude the distance east or west from the prime meridian; measured in degrees (38)

longshore current the movement of water near and parallel to the shoreline (301)

low Earth orbit an orbit located a few hundred kilometers above the Earth's surface (603)

lunar eclipse an event in which the shadow of the Earth falls on the moon (552)

luster the way the surface of a mineral reflects light (64)

M

mafic (MAYF ik) describes relatively dark-colored, heavy igneous rocks that are rich in iron, magnesium, and calcium (88)

magma the hot liquid that forms when rock partially or completely melts; may include mineral crystals (83)

magnetic declination the angle of correction for the difference between geographic north and magnetic north (36)

magnetic reversal the process by which the Earth's north and south magnetic poles periodically change places (176)

main sequence a diagonal pattern of stars on the H-R diagram (578)

mantle the layer of the Earth between the crust and the core (167, 525)

map a model or representation of the Earth's surface (34)

mass the amount of matter that something is made of; its value does not change with the object's location (24)

mass movement the movement of any material downslope (316)

mechanical weathering the breakdown of rock into smaller pieces by physical means (246)

Mercator projection a map projection that is made by transferring the features of the globe onto a cylinder (41)

mesosphere literally, the "middle sphere"—the strong, lower part of the mantle between the asthenosphere and the outer core (169); *also* the coldest layer of the atmosphere (396)

metamorphic rock rock that forms when the texture and composition of preexisting rock changes due to heat or pressure (84)

meteor a streak of light caused when a meteoroid or comet dust burns up in the Earth's atmosphere before it reaches the ground (560)

meteorite a meteoroid that reaches the Earth's surface without burning up completely (560)

meteoroid a very small, rocky body that revolves around the sun (560)

meteorology the study of the entire atmosphere (8)

meter the basic unit of length in the SI system (23)

microclimate a small region with unique climatic characteristics (466)

mid-ocean ridge a long mountain chain that forms on the ocean floor where tectonic plates pull apart; usually extends along the center of ocean basins (175, 339)

mineral a naturally formed, inorganic solid with a crystalline structure (60)

model a representation of an object or system (19)

Moho a place within the Earth where the speed of seismic waves increases sharply; marks the boundary between the Earth's crust and mantle (211)

mold a cavity in the ground or rock where a plant or animal was buried (148)

monocline a fold in sedimentary rock layers in which the layers are horizontal on both sides of the fold (182)

month roughly the amount of time required for the moon to orbit the Earth once (482)

moon a natural satellite of a planet (549)

mudflow the rapid movement of a large mass of mud, rock, and soil mixed with a large amount of water that flows downhill (318)

N

NASA National Aeronautics and Space Administration; founded to combine all of the separate rocket-development teams in the United States (599)

natural gas a gaseous fossil fuel (112)

natural resource any natural substance, organism, or energy form that living things use (108)

neap tides tides with minimum daily tidal range that occur during the first and third quarters of the moon (380)

nebula (NEB yuh luh) a large cloud of dust and gas in interstellar space; the location of star formation (510, 584)

nekton (NEK TAHN) free-swimming organisms of the ocean (342)

neutron star a star in which all the particles have become neutrons; the collapsed remains of a supernova (581)

nonfoliated the texture of metamorphic rock in which mineral grains show no alignment (98)

nonpoint-source pollution pollution that comes from many sources and that cannot be traced to specific sites (285, 352)

nonrenewable resource a natural resource that cannot be replaced or that can be replaced only over thousands or millions of years (109)

nonsilicate mineral a mineral that does not contain compounds of silicon and oxygen (63)

normal fault a fault in which the hanging wall moves down relative to the footwall (183)

nuclear energy the form of energy associated with changes in the nucleus of an atom; an alternative energy resource (118)

nuclear fusion the process by which two or more nuclei with small masses join together, or fuse, to form a larger, more massive nucleus, along with the production of energy (521)

O

observation any use of the senses to gather information (14)

oceanography the study of the ocean (7)

ocean trench a seemingly bottomless crack in the deep-ocean basin that forms where one oceanic plate is forced underneath a continental plate or another oceanic plate (339)

Oort (ort) **cloud** a spherical region of space that surrounds the solar system in which distant comets revolve around the sun (558)

open cluster a group of stars that are usually located along the spiral disk of a galaxy (584)

orbit the elliptical path a body takes as it travels around another body in space; the motion itself (515)

orbital velocity the speed and direction a rocket must have in order to orbit the Earth (601)

ore a mineral deposit large enough and pure enough to be mined for a profit (70)

outer core the liquid layer of the Earth's core that lies beneath the mantle and surrounds the inner core (169)

oxidation a chemical reaction in which an element combines with oxygen to form an oxide (251)

ozone a gas molecule that is made up of three oxygen atoms and that absorbs ultraviolet radiation from the sun (395)

P

parallax an apparent shift in the position of an object when viewed from different locations (575)

parent rock rock that is the source of soil (255)

pelagic (pi LAJ ik) **environment** the entire volume of water in the ocean and the marine organisms that live above the ocean floor; also known as the water environment (345)

period the third-largest division of geologic time (153)

period of revolution the time it takes for one body to make one complete orbit, or *revolution,* around another body in space (515, 539)

period of rotation the time it takes for an object to rotate once (539)

permeability (PUHR mee uh BIL uh tee) a rock's ability to let water pass through it (280)

permineralization a process in which minerals fill in pore spaces of an organism's tissues (146)

petrification a process in which an organism's tissues are completely replaced by minerals (146)

petroleum an oily mixture of flammable organic compounds from which liquid fossil fuels and other products are separated; crude oil (111)

phases the different appearances of the moon due to varying amounts of sunlight on the side of the moon that faces the Earth; results from the changing relative positions of the moon, Earth, and the sun (551)

photosphere the layer of the sun at which point the gases get thick enough to see; the surface of the sun (519)

planetesimal (PLAN i TES i muhl) the tiny building blocks of the planets that formed as dust particles stuck together and grew in size (512)

plankton microscopic organisms that float at or near the ocean's surface (342)

plate tectonics the theory that the Earth's lithosphere is divided into tectonic plates that move around on top of the asthenosphere (177)

point-source pollution pollution that comes from one particular source area (285)

polar easterlies wind belts that extend from the poles to 60° latitude in both hemispheres (405)

polar zone the northernmost and southernmost climate zones (464)

porosity (poh RAHS uh tee) the amount of open space between individual rock particles (280)

precipitation solid or liquid water that falls from the air to the Earth (335, 428)

prevailing winds winds that blow mainly from one direction (455)

primary pollutants pollutants that are put directly into the air by human or natural activity (409)

prime meridian the line of longitude that passes through Greenwich, England; represents 0° longitude (38)

prograde rotation the counterclockwise spin of a planet or moon as seen from above the planet's north pole (540)

psychrometer (sie KRAHM uht uhr) an instrument used to measure relative humidity (424)

pulsar a spinning neutron star that emits rapid pulses of light (581)

P waves the fastest type of seismic wave; can travel through solids, liquids, and gases; also known as pressure waves and primary waves (200)

pyroclastic material fragments of rock that are created by explosive volcanic eruptions (225)

Q

quasar (KWAY ZAHR) a "quasi-stellar" object; a starlike source of light that is extremely far away; one of the most powerful sources of energy in the universe (585)

R

radiation the transfer of energy as electromagnetic waves, such as visible light or infrared waves (398); *also* energy transferred as waves or particles (118)

radiative zone a very dense region of the sun in which the atoms are so closely packed that light can take millions of years to pass through (519)

radioactive decay a process in which radioactive isotopes tend to break down into stable isotopes of other elements (142)

radiometric dating determining the absolute age of a sample based on the ratio of parent material to daughter material (143)

recharge zone the ground surface where water enters an aquifer (281)

reclamation the process of returning land to its original state after mining is completed (71)

recycling the process by which used or discarded materials are treated for reuse (110)

red giant a star that expands and cools once it runs out of hydrogen fuel (579)

reference point a fixed place on the Earth's surface from which direction and location can be described (35)

reflecting telescope a telescope that uses curved mirrors to gather and focus light (497)

refracting telescope a telescope that uses a set of lenses to gather and focus light (497)

relative dating determining whether an object or event is older or younger than other objects or events (137)

relative humidity the amount of moisture the air contains compared with the maximum amount it can hold at a particular temperature (423)

relief the difference in elevation between the highest and lowest points of an area being mapped (47)

remote sensing gathering information about something without actually being nearby (43)

renewable resource a natural resource that can be used and replaced over a relatively short time (109)

residual soil soil that remains above the bedrock from which it formed (255)

retrograde orbit the clockwise revolution of a satellite around a planet as seen from above the north pole of the planet (556)

retrograde rotation the clockwise spin of a planet or moon as seen from above the planet's or moon's north pole (540)

reverse fault a fault in which the hanging wall moves up relative to the footwall (183)

revolution the elliptical motion of a body as it orbits another body in space (515, 539)

rift a deep crack that forms between tectonic plates as they separate (232)

rift valley a valley that forms in a rift zone between diverging tectonic plates (339)

right ascension a measure of how far east an object is from the point at which the sun appears on the first day of spring (492)

rock a solid mixture of crystals of one or more minerals or other materials (80)

rock cycle the process by which one rock type changes into another rock type (82)

rocket a machine that uses escaping gas to move (598)

rock fall a group of loose rocks that fall down a steep slope (317)

rotation the spinning motion of a body on its axis (515, 539)

S

salinity a measure of the amount of dissolved salts and other solids in a given amount of liquid (332)

saltation the movement of sand-sized particles by a skipping and bouncing action in the direction the wind is blowing (304)

satellite a natural or artificial body that revolves around a planet (549)

scientific method a series of steps that scientists use to answer questions and solve problems (13)

sea-floor spreading the process by which new oceanic lithosphere is created at mid-ocean ridges as older materials are pulled away from the ridge (175)

seamount an individual mountain of volcanic material on the abyssal plain (339)

secondary pollutants pollutants that form from chemical reactions that occur when primary pollutants come in contact with other primary pollutants or with naturally occurring substances, such as water vapor (409)

sedimentary rock rock that forms when sediments are compacted and cemented together (84)

seismic (SIEZ mik) **gap** an area along a fault where relatively few earthquakes have occurred (207)

seismic waves waves of energy that travel through the Earth (200)

seismogram a tracing of earthquake motion created by a seismograph (202)

seismograph an instrument located at or near the surface of the Earth that records seismic waves (202)

seismology the study of earthquakes (196)

septic tank a large, underground tank that collects and cleans waste water from a household (287)

sewage treatment plant a factory that cleans waste materials out of water that comes from sewers or drains (286)

shadow zone an area on the Earth's surface where no direct seismic waves from a particular earthquake can be detected (211)

shield volcano a large, gently sloped volcano that forms from repeated, nonexplosive eruptions of lava (228)

shoreline the boundary between land and a body of water (298)

silica a compound of silicon and oxygen atoms (224)

silicate mineral a mineral that contains a combination of the elements silicon and oxygen (62)

smog a photochemical fog produced by the reaction of sunlight and air pollutants (117)

soil a loose mixture of small mineral fragments and organic material (255)

soil conservation the various methods by which humans take care of the soil (259)

solar eclipse an event in which the shadow of the moon falls on the Earth's surface (552)

solar energy energy from the sun (119)

solar nebula the nebula that formed into the solar system (511)

solar system the system composed of the sun (a star) and the planets and other bodies that travel around the sun (510)

space probe a vehicle that carries scientific instruments to planets or other bodies in space (606)

space shuttle a reusable vehicle that takes off like a rocket and lands like an airplane (613)

space station a long-term orbiting platform from which other vehicles can be launched or scientific research can be carried out (614)

specific gravity the ratio of an object's density to the density of water (66)

spectrum the rainbow of colors produced when white light passes through a prism or spectrograph (570)

spiral galaxy a galaxy with a bulge in the center and very distinctive spiral arms (582)

spring tides tides with maximum daily tidal range that occur during the new and full moons (380)

station model a small circle showing the location of a weather station along with a set of symbols and numbers surrounding it that represent weather data (442)

storm surge a local rise in sea level near the shore that is caused by strong winds from a storm, such as a hurricane (377)

strata layers of sedimentary rock that form from the deposition of sediment (91)

stratification the layering of sedimentary rock (94)

stratified drift rock material that has been sorted and deposited in layers by water flowing from the melted ice of a glacier (314)

stratosphere the atmospheric layer above the troposphere (395)

stratus (STRAT uhs) **clouds** clouds that form in layers (426)

streak the color of a mineral in powdered form (65)

stress the amount of force per unit area that is put on a given material (181)

strike-slip fault a fault in which the two fault blocks move past each other horizontally (184)

strip mining a process in which rock and soil are stripped from the Earth's surface to expose the underlying materials to be mined (115)

subduction zone the region where an oceanic plate sinks down into the asthenosphere at a convergent boundary, usually between continental and oceanic plates (178)

sunspot an area on the photosphere of the sun that is cooler than surrounding areas, showing up as a dark spot (523)

supernova the death of a large star by explosion (580)

superposition a principle that states that younger rocks lie above older rocks in undisturbed sequences (137)

surf the area between the breaker zone and the shore (374)

surface current a streamlike movement of water that occurs at or near the surface of the ocean (365, 457)

surface gravity the percentage of your Earth weight you would experience on another planet; the weight you would experience on another planet (539)

S waves the second-fastest type of seismic wave; cannot travel through materials that are completely liquid; also known as shear waves and secondary waves (200)

swells rolling waves that move in a steady procession across the ocean (375)

syncline a trough-shaped fold in sedimentary rock layers (182)

T

tectonic plate a piece of the lithosphere that moves around on top of the asthenosphere (170)

telescope an instrument that collects electromagnetic radiation from the sky and concentrates it for better observation (496)

temperate zone the climate zone between the Tropics and the polar zone (462)

temperature a measure of how hot (or cold) something is (25)

tension the type of stress that occurs when forces act to stretch an object (181)

terrestrial planets the small, dense, rocky planets of the inner solar system (539)

texture the sizes, shapes, and positions of the grains that a rock is made of (86)

theory a unifying explanation for a broad range of hypotheses and observations that have been supported by testing (19)

thermocline a layer of ocean water extending from 300 m below sea level to about 700 m below sea level in which water temperature drops with increased depth faster than it does in other zones of the ocean (333)

thermometer a tool used to measure air temperature (440)

thermosphere the uppermost layer of the atmosphere (396)

thrust the force that accelerates a rocket (600)

thunder the sound that results from the rapid expansion of air along a lightning strike (435)

thunderstorms small, intense weather systems that produce strong winds, heavy rain, lightning, and thunder (434)

tidal bore a body of water that rushes up through a narrow bay, estuary, or river channel during the rise of high tide, causing a very sudden tidal rise (381)

tidal range the difference between levels of ocean water at high tide and low tide (380)

tides daily movements of ocean water that change the level of the ocean's surface (378)

till unsorted rock material that is deposited directly by glacial ice when it melts (315)

topographic map a map that shows the surface features of the Earth (46)

topsoil the top layer of soil that generally contains humus (256)

tornado a small, rotating column of air that has high wind speeds and low central pressure and that touches the ground (436)

trace fossil any naturally preserved evidence of an animal's activity (148)

trade winds the winds that blow from 30° latitude to the equator (404)

transform boundary the boundary between two tectonic plates that are sliding past each other horizontally (179)

transported soil soil that has been blown or washed away from its parent rock (255)

tributary a smaller stream or river that flows into a larger one (272)

tropical zone the warm zone located around the equator (459)

troposphere (TROH poh SFIR) the lowest layer of the atmosphere (395)

trough (trahf) the lowest point of a wave (372)

true north the geographic North Pole (36)

tsunami a wave that forms when a large volume of ocean water is suddenly moved up or down (376)

U

unconformity a surface that represents a missing part of the geologic column (140)

uniformitarianism a principle that states that the same geologic processes shaping the Earth today have been at work throughout Earth's history (134)

upwelling a process in which cold, nutrient-rich water from the deep ocean rises to the surface and replaces warm surface water (371)

U-shaped valley a valley that forms when a glacier erodes a river valley from its original V shape to a U shape (313)

V

vent a hole in the Earth's crust through which magma rises to the surface (224)

volcano a mountain that forms when molten rock, called magma, is forced to the Earth's surface (222)

volume the amount of space that something occupies or the amount of space that something contains (23)

W

water cycle the continuous movement of water from water sources into the air, onto land, into and over the ground, and back to the water sources; a cycle that links all of the Earth's solid, liquid, and gaseous water together (270, 335, 422)

watershed the land drained by a river system, which includes the main river and all of its tributaries (272)

water table an underground boundary where the zone of aeration and the zone of saturation meet (280)

wave height the vertical distance between a wave's crest and its trough (372)

wavelength the distance between two adjacent wave crests or wave troughs (372)

wave period the time between the passage of two wave crests (or troughs) at a fixed point (373)

weather the condition of the atmosphere at a particular time and place (422, 452)

weather forecast a prediction of future weather conditions over the next 3 to 5 days (440)

weathering the breakdown of rock into smaller and smaller pieces by mechanical or chemical means (246)

westerlies wind belts found in both the Northern and Southern Hemispheres between 30° and 60° latitude (405)

whitecap a white, foaming wave with a very steep crest that breaks in the open ocean before the wave gets close to the shore (375)

white dwarf a small, hot star near the end of its life; the leftover center of an old star (578)

wind moving air (402)

wind energy energy in wind (122)

windsock a device used to measure wind direction (441)

wind vane a device used to measure wind direction (441)

Y

year the time required for the Earth to orbit the sun once (482)

Z

zenith an imaginary point in the sky directly above an observer on Earth (491)

Spanish Glossary

A

abrasion/corrosión erosión y desgaste de las superficies de las rocas causadas por otras rocas o partículas de arena (247, 306)

absolute dating/datación absoluta el proceso de establecer la edad de un objeto, como un fósil o una capa de roca, determinando el número de años que ha existido (142)

absolute magnitude/magnitud absoluta el brillo real de una estrella (574)

abyssal plain/llanura abismal la parte ancha y plana de la cuenca de lo más profundo del océano (338)

acid precipitation/precipitación ácida precipitación que contiene ácido por la contaminación del aire (116, 249, 411)

aerial photograph/fotografía aérea fotografía tomada desde el aire (43)

air mass/masa de aire gran masa de aire que tiene temperatura y humedad similares en toda su extensión (430)

air pressure/presión del aire la medida de la fuerza con la que las moléculas de aire empujan una superficie (393)

alluvial fan/abanico aluvial depósitos de aluvión en forma de abanico que se forman en la tierra seca (279)

alluvium/aluvión rocas y tierra depositadas por las corrientes (277)

altitude/altitud la altura de un objeto por encima de la superficie de la tierra; en astronomía, la distancia angular entre un objeto en el cielo y el horizonte (491)

anemometer/anemómetro aparato usado para medir la velocidad del viento (441)

annular eclipse/eclipse anular eclipse de sol durante el cual el anillo exterior del sol se puede ver alrededor de la luna (552)

anticline/anticlinal un pliegue con forma de bol en capas de roca sedimentaria (182)

apparent magnitude/magnitud aparente el brillo que una luz parece tener para un observador (574)

aquifer/acuífero capa rocosa que almacena agua subterránea y que permite que ésta fluya (280)

arete/arista un risco serrado que se forma entre dos o más excavaciones naturales que se insertan en la misma montaña (313)

artesian spring/manantial artesiano un manantial que se forma en donde las grietas ocurren naturalmente en la roca, y el agua bajo presión en el acuífero fluye a través de estas grietas a la superficie (282)

artificial satellite/satélite artificial cualquier objeto hecho por los humanos puesto en órbita alrededor de un cuerpo en el espacio (602)

asteroid/asteroide un cuerpo pequeño y rocoso que da vueltas alrededor del sol (559)

asteroid belt/cinturón de asteroides región del sistema solar ocupado por la mayoría de los asteroides; aproximadamente entre las órbitas de Marte y Júpiter (559)

asthenosphere/astenosfera la capa parcialmente derretida del manto superior en el cual se mueven las placas tectónicas de la litosfera (168)

astronomical unit/unidad astronómica la distancia promedio entre la Tierra y el sol, o aproximadamente 150,000,000 km (516, 538)

astronomy/astronomía el estudio de todos los objetos físicos más allá de la Tierra (9, 482)

atmosphere/atmósfera mezcla de gases que rodea a un planeta como la Tierra (392)

atom/átomo la partícula más pequeña en la que se puede dividir un elemento y aún retener todas las propiedades de aquel elemento (61)

azimuthal projection/proyección en acimut proyección de un mapa que se hace transfiriendo el contenido del globo a un plano (42)

B

barometer/barómetro instrumento que se usa para medir la presión del aire (441)

beach/playa área de la costa formada por materiales depositados por las olas (300)

bedrock/ lecho de roca, la capa de roca bajo la tierra (255)

benthic environment/ambiente bentónico el fondo del océano y todos los organismos que viven en él o sobre él; también se conoce como el medio ambiente del fondo (343)

benthos/bentos organismos que viven en el fondo del océano o sobre él (342)

big bang theory/teoría de la gran explosión la teoría que establece que el universo comenzó con una tremenda explosión (586)

biomass/biomasa materia orgánica, como plantas, madera, y desechos, que contiene energía almacenada (124)

biome/bioma región grande caracterizada por un tipo de clima específico y por las plantas y animales que viven allí (458)

black hole/agujero negro objeto con más de tres masas solares comprimidas en una bola de sólo 10 km de diámetro cuya gravedad es tan fuerte que ni siquiera la luz puede escapar (581)

breaker/rompimiento de olas donde una ola de agua muy grande comienza a rodar hacia abajo, o a romper, al acercarse a la costa (374)

C

caldera/caldera depresión circular que se forma cuando se vacía una cámara de magma y hace que la tierra que está encima se hunda (229)

calendar/calendario sistema para organizar el tiempo; la mayoría de los calendarios organizan el tiempo en una unidad llamada año (482)

cardinal directions/puntos cardinales norte, sur, este, y oeste (35)

cast/vaciado objeto creado cuando los sedimentos llenan un molde y éste se vuelve roca (148)

catastrophism/catastrofismo principio que declara que todos los cambios geológicos ocurren súbitamente (135)

celestial equator/ecuador celeste círculo imaginario creado al extender el ecuador de la Tierra al espacio (492)

channel/cauce la trayectoria de una corriente (273)

chemical weathering/acción geológica atmosférica química la desintegración química de las rocas y los minerales en sustancias nuevas (249)

chromosphere/cromosfera una fina región de la atmósfera solar entre la corona y la fotosfera, demasiado tenue para ser visible, a no ser que haya un eclipse total de sol (519)

cinder cone volcano/volcán de cono de ceniza un volcán pequeño, de paredes abruptas, que se forma de erupciones moderadamente explosivas de material piroclástico (228)

circumpolar stars/estrellas circunpolares la estrellas que se pueden ver durante todo el año y en todo momento durante la noche (492)

cirque/excavación natural una depresión en forma de bol donde el hielo de los glaciares se inserta en las paredes de la montaña (313)

cirrus clouds/cirrus nubes finas, blancas y parecidas al plumón que se encuentran a grandes altitudes (427)

cleavage/plano de fractura la tendencia de un mineral de romperse a lo largo de superficies planas (65)

climate/clima las condiciones promedio del tiempo en un área durante un período largo (452)

cloud/nube colección de millones de gotitas de agua o cristales de hielo diminutos (426)

coal/carbón combustible fósil sólido que se forma de manera subterránea de materiales vegetales enterrados y descompuestos (112)

comet/cometa un pequeño cuerpo de hielo y roca cósmica poco compacta que despide gases y polvo en forma de cola al pasar cerca del sol (557)

composite volcano/volcán mixto volcán formado por capas alternadas de lava y material piroclástico; también conocido como estratovolcano (228)

composition/composición lo que forma la roca; describe ya sea los minerales o los elementos presentes (85)

compound/compuesto sustancia pura formada por dos o más elementos que se han unido o enlazado químicamente (61)

compression/compresión la clase de presión que ocurre cuando un objeto es compactado (181)

condensation/condensación el cambio de estado de gas a líquido (335, 425)

conduction/conducción la transferencia de calor de un material a otro por contacto directo; la conducción también puede ocurrir dentro de una sustancia (399)

conic projection/proyección cónica proyección de un mapa que se hace al transferir los contenidos del globo a un cono (42)

constellation/constelación sección del cielo que contiene una posición de las estrellas que puede ser reconocida (489)

continental drift/deriva continental la teoría de que los continentes pueden separarse uno de otro y que lo han hecho en el pasado (173)

continental margin/margen continental la porción de la superficie de la Tierra bajo el océano formada por la corteza continental (338)

continental rise/elevación continental la base de la pendiente continental (338)

continental shelf/cuesta continental la parte más llana del margen continental (338)

continental slope/pendiente continental la parte más escarpada del margen continental (338)

contour interval/intervalo de las curvas de nivel la diferencia en elevación entre una línea de contorno y la siguiente (47)

contour lines/curvas de nivel líneas que conectan puntos de igual elevación (46)

convection/convección la transferencia de calor por la circulación o el movimiento de un líquido o un gas (399)

convective zone/zona de convección región del sol en que los gases circulan en corrientes convectivas, llevando la energía del sol a la superficie (519)

covergent boundary/límite convergente el límite entre dos placas tectónicas en colisión (178)

coprolites/coprolito excremento o bosta de animales, preservados (148)

core/núcleo la parte central, esférica, de la tierra bajo el manto (167, 525); también, el centro del sol donde se produce la energía solar (519)

Coriolis effect/efecto de Coriolis la manera en que se curva de una línea recta la trayectoria de los objetos en movimiento a causa de la rotación de la Tierra (366, 403)

corona/corona la atmósfera exterior del sol, que se puede extender hacia afuera en una distancia igual a 10 a 12 veces el diámetro del sol (519)

cosmic background radiation/radiación cósmica de fondo radiación que dejó la Gran Explosión, que llena todo el espacio (587)

cosmology/cosmología el estudio del origen y el futuro del universo (586)

crater/cráter un pozo con forma de embudo alrededor de la chimenea central de un volcán (229)

creep/arrastre movimiento muy lento de material cuesta abajo (319)

crest/cresta el punto más alto de una ola (372)

crevasse/grieta quebradura enorme que se forma donde un glaciar se acelera o fluye sobre una altura (311)

crust/corteza la capa fina y exterior de la Tierra, o la capa superior de la litosfera (166, 525)

crystal/cristal la forma sólida y geométrica de un mineral, producida por un modelo de átomos que se repite (61)

cumulus clouds/cúmulos nubes blancas y algodonosas que tienden a tener la superficie inferior plana (426)

D

day/día el tiempo que lleva para que la Tierra rote una vez sobre su eje (482)

deciduous/caducifolio describe a los árboles que pierden las hojas cuando comienza a hacer frío (462)

declination/declinación medida de la posición de un objeto al norte o al sur del ecuador celeste (492)

deep current/corriente submarina movimiento del agua del océano muy por debajo de la superficie (368)

deep-ocean basin/cuenca profunda del océano la porción de la superficie de la tierra bajo el océano que está formada por la corteza oceánica (338)

deflation/deflación cuando el viento levanta y traslada el sedimento fino (305)

deformation/deformación el cambio en la forma de las rocas en respuesta al estrés (197)

delta/delta depósito de aluvión en forma de abanico en la desembocadura de una corriente de agua, donde la corriente fluye en una gran masa de agua (278)

density/densidad la cantidad de materia en un espacio dado; masa por unidad de volumen (66)

deposition/depósito proceso por el cual el material se deposita o se asienta (277)

desalination/desalinización proceso de evaporación del agua de mar para que el agua y la sal se separen (349)

dew point/punto de rocío la temperatura a la cual el aire debe enfriarse para estar completamente saturado (425)

differential weathering/diferencial de acción geológica atmosférica proceso por el cual las rocas más blandas y menos resistentes a los elementos se desintegran, mientras que las rocas más resistentes perduran (252)

discharge/descarga el volumen de agua que transporta una corriente (273)

divergent boundary/límite divergente el límite entre dos placas tectónicas que se separan (179)

divide/cresta divisoria área de tierras más altas que separa cuencas de drenaje (272)

drainage basin/cuenca de drenaje la tierra drenada por un sistema fluvial que incluye el río principal y todos sus afluentes (272)

dune/duna un montículo de arena deposi- tada por el viento (306)

E

eclipse/eclipse suceso en el que la sombra de un cuerpo celeste se proyecta sobre otro (552)

ecliptic/eclíptico el trayecto aparente del sol a través de la esfera celeste (492)

ecosystem/ecosistema comunidad de organismos y su medio ambiente que no está vivo (10)

elastic rebound/rebote elástico el regreso súbito a su forma original de las rocas deformadas elásticamente (197)

electromagnetic spectrum/espectro electromagnético todas las longitudes de onda de la radiación electromagnética (499)

element/elemento sustancia pura que no puede separarse o dividirse en sustancias simples por procemientos químicos comunes (60)

elevation/altitud la altura de un objeto sobre el nivel del mar, y la altura de los accidentes geográficos sobre el nivel del mar (46, 456)

ellipse/elipse curva cerrada en que la suma de las distancias del borde de la curva a dos puntos dentro de la elipse son siempre iguales (516)

elliptical galaxy/galaxia elíptica galaxia esférica o alargada con un centro brillante y muy poco polvo y gas (583)

El Niño/El Niño cambio periódico en la situación de aguas superficiales cálidas y frías en el Océano Pacífico (371)

energy resource/recurso energético recurso natural que los humanos usan para producir energía (111)

eon/eón la división más grande del tiempo geológico (153)

epicenter/epicentro lugar en la superficie de la Tierra directamente sobre el punto donde comienza un terremoto (202)

epoch/época la cuarta división más grande del tiempo geológico (153)

equator/ecuador círculo a medio camino entre los polos, que divide la Tierra en los hemisferios norte y sur (37)

era/era la segunda división más grande del tiempo geológico (153)

erosion/erosión cuando el viento, el agua, o el hielo levantan y transportan materiales (260, 270)

escape velocity/velocidad de escape la velocidad y dirección en que debe viajar un cohete para separarse por completo del arrastre gravitacional de un planeta (601)

evaporation/evaporación el cambio de estado de líquido a vapor (335)

evergreens/perennifolio árboles que conservan sus hojas todo el año (462)

extrusive/extrusivo el tipo de roca ígnea que se forma cuando la lava o el material piroclástico se enfría y se solidifica sobre la corteza terrestre (90)

F

fault/falla grieta en la corteza terrestre a lo largo de la cual los bloques de corteza se deslizan con respecto a otros bloques; la falla se debe a las fuerzas tectónicas (183, 196)

fault block/bloque de falla bloque de corteza terrestre a un lado de una falla (183)

fault-block mountain/montaña de bloque de falla montaña que se forma cuando las fallas hacen que grandes bloques de corteza terrestre se hundan con respecto a otros bloques (186)

felsic/félsica describe a las rocas ígneas de color relativamente claro, y livianas, ricas en silicio, aluminio, sodio, y potasio (88)

flood plain/llanura aluvial área a lo largo de un río formada por los sedimentos depositados por las inundaciones (279)

focus/foco punto dentro de la Tierra donde comienza un terremoto (202)

folded mountain/montaña de plegamiento montaña que se forma cuando las capas de roca se comprimen y son empujadas hacia arriba (185)

folding/plegamiento cuando las capas rocosas se doblan por presiones en la corteza terrestre (182)

foliated/foliada la textura de las rocas metamórficas en las que los granos minerales están alineados como las páginas de un libro (98)

footwall/pared baja el bloque de falla que está debajo de una falla (183)

fossil/fósil cualquier evidencia de vida que se ha preservado naturalmente (146)

fossil fuel/combustible fósil recurso no renovable de energía que se forma en la corteza terrestre a través de millones de años de los restos enterrados de organismos que una vez estuvieron vivos (111)

fracture/fractura la tendencia de un mineral a quebrarse a lo largo de superficies curvas o irregulares (65)

front/frente la línea divisoria que se forma entre dos masas de aire diferentes (432)

G

galaxy/galaxia agrupación grande de estrellas en el espacio (582)

gap hypothesis/hipótesis de brecha establece que las secciones de fallas activas que han tenido relativamente pocos terremotos probablemente van a ser los lugares donde ocurran terremotos fuertes en el futuro (207)

gas giants/gigantes de gases planetas grandes y gaseosos en el sistema solar (544)

gasohol/gasohol mezcla de gasolina y alcohol que se quema como combustible (124)

geologic column/columna estratigráfica secuencia ideal de capas rocosas que contienen todos los fósiles y formaciones rocosas conocidos en la Tierra, ordenados del más antiguo al más moderno (138)

geologic time scale/escala de tiempo geológico escala que divide la historia de 4.6 millones de millones de años de la Tierra en distintos intervalos de tiempo (152)

geology/geología el estudio de la Tierra sólida (6)

geosynchronous orbit/órbita geosíncrona órbita en la que viaja un satélite a una velocidad que iguala exactamente a la velocidad de rotación de la Tierra, manteniendo en todo momento al satélite en posición sobre el mismo punto de la Tierra (603)

geothermal energy/energía geotérmica energía producida por el calor dentro de la corteza terrestre (125)

glacial drift/sedimento glaciar todo el material transportado y depositado por los glaciares (314)

glacier/glaciar enorme masa de hielo en movimiento (309)

global warming/calentamiento global un aumento en las temperaturas promedio mundiales (18, 400, 470)

globular cluster/agrupación globular grupo de estrellas antiguas que parece una bola de estrellas (584)

gradient/declive medida del cambio en sobre una cierta distancia (273)

greenhouse effect/efecto invernadero el proceso natural de calentamiento de un planeta, como la Tierra, por el que los gases en la atmósfera atrapan el calor (400, 470, 540)

ground water/agua subterránea agua almacenada dentro de la roca bajo la superficie de la Tierra (280)

H

half-life/vida media para una muestra radioactiva específica, el tiempo que lleva para que una mitad de la muestra se desintegre (143)

hanging valley/valle colgante pequeño valle glaciar que se une al valle principal más profundo (313)

hanging wall/pared colgante el bloque de falla que está sobre una falla (183)

hardness/dureza la resistencia de un mineral a ser raspado (66)

horizon/horizonte la línea donde el cielo y la Tierra parecen unirse (491)

horn/cuerno pico agudo, con forma de pirámide, que se forma cuando tres o más excavaciones naturales erosionan una montaña (313)

hot spot/punto caliente lugar en la superficie de la Tierra que está directamente sobre la columna magma que sube, llamada columna del manto (233)

H-R diagram/diagrama H-R diagrama Herzprung-Russell; gráfica que muestra la relación entre la temperatura de la superficie de una estrella y su magnitud absoluta (577)

humidity/humedad la cantidad de vapor de agua o de condensación en el aire (423)

humus/humus partículas muy pequeñas de materiales descompuestos de plantas y animales en la tierra (255)

hurricane/huracán gran sistema climático tropical en rotación, con viento a velocidades de por lo menos 119 km/h (437)

hydroelectric energy/energía hidroeléctrica electricidad producida por caídas de agua (123)

hypothesis/hipótesis posible explicación o respuesta a una pregunta (14)

I

ice age/era glacial período en que el hielo se junta en latitudes altas y se mueve hacia las latitudes bajas (467)

iceberg/témpano gran trozo de hielo que se separa de una plataforma de hielo y se desliza al océano (310)

ice wedging/témpano de hielo el proceso de desgaste mecánico en que el agua se filtra en grietas en la roca, se congela, y luego se expande, ensanchando las grietas (246)

igneous rock/roca ígnea roca que se forma al enfriarse el magma (84)

index contour/índice de las curvas de nivel una línea de contorno oscura y más gruesa que generalmente se da cada quinta línea y está marcada por la elevación (47)

index fossil/fósil indicador fósil de un organismo que vivió durante un período relativamente corto y bien definido; se usa para fechar las capas de roca en que se encontró (150)

inner core/núcleo interior el centro de la tierra, que es sólido y denso (169)

intrusive/intrusiva tipo de roca ígnea que se forma cuando el magma se enfría y se solidifica bajo la superficie de la Tierra (89)

irregular galaxy/galaxia irregular galaxia que no entra en ninguna otra categoría; que tiene una forma irregular (583)

isobars/isobaras líneas que conectan puntos con igual presión del aire (443)

isotopes/isótopos átomos del mismo elemento que tienen igual número de protones pero diferentes números de neutrones (142)

J

jet streams/corrientes en chorro cinturones angostos de vientos de alta velocidad que soplan en la troposfera superior y en la estratosfera inferior (406)

K

Kuiper Belt/Cinturón de Kuiper la región del sistema solar fuera de la órbita de Neptuno, ocupada por cuerpos pequeños, helados, y parecidos a los cometas (558)

L

landslide/desprendimiento de tierras movimiento cuesta abajo, súbito, de una gran cantidad de material (317)

latitude/latitud distancia al norte o al sur del ecuador; se mide en grados (37, 453)

lava/lava magma que fluye a la superficie de la Tierra (84, 222)

leaching/lixiviación proceso por el que el agua de lluvia se disuelve y se lleva los materiales y los nutrientes en la superficie de la Tierra (256)

leap year/año bisiesto año en el que se agrega un día al calendario (483)

light-minute/minuto-luz unidad de longitud igual a la distancia que recorre la luz en el espacio en un minuto, o sea 18,000,000 km (538)

lightning/rayo la descarga eléctrica grande que ocurre entre dos superficies con cargas opuestas (435)

light-year/año luz unidad de longitud igual a la distancia que recorre la luz a través del espacio en un año (493, 575)

lithosphere/litosfera la capa rígida, exterior de la Tierra, que consiste de la corteza y de la capa rígida superior del manto (168)

load/carga los materiales que lleva una corriente de agua (274)

loess/loess los depósitos densos de sedimentos de grano fino arrastrados por el viento (308)

longitude/longitud la distancia al este o al oeste del primer meridiano; se mide en grados (38)

longshore current/deriva litoral el movimiento del agua cerca de la costa y paralelo a ella (301)

low Earth orbit/órbita terrestre baja una órbita situada a unos pocos cientos de kilómetros sobre la superficie de la Tierra (603)

lunar eclipse/eclipse de luna fenomeno durante el cual la sombra de la Tierra se proyecta sobre la superficie de la luna (552)

luster/brillo la manera en que la superficie de un mineral refleja la luz (64)

M

mafic/máfica describe rocas ígneas pesadas y de color relativamente oscuro que son ricas en hierro, magnesio, y calcio (88)

magma/magma el líquido caliente que se forma cuando la roca se derrite total o parcialmente; puede incluir cristales minerales (83)

magnetic declination/desviación magnética el ángulo de corrección para la diferencia entre el norte geográfico y el norte magnético (36)

magnetic reversal/inversión magnética proceso por el cual cambian de lugar los polos magnéticos del norte y del sur de la Tierra (176)

main sequence/secuencia principal el patrón diagonal de estrellas en el diagrama H-R (578)

mantle/manto capa de la Tierra entre la corteza y el centro (167, 525)

map/mapa modelo o representación de la superficie de la Tierra (34)

mass/masa la cantidad de materia de que está hecho algo; su valor no cambia con la posición del objeto (24)

mass movement/movimiento de masa el movimiento cuesta abajo de cualquier material (316)

mechanical weathering/acción geológica atmosférica mecánica la desintegración de las rocas a trozos más pequeños por medios físicos (246)

Mercator projection/proyección de Mercator mapa de proyección que resulta cuando los contenidos del globo se transfieren a un cilindro (41)

mesosphere/mesosfera literalmente, la "esfera media" – la parte inferior, rígida, del manto entre la astenosfera y el centro exterior (169); también es la capa más fría de la atmósfera (396)

metamorphic rock/roca metamórfica roca que se forma cuando la textura o la composición de la roca pre-existente cambia a causa del calor o la presión (84)

meteor/meteoro rayo de luz causado cuando el polvo de un meteoroide o de un cometa se quema en la atmósfera de la Tierra antes de llegar al suelo (560)

meteorite/meteorito un meteoroide que llega a la superficie de la Tierra sin haberse consumido por completo (560)

meteoroid/meteoroide un cuerpo rocoso, muy pequeño, que da vueltas alrededor del sol (560)

meteorology/meteorología el estudio de la totalidad de la atmósfera (8)

meter/metro la unidad básica de longitud en el sistema SI (23)

microclimate/microclima una pequeña región con características climáticas únicas (466)

mid-ocean ridge/dorsal intra-oceánica una larga cadena de montañas que se forma en el fondo del océano, donde se separan las placas tectónicas; usualmente se extiende a lo largo del centro de las cuencas oceánicas (175, 339)

mineral/mineral sólido inorgánico con estructura cristalina que se forma naturalmente (60)

model/modelo representación de un objeto o sistema (19)

Moho/Moho lugar dentro de la Tierra donde la velocidad de las ondas sísmicas aumenta en gran forma; marca el límite entre la corteza terrestre y el manto (211)

mold/molde cavidad en el suelo o la roca donde estaba enterrado un animal o una planta (148)

monocline/monoclinal pliegue en las capas de roca sedimentaria en que las capas son horizontales a ambos lados del pliegue (182)

month/mes aproximadamente, la cantidad de tiempo en que la luna completa una vez la órbita de la Tierra (482)

moon/luna el satélite natural de un planeta (549)

mudflow/alud de fango el movimiento rápido de una gran masa de roca o barro y tierra mezclado con una gran cantidad de agua, que fluye cuesta abajo (318)

N

NASA/NASA Administración Nacional de Aeronáutica y del Espacio; fundada para combinar todos los equipos separados dedicados al desarrollo de cohetes en los Estados Unidos (599)

natural gas/gas natural un combustible fósil gaseoso (112)

natural resource/recurso natural cualquier sustancia natural; organismo, o forma de energía que usan los seres vivientes (108)

neap tides/mareas muertas mareas con rangos diarios mínimos que ocurren durante la luna creciente y la luna menguante (380)

nebula/nebulosa una gran nube de polvo y gas en el espacio interestelar; el lugar donde se forman las estrellas (510, 584)

nekton/necton los organismos en el océano que nadan en forma independiente (342)

neutron star/estrella de neutrón estrella en la que todas las partículas se han vuelto neutrones; restos de una supernova comprimida (581)

nonfoliated/no foliada la textura de la roca metamórfica en la que los granos de mineral no muestran ninguna alineación (98)

nonpoint-source pollution/polución con punto de orígen contaminación que viene de muchas fuentes y cuyo origen no se puede trazar a puntos específicos (285, 352)

nonrenewable resource/recurso no renovable un recurso natural que no se puede remplazar, o que puede remplazarse solamente después de miles o millones de años (109)

nonsilicate mineral/mineral no silíceo mineral que no contiene compuestos de silicio y oxígeno (63)

normal fault/falla normal falla en la que la pared colgante se mueve hacia abajo en relación con la pared baja (183)

nuclear energy/energía nuclear forma de energía asociada con los cambios en el núcleo de un átomo; un recurso energético alternativo (118)

nuclear fusion/fusión nuclear proceso por el cual dos o más núcleos con masas pequeñas se unen, o se fusionan, para formar un núcleo más grande y masivo, y para producir energía (521)

O

observation/observación usar cualquiera de los sentidos para reunir información (14)

oceanography/oceanografía el estudio del océano (7)

ocean trench/zanja oceánica una fractura aparentemente sin fondo en la cuenca profunda del océano, que se forma cuando una placa oceánica se ve forzada a deslizarse bajo una placa continental u otra placa oceánica (339)

Oort cloud/nube Oort región esférica del espacio que rodea el sistema solar en la que los cometas distantes dan vuelta alrededor del sol (558)

open cluster/agrupación abierta grupo de estrellas que en general están situadas a lo largo del disco espiral de una galaxia (584)

orbit/órbita la trayectoria elíptica seguida por un cuerpo al viajar alrededor de otro cuerpo en el espacio; el mismo movimiento (515)

orbital velocity/velocidad orbital la velocidad y dirección en que debe viajar un cohete para permanecer en órbita alrededor de la Tierra (601)

ore/mena un depósito de minerales lo suficientemente grande y puro para que se explote con ganancia (70)

outer core/núcleo exterior la capa líquida del centro de la Tierra situada bajo el manto, que envuelve el interior del centro (169)

oxidation/oxidación una reacción química en la cual un elemento se combina con oxígeno para formar un óxido (251)

ozone/ozono molécula de gas formada por tres átomos de oxígeno y que absorbe la radiación ultravioleta del sol (395)

P

parallax/paralaje cambio aparente en la posición de un objeto cuando se mira desde posiciones diferentes (575)

parent rock/ roca madre, la roca que da origen a la tierra (255)

pelagic environment/ambiente pelágico el volumen completo de agua en el océano y los organismos marinos que viven sobre el fondo del océano; también se conoce como el medio ambiente marino (345)

period/período la tercera divisió del tiempo geológico (153)

period of revolution/período de translación el tiempo que lleva para que un cuerpo celeste complete una órbita, o revolución, alrededor de otro cuerpo en el espacio (515, 539)

period of rotation/período de rotación el tiempo que lleva para que un ojeto rote una vuelta completa (539)

permeability/permeabilidad la capacidad de la roca de dejar pasar el agua a través de sí misma (280)

permineralization/permineralización proceso en que los minerales llenan los espacios de los poros en los tejidos de un organismo (146)

petrification/petrificación proceso en el que los tejidos de un organismo son completamente remplazados por minerales (146)

petroleum/petróleo crudo mezcla aceitosa de compuestos orgánicos inflamables de los que se separan los combustibles fósiles líquidos y otros productos (111)

phases/fases las diferentes maneras en que aparece la luna según la cantidad de luz solar que recibe el lado de la luna que se enfrenta a la Tierra; los resultados de las posiciones relativas cambiantes de la luna, la Tierra y el sol (551)

photosphere/fotosfera la capa del sol al punto en que los gases se vuelven lo suficientemente densos para ser visibles; la superficie del sol (519)

planetesimal/planetesimal los pequeñísimos bloques que constituyen los planetas, que se forman al juntarse y crecer las partículas de polvo (512)

plankton/plancton organismos microscópicos que flotan en la superficie del océano o cerca de ella (342)

plate tectonics/tectónica de placas la teoría de que la litosfera de la Tierra está dividida en placas tectónicas que se mueven sobre la astenosfera (177)

point-source pollution/polución con punto de orígen contaminación que viene de una fuente en un área en particular (285)

polar easterlies/vientos polares del este cinturones de viento que se extienden desde los polos a 60 grados de latitud en ambos hemisferios (405)

polar zone/zona polar las zonas climáticas más al norte y más al sur (464)

porosity/porosidad la cantidad de espacio abierto entre las partículas individuales de roca (280)

precipitation/precipitación agua sólida o líquida que cae del aire a la Tierra (335, 428)

prevailing winds/vientos dominantes vientos que soplan principalmente de una dirección (455)

primary pollutants/contaminantes primarios contaminantes puestos en el aire por la actividad natural o de los humanos (409)

prime meridian/primer meridiano la línea de longitud que pasa a través de Greenwich, en Inglaterra; representa 0 grados de longitud (38)

prograde rotation/rotación prógrada la rotación contraria al movimiento de las agujas del reloj de un planeta o luna, observado desde arriba del polo norte de ese planeta (540)

psychrometer/psicrómetro instrumento usado para medir la humedad relativa (424)

pulsar/púlsar estrella de neutrón que rota y emite rápidos pulsos de luz (581)

P waves/ondas P el tipo más rápido de onda sísmica; puede pasar a través de sólidos, líquidos, y gases; también se las llama ondas de presión y ondas primarias (200)

pyroclastic material/material piroclástico fragmentos de roca creados por erupciones volcánicas explosivas (225)

Q

quasar/cuásar un objeto "casi estelar"; una fuente estelar de luz que está extremadamente alejada; una de las fuentes de energía más poderosas en el universo (585)

R

radiation/radiación energía que se transfiere en forma de ondas electromagnéticas, como la luz visible o las ondas infrarrojas (398)

radiative zone/zona radiactiva una región muy densa del sol en la que los átomos estan comprimidos tan cerca uno de otro que puede llevar millones de años para que la luz la atraviese (519)

radioactive decay/desintegración radioactiva proceso en que los isótopos radioactivos tienden a desintegrarse en isótopos estables de otros elementos (142)

radiometric dating/datación radiométrica determinar la edad absoluta de una muestra basándose en la proporción de material original a material hijo (143)

recharge zone/zona de recarga la superficie en la tierra en que el agua entra a un acuífero (281)

reclamation/recuperación proceso de volver la tierra a su condición original luego de haber completado una explotación minera (71)

recycling/reciclaje proceso por el cual los materiales usados o desechados se procesan para volver a ser usados (110)

red giant/gigante roja una estrella que se expande y que se enfría una vez que se le acaba el combustible hidrógeno (579)

reference point/punto de referencia un lugar fijo en la superficie de la Tierra desde donde se pueden describir la dirección y la posición (35)

reflecting telescope/telescopio de reflexión telescopio que usa espejos curvos para juntar y enfocar la luz (497)

refracting telescope/telescopio de refracción telescopio que usa una serie de lentes para juntar y enfocar la luz (497)

relative dating/datación relativa determinar si un objeto o un suceso es más antiguo o más moderno que otros objetos o sucesos (137)

relative humidity/humedad relativa la cantidad de humedad que contiene el aire comparada con la cantidad máxima que puede contener a una temperatura específica (423)

relief/relieve la diferencia en elevación entre los puntos más altos y más bajos de un área de la que se está trazando un mapa (47)

remote sensing/reconocimiento remoto juntar información sobre algo sin estar cerca en realidad (43)

renewable resource/recurso renovable recurso natural que puede usarse y remplazarse en un período de tiempo relativamente corto (109)

residual soil/tierra residual la tierra que permanece sobre la capa de roca de la que se formó (255)

retrograde orbit/órbita retrógrada la revolución en el sentido de las agujas del reloj de un satélite alrededor de un planeta, observada de arriba del polo norte del planeta (556)

retrograde rotation/rotación retrógrada la rotación en el sentido de las agujas del reloj de un planeta o luna, observada de arriba del polo norte del planeta o de la luna (540)

reverse fault/falla inversa falla en que la pared colgante se mueve hacia arriba con respecto a la pared baja (183)

revolution/translación el movimiento elíptico de un cuerpo celeste al hacer órbita alrededor de otro cuerpo en el espacio (515, 539)

rift/falla profunda fractura que se forma entre las placas tectónicas al separarse éstas (232)

rift valley/valle de grietas valle que se forma en una zona de fisura entre placas tectónicas que se separan (339)

right ascension/ascensión recta medida de la distancia al este de un objeto desde el punto en el que aparece el sol el primer día de primavera (492)

rock/roca una mezcla sólida de cristales de un mineral o más, o de otros materiales (80)

rock cycle/ciclo de la roca el proceso por el que un tipo de roca se convierte en otro tipo de roca (82)

rocket/cohete máquina que usa el escape de gas para moverse (598)

rock fall/desprendimiento de rocas grupo de rocas que se desprenden y caen por una cuesta empinada (317)

rotation/rotación el movimiento giratorio de un cuerpo sobre su eje (515, 539)

S

salinity/salinidad la medida de la cantidad de sales y otros sólidos disueltos en una cantidad de líquido dada (332)

saltation/saltación movimiento de partículas del tamaño de granos de arena por una acción de rebote en la dirección en que sopla el viento (304)

satellite/satélite un cuerpo natural o artificial que da vueltas alrededor de un planeta (549)

scientific method/método científico serie de pasos que usan los científicos para encontrar respuestas para preguntas y soluciones para problemas (13)

sea-floor spreading/expansión de los fondos oceánicos el proceso por el que se forman nuevas litosferas oceánicas en las cordilleras en el medio del océano cuando los materiales más antiguos se separan de las cordilleras (175)

seamount/monte de mar montaña individual formada por materiales volcánicos en la llanura abisal (339)

secondary pollutants/contaminantes secundarios contaminantes que se forman por reacciones químicas que ocurren cuando los contaminantes primarios entran en contacto con sustancias que ocurren naturalmente, como el vapor de agua (409)

sedimentary rock/roca sedimentaria roca que se forma cuando los sedimentos se comprimen y se cementan (84)

seismic gap/brecha sísmica área a lo largo de una falla donde han ocurrido relativamente pocos terremotos (207)

seismic waves/ondas sísmicas ondas de energía que se trasladan a través de la Tierra (200)

seismogram/sismograma trazado del movimiento de un terremoto creado por un sismógrafo (202)

seismograph/sismógrafo instrumento colocado en la superficie de la tierra o cerca de ella, que registra las ondas sísmicas (202)

seismology/sismología el estudio de los terremotos (196)

septic tank/tanque séptico un tanque grande, subterráneo, que junta y limpia las aguas servidas de una casa (287)

sewage treatment plant/planta de tratamiento de aguas de cloaca fábrica que limpia materiales de desecho del agua que viene de las cloacas o los caños (286)

shadow zone/zona de sombra área en la superficie de la Tierra donde no se pueden detectar ondas sísmicas directas de un terremoto dado (211)

shield volcano/volcán en escudo un volcán grande, con cuestas poco empinadas, que se forma con erupciones no explosivas repetidas de lava (228)

shoreline/zona litoral el límite entre la costa y una masa de agua (298)

silica/sílice compuesto de átomos de silicio y oxígeno (224)

silicate mineral/mineral silíceo mineral que contiene una combinación de los elementos silicio y oxígeno (62)

smog/smog niebla fotoquímica producida por la reacción de la luz solar y los contaminantes en el aire (117)

soil/suelo mezcla suelta de pequeños fragmentos de minerales y materia orgánica (255)

soil conservation/conservación del suelo los varios métodos por los cuales los humanos cuidan la tierra (259)

solar eclipse/eclipse solar incidente en el cual la sombra de la luna se proyecta sobre la superficie de la Tierra (552)

solar energy/energía solar energía del sol (119)

solar nebula/nebulosa solar nébula que se formó dentro del sistema solar (511)

solar system/sistema solar sistema compuesto del sol (una estrella) y de planetas y otros cuerpos celestes que se trasladan alrededor del sol (510)

space probe/sonda espacial vehículo que lleva instrumentos científicos a los planetas o a otros cuerpos en el espacio (606)

space shuttle/transbordador espacial vehículo que puede volverse a usar que despega como un cohete y aterriza como un avión (613)

space station/estación espacial una plataforma que está en órbita por un tiempo largo, de la que se pueden lanzar otros vehículos o donde se puede hacer investigación científica (614)

specific gravity/gravedad específica la razón de la densidad de un objeto a la densidad del agua (66)

spectrum/espectro el arco iris de colores que se produce cuando la luz blanca pasa a través de un prisma o espectrógrafo (570)

spiral galaxy/galaxia espiral galaxia con un bulto en el centro y brazos espirales muy distintivos (582)

spring tides/aguas vivas mareas con rangos diarios máximos que ocurren durante la luna nueva y la luna llena (380)

station model/modelo de estación un pequeño círculo que muestra la posición de una estación meteorológica junto con un grupo de símbolos y números que lo rodean que representan información sobre el tiempo (442)

storm surge/oleada de tormenta una subida local en el nivel del mar cerca de la costa causada por los vientos fuertes de una tormenta, como un huracán (377)

strata/estratos capas de roca sedimentaria que se forman del depósito de sedimentos (91)

stratification/estratificación las capas de roca sedimentaria que se superponen (94)

stratified drift/sedimento estratificado material rocoso que ha sido dividido y depositado en capas por el agua que fluye del hielo derretido de un glaciar (314)

stratosphere/estratosfera la capa atmosférica sobre la troposfera (395)

stratus clouds/nubes estratos nubes que se forman en capas (426)

streak/color de la raya el color de un mineral en polvo (65)

stress/exfuerzo la cantidad de fuerza por unidad de área que se ejerce sobre un material dado (181)

strike-slip fault/falla de desplazamiento horizontal falla en la que los dos bloques de falla se mueven más allá uno de otro en forma horizontal (184)

strip mining/minería a cielo abierto proceso en que la roca y la tierra se quitan de la superficie de la Tierra para exponer los materiales que están abajo que van a ser extraídos (115)

subduction zone/zona de subducción la región donde una placa oceánica se hunde en la astenosfera en un límite convergente, usualmente entre las placas continentales y las oceánicas (178)

sunspot/mancha solar área en la fotosfera del sol que es más fría que las áreas que la rodean, y parece una mancha oscura (523)

supernova/supernova la muerte de una estrella grande causada por una explosión (580)

superposition/superposición principio que establece que las rocas más nuevas descansan sobre rocas más antiguas en secuencias inalteradas (137)

surf/oleaje área entre la rompiente y la costa (374)

surface current/corriente superficial movimiento de agua parecido a la corriente que ocurre en la superficie del océano o cerca de ella (365, 457)

surface gravity/gravedad de la superficie el porcentaje de tu peso en la Tierra que experimentarías en otro planeta; el peso que experimentarías en otro planeta (539)

S waves/ondas S el tipo de onda sísmica que está en segundo lugar en cuanto a velocidad; no puede trasladarse a través de materiales completamente líquidos; también conocidas como ondas cortantes y ondas secundarias (200)

swells/marejada olas ondulantes que se mueven en una procesión estable a través del océano (375)

syncline/sinclinal un pliegue con forma de hondonada en las capas de roca sedimentaria (182)

T

tectonic plate/tectónica de placas un trozo de la litosfera que se mueve sobre la astenosfera (170)

telescope/telescopio instrumento que junta radiación electromagnética del cielo y la concentra para mejor observación (496)

temperate zone/zona templada la zona climática entre los trópicos y la zona polar (462)

temperature/temperatura medida de cuán caliente o frío es algo (25)

tension/tensión la clase de presión que ocurre cuando las fuerzas actúan para estirar un objeto (181)

terrestrial planets/planetas terrestres los planetas pequeños, densos y rocosos del interior del sistema solar (539)

texture/textura el tamaño, la forma y la posición de los granos que forman la roca (86)

theory/teoría explicación unificadora para una variedad de hipótesis y observaciones que han sido apoyadas con la experimentación (19)

thermocline/termoclino una capa de agua del océano que se extiende entre 300 m y aproximadamente 700 m bajo el nivel del mar en que la temperatura del agua baja con más rapidez al aumentar la profundidad de lo que lo hace en otras zonas del océano (333)

thermometer/termómetro instrumento usado para medir la temperatura del aire (440)

thermosphere/termosfera la capa superior de la atmosfera (396)

thrust/propulsión la fuerza que acelera un cohete (600)

thunder/trueno el sonido que resulta de la rápida expansión de aire a lo largo de un rayo (435)

thunderstorms/tormentas sistemas de tormentas pequeños e intensos que producen vientos fuertes, lluvia torrencial, relámpagos, y truenos (434)

tidal bore/oleada masa de agua que avanza a través de una bahía, un estuario o canal de río pequeños durante la subida de la marea alta, causando una subida muy súbita de la marea (381)

tidal range/rango de marea la diferencia entre los niveles del agua del océano durante la marea alta y la marea baja (380)

tides/mareas movimientos diarios del agua del océano que cambian el nivel de la superficie (378)

till/sedimento desordenado materia rocosa no separada, depositada directamente por el hielo glacial cuando se derrite (315)

topographic map/plano topográfico mapa que muestra los accidentes geográficos de la Tierra (46)

topsoil/capa superior del suelo la capa exterior de tierra que generalmente contiene el humus (256)

tornado/tornado una columna de aire pequeña y rotativa que tiene vientos de alta velocidad y presión central baja y que toca la tierra (436)

trace fossil/fósil vestigio cualquier evidencia de la actividad de un animal que se ha preservado naturalmente (148)

trade winds/vientos alisios los vientos que soplan entre los 30 grados de latitud y el ecuador (404)

transform boundary/límite transformante el límite entre dos placas tectónicas que se deslizan horizontalmente (179)

transported soil/tierra transportada la tierra que ha sido arrastrada por viento o por agua lejos de su roca original (255)

tributary/tributario una corriente o un río más pequeño que desemboca en uno más grande (272)

tropical zone/zona tropical la zona cálida situada alrededor del ecuador (459)

troposphere/troposfera la capa más baja de la atmósfera (395)

trough/seno el punto más bajo de una ola (372)

true north/norte real el Polo Norte geográfico (36)

tsunami/tsunami una ola que se forma cuando un gran volumen de agua del océano súbitamente se mueve hacia abajo o hacia arriba (376)

U

unconformity/disconformidad superficie que representa una parte de la columna geologica que falta en una secuencia de capas rocosas (140)

uniformitarianism/uniformismo principio que establece que los mismos procesos geológicos que hoy en día dan forma a la Tierra han estado presentes a través de la historia de la Tierra (134)

upwelling/corriente ascendente proceso en el cual el agua fría y llena de nutrientes de las profundidades del océano sube a la superficie y remplaza el agua cálida de la superficie (371)

U-shaped valley/valle con forma de U valle que se forma cuando un glaciar erosiona un valle de su forma original en V a una U (313)

V

vent/respiradero agujero en la corteza terrestre a través del cual sube el magma a la superficie (224)

volcano/volcán montaña que se forma cuando la roca derretida, llamada magma, es forzada a la superficie de la Tierra (222)

volume/volumen la cantidad de espacio que ocupa algo, o la cantidad de espacio que algo contiene (23)

W

water cycle/ciclo hidrológico el movimiento continuo del agua de fuentes de agua al aire, a la tierra, adentro y arriba del suelo, y de vuelta a las fuentes; ciclo que une a toda el agua de la Tierra, en su forma sólida, líquida, y gaseosa (270, 335, 422)

watershed/cuenca el terreno drenado por un sistema fluvial, que incluye el río principal y todos sus afluentes (272)

water table/nivel hidrostático un límite subterráneo donde la zona de aireación y la zona de saturación se unen (280)

wave height/altitud de onda la distancia vertical entre la cresta de una ola y su seno (372)

wavelength/longitud de onda dos crestas o senos de onda adyacentes (372)

wave period/período de onda el tiempo entre el pasaje de dos crestas (o senos) de onda por un punto fijo (373)

weather/tiempo atmosférico la condición de la atmósfera en un momento y lugar específicos (422, 452)

weather forecast/pronóstico meteorológico predicción de las condiciones futuras del tiempo para los próximos 3 a 5 días (440)

weathering/acción geológica atmosférica la desintegración de la roca en trozos cada vez más pequeños por medios mecánicos o químicos (246)

westerlies/vientos del oeste cinturones de viento que se encuentran en los hemisferios norte y sur entre 30 y 60° (405)

whitecap/cabrilla una ola con cresta blanca, espumosa, y muy profunda, que rompe en el océano abierto antes de acercarse a la costa (375)

white dwarf/enana blanca una estrella pequeña y caliente que se acerca al final de su vida; el centro que queda de una estrella antigua (578)

wind/viento aire en movimiento (402)

wind energy/energía eólica energía que se encuentra en el viento (122)

windsock/manga de viento aparato que se usa para medir la dirección del viento (441)

wind vane/veleta aparato usado para medir la dirección del viento (441)

Y

year/año el tiempo que toma para que la Tierra recorra una vez la órbita del sol (482)

Z

zenith/zenit punto imaginario en el cielo directamente sobre un observador en la Tierra (491)

INDEX

INDEX

INDEX

CREDITS

Credits

Abbreviations used: (t) top, (c) center, (b) bottom, (l) left, (r) right, (bkgd) background

ILLUSTRATIONS

All work, unless otherwise noted, contributed by Holt, Rinehart & Winston.

Table of Contents: Page ix(tr), MapQuest.com; ix(bl), Uhl Studios, Inc.; x(t), Patrick Gnan; xi(tl), Mike Wepplo/Das Group; xi(bl), Marty Roper/Planet Rep; xii(cl), Yuan Lee; xii(bl), Marty Roper/Planet Rep; xiv(tl), Marty Roper/Planet Rep; xv(tl), Paul DiMare; xv(cr), Dan McGeehan/Koralick Associates.

Chapter One: Page 4(br), Barbara Hoopes-Ambler; 7(br), Craig Attebery/Jeff Lavaty Artist Agent; 9(b), David Schleinkofer; 10(tl), Robert Hynes; 12(b), Barbara Hoopes-Ambler; 14, Carlyn Iverson; 15, Carlyn Iverson; 16(tl, cl), Carlyn Iverson; 16-17(b), Christy Krames, 18, Uhl Studios, Inc.; 19(br), Stephen Durke/Washington Artists; 20(c), Jared Schneidman Design; 25(tr), Stephen Durke/Washington Artists; 26(c), Christy Krames; 28(cr), Geoff Smith/Scott Hull; 29(tr), Sidney Jablonski; 30(c), Uhl Studios, Inc.

Chapter Two: Page 35(bl), John White/The Neis Group; 37, MapQuest.com; 38(tl), MapQuest.com; 39(t), MapQuest.com; 41, MapQuest.com; 42, MapQuest.com.

Chapter Three: Page 60(bl), Gary Locke; 61, Stephen Durke/Washington Artists; 68-69(bkgd), Uhl Studios, Inc.; 70(bl), Jared Schneidman Design.

Chapter Four: Page 82-83, Uhl Studios, Inc.; 85(b), Sidney Jablonski; 87, Keith Locke; 88(l), Uhl Studios, Inc.; 89(b), Uhl Studios, Inc.; 92(bl), Robert Hynes; 96(b), Uhl Studios, Inc.; 97(t), Stephen Durke/Washington Artists; 97(b), Uhl Studios, Inc.; 100(br), Sidney Jablonski; 103(cr), Sidney Jablonski.

Chapter Five: Page 106(tl), Uhl Studios, Inc.; 108(b), Uhl Studios, Inc.; 113(bl), Uhl Studios, Inc.; 114(l), Uhl Studios, Inc.; 115(t), MapQuest.com; 118(cl), Stephen Durke/Washington Artists; 121(tr), John Huxtable/Black Creative; 125(br), Uhl Studios, Inc.; 126(br), John Huxtable/Black Creative; 126(cr), Uhl Studios, Inc.; 129(cr), Sidney Jablonski.

Chapter Six: Page 132(t), Nenad Jakesevic; 134(b), Uhl Studios, Inc.; 136(c), Barbara Hoopes-Ambler; 138(b), Jared Schneidman Design; 139, Uhl Studios, Inc.; 140(b), Jared Schneidman Design; 141, Uhl Studios, Inc.; 142(b), Stephen Durke/Washington-Artists' Represents; 147(br), Will Nelson/Sweet Reps; 148-149(c), Frank Ordaz; 150(cr), Uhl Studios, Inc.; 159(tr), Joe LeMonnier.

Unit Three: Page 163(cr), Terry Kovalcik.

Chapter Seven: Page 166(b), Uhl Studios, Inc.; 167(br), Uhl Studios, Inc.; 168-169, Uhl Studios, Inc.; 170(c), Uhl Studios, Inc.; 171(c), Uhl Studios, Inc.; 172(tl), Uhl Studios, Inc.; 173(tr), Uhl Studios, Inc.; 173(bl), MapQuest.com; 174, MapQuest.com; 175, Uhl Studios, Inc.; 176(cl), Stephen Durke/Washington Artists; 176(cr), Uhl Studios, Inc.; 177(b), Uhl Studios, Inc.; 178-179(b), Uhl Studios, Inc.; 182(tl), Uhl Studios, Inc.; 183(tr), Marty Roper/Planet Rep; 183(cr), Uhl Studios, Inc.; 183(br), Uhl Studios, Inc.; 185(tr), Uhl Studios, Inc.; 186(t), Tony Morse/Ivy Glick; 186(bl), Uhl Studios, Inc.; 188, Uhl Studios, Inc.; 189(cr), Marty Roper/Planet Rep.

Chapter Eight: Page 194(tr), Tony Morse/Ivy Glick; 196(b), MapQuest.com; 197(b), Uhl Studios, Inc.; 198(b), Uhl Studios, Inc.; 198-199, Uhl Studios, Inc.; 200, Uhl Studios, Inc.; 201(cl), Uhl Studios, Inc.; 202(bl), Uhl Studios, Inc.; 203(tr), Sidney Jablonski; 205(b), MapQuest.com; 207(t), Jared Schneidman Design; 208, Uhl Studios, Inc.; 211(b), Uhl Studios, Inc.; 212, Sidney Jablonski; 214(br), Sidney Jablonski; 214(cl), Uhl Studios, Inc.; 216(br), Uhl Studios, Inc.; 217(cr), Sidney Jablonski.

Chapter Nine: Page 224(tl), Uhl Studios, Inc.; 228(l), Patrick Gnan; 229(tr), Uhl Studios, Inc.; 230(b), Uhl Studios, Inc.; 231(tr), Stephen Durke/Washington Artists; 231(bl), MapQuest.com; 232, Uhl Studios, Inc.; 233, Uhl Studios, Inc.; 234(t), Uhl Studios, Inc.; 239(tr), Ross, Culbert and Lavery.

Unit Four: Page 243(tl), MapQuest.com.

Chapter Ten: Page 246(b), Uhl Studios, Inc.; 248(br), Will Nelson/Sweet Reps; 249(r), Stephen Durke/Washington Artists; 252(b), Stephen Durke/Washington Artists; 253, Stephen Durke/Washington Artists; 256(r), Will Nelson/Sweet Reps; 260(t), Uhl Studios, Inc.

Chapter Eleven: Page 271, Mike Wepplo/Das Group; 272(bc), MapQuest.com; 274, Uhl Studios, Inc.; 277(b), Marty Roper/Planet Rep; 280(cl), Stephen Durke/Washington Artists; 281(c), MapQuest.com; 281(br), Geoff Smith/Scott Hull; 282, Stephen Durke/Washington Artists; 286(b), John Huxtable/Black Creative; 287(cl), John Huxtable/Black Creative; 287(b), Sidney Jablonski; 289(c), MapQuest.com; 290(c), Mike Wepplo/Das Group; 293(cr), Sidney Jablonski.

Chapter Twelve: Page 296(t), Paul DiMare; 300(bl), Uhl Studios, Inc.; 302-303, Mike Wepplo/Das Group; 304(b), Dean Fleming; 304(cl), Keith Locke; 306(bl), Geoff Smith/Scott Hull; 307(c), Uhl Studios, Inc.; 313(b), Robert Hynes; 323(tr), Sidney Jablonski.

Chapter Thirteen: Page 328(t), Rainey Kirk/The Neis Group; 331, MapQuest.com; 332(tl), Ross, Culbert and Lavery; 333(tr), MapQuest.com; 333(b), Ross, Culbert and Lavery; 335(b), Mike Wepplo/Das Group; 338–339(b), Uhl Studios, Inc.; 340(b), Uhl Studios, Inc.; 341(br), Ross, Culbert and Lavery; 342, Yuan Lee; 350(tl), Jared Schneidman Design; 353(br), Mark Heine; 357(c), Jared Schneidman Design; 358(c), Bill Mayer; 358(tr), MapQuest.com; 359(tr), Ross, Culbert and Lavery.

Chapter Fourteen: Page 362(t), John Huxtable/Black Creative; 362(bl), Tony Morse/Ivy Glick; 364(tr), Dean Fleming; 365(tr), Stephen Durke/Washington Artists; 365(bl), MapQuest.com; 366, MapQuest.com; 367(c), MapQuest.com; 368, Stephen Durke/Washington Artists; 369, Jared Schneidman Design; 370, MapQuest.com; 372, Jared Schneidman Design; 373, Jared Schneidman Design; 374, Dean Fleming; 376(tc), Uhl Studios, Inc.; 377(t), MapQuest.com; 378(c), Marty Roper/Planet Rep; 379, Sidney Jablonski; 380, Sidney Jablonski; 382(br), Dean Fleming; 382(c), Stephen Durke/Washington Artists; 383(c), Marty Roper/Planet Rep; 385(cr), Sidney Jablonski

Unit Six: Page 388(bl), John Huxtable/Black Creative; 388(br), Annie Bissett; 389(cl), Terry Kovalcik.

Chapter Fifteen: Page 392(b), Sidney Jablonski; 393(br), Stephen Durke/Washington Artists; 394(b), Stephen Durke/Washington Artists; 395(c), Stephen Durke/Washington Artists; 396, Stephen Durke/Washington Artists; 398(b), Uhl Studios, Inc.; 399(b), Uhl Studios, Inc.; 400(c), John Huxtable/Black Creative; 402(bl), Uhl Studios, Inc.; 402(bl), Stephen Durke/Washington Artists; 403(tr), Uhl Studios, Inc.; 403(tr), Stephen Durke/Washington Artists; 404(b), Uhl Studios, Inc.; 404(b), Stephen Durke/Washington Artists; 406, Stephen Durke/Washington Artists; 407, Stephen Durke/Washington Artists; 409(b), John Huxtable/Black Creative; 415(c), Stephen Durke/Washington Artists.

Chapter Sixteen: Page 422(b), Robert Hynes; 427(b), Stephen Durke/Washington Artists; 428(tl), Stephen Durke/Washington Artists; 430(b), MapQuest.com; 432, Stephen Durke/Washington Artists; 433, Stephen Durke/Washington Artists; 435(br), Paul DiMare; 438(b), Paul DiMare; 440(tr), Dan McGeehan/Koralick Associates; 443(cr), MapQuest.com; 447(cr), MapQuest.com.

Chapter Seventeen: Page 450(tr), Will Nelson/Sweet Reps; 453(br), Uhl Studios, Inc.; 453(br), Stephen Durke/Washington Artists; 454(c), Craig Attebery/Jeff Lavaty Artist Agent; 455(tc), Stephen Durke/Washington Artists; 456(b), Uhl Studios, Inc.; 457(c), MapQuest.com; 458(cl), Stephen Durke/Washington Artists; 458(b), MapQuest.com; 459(tr), Stephen Durke/Washington Artists; 459(c), MapQuest.com; 462(tr), Stephen Durke/Washington Artists; 462(c), MapQuest.com; 464(bl), Stephen Durke/Washington Artists; 465(t), MapQuest.com; 467(bl), MapQuest.com; 467(tr), Marty Roper/Planet Rep; 468, Sidney Jablonski; 469(c), Uhl Studios, Inc.; 469(br), MapQuest.com; 470(b), Marty Roper/Planet Rep; 472(t), Craig Attebery/Jeff Lavaty Artist Agent; 472(cr), Stephen Durke/Washington Artists; 474(tr), Terry Kovalcik; 475(cr), Sidney Jablonski.

Chapter Eighteen: Page 483(t), Nenad Jakesevic; 486, Dan McGeehan/Koralick Associates; 489, Stephen Durke/Washington Artists; 490(c), Sidney Jablonski; 491(tr), Stephen Durke/Washington Artists; 492(t), Sidney Jablonski; 493(b), Stephen Durke/Washington Artists; 495, Paul DiMare; 497, Uhl Studios, Inc.

Chapter Nineteen: Page 508(l), Stephen Durke/Washington Artists; 511(c), Stephen Durke/Washington Artists; 512-513, Paul DiMare; 515(c), Sidney Jablonski; 516(t), Mark Heine; 516(br), Sidney Jablonski; 518(c), Sidney Jablonski; 519(br), Uhl Studios, Inc.; 520, Marty Roper/Planet Rep; 521(c), Marty Roper/Planet Rep; 521(b), Stephen Durke/Washington Artists; 522, Stephen Durke/Washington Artists; 523(b), Sidney Jablonski; 525, Uhl Studios, Inc.; 526(bl), Paul DiMare; 527(tr), Paul DiMare; 529(br), Uhl Studios, Inc.

Chapter Twenty: Page 536(tl), Uhl Studios, Inc.; 538(b), Sidney Jablonski; 539(tr), Sidney Jablonski; 544(tl), Sidney Jablonski; 546(b), Sidney Jablonski; 547(tr), Dan McGeehan/Koralick Associates; 548(cl), Paul DiMare; 550, Stephen Durke/Washington Artists; 551(c), Sidney Jablonski; 552(c), Paul DiMare; 553(c), Paul DiMare; 558(tl), Stephen Durke/Washington Artists; 558(br), Paul DiMare; 559, Craig Attebery/Jeff Lavaty Artist Agent; 562(br), Sidney Jablonski; 563(c), Stephen Durke/Washington Artists.

Chapter Twenty-One: Page 568(br), Craig Attebery/Jeff Lavaty Artist Agent; 571(c), Stephen Durke/Washington Artists; 572(tl), Stephen Durke/Washington Artists; 575(c), Sidney Jablonski; 576(tl), Sidney Jablonski; 576(c), Stephen Durke/Washington Artists; 578-579, Stephen Durke/Washington Artists; 587(br), Craig Attebery/Jeff Lavaty Artist Agent; 589(r), Craig Attebery/Jeff Lavaty Artist Agent; 593(cr), Sidney Jablonski.

796 Credits

Chapter Twenty-Two: Page 599(b), Stephen Durke/Washington Artists; 600(l), John Huxtable/Black Creative; 603(br), Stephen Durke/Washington Artists; 606, Stephen Durke/Washington Artists; 607, Stephen Durke/Washington Artists; 608, Stephen Durke/Washington Artists; 609(b), Craig Attebery/Jeff Lavaty Artist Agent; 609(tr), Stephen Durke/Washington Artists; 609(br), Stephen Durke/Washington Artists; 611(tl), Paul DiMare; 617(c), Paul DiMare.

LabBook: Page 631(tr), Mark Heine; 632(cl), Marty Roper/Planet Rep; 640(br), Mark Heine; 645, Mark Heine; 648(br), Mark Heine; 650(c), Uhl Studios, Inc.; 662(c), Sidney Jablonski; 663(c), MapQuest.com; 664(b), MapQuest.com; 666(t), Marty Roper/Planet Rep; 667(tr), Ralph Garafola/ Lorraine Garafola Represents; 671(t), Mark Heine; 673(tr), Mark Heine; 680(cr), Dean Fleming; 683(br), Geoff Smith/Scott Hull; 686(b), Mark Heine; 687(b), Sidney Jablonski; 691(tr), Mark Heine; 693(tr), Mark Heine; 696(t), MapQuest.com; 698(tl), Dan McGeehan/Koralick Associates; 698(br), Mark Heine; 701(cr), Marty Roper/Planet Rep; 704(br), Sidney Jablonski; 704(cr), MapQuest.com; 705(tl), Sidney Jablonski; 705(tr), MapQuest.com; 705(cl), Sidney Jablonski; 705(cr), MapQuest.com; 706(b), Sidney Jablonski; 708(cr), Sidney Jablonski; 712, Marty Roper/Planet Rep; 723(tr), Geoff Smith/Scott Hull.

Appendix: Page 729(cl), Blake Thornton/Rita Marie; 732(c), Terry Guyer; 736(b), Mark Mille/Sharon Langley; 744, Kristy Sprott; 745, Kristy Sprott; 746(bl), Stephen Durke/Washington Artists; 747(tl), Stephen Durke/Washington Artists; 747(c), Stephen Durke/Washington Artists; 747(b), Bruce Burdick; 752-753, Sidney Jablonski.

PHOTOGRAPHY

Cover and Title Page: (tl), Jack Dykinga/Tony Stone Images; (tr), Barry Rosenthal/FPG International; (bl), David Parker/Science Photo Library/Photo Researchers, Inc.; (Earth on cover, title page), Geospace/Science Photo Library/Photo Researchers, Inc., (owl on cover, spine, back, title page), Kim Taylor/Bruce Coleman, Inc.

Sam Dudgeon/HRW Photo: Page v(br), vi(bl), vii(cl), viii(tl), ix(cl), xi(tr), xiii(cl), xiv(bl), xvii(cl), xviii(br), xx, 5, 23(cl), 35(tr), 38(bl), 46(tr), 59(b), 60, 62(cr), 65(tr, bl), 66(bl), 67(tc, cl), 68(c), 69(b), 73(cl), 74(tl), 84, 85(c), 86(cl), 92(c), 95(cl), 97(brt), 98(cl, bl, bc), 105(c), 107, 110(tr), 117(cr, c), 119(b), 124(tl), 135(tl, br, tr, bl), 137(bl), 143(all), 164(tr, tl), 181(c), 195, 209(tr), 210(br), 244(tl, cr, tr, bc), 266, 269(br), 288(bl), 297, 316(bc, br), 329(tl, tr), 391, 395(bc), 412, 421, 423, 424, 429(br), 440, 451, 499(radio, oven), 508(joggers), 509, 569(br), 577(cl), 588(all), 597, 624(cl, tr, br), 626, 627(bc), 628(br, cl), 629(tl, b), 633, 634, 635, 637, 639(hematite, br), 641(tr, br), 642, 643(all), 646(tr), 647(all), 649, 651, 656, 658, 659, 661(all), 664(tr), 667, 668, 669(bl), 676, 678, 679, 681, 682, 689, 690, 692, 693, 699, 702, 707, 713, 714, 716, 717, 719, 720, 721, 725, 729(br, tr), 733(br).

Table of Contents: Page v(tr), E. R. Degginger/Color-Pic, Inc; v(cr), K. Segerstrom/USGS; vi(tl), Jean Miele/The Stock Market; vii(tr), Mike Husar/ DRK Photo; vii(bl), Walter H. Hodge/Peter Arnold, Inc.; viii(cr), Thomas R. Taylor/Photo Researchers, Inc.; viii(bl), American Museum of Natural History; x(tl), Tom Bean/DRK Photo; x(bl), Tom Walker/Tony Stone Images; xii(tr), James B. Wood; xii(bl), Norbert Wu; xii(bc), James Wilson/Woodfin Camp & Associates; xiii(tl), TOMS/NASA; xv(bl), World Perspective/Tony Stone Images; xvi(tl), I M House/Tony Stone Images; xvi(bl, bc), NASA; xix, Peter Van Steen/HRW Photo; xxi(br), G.R. Roberts Photo Library.

Unit One: Page 2(tl), Ed Reschke/Peter Arnold, Inc.; 2(tr), Uwe Fink/ University of Arizona, Department of Planetary Sciences, Lunar & Planetary Laboratory; 2(cr), USGS; 2(bl), Smithsonian Air and Space Museum; 2(tl), T.A. Wiewandt/DRK Photo; 3(tl), Hulton Getty Images/Liaison Agency; 3(tr), Adam Woolfitt/British Museum/Woodfin Camp & Assocites, Inc.; 3(cl), Francois Gohier; 3(bl), Jason Laure/Woodfin Camp & Associates, Inc.; 3(br), NASA.

Chapter One: Page 4(inset), Dr. David Gillette; 4(t), Peter Van Steen/HRW Photo; 6(bl), S. Schwabe/The Rob Palmer Blue Holes Foundation; 6(tr), Earth Imaging/Tony Stone Images; 8(tl), Marit Jentof-Nilsen and Fritz Hasler—NASA Goddard Laboratory for Atmospheres; 8(bl), Howard B. Bluestein; 9(tr), Jean Miele/The Stock Market; 10(bc, br), Andy Christiansen/HRW Photo; 11(tr), Mark Howard/Westfall Eco Images; 11(cr), Annie Griffiths/Corbis; 15(tr), Brian Parker/Tom Stack & Associates; 17, Paul Fraughton/HRW Photo; 19(tr), NASA; 21, Victoria Smith/HRW Photo; 23(tr), Otis Imboden/National Geographic Image Collection; 23(cr), Alan Schein/The Stock Market; 24(tl), Andy Christiansen/HRW Photo; 24(bl, br), Peter Van Steen/HRW Photo; 28(cl), Visuals Unlimited/Ken Lucas; 31(tl), Michael Lyon/HRW Photo; 31(br), NASA.

Chapter Two: Page 32(bkgd), USGS; 32(bl), Victor Boswell/National Geographic Society Image Collection; 32(cr), Scala/Art Resource, NY; 34, Royal Geographical Society, London ,UK./The Bridgeman Art Library; 36, Tom Van Sant/The Stock Market; 40(cl, b), Andy Christiansen/HRW Photo; 43, Aerial Images, Inc. and SOVINFORMSPUTNIK.; 44(bl), 45(br), The American Map Corporation/ADC The Map People; 46(bl), 47(bl, cr), 48, USGS; 51, Tom Van Sant/The Stock Market; 52(bl), Andy Christiansen/HRW Photo; 52(tr), Vladimir Pcholkin/FPG International; 53, USGS; 54, JPL/NASA; 55(tl), Andy Christiansen/HRW Photo; 55(br), Courtesy Lower Colorado River Authority, Austin, TX.

Unit Two: 56(tl), Science Photo Library/Photo Researchers, Inc.; 56(tr), Visuals Unlimited/Science VU; 56(bl), NASA/International Stock; 56(bc), UPI/Corbis; 56(br), Thomas Laird/Peter Arnold, Inc; 57(tr), SuperStock; 57(cr), Francois Gohier; 57(cl), AP/Wide World Photos; 57(br), NASA/Science Photo Library/Photo Researchers, Inc.

Chapter Three: Page 58(t), E. R. Degginger/Color-Pic, Inc.; 58(t), Mike Husar/DRK Photo; 59(tr), Inga Spence/Tom Stack & Associates; 61(br), Dr. Rainer Bode/Bode-Verlag Gmb; 62(bl), Pat Lanza/Bruce Coleman Inc.; 62(cl, c), E. R. Degginger/Color-Pic, Inc.; 63(top to bottom), (top four), E. R. Degginger/Color-Pic, Inc.; SuperStock; Visuals Unlimited/Ken Lucas; 64(tr), Liaison Agency; (tl), Jane Burton/Bruce Coleman, Inc.; Luster Chart (row 1), E. R. Degginger/Color-Pic, Inc.; John Cancalosi 1989/DRK Photo; (row 2), Biophoto Associates/Photo Researchers, Inc.; Dr. E. R. Degginger/Bruce Coleman Inc.; (row 3), E. R. Degginger/Color-Pic, Inc.; Biophoto Associates/Photo Researchers, Inc.; (row 4), E. R. Degginger/Color-Pic, Inc.; 65(br), Tom Pantages; 65(c), E. R. Degginger/Color-Pic, Inc.; 65(cl), Erica and Harold Van Pelt/American Museum of Natural History; 66(1), Visuals Unlimited/Ken Lucas; 66(2,4,5,6), E. R. Degginger/Color-Pic, Inc.; 66(3), Visuals Unlimited/Dane S. Johnson; 66(7), Carlyn Iverson/Absolute Science Illustration and Photography; 66(8), Mark A. Schneider/Visuals Unlimited; 66(9), Charles D. Winters/Photo Researchers, Inc.; 66(10), Bard Wrisley/Liasion Agency; 67(tl, bc), E. R. Degginger/Color-Pic, Inc.; 67(cr), Sam Dudgeon/HRW Photo Courtesy Science Stuff, Austin , TX; 67(cr), Tom Pantages Photography; 67(br), Victoria Smith/HRW Photo; 68(b), E. R. Degginger/Color-Pic, Inc.; 68(tl), Victoria Smith/HRW Photo, Courtesy Science Stuff, Austin, TX; 69(cr, t), E. R. Degginger/Color-Pic, Inc.; 70(c), Wernher Krutein/Liaison Agency; 70(inset), Kosmatsu Mining Systems; 70, Index Stock Photography, Inc.; 71, Historic Royal Palaces; 73(inset), Kosmatsu Mining Systems; 73(tr), Wernher Krutein/Liaison Agency; 74(bl), E. R. Degginger/Color-Pic, Inc.; 76(bl), Peter Menzel; 76(bl), Ralph Wetmore/Tony Stone Images.

Chapter Four: Page 78(t), Ron Ruhoff/Stock Imagery; 78(c), Kreg Photography courtesy Denver Theatres & Arenas; 79, Victoria Smith/HRW Photo; 80(c), Kenneth Garrett; 80(bc), Fergus O'Brian/FPG International; 80(br), Peter Cummings/Tom Stack & Associates; 80(bl), Historical Collections, National Museum of Health and Medicine, AFIP; 81(bl), A.F. Kersting; 81(br), Andy Christiansen/HRW Photo; 81(c), Breck P. Kent; 81(cr), NASA/Science Photo Library/Photo Researchers, Inc.; 85(granite), Pat Lanza/Bruce Coleman Inc.; 85(br,c), E. R. Degginger/Color-Pic, Inc.; 85(cl), Walter H. Hodge/Peter Arnold; 85(bl), Sp. Harry Taylor/Dorling Kindersley; 85(bc), Breck P. Kent; 86(c), Dorling Kindersley; 86(cr bc), Breck P. Kent; 88(br), E. R. Degginger/Color-Pic, Inc.; 88(cl, bl, cr), Breck P. Kent; 89(tr), Laurence Parent; 90(cl), Breck P. Kent; 90(cr), Peter Frenck/Bruce Coleman, Inc.; 91(br), Robert Glusic/Natural Selection; 92(tl), Breck P. Kent/Animals Animals/Earth Scenes; 92(breccia), Breck P. Kent; 92(cl), Joyce Photographics/Photo Researchers, Inc.; 92(cr), E. R. Degginger/Color-Pic, Inc.; 92(br), Breck P. Kent; 93(br), Ed Cooper; 93, Stephen Frink/Corbis; 93(bl), Breck P. Kent; 93(c), SuperStock; 94(cr), Franklin P. OSF/Animals Animals/Earth Scenes; 94(tl), Breck P. Kent; 95(bl), E. R. Degginger/Color-Pic, Inc.; 95(br), George Wuerthner; 97(tl), Visuals Unlimited/Dane S. Johnson; 97(tlc), Carlyn Iverson/Absolute Science Illustration and Photography; 97(tlb), Breck P. Kent; 97(tr), Breck P. Kent/Animals Animals/Earth Scenes; 97(brc), Tom Pantages; 97(br), Breck P. Kent/Animals Animals/Earth Scenes; 98(tl), Ken Karp/HRW Photo; 98(br), Breck P. Kent; 99(tl), E. R. Degginger/Color-Pic, Inc.; 99(bl), Ray Simmons/ Photo Researchers, Inc.; 99(tc), The Natural History Museum, London; 99(bc), Breck P. Kent; 100, E. R. Degginger/Color-Pic, Inc.; 101, Doug Sokell/Tom Stack & Associates; 104(c), Wolfgang Kaehler/Liason International.

Chapter Five: Page 106(t), Greg Vaughn/Tom Stack & Associates; 106(t, b, bl), Kaku Kurita/ Liaison Agency; 106(br), Mark Burnett/Photo Researchers, Inc.; 106(t), Florida Institute of Technology; 108(c), Andy Christiansen/HRW Photo; 108(l), John Blaustein/Liaison Agency; 108(r), Mark Lewis/Tony Stone Images; 109(tc), James Randklev/Tony Stone Images; 109(tr), Bruce Hands/Tony Stone Images; 109(br), John Zoiner Photographer; 109(bl), Ed Malles/Liaison Agency; 110(cl), Andy Christiansen/HRW Photo; 111, Telegraph Colour Library/FPG International; 112(cr, bl), John Zoiner; 114(t), Paolo Koch/Photo Researchers, Inc.; 114(t), Horst Schafer/Peter Arnold, Inc.; 114(b), Brian Parker/Tom Stack & Associates; 114(b), C. Kuhn/Image Bank; 115(bl), Mark A. Leman/Tony Stone images; 115(br), Tim Eagan/Woodfin Camp & Associates; 116(tr), Adam Hart-Davis/Science Photo Library/Photo Researchers, Inc.; 116(bl), James Stanfield/National Geographic Image Collection; 117(tc, tr), Victoria Smith/HRW Photo; 118(bl), Sylvain Coffie/Tony Stone Images; 119(tr), Tom Myers/Photo Researchers, Inc.; 120(c), Alex Bartel/Science Photo Library/Photo Researchers, Inc.; 120(bl), Joyce Photographics/Photo Researchers,Inc.; 121(bl), Hank Morgan/Science Source/Photo Researchers, Inc.; 122, Mark Lewis/Liason International; 123(tr), Craig Sands/National Geographic Image Collection; 123(cl), Tom Bean; 124(cr), G.R. Roberts Photo Library; 128(bl), John Blaustein/Liason Agency; 128(tr), Tom Myers/Photo Researchers, Inc.; 130(t), SuperStock; 130(c), Bedford Recycled Plastic Timbers; 130(b), Kay Park-Rec Corp.; 131, Culver Pictures, Inc. .

Chapter Six: Page 132(tl, c), Louis Psihoyos/Matrix International; 133(cr), M.C. Chamberlain/DRK Photo; 133(br), Bill Patterson, Sr./Patterson Graphics, Inc.; 137(br), Andy Christiansen/HRW Photo; 144, Tom Till/DRK Photo; 145, Courtesy Charles S. Tucek/University of Arizona at Tucson; 146(bl), Francois Gohier/Photo Researchers, Inc.; 146(cr), 147(tr), E. R. Degginger/Color-Pic, Inc.;